ALIEN INK

Other Books by Natalie Robins

Wild Lace (poems)
My Father Spoke of His Riches (poems)
The Peas Belong on the Eye Level (poems)
Eclipse (poems)
Savage Grace (coauthored with S. Aronson)

ALIEN INK

The FBI's War on Freedom of Expression

NATALIE ROBINS

WILLIAM MORROW AND COMPANY, INC.
New York

Library of Congress Cataloging-in-Publication Data

Robins, Natalie S.
    Alien ink : the FBI's war on intellectual freedom / by Natalie
Robins.
      p.   cm.
    Includes bibliographical references and index.
    ISBN 0-688-06885-5
    1. Authors, American—20th century—Political activity. 2. United
States. Federal Bureau of Investigation. 3. Freedom of
information. I. Title.
PS129.R63 1992
363.2'3'0973—dc20   91-25559
                                              CIP

Printed in the United States of America

2 3 4 5 6 7 8 9 10

BOOK DESIGN BY PAUL CHEVANNES

For Christopher,
"guardian of my solitude"

Acknowledgments

I am very grateful to the many individuals and institutions that helped me during the research and writing of this book. If I've left anyone out, it's an oversight, and I ask his or her forgiveness.

For their cooperation, and, in certain cases, their advice and guidance, I thank the following from the bottom of my heart: William Abrahams, Clinton Adlum, FBI Assistant Director Milt Ahlerich, Svetlana Alliluyeva, Karen Alkalay-Gut, Selma Algaze, the American Library Association, Jack Anderson, Raymond Anderson, the Sherwood Anderson Collection of the Newberry Library (Chicago, Illinois), Archives et Centre de Documentation Juive Contemporaine (Paris), the Association of Research Libraries, James Atlas, Perry Baker, William M. Baker, the Bancroft Library of the University of California at Berkeley, Amiri Baraka, Carole Baron, Richard Baron, Jaia Barrett, Fred Bauman, the Beinke Library of Yale University, Susan Bell, Robert Bernstein, Zerina Bhika, June Bingham Birge, Eivind Allan Boe, Joe Boltar, Senator David L. Boren, Kay Boyle, Betsy Bowman, Phillip Brickner, Richard Brickner, the Brooklyn Public Library, Frances Bronson, the Broward County (Florida) Public Libraries, Pat Buchanan, William F. Buckley, Jr., Linda Bunche, Robert Bunn, the Bureau of National Affairs, Edward Burns, Stanley Burnshaw, Gerry Lynn Broyey, Dorothy Byers, Lisl Cade, Angus Cameron, Ina Caro, Bill Carter, Ruth Carew, the Central Intelligence Agency, Mary Cheever, Alan Cheuse, Scott Chafin, Blair Clark, Ramsey Clark, Walter Clemons, Addie Corram, Rob Cowley, Mrs. Malcolm Cowley, the Malcolm Cowley Collection of the New-

7

berry Library, Ester Daniello, Shelley Dattner, Vanya Del Borgo, Neil de Mause, Cartha DeLoach, the Floyd Dell Collection of the Newberry Library, Jim Demsey, E. L. Doctorow, the John Drury Collection of the Newberry Library, FBI Assistant Director (Intelligence Division) Thomas DuHadway, Ulla Dydo, Richard Eberhardt, Congressman Don Edwards, the Dwight David Eisenhower Library, Richard Elman, Franz Enciso, Nora Ephron, Sylvia Evans, Paul Fasana, Bette Fast, Howard Fast, Jon Fast, the FBI Freedom of Information/Privacy Acts Section, the FBI Office of Congressional and Public Affairs, the FBI Reading Room, Bill Fitzgerald, Catherine Fitzgibbons, Maureen Fleming, Jean Frank, Jerry Garchik, Leah Garchik, Isobelle Geffner, George Mason University, Allen Ginsberg, Peggy Girard, Mary Gordon, Dan Green, Judy Greif, Lew Grimes, A. Tom Grunfeld, Nancy Gubman, Elizabeth Guy, Diane Hamilton, Peter Hanff, Roger Hanson, Elizabeth Hardwick, Eleanor Harrison, Diana Haskell, Marilyn Hatch, Tom Hawkins, Julie Hinz, Maurita Peterson Holland, Sven Holmes, Glenn Horowitz, Alex Hoyt, Charlene Hurt, the Information Industry Association, the Inter-Library Loan Network of the New York Public Library, Gloria Jones, the Judicial, Fiscal and Social Branch of the Civil Archives Division of the National Archives, Alice Yeager Kaplan, Leanne Katz, Paula Kaufman, Murray Kempton, Carmela Kibble, Marvin Kitman, Linda Kloss, Nancy Kranich, Judith Krug, Kurt Krumer, Judy Kutulas, Ellen LaConte, Philip Lagerquist, Ellen Lambert, Gerald Lawton, Noah Lehmann-Haupt, Rachel Lehmann-Haupt, Roxanna Lehmann-Haupt, Tamar Lehrich, Harold T. Leinbaugh, Edward Levi, the Library of Congress, Dave Lieberman, Richard Lingeman, Margaret Lippert, the Los Angeles PEN Center, Ira Lowe, Jeffrey Lyons, Sylvia Lyons, Stephen R. MacKinnon, Paul Mahon, Norman Mailer, Kathy Makara, David Malinek, Bob Markel, Linda Martin, the University of Maryland Libraries, Greg Masters, Ray McElhaney, Toby McIntosh, Judith McNally, Michael Meeropol, Joan Mellen, Karl Meyer, Arthur Miller, Leo Milonas, Jessica Mitford, E. J. Montini, Robert Morgenthau, Kathleen Morowitz, Emil P. Moschella, Anthony Mullan, Sophie Mumford, Anne Murray, Tom Murray, *The Nation* magazine, the National Archives, the National Emergency Civil Liberties Committee, the National Coalition Against Censorship, the National Security Archive, Victor Navasky, Helen Ann Near, Helen Nearing, Margaret Neis, Lynn Nesbit, Marjorie Ness, the Newberry Library, the New York Public Library, the New York University Courant Institute of Mathematics and Science, Hugh Nissenson, Marilyn Nissenson, Denuta Nitecki, the Office for Intellectual Freedom of the American Library Association, the Ohio State University Libraries, Richard Ohmann, Congressman Major R. Owens, Michael Pakenham, Grace Paley, Erik Palma, David Payton, William Phillips, Angel Pino, Richard Gid Powers, Linda Resnik, Richard Rappaport, Walter Rideout, Bill Roberts, Stephen Roberts, Alexander Rolich, Mary Ronen, Jack Rosenthal, Judy Rossner, Ellen Rudley, Rex Sabel, Sally and Sandy at the New York State Library, Faith Sale, John Saltmarsh, Pamela Sauer, Ronnie Scharfman, Gracie Schmidt, C. James Schmidt, FBI Supervisory Special Agent Susan Schnitzer, Barry Schwabsky, Leroy Schwartzkopf, the Senate Select Committee on Intelligence, FBI Director William Steele Sessions, Ted Shabid, Karl Shapiro, Quin Shea, Loren Shaver, Carolyn Sheehy, William Shawn, William Shirer, Robert Silvers, Bob Simons, the Charles E. Simon Company, Bernard Stein, Douglas Stumpf, Margaret Sumners, Tad Szulc, Studs Terkel, Mary Ternis, Edith Tiger, Steven Tilley, Robert Treuhaft, Diana Trilling, the Harry S Truman Library, Tracy Tullis, Amanda Urban, Cynthia Wall, Sheryl L. Walter, Robert Penn Warren, Joyce Waters, Barbara Weaver, Erik Wensberg, Linda Welborn, Gerald Whitmore, Sophie Wilkins, Bob Woodward, Herman Wouk, Buzz Wyeth, Gerald Young, Benedict Zobrist.

For counsel beyond the call of duty, I thank again and again: Richard Gid Powers, Victor Navasky, Lynn Nesbit, and most especially, Richard Lingeman, whose skill, energy, intuition, and wisdom helped shape the final version of this book.

Contents

A great part of information obtained in war is contradictory, a still greater part is false, and by far the greatest part is of a doubtful nature.

—*General Karl von Clausewitz,* On War, *1832*

For the FBI to make an error of fact is inexcusable.

—*J. Edgar Hoover, marginal note next to an error in his biographical sketch, 2/29/48*

Stick to the facts. The FBI is not interested in rumor or idle gossip.

— *J. Edgar Hoover,* Masters of Deceit, *1958*

Something deeply hidden had to be behind things.

—*Albert Einstein, jotted on a scrap of paper, undated*

Prologue

In June 1984, while I was in the middle of working on another book, I read an item in the *New York Post* about the *San Jose* (California) *Mercury News,* which had received, under the Freedom of Information Act, a secret FBI file on John Steinbeck. The article said Steinbeck had requested J. Edgar Hoover's "boys to stop stepping on my heels. They think I'm an enemy alien."

I became curious about other writers who might be in the files, and if there were others, did they, like Steinbeck, realize they were under surveillance? So when I finished the book I was working on, I assembled, more or less at random, a list of about 150 authors, and sent it off to Washington. Two or three weeks later, someone from the FBI phoned to say that under the provisions of the FOIA, one may ask only for material on deceased authors, and that files on the living could be requested only by their subjects. (Mysteriously, someone else from the FBI later denied any such call had been made to me.) Thus, I altered my list and sent it off again. I also asked several living writers to request their files for me. Some had done so already for their own purposes and made the material available to me; the others joined the long FOIA request waiting list.

"The FBI had no program of maintaining files on writers or anyone else in the communications profession, unless that individual, or individuals, concerned the subject of a possible legal violation of the law, or else some phase of intelligence under FBI jurisdiction." This statement was made to me by Cartha D. DeLoach, once Director J. Edgar Hoover's number three man at the Federal Bureau of Investigation, a man who joined the Bureau in 1942, and retired in 1970, two years before Hoover's death in 1972.

But is it conceivable that the 148 American writers whose files are discussed in this book could be involved in "some phase of intelligence under FBI jurisdiction," or "a possible violation of the law"? It seems unlikely. My curiosity about the files was turning into bewilderment and dismay, and I became determined to find out what was going on. I began to wonder what the issues were, and why all these files on writers really existed. What did the files' existence say about our history? What was their actual impact? Did they do any lasting harm? Were their effects, if any, visible or invisible? Did they influence writing in America?

What was the real story? I had to find out.

Congress had created the Department of Justice in 1870, and in 1908 it set up the FBI (or Bureau of Investigation, as it was called until 1935), strictly as a law-enforcement operation to aid the Department of Justice in uncovering crimes committed against this country.

The FBI was eventually charged with investigating kidnappings, bank robberies, frauds against the government, acts of sabotage and espionage, and civil rights and security violations. Nowhere are there any statutes that mention intelligence authority. According to *The Lawless State* by Morton H. Halperin, et al., "FBI intelligence has its roots in war and its authority to engage in intelligence activities derives not from statutes, but from executive orders and instructions issued during war time emergency." *FBI intelligence has its roots in war.*

Indeed, I discovered that the FBI's intelligence operations involving writers occurred at points in our history when there was strong feeling about enemies, and it is for this reason that the section titles in *Alien Ink* are named after the larger events that were going on, that is, generally the most prominent war(s) in the particular decade under examination.

The largest group of files discussed in this book—sixty-four of them—comprises those that were started in the thirties, around the time of the Spanish Civil War and on the eve of World War II. The second largest group—thirty-four—consists of files started in the forties, during and right after World War II. Twenty-four files, the third largest group, were started in the twenties, immediately following the Russian Revolution and World War I. Ten files were started between 1911 and 1920, and only ten in the fifties, during the McCarthy years, the Korean War, and the continuing Cold War.

The greatest number of writers—*over 250,* most still alive and unaware—had files begun in the 1960s, after Director Hoover had practiced his trade for almost forty years. But it was not until I had read the files of some living writers—files that contained information from the sixties and seventies—that I discovered these lists and lists of writers (and publishers and editors) who had files started because of their civil rights and/or antiwar activism. Most of them do not even realize they have a file, and will discover the news only after reading their names in Appendix A. In any case, this book focuses on the files opened in the sixties on six writers, whose names were on my original request list to the FBI's FOIA section.

The FBI, I would also learn, helped make J. Edgar Hoover's 1958 book, *Masters of Deceit,* an instant hit—by exerting pressure and buying up copies. "The FBI could make a best seller out of a calculus textbook," a special agent once said. But such manipulations would emerge only as a minor aspect of the Bureau's part in literary history. The massive accumulation of files on American writers would be its greatest—and unprecedented—role.

Was it paranoia? Conspiracy? A case of monumental bureaucratic overkill? Or were they simply doing their job?

The answer is often all four.

Yet one thing is certain: most of the writers were watched because of *what they thought.*

It is important to define what exactly a file *is.* At the point at which the documents reach anyone who has solicited them under the Freedom of Information Act, a dossier consists of separate pages of investigative reports, legal forms, interviews, memorandums, petitions, letters, articles, and news clippings that have been collected and clipped together in one folder by the Federal Bureau of Investigation. But to put those separate references together to create such a file, the FBI goes through 67,744,000 index cards, of which around twenty-seven million are on a computer, the rest being in "manual indices"—that is, in a card catalog. The index cards are the key to defining what a file is; it doesn't matter whether the writer is the actual subject of an investigation or is mentioned in another subject's investigation—what matters is that the writer's name appears in the FBI's indexing system: it is crucial to understand that *to be indexed is to have a file.* There is no other definition. Every file starts with an index card. J. Edgar Hoover himself discovered the significance of indexing when he catalogued books for the Library of Congress after graduating from high school. Decades later, his Bureau invented "Do Not File" files, which meant that the material in them was not to be indexed, and thus could be hidden. Later on a file could also be opened as a "dead" file—"open dead" is the bureau slang for it—and information pertaining to persons agents don't want to investigate is placed there "in case someday you might need to investigate." Today, the FBI also uses the heading "Informal Advice—Not for Retention," instead of "Do Not File," on certain documents. In addition, the Bureau often has *two* files on the same subject—for security reasons. One is hidden under another name, however, and is basically unretrievable from the system except by the FBI agent who created it. As one FBI agent, whom I shall call FBI Agent "X," says, "You have to put informant information someplace, and you don't really want to spread it around to everybody in the world." He also says the information can be spread around in "other files, too," and this is to "protect the identity of the informant" because "developing the informant is one of the foremost things."

Since the 1930s, the FBI has maintained various *types* of indexes, as well. In 1939, it created one first called a Custodial Detention List, and in 1943 its name was changed to the Security Index. This contained the names of potentially dangerous Americans, that is, persons who the FBI felt threatened the country's internal security; there were three categories of "dangerousness." In 1948, a Communist Index was also created, and Hoover later devised a secret Reserve Index of potentially dangerous citizens. The FBI also invented such indexes as an "Agitator Index," a "Rabble-Rouser Index," and a "Key Activist Index." In 1971, the Security Index became the Administrative Index, and this was discontinued in 1976.

For a researcher, one of the problems with the files occurs because, as one special agent told me, "We get conflicting information all the time, so a lot of untrue information gets recorded in our files. A lot of what the story is turns on the questions that are asked by the agent." In addition, as Clarence M. Kelley, director of the FBI from 1972 until 1978, writes in a memoir, "Most reports were written, rewritten, edited, scrubbed, and cleaned and pressed a dozen times before they were put in the mail. Reportorial accuracy was seldom a consideration. Almost everyone in the organization was usually afraid to tell Hoover the truth for fear of upsetting him—and for fear of the inevitable punishment. As a result, Hoover often had to rely on information that had been sugarcoated for him."

Moreover, if "Do Not File" information exists, as well as duplicate files, the dossier compiled by the Bureau may not contain all that has actually been collected on a particular subject. "Do Not File" data can be solicited under the Freedom of Information Act; however, one can't be certain any of it—as well as data from "dead" files—is retrievable, in whole or in part. And then there is the problem of evaluating contradictory and erroneous material. Finally, a good deal of the material is heavily blacked out because it is still classified. In a few of the files I received, only one or two words are left on a page after the excising process. There are eighteen exemptions under the FOIA, but most excisions fall under the exemptions stating that disclosure of the information would harm our national defense or that the disclosure would constitute an invasion of the personal privacy of another person or might reveal the identity of a confidential FBI source.

Despite all the impediments, the files do yield fascinating material for biographers. Since we know that the collecting of information involves selection, the files also tell us about the inner life of the Bureau—what, at a given time, was on the mind of the FBI. They are valuable as a source of raw data because the FBI is, after all, a bureau of investigation, and as such it did—and continues to do—a great deal of admirable investigative work. The files are also absorbing to read simply on the level of gossip because of our inherent interest in the lives of the writers.

"The FBI builds its files somewhat like a newspaperman builds his files," Drew Pearson once commented. "A piece of information comes in from one source which means nothing. Then something comes in from another source, and perhaps from a third source, which taken separately mean nothing. But put together, they begin to tell a story." But the story that emerges from the writers' files is never a complete story.

"All history," Samuel Johnson wrote, "so far as it is not supported by contemporary evidence, is romance." I decided I needed to find some people who could supply some "contemporary evidence" about the information in the files. The people I found and interviewed—and will call "formal witnesses"—are those who once worked for and/or with the FBI or people who currently work for and/or with the FBI; relatives, friends, and colleagues, both well-disposed and otherwise, of the deceased writers; living writers who have been subject to FBI scrutiny; and writers who have lived through dictatorships as well as democracies.

It's quite possible to be misled by the actual files, and in certain cases, unless one does go beyond the official documents to formal witnesses (as well as to evidence such as letters, memorandums, published interviews, pamphlets, essays and biographies), the material can be extremely misleading. (In fact, my definition of the word *witness* includes not only people I've interviewed, but this written evidence as well.) The testimony of "formal witnesses" provides a clearer, and more complete understanding of the FBI records. These witnesses carry the story beyond the official pages; they speak about what is in the files—and even more—and their words resonate beyond specific testimony.

Such witnesses can tell what they know, offering a unique historical as well as social perspective. They can furthermore be freely cross-examined. The testimony of witnesses is also valuable because the FOIA appeal process is time-consuming and very often fruitless, and one way around the blacked-out passages as well as the often biased point of view is to go directly to the people involved in one way or another.

Another source of evidence must also be considered. Richard Gid Powers writes that "one of Hoover's principal ways of managing his bureau was by writing marginal notes on the memos that crossed his desk." A former special agent says Hoover "really wrote those notes thinking they were private, so he was totally candid. It was strictly private within the house, like a man talking to his wife type of thing. It never occurred to him that there would be a Freedom of Information Act."

These marginal notes speak most fully and most tellingly about the hidden agenda and the secret life of the FBI during a certain period of its history, and they help explain how and why the writers' files came into being. They also will be subsumed under the category of witnesses.

FBI AGENT "X":

The lifeblood of the FBI is the index. Every piece of information that comes in that some agent wants to put on paper is very easily retrievable; it was indexed and you knew exactly where to go. There were no loose ends, and as far as investigations that were going on, you knew *exactly* how to find out how to follow it.

A lot of information goes into the files that we don't know if it's true at the time. Maybe we're putting into the file somebody's speculation. Maybe we're putting into the file information that isn't true. Nevertheless, if we have a source for that information we'll put it into the files. I think we do characterize it as such, that this information was received from a particular person. Obviously if Person One says the color of the skin of Mr. X is black, and from Person Two and Person Three we know that the color of Mr. X's skin is white, then the information from Person One is untrue. Nevertheless, it's in the file. Do we pull that information out and say it's never been recorded? No. Somebody gave this as information. One person will say a person is a tremendously loyal American and another person will say this person is suspect. We consider the source—and when we come to any conclusions, we consider the source.

There are different motivations for informing for different people. Some people will inform on the illegal acts of other people for very selfish reasons, namely to be rewarded in terms of monetary payment, or to protect themselves, or curry favor with the courts. In the realm of security it can be very high motives—a person who believes that he's doing it for the sake of his country. Sometimes it's as simple as liking and relating to the agent as a person. But why people want to be informants, or cooperate—it's such a broad psychological topic.

Do we pay a lot for information? It depends upon the information we get. We put a value on it—you're paid for services rendered. It doesn't take away the credibility to pay for information provided. If they are good informants, they're devoting an awful lot of time to doing it—it's almost like another job.

A live informant is the most important investigative technique that the FBI has as a law-enforcement agency. A live informant gives you leads into things. You're getting reasons. You're getting perspectives. You're getting possibilities. You're getting motivations and stories beyond that.

An interviewer can change a story from an unwitting angel just by the questions he asks. Don't ask certain questions, then you know you're not going to get certain answers, and that doesn't come out on paper. It may be a completely inaccurate story only because the agent didn't ask the question that should logically have been asked.

The Files

(In alphabetical order, with dates file was opened by FBI)

Léonie Adams 1921
James Agee 1937
Conrad Aiken 1945
Nelson Algren 1935
Fred Allen 1936
Maxwell Anderson 1938
Sherwood Anderson 1932
James Baldwin 1951
Amiri Baraka (formerly LeRoi
  Jones) 1961
Djuna Barnes 1944
S. N. Behrman 1938
Ludwig Bemelmans 1944
Steven Vincent Benét 1938
Maxwell Bodenheim 1936
Louise Bogan 1937
Jane Bowles 1945
Kay Boyle 1940
Van Wyck Brooks 1935
Heywood Broun 1935
Pearl S. Buck 1937
William F. Buckley, Jr. 1941
Witter Bynner 1937
Erskine Caldwell 1932

Truman Capote 1956
Dale Carnegie 1936
Willa Cather 1947
John Cheever 1965
Malcolm Cowley 1936
James Gould Cozzens 1942
e. e. cummings 1955
E. L. Doctorow 1968
Bernard De Voto 1944
John Dos Passos 1923
Theodore Dreiser 1927
F. W. Dupee 1939
Max Eastman 1912
T. S. Eliot 1949
James T. Farrell 1934
Howard Fast 1932
William Faulkner 1939
Edna Ferber 1935
F. Scott Fitzgerald 1951
Waldo Frank 1932
Robert Frost 1942
Erle Stanley Gardner 1943
Allen Ginsberg 1957
Horace Gregory 1930

John Gunther 1936
Dashiell Hammett 1934
Moss Hart 1938
Gabriel Heatter 1942
Ben Hecht 1941
Lillian Hellman 1933
Ernest Hemingway 1935
Josephine Herbst 1924
Robert Herrick 1935
Granville Hicks 1926
Hedda Hopper 1946
William Dean Howells 1941
Langston Hughes 1925
Fannie Hurst 1930
William Inge 1957
Randall Jarrell 1944
Robinson Jeffers 1935
James Jones 1963
Murray Kempton 1938
Joyce Kilmer 1941
Joseph Wood Krutch 1928
Fulton Lewis, Jr. 1938
Sinclair Lewis 1923
A. J. Liebling 1937
Walter Lippmann 1913
Jack London 1917
Robert Lowell 1943
Leonard Lyons 1935
Mary McCarthy 1959
Carson McCullers 1956
Dwight Macdonald 1936
Archibald MacLeish 1917
Norman Mailer 1949
Thomas Mann 1927
John P. Marquand 1939
Edgar Lee Masters 1938
F. O. Matthiessen 1935
H. L. Mencken 1922
Edna St. Vincent Millay 1923
Arthur Miller 1938
Henry Miller 1945

Jessica Mitford 1939
Marianne Moore 1935
Lewis Mumford 1923
Ogden Nash 1941
George Jean Nathan 1922
Anaïs Nin 1944
Clifford Odets 1935
John O'Hara 1939
Eugene O'Neill 1917
Grace Paley 1941
Dorothy Parker 1927
Louella Parsons 1934
Drew Pearson 1934
Westbrook Pegler 1935
Katherine Anne Porter 1927
Ezra Pound 1911
Ernie Pyle 1937
John Crowe Ransom 1962
John Reed 1917
Quenton Reynolds 1938
Elmer Rice 1925
Theodore Roethke 1941
Damon Runyon 1946
Muriel Rukeyser 1932
Carl Sandburg 1918
William Saroyan 1940
Delmore Schwartz 1961
Karl Shapiro 1940
Irwin Shaw 1935
James Vincent Sheean 1927
Robert Sherwood 1917
Upton Sinclair 1923
Edgar Snow 1931
George Sokolsky 1925
Lincoln Steffens 1917
Gertrude Stein 1937
John Steinbeck 1936
Donald Ogden Stewart 1936
Rex Stout 1920
Booth Tarkington 1936
Allen Tate 1956

James Thurber 1938
Lionel Trilling 1937
Louis Untermeyer 1921
Carl Van Doren 1929
Mark Van Doren 1927
Gore Vidal 1948
Edith Wharton 1945
E. B. White 1956
Thornton Wilder 1933
Tennessee Williams 1947

William Carlos Williams 1930
Edmund Wilson 1946
Walter Winchell 1934
Ella Winter 1927
Thomas Wolfe 1930
Herman Wouk 1941
Alexander Woollcott 1943
Richard Wright 1935
Louis Zukofsky 1935

The Formal Witnesses

(In alphabetical order)

Svetlana Alliluyeva: Writer; daughter of Josef Stalin and best-known Soviet defector to United States

Jack Anderson: Newspaper columnist

Amiri Baraka (the former LeRoi Jones): Poet and playwright

Kay Boyle: Short story writer, novelist, essayist

William F. Buckley, Jr.: Editor-at-Large of *National Review,* newspaper columnist, novelist

Stanley Burnshaw: Poet, critic, and editor

Angus Cameron: Editor

Ramsey Clark: Lawyer, former U.S. attorney general

Roy Cohn: Lawyer; worked for United States attorney's office and helped prosecute Julius and Ethel Rosenberg; chief counsel to Senator Joseph McCarthy

Malcolm Cowley: Poet, critic, and editor

Cartha D. DeLoach: Number three man under J. Edgar Hoover

E. L. Doctorow: Novelist

Richard Eberhart: Poet

Howard Fast: Novelist

Jean Frank: Writer and widow of Waldo Frank

Allen Ginsberg: Poet

Elizabeth Hardwick: Novelist, short story writer, and critic

27

Sidney Hook: Philosopher and social critic
Murray Kempton: Newspaper columnist, essayist, nonfiction writer
Harold T. Leinbaugh: Former FBI official and nonfiction writer
Sylvia Lyons: Writer and widow of columnist Leonard Lyons
Norman Mailer: Novelist and nonfiction writer
Arthur Miller: Playwright
Jessica Mitford: Nonfiction writer
Sophie Mumford: Widow of social critic Lewis Mumford
Grace Paley: Short story writer
William Phillips: Editor of *Partisan Review;* essayist
William Steele Sessions: Director of FBI, 1988–present
Karl Shapiro: Poet and autobiographer
Diana Trilling: Critic, essayist, nonfiction writer
FBI Agent "X": A current FBI agent
Merchant Marine "X": A former sailor and Communist party member

PART ONE

The Russian Revolution and World War I

CHAPTER ONE

Before Hoover

History has forgotten that there were *four* FBI directors before J. Edgar Hoover; what is remembered is the extent to which his name eventually became synonymous with the FBI. But, in fact, when the Bureau was formed in 1908, its first director—"Chief" was the official title—was a financial expert named Stanley Finch, who had been the Justice Department's chief examiner, or auditor, responsible for keeping track of the accounts of all U.S. attorneys, marshals, and clerks. In 1912, Finch was replaced by a lawyer, A. Bruce Bielaski, who remained in the position until 1919, the year after World War I ended, and two years after the Russian Revolution of 1917. A famous Secret Service detective named William J. Flynn became director in 1919, stayed on the job for three years, and was replaced in 1922 by another celebrity from the Secret Service, William Burns.

History has also forgotten that the rudimentary legal framework for investigating political dissent had also been erected by 1908. Congress passed an antiradical law in 1903, when J. Edgar Hoover was just eight years old, and passed another such law in 1911. Also, the 1910 Mann Act (or White Slave Traffic Act), forbidding the transportation of women across state lines for immoral purposes, would, in time, give the FBI another excuse for intrusive investigations.

After the Bureau was created in 1908, and until the beginning of World War I in 1914, more than half a million immigrants came to America's shores. Richard Gid Powers reminds us that "as the numbers of immigrants rose, so did nativist revulsion against the foreigner and his un-American ideas." After the flood of immigration, "a fateful and erroneous identification of alien and radical was firmly implanted in the public mind," William Preston, Jr., writes in *Aliens and Dissenters*.

Most visible of those imported radical ideas was socialism. The Socialist party had been formed in 1901, and its influence was steadily increasing, so that by 1908, as Albert Parry writes in *Garrets and Pretenders*, a history of bohemianism in America, "Socialism was rampant in the labor halls and liberal parlors of New York. . . . It was the central idea, the rallying point."

About this time, the militant Industrial Workers of the World—known as the "Wobblies"—which had been founded in 1905 to link all skilled and unskilled workers to a socialist ideal, was becoming, according to William Preston, "the most feared radical organization in the country." He adds, "Whether [the IWW] deserved this reputation was beside the point; from then on the federal government saw the internal security problem largely in terms of the I.W.W. threat." By the time J. Edgar Hoover, only a year out of law school, joined the Justice Department in 1917, it was already in the midst of "committing some of the most egregious violations of civil liberties in American history," Preston writes in reference to the harassment, and later, the arrest and trial of the entire leadership of the IWW.

During the teens America was being overwhelmed by new people, radical ideas, and sudden changes. A bureau memo describes how "revolutionary remarks are heard everywhere. . . . It is not only foreigners who are affected . . . but also some native-born Americans."

And so the institutional impulses to control writers were already set in motion by a fledgling Bureau when one of Stanley Finch's associates entered a reference sent directly from the State Department in a file that would eventually grow to 1,512 pages: "This bureau has been advised that Dr. Ezra Pound . . . left the United States in February 1911 and proceeded to Rapallo, Italy." That year a notation would be entered in another file that would end up with 833 pages. It would state that "the first issue of *The Masses* appeared in February 1911," and that "it was founded by a group of outstanding liberals and radicals," including

"John Reed." These separate 1911 references mark the very first ones kept on American writers. The FBI's future—most famous—director, J. Edgar Hoover, was a sophomore in high school, and delivering groceries at the time, earning the nickname "Speed" because of the fast and efficient way he carried out this after-school job.

Poet Ezra Pound, a reactionary, and journalist John Reed, a radical, share poetic temperaments, but little else besides having FBI records. Of course, they also share similar fates—Reed was arrested for sedition in 1919, and Pound was arrested for treason twenty-four years later, in 1943. Pound and Reed also share one other thing: both of their first FBI references are inaccurate.

In 1911, Reed, a recent Harvard graduate, was out looking for a job in New York City, but it was not until two years later in 1913, that he actually joined *The Masses,* eventually becoming its managing editor, and concocting this slogan for it with editor Max Eastman: "A magazine with a sense of humor and no respect for the respectable."

Ezra Pound first left the United States in February of 1908, going to England, not to Italy, which didn't become his home until 1925. He returned to America briefly in 1910, but left again that same year. In 1911, when the Bureau reports him as first leaving the United States (it remains inexplicable why the State Department passed this information on), he was already in London, writing "as to twentieth-century poetry . . . it will be as much like granite as it can be, its force will lie in its truth. . . ." In 1911, Pound was not particularly interested in politics, either, although he did contribute to a controversial English magazine called *The New Age,* a periodical not unlike *The Masses.* In any case, it was not until much later that Pound's views turned right and reactionary. His name and initial reference stayed in the FBI's indexes for three decades without any additions. It remained a "dead" file until sometime in the mid-thirties, when new intelligence was received.

As Kenneth O'Reilly writes in his *Hoover and the Un-Americans,* the Bureau, in its early years before the advent of Hoover, was "an undisciplined, somewhat ineffectual. . . . organization." Thus, it was haphazard in maintaining its files, and there was no logic or organizing concept to the files on the writers, and had J. Edgar Hoover not entered the Justice Department in 1917, those files might have remained ineffectual for a lot longer. But Hoover would organize them obsessively out of a great personal and political need to control the flow of information in America. More importantly, his role at the FBI was the one he was always best at and most celebrated for—that of enforcer.

J. Edgar Hoover enforced the laws and regulations (even some which his bureau invented) in such a way that writers were slowly and methodically turned into suspects.

After its first entry, John Reed's file remained "dead" until May 30, 1917 (three months before he would leave for Russia), when the Bureau reported that he "attended the First American Conference for Democracy and Terms of Peace" at Madison Square Garden in New York. The sponsor of the conference was not noted by the Bureau, but it was, no doubt, a socialist one, since the Communist party was not formed until 1919.

In 1918, the Bureau seized the notes for Reed's book on the Russian Revolution, *Ten Days That Shook the World*. Reed had been an eyewitness to the October revolution, and agents interrogated him; "Mr. Reed states that he has a lot of material bearing on the revolution." The Bureau also collected "stenographic reports made of his speeches," and reported that he was "named as Russian Consul General of the Russian Soviet government," though this "status" was not "recognized by the United States government."

In his voluminous file, Reed is called many things, ranging from "one of the earliest Communist leaders in the United States," to "not only a fanatic Communist but also an eccentric romantic." He was also considered a *Russian* intelligence "asset," or informant, receiving the many privileges and interviews he did because of his value to the Soviets in publicizing their revolution. His FBI file states, "While under cross-examination . . . John Reed frankly admitted that he had been in the employ of the Foreign Office of the Lenine [*sic*] Trotsky government while in Russia."

But, wittingly or not, Reed was also a Bureau "asset." In 1919, a year after the United States government put him on trial for sedition, and a year before he fled the country on a false passport, a Bureau operative entrapped him into giving intelligence.

On March 19, 1919, a Bureau report discloses that "our informant, Mr. Aubrey Meyerheim, was successful in obtaining an interview with John Reed." This astonishing interview, in which Meyerheim tricked John Reed into believing he was a Norwegian political official (Reed, at the time, was looking for a way to escape to Russia via a Scandinavian country), is included in a report entitled "Bolchevik [*sic*] Activities in United States."

It explains that "on March 13, I [Meyerheim] received a telegram from John Reed to the effect that he would telephone me on the following day. Evidently the note which I left in his room the day before had aroused his curiosity and he was therefore desirous of seeing me.''

The report continues, ''On Friday March 14 I received a telephone call from John Reed to the effect that he would like to speak to me at his room that evening.

''I called at the home of John Reed at 7:00 on Friday March 14th. His home is located on the top floor front of One Patchen Place. The room into which I was ushered was approximately 12' x 16' & contained a [*unintelligible*] of Bolshevik literature and papers. Outside of his room was the trunk that had carried his personal effects from the other side and still bearing the label of Christiansand, Norway, which was the last place he visited before returning to America.

''After talking matters over in general for a while, Reed was desirous of learning what credentials I had as he stated the Bolsheviks in this country were pretty closely watched by the Police officials and the Department of Justice and therefore they could run no risk. My affiliation with the Norwegian Working Party evidently met with his approval.

''Reed corroborated in the main the facts that had been stated in my report submitted to Military and Naval Intelligence at Washington D.C.[*] He corroborated that the Bolsheviks in this country to-day have no reliable means of securing information from Russia and from many other countries. Reed stated that the only means that they had of securing information from the foreign countries was through underground channels.

''Reed is very desirous of establishing relations, if possible, direct with Russia. Trotsky has what Reed described as a personal 'official agent.' Reed intends to prepare a statement for me, that I am to take across, as to the best methods of cooperating between the countries. . . .'' [*The next page is entirely unintelligible, but the report then continues.*]

''He [Reed] further stated that I was absolutely safe in sending anything through the mail in New York City to him as the Postal Authorities here do not interfere with his mail. My story appealed very much to Reed and he will attempt to use me.''

Yet who used whom? According to historian Theodore Draper, in 1932, Reed's wife, Louise Bryant, told the ''incredible story'' that her husband had been, all along, an American secret agent; considering the

---

*This report has disappeared.

Meyerheim interview, which is not mentioned in any biography of Reed, perhaps her story is not so incredible after all.

After Meyerheim had gained Reed's confidence, Bureau agents began a daily log of his activities. A report dated May 16, 1919, mentions that Reed was even "observed shaving." Another report says that he was about to get evicted from his apartment because of the noise he created, "but the bureau stepped in to prevent it since it would hurt the case." This probably refers to either *The Masses* trial, in which the government attempted to suppress the magazine, charging it with sedition and preaching resistance to the draft, or to the 1919 Senate subcommittee hearings on radical activities, where Reed, who founded the Communist Labor party in 1919, was subjected to very heated questioning.

In April of 1920, the Bureau reported that he "had in some way escaped the vigilance of American port authorities" and "was in jail in Finland charged with smuggling." (After being indicted for sedition, Reed fled America, using a false passport.) The report told the then Bureau director, William Flynn, that Reed "had been found in the coal bunker of a steamer bound for Sweden" and had "on his person" not only "a large amount of money," but also letters from "Russian Soviet leaders."

Six months later, on October 17, Reed died of typhus in Moscow, and was buried in the Kremlin wall. But for the FBI, John Reed, prototypical American radical, never died. References continued to be collected about him for fifty-four years after his death, and sixty-six references remain classified under that all-sheltering umbrella, *national security*. Any association with Reed, however remote, however posthumous, was grounds for suspicion. An August 25, 1940, memo about Ambassador William C. Bullitt, who was sent by President Woodrow Wilson on a special mission to Moscow in 1919, accompanied by Lincoln Steffens, comments on Bullitt's private life: "One of his former wives [Bryant] was at one time married to John Reed." Another memo, dated April 17, 1944, discusses a library that is "filled with propaganda of communist nature"—including one of Reed's articles—and still another report, dated September 10, 1956, states that "Russia announced it is preparing to republish *10 Days That Shook the World,* a history of the Soviet Revolution suppressed by Josef Stalin because it did not mention his name." During the early sixties, the FBI added to Reed's file a surprising revelation from a Russian-language newspaper article that had been published in Germany and translated in Washington: ". . . John Reed . . . took advantage of the rivalry between the American political parties and of sensation-loving American press to get a Soviet note to President Wilson, and the Soviet constitution published in American newspapers.''

Reed's last words to editor Max Eastman were, supposedly, "This class struggle plays hell with your poetry." However, for the FBI, Reed's writing played hell—and continued to do so for many decades—with the view of the class struggle they wanted publicly presented.

The Bureau expected all Americans to realize that although the "originator of Communism," Karl Marx, had a "sharp and keen" mind, he was also "perverted," "biased," and full of "arrogant pride." The Bureau insisted that the "false reasoning" behind the 1917 revolution be included in all descriptions or discussions of it, and any writer who failed to present the Soviet system in this way would be regarded, like Reed, as an American turncoat.

In 1912, the year Woodrow Wilson was elected President and Vladimir Ilich Lenin became editor of *Pravda,* the Bureau, now under the leadership of lawyer A. Bruce Bielaski, began a 112-page file on one of America's most influential journalists, Walter Lippmann, reporting that "he was secretary to the socialist mayor of Schenectady, New York." An undated reference in his file states that while he was in college (Harvard, class of 1910), he was "active in the Harvard Socialist Club."

In 1914, the Bureau reported that Lippmann was an associate editor of *The New Republic,* which had been founded that year as a liberal weekly. Two years later, in 1916, the Bureau reported that Lippmann was a charter member of a club "dominated by a radical element"— the Civic Club of New York. The Bureau also noted that "during World War One, Lippmann assisted Roger Baldwin, Director of the American Civil Liberties Union[,] in his anti-draft propaganda, for which[,] it is noted, Roger Baldwin was sent to prison." It does not mention that Lippmann also assisted President Wilson in conceiving the League of Nations.

The following year, in 1917, the Bureau put in the record that Lippmann was an "assistant to the Secretary of War." While serving in that capacity, he was, in fact, once part of a secret military intelligence unit authorized by Secretary of War Newton Baker (to plot peace—not war) that met clandestinely at the New York Public Library on Forty-second Street. Lippmann biographer Ronald Steele discloses that "even the head librarian was pledged to secrecy."

*   *   *

In 1913, John Reed was reporting on the Paterson, New Jersey, silk strikers for *The Masses*. That same year, the Bureau began its 369-page file on the magazine's flamboyant editor, Max Eastman, a well-known New York bohemian whom the Bureau called "one of the most dangerous radical socialists [*sic*] in America, a true believer in free love." Eastman had recently published *Enjoyment of Poetry*, but the Bureau was not interested in his opinions on poetry, only his opinions on politics and society, especially as they were expressed in *The Masses*, which he had begun editing in 1913.

A file entry explains: "Concerning Eastman's connections with the Communist movement in the United States and Europe, this bureau's files reflect that from 1913 to 1922 he was editor of the Communist weeklies, *The Masses*, and *The Liberator*." (After it was banned in 1918, *The Masses* became *The Liberator*.) Another entry asserts that he is "a very radical Marxian Socialist, as well as a founder of the Communist Party, USA." Eastman was a radical, but was not a founder of the party. He once wrote to another *Masses* editor, Floyd Dell, "We were class struggle socialists—at least the magazine was, thanks largely perhaps to Jack Reed and me, but also largely, I believe, to you." Eastman also wrote Dell that "I was never attached to or committed to the detailed support of any party or program in my life—least of all the program of an orthodox Marxist. . . ."

Daniel Aaron argues in *Writers on the Left* that *The Masses* editors and contributors "were not 'party' people. What distinguishes them from the 'hard' communists of the twenties and thirties was their refusal to subordinate their art to politics." But the FBI made no such distinctions.

A memo entitled "Revolutionary Movement" scrutinizes Eastman's New York life, stating that he is "a frequenter of the Liberal Club on Washington Square, New York," that "he eats frequently at 'Dutch Oven' in the basement of the Club, at Polly's, etc.," and goes on to relate that he "is married, but the general consensus of opinion around Washington Square is that he is a dangerous man where women are concerned. Even experienced literary and stage women 'shy clear' of handsome Max Eastman."

Eastman lived in Russia for two years, beginning in 1922, and the Bureau, under the direction of William J. Burns, kept track of him the entire time he was there, recording such events as the following: "On September 16th [1923] there was a gathering at Max Eastman's house in Moscow. . . . The gathering was more in the nature of a party than a political meeting."

Actually, Burns's Bureau kept track of him even before he had reached Russia. While he was in Paris, where he had gone first, there are detailed reports "received from a strictly confidential source" of his every movement: "About March 25th [1922] certain unknown people with a pronounced Toutonic [*sic*] accent came to Hotel Marceau [where Eastman had been staying] to take him out in a luxurious automobile." But by 1923, the Bureau would report that Eastman "had high hopes for the Russian Bolshevist experiment until he saw how it actually worked out," and by 1927, it would be reported that "this bureau's files further reflect that Eastman has been one of the foremost writers attacking the Communists and the Soviets."

John Reed's 1911 reference is significant not only because it began a writer's file but because it also began a file on that "journal of fun, beauty, realism, freedom, peace, feminism, revolution," *The Masses*. Starting in 1911, the Bureau began to track the magazine's contents and all of its editors and contributors—the list "reads like a who's who of artistic and literary America" according to Theodore Draper—until they all had files.

The August 1917 issue of *The Masses* was barred from circulation by the postmaster general. It was not alone that year; about fifteen other publications had also been found seditious and therefore unmailable. Max Eastman even went to Washington to see President Wilson and ask that the ban be lifted. Wilson was cordial but not cooperative.

Meanwhile, the Bureau decided to try to prove that the editors had conspired to interfere with the draft in violation of the Espionage Act. A November 30, 1917, letter in Eastman's file from the U.S. attorney from New York, Francis G. Coffey, to the attorney general explains that "it will be possible to satisfy the jury that the objectionable articles and cartoons were published with the specific intent of obstructing recruiting and enlistment, and of promoting disloyalty in the enlisted forces." It turned out *not* to be possible to satisfy the jury in question: two members of it refused to find the defendants guilty.

According to a document in Eastman's file, "The failure to obtain a verdict was due to the disloyal and un-American frame of mind of . . . two jurors." These jurors are described in the letter from Coffey to the attorney general; one lived in New York's Greenwich Village, "which is the center of the activities of the *Masses* group," and was also opposed to the war, and the other was an Austrian-born alien who had lived in America for five years and "did not think the government had any right to send him to fight his own people or send anybody out of the country to conduct a war." The letter concludes by saying "there will be an additional defendant placed on trial by the name of John Reed who has just returned from abroad. . . . I have every confidence that the government will be successful on the re-trial of the case."

The government decided to attempt a second trial. Another letter from Coffey to the attorney general describes new evidence: "A telegram [sent by] Max Eastman on April 6, 1917, in which he stated that he hoped riotous resistance would follow any attempt to conscript for service abroad" as well as "a speech by Max Eastman in the Madison Square Garden on August 1, 1917, in which he referred to 'we bloody-handed Americans' as pretending to be fighting in the cause of democracy, and stated that the only war in which he was willing to engage was the war of the working classes against the capitalists." U.S. Attorney Coffey also mentions an interview in which the business manager of *The Masses*, Merrill Rogers, "stated that nothing would give him greater pleasure than to see the entire naval and military program of the United States go to smash."

The government failed again in the second trial. Eastman's file acknowledges that he personally "was prosecuted by the Department of Justice with negative results," although that hardly mattered to the Bureau, since it was also known and reported, of course, that the magazine, "was suppressed by the United States government for its subversive policies" since it had been banned from the mail.

(Anarchist Emma Goldman and her magazine, *Mother Earth,* had also been an FBI crusade; in fact, Goldman's 1919 deportation was one of Hoover's earliest triumphs.)

Three months after turning *The Masses* into the slightly toned-down *Liberator,* Eastman wrote in a letter that appears in his file: "What the Department of Justice wants to do is make us crawl on our knees and beg for mercy." He added that "with many other radicals I failed at the beginning of the war to realize the greatness of [President Wilson's] international idealism, and I should be glad of an opportunity to acknowledge that to him—as I have in the *Liberator*. But that is not what the Post Office and the Department of Justice want. They want me to submit to a chastening from them as a self-confessed criminal. I decline to so mishandle the truth."

In 1916, Jack London, the "world-famed radical," as his file calls him, the author of *The Call of the Wild, White Fang,* and *The Sea Wolf,* adventures that made him one of the best-known and highest-paid writers in the world, committed suicide on his ranch in Glen

Ellen, California. Twelve years earlier, in 1904, he had covered the Russo-Japanese War as a correspondent, and in 1914 he had covered the U.S. Marine occupation in Veracruz, Mexico. London, who "fought with his pen," according to the Bureau, was a long-time member of the Socialist party. He resigned the year of his death.

Inexplicably, the Bureau kept no account of any concern they might have had about London until 1917, the year after his death. In fact, the work of his that brought him to the Bureau's attention was probably a forgery.

On August 23, 1917, one month after Hoover's arrival at the Justice Department, the postmaster general barred from the mails "a printed circular entitled 'A Good Soldier.' " The first line of this leaflet, which was subtitled "an anti-draft matter," said: "Young man, the lowest aim in your life is to be a good soldier," and its concluding line said, "No man can fall lower than a soldier—it is a depth beneath which we cannot go." An unsigned note attached to it, presumably written by someone in the postmaster's office, stated, "This certainly violates the Espionage Act. . . . The responsibility for getting out and distributing [this] should be run down and prosecutions instituted."

However, there is no record of the steps the government did take, because there are only two other brief references to the matter. One is dated May 21, 1918, nine months after the original complaint, and reports that "Mrs. Jack London states husband did not write article in question and was very much annoyed on account of it. Wrote denials to various parties, including army officials. Mrs. London worked with him and knows he did not write article as does Mrs. Shepherd, his stenographer."*

Another item in London's file provides a hint of another of the Bureau's obsessions. A 1917 report discusses how London helped form the Pan-Pacific Club, whose "declared objective was seeking a solution to the racial problem." This is the earliest indication that the Bureau believed a "solution to the racial problem" had an intrinsic subversive component.

Lincoln Steffens, the author of the 1904 *Shame of Our Cities,* was not examined by the Bureau until 1917, when the muckraking

---

*"A Good Soldier" had a curious career. It resurfaced in a 1942 Los Angeles case report entitled "Internal Security—Selective Service." The report quotes the whole of "A Good Soldier," although the last line is altered slightly from the 1917 version; "We" becomes a "Human" in 1942.

movement—of which he was the prophet—reached its crest. The term "muckraking" was first used in 1906 by Steffens's friend, President Theodore Roosevelt, who had also first proposed the idea of creating an FBI.

Early in 1917, Steffens had made the first of several trips to Russia, but the Bureau did not record anything about the "Communist writer," as they referred to him, until his return to America later that year.

On October 9, 1917, a report about his activities titled "IWW Agitators, Pittsburgh District," describes a speech he made "at Soldier's Memorial Hall, given under the auspices of the Single Tax League." Bureau agent L. M. Wendell explains that "Steffens lectured on the New Russia, and from his talk it was very plain that he viewed the accomplishments of the Russians from a Tolstoian, Syndicalist, Anarchist viewpoint. The only allusions to this country were a few sarcastic comments when making a comparison of the Democracy and Free Speech of Russia with the United States. Steffens told [Joe] Mountain [secretary of the People's Council] and [unintelligible] that he was working in conjunction with President Woodrow Wilson when he went to Russia." (This was a secret fact-finding trip he made with future Ambassador William C. Bullitt after the revolution.)

In 1919, the year the American Communist party and Communist International, or Comintern, was formed, as well as the year Steffens returned to Russia in order to evaluate conditions there, the Bureau placed him on its list of radical leaders. But communism was always more of an intellectual adventure than anything else for Lincoln Steffens, who was never a party member, even though he did say after his return from Russia, "I have been over into the future and it works."

A June 23, 1919, report reveals that Steffens's mail was checked by the Bureau, making him—as well as Max Eastman, who is also mentioned—the first American writers to be subject to what FBI historian Sanford Ungar calls "the art of postal espionage." Such "art" involves either a mail "cover," wherein all the correspondents of the person under investigation are recorded by post office officials, or a mail "intercept," when the mail is actually opened and read by the FBI. In practice, however, the terms are often used interchangeably.

Special Agent J. F. McDevitt wrote about Lincoln Steffens that "for sometime [sic] past I have been having tracings made of the mail going to the homes of several well known Philadelphia radicals." It is not really clear whether "tracings" means the mail was copied and read or that just the names of the addressees and senders were recorded. In any case, some other names found in those "tracings" include the radical sociologist Scott Nearing, whose file began in 1917 when the Bureau became suspicious of his antiwar agitation, and the American Socialist leader Eugene V. Debs, who was jailed for violating the Espionage Act.

When the Bureau placed Steffens on the radical leaders list in 1919, it said that "no radical leaders are aliens. The aliens who would be radical leaders have naturally (since the declaration of war) taken a rear seat and allowed radicalism to be spread by regular born citizens or aliens who have become naturalized." But J. Edgar Hoover, now head of the Radical Division, would confer new meaning on the word alien. He would equate it with "writer."

In 1913, the Bureau stepped up its surveillance of writers by opening a file on one of their organizations, the Authors League of America. Ironically, though, the file was opened because the Authors League was a union "formed for the purpose of promoting and protecting the general professional interest of all creators of literary, dramatic, or musical materials." The Bureau, of course, feared such objectives because of its deep suspicion of the IWW, of which it noted a little later, "agents of the Bolsheviki and I.W.W.'s are active everywhere." Another memo helps explain the Bureau's excitement: "All organizations of labor are being honeycombed with revolutionary radicals who have 'burrowed from within' and assumed positions of tactical advantage in carrying out the general plan of the revolutionists for the establishment of the 'One Big Union' " favored by the IWW. Later, Bureau chief Bielaski observed that the Authors League "is an independent organization operating as a labor union but not considered in the same status as a union . . . ," an important distinction for the Bureau, and one that serves to illustrate that after opening the file on the Authors League, the Bureau soon realized exactly what it had on its hands: an organization representing most of the writers in America—an organization that could be watched and controlled.

Forty-nine days after the Armistice was signed between the Allies and Germany on November 11, 1918, an angry telegram was sent by the editor in chief of the Newspaper Enterprise Association, S. T. Hughes, to Secretary of War Newton D. Baker. It expressed outrage over the government's confiscation of poet and biographer Carl Sandburg's notebooks and manuscripts, a step that would begin his thirty-one-page file. Hughes told Secretary Baker that "our staff correspondent Carl Sandburg returning from Sweden has been held up by the customs military naval and secret service authorities in New York and all of the property of the Newspaper Enterprise Association taken from him. This property consisted of notebooks and manuscripts which he had gathered in a neutral country for this organization. Much of it referred to Finland and to Bolshevism in Russia and it was gathered for the purpose of publishing such of it as seemed proper in our judgement. Is it the purpose of the Government to seize and search a reputable correspondent of a reputable news organization upon his return to United States from any country on earth and also to censor and confiscate and prevent publication of news material brought to this country for a reputable news organization by a reputable correspondent?''

The answer, of course, was yes, although Secretary Baker, in his reply fifteen days later, didn't quite come out and say so. For the American government, especially the Bureau, the Russian Revolution was a terrible trauma, and neighboring Finland was another dangerous place, even though the short-lived communist people's republic there had been overthrown after a few months.

In Russia, Josef Stalin, beginning his rise to power, was the People's Commissar of Nationalities, and his future rival, Leon Trotsky, had recently spoken of Russians and Americans traveling together ''in the same car, each having the right to alight when so desired''—thus, of course, giving rise to the term ''fellow traveler,'' which would become a term denoting disloyalty in America.

Secretary Baker's letter of reply on January 14, 1919, told Hughes that ''there has been an unavoidable delay in answering your telegram of December 30th, due to the necessity of ascertaining facts in the case of Mr. Sandburg. In reply to your specific inquiry you are advised that the Government has no disposition to subject correspondents to any examinations other than those given to ordinary travelers. It is not understood that you claim for correspondents privileges and immunities superior to those of citizens in general. Mr. Sandburg, in passing the routine examination, declined to inform the government of the source of $10,000 which he carried in drafts, payable to Anteri Nuorteva, the representative in this country of the Finnish revolutionists, and Mr. Nuorteva is equally reticent upon this point. Mr. Sandburg further has admitted that a large portion of the revolutionary literature contained in his baggage and for which he is unable to furnish translations would, if published in the United States, violate the emergency legislation. It is clear that these circumstances, created by Mr. Sandburg himself, have delayed the government in reaching a determination in this case, and caused any inconvenience to which you may have been put. I feel sure that we may rely on your patriotic cooperation in this matter, as in others, pending the translation of the documents and the decision of the United States Attorney who is handling the case.''

Meanwhile, on January 28, 1919, two weeks after Secretary Baker's answer, Sandburg—who would win the Pulitzer Prize later that year for his book of poems *Corn Huskers*—wrote his editor in chief a remarkable letter. He told his boss that ''the authorities have given me one suit case of stuff tho they still hold all Swedish and Norwegian socialist and labor papers, and a mass of Russian pamphlets, books, newspapers, and all my written notes. I'm planning to get back to Cleveland this week and spill all I've got and then see about the rest of the stuff. I have some live ones on hand. A letter of the czarina to her man, her last words to him while he was czar. I will match it for human interest with the wildest confessions of a wife you ever ran.''

His letter continued,

American and British intelligence officers and an assistant district attorney spent three hours asking questions. Sample interrogations and replies:

''Which group do you personally favor, the Liebknecht-Luxemberg [*sic*] Spartacans or the Ebert-Scheidamann [*sic*] government?''

''Well, I can't say I favor either of them.''

''Well, who do you favor? Why are you so reluctant to tell us?''

''If I favor—as you put it—if I favor any one group, it is the Haase-Lebedour Independent Socialist group.''

''That is not answering our questions strictly. As between the Ebert-Scheideman [*sic*] group and the Liebknecht-Luxemberg [*sic*] group, which do you favor?''

''I would answer that question by saying I regard Liebknecht and Rosa Luxemberg [*sic*] as honest fanatics while they lived and martyrs now that they are dead. And I have no other opinion than that Ebert and Scheideman [*sic*] are the same kind of crooks in the present government that they were in the government of the kaiser.''

So it goes.
Carl

The next day, Sandburg's even more outraged editor in chief wrote another letter to the secretary of war, saying, in part: ''. . . All I have to say is that I shall instruct Sandburg to write exactly what he thinks proper as our correspondent and I propose then to print what I please of his writings regardless of all the censors in the country and regardless of all the district attorneys in the country. The trouble is largely that these fellows don't know who Sandburg is. They have learned that he has been a socialist in his earlier days and they think his name is German. He is, in fact, the son of a Scandinavian father and mother; he is himself a veteran of the Spanish-American war; he has been a newspaperman for years on Neg Cochran's Chicago Day Book and Victor Lawson's Chicago Daily News and today the best known critics in America such as Amy Lowell, declare in such magazines as The Outlook and Review of Reviews that Carl Sandburg is America's coming poet. Isn't it fine for the government to treat such a man like a dog of a traitor? . . .''

Nonetheless, the FBI file does confirm the story that Theodore Draper recounts (without access to the file) in his *Roots of American Communism*, in which he concludes that one of Comintern's first couriers to the United States ''had to find an intermediary. By a strange combination of circumstances, his choice fell on the famous American poet and biographer, Carl Sandburg.''

This episode would haunt Sandburg's career and would be used by the FBI as ammunition to attempt to control some of his activities decades later. In 1959, when Sandburg was eighty-one years old, the FBI would try to prevent his going to Russia as part of a cultural exchange group by deciding that ''activities that occurred after the first World War'' would make it ''extremely undesirable to permit him to go to Russia.''

CHAPTER TWO

The Arrival of Hoover

It was against the backdrop of America's April declaration of war against imperial Germany, the impending October Bolshevik revolution, and the continuing IWW conflicts that John Edgar Hoover, only one year out of George Washington University Law School, joined the Department of Justice as a clerk on July 26, 1917. By that time German spies were thought to be everywhere—behind every cabinet, table, chair, and bed in America—and twenty-two-year-old Hoover diligently joined in the search. America was defending itself—an Espionage and Sedition Act had been passed, and a second one would be passed a year later, in 1918, as would more antiradical laws. These laws would punish "disloyal utterances."

During the winter of 1917–1918, Hoover became part of the War Emergency Division's Alien Enemy Bureau; his quickness, eagerness, and efficiency at compiling lists, reports, summaries, and recommendations concerning aliens were immediately noticed by his superiors. More importantly, as Richard Gid Powers writes, this wartime experience "did more than simply give him a foothold in the Justice Department. It accustomed him to using administrative procedures as a substitute for the uncertainties and delays of the legal process. The enemy status of the aliens Hoover supervised had stripped them of the protection of the Constitution, and so he got his first taste of authority under circumstances in which he could disregard the normal constitutional restraints on the power of the state.''

In 1919, the Justice Department's Alien Enemy Bureau was dismantled, even though its modus operandi would be retained for decades. But after the armistice was signed, the Labor Department's Immigration Bureau resumed authorized alien responsibilities.

Hoover was rewarded for his diligent alien work: he was named head of the Antiradical Division, the largest section of the Bureau. He went into battle with his gear in tiptop shape. The ''Red Scare'' and the Palmer Raids—the roundup and deportation of alien radicals during the summer of 1919—had been the Justice Department's response to a bomb explosion at the home of Attorney General A. Mitchell Palmer. Powers reports that by November 1919, Hoover's division ''had completed a classification of over 60,000 'radically inclined' individuals. . . . He organized and trained a team of forty translators, assistants, and readers to monitor 471 radical periodicals published in this country and abroad.'' The Alien Act of 1918, under which ''members of the anarchist classes'' could be expelled from the United States, allowed the Bureau to proceed under a cloud of legitimacy.

Massive strikes all around the country contributed to panic in the nation, and by the fall of 1919, all labor conflict was perceived as a Red plot. The Bureau saw this as an indication that a great conspiracy was at work against the government. On November 17, 1919, Hoover organized a raid on the Union of Russian Workers headquarters in New York, as well as at branch offices in twelve cities across the country. According to Powers, ''It was at this stage that Hoover began his research on Communism. . . . [His] 1919 studies of Communism were, with little exaggeration, fundamental texts in the evolution of the anticommunism that was American orthodoxy for the next fifty years. . . . A year after the organization of his division, Hoover had at his disposal a Publications Section that scanned 625 papers for information . . . and a card catalog of 200,000 entries on 'various subjects or individuals.' ''

J. Edgar Hoover never changed his first important job description. His experiences with the Justice Department's Alien Enemy Bureau in 1917 were crucial in forming his ideas; that early bent hardened into an attitude. ''With the nation troubled by a vague dread of change,'' Powers writes, ''Hoover had identified the source of evil as those who were different in appearance, culture, and belief . . . despised aliens.'' For Hoover, that meant foreigners; but it would also mean poets, playwrights, novelists, short story writers, essayists, critics, and journalists. They would be just another group of aliens—''alien enemies''—to be watched, rounded up, or controlled. Early in his career, Hoover discovered his most important technique of control—what this book calls ''the power of suspicion,'' what the FBI calls ''the chilling effect,'' and what we all call by a simpler, more universal term: *intimidation.*

During his FBI career, Hoover imitated what he scorned—and feared—and this pattern of behavior became responsible for producing many of his uncompromising points of view. He feared the Soviet Union, yet when he became FBI director in 1924, he ran the Bureau as if it were a Soviet state. He used fear as an ''enforcement technique,'' while chastising the Soviet Union for the identical thing. In 1920, Lenin wrote that it was necessary ''to resort to all sorts of devices, manoeuvres, and illegal methods, to evasion and subterfuge,'' and J. Edgar Hoover applied the very same ''rules'' in running the FBI. Former FBI agent Joseph L. Schott writes in his memoir, *No Left Turns,* that Hoover ''got his ideas about Bureau discipline from the Commonist [*sic*] party.'' (Schott deliberately spelled the name the way his boss pronounced it.)

William Z. Foster, a former chairman of the Communist Party, U.S.A. (CPUSA) once said, ''A Communist Party will be able to perform its duty only if it is organized in the most centralized manner, and only if iron discipline bordering on military discipline prevails in it. . . .'' Iron discipline was the guiding principle of Hoover's FBI, and the director enjoyed running his agency with strict rules, instilling fear in those who worked for him as well as in those Americans he suspected of unpatriotic acts. Agents had to submit to a dress code: dark suits, unobtrusive ties, and white shirts. Former FBI Director Clarence Kelley writes that Hoover's ''compulsion to control was extreme. He, for example, fiercely opposed drinking coffee in the office. There were times when people who were caught drinking coffee in the office were penalized.''

Hoover utilized other Communist party tactics: for instance, the use of code names for individuals, groups, and organizations. He berated Marx for using ''invective, anger and abuse,'' yet Hoover also used these ''weapons.''

Hoover also feared—and envied as well—the power of the writers he decided very early in his career to try to control. He especially envied journalists because of their instantaneous access to print and airwaves, and he often imitated them by contributing many guest columns to their newspapers and magazines, as well as by writing books he—and his Bureau—made sure reached millions of readers.

The Publication Section, founded in 1920, and later known as the Book Review Section, gave Hoover convenient and timely access to what Americans were writing, and offered him the opportunity to monitor the written word and discover writers who should be deemed suspicious. The Publication Section was part of the Domestic Intelligence Division. Its functionaries read books "for the purpose of propaganda analysis." Hoover believed that writers had the potential to become, in his words, "Communist thought-control relay stations" because they were more susceptible to radical propaganda than ordinary people, and more adept at communicating ideas.

Once, to illustrate that some unnamed teacher was a Communist sympathizer, Hoover reported that the teacher had assigned Sinclair Lewis's satirical novel *Babbitt* to his class and had described it as a "masterpiece." Another time, he reported that John Dos Passos's short story "Facing the Chair" dealt with the "framed" trial of Sacco and Vanzetti. The FBI also singled out the following complex line, by poet Robinson Jeffers, as being subversive: ". . . and patriotism has run the world through so many blood-lakes: and we always fall in . . ." J. Edgar Hoover was offended that patriotism could be presented in such a manner, even though Jeffers is expressing disappointment not disloyalty.

The one writer Hoover revered, it seems, was Mark Twain—whose framed autograph hung on the wall of a hallway in his house in Washington, D.C. Hoover also read G-Man and Tarzan comic strips and westerns (which he swapped with President Dwight D. Eisenhower), and his personal library included such advice books as *Are Your Troubles Psychosomatic?, Modern Sex Life, Roses, Eat and Stay Well, Dogs, Health in the Later Years,* and *How to Overcome Nervous Stomach Trouble.*

Excerpts from *The Communist Party of the United States of America: A Handbook for Americans:*

From its very inception, the Communist Party USA has received instructions and directives from Moscow . . . on such important matters as the merger of the Communist Party of America and the Communist Labor Party (1920), combining legal and illegal work (1922), campaign in behalf of political prisoners (1923) . . . trade union activity (1925) . . . removal of *Daily Worker* and party headquarters from Chicago to New York (1926) . . . work among the miners (1929). . . .

There is no doubt that the Communist network holds an attraction for adventurous spirits who thrive on the conspiratorial atmosphere within the party . . . those who have a tendency to rebel against tradition and convention. . . . The Bohemians and the nonconformists of all stripes . . . are naturally attracted to the Communist movement. A Communist writer, who is himself a temperamental coward, will find considerable delight and satisfaction in writing in the columns of the *Daily Worker* resounding and defiant tirades against the monopolies and those in high places in the government.

The party is, in a sense, a vehicle for anyone with an axe to grind, for anyone who has become embittered either by some unfortunate personal or emotional experience . . . a writer without an outlet . . .

—from handbook published by the United States Senate Internal Security Subcommittee, James O. Eastland, Chairman, 1956.

**

SVETLANA ALLILUYEVA:

Really, what can writers do? I mean, what can they do? How can writers be more dangerous than some kind of military people? Well, there can be military plots, all right, people have arms—they are plotting—but why this *constant* persecution against writers and poets and artists? Because it's the hatred! Hatred of those who can't do that—so they hate others who are creative. I think it's been that way for centuries. It has been done in Russia for more than a century—much earlier than that. There were always files against writers in the Soviet Union. Even in the time of Pushkin. God, so long ago! And there was no Marxism, no communism, no fascism—nothing of that. But there were always writers and poets suspected of being disloyal.

You see, it has something to do with the fact the human nature doesn't change. The ideas change, and social phenomena change, but human nature remains the same. And this surveillance over other people is based on fear. And on hatred. Hatred of a mediocre bureaucracy toward creative people. What are they creating there? We don't understand! We don't know! Why are they doing that? It is fear and hatred and envy. And it is one thousand years old.

Well, first I thought, that project—the FBI and its files on writers—what does it have to do with me? Or why should I be interested? I don't care, you know, if there are files on writers or not. But then I thought that it really is not a separate question. It is something that exists not only here, in America, not only in fascist Germany, and not only in the Soviet Russia these days, but it existed long ago in Old Russia, in the early nineteenth century—when there was no Marxism, no Nazis, and no FBI.

But artists and writers and poets were supervised anyway, probably by more primitive methods. I think somebody was just reading their papers—there couldn't have been electronic things. But I think their mail was checked and their homes were checked. Because of the fear of free-thinking! It was dangerous that artists, poets, and writers think what they want and not what they should!

Probably the FBI is looking for Communists and the Soviet KGB is looking for some sort of Western penetration—I don't know—anti-Soviet ideas. But actually, they are looking for freethinking! It's very sad because they can't admit they are afraid of it. The government and police aren't concerned about the importance of *ideas,* but it's the freethinking *people*—that's the dreadful thing. The freethinkers are like a mysterious force, and that is why the police are always chasing them and watching them and bugging them and getting into their private papers and all that.

You can't get files on writers or anybody in Russia, it would never be made public. Even ten or twenty years later they wouldn't give it to you.

Because there is no information in Russia, there is no source of knowing anything from the press. Gossip is very powerful because it's the only way you hear anything. Word of mouth. Sometimes it's true and sometimes not. But people listen anyway. How it works in America I really don't know. But I think I gossiped when I lived in Russia and I knew literary circles well. I knew what to gossip about; here, in America, I simply don't know too many people. You have to know your subject to be able to gossip.

In Russia I think people would be scared to be taped in an interview. They would be scared to do that because it could be printed or published. In Russia it never comes out in print, it remains in the domain of the spoken word—word of mouth. People might say anything, but then say, "Oh, don't quote me," you know, or "Don't write it down."

I've accepted America with open arms, but they can't forget who my father is. Maybe they'll look further and see that I have a mother, too. Everyone wants me to say how happy I was in America. Well I was, in a way, but in a way I was not. And that was one of the things—I lost my face, I became not what I am.

But I think that the great blessing of America is the variety—you can find anything and anybody. And one of my favorite characters is Georgia O'Keeffe. She certainly was quite unlike anybody else. There was a very good book written about her. And when I think about Americans, somehow certain women come to mind. Like Georgia O'Keeffe—or Bette Davis! I like her very much. She was so strong and *bitchy!* She was never afraid to portray bitchy, unpleasant women—which is good—because usually women are terribly afraid of doing that.

PART TWO

The 1920s:
Undeclared Wars,
the Rise of Fascism,
and the Sacco-
Vanzetti Case

CHAPTER THREE

The Arrival of New Aliens: 1920–1929

In 1920, J. Edgar Hoover changed the name of his Antiradical Division to the General Intelligence Division, or GID. This change marked a broadening of Hoover's literary interests, and he would add the names of many writers to his index, even though not much was collected on any of them until the 1930s.

There were approximately fifteen thousand members of the Communist party in 1920, and later he would write in his best-selling *Masters of Deceit,* "Never has the American Communist movement expressed itself in more revolutionary, violent, and bitter terms than in the early 1920's." J. Edgar Hoover was prepared to fight a party that "in the beginning seemed little more than a freak," but would soon display "complete and unquestioning subservience . . . to Soviet Russia." He would become suspicious of any group or individual that evinced any sign whatever of friendship toward Russia.

Hoover's GID gained momentum from the Immigration Act of 1920, which made it illegal for aliens to belong to or even contribute money to any radical group, or to possess radical literature.

Anarchists Nicola Sacco and Bartolomeo Vanzetti were arrested for murder in 1920, and their trial and legal entanglements would become a cause célèbre and a radicalizing issue for many young writers later.

Daniel Aaron observes in *Writers on the Left* that during the twenties "only a few [writers] dared to join the party. The majority camped on the "intellectual outskirts" of communism as friendly neutrals protected by their liberal labels and functioning as the conscious or unconscious auxiliaries in those numerous committees, groups, leagues against this and that which constitute the party periphery and which permit the leftward liberal to dabble safely in the class struggle." Hoover's agents carefully monitored all those various "committees, groups, leagues against this and that" and placed informants in them whenever they could. The Bureau even had "informants reporting on informants."

But many writers were also apolitical, in keeping with the prevailing cynicism of the postwar years. Many fled to Europe—the expatriates like Hemingway and Fitzgerald (whose *Tales of the Jazz Age* would, of course, become the symbol of the youthful rebellion of the decade). Kay Boyle says, "The recovery of the self was what we were seeking in Paris in the twenties, although we never gave it such a grand-sounding name. Our daily revolt was against literary pretentiousness, against dreary, weary rhetoric, against the worn-out literary convention. We called our protest the revolution of the word. There is no doubt that it was high time that it took place."

On September 5, 1922, the year the Soviet states would merge into the USSR, the Bureau had received from the Department of State a report entitled "Decreasing Influence of Bolshevism." It disclosed that "former adherents" of the cause, such as Eastman and Steffens, "are deserting." The year before, reeling from persecution during the Red Scare, the American Communist party had gone underground, but to J. Edgar Hoover that made it even more of a threat. The secrecy both frustrated and worried him. As he later wrote in *Masters of Deceit*, "Identifying Communists is not easy. They are trained in deceit and trickery and use every form of camouflage and dishonesty to advance their cause."

In 1924, the year Calvin Coolidge—who seemed to epitomize the conservative, provincial, small-town values the young were rebelling against—was elected President, Hoover at last became director of the Bureau. He was appointed by the new attorney general, Harlan Fiske Stone (who had been an opponent of the Palmer Raids), to reform the Bureau and end its police-state tactics and operations. Stone got rid of Hoover's GID and announced that from then on the Bureau was not to be "concerned with political or other opinions of individuals. It is concerned only with their conduct and then only with such conduct as is forbidden by the laws of the United States.''

Twenty-nine-year-old Hoover *did* begin to concentrate his prodigious energies on bona fide criminal investigations—for instance, the Dyer Act of 1919 empowered the Bureau to police the interstate transportation of stolen automobiles. But despite Stone's mandate not to investigate what was on American minds, Hoover never stopped keeping track of American writers.

The year he became the Great Enforcer was also a significant year for the rest of the world; Lenin died, and at his funeral Stalin announced: ''We Communists are people of a special mould.'' Indeed, Stalin, Zinoviev, and Kamenev united against Trotsky later that year. Britain recognized the Soviet Union, sixty-five percent of the Italian electorate supported Mussolini, and the Pan-American treaty to prevent conflicts between nations was signed in 1924, as well.

In 1920, the creator of the Nero Wolfe detective novels, Rex Stout, who was also once chairman of the Writers War Board and president of the Authors Guild and the Authors League, joined the League for Mutual Aid, which had been founded that year to give financial help to ''political prisoners and radical agitators and workers temporarily in distress.'' Bureau agents spotted his name on the letterhead and began his 186-page file. It remained ''dead'' for six years, until 1926, when agents discovered he was a member of the executive board of *The New Masses,* which began that year (two years after *The Liberator* ceased publication). Actually, Stout had resigned when he learned there were Communists on the board of *New Masses,* but this reference would follow him for four decades.

Poet and anthologist Louis Untermeyer's seventy-nine-page file was begun in 1921 when the Bureau discovered Untermeyer's name on the letterhead of *The Liberator,* successor to the old *Masses.* In his autobiography, Untermeyer writes that ''the aims of *The Liberator* were less revolutionary'' than *The Masses,* which was quite true, but the Bureau hardly noticed. The Bureau kept Untermeyer under close scrutiny, noting not only that ''he has a small pot belly,'' but that he ''has been of great help to the Party in raising finances among certain wealthy people who are devoted to him as a personality.'' Untermeyer was not a Communist, but was on the political left, and his file continued until his death. Hoover was determined to prove that Untermeyer was a Communist because a ''highly confidential source'' once told him in

1951 that he was—despite Untermeyer's statement that he was "un-equivocally opposed to communism."

In 1922, the year Mussolini marched on Rome to begin his fascist government, the fifty-five-page file on editor and writer H. L. Mencken was opened. Mencken, whose book *The American Language* made him the leading authority on American English, drew the Bureau's attention on October 14 because of an "alleged" interview with the German crown prince Friedrich Wilhelm, who was in exile in Holland. This interview, which appeared in the *Baltimore Sun* four days earlier—on October 10, 1922—was evidence, according to the Bureau, that "Germany is planning still to regain the power she had prior to 1914, with sinister motives regarding America."

J. Edgar Hoover, fresh from investigating German aliens in World War I, thought that Mencken might be a spy. However, the file later states that although during World War I Mencken "was deemed by some to be a suspicious person and information was received that he was of pro-German sympathies . . . he was not involved in espionage activities."

In 1919, Mencken and drama critic George Jean Nathan had started a monthly column entitled "Repetition Generale" in *Smart Set* magazine, which they coedited. Their biting editorial comment hit hard, and as Carl Dolmetsch writes in his history of the magazine, "Its overriding theme was simply that America was one great human comedy and that humor was the intelligent man's only defense. . . ." Most of the column was written by Mencken, although Nathan contributed from time to time, but both editors always signed the feature, which lasted until they founded *American Mercury* in 1924.

Two years before Hoover would become director, "Repetition Generals" [*sic*] "was read by [Director] William J. Burns, September 22, 1922," and because he did not like or appreciate what he read, a fifteen-page file was started on George Jean Nathan.

The selection that offended Director Burns concerned Prohibition, which had been established in 1919 by the Eighteenth Amendment to the Constitution. Nathan and Mencken wrote that "the fact that a Prohibition enforcement officer is universally regarded in America as a licensed blackmailer and scoundrel, even when he shows all the outward signs of integrity, is due to a sound instinct in the common people. They sense the plain fact that his business is unescapably anti-social—that it is, in fact, quite as anti-social as that of the porch-climber, pickpocket or private detective. Decorating him with a badge and a pad of black warrants doesn't change him in the slightest. He is intrinsically a criminal, and before many moons have waxed and waned mob justice will begin to deal with him as such.''

Perceiving a genuine threat to "enforcement officers" instead of seeing that Nathan and Mencken were poking fun at them, the Bureau began an investigation of Nathan, even though, if it had been an actual threat to Prohibition, the Bureau had no authority to protect it until 1930, when the Prohibition Bureau became part of the Department of Justice. But calling an "enforcement officer" a "criminal" and then predicting "mob violence" against him was the FBI's only interest, of course, not Prohibition per se.

In 1923, when the CPUSA had close to thirteen thousand members, and had emerged after two years underground, the Bureau began a file on poet Edna St. Vincent Millay.

Bureau agents found her name among those entered in a "Free Trip to Russia" contest sponsored by the Friends of Soviet Russia, which at the time was trying to raise $40,000 to buy tractors for Soviet peasants. Her ninety-four-page file remained "dead" for a decade (when, among other things, it was reported that "Miss Millay used the analogy of the mole boring under the garden in her exposition of the alien menace"). There were no reports of her connection with Sacco and Vanzetti's defense. H. L. Mencken was a leading member of the Sacco and Vanzetti Defense Committee, but there is nothing in his file concerning this affiliation, evidence of the Justice Department's early reluctance to get involved with the case because, as Richard Gid Powers writes, it "saw nothing to gain in continuing its antiradical campaign after the collapse of the Red Scare."

It was not until 1927 that the Bureau finally recognized that the case was a watershed—the radicalizing issue of the 1920s—and that raiding the list of supporters who crusaded for the men until the bitter end was a productive way of adding new "aliens" to the index. Katherine Anne Porter's eleven-page file was begun after agents discovered her name listed in a 1927 newspaper article describing a telegram that the Citizens National Committee for Sacco and Vanzetti had sent to President Coolidge requesting that he intervene and stay the execution of the two anarchists. Another writer whose support for Sacco and Vanzetti brought her into the files was the illustrious wit Dorothy Parker. In 1927, Parker was a book reviewer at *The New Yorker* and was part of the famous Algonquin Hotel literary Round Table, along with Robert

E. Sherwood, Robert Benchley, George S. Kaufman, and Alexander Woollcott. Agents discovered that she and John Dos Passos had been jailed "because of a demonstration in which they were involved protesting the execution of Sacco Vanzetti [sic]."

When a high school student writing a term paper on Parker wrote to J. Edgar Hoover in 1965 to ask if the author and critic was ever a Communist, the Director told the student that "FBI files are confidential," thus indirectly telling the student that a file did exist, since he didn't say Parker had no file at the Bureau. Hoover also sent the student a list of subversive organizations, as well as an assortment of articles with such titles as "Communism—the Incredible Swindle" and "What Young People Should Know About Communism." These unsolicited enclosures may have seemed to this high school student that the answer to her question "Was Dorothy Parker a Communist?" was a resounding "yes."

"Probably December, 1928," according to the record, an unidentified informant sent a circular to the Bureau announcing that "The Letters of Sacco and Vanzetti," published by the Viking Press, was "sponsored by an international committee, of which Sinclair Lewis was a member." But Lewis's name had been indexed five years earlier, in 1923, the year of the Teapot Dome oil fields scandal hearings. Hoover was still one year away from becoming director of the Bureau, but his influence was growing steadily. Agents not only continued scanning lists searching for new "aliens," but increasingly, the many informants on the payroll told the Bureau where to look for them as well. On April 30, 1923, an informant reported that "Sinclair Lewis was one of the original organizers of The Penguin Club, a literary and artists club," opening his 150-page file. In 1929, which was just one year before Lewis would win the Nobel Prize, the Bureau reported that he had published a pamphlet on labor that said there was only "one answer on the part of workers—a militant and universal organization of trade unions." The Bureau also discovered his name on another list that year, this time on the book committee of the American Society for Cultural Relations with Russia.

Daniel Aaron comments in *Writers on the Left* that John Dos Passos was "an observer rather than a joiner, never belonged to the Communist Party, never organized a strike, never fought in Spain, but he watched these events with his own eyes."

To the Bureau, however, that was close enough. In 1923, his eighty-two-page file was started because his name was listed on the letterhead of the American Committee for Relief of Russian Children. From that time on, until 1974, four years after his death, over one hundred items concerning the activities of the author of *Manhattan Transfer, USA,* and *The Big Money* were collected.

Was he ever a communist? In 1937 the FBI "reliably reported" that he was "close to Communist Party Headquarters in New York City." Contrary to what biographers and historians have maintained, Howard Fast said in 1988 that "Dos Passos was known as a member of the Communist Party until he turned against the party. When he wrote *USA,* he was a member."

On June 3, 1952, Dos Passos, who had by then moved to the far right, described his radical curriculum vitae in the 1920s to two FBI agents: "At the outset of the interview, Dos Passos informed that he was never a member of the Communist Party, although he related that he had close associations with the Communist Party at various times. He pointed out that inasmuch as he was never a member . . . he was not in a position to definitely state that a person was a Communist. . . . He declared that the first time he came into contact with the Communist Party was during 1924 and 1925, at which time he was vitally interested in the defense of Sacco and Vanzetti. He pointed out that as a writer he was interested in seeing that the true facts concerning the Sacco Vanzetti case appeared in the newspaper and since 'the Daily Worker' was the only publication which appeared desirous of printing the true facts in this case he became closely associated. . . . Dos Passos further related that he was interested in the reorganizing of the 'Old Masses' which went out of existence during World War One and had been sponsored by John Reed and Max Eastman. He declared that in 1922 or 1923 when the New Masses was re-organized they had no idea of affiliating with any political party and the theory behind the magazine was to make it 'a native American thing.' . . .

"He remarked that he had been to Russia . . . in the fall of 1921 at about the time the Soviets took over. He claimed that he was traveling at this time as a tourist and was attracted to the country. . . . He recalled that in the spring of 1929 he went to Russia to study the Russian theatre. . . . Concerning various front organizations organized during this period such as the American Committee for Relief of Russian Children, Dos Passos claimed that he could not recall specifically this organization but he did lend his name . . . because he was interested in cementing relations with the Soviet Union and seeing that the Soviet Union was recognized. . . . He pointed out, however, that there were occasions when his name was used without his authorization. . . . During the interview Dos Passos appeared to be cooperative but was hazy concerning details. . . .''

The Bureau started a file on its first Nobel Prize winner, playwright Eugene Gladstone O'Neill, ''in the early part of 1917,'' the same year his one-act play, *The Long Voyage Home,* was being staged in Provincetown, Massachusetts.

The Bureau believed that ''O'Niel'' (as it was spelled in the report) and a friend, ''Harold DePolo,'' might be ''espionage suspects'' because ''some person alleged that he had seen them in the vicinity of the Provincetown lighthouse.'' The document reveals that ''they were released, there being no foundation for any charge.''

However, once suspicious, the Bureau remained vigilant, and two years later, in 1919, the year President Woodrow Wilson won *his* Nobel Prize, the Bureau noted that ''one E. O'Neil'' (as the agents tried spelling it this time) was an associate editor of a little magazine *The Pagan.*

Both of these references—the one in 1917 and the one in 1919—are included in a confusing April 22, 1924, report entitled ''Memorandum in R. E. Eugene O'Neil''[*sic*]. There is no identifying data on the memo—to whom or from whom it was sent or why—other than a stamped date reading ''Bureau of Investigation May 6, 1924.'' There is also a reference in the memo to a previous memorandum that is not included in O'Neill's short, two-page file; one unidentified person informs another that ''The play referred to in your memorandum I believe is entitled 'All God's Chillun Have Wings' [*sic*]. My recollection is that it was never produced owing to the notoriety the incident you refer to received in various publications.''

The play is, of course, *All God's Chillun* Got *Wings,* and contrary to the Bureau's memory (or wish), it was produced—the very same year as the mysterious memo about the playwright. The rest of this memo points out that ''Eugene O'Neil [*sic*] is a well known playwright. He is the son of the late James O'Neil [*sic*], the noted tragedian who played in 'The Count of Monte Cristo' for many years. I believe he is a Harvard graduate. He has written several plays that have achieved world wide notice, among them being 'The Emperor Jones', 'Beyond the Horizon', 'The Moon of the Caribees' [*sic*], 'The Hairy Ape', 'Anna Christie', etc. He has produced two plays this year; one of them 'Welded', and the other a dramatized version of 'The Rhyme [*sic*] of the Ancient Mariner.' Both of the latter two have been failures. The central figure of 'The Emperor Jones' is a negro, this seeming to be a favorite theme of O'Neil's. O'Neil's plays have been produced by the Provincetown Players and the McDougall [*sic*] Street Players, as well as on Broadway. 'Anna Christie' has been produced abroad. 'The Hairy Ape' could easily lend itself to radical propaganda, and it is somewhat surprising that it has not already been used for this purpose. It possesses more inferential grounds for radical theories than 'R.U.R.' by Karel Capek, which has lately been adopted by the radical fraternity.''

There can be little doubt that in this 1924 document, the FBI reveals its intended role as a police force against writers. Yet despite this evidence of intent, the FBI collected very little information about O'Neill, so we have to conclude that he was not considered a threat to the republic.

However, the object of the file was not to police O'Neill in any sustained way; rather, it was to produce a cumulative effect within the FBI. In other words, the more the Bureau learned about "writing that could easily lend itself to radical propaganda," or writing with "negro themes," the better it could discern dangerous tendencies in the other writers. O'Neill's file crossed an invisible boundary; it shows the FBI entering the terrain of a writer's *mind* and finding danger in the art and ideas that mind produced, apart from any criminal acts. With O'Neill, as with other writers, the FBI's purpose was simply to be on the alert for ideas that could threaten J. Edgar Hoover's notion of what was best for the nation.

"The Negro radicals held their usual meeting . . . all of them picture a Soviet America similar to Russia," an agent wrote in his 1920 report to Hoover entitled Negro Activities. It is not known when Hoover's personal belief that racial unrest could be equated with Communist agitation began, but Richard Gid Powers writes that Hoover had "a racial hostility so strong it could overwhelm any sense of fairness or justice," and that he held "the dangerous conviction that Communist agitation, and not the objective racial situation, was the cause of unrest among American Blacks." (Of course, the *Bureau's* attitude toward this matter was first seen in 1917, according to the file of Jack London.)

In 1925, five years after that 1920 report, the Bureau discovered that Langston Hughes, whom they later would demean with the title "Negro pornographic poet," had belonged to a group called the All America Anti-Imperialist League when he was working as a busboy for a Washington, D.C., hotel. This reference began the poet's 559-page file, the same year Hoover was finally successful in imprisoning Marcus Garvey, the Jamaican-born black nationalist he had begun to investigate in 1919. As Powers writes, "The desire to destroy Garvey as a black leader came first, the search for a crime came later."

Garvey had founded the Universal Negro Improvement Association—with branches all over the United States—and his many ideas (he urged blacks to accept a black deity) were repugnant to Hoover. Garvey was eventually indicted for fraud involving the Black Star Steamship Line, which he owned. He was sent to prison until his deportation in 1927.

In a 1941 report in Hughes's file, the FBI says that "United Negro movements began in 1920 under Communist supervision." The Communist party did take on black rights as a cause, but not until 1928. When Langston Hughes became president of the National Negro Congress in 1930, the Bureau called it "an official Communist subsidiary."

In 1933, a confidential informant told the Bureau he "had loaned" Langston Hughes "a pamphlet entitled "An Election Appeal to the Negro Voter," and still another confidential informant told the Bureau that Hughes "admired the Soviet system for its non-race prejudice [*sic*]."

The following year, in 1934, the FBI reported that Hughes was on the National Committee of the American League Against War and Fascism, and three years later, now calling Hughes an "alleged poet," the Bureau reported more "Communist front" activities, noting that "Negroes are growing in international consciousness."

AMIRI BARAKA:
If the FBI's going to call Langston Hughes a "Negro pornographic poet," what can you expect? Now, when you see *that* kind of antagonism, I know Hoover's sick.

Langston used to put me down all the time for using dirty words. Like my father: "LeRoi, why do you want to use bad language?" The only thing you ever find in Langston is a "hell" or a "damn." You aren't going to find nothing else—definitely not pornography. Whose pornographic mind does the FBI have in mind? "Negro pornographic poet"! And that's a description of our greatest poet.

Langston is saying the same thing the people want to say, only he can say it better. And that's why the FBI is opposed to writers—because they're saying the same thing people feel—only the writers can say it better.

**

"Wears glasses, Jewish appearing features" is how the Bureau described playwright Elmer Rice, whose file was started in 1925 when agents discovered his name on an advance letterhead of *The New Masses.* As William Preston, Jr., writes in *Aliens and Dissenters,* during the twenties anti-Semitism was part of "the general atmosphere of hate that was directed more specifically against aliens." Hoover was concerned about close-knit groups of any kind and was particularly worried that Jewish intellectuals would be susceptible to Communist propaganda, especially since his Bureau had reported that "Moscow" sent its propaganda literature to, among other places, "the Union of Jewish Authors and Propagandists," and "The Jewish Workers' Revolutionary Theatre."

The columnist George Sokolsky had once called Hoover's attention to an article by Michael Blankford called "The Education of a Jew," which said that for many Jews, Marxism had replaced religion. Hoover admired the article, which also said that "Judaism must reject Communism because Communism is ready to sacrifice more to attain its ends." In fact, Hoover was so pleased with the article that he invited Blankford to become an FBI informant. There is no indication in the file if Blankford ever accepted.

It is possible to trace the Bureau's attitude toward Jews in other files as well. For instance, journalist Drew Pearson's file contains a memo indicating that information "from a reliable source" that his cowriter Robert Allen's "true name" is "Ginsberg" should be used in a derogatory manner.

Among the organizations Hoover—who referred to the clock in the dining room of his house as a "Jewish bronze clock"—felt were "Communist types" were the American Committee of Jewish Writers, which the FBI called "A Communist front for racial agitation" and a "money-collecting media, [*sic*]" and the American Jewish Congress, which the FBI considered one of "the special political organizing centers for the racial minority they pretend to champion."

In 1929, the year Elmer Rice's *Street Scene* won a Pulitzer Prize, the Bureau noted that he changed his name "from Elmer Leopold Reizenstein and that he had never to that time voted in any election." From 1929 on, the Bureau referred to the playwright—described as "a trifle to the Left, recently a liberal, never orthodox in his radicalism"—as "Elmer Rice, with aliases."

Although the Bureau eventually reported that Rice was "inclined more toward those who have renounced the revolutionary attitude in favor of one more moderate to our native tradition," they continued to check his activities, noting that in 1932 he was "one of the supporters of an injunction to prevent interference with the Hunger March to Washington,'' and that two years later, in 1934, he told some students at Columbia University that ''Russia is the only place where the theatre is really important.''

ELMER RICE:

Politically, I have always been left wing. I won't say Communist. Communist is amorphous. No Communist is capable of too elastic a definition. But I have been a Socialist since I was seventeen or eighteen years of age. Not a member of the party, you understand, but a Socialist.

I have a friend who went to see his aunt and found she had discharged her maid. "She was a Communist," the old lady explained. "How do you know?" asked my friend. "Well," the old lady told me, "she was rude to me and if that is not being a Communist, what is?"

—From the *New York Journal-American*
December 17, 1938
as reported in his FBI file

**

As the twenties headed toward the stock market crash of October 24, 1929, Hoover moved toward the goal of making his Bureau family complete.

In 1928, Clyde Tolson joined the Bureau. His application had stated ''applicant's experience in the office of the Secretary of War would appear to be an asset to him in the work of the Bureau.'' Clyde Tolson's personnel file has 1,720 pages and spans from 1928 until his death in 1975. It contains his original Bureau job application—where Secretary of War Baker describes him as ''a capable and efficient stenographer, and of good reputation and habits''—and holds his fingerprints, as well as salary information and copies of all his office memos.

''Just the slugger at his best,'' Hoover once wrote in the margin of a memo praising a radio broadcast Tolson made. Tolson, aka ''the Killer,'' was especially at his best when performing duties Hoover could trust to no one else. As associate director of the FBI, he was the hatchet man.

In time, Tolson and Hoover went to and from work together, ate all their meals together, and were never out of one another's presence or thoughts. Even in official FBI letters, Hoover would write ''Clyde joins me in sending our best wishes to you.'' Columnist Walter Winchell would address his letters ''To Mr. Hoover and Clyde.'' They even took vacations together. The two men had what Richard Gid

Powers calls a "spousal relationship" and what former FBI Director
Clarence Kelley calls a "mentor-protégé relationship."

In his personal life, Hoover seemed to imitate what he scorned and
feared—homosexuality. He was obsessed by any suggestion of it being
in his own life—as well as in the lives of others—and kept a record of
all such rumors regarding himself and other prominent officials. His
Official and Confidential files are filled with such items as a 1944
"rumor to the effect Hoover was 'queer.' " Next to this piece of
intelligence, the Director wrote, "I never heard of this obvious de-
generate. Only one with a depraved mind could have such thoughts."

In 1925, Hoover had begun isolating from his Bureau's general files
certain derogatory information on important people; he kept this very
special material in the privacy of his office—a suite that contained nine
offices and a reception room. "Those files were not kept in Central
files," says former number three man under Hoover, Cartha DeLoach,
"because any clerk who had access to them might go out and gossip."

Hoover also started an "Obscene file" in 1925, which, according to
Athan G. Theoharis and John Stuart Cox in their book *The Boss,*
"contained, principally, printed pornographic literature, the publication of which might in extreme cases be adjudged a federal offense."
Eventually, the "Obscene file" became the excuse—and offered the
opportunity—to pass on gossip, primarily of a sexual nature, about
prominent people, and Hoover was able to use this file as a "cover"
for his own private interests, as well. Theoharis and Cox write that
Hoover "identified political radicalism with filth and licentiousness,
neither of which ever failed to arouse in him almost hysterical
loathing."

PART THREE

The Spanish Civil War

CHAPTER FOUR
Images in Their Minds

Alfred Kazin writes in *On Native Ground,* ''The appeal of Marxism to writers in the thirties was rarely founded upon their conscious and intelligent acceptance of it as a doctrine; rather it found converts and stimulated zeal by setting up an image in their minds, by giving their thinking a new sense of order and their everyday lives the excitement of a liberation. It did not always produce the sense of incipient revolution that it did in the mind of the European working class up to the First World War; but it did give them an indefinable yet inexhaustible assurance of the significance of their thought, an assurance of their function as intellectuals; and that was enough.''

The FBI could never understand the attraction communism had for so many writers in the depths of the Depression in the early 1930s. To those who ''went left,'' Marxism offered a solid diagnosis of the economic malaise and a program for action, in contrast to the futility of two mainstream political parties. It also provided a quasi-religious faith or a cause, an ideology of solidarity with the dispossessed in the struggle for social justice. To be sure, for many converts communism was nothing more than a ride on an intellectual Ferris wheel.

Indeed, most intellectuals' infatuation with communism was brief, and their participation in party affairs was minuscule. Few major writers actually joined the Party, and for its part, the Party did not encourage them, at least in the early 1930s. At that time, the CP was suspicious of intellectuals, because it feared it could not control them. They were considered more useful outside the Party, on call, as it were, to adorn a letterhead, chair a committee, swell a protest march, write a sympathetic article.

The case of one of the few prominent literary figures who sought to join the party, the novelist Theodore Dreiser, was typical. His application in 1931 was declined by party leader Earl Browder himself. Although somewhat hurt by the rejection, Dreiser soon became disillusioned with left-wing sectarianism and went his own political way. Sinclair Lewis, known as "Red" in his youth for his socialist ideals as well as for the color of his hair, grew downright hostile to the American comrades and scorned fronts. As he said in 1937, "It's an old trick of the Communists, and a good one, to coax an illustrious innocent to serve as show-window dummy." Ernest Hemingway swung left during the Spanish Civil War, then went his way. Lillian Hellman, who admitted Party membership between 1938 and 1940, was watched by the Bureau as early as 1933 because she belonged to a John Reed Club in New York. Poet Muriel Rukeyser's name first attracted the Bureau's attention in 1932 when she was a nineteen-year-old student who "took two courses, one entitled *The Revolutionary Spirit in Literature* and another entitled *The History of International Sociology,* at the Rand School of Social Sciences, which has a reputation of being communistically inclined." So it went. As Daniel Aaron comments in *Writers on the Left,* "The strongest writers of the thirties used politics and were not used by it. The party could not have dictated to a Dos Passos, a Hemingway, a Lewis, a Dreiser, a Steinbeck, a Wolfe even if it had tried to do so." Yet Lewis as well as Dreiser, not to mention Dos Passos, Hemingway, Steinbeck, and Wolfe all had FBI files. Hoover and his agents did not recognize degrees of commitment, or even hostility, as in Lewis's case. The Bureau kept files on everyone connected to the Party, or one of its auxiliaries, no matter how weak the tie. A majority of writers were instinctively liberal in their politics, and most of them joined a "front" or supported or contributed to it or signed a petition in behalf of a cause supported by the Communist party, and their names were indexed and a file accumulated.

Such fronts as the National Committee for the Defense of Political Prisoners or the League of American Writers had been founded by the Party and were dominated by a Communist "fraction," according to the Bureau. As Maurice Isserman writes in *Which Side Were You On?*, "In the classic pattern, front organizations had a well-known but relatively inactive non-Communist president, and an obscure but extremely hard-working Communist executive-secretary." But, as Isserman points out, "The 'innocents' who filled out membership rolls had their own purposes for joining, and proved quite resistant to Communist efforts to change organizational priorities in mid stream."

Still, many Americans worried about a revolution, and conservatives pressed for laws to deal with the Red menace. In 1930, Hoover appeared before a special House committee chaired by Hamilton Fish of New York that was looking into Communist activities, and his testimony convinced the members to urge legislation that not only would create a new division within the Bureau to investigate revolutionary activity, but would forbid Communists from utilizing the U.S. Postal Service. But, as Kenneth O'Reilly writes in *Hoover and the Un-Americans*, "None of the Fish Committee's proposals were enacted. Even Hoover opposed the recommendation that Congress grant the Bureau of Investigation formal authority to investigate subversive activities."

The lack of a firm statute or official sanction had never really stopped Hoover from gathering information he believed was essential; in fact, he preferred to work in secrecy. Nonetheless, because he was also a careful bureaucrat, he wanted to be perceived as someone who acted under the law. Eventually, he would receive the authority he needed from the most liberal American president in history.

On March 4, 1933, Franklin Delano Roosevelt, who promised a New Deal for the American people, was inaugurated as the thirty-second President of the United States. His advent marked the beginning of a new deal for the FBI. The following year the President issued an executive order giving the Bureau authority to track the U.S. Nazi movement. Then, in 1936, and again in 1938, the President issued secret oral instructions to Hoover to investigate *all* subversive activities, including communism.

In 1959 Hoover would write, "On September 6, 1939, the President of the United States directed the FBI to take charge of investigative work in matters relating to espionage, subversive activities and other related matters." Hoover knew how to keep a secret and he had kept the secret of FDR's confidential order well.

Although FDR the politician might court the far left, including the Communist party, especially during its Popular Front phase in the mid-1930s when it supported the New Deal and other progressive causes and groups, he was not averse to secret initiatives against radicals. As early as 1919, when he was assistant secretary of the navy, he sent Attorney General A. Mitchell Palmer "a confidential report on a speech of Max Eastman at Seattle"—the quote is contained in a document in Eastman's file—and expressed the hope that Palmer would find it useful in his "investigations." FDR's report told Palmer that "revolutionary literature is now printed by the tons in English and foreign languages, the majority of it in Chicago and New York. . . . The injustice of our present government is strongly pointed out . . . and the beautiful ideals of Bolshevism and I.W.W. are painted in the brightest of colors. . . ."

As an early foe of Nazism, to his undying credit, Roosevelt sought to curb its spread to the United States. But he was not finicky about the means used. David Wise writes in *The American Police State* that "Roosevelt used the Nazi threat to justify illegal wiretapping by the government. This was the beginning. . . . He directed that the tapping be limited as far as possible to aliens, and there is no indication that he expected the practice to continue after the war." He probably did not foresee that it would be used against Hoover's brand of "aliens"—writers.

As the political situation in Europe grew more ominous, the President authorized more drastic measures. As he said in one of his famous public fireside chats, "When you see a rattlesnake poised to strike, you do not wait until he has struck before you crush him." William C. Sullivan, who served as an assistant FBI director under Hoover, comments: "Such a very great man as Franklin D. Roosevelt saw nothing wrong in asking the FBI to investigate those opposing his lend-lease policy—a purely political request. He also had us look into the activities of others who opposed our entrance into World War II, just as later administrations had the FBI look into those opposing the conflict in Vietnam. It was a political request also when he [FDR] instructed us to put a telephone tap, a microphone, and a physical surveillance on an internationally known leader of his administration. It was done. The results he wanted were secured and given to him. Certain records of this kind . . . were not then or later put into the regular FBI filing system. Rather, they were deliberately kept out of it."

Cartha DeLoach says, "A complete review of the FBI files would reflect the fact that President Roosevelt used the FBI far more than any other President—and for things that were *not* within our jurisdiction."

Paradoxically, although J. Edgar Hoover owed his increased authority to Roosevelt, he never liked or trusted the President, whose policies were too liberal for his taste, or the First Lady, whom he considered even more liberal than the President. Roy Cohn recalled, "Mr. Hoover and the FBI always regarded Eleanor Roosevelt as the leader of the left-wing thought movement in the United States." Cartha DeLoach comments that the Director also regarded her as "a somewhat sad social butterfly."

According to Sullivan, in 1936, "Hoover got the idea that he should run for President against FDR. . . . He thought that if he had the support of the entire law enforcement community . . . he could run as a Republican and turn Roosevelt and his crew of liberals out of office. He sent . . . some of his most trusted veteran agents . . . on a top secret mission to test the political waters. . . . Much to Hoover's surprise, the response to his presidential ambitions was overwhelmingly negative . . . when he learned the results of his informal poll, he never again mentioned running for President." Some would say he didn't need the job. Armed with the authority conferred on him by Roosevelt, he had acquired enough power for any man.

The number of files on writers increased after 1935. Out of a total of sixty-four files begun on writers in the 1930s, almost half were opened after 1935. Hoover's general files grew as well, including his ultrasecret Official and Confidential files, which were kept in the privacy of his office. In 1937 he also began compiling a "Congressional" file, keeping in it such things as threats against members of Congress, but including in addition such information as that an unnamed member "was having an affair with a woman" and therefore an allegation that he was a homosexual was "unfounded."

There are five U.S. Presidents with "O and C" files: Roosevelt, Eisenhower, Kennedy, Johnson, and Nixon. In 1937, a file on "Nixon, Richard M." of Whittier, California, was opened. It contains, according to the summary, "investigation re Nixon and follow-up correspondence from interested parties asking why he was not appointed to the FBI." It is by now common knowledge that Nixon's application to become an FBI agent was rejected, and the O and C summary confirms this fact; nonetheless, Cartha DeLoach insists that "he wasn't turned down, he was accepted, and *he* turned it down."

In 1937, Hoover also began an O and C file entitled "Wiretapping, Use of in FBI."

In the files opened during this period, one often sees the far-left political activities of writers ignored in the early 1930s while the tamer liberalism of their later years was scrupulously chronicled. The file of literary critic Edmund Wilson was not opened until 1946, although he was most active in Communist causes at the beginning of the thirties. Another example is the critic and novelist Lionel Trilling, whose file was opened in 1937. When his widow, writer and critic Diana Trilling, was apprised of this years later, her reaction was: "Why as late as that? Why not in '32, in '33? That's very stupid of them. He was a member of the National Committee for [the Defense of] Political Prisoners. Nineteen thirty-two–thirty-three was the period of his most ardent commitment, although he was never a member of the Communist party. He was a fellow traveler."

One of J. Edgar Hoover's most useful aids to compiling his files was a book published in 1934, *The Red Network,* by Elizabeth Dilling, described by Richard Gid Powers as a "compilation of rumors." *The Red Network* recklessly accused more than thirteen hundred people, including Eleanor Roosevelt, Mahatma Gandhi, Albert Einstein, and Sigmund Freud (described as a "sex psychoanalyst" who "says religious ideas are illusions"), and five hundred organizations of being a part of an international Communist conspiracy.

Most historians contend that Hoover did not pay much attention to *The Red Network* (they believed that he understood how intellectually polluted the material was), but its findings are, in fact, liberally peppered throughout the writers' files. In many files, the language of Dilling's book is used, word for word. Novelist Josephine Herbst's file indicates that the book had been checked to see if she was listed, which she is, along with Fannie Hurst, Malcolm Cowley, Sidney Hook, Edmund Wilson, and Stanley Burnshaw. Burnshaw's entry says, "A Communist poet and author, *New Masses* staff, 1933." Burnshaw was on the *Masses* staff, but he was never a Communist party member. In Lillian Hellman's file, information from the book is attributed to a "confidential source." And Hellman, herself, is not in Dilling's book. In Dashiell Hammett's file, the entire book is reproduced, though Hammett is also not listed in it.

The lodestar of the decade was the Spanish Civil War, which began in July 1936 and galvanized American intellectuals. "Spain was the passion of our generation," says Howard Fast. "This was a great conflict, where fascism could be stopped. I guess every writer of the time was deeply moved by Spain. No doubt about it."

Most of them who were on the left supported the Loyalist or Republican side, a loose alliance of liberals, anarchists, Socialists and Communists, against the right-wing Nationalists, which represented military leaders, landed aristocracy, Catholics and the fascist Falange party. In starker terms the war pitted the Left against the Right, socialism against fascism. More than 2,800 Americans volunteered to fight in the Abraham Lincoln Brigade on the side of the Loyalists.

To the FBI anyone who supported the Loyalist side was automatically suspect. Those who signed petitions, contributed funds, attended banquets, joined organizations devoted to the cause were indexed. Pearl S. Buck, the 1938 Nobel Prize–winning novelist, author of *The Good Earth* and other best-selling books, and certainly no radical, had her file opened in 1937 after she attended a dinner in support of the Loyalists. And in the file of novelist Edna Ferber, popular author of *Show Boat, Cimarron,* and other novels, beside a mention that she belonged to a committee to help the Loyalists, appears a handwritten notation "Writers Spain," indicating that the bureau had come up with a helpful formula: writer + Spain = Communist.

During the years the FBI was monitoring Communists and their "dupes," it was also on the *qui vive* for spies. Espionage had always, of course, been a staple item in its investigative storehouse, but now there were Nazi and Communist spies out there, and anyone suspected of sympathizing with either of those philosophies was potentially a spy. Occasionally, though, an innocent writer got caught in the gears. What made writers particularly vulnerable was the fact that they wrote books. What was so suspicious about that? It seems that spies sometimes devise codes keyed to certain pages and lines of a previously agreed-upon title. Howard Fast, whose 1944 novel *Freedom Road* was suspected of being a code book, explains: "*Any* book could become a code book. . . . There's a pattern to the use of certain words. Suppose you want a word that's on page thirty-one, fifth line. So your code for that word can be 31-5. . . . A code based on a code book cannot be broken unless the person can decide which of the million books that exist *is* the code book." As for his own novel being one, Fast, a former CP member, says, "The FBI's totally crazy! Who are we having codes with? Russia?" Cartha DeLoach says Steinbeck's *Grapes of Wrath* "was used as a code book in some espionage cases—not written purposely for that, but *used.*"

Another victim of guilt by authorship (and a posthumous one at that) was the novelist Thomas Wolfe. In 1944, six years after he died, an item in his file says that a copy of *The Web and the Rock*—"with no visible markings or writing"—was "a possible code book," along with John Dos Passos's *The Big Money, Beards Basic History of the*

United States [*sic*], and a copy of ''Collier's issue of 10/21/44, open at pages 70 and 71, a story of an underground agent of the United States operating in Mexico.''

In 1941 an informant told an FBI agent that a mystery by Rex Stout, *Sisters in Trouble,* might be ''a deliberate attempt to convey a meaning other than the solution of a mystery story . . . note the almost exclusive German cast of characters.'' The cryptic effusions of poets were also considered likely repositories of secret messages.

If the Spanish Civil War was a defining event for politically concerned writers and intellectuals, the Moscow treason trials of 1936–1938 were a severe test of their faith. The trials were based on Stalin's paranoid theory that his old enemy, the exiled Leon Trotsky, was plotting the overthrow of the Soviet state. Trotsky's opposition to Stalin had already caused fissures on the American left. As Harvey Klehr writes in *The Heyday of American Communism,* ''For some radical intellectuals, the Communist party's increasingly moderate policies were as disconcerting as its cultural and literary judgments. More and more of them began to look to the figure of Leon Trotsky. In opposition to Stalin's doctrine of socialism in one country, he had continued to stand for worldwide revolutionary militancy. . . . A handful of distinguished intellectuals had previously dabbled around the fringes of the Trotskyists or been allied with them, including Max Eastman [and] Sidney Hook. . . . But it took Stalin's full assault on Trotsky to rally larger numbers of American intellectuals to his defense.'' The trials polarized American intellectuals; in addition to Eastman and Hook, John Dos Passos, James T. Farrell, and Edmund Wilson took Trotsky's side. Others, such as Granville Hicks, Malcolm Cowley, Theodore Dreiser, Dorothy Parker, and Lillian Hellman, stuck with Stalin.

Another wave of intellectuals left the Party when the Hitler-Stalin nonaggression pact was signed in 1939. The American CP, as usual, sided with Moscow and abandoned its antifascist campaign, which had inspired many of its members to fight for the Loyalists in Spain. When World War II commenced after Germany and the Soviet Union invaded Poland in September 1939, the Party labeled it an ''imperialist war'' that was of no concern to the progressive forces, and preached isolationism.

In 1938, Congressman Martin Dies, a former FDR supporter, organized a special committee to investigate un-American activities. J. Edgar Hoover now had a congressional conduit for leaking information from the Bureau's files; his years of collecting references on Americans he had labeled un-American would begin to pay off in a more public way.

On August 12, 1938, Congressman Dies convened his House Committee on Un-American Activities. In his opening statement he pledged that his committee "will not permit character assassinations or any smearing of innocent people," but that promise was soon broken. By then the FBI had files on over one hundred writers, and Hoover leaked to the committee information to use against people called for questioning. From 1938 until 1944 it was Dies and Hoover, and until 1969, when the committee was disbanded, it was Hart and Hoover, Wood and Hoover, Thomas and Hoover, Velde and Hoover, Walter and Hoover, Willis and Hoover, and Ichord and Hoover.

In Martin Dies, who said that "communism is nothing more nor less than organized treason and those who abet it run grave risks of being *particeps criminis*," Hoover had found a soulmate.

The 1930s ended with Hoover at the peak of his considerable powers. In 1939, as war loomed in Europe, the Bureau readied itself for an emergency. The Security Index was begun under its original name, the Custodial Detention List. Those on this list were considered candidates for internment in wartime. From 1939 until 1941, when the United States entered World War II, J. Edgar Hoover would send Franklin Delano Roosevelt two or more reports every single day. And most important, in 1939, the old Antiradical Division was officially reactivated.

If the Communist party feared it could not control writers, so did Hoover. He developed his power of suspicion as a means of controlling this basically uncontrollable group. For a long while, at least during the mid-thirties, the forties, and the early fifties, the CP *was* a potential danger worthy of much of Hoover's concern—although certainly not worthy of the resulting abuses, not only in the FBI, but in Congress and the rest of the government and nation. But the truth was that the CP did want to get rid of American democracy, and was willing to defraud even its friends and acquaintances in an attempt to accomplish its goals. Communist International was at its peak during the thirties, and although its influence diminished after 1939, membership in the CPUSA rose until it reached eighty thousand members in the mid-forties. But the danger did not last as long as J. Edgar Hoover believed it did, and his preoccupation and obsession with a Communist conspiracy eventually became more dangerous to American liberties than the conspiracy itself.

CHAPTER FIVE

The Search for New Aliens— the 1930s

"A great American novelist, but not a great American," is how the FBI characterized Theodore Dreiser, the author of such novels as *Sister Carrie* and *An American Tragedy*. The Bureau had opened Dreiser's 209-page file in 1927 when he endorsed Workers International Relief, a Communist party–sponsored group under whose auspices Dreiser visited the Soviet Union that same year.

The following year, the FBI reported that Dreiser was a member of an international committee for the defense of Sacco and Vanzetti. One of Dreiser's biographers, Richard Lingeman, says that the novelist had earlier felt that the two anarchists were guilty, but by 1928 he had changed his mind. Always a dissenter and quasisocialist, his trip to Russia made him sympathetic to communism, and after the crash of 1929, in which he lost half of the fortune *An American Tragedy* had brought him, he became outspokenly radical.

In 1930 the FBI reported that Dreiser told the Soviet newspaper *Izvestia* that there was "a possibility Russia in the near future would overshadow Western capitalism in importance." The following year Dreiser became chairman of the National Committee for the Defense of Political Prisoners, one of the first front groups set up by the Party to attract intellectuals. That year he and five other writers, including John Dos Passos, went to Harlan County, Kentucky, to investigate conditions among the striking miners who were being terrorized by local authorities acting in league with the coal mine operators. The CP-dominated National Miners Union had begun organizing the miners after John L. Lewis's United Mine Workers pulled out. Dos Passos recalled in an interview with the FBI in 1952 that "he got the impression that the National Miners Union was controlled by the Communist Party" and was "trying to make a monkey out of him" and "was not sincere in their help."

A Harlan County grand jury indicted Dreiser for adultery (an inveterate womanizer, he had brought along a young woman as his "secretary"), but the indictment was dropped in 1933 because of lack of evidence. Dreiser, who had fled Kentucky before the indictment was handed down, told the press "he could not have committed adultery because he was impotent." According to the FBI's version of the incident, "In Kentucky . . . the employing corporations were opposed to Dreiser and upon finding out that he had brought a woman down there with him, took steps to have [him] indicted. However, through friends he was able to escape from the state just prior to being arrested." To Hoover, Dreiser's unconventional love life was distasteful; the Kentucky prosecution also suggested a way to use such a life against the novelist in the future.

Although Dreiser was rejected for CP membership, the FBI continued to keep him under close watch. In 1934, agents scanned an issue of the Moscow-based magazine *International Literature* to which Dreiser had contributed, along with other American writers, as part of a symposium called "Where We Stand." The next year, 1935, the Bureau recorded that Dreiser was one of the signers of the Call to the First Writers Congress sponsored by the League of American Writers.

In 1938 it was considered worthy of note that Dreiser and Ernest Hemingway "are turning away from individualism" (Dreiser had actually made the shift a few years earlier). For Hoover "individualism" represented a basic American principle, yet in practice Hoover disdained it not only in his attitude toward exotic dress on young people, but in the way he ran his office. FBI agents had to submit not only to a unified behavior code, but to a weight and height code.

In 1939, an informant reported that Dreiser had told a group of writers, "We are intellectual shock troops that should speed the gospel of Moscow." Lingeman believes this is an inaccurate paraphrase, since Dreiser was opposed to writing novels to spread a political "gospel" or party line.

In 1939 an FBI agent interviewed Dreiser, who was then living in California. According to the agent's report, the interview had to do with a "registration matter involving the American League for Peace and Democracy," though that may have been a pretext according to Lingeman, since Dreiser had never belonged to the organization in question. The FBI also listed Dreiser as a member of the American-German Aid Association, but this also seems dubious, according to Lingeman. A second-generation German-American, Dreiser had been pro-German during World War I and during the early 1930s had been fascinated with Hitler as a leader who would revive a Germany prostrated by the harsh terms of the Treaty of Versailles. But he eventually decided Hitler was crazy and turned violently against him when the Wehrmacht invaded his beloved Russia in 1940.

Dreiser told the special agent who interviewed him on June 13, 1939, that "he is not a member of any organization of any kind or character" and "that he does not belong to any club or lodge of any kind," which was true. Lingeman says that "after 1933 he was very wary about joining any groups on the left. He disliked the way the Party fronts used his name without his permission."

In 1938 Dreiser had gone to Barcelona to meet with officials of the Republican government, and he told the FBI agent that upon his return he "conferred with President Roosevelt personally" to relay a request for humanitarian aid. The President told him to "go out and find a strong committee composed of Catholics, Protestants, Liberals and Conservatives" in order to help "the starving people on both sides." But, Dreiser told the agent, "he [Dreiser] had been unable to interest persons who were suitable for such an undertaking." However, "as a result of the agitation in this matter, 5,000,000 bushels of wheat were sent to Spain in November 1938," via the Red Cross. The interview concluded with Dreiser telling the agent that "he is not a Communist and has never engaged in any Communistic activities and has never been a member of any group which was engaged in radical activities, but that it is well known that he has always been a liberal in all his thoughts and actions." Lingeman adds, "After this 1939 visit, Dreiser became aware of the Bureau's interest in him. He was also wary of Martin Dies, whose House Committee on Un-American Activities was conducting noisy public investigations of Communist party activities at this time. He sometimes referred to the FBI caller as an investigator for the Dies Committee. He also complained of an FBI 'blacklist' of his books, and spoke of an 'International FBI' banning his books in South America. Paradoxically, all this attention, while worrying him, revived his interest in Communist causes on the West Coast during World War II, when, of course, the Soviet Union was our heroic ally. He issued statements praising Soviet communism and the brave Red Army. He made speeches against U.S. involvement in World War II, and became critical of FDR, accusing him of leading the United States into war (yet when Roosevelt died in 1945, Dreiser wept). He also spoke out for the right of the Communist party to be on the ballot in 1940.''

The FBI continued to list him as an ''intellectual Communist'' and issued a ''custodial detention'' card for him in 1941, which meant that in the event of a national emergency he would be detained.

In 1945, a few months before his death, Dreiser did join the CP. His file includes the letter that explains his decision, a letter that Lingeman says was actually written by Party members in Hollywood, where Dreiser was then living, though Dreiser did approve the statement, which was published in the *Daily Worker* on July 30, 1945. Lingeman explains that joining the Party at that particular time was a ''symbolic gesture.'' Dreiser was ''concerned about economic justice for the common man in the post-war world.'' The statement was also a kind of last testament, an affirmation of what he saw as the ideals of communism. Finally, joining the Party gave him a ''sense of belonging to a higher cause.''

The FBI, while concluding that Dreiser ''is not believed to have ever been an actual Party member,'' put his name on the Security Index in 1943, showing again how little Hoover cared about degrees of commitment to the cause. The report also points out that Dreiser's books were widely published in Russia, perhaps accounting for the ''tentative dangerousness classification'' he was given. The Bureau believed that the royalties paid to Dreiser were a way of ''buying'' him. Actually, Dreiser complained about unpaid royalties, and in 1944 wrote to Stalin himself asking for an accounting. His plea was successful, for a sizable sum arrived to settle the account.

The year before he was placed on the Security Index, Dreiser had made an anti-British speech in Toronto, which caused such an uproar that he feared arrest and was forced to flee the country. In the aftermath, Hoover considered having him prosecuted under the White Slave Traffic (Mann) Act, as a way of silencing him. According to one FBI report, the novelist had ''transported'' a woman, whose name is blacked out, ''for immoral purposes'' from Canada to Michigan. (The woman, Lingeman says, was an American living in Canada with whom Dreiser was having an affair. She had helped him flee to a town just across the border and stayed with him in a hotel there.) The report notes that "Dreiser is 71 years old and the possibility of his having natural relations seems unlikely."

No prosecution was ever brought, although Dreiser's potency, or alleged lack of it, was not the reason. The Justice Department refused to take any action, and Hoover himself was worried that a trial would receive "extensive publicity because of [Dreiser's] fame as a writer" or that "some Civil Liberties Group will interest itself in [his] case."

Later, the FBI placed Dreiser's name on the "censorship watch," meaning that his mail was monitored. And after he joined the Party, the FBI watched his home, noting visitors' license plate numbers and makes of cars. They even reported that he told a female friend, "I am a Red and hope I die a Red," which he did.

Waldo Frank was the archetypal literary radical of the 1920s: managing editor of the pioneering little magazine *Seven Arts,* author of the 1919 manifesto book *Our America,* and the 1925 *Virgin Spain,* profiler for *The New Yorker,* champion of new writing. In the thirties, he became almost the archetypal literary *political* radical. Frank saw no contradiction between those roles. In the September 1932 issue of *The New Masses,* Frank explained that his "movement toward the left" was "a steady, logical evolution."

The FBI first discovered Frank's name when he was a member of Dreiser's National Committee for the Defense of Political Prisoners in 1932. That year Frank made the ritual journey to Harlan County, with Edmund Wilson and other intellectuals, and was beaten up by sheriff's deputies. After he became president of the League of American Writers in 1935, the FBI pursued him vigorously, and his file would grow to 565 pages by the 1960s.

Frank, who never hid his Communist sympathies, once addressed a letter to the executive committee of the league with the salutation "Dear Comrades." In this May 4, 1935, letter, Frank explains that the league's work should "be constructive, rather than that of protest and agitation"; writers should write about strikes, rather than join the picket lines. Malcolm Cowley and other members of the executive committee received this missive, but not the FBI.

*   *   *

The 1906 success of Upton Sinclair's sixth novel, *The Jungle,* and the subsequent passage of the Meat Inspection Act of 1906, which the book's publication brought about, occurred seventeen years before the FBI took notice of its author. In 1923, agents searching for new names found his on the advisory committee of the Friends of Soviet Russia, a Communist front, and this reference began his 211-page file.

There are, however, no further reports about the famous social reformer–writer, whom the FBI often called a "Communist dupe," until 1934, when he was running for governor of California on the Democratic ticket. On September 13, 1934, at 1:30 P.M., the FBI monitored a phone conversation concerning Sinclair that took place between J. Edgar Hoover and President Roosevelt. This is the only one of the many conversations between the director and FDR of which there exists a transcript.

President: Hello—Edgar Hoover.

Mr. Hoover: Yes, Mr. President.

President: I have got a thing here which, strictly speaking, is not our concern, but in view of all the facts, I suppose we ought to do something about it. Sinclair—Upton Sinclair—was in the East last week, and on Sunday, on the New York Central train, near Chicago, he wrote a letter to Mrs. Roosevelt which she didn't get because she was away, and we have only just got it. And the letter reads as follows:

"Dear Mrs. Roosevelt:
Please pardon the bad writing on a jolting train. This is probably the most important letter I ever wrote and I hope that your secretaries will get it to you at once. Last night I received from an underworld source information of a kind I cannot neglect. It comes through an old trusted friend who talked directly with [*four lines are blacked out here*] There is no use in going to any California police about such a matter—where they are not crooked they are dumb, but the Federal Government has a real service if the President will say the word and can protect me. I have known that this was coming. Two months ago a detective agency in San Francisco, secretly our friend, told me of a decision that had been taken to use a little German frightfulness and publish this in our papers and warn our friends. But this matter is too direct and too urgent to handle that way. These men do not mind talk, but they do fear Federal men, and so indicate that. Of course, we are going on with our job, but we don't crave martyrdom, nor is it what the country needs in this crisis. If the President sends some-

one to me I will tell the whole story. Please wire me on the Chicago Northwestern train leaving on Sunday evening. The secretary may sign the wire. I just want the word that action will be taken.''

President: Well, of course, it is one of those things that we can't tell if there is anything in it or not.

Mr. Hoover: I think we ought to have somebody see him, Mr. President.

President: I think you ought to have somebody see him.

Mr. Hoover: I'll call out in California right away.

President: That's fine.

Mr. Hoover: And have somebody see him—

President: I'll send this letter down to you.

Mr. Hoover: That will be very nice of you, and I'll get the details right away.

President: Yes, that's fine.

Mr. Hoover: I'll be glad to, Mr. President.

President: I'll send the letter down through the White House.

Mr. Hoover: All right. Thank you very much.

President: Goodbye.

Mr. Hoover: Goodbye.

It is interesting that the President calls Hoover ''Edgar,'' as did most of the Director's colleagues. However, his oldest and most counted-on friends called him ''John.''

In any case, Hoover immediately called his attorney general to tell him about the conversation, and then contacted his agent in charge of the Los Angeles office to begin an investigation in conjunction with the agent in charge of Chicago, Melvin Purvis, of Dillinger fame, who said ''the story is rather wild.''

The story, as pieced together from other reports in Upton Sinclair's file, involves ''alleged threats'' on the writer's life by ''a former playboy,'' ''an extremely dissipated youth of many years'' who had been staying at the Algonquin Hotel in New York.

Because Hoover knew that Roosevelt was following this case, he told his agents not to ''upset Sinclair''; Hoover himself also followed the case closely, even jotting in the margin of one report: ''Find out where this is. It is now 5:30 pm Sunday and I haven't received it yet.''

Eventually, Hoover decided against guarding Sinclair, ordering his agents in very firm language not to do it. But toward the end of October, he received a letter telling him that someone ''who stated he was a very close friend of Mr. Louis Howe, Secretary to President Roosevelt . . . advised that he had received information of a plot to bomb the State Capitol at Sacramento . . . and that the bombing was to embarrass the Sinclair forces, and to make it appear that Sinclair sympathizers were behind the plot . . . whereas, in fact, the plotters were actually enemies. . . .''

Hoover and his FBI were not concerned with the bomb threat, but rather that ''the newspapers would give publicity to aid the Sinclair forces,'' an indication of just how far Hoover's zealotry could go.

For Hoover, the ''explosion'' caused by the election of a Socialist Governor hiding in a Democrat's clothes may well have seemed more dangerous than the explosion caused by a bomb.

Another prominent American writer, Sherwood Anderson, the author of *Winesburg, Ohio,* first came to the attention of the Bureau when agents read his contribution to ''a symposium of articles'' that appeared in *The New Masses* in 1932. The subject was ''How I Came To Communism.''

Anderson biographer Walter Rideout says that in this article, Anderson ''was simply saying that in *Winesburg, Ohio* he dealt with poor and working-class characters whom American literature had pretty much ignored before, and so that book was 'revolutionary.' It was in a literary sense, and maybe indirectly in a political sense, too.''

But the FBI did not share that opinion, though a report from John Reed's file mentions that Anderson ''violently disliked'' Reed, an opinion they *did* share. In any case, more than eighty additional ''subversive'' references were collected about him.

Anderson, like so many of his contemporaries, flirted with the Party, but never joined. In 1952, when John Dos Passos was interviewed by the FBI, he told the agents that Anderson had never been a member, but the FBI continued to collect references until 1956, fifteen years after his death.

The radical career of the novelist John Dos Passos began in the 1920s, as it has been shown. During the 1930s he continued to be active in support of Party causes, but grew increasingly critical of the Party in the United States and of Marxism itself. His radical journey is detailed in a memo the FBI prepared for President Richard M. Nixon in 1970. Nixon's staff had requested a file check before sending out a White House dinner invitation to Mr. and Mrs. Dos Passos.

According to the memo, "The files indicate that Dos Passos first had sympathy for the Soviet Union in 1923. He next showed an interest in the Civil War in Spain." But even before the conflict in Spain, Dos Passos had become skeptical, and the memo notes, "In 1937, Dos Passos was reported to be sympathetic to the Trotskyites." His disillusionment with communism was intensified during a visit to Spain. Ernest Hemingway, who prided himself on his language abilities, told Stanley Weintraub, author of *The Last Great Cause,* that Dos Passos "spent his whole time in Madrid looking for his translator."

In an interview with the Bureau in 1952, Dos Passos confirmed that while in Spain he had "little contact with the Abraham Lincoln Brigade and most of the persons [he] contacted were those attempting to get out of Spain due to Russian treatment they were receiving." In the same interview he said that although he had been "instrumental in helping organize a committee to see that arms were sent to the Spanish Republic Government . . . he had kept the Communists off the committee." He also said that "at the time of his going to Spain," he was "unaware of the complete job of infiltration which the Communists had completed." Dos Passos would expose the Communist infiltration of the Loyalist forces in his book *Travel Between Wars.*

The memo continues to trace Dos Passos's rightward swing, reporting, "Later Dos Passos indicated [an] anti-communist attitude. He has since written numerous articles which were extremely critical of communism." By 1947 his right turn was complete: "Dos Passos indicated to a bureau agent in Boston that his political sympathies were now 'to the right.' " By 1959, Dos Passos was writing the introduction to a polemic by right-wing editor William F. Buckley, Jr., *Up from Liberalism.* But that was not sufficient expiation for Hoover, and Dos Passos's file continued until 1974, four years after the writer's death.

The League of American Writers was also formed in 1935 as a successor to the John Reed Clubs, which were "liquidated by the Party." After 1935, the Party announced it wanted writers "to be good writers, not bad strike leaders." Malcolm Cowley told the First American Writers Congress, where the league was created, that the writer stood to gain more from the revolutionary movement than the movement from the writer.

At one point it was reported that *Partisan Review,* which began in late 1934 under the aegis of the New York John Reed Club, was going to become the official organ of the league, but this idea never worked out, according to Alan M. Wald, author of *New York Intellectuals,* because its editors, William Phillips and Philip Rahv, did not agree with the slogan "Art as Weapon." But William Phillips says "the League of American Writers was a front for the Communist party. They never asked us to be an organ of it. Why should they have asked us? It doesn't even make sense . . . we broke with the Communists. We'd been an organ of the John Reed Club."

Although Phillips and Rahv had taken *Partisan Review* out of the John Reed Club and the Communist movement, the magazine remained suspect to the FBI, which continued to use its masthead as an investigative tool. For example, on May 13, 1939, agents indexed the name of critic and biographer F. W. Dupee after they found it on the letterhead of the *Partisan Review,* where he had been an editor since 1937. Although the FBI noted that the magazine was "formerly associated with the Communist Party," but now has "no commitments to any political party," it also reported that the editors were "a group of self-styled revolutionists" who "still adhered to their Marxian revolutionary theories."

The FBI's deep and long-lasting suspicions concerning the magazine continued well into the 1950s, as witnessed by the inclusion in Dupee's file of a 1955 Navy Intelligence report on a person who is "a subversive and possible homosexual suspect." Among the reasons given for suspecting subversion is that the "subject received *The Partisan Review.*" Why is this six-page document in F. W. Dupee's file? Because the Navy Intelligence report lists him, along with Dwight Macdonald, William Phillips, and Philip Rahv, as editors, and reports on the magazine were spread around in many different files.

WILLIAM PHILLIPS:
The League of American Writers started when the Communist line changed, as I recall, because of the popular front, and it was created to replace the John Reed Clubs. They were considered too sectarian, and they were dissolved, I always assumed, on orders from Moscow, but one never knew those things. One sort of smelled them, but didn't know them.

Philip Rahv and I actually went to one meeting of the League of American Writers—and created a rumpus—it must have been '37. We were against the League of American Writers and they were against us.

There was once a shindig to raise money for the *Partisan Review* and the John Reed Club. I was entrapped by a cop and arrested for selling liquor without a license, and Rahv was arrested with me—he was arrested for running a dance without a license! The cop was a liar. He said to me—I guess he was afraid of a disturbance or something—"Just come with me down to the jail, and the officer there will ask you a few questions and then you'll leave and come back here." We spent the night in jail! And then there was a trial and we got off. Years later I was told that my name was proposed to be a member of the National Endowment for the Arts—and I was turned down because of an FBI check. Maybe it's because of that arrest in the John Reed days. Who knows?

I'm for an intelligent FBI. I'm not against an FBI, I'm against a stupid FBI. If the FBI is investigating foreign agents, I'm not opposed to that. Also, I don't share a position that is prevalent in some parts of the left today—a position which seems to me just as stupid as the FBI was on occasion—and that is total opposition to the FBI and the CIA. To expect the country to be without an intelligence service seems to me to be a form of stupidity—well, it's ideological stupidity.

When I was a member of the John Reed Club and when I was a fellow traveler as a Communist for a very short time—I think it was a year, a year and a half, maybe two years, I've forgotten exactly—the FBI never bothered me. They never bothered the magazine. As a matter of fact I've wondered why they never bothered us. And so far as I know they never bothered the John Reed Club, but maybe they did and I didn't know about it.

But afterwards, after I had broken completely with the Communists, I became what is called an anticommunist, an anti-Stalinist, the FBI tried to get information from me. Once the FBI came to me and wanted me to verify that Anna Rosenberg, who had been the assistant secretary of defense, had been a member of the John Reed Club. I honestly had no recollection that there was anybody by the name of Anna Rosenberg in the John Reed Club, and I told them the straight story that I didn't know *anything* about this—to my knowledge she was never a member of the John Reed Club; if she was, I'd forgotten it. And then they came to see me about somebody—I'd been teaching at New York University and he was a member of the English department—I don't even remember his name. They didn't tell me, but I think they suspected him of being an agent, and I knew nothing about him. The FBI agents kept asking me questions about him, and I kept saying I really don't know anything about him, I don't know why you're bothering me, you obviously know more about him than I do! I made one remark: I said all I knew was he was supposed to be homosexual—but I'm not saying that in criticism, I'm just saying it factually.

And the last time the FBI came, it was sort of irritating. They came to question me about some people who had actually been members of the John Reed Club, I think, as far as I could recall. How could I know who was a Communist party member, since I wasn't one myself? They were talking about people who were members of the John Reed Club. But anyway, I said, I don't want to cooperate with you because I'm not anti-Communist in the way you are, and I don't believe you're serious in your anticommunism, and what you're doing makes no sense, so I just won't cooperate with you. They had been fairly polite before, but this last time they tried to get a little tougher. They tried to threaten me. They said they would haul me into court and put me on the witness stand. I said, all right, do that. But they never did. That was the end of it.

Rahv and I were once subpoenaed—I assume the FBI was the source. We were subpoenaed to a grand jury in Washington, and I think that must have been the occasion they pestered us about Anna Rosenberg. Rahv and I were examined separately, and the district attorney kept badgering me about what I knew about Communists. I kept telling him I had never been a member of the Communist party so I didn't know who was and who wasn't a Communist. And he wanted to know what happened to the records of the John Reed Club, and I really answered truthfully—I had forgotten what happened to them. I didn't remember how they were kept or where, and they tried to trap me. And at one point I got very irritated because the tactics were very annoying. I had said several times, I'll tell you all you want to know about myself. I've never been secretive about my activities. I believe in being open about myself. So they kept asking me when I broke with the Communists, and I told them, and they said, "What happened?" and "How did the Communists treat you?"

I said, "Well, very badly. They refused to talk to me and they refused to even acknowledge that they knew me, and I was abused in the Communist press."

And the district attorney said to me, "Who were the 'they'? What names can you attach to the word 'they'?"

And I got terribly irritated at that, because I had told them before that I didn't know who were Communists, it would be irresponsible of me to speculate—and by Communist I meant people who were sympathetic to the Party and may have been members, but I had no way of knowing. I started to give a lecture on Freud and psychoanalysis and the phenomenon of projection. And I said this was a projection of mine and I can't assign names to projections. They got completely disgusted with me and dismissed me.

In the fifties, I was asked by high-level CIA agents to work for the CIA. I was in Paris on a Rockefeller grant when I was approached, the CIA contact told me he was in charge of the CIA for all of Europe. He wanted me to be able to travel to Paris and hand out American dollars to various anti-Communist individuals and organizations.

And he said to me, "You'd have a perfect cover as a writer and as an editor of a magazine—your coming to Paris would be legitimate," and I said, "No, I won't do it," and he said, "Why not?" and I said, "It's not my line of work."

**

Clifford Odets (sometimes spelled "O'Dets" by the FBI), the author of such socially conscious plays as *Waiting for Lefty, Awake and Sing!* and *Golden Boy,* came to Hoover's attention in 1935 when agents noted his byline on an article in *The Daily Worker.* Two years later, the FBI reported that "the darling of the left" had volunteered to help the Citizens Committee to Aid Striking Seamen and was also active in the New Theatre League and the National Writers Union, both politically suspect groups.

Odets later testified to the House Committee on Un-American Activities that he had joined the Party in 1934, but quit in 1935 because he found the CP meetings "silly" and resented the Communists' trying to steer his writing. Odets also told the committee that the CP "drove all the good writers away. So far as I know offhand, they don't have a first-grade writer, and they haven't for years, because of [such] tactics as . . . you read some pamphlets, you listened to someone talk, and finally a person would ask you if you didn't want to join." Odets elaborated that "in my case it happened: 'No, I don't. When I am ready, I will.' I was not ready that month, I was ready a month or two later," adding "the Communist Party functionaries, when they are such, are always secretive. They never announce themselves . . . but they have a quality of authority, a quality of talking with knowledge, and one makes the surmise that this is some kind of functionary. . . .''

When he gave that testimony in 1952, Odets had abandoned socially conscious dramas and become a Hollywood screenwriter. His appearance as a friendly witness shocked many of his colleagues. Howard Fast, a Party member at the time, recalled attempting to dissuade a weeping Odets from cooperating: "He kept crying, and I kept saying, 'You don't have to do it. Nothing will happen to you. All you do in Washington is tell them to go to hell.' And he said, 'They'll send me to prison.' I said, 'They don't want to send Clifford Odets to prison.' I begged him. I pleaded with him. I couldn't get to him.''

Arthur Miller writes in his autobiography, *TimeBends,* that Odets displayed a deep ambivalence during his testimony. "He roundly castigated [the committee] at one moment and without at all changing his indignant tone proceeded to corroborate for them the names of people he had known in the Communist Party.''

In defense of his political views Odets told the committee that "a liberal has no place to go" but to some of the questionable organizations. Neither that explanation nor Odets's willingness to name names was good enough for J. Edgar Hoover, who endorsed a 1952 editorial in the New York *Mirror* commenting on the HUAC hearings. The editorial, on which Hoover wrote the word "Excellent," said writers should renounce "organizations established to harm America" and join "a picket line of patriotic Americans." Odets's file would continue until 1964, a year after his death.

The FBI began its 915-page file on the novelist and screenwriter Donald Ogden Stewart in 1936, when they learned "he was one of the principal leaders of the Communist element in the motion picture industry.''

Stewart, the author of several obscure satirical novels and the collaborator on such screenplays as *Dinner at Eight, Holiday,* and *The Philadelphia Story,* became "a secret party member" in 1936, and the following year became president of the League of American Writers.

Compounding the FBI's uneasiness about Stewart was his marriage in 1939 to writer Ella Winter, identified in a report as "the wife of Lincoln Steffans [*sic*], the Communist writer." In fact, Winter's own file is included with Stewart's file, making theirs the only "his-her" file.

The FBI had been collecting references on Winter since 1927, when she was still married to Steffens, whom she divorced in 1929. The Stewart-Winter files contain copies of letters Winter wrote to Steffens. One 1927 letter mentions the radical sociologist Scott Nearing, saying he ''is doing a lot of talking. He is supposed to be the best and clearest Communist speaker now.'' In another letter, the FBI reports that Winter wrote her first husband, ''Stef, Communists have to be sons of b's because the capitalist system *is* a son of a b. The nature of the beast is coming out more and more.'' Winter's passion for the cause is evident in another hortatory letter to Steffens: ''You say you want communism in the USA. But how is it to come unless there's a fight for it? And who is to do the fighting? You know that there's a vast difference between saying in your drawing room you believe in something, and going and putting yourself at odds with society for fighting for it. You never mention class struggle, you never say in your lectures, 'if it's communism we want we must help the workers and farmers get it . . .' Intellectuals alone won't make a revolution, you know that.'' And in another letter she writes: ''I'm keeping a diary of things to tell you. I'm afraid to write much. Do you think letters may be opened? I always keep that possibility in mind. I'm sure wires are tapped—many people are sure.''

The mail intercepts continued after the Stewarts were married. When the couple defended their close friend, radical labor organizer Harry Bridges, the FBI scanned their mail, seeking incriminating information. They found little. In one 1941 letter, Stewart tells his wife that Bridges ''sends you love,'' and that ''the more I read re Bridges, the more I fail to understand the strategy. The worst red baiter could not talk worse than Bridges. Why? Why?'' It is not clear what strategy Stewart does not understand.

The Stewarts eventually became aware of the snooping. A June 4, 1944, FBI report says, ''In one letter Mr. Stewart asked if she could think of some way to work out a code which they could use, and which would circumvent censorship in future correspondence.''

The Bureau continued to monitor their mail for decades. The letters range from Stewart writing about his politics—''In the future I shall work with Communist Party members, but I shall not front for them blindly''—to his talking shop, always with shades of politics, as in this about a producer who ''asked 'How could anyone think a guy that looks like you could be a Communist?' (he had just read the script)'' or ''I forgot to tell you that I phoned Joanie Payson on their anniversary—in the midst of writing the great movie to expose the

Charlie Paysons of America I pause to assure them of my undying affection.'' (Wealthy socialite Joan Whitney Payson and her husband, Charles, owned race horses and the Mets baseball team.)

But in 1944, after Ella Winter received a letter written in Russian that contained ''a German game of Guess the Numbers,'' which the FBI believed was going to be used to transmit secret messages, the Stewarts became the subject of a ''highly confidential Comintern case'' and the FBI stepped up its surveillance, even somehow expropriating Winter's private diary in order to discover her plans.

The couple was watched around the clock, and many informants were used, including ''a delivery boy from the University Cleaners'' and a hotel maid. In addition, agents kept them under surveillance. They reported when Stewart went to sleep at night (''surveillance was . . . discontinued when the lights in the Stewart residence went out''), when he got up in the morning, when he walked his dog (''a brown and white setter''), when Ella Winter went shopping (''around 4:00 pm she went to a neighborhood store''), and when they went out for an evening of entertainment (''both subjects proceeded to the Astor Theatre . . . to see the picture 'Lifeboat'.'').

In 1945, the year the FBI believed Stewart left the Party, an informant told the FBI that Eleanor Roosevelt and Ella Winter had addressed one another at a dinner as ''Ella'' and ''Eleanor.'' The informant also reported that ''Mrs. Roosevelt asked Miss Winter if she would assist in having Elliot Roosevelt's forthcoming book published. Miss Winter immediately contacted editor Angus Cameron,'' described as ''responsible for the selection of numerous works by Communist authors for publication by Little Brown Company.''

By 1950, three years after ''movie director Sam Wood named the subject as a Communist in testimony before HUAC,'' Stewart was put in a ''special section'' of the Security Index, along with two hundred other people who are not mentioned. Stewart was placed in the ''Prominent Individuals'' section because he was ''a nationally-known playwright, actor and author''; the other five categories were espionage subjects, government employees, atomic energy employees, foreign government employees, and United Nations personnel.

The following year the FBI warned nine field offices that the Stewarts' names had been discovered on a ''VIP list'' for an invitation to the Soviet Union; the list had been uncovered during a search of Tass News Agency's New York offices.

In 1952, the FBI reported that Stewart and Winter moved to England, and the U.S. State Department confiscated their passports so they could not travel around.

"What about this?" J. Edgar Hoover jotted in the margin of a 1955 memo. The memo told him the Bureau was having trouble getting the exact issue of the *Daily Worker* in which Stewart was quoted as saying he would honor the Hollywood Ten "for the rest of his life."

In 1957, the Stewarts' passports were renewed, although the FBI asked the embassy in London to monitor their activities from time to time; the last FBI report is dated June 18, 1970.

ANGUS CAMERON:
I never published that book by Elliot Roosevelt that Ella Winter talked to me about. In fact, I don't even remember that she did take it up with me, because I don't ever remember considering the project, though obviously I must have. I'm certain that if Mrs. Roosevelt asked her to help get it published, the first one she would have come to would have been me, because I was her publisher. I published one book of hers. It was called, I think the title was, *I Saw the Russian People*. She was not primarily a writer, she was primarily a political person.

The last time I saw Ella Winter, I asked her what she'd been doing, and she said, "I've been taking stuff out of my files." And I said, "What do you mean?" She said, "Some of it is scandalous—I'm not talking about politics, I'm talking about sex." And I said, "Well, I think *that's* scandalous—for anybody who has a respect for history, to cut anything out of your papers is not fair to future social historians." So she said, "All right, I'll restore it," but I don't know whether she did or not because I haven't seen her papers. She just knew *everybody*. Beginning at the end of the first world war.

I don't think she was aware of the FBI surveillance that much. Oh, it wouldn't have bothered her, of course. She wouldn't have been very concerned—she would have been indignant, but not concerned because she didn't have a scared bone in her body. Don was scared, and he told me—he was a good friend of mine—he said, "I'm just too scared to testify," so he left. And of course he moved to England. My memory is that he was subpoenaed but left instead of testifying. He came back once in the late fifties—Ella came back more than once—but he came back at the time he was writing his autobiography.

It was a fascinating thing: for one of the funniest men that ever lived, it was the *dullest* autobiography. Don didn't realize the two sides to the mask when he wrote his plays—that comedy was as socially useful as tragedy, and he always felt kind of guilty about being a comic writer, whereas that's what he should have done, you see, because he was really a very funny guy. At one stage, I was kind of the editor at large for his autobiography, and he expected me to publish it, which, of course, I expected to do, until I saw it. It was so dull, and of course, he waited too long to write it. My memory is that he devoted four paragraphs to the story of the week he and Hemingway—and two or three others—went to the bullfights that figure as the basis for *The Sun Also Rises*. And Don's one of the characters in that novel! I began to repeat to him what he had told me, and I said this is what you *should* have here. I said you devote three *chapters* to getting into Skull and Bones at Yale—which really impressed him, you see. And he said, "Well, you know, I forgot about those Hemingway details, but now of course I remember."

At the end of the week in Spain, they all got in an argument over the bill, and Don was the only successful one among them at the time. Hemingway wasn't very successful, and Don had a play on Broadway and a best-seller—so *he* paid the whole bill for *everyone.* And Don had forgotten all about it, and hadn't included that in his autobiography!

Hemingway considered Don a very able writer, and their friendship broke up over the fact that Hemingway believed Don had sold out. And Don said, "I *had.*" He always felt very guilty about being the most successful writer in Hollywood. What a lovely guy he was—what a wonderful man. Don told me the story of his break with Hemingway, who said something quite crude to Don—something to the effect that "our relationship is finished because you sold out." Hemingway told him he had the capacity to be a great comedy writer—and he sold out just to make money. I never could tell how much of that was moral principle on Hemingway's part and how much it was envy.

**

Sometime in 1937 or 1938 the FBI opened a letter Ella Winter had written to John Steinbeck that attacked him for his denunciation of her position vis-à-vis a strike in San Diego, California. According to the report, which is in Donald Ogden Stewart's file, Winter's tongue-lashing "is in part obscene," presumably for its ending: "Really, haven't you gotten out of the stage of wetting your didies yet?" The FBI also quotes other parts of the letter: "I wrote [*blacked out, but it is probably Sam Darcy, a CP official*] what do you want to attack Steinbeck for on labor matters when he's sympathetic to labor? You were a friend of Steffens, you told me you liked Don—Don and I made it possible for you to meet [*blacked out*] and make your Mexican movie, and in addition for years I protected you in every way possible from being asked to do things for the Left, because they tend to admire and like you and wanted you to do many things." Clearly, Winters is here reminding Steinbeck she was responsible for shielding him from dupe assignments on behalf of the CP.

Steinbeck's 139-page file was started in 1936, the year after *Tortilla Flat* became a best-seller, because he participated in a western writers conference, and contributed to *Pacific Weekly,* a West Coast magazine the FBI labeled "Red."

In 1939, the year *Grapes of Wrath* was published, Steinbeck contacted the FBI after he had received a letter demanding money. After an investigation, the FBI found no grounds for initiating extortion charges against the letter writer. At the time, Steinbeck probably had no idea that the FBI was more interested in him, but by 1942 he had found out, and had protested in a letter to Attorney General Francis Biddle. The attorney general forwarded the letter to Hoover, who lied when he replied, "Steinbeck is not being and has never been investigated by this Bureau."

Hoover believed there was "substantial doubt as to the loyalty and discretion" of the writer, and in fact, had recommended that he not receive a commission in the U.S. Army in 1943. But according to Department of the Army records, Army Intelligence agents who investigated Steinbeck called him "a candid and powerful writer," and recommended that he receive a commission "if he can be placed where his writing ability may be utilized." However, this recommendation was overruled by the lieutenant colonel in charge of the investigation, who was influenced by the FBI's reports.

In 1944, the FBI learned that American merchant marines were being supplied "with libraries for the seaman to read while at sea," and that "*Grapes of Wrath* is naturally present, as it would be in any Communist's selection."* The FBI had once received a report that told them that Steinbeck's "writings portrayed an extremely sordid and poverty-striken side of American life," and thus "were reprinted in both German and Russian and used by the Nazis and Soviets as propaganda against America."

In 1946 the FBI was told by an informant that Howard Fast "approved" of Steinbeck being invited to a reception sponsored by the National Council of American-Soviet Friendship, a party that "Fast declared anti-Soviets and Trotskyites should not be invited to" because "they would make things very uncomfortable."

Fast says Steinbeck never came to that reception in 1946: "He never came to anything. But he was a CP member when he wrote *In Dubious Battle*," which was published in 1936, the year his file began. Although no biographer has ever placed Steinbeck directly in the Party, Fast says he belongs there. He adds, "I suppose he left the Party when he hit it with *Grapes of Wrath*. But we all knew he was a Party member. It was widely known. And then he sold out."

In 1963, the FBI reported that although Steinbeck said he wanted "his fellow American writers to be 'for' not merely 'against' something," and that "some American writers give too much attention to denouncing everything in the past," he was "impressed by the changes" he saw in Russia since his visit there twenty years earlier. In 1964, the Bureau recorded that Steinbeck "had received the sum of $420 as an author's fee from the Soviet publication, Novyi Mir."

---

*A former merchant marine seaman who joined the Communist party in 1938 says the ship's libraries "were not worth investigating because they didn't amount to much." This merchant marine, who wishes anonymity, says, "The CP was the only one that did anything—raised the question of unemployment insurance, social security, and medical benefits. The Communists were the kindest, softest, most unbusinesslike people I knew."

In 1964, the propaganda report about his writing came up again, but with some changes. It used broader language and said his books were "translated into foreign languages and distributed by enemies of the United States," and added that "the Communists were at odds" with Steinbeck for not "adequately portraying American Communists or life in America." Here, twenty-nine years after beginning his file, and six years after he won a Nobel Prize, the FBI acknowledged that perhaps he is no longer a Communist, although Hoover continued to "step on the heels" of his fourth Nobel laureate until 1968, the year of his death.

The year agents reported somewhat belatedly that the "Communists were at odds" with Steinbeck, they also reported that he was mentioned on a wiretap at the Chicago headquarters of the Students for a Democratic Society. An unidentified person suggests "that they get John Steinbeck to speak. Trouble is that he is Conservative." A second person replies, "Okay then drop that. Try to change him."

Maverick poet Maxwell Bodenheim, once a leading figure in Chicago literary life, and a hard-drinking, flamboyant member of New York's Greenwich Village scene in the late teens and early twenties, went to work for the Federal Writers Project in 1938, but was fired in 1940 because he had "falsely executed" the application form by not admitting his Communist past. Bodenheim had first come to the attention of the FBI in 1936, when agents reported that he had been a contributor to an issue of *The New Masses,* and that "on May 1, 1936 he was photographed at the May Day Parade carrying a Communist flag and selling the *Daily Worker.*"

According to one report, Bodenheim told officials he had been a Party member in 1938 and 1939; but informants in the WPA told the FBI he was a member of the Party from 1932 on, and was still a member as late as 1940. One of the informants said he had seen the poet's "Communist dues book" and a copy of Earl Browder's book, *The People's Front,* which Bodenheim had marked with "the Communist symbol, the hammer and sickle, after his name." Still another informant told the FBI that he "doubts whether he was ever sober enough to attend the [CP] meetings."

In another report, Bodenheim himself told the FBI in 1940 that he had resigned from the Party that year "because of the Russian-Finnish War." He also confessed that he had "belonged to several units of the Communist Party in New York, Chicago, and the West Coast, but all the time he had been more of a socialist than a Communist." Bodenheim also admitted that he "still believes in Socialist principles," and that he "has only twice written anything which might be construed as having a Communist tinge"—a "sonnet . . . which tells the story of police brutality towards members of a picket line," and a novel, *Run, Sheep, Run.* Bodenheim told the FBI "he had never completed his novel on the class conflict in the United States." The interviewing agents added a note to their report in the sixty-three-page file, saying that "Bodenheim stated that he desired to leave after the interview but would return in two or three days to sign the statement, but he did not return."

A clue as to why Bodenheim chose to stay away can be found in a letter he wrote his Chicago colleague, Ben Hecht, in 1940: "The galoriously [*sic*] democratic FBI has threatened me with arrest and a trial for perjury unless I turn stool pigeon and informer and give reams of information regarding names of Party members, places where members recruited others, etc., in return for which the government would restore my $21.90 WPA job (just a little deal between friends). If I do not sign certain papers the F. B. I. declares that I will be arrested."

The last reference in the file concerns the 1954 murder of Bodenheim and his wife in New York City by a man named Harry Weinberg, who shouted after his arrest, "I killed two Communists, I ought to get a medal."

J. Edgar Hoover telegrammed his New York agent not to give out any "information concerning subversive behavior" of the Bodenheims to the New York City police department without first checking with him. There is no indication why Hoover issued this order, or what plans he had for the subversive material, or how much he planned to release, but it seems likely that what was really behind his order was the fact that he didn't want it known that the FBI had been investigating Bodenheim. Still, the Director's real motive—like the motive of the man who murdered the Bodenheims—remains a mystery to this day.

Sinclair Lewis, whose file was started in 1923, as has been shown, won his Nobel Prize in 1930, yet the FBI's only real interest in him that year was that he was "a member and correspondent" of the *Labor News,* as well as a member of the National Council of the American Birth Control League. Agents also reported that four of his books—*Elmer Gantry, Main Street, Babbitt,* and *Arrowsmith*—were part of The Workers Library, which offered "literature most essential to the class-conscious, militant worker in his task of awakening, organizing, and leading the masses. . . ."

Despite Hoover's mistrust of Lewis, in 1936 when the writer requested a tour of the Bureau, Hoover arranged it. He wasn't going to
let politics totally interfere with the publicity that a Nobel Prize visitor
could bring to him. However, Lewis didn't make it until three years
later. An FBI agent's report on the visit is dated 1939. It says, "Mr.
Lewis stated that Mr. Hoover would make a great fictional character
for a novel depicting what can be done through the application
of intelligence, training, and science. He stated that he had long contemplated writing a novel based upon a policeman. I expressed the
hope that it wouldn't be another *Elmer Gantry*." But the part of the
report that Hoover liked best, no doubt, was this: "Mr. Lewis pointed
out that he had always classed himself as a Liberal but that there was
a line between Liberalism and Communism, and while he had always
believed 'to live and let live' nevertheless two years ago, following his
novel, 'Prodigal Son,' [actually *Prodigal Parents*, published in 1934]
which characterized a Communistic family, his eyes were opened by
what some of the Communists had done; and now he feels badly if they
do not castigate him in the *Daily Worker* at least once a week."

Lewis also told his guide that "a lot of liberals are against finger-
printing, but I've been wondering whether or not those who have been
shouting the loudest don't have something to cover-up."

Hoover's relief over Lewis didn't last for long, because the following year, in 1940, he received a wildly inaccurate report that told him
that the writer was "active as an organizer for the Communist Party."
Howard Fast says, "Sinclair Lewis was never a member of the Party."

In 1947, the FBI was flooded with letters denouncing Lewis's
Kingsblood Royal. The Bureau found ample grounds for concern, for
as one FBI report put it, the book was "very inflammatory due to its
references to the question of Negro and White relations." Another
report said, "The book was stated to be propaganda for the white
man's acceptance of the negro as a social equal." The Bureau's response to the book betrayed its deep-seated racism.

In 1949, the FBI reported that Sinclair Lewis had attacked the
United States at an international meeting; however, after questioning
him, it was determined that the report had placed him on the wrong
side, and he had, in fact, spoken against the Soviet Union, not the
United States.

In 1951, the year of Lewis's death—after the FBI had collected over
one hundred references to him and had employed one phone tap—the
Senate Internal Security Subcommittee, known by its chairman's name
as the McCarran Committee, sent Hoover what he later referred to as

"information that should be credited to a highly confidential source." The information had come from Army Intelligence, but Hoover did not want to acknowledge the source, and whatever information this was—it is not revealed—Hoover also said, "No reference should be made to the McCarran Committee."

SINCLAIR LEWIS:
Hoover is a mere infant. His best years are ahead of him.

—*Comment recorded by FBI during his tour of headquarters, October 24, 1935*

**

The creator of the Studs Lonigan trilogy, James T. Farrell, who supported the Communist party from 1932 to 1935, was discovered by the FBI in 1934 when a confidential informant told the Bureau the author had signed a protest sponsored by the National Committee for the Defense of Political Prisoners. The following year agents recorded his name as one of the members of the first American Writers Congress.

By 1937 Farrell had joined in the defense of Trotsky, and his name soon became anathema to the Party regulars. It also became anathema to non-Party regulars, such as Malcolm Cowley, with whom he had a literary and political feud for many years. But during the early thirties, when Cowley and Farrell were guests at the artists' colony Yaddo, in Saratoga Springs, New York, it was Farrell who "exerted the most influence. It was the tough, Studs Lonigan time," Cowley explains, adding that he "tried to stay out of the quarrels on my brief fall visits, but that required an effort."

The FBI didn't much care whether an individual was a Trotskyist or a Stalinist, although one report states that Farrell "was aiding the Trotskyists even more than if he were an enrolled Party member."

In 1943 the FBI reported that Farrell was a member of the Civil Rights Defense Committee, and in 1944, a confidential informant told the Bureau that Farrell "was the recipient of a shipment of books" from a Socialist group. Four years later, in 1948, the FBI reported that Farrell had contributed to a fund for "drugs and medicine" for the "Vietnamese in their war against the French," which makes him the first writer cited by the FBI for becoming involved in the politics of Vietnam.

In 1950, the FBI put an article entitled "Speaking of Trotskyites" that he wrote for *The New Leader* into his file, and, four years later, opened a "new" investigation of him, although no reason is given for doing this. It is especially puzzling because the following year, 1955, the FBI reported that Farrell, along with John Steinbeck, Robert Penn Warren, and Lionel Trilling, opposed the repeal of the 1950 Internal Security Act, as did the FBI. The Bureau even reported that Farrell said the protesters "overlook or ignore the fact that the association of American Communists with Communists of other countries is for the avowed purpose of overthrowing democratic government by any means, including force and violence." Farrell also announced, the FBI reported, that there was a conspiracy among Communist sympathizers, thus expressing exactly J. Edgar Hoover's thoughts.

The Director, finally satisfied, ended his inspection of the writer.

MALCOLM COWLEY:

I can't answer why Farrell exerted the most influence at Yaddo in the early thirties. I wasn't jealous of his influence. He was *there* more, and he was energetic. He played baseball.

His politics were very radical until 1935.

It was pretty rough for a while. I attacked him in *The New Republic*. But we ended up on good terms, Jim Farrell and I. When he was over the Trotskyites, he lived in this part of the country for a couple of years. He had a place over in Gaylordsville—not Gaylordsville, I can't remember the simplest name—it was right over here in New York State. He thought everybody was cheating him.

I had an enormous—not enormous, I'd say large—file of correspondence with him, and it's at the Newberry Library.

What brought about our ending up good friends? Time. And finally, I came to be of a more forgiving mood, and yes, so was he.

Finally.

**

Novelist and critic Granville Hicks was one of the first writers to recant his Communist party involvement in a way that would completely satisfy J. Edgar Hoover, becoming what Max Eastman had termed in 1918 "a self-confessed criminal." But Elizabeth Hardwick comments, "He shifted later with great torment to himself, I think."

Hicks's forty-three-page file was begun in 1926, the year a convicted murderer confessed to being the mastermind of Sacco and Vanzetti's crime—a confession that nonetheless did not change the death sentence of the pair. Hicks was a recent graduate of Harvard Theological School when the FBI reported that he spoke to "a mixture of Communist Party members and intellectual sympathizers" at a "convocation of 'Youth for Training in Peace Leadership,' " held in Concord, Massachusetts. The FBI said, "Hicks spoke on 'Is International War Implicit in a World Organized for Private Profit?' "

His name remained "dead" in the Bureau index for almost a decade without further references until 1934, when J. Edgar Hoover read in files agents gleaned from Elizabeth Dilling's *The Red Network* that Hicks was a member of the Communist party. Hoover's agents used this reference work to fill in missing details as often as they used *Current Biography*.

The Red Network reminded the FBI that Hicks was a book reviewer for the *Daily Worker,* and a member of the Friends of the Soviet Union. The following year, 1935, the FBI reported that Hicks gave a lecture entitled "Dialectics in the Development of Marxist Criticism" at the Congress of American Revolutionary Writers, and in 1936, it reported that he had written a book about John Reed.

In 1937, it was recorded that *Soviet Russia Today* had referred to him as a "Communist author," and that he had also recently contributed to a Marxist quarterly called *Science and Society*. Granville Hicks was a marked man in Hoover's mind, a writer to be carefully observed and a writer to worry about.

But the Director need not have been so concerned, because just two years later, in 1939, Hicks would become "a self-admitted former [CP] member."

Hoover surely was gratified to hear that Hicks believed "the Communism to which I was devoted was not the same as the Communism I now hate." His "confession of error"—he was a Party member from 1936 to 1939—plus his willingness to aid the Bureau in its anticommunism campaign is the major reason his file is relatively brief. Most of the references after 1939 pertain to his cooperation with both the Bureau and HUAC, where he was a friendly witness in 1953. In fact, because he was a friendly witness, the FBI wrote in his file that in any future investigation of him "consideration should be given."

Hicks had told HUAC what the FBI had always believed, that "the Communist Party in the United States was wholly under the domination of the Soviet Union," and that "every member . . . is an actual or a potential agent of the Soviet Union."

Theodore Draper writes in *The Roots of American Communism* that during the twenties "there were so many code names for different groups in and around the Party that the papers and documents of this period cannot be understood without a key for deciphering them." In most cases, the FBI could not decipher them, and that is one of the reasons a suspected Communist often became a confirmed Communist to them. In the absence of documented proof, circumstantial evidence like membership in a front was J. Edgar Hoover's passkey. Such evidence, risky but necessary for a time, would eventually contribute to the abuses that mounted later on. But particularly in the case of writers, Hoover never cared if proof of actual Party membership ever existed.

Even though informants were his best tools, Hoover relied a good deal on—and put a good deal of hope in—"self-confessions." He was particularly grateful to Granville Hicks, and in the fall of 1954, a year after Hicks's friendly HUAC testimony, he even sought the writer's advice about how to conduct an espionage and internal-security investigation, and received extremely valuable counsel from him. The result of this only known interview in which a writer virtually evolves into an FBI operative is included in his file, and while one has to take into account FBI paraphrasing, the document is still unparalleled for the insights it provides into the mind of a repentant ex-Communist.

The report of the interview contains one paragraph that the Director felt moved enough by to underline with his thick blue pen: "Hicks commented regarding the orientation given to Communist Party members concerning their hatred and fear of the FBI. He was of the opinion that this would be a very difficult barrier to overcome."

GRANVILLE HICKS:

"Granville Hicks . . . furnished the following information: He felt that a person would have to be on the verge of breaking with the Party in order to be contacted and furnish information. He thought there were two types of Communists who might break with the Party; the first, being the extreme repenter who, on breaking from the Communists, immediately returns to the church, and he, of course, would be cooperative with the Bureau. The other type would be a Communist who is somewhat disillusioned over one specific issue, perhaps a party line.

"To approach the second type of person, it was Hicks' opinion that an Agent upon making the first contact should merely state that we know about the person's background and activities, and that someday soon, it will get him into a great deal of trouble. The Agent should then leave a telephone number and name, merely stating that this person should think it over and contact us. Hicks thought that a few weeks hence, the same type of contact should be made, but no attempt should be made to converse with the individual at any length until the individual himself voluntarily initiates the conversation. Above all, Hicks thought the approach should be a [sic] friendly, and an attempt should be made to show the individual that the FBI Agent is not hostile.

". . . Concerning another point, Hicks thought that if the Agent could convey to the Communist that he might be able to clear an innocent person of a Communist taint, then the Agent might be able to persuade the Communist to state that he did not know a particular person as a Communist. Hicks felt that once you could get the Communist to state one specific thing, it would be easier to persuade him to continue his conversation. Hicks stated that it was the thought of possibly helping innocent people that he originally made up his own mind to assist the FBI.

"Another point brought up by Hicks, was to bring out the inefficiency of the Communist Party leadership. This could be done by asking the Communists what, after all these years, has the Party accomplished in this country, and what has it done for the individual.

"In general, Hicks felt that the biggest problem the Agent would have with the Party member would be to convince the Communist that the Agent is not the "Fascist" Agent that the Party had led the individual to believe. The Agent should attempt to impress on the Communist a feeling of friendliness and sympathy. . . ."

—*From an FBI report to J. Edgar Hoover,*
October 27, 1954

**

MURRAY KEMPTON:

There's a certain kind of mind which essentially will not admit that it was wrong—and even the people who broke with the Communists, most of them had the same mind. You know that wonderful line of Malraux's—which I think says everything you need to know about Malraux—he said, "I didn't change. Communism did." Thus meaning I was right all along. I was right when I was a Communist.

Communists really only lie to fellow travelers, and fellow travelers lie to everybody. I think fellow travelers ought to have joined the Party. I have tremendous respect for a lot of people who stuck with the Party. I love Party people. I can't tell you how many Communists I liked. Fellow travelers are dishonest. If they were honest, they'd be Communists.

One thing that has struck me is that people did not leave the Party for the reasons they said they left the Party. It's very, very important. I don't mean they lied. But you would be astounded how few Party members—and for that matter, even fellow travelers—left because of the Nazi-Soviet pact. Very few people left for that reason. The husbands leave, the wives leave with them. I mean, husbands are expelled, wives leave.

It's an interesting business because the whole idea that you're part of the cosmos and that you are moved by historical events just isn't true. You're moved by the pettiness of somebody. Or you're moved by the pedantry or the pomposity. You meet a girl from someplace else, or you meet a guy from some other Party. But then everybody has to explain this as though it was the result of intensely serious feelings.

I don't think I ever got over trying to explain myself and my motives in cosmic terms until I got ambushed in the Philippines. I mean, you can take your personal feelings very seriously, but the idea that you have some special identification, some special concern with world history is something you just don't have. I mean you keep saying to yourself, finally, why does Jeane Kirkpatrick take herself so seriously? I mean, I'm not picking on her now, but why does she take herself *all that seriously?* Once you regard yourself that way, your judgment is always wrong.

I mean, if you take most of the prediction record of most of these people who take themselves seriously as commentators and observers of the world scene, *most* of them are consistently wrong.

**

MERCHANT MARINE "X":

The libraries on the ships were *lousy*. It was just a collection of some 1910 and 1920s obscure novels no one ever heard of, and some cartoon books, old *Popular Mechanics* magazines, and one or two classics, like Dostoevsky. And the books were just piled up in some room. It was a joke. And they all had a moldy smell, I remember that. And you could keep the books out as long as you wanted. I rarely used it because I'd buy fifty to a hundred dollars worth of books myself, before I shipped out. They cost a dollar, and for longer books, $2.45. They were part of The Living Library, and I remember you could get *Tale of Two Cities, The Scarlet Letter,* and Fast's *Citizen Tom Paine,* Dreiser, Hemingway, Pearl S. Buck.

You know, I never heard the expression "fronts" while I was in the Party. It's a right-wing term. The Party was always broke, so it didn't create any organizations—except many unions. But it's a myth that the CP infiltrated unions—because the members were there to begin with!

I didn't want to overthrow anything and neither did the leadership of the Party. Terrorism doesn't work. If you can't do it politically, forget it.

And the only time I heard Stalin's name mentioned was in the CP literature, or if you took a class. In day-to-day things, no one said Stalin said this or that. It was a myth. And another myth was that there was a lot of discipline in the Party in the United States. There wasn't. Maybe in France, but not here, at least not in New York.

One time, though, a person was expelled for political reasons—because he decided the Trotskyites were right. We saw Trotskyites as counterrevolution-aries. You can't have revolution in one country, Trotsky said. They were more concerned with destroying the Party than with the goals of the Party. But I realize we forced them into that position. There was a Party line and Stalin got rid of Trotsky. There was a joke going around, "That's what you get for hanging around Trotskyites."

I didn't believe Stalin murdered him until 1980. You continue to read, and some of the things start to seep in.

In the beginning, I belonged to a local branch—and they weren't called "cells"! That's an FBI term! They were called "branches," and were within the framework of "sections." The branch meetings were in the evening and lasted one or two hours. They were very boring—"Who's-going-to-distribute-the-*Daily-Worker*-this-Sunday" kind of thing. Most of the talk was concerned with local problems. But when I got to the waterfront, it was more interesting. When I went to sea, I was in an industrial branch. We had guest speakers, and we were trying to organize a group to oppose national legislation.

Once we were organizing in Buffalo—in 1947—and I was aboard a ship illegally, distributing literature. A couple of guys threw me over the ship's side— about ten feet!

And we didn't hush up at meetings—no one cared if the FBI was there. The FBI infiltrated the union, and this one guy in New Orleans, he almost told us he was an FBI agent. He had no shipping time and he shows up in the hiring hall. Four or five out of fifty seamen were CP members—or none were. But some were "anti" and some were "pro"—but they didn't care. They saw the conditions change for the better.

The shape-up system of getting hired was destroyed—where guys were just picked out at "crimp" joints and in most cases used bribes to be hired. Hiring halls were developed, based on honest competition and seniority. The CP was the first to scream about unemployment insurance and social security, too.

A few Party members had different names, but most people used their real names; the concealed members were afraid they'd lose their jobs. And you were expected to give a certain amount of your salary to the Party, but it's a myth that you *had* to give, because if you didn't give it was all right.

The Communist party said in order to alleviate conditions, you have to change the system. I never did anything illegal as a CP member. And I heard all my life that Moscow gave money to the CPUSA, but I *never* saw it documented. It doesn't make sense—you've got to conduct your own revolution.

I knew Lillian Hellman was a member. I just knew. You *knew.* Dashiell Hammett was a member. Someone like Arthur Miller just hung around. He never was a member.

Naval Intelligence wasn't too sure of me. In 1942, I was on a troop ship and somebody came to see me. I was twenty-four, twenty-five years old. They asked if I was in Spain. They knew I wasn't, but it was a trick question. I said, "No, there are no ships going to Spain now." But *they* wanted me to answer it politically—about the Spanish Civil War.

I left the Party around 1953. I didn't leave because of pressure or the FBI or disagreement. It was personal. I broke up with my wife, I was driving a cab, and I was tired of fighting with the system. I stopped going to meetings, although I would still give them some money. I just drifted away. I still have friends that may or may not be Party members.

When Howard Fast left the Party, it was philosophically floundering around. The Party was mad at him for quitting. A guy like that was important to the Party—he was a famous author.

What did I achieve as a CP member that I couldn't have achieved otherwise? Two things. Some of the slogans were picked up by other groups—that there are those who own the means of production and those who do the producing, and based on that there's always going to be a struggle, which is a Party slogan, more or less. And two: unemployment insurance.

The CP made a lot of mistakes, and it had the wrong programs. It's too sectarian. But they didn't fail yet.

They're not dead yet.

CHAPTER SIX

"A Little Bit in Awe of Them"

American journalists were writers J. Edgar Hoover particularly feared and envied. Their power to communicate with the public quickly and directly—through airwaves and print—both fascinated and concerned him. He knew, of course, what words could do.

Hoover played the leaking game with the best. As Cartha DeLoach says, "You name me any senator and any congressman in the United States or the head of any federal agency that doesn't play the same game. They're playing the oldest game in Washington." Hoover used it to plant damaging information about his enemies in both his war on communism and in his war to keep the FBI's image untarnished by any criticism. He maintained both a "Special Correspondents" list, composed of "friendlies" such as Walter Winchell, George Sokolsky, and Louella Parsons, who could be counted on to do a favor or two, and a "Do Not Contact" list, composed of "unfriendlies" such as Drew Pearson, Bernard De Voto, and Murray Kempton, whose attitudes toward the FBI ranged from ambivalent to hostile. For Hoover, those who were anti-FBI were as dangerous as those who were pro-Communist, and this conviction created a side to his personality that turned him into a full-fledged bully. If you don't like me, he believed, then you can't like this country, and I'll get you. *I'll get you.*

For example, in 1949 Hoover had written a note saying, "Another attack in a new and very effective smear of FBI—article in *LOOK*; Sat. Review of Literature; Harper's; Merle Miller book; Tex McCrary broadcast; Mrs. Roosevelt's column; Col. McCormack's [*sic*] broadcast; Amer. Civil Liberty [*sic*] report & St. Louis incident resulting in charge of anti-Semeticism [*sic*]. And we are doing absolutely *nothing* to combat it or challenge it." Hoover's handwritten marginal notes on FBI documents always expressed his most personal and urgent thoughts.

Cartha DeLoach says, "Mr. Hoover didn't have such a thing as a list of sources. He had a list of friends. And a lot of columnists were his friends. He was in California during the summer vacation period, and he would get to know all these people. And when he would come to New York, which was once or twice a week, or something like that, he would always end up at the Stork Club, with Walter Winchell, Leonard Lyons, people like that. And a lot of columnists were his enemies . . . those who were of ultraliberal persuasion and disagreed violently with him politically."

According to DeLoach, Hoover "cultivated writers and reporters and television personnel" and this "was a *conscious* effort." He adds, "It was routine. As a matter of fact, at every field office I inspected, I was told to call upon newspapers and ascertain their relationship with the FBI. Was the FBI treating them all right? We wouldn't have done that unless there was a conscious effort to cultivate the newspapers—we attempted to cultivate all communications media. The FBI was a little bit in awe of them."

In 1925, after Hoover began segregating derogatory information on important people, keeping this material under lock and key, and after he started the "Obscene" file, which held sexual tidbits about the lives of important people, the Director realized that information was power: He commanded the necessary facts (or gossip) for intimidating anyone who dared to cross him.

In the same way that Hoover would hide material in his "Do Not File" files—where information was not indexed and thus there was no record of its ever existing—Hoover could hide material in his "Obscene" file. According to Athan G. Theoharis and John Stuart Cox, in *The Boss,* "When creating the Obscene file, Hoover recognized the value of gossip, which could be used either to discredit his adversaries or to curry favor with his ostensible superiors . . .''

"For a few centuries the word gossip retained its unpleasant connotation," St. Clair McKelway writes in *Gossip: The Life and Times of Walter Winchell,* but goes on to say that "around 1925, in this country, the word began to climb onward and upward to a position of eminence. . . .'' Hoover liked to leak items to friendly gossip columnists like Winchell, Parsons, and Hedda Hopper, but he also liked to leak them to political columnists as well. These leaks enabled him to control the depiction of the FBI in the media, but also, in a trade-off, they gave the columnists who received them exclusive "inside" information.

Cartha DeLoach says, "Hoover may have pretended with certain friends that he liked gossip, but he was a no-nonsense-type individual. When you went into his office—as I did every day, sometimes more than I wanted to—our conversation was strictly official in nature—formal—and on rare occasions, we would tell jokes. Mostly I would tell *him* jokes. But if he had an interview with George Sokolsky or Walter Winchell—and I've been in there on such occasions when he did have such interviews—they would tell him something, and he would tell them something back and, you know, gossip like that. But he was not a gossip, he was not a gossipmonger, no. He was too formal and too stiff. He was not the man to indulge in petty gossip.''

From the time he took over the Bureau in 1924, Hoover used the power of the FBI to make and break relationships between individuals and organizations. He used gossip, lies, and sometimes even the truth to further his objectives.

ROY COHN:
The FBI did exist in part on gossip, that was part of its job—to collect it, not to start it. Gossip very often led to useful things. And agents on the lower level made the decision it could lead to a useful thing, not Mr. Hoover, but also not some guy who was pounding the pavements. But it was part of their job to pass along what they would pick up in the course of their daily routine.

You could write about the power of gossip in the Reagan administration, or you could write about the power of gossip on the part of Eleanor Roosevelt. I mean that Presidents—leaders of the country, people who wield power—are gossips! They love it! Did you hear that so and so and so and so are involved—they love it. Jackie Kennedy loved it. John F. Kennedy loved it. Everybody knew that. This myth about the adoring couple—I'd be surprised if they crossed each other's paths once in three weeks during the time he was President. The American people are the most gullible people in the world for being handed and buying and believing and not checking gossip. And that goes right to the top—because the leaders of our country are isolated, and it's a dull, boring life.

**

FBI AGENT "X":

Harm comes, of course, when you disseminate false information—then I think we'd be held accountable. But dissemination of information, especially *false* information, is a thing to guard against.

Believe me, when you talk about gossip, agents traditionally gossip more than any other group of people I know—as far as getting information and trading information.

I've heard stories that someone kept a file on Hoover. It was a personality conflict, basically. But the notes were thrown away.

CHAPTER SEVEN

The "Friendlies"

J. Edgar Hoover and Walter Winchell had a great deal in common: both preferred power to wealth, both had an obsession to know backwards and forwards everything that was happening everywhere, both became vicious when attacked, both despised disloyalty of any kind, and both enjoyed playing "cops and robbers." They even died the same year, 1972.

Winchell's file contains an unsigned article about him that describes even further similarities: "Both men have a sense of insecurity. . . . They both have deep persecution complexes and are always visualizing dark conspiracies fashioned by invisible enemies . . ."

There were some subjects Hoover and Winchell did not agree upon. One was President Roosevelt, whom Winchell supported. In fact, Roosevelt and J. Edgar Hoover were the only two people he never attacked in his column.

Winchell did not turn to the right until Truman became President, yet during the years Winchell's politics were still left, Hoover played along because Winchell was so much in the center of a world of information that Hoover admired. Still, it must have stung when

Hoover learned that his friend was writing under the pseudonym Paul Revere II for *PM,* a newspaper Hoover abhorred because of its liberal editorial policies.

Hoover kept tabs on Winchell to the very end in a file that contains nearly four thousand pages (not including the thirty-one volumes of Winchell's gossip columns also kept on file, which would make the total file amount to approximately one hundred thousand pages).

Winchell's file was begun on May 2, 1934, the year the FBI gunned down bank robber John Dillinger in Chicago—a highly publicized coup for the Bureau. Hoover received a memo telling him that two agents had been "assigned to accompany Walter Winchell while he is in Chicago." At this point, the Director knew the columnist only by reputation; Winchell, who would later be called the FBI's "mouthpiece," had been a gossip columnist on the New York *Evening Graphic* from 1924 to 1929, when he joined the New York *Mirror,* and began a nationally syndicated column that he wrote for thirty-four years. Winchell also had a popular radio show.

No reason for the guards was given, but two weeks later, Hoover wrote a letter to the agent in charge of his Los Angeles office and told him that Winchell "has been very active in an anti-Nazi movement and feels there may be some efforts made to cause him harm or embarrassment." Although protection was not needed this time, Hoover asked his agent to stay on the alert, telling him that "Mr. Winchell also is in possession, from time to time, of considerable information" that could help the Bureau.

Hoover requested that Winchell be "placed on the list of persons to receive all releases," and a relationship developed in which Winchell considered himself an adjunct of the FBI. Indeed, Hoover considered the columnist the equivalent of an FBI agent; one such example of this occurred on February 7, 1943, when Hoover told Clyde Tolson to "call Walter and ask for details as it is news to us and we would want it."

Cartha DeLoach says, "Winchell was friendly and unfriendly. He went both ways. I recall that Winchell called me and insisted that the FBI obtain a license for a gun because he was afraid for his life. He'd received threatening letters. But I refused to do it. He indicated that he would write a nasty column concerning the FBI and he was going to have my job! I told him to go right ahead and report me to Mr. Hoover, but I wasn't going to get him a gun or a license. He did write a nasty column about the FBI."

Although Hoover fed Winchell an enormous amount of material, he remained sensitive to any charge that he did this. For instance, after receiving a phone message telling him that General Joseph P. Battley, chief of public information of the War Department, had inquired about a Winchell item that a Russian plane had been shot down in the Aleutians, Hoover scribbled next to the message: "He certainly has his nerve. We are not W. W.'s keeper and we should in no unmistakable manner get this over to such upstarts." On February 11, 1947, next to an article that reported "Navy Department officials said . . . that the FBI be contacted 'since everyone knows J. Edgar Hoover feeds . . . stuff to Mr. Winchell,' " the Director jotted "If *New York Tribune* is going to support such rat-trap journalism . . . then it must be judged accordingly. I am amazed that such a paper would indulge in such tactics." That same year, when *Collier's* magazine wanted to interview Hoover about his relationship with Winchell, Clyde Tolson suggested to his boss that he "not be available," and Hoover "agreed."

Hoover, of course, could also be friendly and unfriendly to Winchell. After a January 21, 1940, Sunday-night broadcast Hoover particularly liked, he wired Winchell, "Your editorial tonight was a masterpiece." After a September 12, 1943, broadcast that predicted the Gestapo would blow up many U.S. railroads, Hoover wrote an angry note about Winchell: "I am getting fed up with his hysterics— they in fact do more to sabotage the war effort than saboteurs have ever done."

Sometimes Hoover absorbed Winchell's very occasional barbs. On a letter the columnist wrote him on March 8, 1943, Hoover scribbled "Subtle sarcasm, but maybe deserved." Once when Winchell wrote the Director that someone told him "America's favorite spy-catcher" had received a knife wound while protecting "a little lady's honor and zip," Hoover wrote back, "This is news to me unless my hide is so callous I can't feel a knife." Hoover could also be naive about certain matters. After Winchell suggested that "the best defense against germ warfare is a toothbrush and a bar of soap," Hoover asked: "Is there any basis as to reliable value of the suggested antidote?"

Hoover wanted the information he received from Winchell to remain a private matter between the two men. A March 25, 1943, letter reprimands Winchell for sending a copy of a letter "concerning a bartender employed in the Stork Club" to the attorney general. Hoover told Winchell he was "considerably surprised" he had done this. A May 7, 1947, scolding concerns Winchell's asking the Anti-Defamation League to investigate an anti-Semitic charge; Hoover wrote: "If W. W.

wants to know he should ask me and not have an outfit like ADL investigating alleged acts of mine."

The Director often received literary tips from the gossip columnist. On September 13, 1942, after Winchell talked about a book entitled *Sabotage: The Secret War Against America,* Hoover said: "Let me see review." The following year, Winchell told the Director to read *Betrayal from the East,* which "exposes the Japanese spies and their American helpers."

Winchell's file says that "a Hoover friend and Winchell foe reported that Hoover 'regretted' the extent of his involvement with Winchell." Former Hoover assistant William C. Sullivan writes in *The Bureau* that Winchell "became so obvious after a while that he finally lost his value" to the FBI. In 1969, with no reason given, Clyde Tolson suggested that the Bureau take the columnist "off the mailing list." Hoover wrote next to his suggestion: "Yes."

The following year, Hoover, who wrote in 1971 that "I know Winchell as well as any other living person," sent him a telegram of condolence after the death of his wife, and five days later restored Winchell to "the Special Mailing List" because "he has not been well and he took his wife's death very badly." Richard Gid Powers comments that for Hoover, this is "a surprising and almost unprecedentedly human reaction."

J. EDGAR HOOVER:

"Just who is [*blacked out*]? Maybe our files know."
—*marginal note scribbled on letter from Winchell saying, "The lies he writes about me I don't bother to combat"; February 13, 1947*

"It looks as if W. W. has got us this time. Hereafter it certainly seems to me we ought to be able to utilize music by someone other than that of a well-known Communist. . . . Please get together on this and *quickly.* I understand Prokofieff's music is used on our program 'This is Your FBI.' "
—*note on column; April 23, 1947*

"Absolutely no comment."
—*note on column item saying the "Director had been offered a million dollars for the next ten years as a czar of boxing"; January 5, 1953*

"All of the above has been printed before. Because it appeared in N.Y. *Post* it is significant."
—*note on phone message concerning book* The Secret Life of Walter Winchell; *October 26, 1953*

"See that we get all the cards and promptly analyze them."
—*note on Internal Security memo stating that a source gave Winchell "12 names contained on 3x5 cards"; March 1, 1954*

"I completely agree."

    —next to Clyde Tolson's note "We better be careful about telling Winchell anything," re information received about a kidnapping; July 25, 1956

"Did we disseminate this to the Dept. and if so when?"

    —on broadcast item stating that informer Elizabeth Bentley was going to tell publicly for the first time something she had secretly told FBI; February 28, 1955

"I can't do either as I am already committed to both lunch and dinner."

    —on telephone message from Winchell inviting Hoover to lunch or dinner; November 5, 1956

"No."

    —on memo from Louis Nichols asking if he should query Winchell on an item that Roy Cohn had talked to him about; June 24, 1957

"Yes."

    —marginal note agreeing with memo saying Bureau should not advise Walter Winchell about whether to go to Cuba to get Castro's "side of the story"; March 20, 1958

"Dear Walter, It has been some time since we last saw each other. If my memory is correct, it was a night at the Stork Club. . . . I noted with great interest your remark about 'Waiting for Godot.' This is not all of the dirty work produced and authorized by our State Department . . ."

    —letter; July 16, 1958

"Dear Walter, I want to congratulate you on your forthright presentation of the news Sunday evening relative to Mr. Khrushchev's junketeering—most certainly I share your opinions regarding the disgusting displays on the part of some of the Hollywood colony . . ."

    —letter; September 22, 1959

"Many thanks for giving me the opportunity of reading the information from Walter's anonymous friend . . ."

    —letter to Winchell's secretary acknowledging such tips as "I'll show you how big dope shipments get into New York with no trouble. So simple it will amaze you. . . . how Costello was so relieved he wasn't going to be hit he gave me a horse that won and paid $42.00. . . . a fireman who is worth about 3 million in cash . . ."; February 26, 1960

"Dear Walter . . . the rumor about my quitting certainly is not true but it keeps cropping up periodically . . ."

    —letter; February 5, 1962

"It will be a 'stinker.' "

    —on Winchell column stating that the Saturday Evening Post *is doing a cover story about Hoover; March 19, 1965*

"In fact, in 1939, Mr. Winchell was responsible for having the notorious Louis (Lepke) Buchalter surrender to me . . ."

    —letter to the White House; October 11, 1966

"Write note."
—*on memo from Cartha DeLoach telling Hoover that Winchell came by "to kill time" while waiting for a White House appointment and that he had hoped he'd be able to say hello to "the Director and Mr. Tolson"; May 1, 1968*

"Dear Walter . . . it was indeed thoughtful of you to send me this material . . . concerning the literary figures who reportedly had an interest in the recent disturbances in Chicago. . . ."
—*letter acknowledging information about activities of "literary figgers" Alan [sic] Ginsberg, Jean Genet, and William Burroughs at democratic convention; September 13, 1968*

**

WALTER WINCHELL:
"The 'cops and robbers' pattern is always good . . ."
—*letter to Hoover; September 4, 1934*

"I find that the only way I can get a vacation this year is to have some guest columns. . . . I have read some of your speeches and none of them are dull. . . ."
—*letter to Hoover; June 6, 1935*

"Dear John . . . I think you're crazy not to go down South, even for a week, and enjoy a little life and pleasure. . . . Regards to Clyde . . . affectionately, Walter."
—*February 9, 1936*

". . . Well, Doctor, it was nice writing you again. S'long, Doc. Haw!"
—*letter to Hoover; May 29, 1942*

"Memorandum for Mr. Hoover: R. E. The Unnamed Tugboat Executive . . . who was overheard in the Stork Club while under the influence of liquor saying so that nearly everybody could hear him, 'The Navy is driving me crazy, changing the channel [invasion] plans from week to week . . .' "
—*memo; September 10, 1942*

"A new and very exciting book has just been published . . . *Passport to Treason* . . . [which] reveals that many disloyal Americans are right now holding good jobs in various government agencies in Washington . . ."
—*FBI broadcast summary; May 2, 1943*

"What is this? Tell Hoover it may be a clue! To do something about it please!"
—*to his secretary concerning a suspicious letterhead Winchell received in the mail; June 28, 1943*

". . . Phone Mr. H. Ask him if it is Commy and may I accept it?"
—*note to his secretary concerning a speaking assignment; April 19, 1944*

"We published as a fact, but you can use if you wish."
—*note to Hoover on his column that states, "Isn't it true that Earl Browder has phfft with the Communist Political Association?"; June 18, 1945*

"To Hoover"
—*on anonymous letter Winchell received and forwarded to Hoover, de-*

tailing that "former lover and protégé of Adolf Hitler now in Hollywood seeking movie career"; February 14, 1946

"Dear John, Is this true? I don't believe it. The FBI can't do that or can it. WW."
   —on tip Winchell received telling him "The FBI has given one of Hollywood's top stars (Judy Garland) ninety days to give up dope or else face public prosecution. Drugs have aged her so badly that she can barely stand a close-up despite the fact that she's still a blooming youth"; October 1, 1948

"Hoover—true? Not for publication. I want to know if source is ok."
   —on tip Winchell received telling him "The wife of a NY morning paper's editor is under scrutiny of the FBEye. She has an important atomic energy group post"; October 24, 1949

"H:"
   —handwritten initial on blind item forwarded to Hoover that asks Winchell to "check with the FBI on Johnny Ray–Marilyn Morrison marriage???? Have reliable information that this marriage occurred and was greatly publicized to cover up a 'messy' episode with a fourteen year old boy"; December 14, 1952

"Dear John, Can you please help check this group and man [National Television Review Board and Robert Kubicek]? Seems like a racket to me. Could be a Commie front, maybe?"
   —March 31, 1953

"Dear John . . . I would like some anecdotes on *things I never knew till now items*. . . . Can your researchers dig such a column for me?"
   —letter, October 22, 1953

"A sure best-seller coming out in March is *McCarthy and His Enemies*. The author is William Buckley of Yale University."
   —FBI broadcast summary, in which FBI comments that his first book "caused quite a sensation"; February 7, 1954

"Random House will soon publish a very great book about the FBI and John Edgar Hoover by Don Whitehead . . ."
   —FBI broadcast summary; September 16, 1956

"Arthur Miller a prize-winning playwright and the husband of a well-known movie star was indicted this week. . . . [His] pro-Red leanings are stale news to you listeners. I was the first to make them public. . . ."
   —FBI broadcast summary; February 24, 1957

"Every literate man, woman and child in the United States should read . . . *Masters of Deceit* . . . a blueprint on how to defend the moral foundations of our country . . ."
   —column; April 9, 1958

"Dear John, Thanks again for another letter that lights me all up when I get it . . ."
   —letter; November 20, 1959

"Ask J. E. Hoover if true?"
   —to his secretary on item killed by his editor about a possible Russian-Chinese war. Another note at bottom adds, "Exactly what the Commies want

*us to believe. Really, it's Red propaganda. China has no modern arms—
except those Russia doles out to her"; December 21, 1959*

"John—who is this pamphlet sender? or Printer? Are these people listed Pinks,
Reds, Commies? . . ."
    —May 31, 1960

"Dear John, The rumor about you quitting is around again. I hope it is not
true . . ."
    —letter, February 2, 1962

"Ignore WOW!!!"
    *—on letter saying John F. Kennedy and Lee Harvey Oswald are still alive;
December 11, 1963*

"Dear John . . . I met several Secret Service men today. . . . I introduced myself
as 'Walter Winchell of the F. B. I.' It didn't get the laugh I anticipated. One man
said, 'we are not F. B. I.' I said 'You don't have to tell me, I can SMELL' . . ."
    —letter; June 12, 1964

"To J. E. Hoover"
    *—on letter congratulating Winchell for "being the one columnist in New
York who dares to mention the Communist influence in the civil rights movement"; March 25, 1965*

"A sidewalk peddler in Times Square, NYC, is selling novelty wooden outhouses calling them 'LBJ' outhouses. Notify the Director."
    *—phone call to special agent in charge of New York office, October 1,
1967*

"I'm feeling well and continuing to 'charge' as a good newspaperman should."
    *—in-person message to Cartha DeLoach (to be passed on to Hoover);
May 1, 1968*

"Irving Mansfield heard some revolting news about Mr. Hoover—he said that
Bernard Geis is publishing a book in which he will name Mr. Hoover as a
homosexual. Bureau should get in touch with Mansfield—who is married to
Jacqueline Susanne [*sic*], author of Valley of the Dolls."
    *—phone message to special agent in charge of New York office, who wrote
Hoover a memo telling him about the phone call; May 13, 1968*

"Dear Clyde . . . Please stop sending the FBI booklets, etc. to Arizona. I am
back in New York. . . . But thanks for sending them all these years. Best to you
and John."
    —letter; April 30, 1969

" 'Attack on Terror: The FBI against the Ku Klux Klan in Mississippi.' Don
Whitehead's latest eye-holder . . ."
    —column in file; January 6, 1971

**

Winchell biographer Bob Thomas whom Hoover once called "a
scavenger," wrote that during the fifties Roy Cohn "became McCarthy's go-between with Walter Winchell," and that "each Sunday

night, Cohn telephoned information on the revelations McCarthy planned to make the following week. Walter Winchell broadcast the news to the nation.''

But this relationship between Winchell, McCarthy, and Cohn also involved a fourth: J. Edgar Hoover.

ROY COHN:
Walter Winchell and Hoover were very cozy, and Hoover would feed Winchell items, particularly over the weekends so Winchell could use them on his Sunday-night radio broadcast, which had an enormous circulation. *I* would feed Winchell items. There were maybe five, six of us when I was a kid—that's how I got to know Winchell—in the U.S. attorney's office. But I had access to a lot of information that didn't really matter whether it was public or not—about McCarthy.

I used to feed Winchell, Mr. Hoover and the FBI used to feed Winchell, and it developed into a close, personal friendship. They used to go away every summer to a resort in California owned by Clint Murchison, who was one of the really rich people in this country—he was maybe the third or fourth wealthiest oilman in Texas. A great friend of Mr. Hoover's and good friend of Winchell's. Every summer, Winchell and Mr. Hoover, who was accompanied by Clyde Tolson, would rendezvous at this place in California, and would spend about two weeks together.

In a typical summer, Murchison's guests would be Mr. Hoover, Mr. Tolson, Senator Joe McCarthy, and when Mrs. McCarthy came along, Mrs. McCarthy, me, and so on and so forth. I'm sorry, I left out Winchell. And Walter Winchell.

And we were all together in this one compound. Mr. Hoover would go in the mornings to Scripps Clinic for a checkup—he'd have it spread out, he always used to finish about twelve, one o'clock—and then he would go over to the racetrack. Every day. Because Mr. Hoover, of course, loved the races. And we would all go to the track together in the afternoon.

Mr. Hoover was a very good friend of mine. He called me Roy and I called him Edgar. He was called by his good friends John, but called by most of his friends, Edgar. Every letter from him to me is "Dear Roy," signed "Edgar." Not John. All through my criminal trials, when the FBI was the investigating agency against me, every single birthday and Christmas I would get a box of cigars, two or three books, or something.

I think Mr. Hoover said there was no organized crime in America because he felt that the quantity of the dramas on the radio, in the newspapers and the columns—on Al Capone and on Dillinger and all of that—represented such a *small* element of American life and American crime and that it did not qualify for an exalted place such as it is given by the press. I view Mr. Hoover as a guy who if he were alive today would be watching one of the television playback systems—Betamax or VHS or something like that—getting a certain degree of amusement out of it.

You've got to remember how different those days were. I don't know if he would have stood by that statement that there *is* no *organized* crime—Mafia. Now those were the days when Dillinger would surrender, when the streets would be lined for five blocks on each side and it would all be a setup because Walter Winchell would have arranged the whole thing! And Hoover was very conscious of that, and he had a great sense of public relations.

**

J. Edgar Hoover was fascinated with the glamour of Hollywood, and its gossip columnists were a special breed because of their immense power. Hoover recognized, naturally, the tremendous influence of movies, and wanted to control the cinematic portrayal of the FBI; during the McCarthy era he also sought to purge "subversives" from the movie business, as well as television. (A well-known and popular TV show about government agents, *The Untouchables,* was considered "rotten from every viewpoint" by Hoover.)

Eventually, the Great Enforcer would achieve many of his goals with the help of such cooperative columnists as Louella Parsons and Hedda Hopper. For over forty years—from 1925 until 1965—Parsons's gossip columns about movie stars made *her* a Hollywood star. She was as feared in Hollywood as J. Edgar Hoover was in Washington—and it seems inevitable these two would meet.

They did in 1934 when Parsons wrote an item that Paramount Pictures was going to "dramatize the life of [FBI agent] Melvin Purvis," who killed gangster Pretty Boy Floyd, and that the project had the Bureau's "authorization."

An FBI memo indicates that "Purvis himself did not know anything about [the movie] until he saw it in the papers," and that "it was one of the most contemptible things the motion pictures had ever tried to do." J. Edgar Hoover told Purvis "if anyone asked him about it" he was to say that the whole "idea was most distasteful and unpleasant," and then Hoover immediately wrote the attorney general that the FBI had not "issued any permission," and that the public might get the idea from such a movie that FBI agents go in for "cheap, nauseating publicity."

Hoover added that while "we have to stand for some literary license," the "trend" of the press has recently been "repugnant." Hoover cited an example involving Agent Purvis. After Pretty Boy Floyd was killed, there was one "lurid" story of how Purvis "personally interviewed Floyd as he lay on the ground dying, whereas, as a matter of fact, Mr. Purvis never spoke one word to Floyd."

Eventually, Paramount Pictures backed down and said Parsons's item was "unauthorized," and the studio had "no definite plans" to make the picture on Purvis.

But the incident began Parsons's 178-page file, a small one compared to that of her male counterpart, Walter Winchell, but women, no matter how powerful or how helpful to the FBI, just didn't count as much. (Hoover once chastised Winchell for saying that "Marge Conors, running against Clare Luce, was the first femme FBI agent" by firmly informing him that "the bureau does not employ female special agents."

Louella Parsons started a radio interview program called *Hollywood Hotel* the year her file began, and between her column and her show, she had the movie industry at her mercy. But Hoover did feed her tips after Parsons began mentioning the Bureau or Bureau-related matters in a favorable light, although most of his "tips" were related to items she had gotten wrong and Hoover wanted corrected. (Once, when she mentioned on an April 1, 1951, broadcast that a certain spy was "missing," Hoover demanded a "retraction," which he got. Parsons wrote that the spy's family knew exactly where he was, after all.)

In 1940, after being impressed by a visit to FBI headquarters, she wrote in her column, "I'm going to keep to the straight and narrow . . . they showed me how quickly they trace a criminal by fingerprints." Parsons was always glad to promote the Bureau. In 1945, her column announced "a scoop on the atomic bomb," the film *The House on 92nd Street,* which showed "how the FBI protected the secret from the enemy." She wrote that "she had talked to Mr. Hoover about it and he had told her that it was one of the best shows he had ever seen." Here, in a movie favorable to the FBI, Hoover was more than willing to give a plug.

In 1947, she wrote, "I ran into Walter Winchell having dinner with J. Edgar Hoover, who is in Hollywood on business. I asked if it was Bugsy Siegel's murder that brought him to Hollywood. He said no . . . but he is investigating certain activities . . . [of Siegel's] before he was murdered. . . . He [Hoover] is also here to find out about the subversive element . . . that . . . should be brought out in the open." Clearly, in this "tip," Hoover has manipulated Parsons away from a discussion of the Hollywood gangster's murder in order to use her to create the idea that "the FBI is watching *you.*"

In 1949, Hoover became upset after Parsons wrote that Dore Schary's movie, *Big Country,* would "stress feats of the foreign-born," and so he began an investigation of the film. He was also concerned that year when she broadcast an item that "the FBI is keeping very close watch on a certain little theatre group . . . infested with Communists." At the time of her broadcast, an investigation of such a group—the Actors Laboratory—was "in pending status," according to a memo in Parsons's file, but the next day a new investigation was opened, perhaps because of Parsons's prodding.

In 1950, the columnist reported that FBI agents were taking down the names of people who attended every performance of a "pro-Communist picture called Speak Your Peace." Although the Bureau discovered that, in fact, "no names were taken" and that the film was merely "observed to ascertain its nature," it also reported that the "two or three" agents did not attend "every showing," as Parsons said. Hoover did not correct her. In fact, he welcomed her hyperbole because it contributed once again to the idea that the FBI was "watching" Hollywood.

In 1951, Parsons sent Hoover the "research script" for a program she was doing on "What possessed a young man like Larry Parks to make him become a Communist?" and "How was intelligent Sterling Hayden trapped in the reds' slimy coils?" At the point in the script where one of the guests says, "The Commies always work underground and anything that brings them out into the open hurts them, that's why Hollywood must support Parks and Hayden—to encourage more people to speak out," Hoover scrawled on the script: "This is sickening." It is unclear whether he is "sickened" by the "Commie" underground or by the naming of names, since the whole paragraph is marked with his penned parenthesis.

Hoover made a deal with Parsons that year that she would announce his West Coast visit as one "to check on subversive matters," once again using her to spread his power of suspicion. According to the file, Hoover also made up his mind that if she decided not to "adhere" to the planned wording, he might give out another comment that could make her "look bad." But of course, there was no need for that—she had been on his side for a long time. Louella Parsons was happy to "adhere." She might need him one day.

Indeed, two years later, in 1953, Parsons sought the Director's help when she began receiving threatening letters, along with Gary Cooper and John Wayne. Hoover had an investigation started immediately, which resulted in the discovery that the letter writer was "a mental case" and that the letters "do not violate the extortion statute."

In 1960, Parsons's name (as well as that of rival columnist Hedda Hopper) was overheard on an FBI wiretap of two Las Vegas gangsters, who speak of hiding an unnamed Mr. Big in "Louella Parsons's suite" at the Tropicana Hotel.

Whoever it was that hid out in Louella Parsons's suite "was the big boss there at one time, 'cause he used to sit with Bugsy Siegel when Bugsy was building that joint."

Louella Parsons might have gotten a headline out of that; on the other hand, she might not have wanted the information that she had a presumably free suite at a gangster-run hotel made public.

ROY COHN:
Hoover was very close to certain columnists. I mean he didn't go about cultivating Louella Parsons or Hedda Hopper—it just happened by virtue of his existence.

**

J. EDGAR HOOVER:
"Tell Hood [an FBI official] to specifically deny this."
—*on Parsons's item that FBI was guarding the home of a potential kidnap victim; February 11, 1939*

"Of course we will *not* designate our L.A. Office to assist. I want to keep tight control of this project *here*. I still doubt their sincerity."
—*on memo telling him that 20th Century–Fox is "dilly-dallying" over a film project involving Bureau; May 6, 1947*

"Write Louella."
—*on Parsons's remark that Hoover "remains untouchable"; December 14, 1961*

**

Syndicated columnist and radio personality Hedda Hopper, who had been dishing out her chatter about movie stars since 1938, became the second member of the FBI's gossip auxiliary in Hollywood. Her 116-page file was opened in 1946 after she wrote a letter to the Director praising him for one of his speeches.

Hoover scribbled "Write Letter to Hedda Hopper" in the margin of the letter, beginning another important relationship, in which the Bureau would feed her material and she would continue to gush praise for the FBI in return. Hoover sent Hopper, who became "an adjunct of the blacklist process," as Victor Navasky has written in his book *Naming Names,* blind memos* on people she suspected were Communists, and Hopper, like her competitor Louella Parsons, smeared them in her column and on the air. "The line between name-dropping and name-naming" was "thin," Navasky explains.

In 1947 Hopper wrote Hoover an effusive letter about his book *The Story of the FBI.* "I loved what you said about the Commies in the motion picture industry," she told the Director, adding, "I'd like to

---

*Memos "without a cover letter so as to definitely eliminate any possibility of retracing the memorandum back to the Bureau."

run every one of those rats out of the country, starting with Charlie Chaplin." The Director immediately had agents prepare material on Chaplin for Hopper, including a report that "The Pravda" gave a great boost to "Comrade Charlie."

Agents were unable to locate the *Pravda* article supposedly saying that Chaplin "had recently joined the Party," and so they told Hoover "an effort is being made" to search for it at the Library of Congress. Hoover, however, was not impressed with this effort or with the Chaplin references so far collected for Hopper, and wrote on the memo: "Certainly a much labored effort brought forth a miserable product."

The following year, in 1948, Hopper reported in her column that she had "an off-the-record talk with J. Edgar Hoover at the Stork Club."

In 1958 Hopper wrote an item about movie star Kim Novak's "new boyfriend," whose identity could embarrass the Bureau. The FBI did some "research" and discovered it was someone close to the FBI and "if a scandal breaks we might not look so good."

Two years later, in 1960, Hopper telephoned the Director for "informal guidance" regarding two unnamed movie stars "who had been entertained in Moscow by Stalin before his death." In 1961, the FBI leaked to Hopper testimony (whose is not mentioned) made before the House Committee on Un-American Activities, telling her that it had been "obtained on a highly confidential basis and the fact that we have it should not be disclosed."

Hedda Hopper knew how to keep the FBI's secrets, but she had some of her own. According to her file, her name was on the mailing list of the American Nazi party.

EXCERPT FROM FBI WIRETAP LOG:

FIRST: I was getting worried because of the rain, you know. There was a lot of people coming from all over.

SECOND: He did a lot of work for people.

FIRST: He had a bad heart for a long time.

SECOND: The good people are going to the Stardust, the Sands, the Flamingo, the Desert Inn, the Riviera.

FIRST: I walked into the Riviera, I walk in there, get a front table, and no check. That Tropicana could be a ball of fire, if somebody could get in there.

SECOND: It's the worst run joint in the world.

FIRST: If Hedda Hopper . . . walks in, or anybody walks in, nobody knows them.

Nobody buys them a drink. When the place blows, you or somebody can step in and take over . . ."

—*from transcript of conversation between two unnamed gangsters; 1960*

**

One of Hoover's favorites was George Sokolsky, the right-wing columnist who was called "a member of our FBI team" by J. Edgar Hoover in 1958. His 906-page file was begun in 1925, ironically because he was suspected of being a Communist spy. On January 30, 1926, the Department of State sent Hoover a copy of an article from the *North China Daily News* entitled "The True Significance of the Student Movement," by George E. Sokolsky. The accompanying "despatch" from the American consul general at Shanghai advised the FBI that "except for this, the Department has no information which would indicate that Mr. Sokolsky is a Bolshevik agent." Hoover was also told "it is a matter of common knowledge that Mr. Sokolsky has been intimately associated with various officials of the Nationalist Government of China and that he is a close personal friend and confident of the present Minister of Finance."

In 1930, the FBI had received word that Sokolsky, now regarded as "very active in Communist work," was planning to conduct "a propaganda tour in the United States."

Four years later, in 1934, the Bureau received information that Sokolsky, who would join the New York *Herald Tribune* the following year, was a Japanese spy "endeavoring to obtain information about the fleet in New York."

By 1942, Sokolsky's checkered past was forgotten. He had moved far to the right, and the FBI dismissed its previous information as "rumor," adding, however, that "it was common gossip that Sokolsky had been kicked out of China for being on the Japanese payroll."

Two years later, when Sokolsky was a columnist for the New York *Sun,* he was receiving laudatory letters from Hoover. Now a staunch defender of the FBI, Sokolsky wrote Hoover: "Your work is of the highest order because you have not used great power for unworthy causes or to hurt innocent, even if mistaken, individuals." Actually, both men did use great power for unworthy causes and both men hurt innocent people. Sokolsky used his column to smear people he—and Hoover—considered suspect. As Victor Navasky writes in *Naming Names,* Sokolsky "indicted, convicted, pardoned, paroled, and granted clemency according to his own rules of evidence."

At first, though, Hoover did not totally trust Sokolsky, and in 1947 decided to test him. Sokolsky had suggested in a column that the FBI had allowed two espionage agents to escape. Hoover wrote a marginal note that the columnist should be "straightened out." An unnamed assistant was sent to interview Sokolsky, and later reported that the columnist "had learned he was in error . . . and apologized." Sokolsky had passed the test. When he mentioned to Hoover's emissary that "Congress should investigate the FBI to point out who was responsible for tying the Director's hands" regarding Communists, the FBI man advised him that this "would play into the enemy's hands," and was "the last thing he should do if he wanted to help [the FBI's] cause." Instead, Sokolsky was told "rooting out communism in the schools, the churches, publications, and thinking . . . was the real field where writers such as he could lend a great service." A congressional investigation *was* the last thing Hoover wanted, because his illegal activities and methods of hiding information could be uncovered.

Satisfied, Hoover wrote in the margin of the report, "This shows value of making such contact and cleaning up misunderstandings." It also shows how Hoover controlled the press.

By the 1950s Sokolsky was regularly forwarding Hoover confidential information, usually about Communist infiltration in the movie industry. He always warned the Director that what he was sending him had to be "treated confidentially." In time, Sokolsky supplied the Bureau with so much information about alleged Communists that a "special procedure" for handling it was "approved." This "special procedure" consisted of a simple Bureau order: upon receipt of anything from Sokolsky, "initiate a security investigation, if warranted."

By 1953, Hoover was gushing to Sokolsky that "reading your column each day is a 'must' for me," and "you have done an exceedingly effective job over the years in arousing public interest in the menace of Communism." But Hoover continued to keep tabs on the columnist because Sokolsky wasn't one hundred percent behind the Director. In 1956, he had questioned a Bureau technique in a column and Hoover noted, "I am getting a little fed up over the way some people harp upon FBI shortcomings and that includes Sokolsky."

In 1961, Sokolsky mentioned to Hoover that a typist in his office seemed to know some unnamed but very high government official. Fearing she would reveal what he was up to, Sokolsky told Hoover he planned "to get rid of" her to seal the potential leak. Hoover instructed his staff "most certainly" to be "careful in dealing with George until this girl has been removed."

Cartha D. DeLoach was an honorary pallbearer at Sokolsky's funeral on December 14, 1962. Richard Gid Powers says that Roy Cohn and Robert Kennedy were also among the pallbearers, illustrating that "anticommunism overpowered some of the hatreds" among certain Washington factions. In a lengthy and gossipy memorandum written three days after the funeral, DeLoach told Hoover that "the funeral lasted fifteen minutes" and "the service was beautiful by its simplicity." He also reported that "George had left a note to Roy Cohn to be opened upon his death; giving specific instructions as to the funeral and the burial," adding that "George left approximately an estate of $200,000 to his wife" and that "Roy Cohn owns the apartment that George lived in. He plans to deed it immediately to the widow."

DeLoach also wrote that "Roy Cohn approached me after the funeral and told me that the Attorney-General had greeted him very cordially outside the church and had mentioned don't worry about this case involving you [Cohn]. Just keep up the practice of law rather than 'maneuvering' so much."

The case in question was a 1962 obstruction of justice proceeding against Cohn. According to a memo in Roy Cohn's FBI file, Sokolsky told DeLoach about nine months before he died that Cohn "was extremely worried about the possibilities of being implicated in a stock rigging case," and that "rumors concerning his possible indictment have emanated from unfriendly sources."

The memo indicates that DeLoach felt "George was doing a little fishing," since Cohn was not named in the indictment, although De-Loach also said that "indications are that [Cohn] participated to a degree in the over-all scheme as [a] hidden principal."

A few months later, Sokolsky was still trying to help Cohn, who was being investigated by the FBI. Sokolsky told DeLoach that he was "considering writing an article about the impropriety of the FBI harassing innocent people," and also mentioned that an unnamed FBI agent told some woman he had interviewed that "Roy Cohn is in great trouble." An immediate investigation of the agent in question was launched; it revealed that the report was not true. Sokolsky was eventually shown some secret evidence about Roy Cohn that made him realize "he had been used by Cohn, and he resented it very much." No anti-FBI or anti-FBI-agent column was written by Sokolsky. Hoover had cleaned up another "misunderstanding."

On another occasion, George Sokolsky did use his column in Cohn's behalf. Cartha DeLoach recalled the incident: "George Sokolsky at one time indicated that if I didn't go to Roy Cohn and tell him to stop doing what Sokolsky indicated were immoral acts—he was sleeping with some hoodlum's wife—that he was going to write a nasty column concerning the FBI. I told him I wouldn't do it; that was not our jurisdiction and I refused to do it. I realize that Roy died of AIDS and was reportedly a homosexual, but at the time Sokolsky indicated that he was bisexual and the hoodlum would probably kill him if he didn't stop sleeping with his wife. I refused to have anything to do with it. George Sokolsky, who was one of our best friends, wrote a nasty column concerning the FBI.''

George Sokolsky used the FBI, too, but the FBI used him even more. One of his most important public relations statements was one he made in 1957 when he told the American public that ''the FBI does not maintain a 'blacklist.' '' Hoover told his friend that the blacklist idea was started by people who wanted to ''injure'' America, or ''persons who simply don't know what they are talking about.''

CARTHA DeLOACH:
Well, I liked George Sokolsky very much. I thought he was a grand old man, and I helped him—from the standpoint of when he came to Washington I'd always have dinner with him, and I'd talk to him quite frequently.

Mr. Hoover felt that the FBI was pretty much his fiefdom, his turf—and any derogatory comment concerning the FBI was somewhat taken personally by him. Now to a certain extent that was good. Why? Let's take the false accusations made about the FBI during the Civil Rights era of the 1960s. It was very difficult for the FBI to go out and investigate violations of civil rights cases—although we did it. But people did not want to furnish information. You had the Ku Klux Klan on one hand battering at us and criticizing the FBI and planting snakes in our cars. I participated in the investigation of the three missing Civil Rights workers down in Mississippi—they refused to serve us food in restaurants. Once they brought a casket to the door of the wife of an FBI agent and said, "Your husband is dead, and inside." Of course, it was empty. But the point I'm trying to make is that on the one hand you had the extreme right wing and on the other hand you had the extreme left wing, and then you had many Blacks who were somewhat polarized because they thought the federal government was not helping them enough. We didn't have the manpower to protect them. It was not within our jurisdiction. But we did have the authority and need to get out and investigate those cases. So we needed the cooperation of the general public as much as we could. An informed, cooperative public is the greatest tool you can have for investigative purposes. Now, where the FBI was criticized, and people lost faith in us, it made it that much harder. So that's why the FBI was sensitive and perhaps Mr. Hoover went a little overboard from time to time in his sensitivity.

We always fought against the FBI becoming a national police force. We were encouraged time and time again by certain people—particularly congressmen and senators—to make the FBI independent of the Department of Justice. We thought it was wrong. We thought it was better to be under the wing of the Department of Justice, and have the public on your side—and informing—not a nation of informers, not a national police force, but helping us in specific cases.

Our more bitter enemies had a built-in hatred toward the investigative process. They felt it was strictly an invasion of privacy and therefore had no place in American society. They failed to understand that the FBI was actually protecting them—keeping them from being victims of crime and keeping them from being overrun by certain of the revolutionary elements.

CHAPTER EIGHT

The "Friendlies,"
Continued

Fulton Lewis, Jr., had been reporting since 1923, but his name wasn't placed in the FBI's files until 1938, when he requested some information about "a spy case." A week later, on July 1, he was put on the "general mailing list," and later, when he had done enough favors for the Bureau, he was put on the Special Correspondents list.

That same month, July 1938, J. Edgar Hoover told a radio audience that Fulton Lewis, Jr., had "placed patriotic duty above personal gain and recognition" and had turned over "sensational" information involving an "espionage plot" to the FBI. The Director told his audience that he urged all members of the press "to cooperate with law enforcement officials." He meant secretly as well as publicly.

Hoover wrote Lewis that he "would not be at all surprised" to learn that "Communistic forces" were behind the attempt to smear him and the FBI. In his correspondence with Lewis, he became almost reckless in his description of those who were opposed to him. His accusations ranged from calling the criticism merely an "annoyance" to "a racket." He and Lewis both believed "Moscow" was behind a great deal of the criticism directed against him. Even if this accusation were true, and so far history has not proved it to be, Hoover, as usual, overreacted.

On July 13, 1938, thirteen days after he was put on the mailing list, Lewis invited the Director to offer his "point of view of the day's news" on his radio program. Hoover, of course, was "happy to make this broadcast."

By July 24, 1939, the Justice Department was complaining of leaks in Lewis's column that could only have come from the FBI because "only one or two agents knew of the information." It is not known if the Justice Department actually followed up on this.

A year later, Lewis was writing Hoover that he had heard "many favorable comments" about him, "even from your strongest newspaper critics," and "we have managed to squelch" a "smear" campaign. Lewis announced on a broadcast that "radical reporters" who had been "very active in support of the Spanish Loyalists" were trying to discredit Hoover as a "publicity seeker."

Lewis's King Features syndicated newspaper column, as well as his radio and television broadcasts, made him a very valuable friend, indeed. According to Victor Navasky the writer and *Nation* editor, Lewis became "a professional hatchet man" who "would get on a case and not let go." A steadfast right-winger, he "was always very favorable to the FBI," Cartha DeLoach says. A 1963 document calls Lewis one of the "anti-Communist writers who have proved themselves to us." In fact, like Walter Winchell and George Sokolsky, Fulton Lewis, Jr., behaved like an adjunct FBI agent.

"I knew him well. Mr. Hoover knew him well," Cartha DeLoach says. "I was in his home on many occasions for dinner, and he was in my home on occasion. I thought he was a little loose sometimes with his facts, but nevertheless, I knew him well, and he was always very favorable."

In 1949, Lewis turned to Hoover for help when an unfriendly article about him was about to appear in the *Princeton Public Opinion Quarterly Review*. Lewis termed the author of the article, a "character assassin." Breaking the law, Hoover checked his confidential files, and later told Lewis he had nothing on the individual, a speech professor at Cornell.

The following year, in 1950, an assistant to President Truman wrote Hoover that Lewis had said a secret document in his possession, a memorandum "prepared by the White House" that asked the Kremlin to "direct the North Koreans to cease and desist" had been confiscated from the Philadelphia headquarters of the Communist party. The presidential assistant told Hoover that the material Lewis referred to was not prepared by the White House, but by the "State Department."

Hoover initiated an investigation of ''White House leaks,'' but he was mainly interested in finding out if the leaked information was also in the Bureau files. As it turned out, some of it was and some was not. According to Lewis's file, Hoover attributed the leaks to Joseph and Stewart Alsop of the *Herald Tribune*.

A former high government official says that ''one of the Alsop brothers'' was once ''compromised by the Soviets'' because of homosexual behavior, and ''came to the FBI and CIA and said the Soviets would expose his homosexuality unless he worked for them.'' It is possible that Hoover's blaming the White House leaks on the Alsop brothers is somehow, even if remotely, linked to this.

In 1950, Hoover enlisted the help of Lewis in his assault on lawyer Max Lowenthal, who had written a book attacking the Bureau and Hoover. That same year, Lewis supplied the FBI with a list of people who were to attend a screening of the movie *Walk East on Beacon,* which Hoover and Clyde Tolson were also attending.

A February 1954 memo reports that Roy Cohn was a guest on one of Lewis's broadcasts, and said that Senator McCarthy's committee ''gives witnesses greater rights than they would get in a court of law.'' Another memo written two months later reports that ''McCarthy and Lewis are 'thicker than thieves and that Lewis furnishes McCarthy with information from Mr. Nichols of the FBI.'' The conduit for the leaks was probably Roy Cohn, who met regularly with Nichols, according to Cartha DeLoach.

Hoover maintained a file on Lewis that reached 1,754 pages by 1968, two years *after* his death.

ALLEN GINSBERG:
I mention Fulton Lewis, Jr., in a poem of mine—because I remember listening to the radio when the Rosenbergs were executed and he announced that they smelled bad. And that struck me when I was a kid: it was such an anti-Semitic, overtly racist remark—that Jews smelled bad—as a reason for killing somebody.

But it stuck in my mind.

**

ROY COHN:
Fulton Lewis, Jr., was a good friend of Hoover's in sort of a circle consisting of Hoover, Richard M. Nixon, Edward Nellor, who wrote most of Lewis's stuff, and Louis Nichols, the associate director of the FBI.

**

J. EDGAR HOOVER:
"I want *very* special attention given to this."
—*response to tip Fulton Lewis gave FBI involving an overheard conversation "discussing the numbers 1106 and 686" which, "he felt, referred to either radio tubes or numbers of government contracts"; July 19, 1945*

"Right, I certainly am not doing any research work for Mrs. R."
—*on memo requesting information for Eleanor Roosevelt; February 6, 1951*

"What do our files show on this?"
—*on memo from Lewis telling Hoover that Ford Foundation was "a left-wing propaganda operation"; October 21, 1955*

"Lewis told me one of the researchers [of Ford Foundation Fund for the Republic Study of CP] is now employed by the [Justice] Dept's anti-trust div. Was her name mentioned last evening? If not, have Nichols get it from Lewis."
—*on memo criticizing Ford Foundation for not including enough anti-Communist material in its research; November 1, 1955*

"I certainly have no intention of getting into politics."
—*on Lewis item suggesting Hoover run for President; November 9, 1955*

**

Quentin Reynolds, an editor at *Collier's* magazine, entered the files in 1938 as a supporter of Loyalist Spain. The following year the FBI also found his name on the letterhead of the American Union for Concerted Peace. Eventually, however, Reynolds would "cooperate" and become a Bureau friend.

Best known as a World War II correspondent, Reynolds wrote celebrated books on combat, including *The Wounded Don't Cry,* and *The Curtain Rises,* a 1944 best-seller. Two years after the latter's publication, Reynolds was classified an Internal Security threat after agents reported that he had praised the Soviet Union during a town hall meeting in Phoenix, Arizona. That same year, however, Reynolds and his wife were given a tour of headquarters, and a report of the visit described their "enthusiasm," as well as the fact that "Mr. Reynolds stated that he probably is the only person who calls the Director "John," as everybody else either calls him 'Speed' or 'Edgar,' " suggesting that he and Hoover had become close friends. (Nonetheless, only two of Reynolds's letters in the file use "Dear John"; the rest are addressed "Dear Edgar.")

Close friend or not, Hoover cooperated with the secretary of defense's request, in 1947, to investigate Reynolds (no reason for the inquiry is given in the file). The Bureau sent a blind memo "reflecting all pertinent information" on Reynolds to the Defense Department. This extreme measure to protect the FBI's identity was odd, considering that the request for the investigation began with the Defense

Department. But Hoover was not supposed to be keeping a file on Reynolds, and didn't want anyone to know that he had one.

What did this blind memo contain? Information that although Reynolds was "closely associated with a number of Communist front organizations," he "is definitely not a Communist." In fact, the memo said Reynolds "despised" communism, and "had been commendatory in his remarks relating to the Bureau." The worst thing Hoover found to say about the journalist was that he was a "confirmed liberal." It may be that a letter Reynolds wrote around this time had something to do with the Director's tolerant attitude in not holding Reynolds eternally suspect for his front activities, as he did with other writers. Reynolds had written: "I hate to bother you with this, and feel like an awful ham asking you to read a story of mine. However, the remark Ronald Reagan made the other night at dinner has bothered me a little. You will recall he said, maybe kiddingly, that a few people down in Washington have told him that I was a Communist. You might have heard the same thing. I value your opinion of me, and Clyde's opinion, so much that I would like to go on record as to exactly how I feel. I think this piece I did for PM explains just that.   . . ."

In 1953, when he was asked to write a children's book about the FBI for Random House, the FBI prepared a memo of possible cases Reynolds could use. It is doubtful Reynolds ever saw this particular memo, because it "contained material not suitable for dissemination in its present form," and also contained some cases marked with a "no" that associate director Louis Nichols felt the FBI should not suggest to Reynolds.

Bennett Cerf, the president of Random House, wrote Hoover in June of 1953 that "I am convinced that Quent will turn out a book of which all of us may feel justly proud." Journalist Murray Kempton comments on Cerf's statement: "I think by and large dealing with the Director was an insurance policy." Cerf understood this principle well. He once said: "If you publish J. Edgar Hoover, you can publish anyone."

Two months after "choosing" the cases Reynolds could use in his children's book, the Bureau wrote a follow-up memo about the "general format" he "worked out." Louis Nichols told Clyde Tolson the "techniques" to be used in the "story," and even commented that Reynolds "is very much enthused about the book."

At the time, Reynolds was also involved in preparing a libel suit against Westbrook Pegler, who had challenged his record as a war correspondent in a column written in 1949, and had also called him pro-Communist, immoral, and a coward. In another column written that year about Reynolds's book review of a recent biography of newspaperman Heywood Broun, Pegler had said that "Reynolds was a coatholder for Broun and imitated his morals." (Interestingly, Hoover liked this put-down of Reynolds, for he wrote in the margin: "This is terrific, particularly as to Quentin Reynolds.")

Nichols mentioned in his memo to Tolson about the children's book that Reynolds "is boasting how he has Pegler over the cracker barrel" in the suit. A year later, in another memo, Nichols told Tolson that some unnamed person told him that "Pegler thinks that he has Reynolds beat," and Nichols commented that that means the case is "probably going against Pegler," which it did; Reynolds was awarded $175,000 in damages. In fact, for unknown reasons, but possibly because of the suit, Reynolds's file, which was kept until 1966, the year after his death, has more unreleased, classified pages (330) than unclassified ones (250).

In December of 1953, Quentin Reynolds submitted his Random House book to the FBI to be checked for "factual inaccuracies and errors in Bureau policy." The FBI reprimanded Reynolds's editor for choosing a title, *The Story of the FBI,* that had already been used "a few years back" on another book that had been published by "the editors of *LOOK* magazine," and suggested that another title be selected. The book was retitled *The F.B.I.*

An eleven-page memo was also written, containing such criticisms as "this paragraph leaves the impression that Mr. Hoover was in the Bureau of Investigation during World War I, when, in fact, he was in the Department of Justice, 1917–1921" and "the discussion between the Attorney General and the Director is not realistic" and "the story depicted in this entire chapter is contrary to Bureau policy." In a later memo, Nichols told Tolson that although the first draft was "impossible," the "second draft was excellent, although chapters three and four of the second draft will have to be rewritten. I think the book will then be in excellent condition and will serve a useful purpose."

Reynolds was eager to cooperate. While his book was in progress, he had written Hoover: "Just a note to thank you for the wonderful cooperation I received from the Department when I went to Washington last week to gather information for a juvenile book I am writing on the FBI. . . . I'll finish the book in a month or so and will send it to Lou [Nichols]. I've asked him one favor—if after reading it he does not think it will be useful to the Department, to drop it into the nearest waste paper basket." (In 1960, Reynolds would write another flattering letter: ". . . Guess I've met fifty of your agents by now, but I never met a more intelligent, decent, co-operative man than [*name blacked out, but a memo indicates it is probably M.A. Jones, who worked under Cartha DeLoach*]. He was wonderful. His respect and admiration for you and Clyde warmed my heart. . . . Congratulations for molding him to your image. My regards to the 'Killer.' ")

The Director wrote a foreword to *The F.B.I.*, and also "asked" for a discount price for all FBI employees. Bennett Cerf complied, and according to the file, the FBI kept track of every single copy bought.

Reynolds later wrote Louis Nichols that it was "the most popular book he has ever written." Quentin Reynolds was now referred to as "an old friend of the Bureau," and all of his 1930 and 1940 Communist front references were forgotten.

Nonetheless, when the editor of Reynolds's 1963 autobiography wrote Hoover for "at least one anecdote" to be included in the book, to be published by McGraw-Hill, Hoover's response was to open a file on the editor and to decline his invitation to contribute to the book.

Journalist and radio announcer Gabriel Heatter, the man who made "Ah, there's good news tonight" a national catchphrase during World War II, had only that kind of news in mind for the FBI on his December 27, 1942, broadcast when he said Hoover had "done a marvelous job," and that the country "owed him a debt that could not be repaid." The Director wrote a thank you note, and Heatter became an instant, if neglected, Bureau friend. Over a decade later, Clyde Tolson had to remind Hoover that the commentator "be kept in mind as a special friend who can be helpful." Hoover wrote next to that observation: "Yes. I am at a loss as to how we have overlooked him all this time." From then on, Heatter was given insider tips "from time to time," including "the highlights" on the "solution of the Brink's case."

Heatter later told an FBI official that he "wanted to be sure that the Director knows that he stands ready to do anything for the FBI at any time." The FBI official reporting this to Hoover added that Heatter "emphasized *anything*."

**

In 1935, newspaper columnist Leonard Lyons, who wrote "The Lyons Den" gossip column for the *New York Post* from 1934 until his death in 1976, ran an item that "revenue agents were exacting graft from night club owners," precipitating the FBI to interview him about his sources, but he told the agents he could "not divulge the names unless [the owners] authorized him to" and later said the owners said "no." The exchange began a relationship among the FBI, Hoover, and Lyons that lasted for over thirty years.

Roy Cohn says that Lyons was "an intimate personal friend of Hoover's," but Lyons's widow, Sylvia, explains that "Mr. Hoover was an acquaintance, not a friend. We never went to his house and he never came to ours." She adds that her husband and Roy Cohn "weren't friends. When you're a columnist, you talk to all sorts of people."

Indeed, these men were sources for Lyons, and he used them to fill up his column with up-to-date morsels of gossip and news.

From 1935 to 1970, J. Edgar Hoover amassed a thousand-page file on Leonard Lyons, recording all letters received and all conversations held, plus a detailed summary of every single column item of relevance to the FBI.

Jeffrey Lyons, the movie critic, says his father "would have been surprised he had a file," adding that he doesn't believe the FBI caused "any professional detriment" to his father's career. Sylvia Lyons says that J. Edgar Hoover once told her that it was just "raw material" in the files, and that "they collected everything—gossip, everything— and perhaps someday it would be used, if needed." At the time Hoover told her this, she had no idea her own husband had a file, too. "My God, they must have spent a lot of time on that," she says. "I always thought Hoover had something on every President, or every President feared that he might have something. Hoover was an odd character. He thought there were Communists under the bed. And he knew how to get very good publicity for himself. It's interesting how closely Hoover watched Leonard."

Mrs. Lyons, who is writing her husband's biography, also says, "I think a lot of people were curious about his sources." Jeffrey Lyons explains that "my father was a lawyer—and was very careful about sources."

Hoover understood how careful he was, but never gave up trying to discover some of them. In fact, sometimes Hoover was relentless in his attempt to get to them, once going all the way to the front door of the Supreme Court. A 1943 memo indicates that "Supreme Court Justice William O. Douglas advised regarding Leonard Lyons's story on 'Disappointing Clubs' that he heard the story as anecdote and repeated it to a friend whose identity he didn't recall, but thought was a New Yorker, and apparently that was how Lyons got the story."

Sylvia Lyons says that during the fifties her husband "almost went to jail in the Rosenberg case. They wanted him to reveal his source of information. They didn't argue about the accuracy of it, they wanted him to reveal his *source.*"

Lyons had written that Ethel Rosenberg was imprisoned in Sing Sing Prison's death house pending her appeal rather than in a federal house of detention in an effort to make her talk.

In 1938, when Lyons wrote that "the G-Men now have forty thousand sets of [civilian] fingerprints submitted," Hoover wrote him that the number was actually "over 750,000," and that same year when Lyons wrote about the facts in a murder case, a special agent wrote to the Director "that only one or two agents" knew such information and he wondered about Lyons's source. The special agent felt that Lyons would not divulge it, but urged Hoover to put Lyons before a grand jury. Hoover agreed, although the matter was later dropped.

In 1940, someone whose name is blacked out, but who is clearly a journalist, complained to the FBI that Walter Winchell and Lyons were always getting the scoops. The grumbling journalist was told that "he was just wasting his time trying to make something out of nothing." Sylvia Lyons says that "any columnist would have been jealous—if that's the right word—to have a pipeline, so to speak. . . . Winchell was Hoover's Number one outlet."

According to his file, Lyons often checked information with Hoover. A 1944 letter from Hoover to Lyons answers Lyons's "request for information on the enforcement of Selective Service during World War I and II," and ends with a "it is a pleasure to work with you in this matter."

In 1945, Lyons telegrammed a request that Hoover "rush" a security clearance so he could be accredited as a war correspondent "immediately." Hoover replied that as soon as he was asked for his recommendation it would be "immediate and favorable."

Roy Cohn also says that Lyons "was an intimate personal friend of Ernest Hemingway's," and that Lyons brought Hemingway and Hoover "together." Sylvia Lyons says, "My husband and he were friends. Somebody introduced them—probably at the Stork Club. We visited Hemingway in Havana."

According to the file, Lyons once asked the Director to be a reference when he was applying for an apartment. "I don't remember that," Mrs. Lyons recalls. "That must have been funny for the landlord! A landlord must have been flabbergasted to see that." ·

In 1947, Lyons asked Hoover to write a guest column while he was on vacation, and in a letter that ends "With all best wishes to Sylvia, to you, and the family for a happy Holiday season," Hoover enclosed a "draft of a column based upon the Federal Employee Loyalty Program." Two years later, Lyons requested another guest column, and suggested that Hoover write about "FBI sources." Hoover wrote one entitled "The Power of Facts." Lyons, in his thank-you note to the Director, said it was "perfect," and mentioned an up-and-coming trip to Sweden, "where our main mission will be to acquire the royal crown cuff-links which you and Clyde admired."

In 1953, J. Edgar Hoover created a "Secret Correlation Summary" of all references on "Leonard Lyons," or his "aliases": "Len Lyons," "Lennie Lyons," "L. Lyons," and "Lenny Lyons."

The secret summary divulged that Lyons's contacts "are principally with the night life and cafe society groups in N.Y.C." —hardly a secret. The summary also lists the subject matter of every column of "interest to the Bureau," as well as a summary of secret intelligence concerning Lyons. In this latter category is a 1936 memo that Lyons " 'plays around' with the radicals in the newspaper profession and was one of a group who protested against the playing of the national anthem on radio programs." A 1938 memo in the Secret Summary mentions that Lyons's name was "not removed" from the Bureau mailing list. The implication is, of course, that Hoover was once thinking about using his favorite form of banishment, but then changed his mind for reasons not given—although another memo, dated two years later, explains that "Lyons was on the mailing list although employed by the New York Post, which has indicated unfriendliness to the Bureau through their editorial policies." And Hoover once noted that the *Daily Worker* picked up a 1944 Lyons item about Stalin wanting to see the War Department's film *Battle of Russia*. In 1941, the secret summary reports that the columnist "age 34, traveled from N.Y.C. to Mexico." The reason for including this information is blacked out, although the next line reads "Espionage G," or German. Surely Hoover did not really believe Lyons was a spy, although that is the implication from the reference, especially since the next summary item states that Lyons "boarded plane at San Jose, Mexico to Brownsville, Texas." Why was Hoover following him? The next eight items are blacked out, so it is not possible to know.

Lyons's file disclosed that Hoover was not above tapping his phone. A 1944 document reveals that the FBI bugged Lyons, as well as Winchell and columnist Ed Sullivan. Another document establishes that at one point the FBI also kept track of Lyons's name in the conversations of others being tapped. A 1945 report states that he "had a 'pipe line' into the White House." Leonard Lyons would be "aghast," at the FBI's tactics, his widow says, adding that she believes his "file isn't damaging—it's just that they could spend so much time—or be suspicious about him. I think Hoover always felt that the *Post* was a Communist paper." The file might not be "damaging," but it is ugly. One report refers to "that Jew columnist, Leonard Lyons."

A 1943 memo says someone whose name is blacked out "was thinking of making up an item and make it exclusive to someone like Leonard Lyons." Sylvia Lyons says, "It was very hard to get into a Lyons column. Of course, someone could put one over him. If you're writing a thousand words a day—and if he trusts the source—who knows? Maybe the source is disloyal or trying to plant something. But Leonard, if at all possible, would check if someone he knew had given him an item."

As late as 1960, Hoover recorded remarks made by Jeffrey Lyons when he visited the Bureau with his classmates: "You won't have any trouble with me. I can see that crime doesn't pay especially where the FBI is concerned." Why was it necessary for the Bureau to record a schoolboy's remarks?

In 1970 Lyons sent Hoover a copy of a black hate letter containing such phrases as "power crazy Blacks" and "the new red front—liberals" that had been forged with his signature and sent to presidential assistant John Ehrlichman at the White House. Ehrlichman, President Nixon's authority on domestic affairs, had not recognized it as a fake letter, and routinely answered it. His reply is not included in the file, although there is a brief, nonchalant note to Lyons included. This note says "Enclosed is a xerox copy of the letter received—supposedly—from you. . . . Evidently someone had taken the liberty of signing your name to this letter, and we, in turn, replied." There is no indication given as to how or when Ehrlichman learned the letter was not written by Lyons, but Lyons may have been exploited in a COINTELPRO (Counterintelligence Program) operation.*

Sylvia Lyons says she had never heard about the letter, so could provide no further information on this final, ominous reference in her husband's file.

J. EDGAR HOOVER:
"Is there any truth to this? If not, write and tell Lyons."
—*comment next to item stating that the Department of Justice purchased, for $3.50 each, photos of people making anti-American speeches at German-American Bund meeting; 1939*

---

*These were manufactured disruptions. See the discussion in Chapter 16.

"My, my this joke has whiskers on it."
    —*note on item mentioning that "even if you were J. Edgar Hoover himself you can't get in [to the Justice Department Building] without a card"; 1940*

"Send Regrets."
    —*scribbled on invitation to Warren Lyons's Bar Mitzva; 1953*

CHAPTER NINE

The "Unfriendlies"

Just as J. Edgar Hoover had his favorite journalists, he also had his unfavorites. These "unfriendlies" were not all liberals; in fact, quite a few were rightists. There was a transgression much worse than any political one: this was the crime of criticizing J. Edgar Hoover.

Drew Pearson wrote a daily syndicated column entitled "Washington Merry-Go-Round" from 1932 until the year of his death, 1969. Cartha DeLoach says that "he and Mr. Hoover had a *passionate* dislike for each other." The only writers in Hoover's Official and Confidential files are Pearson, Winchell, Eleanor Roosevelt biographer Joseph P. Lash ("5 in-house memos dealing with his relationship with Eleanor Roosevelt, plus 200 pages, information highly derogatory!!!"[*sic*])—and Fred J. Cook, author of a highly critical special issue of *The Nation* on the FBI, later published as a book, *The FBI Nobody Knows* (six pages of "background data"). (There is also a 1970 O and C file on an unnamed "reporter for the Los Angeles Times" who "was planning to write some article critical on Mr. Hoover including information that Hoover was a homosexual.")

In addition to his 3,260-page general file which runs from 1934 until 1968, Pearson's O and C file contained five pages, though oddly it included "no derogatory information." What it did include, according to the FBI's own description of it, were two mysterious letters "to person in Rome, Italy" and "one letter vice-consul Rome to Mr. Hoover enclosing one of the above letters." Columnist Jack Anderson, who once worked with Pearson, has "no clue," as to what those letters contain, adding that Pearson "was very secretive. He knew people were spying on him. He knew that Naval Intelligence was spying on him in World War II, and he knew the FBI didn't trust him. He had decided that the best way to protect his sources himself was to tell nobody."

Pearson also had an FBI "June Mail" file—which is a code name for files that were separate from the main file and held intelligence gathered from wiretaps, microphone surveillance, and burglaries. His June Mail file was begun in 1958, after Pearson was accused of receiving leaks from a secret congressional meeting held by President Eisenhower. This investigation of Pearson was also secret, to avoid the FBI receiving "vicious Congressional criticism for failure to trust members of Congress."

Pearson, who, like Winchell, had a popular radio show, was praised by most of his fifty million readers and listeners for his muckraking that led not only to the exposure of much corruption, but to the conviction of many politicians. Yet J. Edgar Hoover called Pearson a "psychopathic liar" and an "eel." He also referred to the columnist's "muckraking yellow dog style of journalism for which he has become notorious." In 1961, twenty-seven years after he began the file, the Director wrote a marginal note, "This whelp still continues his regurgitation," on a Pearson column suggesting that Hoover might retire. In 1939, Pearson had printed a similar rumor, but when he discovered his source was wrong, he apologized to Hoover. In his apology Pearson requested a tour of headquarters for some unnamed person (and possibly himself, too—it is not clear); Hoover agreed, as long as the "cells in the basement" weren't shown. Hoover wasn't taking any chances with what Pearson might write of their presence. (He may have been joking, but very little is known about the presence and/or use of such prison cells in the FBI building.)

Jack Anderson says that Pearson told him that "at the very beginning" of his career, Hoover "persuaded" Winchell and Pearson that "it was in the public's interest to have this powerful FBI that could crack down on organized crime and the other evils that were going on." At first Pearson cooperated with the Director, much as Walter

Winchell did. Anderson says, "Winchell and Pearson helped build up Hoover's bulldog reputation. Winchill never got off the bandwagon, but Pearson began to find out that Hoover was abusing some of his powers and turned against him. Drew *fought* McCarthy, and began to worry that he had helped create a monster in his earlier cooperation with Hoover."

Pearson was relentless in his criticism of the Bureau, and J. Edgar Hoover never stopped believing that it was because Pearson was "brainwashed" by the Communists, especially whenever he stated that the Red threat was diminishing. From 1951 to 1953, Hoover even kept precise records of every time Westbrook Pegler "discredited" Pearson in a column.

In his diaries, Pearson writes that an ex-employee of his was questioned by the FBI about his "commie" ties, and when he balked at cooperating, agents told the man that he was "an American first," and an "ex-Pearson employee second." He says that the agents also referred to the "huge file" on Pearson.

Hoover could also, surprisingly, absorb certain rebukes. When Pearson mentioned "government gobbledy gook" in a column about the often tangled bureaucratic process, Hoover scribbled on the side, "We should take a lesson from this. Even InterDivision memos and inter-office memos are so foggy I am thinking of getting an interpreter." In 1963 when Pearson criticized the Bureau for the role it played in failing to protect President Kennedy in Dallas, and Cartha DeLoach told Hoover that "many of our news media friends have offered to 'take Pearson apart,' " Hoover replied, "Unfortunately, we are not in a position to completely contradict Pearson," thus acknowledging within the FBI what he denied publicly: the FBI's negligence in Dallas that day in November.

Part of Hoover's animus against Pearson arose out of jealousy; he disliked muckraking journalists who uncovered wrongdoing before the FBI did. In 1937, he was furious because Pearson and his cowriter Robert S. Allen had written about an investigation in the tire industry, when his own Bureau's files showed nothing. It wasn't just muckraking that bothered Hoover. In 1938, Hoover was furious again when Pearson and Allen wrote that a Guatemalan diplomat said Hoover "uses a distinctive and conspicuous perfume." In fact, Hoover was so mad about this he tried to get the diplomat fired.

Hoover also attacked Pearson's partners, beginning with Robert S. Allen. He orchestrated a smear campaign against Allen, whom he called the "worst of the two," by leaking the information that "a reliable source" had told him Allen's real name was Ginsberg. "That's the sort of games Hoover played," Jack Anderson says.

In 1947, after Jack Anderson became Pearson's chief investigative reporter, a file was begun on him. Anderson says, "Somebody once showed it to me," and he was "outraged." When Anderson protested, an FBI official named Tracy said blandly, "What file?" Anderson replied that "I've seen it," and gave the file number. Anderson remembers that Tracy looked "alarmed," but said he couldn't talk about it because "it was over his head and I have to go to the Boss." Anderson was temporarily mollified after Hoover called Pearson and told him "the White House had ordered it and that the FBI had to carry out instructions." But that was a lie, and it fooled neither Pearson nor Anderson.

Cartha DeLoach says he and Anderson were "very close friends, and still are," adding that "we had lunch together about once every two or three weeks at the Madison Hotel, for many years." DeLoach recalls that "he would moan and groan about working for Drew Pearson and I would moan and groan about working for J. Edgar Hoover."

"DeLoach was a good official source," Anderson says, "and he was very loyal to Hoover. I had to explain Drew, who had turned against Hoover by that time." Anderson says he had "his own FBI sources," but that DeLoach was "very useful. In fact, he would get very upset at some things that didn't come through him. He wanted to control the leaks, which was Hoover's game. We had a good relationship even though we were on opposite sides."

As he always did with journalists, Hoover tried to discover sources, and Pearson's file contains detailed summaries of private notes that the FBI stole from his office.

Hoover once accused Secretary of the Interior Harold Ickes of leaking information to Pearson, and he also believed that President Truman, who also disliked Pearson (one memo says Truman called Pearson "poison to him"), nonetheless leaked information to him. Another memo indicates that because Truman had once said Attorney General Tom Clark "was too close to Pearson," Hoover believed Clark was also leaking information. Other documents reveal that Hoover believed Harry Hopkins might have cued in Pearson about his conversations with Stalin; and during the investigation of President Kennedy's assassination, Hoover believed that Chief Justice Earl Warren leaked "certain information."

Naturally, the leaks went both ways. A "late October 1946" report indicates that Pearson told the FBI that "he understood some secret code was utilized by John L. Lewis in getting word to his mine workers when to strike." Two months later, Pearson sent the Bureau "a photostat" of the "announcement of courses" for a suspected subversive school in California. In fact, five years earlier, in 1941, Pearson even deleted an item in his column at Hoover's request. According to the file the item concerned something that Archibald MacLeish "had called the Director about," and Pearson and Allen "agreed" it should not be published.

As the Director did with Walter Winchell, he also monitored Pearson's radio broadcasts, looking for information that the Bureau didn't have or information that was critical to the FBI. The radio summaries often included such comments as "we expect him to distort the facts," and when Jack Anderson substituted for Pearson in the broadcasts, these, too, were monitored. In one 1968 broadcast when Anderson stated that the Justice Department would investigate George Wallace's campaign spending, the Bureau said "no such request has been received."

In the FBI's summary of a series of confessional articles that Pearson wrote in 1956, the Bureau was less concerned about the confessions ("Denounced by fifty-four senators and congressmen, called a liar by two Presidents, officially investigated a dozen times for news leaks") than it was that the series, entitled "Confessions of an S.O.B.," did not mention the Bureau or its Director a single time.

A 1963 document in the file entitled "Relations with the CIA" begins: "Information developed by Mr. DeLoach has indicated that John McCone, Director, CIA, has attacked the Bureau in a vicious and underhanded manner characterized with sheer dishonesty." The memo suggests that the FBI have a "firm and forthright confrontation" with McCone, who, it was said, passed false information about Lee Harvey Oswald to Drew Pearson. It was hoped that McCone could be chilled into never attempting another "attack against the Bureau."

"OK," Hoover wrote, thus giving permission for the director of the CIA to be intimidated.

Jack Anderson suggests that what could be behind this memo "is part of the very involved plot" concerning the assassination of President Kennedy in Dallas on November 22, 1963. He explains: "I got a tip that he was killed on the orders of Castro because the CIA had been trying to kill Castro. I would imagine that Hoover found out something was going on there and the FBI was inquiring about it—and that's why there's the "Relations with the CIA" memo.

"Lyndon Johnson got a debriefing from the CIA, and was told that the CIA had used the Mafia to try to kill Castro, and Castro had found out about it and it was likely that he had retaliated. The next morning Johnson called J. Edgar Hoover. Now, only Hoover and Johnson know what occurred in that telephone call, but I knew both men and I can almost figure out what they said. Lyndon, who had also been warned by the CIA that Khrushchev was a loose cannon, would have said, 'Edgar, I need your help to save the country.' Johnson had also been told he couldn't have another Cuban missile crisis because Khrushchev might do something reckless, he was so humiliated by the first one. So Lyndon asked for Hoover's help, probably saying something like, 'I'm going to have to set up this commission to look into the assassination and they'll get their information from you, and you've got to make sure they conclude that it was the work of Lee Harvey Oswald.' And that is very likely what was said. That *is* what the FBI did. I don't think anyone in the FBI could do that today—withhold information that might have led them to the Castro connection—but *Hoover* could do it. He could control the investigation.''

J. EDGAR HOOVER:
"Well handled. Now keep on top of it."
—on memo telling him that Truman is "personally interested" in an FBI "espionage" investigation of Pearson and the possibility that Pearson placed "a microphone in the Cabinet room"; December 14, 1951

"Drew is now 'mouthing' the same suggestions the Communists and the 'bleeding hearts' always advance when 'on the ropes.' "
—December 10, 1953

"This is obviously a complete fabrication and typical of the pathological liar Pearson is."
—January 12, 1955

"This is pure bunk. I have never been in touch with anyone in R.N.C."
—note in reference to the Republican National Committee; May 16, 1955

"This wish is Father to the thought."
—note on broadcast summary item that Hoover will resign to head a foundation on juvenile delinquence; June 6, 1955

"Ok." [*next five or six words are blurred*] "Stupid."
—words on memo from William C. Sullivan offering to have "close friends" write Pearson's boss "discreet" protests of "Pearson's criticism of the Bureau"; August 21, 1957

"Pearson sounds like a real stooge for Khrushchev!"
—note on column; October 21, 1961

"I think Pearson ranks over [Martin Luther] King as a liar."
   —December 7, 1964

"If we ever resume use of microphones, I never want any installed in a bedroom."
   —re Pearson's allegation that an FBI tap was discovered in the bedroom of a Las Vegas resident suspected of mob connections; February 7, 1966

"Beware! Praise from this source is like a brickbat!"
   —on Pearson column saying FBI "had done a good job" in investigating the murder of Martin Luther King; March 17, 1969

**

In 1926, Chiang Kai-shek, aided by the Communists, finally ousted the Chinese warlords. The following year he banished the Communists who had helped him, thereby starting a civil war that ultimately brought into being the People's Republic of China in 1949, as well as the Nationalist Republic of China in Taiwan, which Chiang Kai-shek established after fleeing the communists who had taken over the mainland.

In 1927, the FBI began its 338-page file on (James) Vincent Sheean, one of the few journalists who was in China during those early days of the political upheaval. Sheean's name got into the files because of a conversation he had with someone in the American embassy in Berlin, but what exactly was said is not in the file. Yet whatever it was, it was enough to keep his name in the indexes for future reference; he was "open dead."

The Bureau did not oversee Sheean for a full decade, after files on two other writers whose work is associated with China were begun—those of Edgar Snow in 1931 and John Gunther in 1936.

In 1937, the FBI recorded Sheean's membership in a variety of suspect groups: the League of American Writers, the Abraham Lincoln Brigade, the American Committee for Yugoslav Relief, and the Committee for a Democratic Far Eastern Policy. In the forties, two more groups concerned Hoover: the India League of America and the Council on African Affairs.

The Bureau used confidential informants and mail and "trash" covers—that is, agents literally sifted through his household garbage. Once, in 1943, the year Hoover decided that Sheean's book *The Thunder and the Sun* was subversive, agents infiltrated a birthday party in honor of Paul Robeson, and noted Sheean's presence.

Although Hoover seems to have known that Sheean was not a Communist, he was interested in his "links" to the Party. It must have given him great satisfaction when Sheean's name appeared on a 1947 "Master Sucker List" that had been published in the New York *World-Telegram,* listing people "who had been used by the Communist Party." Sheean, in his file, is variously called "a liberal," "a Communist," and "the most pathetic figure in the whole gang of pink intellectuals."

Unlike the majority of writers, there is evidence that Sheean was aware of his FBI coverage. One 1948 report states that he "did not think much of these agents," and that "their reports meant nothing."

A 1950 report states that Sheean, who was watched until 1973, two years before his death, "was poisoning the wells of information in America about the Communists and about the Chinese Communists in particular." This report also said that he was part of a "clique of friends of the Chinese Communists, which included State Department officials as well as well-known journalists and others." Hoover believed that "this clique" had a "monopoly in book reviewing in the China field." One 1951 report indicates that additional names were collected after "an examination of the index cards maintained by the House Committee on Un-American Activities."

A report of an FBI interview with Sheean about an unnamed State Department official (no reason is given why this interview was held) states that "in order to give full information regarding Sheean, information has been used from serials which were not indexed." In other words, here the FBI is admitting that it used information that was previously "hidden," in order to discredit Sheean's testimony.

Hoover had safeguards in place to prevent such hidden material from straying too far from its "cover." A 1949 report in Sheean's file states that "this information [is] marked for deletion in case of dissemination to outside agencies." This procedure assured the FBI that no "outside agency" could discover that the FBI had such information on a subject. The FBI also didn't want outsiders to learn the identity of an informant.

In 1931, the FBI began its file on another China hand, Edgar Snow, one of the few journalists to have frequent access to China. The first entries on Snow, who was a close friend of both Mao Tse-tung and Chou En-lai, were received from a confidential informant, who "obtained" them "from the files of the Shanghai Municipal Police," which reported that Snow, who had been in China since 1928, was a "radical journalist" and "believed to be receiving Communist literature from CP agents in Shanghai."

"Snow is an ingenious fellow-traveler," J. Edgar Hoover later wrote in the margin of a May 1945 memo analyzing an article by Snow entitled "Must China Go Red?" which appeared in the *Saturday Evening Post*. A month earlier, the FBI had sent a blind memo to the State Department in an effort to cancel his passport. The Bureau also used "technical surveillance in its attempt to implicate him in a plot "to dominate completely the Government of China and turn it into a Soviet state."

The FBI read and reviewed most of Snow's books, and said of his 1937 best-seller that "anyone who would write a book entitled 'Red Star Over China' would definitely be referring to the Soviet government."

The FBI was wary because "Snow liked everything that the Chinese did," and had called them "fine people." After Snow had interviewed President Roosevelt, agents attempted to find out exactly who initiated the interview, because "Snow had considered China to be divided into two parts," and "it was reported that the President agreed to this theory." The FBI foreign policy evidently was opposed to the "Two-China" scheme.

The FBI kept track of Snow until 1971, a year before his death, because "although he was not an actual Party member, the Party knew just how to use him."

Nonetheless, despite Hoover's strong reservations, Snow was a valued expert to the State Department. For instance, an April 2, 1965, Department of State "Memorandum of Conversation" for "Limited Official Use" (fourteen copies were circulated, including one to President Lyndon B. Johnson) included such observations as "in general the officials all seemed far more confident and assured than in 1960. . . . Mao's health seemed quite good although he had aged quite visibly since I last saw him in 1960. His mind was very alert throughout the interview. He delivered himself somewhat pontifically, more so than in 1960, reminding me of Churchill's manner in the latter part of World War II (whom I interviewed at that time). Mao recognized me at some distance as soon as I came into the room and I could see no evidence of rumored difficulties with his eyesight. Neither did I notice any trembling. . . . Chou was in excellent shape. . . . I saw no infirmity of any sort. . . . Mao's interview, of course, came after Chou's. The difference between the way each handled my Vietnam questions is puzzling. I can only guess that Mao feels free to say anything he wishes, whereas Chou hewed more closely to the regular line. . . . On Kennedy's assassination, several of the leaders asked me what I thought was 'the real story' behind it. Ch'en I [unidentified person present at interview] recounted the view he had heard 'abroad' as one in which he believed; namely that the assassination 'must have been a conspiracy including members of President Kennedy's own entourage.' Parenthetically, I might add that if the Chinese leadership fears assassination, it has not prohibited the public sale of sporting rifles which I found possible in Shanghai. . . ."

I talked as much as I could with students, doctors, nurses, teachers, etc., but really had no chance for extended private conversations and could not claim any 'feel' for public opinion. But the question of youth was clearly on the minds of virtually all top officials with whom I spoke. When I didn't bring up the subject, they did, and always in terms of concern over ways of instilling the correct revolutionary concepts and linking theory with practice. . . ."

Hoover's scrutiny of his critics in the press went beyond mainstream columnists like Pearson. It extended to writers for small-circulation journals as well. One of these gadflies was Dwight Macdonald, a former editor of *The Partisan Review,* a *New Yorker* staff writer, as well as the author of such books as *Memoirs of a Revolutionist* and *Against the American Grain.* He was first noticed by the FBI "when he enrolled under the Communist Party Emblem in the 1936 Election Registration." The name of "the ruddy journalist" was also found that year "on the letterhead of the League for Southern Labor." The Bureau reported in 1937 that Macdonald was "well-known in Communist circles in Washington D.C.," and that he "joined the Socialist Workers Party in 1937 or 1938."

But the FBI's interest in him really grew in 1944 when he founded, edited, and published the first issue of *Politics,* whose stated purpose was to "create a center of consciousness on the Left."

The FBI opened his mail, followed Macdonald and his wife, Nancy, and employed informants to keep track of the magazine. By March 6, 1946, the FBI was reporting that "POLITICS is an intellectual set-up and part of the Communist transmission belt in this country."

The following year, on April 15, 1947, Clifton Bennett, a *Politics* staff member, wrote the Director asking for an interview for an article he was writing on the Bureau. (Bennett's name is blacked out on their correspondence, but left in on the copy of the article in the file.) Hoover refused to see him and told Clyde Tolson to begin "a discreet investigation of the outfit."

During the winter of 1947–1948, *Politics* published Bennett's critical article, which contained certain almost deliberately inaccurate details that inflamed Hoover. Bennett wrote that "at George Washington University, J. Edgar Hoover committed The Perfect Crime. Although the Office of the Registrar will affirm that he did attend a night school law course, obtaining an L.L.B. in 1916 and L.L.M. in 1917, there is no other visible record of his passage. According to the university library, he wrote no thesis for either degree. And the annual classbook for his year was omitted because of a financial crisis." Bennett also wrote that while in high school, "although the smallest boy in his cadet company, it has been claimed that during drill he displayed the loudest voice in the school," and that "he is obsessed by a persecution complex . . ."

Hoover wrote on a memo, "I think we should keep an eye on McDonald [sic] & his publication. He must have some resources to put this out. He could easily be used by Commies even though he may claim to be pacifist." By the spring of 1948, he was still so angry that he requested Macdonald's tax returns from the secretary of the treasury "to determine if the Communist Party and its satellite groups" were financing the magazine, and on April 26, Macdonald's name was put on the Security Index as a "Native-born Communist."

During the summer of 1948, Hoover found out that Haldeman-Julius Publications, in Gerard, Kansas, was reprinting Bennett's article as a booklet entitled *The FBI—The Basis of an American Police State.*

But by the next fall, he had laid aside his plans for outright war when he was told on November 22, 1949, that *Politics* had been "discontinued" because of lack of funds. Not believing the good news, he had an agent confirm it with a pretext phone call, and although he was relieved when it proved to be true, he did not stop watching Macdonald.

In 1957, he monitored Macdonald's association with the British magazine *Encounter,* reporting that in the two issues his agents had read, Macdonald humorously "scoffed" at the U.S. Trotskyist leadership, and his articles "left the impression that the years he spent with these ineffective movements was a tremendous waste of time and energy."

By 1958, he seems to have forgotten all about Macdonald. After reading a "letter to the editor" about a review of *Masters of Deceit* in which the letter writer cites Macdonald as a source for some Communist membership statistics, he wrote, "Who is he?"—meaning Macdonald—in the margin.

On November 5, 1963, Hoover's primary concerns again surfaced.

On that date it was reported that Macdonald had written in a film review in *Esquire* magazine that a movie's FBI agent "is even a greater bungler than the real article."

In 1967, the FBI reported that Macdonald was one of the fifty persons who walked out on a speech by Vice-President Humphrey at "the National Book Ceremonies on the evening of March 7." Two years later, in 1969, the Bureau reported that he turned in his draft card at a Washington, D.C., rally and a request was made for "a discreet inquiry" which lasted until 1975, when Macdonald requested his file under the Freedom of Information Act.

But according to one report, by November 17, Macdonald had not sent the Bureau his notarized signature, so a note on the bottom of a letter of reminder from FBI director Clarence Kelley says, "Location and processing of records is not required by law and would be wasteful if the requester is not entitled to the documents and the request is spurious."

Another on Hoover's unfavorable list was Abbott Joseph Liebling, better known as A. J. Liebling, and best known as a writer on food, boxing, and the press for *The New Yorker* magazine, which the FBI considered "unreliable" and liberal. He was indexed on two separate occasions in 1937; once for being the research assistant on a feature about the Director that appeared in *The New Yorker,* and once for writing a "nasty dig at the Director and the Bureau" for the New York *World-Telegram*—a satire which portrayed Hoover as "A. Edwin Doover."

Liebling's file grew to eighteen pages for reasons ranging from his being suspect in 1947 for receiving a complimentary copy of a book on the National Maritime Union by a fellow *New Yorker* writer, Richard Owen Boyer, to his attendance at a Progressive Citizens of America meeting, which a "confidential and reliable source" who was working for the FBI said had protested "the action of the Un-American Committee against Howard Fast." The following year, 1948, the FBI reported in Liebling's file that Fast was going to jail for refusing to submit the records of the Joint Anti-Fascist Refugee Committee, and was also going to write an article for a Russian publication on the "state of American literature," if "jail officials will let him." Curiously, this latter information is not in Fast's file, or if it is, it is blacked out there.

Liebling is called "a careless journalist of the *New Yorker* smart set" who displays "compulsive fellow-travelerism" in another 1948 reference that says he "disregards the [Whittaker] Chambers evidence" and "adopts a ridiculing, deriding, laughter-provoking 'poohpoohisms' attack on [Elizabeth] Bentley and Chambers and the House Un-American Activities Committee." The FBI also reports that Liebling "became an unofficial member of the defense in regard to . . . Alger Hiss . . . [and] in the guise of collecting material for an article, borrowed from Professor Mark Van Doren of Columbia University a letter Chambers had written 25 years ago in which Chambers admitted he had lied on one occasion." The Bureau said that the very next day "Liebling presented the letter to Hiss's lawyers who eventually used it in court. . . . Liebling also tracked down Malcolm Cowley, a writer 'who had an old score to settle with Chambers' and Cowley was presented to the defense and used as a witness."

In 1950, the Bureau reported that Liebling requested accreditation as a military correspondent, and four years later, in 1954, it was reported that he "wrote an unfavorable article to [sic] Senator McCarran," in which he "infers [sic] McCarran is a liability to the Democratic party." This report contains all of Liebling's previous references, plus six new ones. Another report says that Liebling's book *The Wayward Pressman* was sold at a Communist bookstore, along with books by Howard Fast "and others who have been identified with Communists," and that Liebling was responsible "for the pinko infiltration of *The New Yorker*."

**

One of the FBI's chief bête noires was editor and critic Bernard De Voto, all because of an anti-FBI article he wrote in the October 1949 issue of *Harper's* magazine. In his column, "The Easy Chair," De Voto charged that the FBI "shatters the reputations of innocent and harmless people" with its "hash of gossip, rumor, slander, backbiting, malice, and drunken invention." He also wrote how this material "is permanently indexed in the FBI files."

De Voto was one of those indexed. In 1944, the FBI reported that he was on a committee against censorship, and to make a test case had bought a copy of Lillian Smith's *Strange Fruit*, which "championed Negro rights." The following year, in 1945, the FBI noted that De Voto attended a Win the Peace rally. However, the majority of his 207-page file concerns his October 1949 column.

The Director received a great deal of mail telling him readers "were shocked" by the appalling revelations in De Voto's column, and so, despite his "long standing" policy of reacting only to material written by "Bureau personnel," Hoover replied to his correspondents that he too was "shocked by the article," and that there was no "factual basis" to any of it.

De Voto had also charged that FBI agents asked interviewees whether they read *The New Republic, In Fact, Russia Today,* or *The People's Voice.* In a letter to Daniel Mebane, publisher of the *New Republic,* De Voto explained: "I am prepared to establish that the FBI has asked even sillier questions. In the mind of at least one FBI investigator it was suspicious that the person he was interviewing had published a review of a book about Communism."

The FBI said De Voto "urged the public to refuse to answer future FBI questions except in open court under oath and before witnesses," and wrote that "honest men are spying on their neighbors for patriotism's sake," and "it has gone too far."

Hoover went wild. He announced that De Voto "had among his collection of books a copy of *Das Kapital* which he prized very highly," and that he "was the son of a fallen away Catholic priest . . . and that he himself was a fallen away Catholic." Hoover, a lifelong Presbyterian, was also a lifelong moralist, and the very act of becoming a fallen-away Catholic (or rejecting any religion) would be unacceptable behavior to him.

A 1948 interview of De Voto regarding the security clearance of some unidentified person was dredged up and must have given the Director comfort. In contrast to FBI agents with their strict dress code, De Voto "was unshaven, wearing a loose and somewhat soiled sport shirt and a pair of baggy summer slacks of dark hue." He looked like a dreaded alien.

Hoover put De Voto and *Harper's* on his "Do Not Contact" list. The magazine was even maneuvered into running a letter to the editor from the Director, although the editor had the last word: "We will continue to urge that American citizens refuse to answer FBI questions."

The Bureau continued to attack De Voto after he died in 1955. In 1959 it encouraged the publication of a pro-FBI article by John Shuttleworth that said "De Votos are at work today." However, when Shuttleworth called De Voto "a professional Communist worker," the FBI got cold feet and suggested it be changed to "a professional apologist of Communism or misguided innocent." There is no indication in the file where or whether the article was ever published.

J. EDGAR HOOVER:

[*Blank*] after his first crack should not have been interviewed subsequently. He should never be approached in the future. If one wishes to align himself with the De Voto school of thought as against his country's interest then he is privileged to do so and should be so listed.
—*Memo, November 17, 1949*

let us get what ONI [Office of Naval Intelligence] has on De Voto.
—*Memo, 1949*

**

Murray Kempton is the winner of a 1985 Pulitzer Prize and the 1989 George Polk Career Award "for forty-five years of newspaper work that represents the highest standards of journalism."

Kempton was a reporter and columnist for the *New York Post* from 1942 to 1969 (with intervals at the *Wilmington* [N.C.] *Morning Star, The New Republic,* and the New York *World-Telegram and Sun*), and is the author of *Part of Our Time,* in 1955, a collection of columns entitled *America Comes of Middle Age,* in 1963, and *The Briar Patch,* in 1973, a study of the prosecution of the Black Panthers. He is now a columnist for *New York Newsday.*

When Kempton was a columnist for the *Post,* he was not popular with J. Edgar Hoover. The FBI summed up Kempton this way in 1968: "It is to be noted that while [Kempton] rarely makes statements in his column which directly criticize or accuse the FBI or the Director of misfeasance or malfeasance, his 'tongue-in-cheek' style of satire leaves little doubt as to the contempt and animosity he feels."

Writing in the December 7, 1989, *New York Review of Books* about the Bureau's long-time secret investigation of the National Lawyers Guild, Kempton referred to Hoover's "distaste for Americans who criticized their government" as being "tepid beside his hatred of those who criticized him." Nowhere is this more apparent than in his own 401-page file.

Kempton was on Hoover's "Do Not Contact" list for twenty-three years. He was called a "rat" and a "snake" in the private scribblings of the Great Enforcer. Once when Kempton criticized the Catholic Church, Hoover wrote: "This vitriol tops the jackal's previous column." Told of this, Kempton said, "That's the thing that shocks you, that you can be so hated."

In a detailed summary of "mere highlights" of some of his columns, the FBI added, "Apparently, if Kempton cannot say something bad about the subject, he will not write a column about it at all." Other memos call him "completely unscrupulous" and someone who "has performed acts which benefited Communists."

The FBI began Kempton's file in 1938, when he was a student at Johns Hopkins University. A "promotional-type pamphlet issued in connection with the National Youth Anti-War Congress" was brought to the attention of the FBI, and agents indexed his name because he was listed as one of the sponsors of the congress. Kempton says, "I think this information came to them from the front pages of the *Baltimore Sun*. It was unlikely to have been the product of any underground informant, because I testified rather inanely before a congressional committee and the papers picked it up—and the agents clipped it. And it was the American Youth Congress."

In an interview with the FBI in 1953, in which agents questioned him about two friends who had been members of the Young Communist League, Kempton told agents that he had been a member of that group from June 1937 until April 1938, and a member of the American Youth Congress during the late 1930s and early 1940s.

Kempton recalls, "I had never dealt with the FBI before. They had never contacted me, and my inclination would have been to plead ignorance of everything. But one of these friends called me up and said would I talk to the FBI—I mean, can I give your name to the FBI? And I said sure, in an offhand way, without really realizing how *delicate* it would be. I'm smarter now than I was then—tactically I'm a little shrewder. Anyway, the FBI guys came and we had this conversation and I told them when the friends had left the YCL, and when I was in, when I had joined, when I left. Actually, I joined in 1936 when I went to sea, and I left in the summer of 1938."

But the FBI knew nothing of Kempton's political life in 1936. Kempton says, "I *joined* the Communist party and the FBI doesn't even know my deep, underground revolutionary history! If you wanted any kind of job at the port, you almost *had* to join the Communist party. The Communist party and the National Maritime Union were really the port officials. I mean talk about vanguards, it was *the* office structure. And I was doing a little work on the rank-and-file strike in '36 and I was recruited. And you would go to meetings of the Party.

"We were also known—with hyperbolic romance—as the Traveler's Club. So every time you'd run into a guy who belonged, he was just back from Hamburg from delivering an underground message to the anti-Nazis, or something like that. Rather Lillian Hellmanesque as a matter of fact in terms of high romance. But we had a fearsome reputation, that is, the Traveler's Club did. I can hardly consider myself a traveler of a major sort, but anyway—the meetings always had an air of high international intrigue which we never got in the National Maritime Union. But that was the only truly revolutionary organization to which I ever belonged—at least it felt like one—and nobody ever knew I was in it!

"I remember one meeting in which we had this rather nice guy with a central European accent who got up and said the International— which meant Moscow—has asked that you collect the addresses of all the Trotskyites! None of the guys there knew any Trotskyites who weren't sailors, therefore they had no addresses, so you couldn't possibly comply with this order. I knew a lot of Trotskyites, but I really felt it wasn't up to me to provide their addresses. That was shortly before I left.

"I quit fairly rapidly. At the time of the Munich pact [1938] I was out of the YCL. I think I quit over the Moscow trials. They were earlier, but they didn't particularly sink in.

"So that was it, and then I joined the Young People's Socialist League. Anyway, that is my revolutionary history, such as it was."

Although the FBI never knew Kempton had been a Party member, it did know he joined the Young People's Socialist League. The FBI's Publication Section had a copy of an "undated" pamphlet he wrote for the league, and a report quoted from it: "There is no anti-Fascism but Socialism . . ."

Kempton recalls the pamphlet, called *Socialism Now,* and says he wrote it in 1940. "It coincided with the Nazi-Soviet Pact, although it had nothing to do with what we pompously referred to as 'the war question'—which is the reason why I think I left the Party. I mean that was the reason I gave for leaving the YCL. I'm sure my reasons were far more trivial than that. I got out of the Young People's Socialist League on the war question, because I had a kind of silly, utopian, revolutionary view of the war. I was against collective security. But then I wanted to see France rescued so I changed my position on the war and I left the Socialist party rather pompously. I did this act two days before Hitler invaded the Soviet Union and the Communist line changed. I always wondered why some lunatic didn't announce me as a *mole* inside the Socialist party."

There are no further references to Kempton until 1947, when he was working as an assistant to *New York Post* labor columnist Victor Riesel, and wrote a letter to Hoover thanking him for the guest column the Director had written during Riesel's vacation. The file records that Hoover acknowledged the letter.

In 1956, Riesel's name came up again after Kempton had written a series of articles on Johnny Dioguardi, the labor organizer who was indicted in an acid attack on Riesel. In one of his articles, Kempton wrote that Teamsters Union head Jimmy Hoffa, upon learning Riesel would be blind for the remainder of his life, had said, "they should have gotten him in the hands." The FBI wanted to know how Kempton "got this statement."

Kempton says, "The FBI could have called me and I would have told them. Actually, they had the information. I got it from Sam Romer, who worked for the Teamsters. He broke and became an informant for Bob Kennedy. I'd known Sam for many years and he told me that the night Riesel got hit, Jimmy Hoffa had taken the elevator two floors down and knocked on Sam's door and said, 'Your friend Riesel got acid thrown in his face—I wish it had been thrown on his hands.' At the time I wrote it, I did not know what actually happened. It makes Hoffa look a little better, although it's still pretty awful. But what had happened was the acid was thrown in Riesel's face because he had taken a pass at Johnny Dio's wife, at least Johnny Dio thought he had; so Hoffa wasn't talking about Riesel's writing, he was talking about his making a pass."

In 1949, the FBI reported that Kempton "agreed" with Bernard De Voto's contention that "people interviewed in the loyalty program should refuse to give any information to FBI agents." In fact, Kempton's appearance on Hoover's "Do Not Contact" list dates from this time.

Kempton believes Hoover was "stark, raving mad," and has written that Hoover's "nights were haunted by the suspicion that somewhere there might be someone who didn't revere him." Indeed, Hoover considered himself the FBI. "The whole thing was so totally personal," Kempton says. "My file is all about Hoover."

Interestingly, the same year Hoover was so outraged that Kempton had defended De Voto's attack on him, the FBI also reported that in an article in *Plain Talk*, Kempton was "not sympathetic toward the Communist cause." Kempton says, "Not only *that*, but *Plain Talk* was just this side of the John Birch Society. It was run by Isaac Don Levine, an old anarchist and a friend of mine. Any magazine called *Plain Talk* is fascist by definition!"

Indeed, after the FBI's 1953 interview with Kempton, it decided to take "no further action" concerning him, because, as an agent put it, "He appears to be an effective writer who could be influential at a time of national emergency." But such "clearance," if that is what it can

John Reed (*pictured*) in advertisement for *The Liberator*, 1918   FROM MAX EASTMAN'S FBI FILE

RIGHT: Assistant Navy Secretary FDR's 1919 letter about Max Eastman's subversive activities
FROM MAX EASTMAN'S FBI FILE

March 10, 1919.

My dear Mitchell:

Let me congratulate you very sincerely on your new dignities.   I am delighted with the President's choice.

I am sending you a confidential report on a speech of Max Eastman at Seattle, together with some other information.   Eastman would seem to be well worth looking after, and while details of the general situation there have doubtless been brought to your attention, I am in hopes that some of this information may be of use to you in your investigations. This report is, of course, quite confidential.

Sincerely yours,

Franklin D Roosevelt

Hon. A. Mitchell Palmer,
    The Attorney General,
        Washington, D. C.

Carl Sandburg shown holding his newborn kid. His file was opened in 1918. PHOTO COURTESY OF THE NEWBERRY LIBRARY

BELOW LEFT: Edna St. Vincent Millay, whose file was opened in 1923 PHOTO COURTESY OF THE NEWBERRY LIBRARY

BELOW RIGHT: Katherine Anne Porter, whose file was opened in 1927 PHOTO BY ROBERT PHILLIPS

Thornton Wilder, whose file was opened in 1933 PHOTO BY ROBERT PHILLIPS. COURTESY OF THE NEWBERRY LIBRARY

BELOW: Ernest Hemingway, whose file was opened in 1935
THE BETTMANN ARCHIVE

Clyde Tolson (*left*) and J. Edgar Hoover play games with an unidentified woman on New Year's Eve at New York's Stork Club, 1935.   PHOTO BY GUSTAVE GALE. NATIONAL ARCHIVES

LEFT: Malcolm Cowley, whose file began in 1936   PHOTO COURTESY OF THE NEWBERRY LIBRARY

Maxwell Bodenheim, whose file was opened in 1936   PHOTO COURTESY OF
THE NEWBERRY LIBRARY

BELOW: J. Edgar Hoover (*center*) listens intently as Al Jolson (*right*) offers Walter Winchell some Hollywood gossip.   NATIONAL ARCHIVES

LIBRARY OF CONGRESS GETS "TOBACCO ROAD"—Archibald MacLeish (left), librarian of Congress, is shown inspecting a manuscript of "Tobacco Road" presented to the Library today Erskine Caldwell, author of the book from which the long-lived play was drawn.—Star Staff Ph

Gertrude Stein (*walking dog*) with her companion, Alice B. Toklas, in France, 1944   THE BETTMANN ARCHIVE

BELOW LEFT: Ezra Pound, at the time of his arrest, 1945   AP/WIDE WORLD PHOTOS

BELOW RIGHT: Assistant FBI Director Cartha D. DeLoach   J. EDGAR HOOVER COLLECTION, MARTIN LUTHER KING LIBRARY, WASHINGTON, D.C.

Howard Fast delivering street speech, New York City, 1948

be called, did not keep the FBI from constantly criticizing his work.

In 1955, the Bureau noted that Kempton wrote "a number of columns about paid informant Harvey Matusow, who provided the names of many supposed Communists to both the FBI and HUAC. The Director underlined these lines from one column: "Couldn't we try now to find out just which government servant coached Harvey Matusow?" Another report said "these columns reflected critically upon Roy Cohn, the Bureau, and the Department," billing Cohn, for the first time, before the FBI.

In another reference, the FBI noted that Kempton received an advance copy of Harvey Matusow's book. Kempton remembers "the last time I talked to the far right was during the Matusow case. And I don't think it's in the Bureau files, because I don't think they apparently told the Bureau. I was in the press room during the Matusow trial, and I get this phone call—a conference call from Ben Mandell, who at that time had risen to be head of [Senator James O.] Eastland's Internal Security Committee, and Raymond Tompkins, I think that was his name, who was then assistant attorney general of the U.S. in charge of security. Tompkins says, 'Mr. Kempton, I'd like you to tell me something about your connections with Harvey Matusow,' and I said, 'Of course, I'd be delighted. Matusow came to me at one point because he was interested in selling his story, so I sent him to the *New York Post,* which wasn't interested, and then I sent him to Simon and Schuster, and they weren't interested. And then Matusow said he had this Communist fellow, Kahn, and I said we all know Kahn and company [Alfred E. Kahn and Angus Cameron had formed Cameron and Kahn, publishers] are Stalinists, and Matusow said to me, 'Do you think I should do this? Should they publish my book?' And I said, 'I think you should publish wherever you possibly can.' "

Kempton recalls that the Internal Security Committee "wanted to know *why* the *Post* and Simon and Schuster turned Matusow down" and he told them they didn't trust him. Kempton mentioned that *he* trusted Matusow and said, "Well, I am the conduit for this particular conspiracy" but Ben Mandel told him, "Oh, I don't take you seriously."

Kempton says, "So ever since then, I had this awful feeling, *what is said about me in those goddamn files?*"

In 1958, when Kempton studied in Italy under a Fulbright scholarship, Hoover wanted to know the members of the commission that picked him, and 173 pages of the file are reprints of Fulbright program reports and guidelines. Hoover was determined to find out how a "pseudo Communist" like Kempton "who belittles the Bureau" could have been selected.

" 'We must find out who's a member of this commission!' As if this commission sat down and it was a conspiracy," Kempton says. "Well, see, Hoover always did that. We must *get* to *our* friends at this place," Kempton adds, referring to the time when he joined the staff of *The New Republic* in 1964, and Cartha DeLoach suggested that the Bureau "discreetly" alert their "good" friends about Kempton's "background"; and Hoover scribbled back: "Yes, do so."

That same year, after Kempton wrote what Hoover told the attorney general was an "inexcusable" and "vicious" attack on the Catholic Church, the FBI prepared a sixteen-page blind memo on the columnist. This memo was more balanced than most; included was a review of Kempton's *Part of Our Time* that said "as a journalist he has fought both Communism and the excesses of Communism," and a reference that *The Daily Worker* had criticized the book for not giving "sufficient credit to the Communist Party." The memo also contained brief reviews of certain columns written between 1949 and 1958 that Hoover considered un-American; after noting that Kempton thinks of Communists "as people" someone in the FBI—probably Tolson or DeLoach (it is not the Director's handwriting)—scrawled on the side, "He is a *real* stinker."

Kempton jokingly comments about the blind memo: "I like this summary. I mean I'm not going to listen to any condescension from the friends of Lillian Hellman about my record during the terror."

The FBI kept up its reports on Kempton all through the sixties, and there are as many references from this decade as there are from the fifties. All concern either his passion for constitutional liberties—or as one memo put it, "his expressing sympathy for sufferings being endured by Communists in America"—or his criticism of the FBI. One 1961 reference tries to smear some unnamed person for being an "admirer" and "friend" of Kempton's, while another notes that his name was found at the "headquarters" of the Fair Play for Cuba Committee.

When he began writing a column for the New York *World-Telegram* in the fall of 1964, Hoover wrote "I am surprised that Scripps-Howard are taking on this rat" next to a column. Shortly afterwards, the FBI wrote that a Kempton column was "extremely critical" of a meeting of ex–FBI agents and reached "a new low of vilification." The Director added his thoughts to the report, writing that "when a newspaper hires a snake like Kempton they can expect the worst."

In 1969, when Kempton was working on *The Briar Patch,* his book about the Black Panthers, the FBI, in an urgent telegram notified five field offices that the Black Panther party had a "fund raising arrangement" with Kempton. Hoover also wrote the attorney general that the "violence-prone" Black Panther party "is having financial difficulties," and that the New York FBI office "has determined that Kempton is working for the Black Panthers raising funds through personal contacts with persons of some affluence."

On December 30, 1969, the FBI sent a memo "concealing confidential sources" to eleven unnamed government agencies, including the information that "the Panther leadership does not believe the subject, Kempton, is capable of performing any useful service" for them. In fact, a confidential informant had told the Bureau that the columnist "is merely using them so he can 'write his book,' " and it was reported to Hoover that the only thing Kempton had done for the Panthers was lend them a typewriter for three days. Kempton says he did lend them a typewriter, and they "used it for a week to type letters. Lots of S.D.S. kids from Columbia were working on the fund-raising appeal, and they needed an electric typewriter. I was working with the S.D.S. kids, we had sort of a committee. The Panthers didn't have much to do with them. But anyway, that was it."

Eventually the Bureau learned that the Panthers "had evidenced distrust of Kempton," so it decided to close the case, while at the same time remaining "alert" to any new developments. A confidential informant also told them that Kempton "was pretty scared actually."

Kempton says, "I had no reason to be scared, and I scare easily. The Panthers said I was just doing it for my book, which was largely true, although I got rather fond of these people. Well, whoever the Panther was who was giving the FBI information, the information seems very strange. I mean, I'm sure that they said I was just trying to write the book, because that's what I told them. I didn't think I was exploiting them by doing this, and I never got very much out of them, anyway. I mean, I never really tried."

During the fall of 1968, it was reported to Hoover that Kempton was arrested in Chicago and charged with disorderly conduct during the Democratic National Convention in August. The FBI decided not to interview him because of his "hostility" and "animosity," and although they considered prosecuting him for violating antiriot laws, this was never followed up because the attorney general decided that what Kempton did was not "a prosecutable violation."

In the spring of 1969, the FBI monitored Kempton's participation in a Vietnam Peace Parade Committee, and during the summer of 1969 noted that he had "criticized FBI agents' interference with New York reporters covering events."

But in 1971 the most horrific reference in any file came into being. That November, Murray Kempton's son, James Murray Kempton, Jr., a writer, and daughter-in-law, Jean Goldschmidt Kempton, a poet, were killed in an automobile accident in Virginia, and J. Edgar Hoover clipped the obituary and requested "subversive references only" on them.

MURRAY KEMPTON:

I've always felt most of us survived this very well, that most people got through life pretty well. With some things, Hoover's perfectly right, they *are* subversive. In my file there are *constant* references to "let's get the son of a bitch"—and nobody ever caused me any trouble. On the other hand, I have to confess that I had a lot of right-wing buddies, and that may have helped me. You know, it's sort of nice to have Bill Buckley decide to be hyperbolic about you.

I knew guys in the fifties whose kids were followed to school by the FBI. I think the harassment of the Communists was really disgusting. I mean, most of us can take care of ourselves. What they were doing to Communists as against what they did to people who were essentially unassailable. I mean, at the height of the blacklist, Arthur Miller sold *Death of a Salesman* to Hollywood! The blacklist, well, it worked so universally that *Death of a Salesman is* an exception—not the rule. But there were people who had something uniquely commercial to offer. *Death of a Salesman* is uniquely commercial.

These files are so goddamn inept. I mean, my revolutionary record is awfully meager, but it isn't even *described*. The paraphrasing in the files is just a hopeless job; well, of course, a lot of times you tell people things and then you say, "Oh, I never said that," and you did. I remember the FBI guys from Newark, in 1953, when I started talking about when my friend broke with the Party—and my friend had given them all the information, anyway—and the agent stopped writing. I told them to go on writing. I said, "Look, I'm very sorry, I think you better write *everything* down." So then the agent went back to writing. But these little things really make you feel very wary.

My wildest experience in the late forties was when I was working for Victor Riesel—and he knew an awful lot of these Dies Committee types. One time the Hiss case came up and I said that I read somewhere that Hiss had belonged to a Marxist study group, and I also read somewhere that his wife belonged to the Morningside Heights branch of the Socialist party. Anyway, that is what I said— that Hiss had been to a Marxist study group, and people who go to Marxist study groups are all Communists. I also said Chambers looks to me like he's telling the truth. (Actually, I believed Chambers because I thought the whole story had artistic credibility.) And the next day I get this phone call from the Un-American Activities Committee and my friend Ben Mandell, who was the chief investigator. He says "We have been informed" that *I had taught* Alger Hiss at a Marxist study group! This is what the story had become in a week! I said "That just isn't so. None of that's true. I mean, when I was in the Party I was nineteen years old—would I be teaching Alger Hiss? I mean, would I be traveling to Washington and teaching in a Marxist study group with distinguished members?" And I suddenly realized that he did not believe a word I was saying—*not a word*. It was just very strange. He didn't believe me. And Victor Riesel said to me afterwards, "Ben thinks you're not coming clean." And I said, "Well, Victor, it's not a matter of coming clean—I'd probably come clean if I could—but what I said to him in this case was pretty innocent in terms of claiming intimacy with Hiss." But they always figured that I was holding out.

I have led far from a blameless life, but there is not one thing in my file of which I am ashamed. And believe me, there are a number of things of which I am ashamed. If my file is typical of what these files are—that steady, steady collecting—it is the real evil of people like J. Edgar Hoover. What is the crime? The crime is criticizing the Director.

You think of this lunatic sitting there and saying "off with their heads"—and there's no axe. There's no executioner. I mean, he presses this button and he says destroy this man's career and the career is not destroyed. Thank God.

CHAPTER TEN

The "Unfriendlies," Continued

The FBI's relationship with right-wing political columnist Westbrook Pegler was a rocky one. His 810-page file was begun in 1935 when his name was added to the FBI's mailing list at the Director's request, a sign he was eligible for the club. Pegler had earned his welcome by writing a column for the New York *World-Telegram* in which he said: "The Department of Justice has become the most fascinating of all the government bureaus to those who like adventure stories and detective comic-strips . . ."

His name was removed a month later after Hoover read that Pegler had called special agents "trigger men." "They have never been instructed to 'shoot to kill,' " Hoover wrote the columnist, after issuing orders that he be taken off the mailing list as punishment. By May 1936, Pegler was back on the list, and the file indicates that he requested a tour of headquarters, but by June 3, he was out of favor and off the list again. This pattern lasted for thirty years.

Nothing could deter the columnist from continuing to attack and offend not only the FBI, but also President Roosevelt, and even Walter Winchell, whom he called "dangerous." Winchell, in turn, called him "Peglouse." The FBI sided with Winchell; Pegler was known as

"Worstcrook Pegler," and a "creature" who "suffers from mental halitosis."

In 1938, after Winchell lambasted Pegler in a column, the Director wrote Winchell that he "frequently judges a man by who calls him a 's.o.b.' rather than the fact that he is called. It is often a compliment to be damned by some and certainly this is true in regard to poor old 'Mental Halitosis' Pegler."

Yet despite his hostility to Pegler, Hoover used him on occasion. In 1947, Louis Nichols suggested that the FBI "furnish Pegler for use without attribution" damaging information about a mobster-owned Las Vegas Hotel, the Flamingo.

In 1942, the FBI received information that Pegler was "either in contact with Nazi sources or obtained certain information therefrom." Some of the FBI's information came from letters the President and Mrs. Roosevelt passed on to Hoover. One addressed to Eleanor Roosevelt had suggested that she "see if the OWI [Office of War Information] is interested in exposing Pegler." Although the key passages in this report are blacked out, a later memo mentions the possibility that Pegler's Nazi source may have been a worker at a locomotive plant in Philadelphia. The FBI's source for this particular piece of intelligence, however, was an article that appeared in the *Daily Worker*.

The following year, in 1943, the special agent in charge of the New York office wrote Hoover that an unnamed reporter at the New York *Journal American* had told him that a member of the Czechoslovak Information Service has "documentary proof" that "Pegler is in the pay of the German government." Hoover was told that "Nazi officials bailed him out" in 1936 when the columnist was in some kind of financial trouble. It is not known whether this is actually true.

Hoover often used an untypical sense of humor when dealing with Pegler. In 1951, when Pegler mentioned to Assistant Director Nichols that he had "hurt his leg," Nichols wrote Pegler that "the Director asked me to give you his regards and to give you a word of caution about not hurting the other leg." On one Pegler column the Director scribbled, "This is terrific! When Pegler keeps to humor he is good."

Louis Nichols had told Clyde Tolson, "The way to handle Pegler is to completely ignore him and ignore the articles," and so every now and then, Hoover tried the silent treatment. But in 1944, when Pegler attacked the FBI for not doing its work "before Pearl Harbor," Hoover spoke out privately, commenting that the article is "no surprise" to him. But he also said that "a careful reading" of it shows that the FBI was "unable to act at Pearl Harbor" and that Pegler "inquires as to who put restrictions on the Bureau." Eventually, though, Hoover decided to make "no public statement on the Bureau's work at Pearl Harbor," especially "in view of the manner in which Pearl Harbor has been injected into the current [Presidential] campaign," as well as "the current inquiries being made by the special army board."

In 1947, in an effort to find something scandalous to use on Pegler beyond the 1943 Nazi allegations, the FBI learned from an unidentified source that Pegler was once arrested in New York (the charges are blacked out). But the Director could not find verification of the complaint, so he let the matter drop.

One of Hoover's "friendlies," columnist George Sokolsky, suggested to the FBI in 1953 that "somebody should try to set Pegler straight about his columns against the Bureau and its work in the Civil Rights field, although this is a problem because once Pegler starts on something, it becomes an obsession with him." Soon after this, Pegler began attacking Sokolsky in his column, and Clyde Tolson wrote to Assistant Director Nichols that "George has told me that he is patiently waiting to pay Pegler back in kind."

But the file also indicates that in 1953 the FBI did "try to set Pegler straight" at least once more. A memo indicates that "Ambassador Joseph Kennedy" had "completely straightened Pegler out as to the facts" in a column criticizing the FBI in civil rights cases. Kennedy's intervention was not happenstance. Cartha DeLoach says, "Mr. Hoover and Joseph Kennedy were the closest friends," and he "highly thinks it true" that Kennedy would intervene on the FBI's behalf. Roy Cohn too says that "Ambassador Kennedy and Hoover were very close," and definitely had the kind of relationship in which Hoover would ask him to influence Pegler.

In 1962, Cartha DeLoach reported that "Pegler as usual was most incoherent in conversation," and did not follow up a tip he received from the columnist.

By 1964, when Pegler had been writing for the publication of the John Birch Society for two years, the FBI had completely given up on him. His "reference card" was transferred to the Crime Records Section, the "chief producer of FBI propaganda." When Pegler asked for some information that year, he received only a press release, and someone noted on one of his last "limited" communications that "over the years our relations with Pegler have become strained." Despite their right-wing bond, the Director thought Pegler's brand of conservatism excessive and unpalatable; also, Pegler was too erratic and unreliable to be made an adjunct FBI agent.

CARTHA DeLOACH:
Westbrook Pegler did not like the FBI at first. I think it was because we had refused to give him information in a certain case, and therefore he had a hatred for the Bureau.

If Joseph Kennedy knew about that hatred, he may have automatically gone to Pegler and said, "This is a bum rap." Or Mr. Hoover may have asked him to do it. I don't know.

Later on Pegler did become friendly with the FBI, and as near as Pegler could, considering his personality, he was favorable to the FBI.

**

ROY COHN:
What can anybody's relationship with Pegler be?

He had a brilliant mind. I agreed with him basically on politics, but I did not agree with the extremism that would push him a little too far on issues like anti-Semitism and things like that. But he was married to a Jewish woman. His wife, Julie, was Jewish—nevertheless, Pegler was widely accused of being an anti-Semite. Peg was a guy, who if he was anti-Semitic, it was a matter of principle and not personal. It was something he couldn't help.

We knew each other very well. When I was under severe attack and all of that, Pegler wrote two or three columns defending me very strongly, and based on those alone I would not have publicly attacked him, I suppose.

**

J. EDGAR HOOVER:
"Be very circumspect in dealing with Pegler. The rat will twist anything around to serve his own purpose."
—1940

". . . it is just as important that sports appear honest as to actually be honest."
—from a letter to Pegler; 1947

"I only saw [*named blacked out*] at the Hollywood Race track on a Sat., and merely exchanged greetings. At no time was Pegler's name mentioned by either."
—note on memo telling Director that [name blacked out] *told someone at headquarters that Hoover said on "Sunday August 5" that "he wanted to get" Pegler and "would like to hang something on him"; 1951*

"Pegler is no bargain."
—1953

"Pegler is acting as if he was 'touched.' "
—1954

**

In 1941 Hoover wrote a letter to Attorney General Francis Biddle answering poet Archibald MacLeish's complaint that FBI agents were "out of touch with intellectual currents." Hoover told his attorney general that the FBI's main problem was "steering a middle course," and that accomplishing this—what with someone like Martin Dies on one side and someone like the liberal MacLeish on the other—was "as difficult as steering a course between Scylla and Charybdis." This is a particularly illuminating insight to Hoover's conception of his political role.

For the Director, both the left and the right could be equally harmful to his vision of America. Ultimately, though, Hoover was harder on, and thus more detrimental toward, left-wing causes because he naturally favored and agreed with right-wing causes. Overall, he was also much harder on the left simply because there are more writers on the left.

In 1990, publisher, editor, journalist, novelist, and playwright William F. Buckley, Jr., said that "the United States' protracted opposition to Communism is one of our truly ennobling experiences." This, of course, is a belief that most American conservatives share. Coming from the editor of *The National Review,* the country's leading journal of conservative political thought, it addresses the coming new century in a vein that would have made J. Edgar Hoover proud.

But J. Edgar Hoover did not always appreciate what Buckley said or wrote. Hoover's treatment of right-wingers he didn't like was basically no different from his treatment of left-wingers he didn't like. He was just as skeptical, just as scornful, and just as vindictive toward William F. Buckley, Jr., as he was toward Murray Kempton. When Hoover was displeased with a person—especially if the person criticized the FBI—he would even risk *hurting* the right in order to achieve a personal revenge. The Director "punished" no matter what the politics were because the personal was far more important than the political.

Buckley's name first entered the FBI's indexes when he was just sixteen years old. A November 22, 1941, Internal Security report concerning his father, "President of the Pantepec Oil Co. of Venezuela, a foreign corporation," includes the incorrect information that the senior Buckley gave the junior Buckley a farm in Connecticut in 1938. This very brief mention evoked a check mark next to the teenager's name and marks the beginning of a 690-page file. (Two decades later, a *1921* report on his father's interest in Mexico's politics became part of a 1969 FBI summary of Buckley's activities.)

Had Buckley's name not come to Hoover's attention in 1941, it would have come up seven years later, when the FBI indexed the names of all the college representatives of the National Student Association, and noted that Buckley attended an interregional convention in Boston on February 7.

The following year, in 1949, when Buckley was chairman of the *Yale Daily News*, he asked an FBI official to participate in a student debate about the Bureau, a request prompted by some anti-FBI articles that had appeared in the *Harvard Crimson*. Buckley told the special agent in charge of the New Haven office that these articles "were journalistically poor" and "vicious." It was eventually decided at headquarters that the New Haven SAC and Associate Director Louis Nichols would participate in the forum, although J. Edgar Hoover was not happy about this arrangement. In a very lengthy marginal note, he wrote: "I don't like this at all. As I understood originally they wanted us to meet informally and to outline our policies and problems and answer questions for honest enlightenment. Now it has degenerated into a public assembly as a debate. We can't arbitrarily set up conditions other than not discussing pending matters and we can't very well say who is to be invited and who can ask questions. I will approve Nick going but I will do so reluctantly."

The forum was a great success, however, and Nichols later wrote Buckley how pleased he was with "his kind references to the Director," concluding "I hope that we will never let you down."

WILLIAM F. BUCKLEY, JR.:
That's interesting that Hoover was never really in favor of Nichols coming up to Yale, because I got a letter from him after the debate was over which is just oleaginous—he was so pleased the way it went. That letter is in my scrapbook, which, incidentally, has been missing for ten years. But he was unbelievably pleased, and then he invited me to come down and see him next time I was in Washington.

When I mentioned to Lou Nichols that I was not going to graduate school, he said, "Well, why don't you come in to the FBI?" And I stalled or said something or other, because I was deep cover at the time with the CIA, bound for Mexico City. I had a good cover; they liked very much the fact that my father had lived in Mexico and had extensive connections there.

But I was offered a job in the FBI, in 1951. Lou Nichols told me that they would be willing to waive the obligation of agents being lawyers if I were immediately to join the Bureau, and I said, "Gee thanks, but I've got other things on my mind." I think I said that I was terribly mixed up with the aftermath of *God and Man at Yale* and was trying to write another book, and was thinking of going to work for the *American Mercury*.

We had a tour of the Bureau when I was receiving my CIA secret training. I didn't tell Nichols I was working for the CIA, because people are terribly solemn about that—I wasn't even supposed to tell my wife for six months, until she was cleared. And I worked in Mexico for about nine months; I finally just quit, because I was bored. You would have been, too.

**

On October 26, 1950, the FBI reported on the special tour of head-quarters given the day before to the Buckleys, who met with the Director "within a matter of minutes after their arrival at the Bureau." The report even includes a comment Mrs. Buckley made afterward: "I just can't get over it and he is so busy," and details how both Buckleys fired Thompson machine guns, and "asked a number of questions." Mrs. Buckley, however, says, "I have never fired a machine gun in my life."

The following year, in 1951, the FBI added to the file a copy of a letter addressed to a "Dear Harry"—not further identified except as "a personal friend" of the letter writer—a Robert Donner (whose name is blacked out in this copy of the letter, but left in when the letter is referred to later on). The letter commends *God and Man at Yale,* and tells "Harry" that "a house cleaning in education is long past due and 'academic freedom' and 'tenure' are the terms behind which educational conspirators hide."

Buckley says that Donner "was a terribly wealthy Colorado steel scion who got mixed up in the John Birch Society. He was very enthusiastic about the launching of *National Review,* but the minute we attacked the John Birch Society, he cut off all ties."

Obviously, Donner sent a copy of his letter to Hoover.

In 1954, the FBI reported that Walter Winchell had broadcast that "a sure best seller coming out in March is *McCarthy and His Enemies.* The author is William Buckley of Yale University." The Bureau commented that his 1951 best seller, *God and Man at Yale,* "caused quite a sensation." That year, the FBI also noted that Buckley was to be a guest speaker at a "new" group, the Foundation to Defeat Communism.

In 1955, the FBI reported that Buckley had recently launched *The National Review,* and on November 23, a Bureau official wrote a memo saying, "I think the Director would be interested in looking at it. . . . It is believed that this journal and the writers connected with it may be of some value to the Bureau."

Buckley acknowledges that the FBI's reaction startled him when he first read about it in his file. "I guess it's a surprise to me that they even reported on the publisher's statement of a new magazine," he says.

According to Buckley's file, the FBI also opened "a main file on *National Review.*"

That same year, the special agent in charge of the New York office sent Hoover the August 12 issue of *Counter-Attack,* which called the thirty-year-old Buckley "an effective foe of Communism." The following year, in 1956, a memo was sent to Hoover telling him that a recent Buckley speech was entered into the Congressional Record.

In 1957, Buckley sent Louis Nichols a copy of the press release announcing that Whittaker Chambers, Alger Hiss's accuser, had joined the staff of *National Review;* it was accompanied by a note: "I wanted you to know ahead of the gang."

Later that same year, Buckley also wrote Nichols that "my family has dealt during the last couple of years with Col. Emiliano Izaguirre in connection with various business matters in Venezuela," and that Izaguirre has asked to be introduced to Hoover in his capacity as "a personal agent of Perez Jimenez, the president of Venezuela."

Nichols told Buckley that "Izaguirre should go to CIA," but Buckley had already approached the CIA, and it had told him to go to the FBI. Nichols later told Buckley, "for your personal and confidential information," that the CIA denied saying Izaguirre should contact the FBI. Nichols also told Buckley, "my hunch is that either you or the Colonel may have heard from CIA," implying that the agency was playing some sort of double game. Elsewhere in the file it states flatly that the CIA "refused" to see Izaguirre.

In 1959, two FBI agents "discreetly covered" a debate between Buckley and James Wechsler, editor of the *New York Post.* A detailed report to Cartha DeLoach told him that Buckley was better prepared than Wechsler, and that Wechsler said "liberals were just as interested in halting communism as conservatives."

About six months later, Buckley sent Hoover an inscribed copy of his book, *Up from Liberalism.* Typed at the bottom of a copy of Hoover's thank you letter is a note, possibly from the FBI's Publication Section, that says that "a quick review" of the book "indicates that it is neither a balanced nor an effective presentation."

Over the years, Buckley continued to send Nichols releases, articles, and other items of interest; all of these were warmly and politely acknowledged, either by Nichols or by the Director himself.

"Buckley is the outspoken anti-communist" was the identifying wording always typed next to copies of anything received from Buckley, a description implying that the Bureau approved of him, and he always approved of it. He continued "a very close association" with Nichols, whom he had met at the Yale forum in 1948.

Buckley explains: "A man named Gaty, a bachelor—a Wichita man—left around five million dollars, about three and a half million to sort of Red Cross things, and a million and a half dollars to sort of right-wing-type things. He named ten trustees, and J. Edgar Hoover was one of them. But Hoover said, no, he couldn't serve—because he wouldn't serve on anything—so I then nominated Nichols, saying, obviously, the guy who left the money wanted someone representing the FBI. So as a result, we had one meeting a year, the bylaws specified that if you attended the annual meeting you had the absolute right to assign $10,000 to your favorite charity—so everybody was always there. Nichols was elected and so we went to ten meetings together—the idea was to exhaust the corpus within ten years. So I saw a lot of him during that period. Nice guy. Not a very secure sense of humor."

In 1962, the FBI reported that Buckley—"a controversial figure"—and his son, Christopher, toured the Bureau, and "visited briefly" with Hoover, who autographed a copy of his book *A Study of Communism* for them. The report includes Buckley's observation "concerning the excellence of [the] communism exhibit." The file also includes ten-year-old Christopher's thank-you note to Hoover.

That same year, Buckley sent the Director a copy of his book *Rumbles Left and Right,* which Hoover said he was "looking forward to reading." (There is no book report in the file.)

Two years later, in 1964, the FBI reported that Buckley began a syndicated newspaper column called "On the Right," though in fact this column had begun two years earlier. The Bureau also made inquiries as to the identity of "Quincy," the pen name of a *National Review* columnist. The FBI was told by a member of the magazine's staff that the column was usually written by Ralph de Toledano, but that he had not written the "portion" the FBI was interested in, which concerned the "identity of a former Russian national" possibly involved with Lee Harvey Oswald.

Buckley comments, "It's very fishy. There was never a point at which you'd say, 'I don't know who wrote that Quincy.' I can't understand so ambiguous an answer. Only one person wrote Quincy. It just sounds like sloppy work on the part of the FBI. Why didn't they just call me?"

The FBI also noted—but did not follow—Buckley's campaign for mayor of New York City in 1965. The file also reports that in the spring of 1965, the FBI investigated a bomb threat to Buckley's offices, but no explosives were found there.

But then Buckley committed the unforgivable sin: he ridiculed Hoover. The May 30, 1967, issue of *National Review* parodied the *New York Times,* and on the mock front page was an article saying that J. Edgar Hoover had submitted his resignation as director upon his arrest on a morals charge. On May 25, 1967, Buckley was removed from the Special Correspondent's list because the FBI said he "attempted to be humorous at the expense of the Director." Hoover called the article "a new low in journalism," and never forgave him. From that time on, every reference to Buckley mentioned the parody. With Hoover's distaste for charges of homosexuality, that "morals charge" must have been especially wounding, and he overreacted.

But Buckley never noticed that he had been taken off the list, because, he says, "I didn't know I was *on* the list."

According to the file, Hoover had been so angry in 1967 that he had Cartha DeLoach call Buckley at home after the parody appeared. When DeLoach was told that Buckley was "very ill" with the flu and was in bed and not able to take calls, he insisted that the matter was urgent, and that Buckley must call him back, which he did. DeLoach lectured Buckley that "there would be many people who would accept the article at face value" and "the entire FBI was outraged." Buckley told DeLoach that he had heard no complaints from anyone about what was clearly satire.

Hoover even pursued the possibility of taking legal action. He was advised against it. Two years later, in 1969, in the course of investigating Buckley for a sensitive government position as a member of the United States Advisory Commission on Information, when Hoover was told that Buckley "thought and wrote a generation ahead of the times," the Director would not be convinced (though Buckley got the job). Hoover didn't like Buckley's wit, and couldn't accept or appreciate what Murray Kempton describes as his "keen sense of the ridiculous," adding, "I think the ridiculousness of Hoover must have struck Buckley." In 1970, when the Director was invited to be a guest on Buckley's television show, *Firing Line,* he declined, pleading a scheduling conflict, but a note he wrote in the margin of the letter inviting him to be on the show gives the real reason: "No. Buckley recently wrote a vicious column on the FBI."

"I'll be damned," says a surprised William F. Buckley, Jr., who never knew of Hoover's anger until he read it in his file. Buckley added that he was also "surprised" that Hoover never "eliminated" his marginal notes from the master file "because these notes are his personal business, aren't they?"

In February 1968, the FBI wrote a memo expressing disapproval of a remark made on *Firing Line* by Leo Cherne, then the director of the Research Institute of America. According to a memo, Buckley "indicated he would delete" the offending remark, in which Cherne said that he had opposed Senator Joseph McCarthy in 1946 because McCarthy "was supported by Communists" according to Louis Nichols, who had advised him about this.

The memo then reported that "no reference to this incident was contained in the show as broadcast in Washington." However, Buckley says that "the only time in the history of *Firing Line* that something was deleted was a libel by Roy Cohn—who was on the show with Cherne. Roy had once called someone a Communist and my ear twitched—because I had a pretty good memory on the question, and he had gotten the wrong guy. So we pulled it out as a matter of slander. And then, one other time we pulled out something that Howard Hunt said. I remember no third time we pulled anything out."

A few months later, Buckley sent Hoover a copy of his 1968 book, *A Jeweler's Eye,* but it was not acknowledged, because of the parody written the year before. "So *somebody* must have had it in for me, I guess," Buckley says.

In early June of 1969, the FBI was asked by the White House to do a hurried investigation of Buckley, who had just been named a member of the U.S. Advisory Commission on Information. Hoover requested that the case be assigned "to experienced agents," and that no "neighborhood" investigation be done.

Most of the people interviewed praised Buckley to the agents, calling him such things as a "clean-thinking American," "an excellent father and husband," a person "endowed with a unique vocabulary which he uses in a proper manner," a person with "no religious or racial prejudices," and "one of the fastest minds ever witnessed." on the negative side, one unidentified person told the agents that Buckley "received one parking ticket," "his views are too far to the right," and "that he turns himself on for his television appearances and therefore does not succeed in presenting a true image of himself." Agents also reported that he had been sued for libel and that "currently he is suing Mr. Gore Vidal for alleged libelous statements made by Mr. Vidal during a television debate with Mr. Buckley." The FBI report sent to the White House quoted *Time* magazine's commentary on this case: "It has to be the most bizarre writer vs writer confrontation since

Westbrook Pegler took on Drew Pearson. . . . Buckley filed suit asking for $500,000 in damages [after] Vidal called Buckley a 'crypto-Nazi,' to which Buckley replied: 'listen, you queer, stop calling me a crypto-Nazi or I'll sock you in your goddam face and you'll stay plastered.''

Buckley served on the commission from July 8, 1969, to January 27, 1972, when his term expired. (In a later investigation, an unidentified government official told the FBI that "Buckley was not reappointed to another term because of his disagreement with President Nixon's policy of detente with the Soviet Union and Red China." Buckley comments that "after returning from China, February '72, I wrote that I would not accept another term.")

During the summer of 1969, Buckley invited Hoover to join him and seven others—Jack Benny, Leonard Bernstein, Robert Graves, Paul McCartney, Roddy McDowall, Archibald MacLeish, and Mickey Rooney—in a libel suit against the Olympia Press for listing their names in *The Homosexual Handbook,* what the publishers called "a hearsay reference work." Although Hoover agreed there was a case, he declined to be part of it, partly because of the publicity that would ensue, partly because the records could not be sealed, and partly because "Buckley indicates no financial target that would make the lawsuit profitable in the money sense." Interestingly, Hoover does not mention any financial concern in the letter he eventually wrote Buckley, a letter he "okayed" over Tolson's "Suggest no reply." Some of the *Handbook*'s other "hearsays" ranged from Alexander the Great, Sir Francis Bacon, and Johannes Brahms to the Rolling Stones.

In October 1969, Buckley told the FBI that his office had "just received" a phone call saying there was going to be an assassination attempt made on Senator Edward Kennedy. The caller said Kennedy should stay away from all anti-Vietnam War demonstrations. Agents immediately interviewed Buckley's secretary, Frances Bronson, who had received two calls from a Dorothy Ruiz, who is not otherwise identified. Ruiz told Buckley's office that the plot "was being formed in Havana" and was going to occur on November 15. She also said that "the plot is Communist in nature" although the killers want it to appear that it was done by the "Right." The FBI contacted the Secret Service and Senator Kennedy's office, and, Buckley says, "It was kept quiet, and never appeared in the newspapers."

In the fall of 1969, a prank letter Buckley wrote to *Life* magazine somehow made its way into his FBI file. The letter is written "in behalf of Roy Cohn" who is offering "to lend *Life* money at modest rates of interest provided *Life* will consent to move its editorial offices from Delaware to Illinois.'' Buckley explains that ''what happened was that somebody wrote a feature story on Roy Cohn, and I occupied one paragraph of it, and in that paragraph it said I had borrowed money from Roy Cohn's Illinois-based bank to buy my schooner, which is absolutely correct. They then went on to say Buckley's boat is registered in Illinois—which it had to be, because of the bank loan—'even though he cruises in Connecticut.' So my letter to *Life* was a tease. *Life* is situated in New York, but is based corporately in Delaware. It's an odd thing to be in my FBI file. But I obviously sent Roy a copy and he probably sent it to an FBI buddy to amuse him—because he was very tight with all these guys.''

Two years after the parody that provoked Hoover's wrath, the Director showed just how far he could take his vengeance. The FBI used Buckley as part of a ''Black Nationalist–Hate groups'' COINTELPRO operation. This is the first known instance of a prominent person on the right being used this way.

During the fall of 1969, the FBI mailed Buckley an anonymous letter ''setting forth Yale University sanctions of Black Panther Party activities on the Yale campus during May 1969.'' The FBI's goal, of course, was to stir Buckley up so he would write something negative about the Panthers, or about the recent arrest of Bobby Seale for murder and kidnapping.

''The idea was to inflame me?'' Buckley asks, adding, ''I had a pretty low opinion of Bobby Seale anyway.'' His office usually keeps anonymous letters, but it could not locate the one the FBI supposedly sent regarding the Panthers. Yale University, which houses Buckley's letters and papers, also conducted an unsuccessful search. Either it was composed but never actually sent, or else it disappeared. In any case, Buckley did write a column on November 13, 1969, about Bobby Seale's trial, saying among many things that ''Seale is engaged in traditional revolutionary strategy,'' and that he is trying ''to distract attention'' from his murder and kidnapping charges. ''I do believe Seale was guilty,'' Buckley comments, ''and he *did* adopt those strategies.''

Buckley, who knew nothing about the COINTELPRO scheme, or about being on Hoover's ''enemies'' list, carried on as usual with the FBI. In June of 1970, he ''confidentially'' forwarded a letter he had received to Cartha DeLoach; its contents involved a student bomb factory in Maryland. The letter writer described in graphic detail what he had seen at this factory and asked Buckley not to contact the police,

although the FBI managed to contact the letter writer without impli-
cating Buckley. The results of the Bureau's investigation are not included in the documents in the file, and Buckley says he never received
any follow-up.

In 1970, the Air Force conducted an investigation of Buckley for
membership on the National Security Forum. The earlier 1969 report
was forwarded to the Air Force. Agents also clipped Hugh Kenner's
New York Times Book Review essay on Whittaker Chambers's letters
to Buckley, and put it in the file that year.

In 1971, another *National Review* parody was misunderstood by the
Bureau. This one, called "The Secret Papers They Didn't Publish,"
purported to be some missing pages from the Pentagon Papers. The
FBI *seriously* analyzed the article in a seven-page memo, calling it
"disjointed and lacking in continuity" and nowhere indicated that they
recognized it as the put-on it was.

Buckley recalls that *The Washington Post* also did not know it was
a put-on. He adds that "I met the press five days after the 'Papers'
appeared and said it was all a hoax." He says it is "extraordinary" that
the FBI report took it so seriously, although he admits that it was
"ingeniously done, and we got from James Burnham, Jr., who had
been in Naval Intelligence, the actual series of secret code numbers
used by the Navy—so the FBI must have been astonished, if they had
checked those out. I can't believe it! I simply can't believe they didn't
know it was a hoax. Among other things, one of them might have
called me up, right?"

In 1971, Hoover thanked Buckley for a favorable FBI column which
attacked Lillian Hellman's Committee for Public Justice seminar at
Princeton University. Buckley remarks that "in fact, we now know she
was an active Communist. But she was recognized then as a fellow
traveler, dating to the early forties, so if she started the committee,
that would tend to have thrown all of us off it. Hellman was the
dominant figure in the invitation to that seminar—so a lot of people
would have said, 'Well, this is a Communist-front organization—the
hell with it.' "

Two years later, in 1973, the State Department requested a new
investigation of Buckley, "for a Presidential appointment, position not
indicated."

During the investigation—the post was public member delegate to
the United Nations—there were some new compliments (that he was a
"saint," and was "loved and respected by his friends and enemies
alike") and it included a statement by a Democrat, saying he would

vote for Buckley for President. Buckley says the Democrat "must have been Clarence Mannion, the dean of the law school at Notre Dame, a trustee—however inactive—of the John Birch Society. But he always insisted on being a Democrat." The comments also included some new criticisms—that he was "an arrogant egomaniac with a very overbearing personality" and was "loyal to the United States government to an obsessed degree." Buckley comments that whoever said that was "probably somebody who's punishing me for being a McCarthyite." Another interviewee told the FBI he questioned Buckley's friendship with Watergate burglar E. Howard Hunt; a marginal note from an FBI official recommends that this information be omitted from the final report. Hunt had been Buckley's boss in the CIA and had recruited him to work in Mexico City, and Buckley says he "assumes" that is why the FBI wanted to omit it. He adds that whoever told the FBI about Hunt "figured anybody that was that close to Howard Hunt was a security risk of some sort."

In 1974, *Firing Line* asked FBI director Clarence Kelley to be a guest, and although this time the memo stated that "over the years the Bureau has had a cordial relationship with Buckley," nonetheless, the 1967 parody—or, as Buckley calls it, "the event"—was mentioned once again. In addition, other reasons were given for Kelley not appearing: that the show was seen on non–prime time and, surprisingly, that it was too much a "sounding board" for conservatism, and the Director should not be "affiliated as a partisan."

Buckley's final reference is a letter Director Kelley wrote him thanking him for a recent pro-FBI column.

WILLIAM F. BUCKLEY, JR.:

I've always thought that the essential distinction is widely ignored—or basically is—namely, that the FBI is a data-collecting agency, and it's on the basis of the data collection that they get *clues*. For instance, on fingerprints. In the Lindbergh kidnapping, if they hadn't collected fingerprints for years, they wouldn't have found Hauptmann.

What they're not supposed to do is *evaluate*. So if, say, you were thinking of hiring me, it would be up to you, surveying these sources to find out whether or not you thought I was safe to be a covert agent in the CIA. So there's nothing in my file that *shocks* me.

The distinction I belabor in my book on McCarthy is the difference between a security risk and a loyalty risk. Inevitably when your mandate is to keep security risks out, you're going to keep some people out that you shouldn't keep out. But you're *absolutely* wrong in saying that anybody who's a security risk is, for that reason, a loyalty risk. You can be a security risk if you drink too much—even though you're obviously loyal.

Inevitably, also, you get changing ambient situations. Right now we are suffering terribly as a result of spies. I was told confidentially by Richard Helms that the damage done to America by the Walker spy ring is just *unfathomable.* In situations like that, you say, well, security's not tight *enough*—so where in the hell was the FBI when these people were being checked?

I assumed my file would be pretty copious because every third person I ran into in 1969 and 1973 said they had been asked about me, and so I assumed it would be bulky. I didn't know about the Hoover rebuff at all. Nor did I know I was an insider. I don't know what service Hoover suspended because I don't remember receiving FBI service. It must have been disappointing to him that I didn't know I was in Coventry.

It's really spooky that agents monitored certain *Firing Lines* and so forth. It sounds as though someone was sort of deranged—giving out these wild orders. Would that have been Hoover?

As for the 1969 COINTELPRO, was Hoover otherwise only using left-wingers? That's fascinating, if I'm the only right-winger whom he victimized like this. So he was just playing games with me! Oh well, I'm not entirely opposed to what would be the equivalent of a CIA-type activity intended to confuse communications among a crystallizing front—people whose intentions were clearly subversive. If you find out they cause riots in Watts or Philadelphia or in Washington by intending to burn down a house, and then disrupt schooling, et cetera, then they become enemies of the state. Now, what is licensable activity in situations like that is a fine line and not easy to draw. If an effort was made to confuse, then, and there was prima facie evidence that the people being watched were bent on disruption and maybe even violence, then it is something that wouldn't shock me.

The idea of being *personally* victimized is simply an aspect of Hoover's lack of any sense of proportion. My satire, in 1967, was something he should have applauded—even though he was entirely an incidental figure. I was astonished that he should have reacted as he did, and it must have been known to his sidekick, Louis Nichols, because we soon after began meeting every year for ten years to disburse that foundation's money—so Nichols must have been embarrassed to have been on such convivial relations with me, even when he knew what his boss was up to.

So, people who don't have a sense of humor should not be in charge of national security—their perspectives are dim, they are not reliable. Hoover was obviously a person without any sense of humor—without any sense of perspective.

The FBI hasn't interfered in my life, so far as I know. The only thing that Hoover did that I find impossible to rationalize is that business involving Bobby Seale.

**

As Hoover's fury at his critics in the press escalated, he began to seek ways to channel it. Evidence of the lengths to which he might go can be found in the file of Walter Lippmann. As it has been shown, the Director had tracked Lippmann since 1912. By the 1930s, the columnist had moved considerably to the right; nevertheless, there is a 1937 report on his book *The Good Society,* which says, "It has been stated that this book attempts to evaluate the conditions of life under a planned economy," which presumably was not a method approved of by Hoover. The year before, after a special tour of the Bureau had been arranged for Lippmann, he had told his tour guide that Hoover "must be an administrative genius," and that he thought the FBI was "the greatest organization he had ever visited." At the time, he had no idea the "genius" was also managing his books.

According to the file, the FBI also once somehow managed to plant an informant in an interview Lippmann conducted with Alger Hiss in 1947. There is no clue as to how this covert feat was accomplished.

The following year, the FBI was appropriately troubled when a former secretary of Lippmann's, Mary Price, was accused of being a Soviet spy who "ransacked Lippmann's files." Her background, the FBI remarked, "was perfect for an undercover agent since she belonged to an old Southern family and Southerners were the last people suspected of being Communists."

But it was not until the 1950s that Hoover found an outlet for his rage against "coyotes of the press" and "men like Walter Lippmann" who criticize the FBI. A 1962 report telling Hoover that Lippmann denounced the Bureau in a television interview provides a hint as to why two very damaging memos from the 1950s were placed in his file.

The first report is dated March 8, 1957, and is still considered so controversial that the name of the FBI official who sent it and the name of the official who received it are blacked out, as is part of the title. What is left of the title reads "RE INFILTRATION OF FABIAN SOCIALISTS INTO HIGH POLICY-MAKING AREAS OF THE UNITED STATES GOVERN-MENT." The FBI devotes two paragraphs to discussing the origins of Fabian socialism, explaining that "the name Fabian was derived from a Roman general . . . who became famous by his military tactics of avoiding direct battles," and concludes its description by stating that "the aim of fabian socialism is to permeate every segment of society with socialistic ideas, words, attitudes, tendencies, and modes of thinking."

Presumably, Walter Lippmann was believed to be using such military tactics as "concession, compromise, and avoidance of conflict," since his name is the only one of the 122 other suspects that is left intact on the document.

The language of the memo is blunt, arguing that "a considerable amount of 'smoke' surrounds" all these people, who among their many crimes have described "Chinese communists as being harmless 'agrarian reformers' when they should have known that they were actually communists," or that they have either "suppressed information unfavorable to communism," written "slanted reports favoring communism," or "have minimized the threat of Soviet Russia to peace and democracy."

Just how many infiltrators were caught is not disclosed.

But the most disturbing item in Lippmann's file is the second report, written two years later, on March 18, 1959. The subject of it is "MOLDERS OF PUBLIC OPINION IN THE UNITED STATES," and reads in part: "On March 6, 1959, the Director expressed to Mr. [blacked out] and myself [blacked out] his concern about the prevalence of articles in publications which are severely and unfairly discrediting our American way of life and praising directly or indirectly the Soviet system. The Director questioned whether there might not be some subversive factors in the backgrounds of some of the prominent columnists, editors, commentators, authors, et cetera, which could be influencing such slanted views."

The memorandum continues, "In accordance with the Director's concern in this matter, immediate research was conducted concerning a representative cross section of prominent molders of public opinion. One hundred names of prominent individuals were considered. A preliminary analysis resulted in the immediate elimination of twelve individuals who had no known subversive connections."

The list of one hundred names that were first considered is not in the file, nor are the names of the twelve nonsubversive writers. The report then explains that "file reviews" were conducted on the remaining eighty-eight names, but this list is also not included.

The FBI does specify, however, that forty out of the list of eighty-eight "were determined to have pertinent factors in their backgrounds which could have a bearing on their reporting of political, economic, and social aspects of world affairs."

This list is included with the report, but, again, the name of Walter Lippmann is the only one not blacked out. (Both the 1957 and 1959 memos do not appear in any of the other writers' files, so it is not possible to determine exactly who the other 121 suspected Fabians or the other 39 subversive molders are.)

The official responsible for the Fabian memo brags that "over 5,500 references were reviewed," while the official responsible for the molders memo boasts that "nearly 4,000 references were reviewed in five days," also admitting that "public source material was used wherever possible; however, confidential material from bureau files was also necessarily utilized." It is likely that all of the material came from the files, and the FBI official did not want to put in writing just how extensive the Bureau files were. Evidence of this possibility is in the next sentence, "The material was carefully paraphrased and prepared, with a brief introduction, in blind memorandum form to conceal the Bureau as the source. This was done in the event the Director should desire to make available to appropriate persons some of the information on an informal and confidential basis." A blind memorandum, of course, is written on a plain piece of paper, not unlike an anonymous letter. It can be circulated among high officials, or even friendly people in the press, and whoever is reading this negative and highly biased material about molders of public opinion that J. Edgar Hoover feels are destroying the American way of life has no idea where it originated. It is a convenient and advantageous way to utilize the power of suspicion, and this 1959 memo shows Hoover at the summit of such powers.

Cartha DeLoach dismisses the document, saying it was "simply for the Director's information as to what caused these people to write that way—you know, what makes Sammy run—that type of thing." But such an explanation seems bland, misleading, and over-simplified. Enormous—and urgent—effort went into the preparation of both reports, and even a cursory look at Hoover's relationship with members of the press would lead to a strong belief that he intended to use the reports at the very least to discredit the "unfriendlies." It has a shocking intent, and although there is no proof these documents were actually used to activate censorship, they were clearly much more than a private exercise.

Nearly forty years after his first Red Scare, Hoover was hoping to create another by sowing suspicion and distrust about certain people he disagreed with and thus believed were poisoning public opinion.

PART FOUR

World War II and the Cold War

CHAPTER ELEVEN

A Broader Net

On New Year's Day, 1940, a year in which the CPUSA would reach fifty-five thousand members,* J. Edgar Hoover turned forty-five. The war in Europe had created a national emergency, in which his personal war on subversion would prosper. The House Un-American Activities Committee was wildly active. In June, the Alien Registration Act was passed. As Maurice Isserman writes in *Which Side Were You On?*, "Congress, in an election year, needed little persuasion to solve the nation's security problems in a time of international menace at the expense of the traditional scapegoats, aliens and radicals." This law, commonly known as the Smith Act, made membership in any group that advocated the forceful overthrow of the government illegal. Hoover would use it to justify many heretofore illegal investigations into political beliefs. His broader net would catch hundreds and hundreds of innocent people, including many writers who had been dramatically swept up in the political passions of the 1930s. Even those who had dropped by the wayside after the Moscow trials and the

---

* Not "card-carrying" members. "There were no *cards*," says novelist Howard Fast. "Membership cards were an invention of the FBI." But there were dues cards.

Hitler-Stalin nonaggression pact still needed to be controlled, as far as Hoover was concerned.

In August of 1940, Leon Trotsky was murdered in Mexico by Stalin's agents. In exile, the old Bolshevik had been a rallying point for anti-Stalinists in the United States, but the distinction had been lost on many FBI agents, who put Stalinists, Trotskyites, Socialists, Liberals, and so forth, into one subversive mold. But there were signs that it was changing, at least somewhat: for instance, in playwright William Saroyan's file, he is identified in 1943 as a "Trotskyite and a Social Democrat."

In November the FBI began using the American Legion, which had been founded in 1919 and had done yeoman work in the Red Scare that year, as an official "confidential source" of information. (In the fifties, Hoover would ask Cartha DeLoach to join the Legion to make sure it continued its strong anti-Communist work.)

In 1941, the Legion passed a "resolution of protest" against the Free Company, a group formed by Saroyan and other writers "to prepare dramatic broadcasts as a counter-attack against foreign propaganda in the United States." But the Legion accused it of planning to broadcast "Red plays designed to encourage radicalism in the United States."

In another boost to Hoover's power that year, President Roosevelt officially authorized the use of wiretaps. Of course, the Bureau had been tapping phones surreptitiously since at least 1937.

Even before the Japanese attack on Pearl Harbor on December 7, 1941, the U.S. economy had been gearing up for war. In the frenetic buildup that followed America's entry into the conflict on the side of Great Britain and the Soviet Union, the defense industry boomed, and so did the FBI's responsibilities—agents now had to investigate every employee working on government defense contracts. In the early months of the war, fears of sabotage swept the country, but as Clarence Kelley writes in his autobiography, "Not one case of foreign-directed sabotage took place in the United States during all of World War Two." When eight German saboteurs actually landed in Florida and New York in 1942, they were immediately captured by the FBI.

The success of the war against saboteurs spurred Hoover's agents on to add new material to existing writers' files and to open new ones as well. In 1941, the FBI decided that Langston Hughes's poem "Goodbye Christ" "appears to be of a Communistic nature." Two years later, he was placed on the Security Index, even though an unnamed informant who "was among the first Negro intellectuals to join the

Communist Party" told Hoover that "Hughes had never been known generally, not even in the Party circle, as a member." Howard Fast agrees: "Langston Hughes would appear in any Communist event, but he wasn't a Communist."

Just about every single member of the Writers War Board, created in 1941 by the Authors League of America to enable writers to "pour their talent and their labor into the country's fight for freedom," had files begun one or two decades earlier. (Clifton Fadiman, the only still living member of the board, says that he has "no recollection whatsoever of any FBI surveillance at any time.")

The Authors League (first indexed in 1913) was an affiliate of the Authors Guild, along with the Dramatists Guild, the Radio Writers Guild and the Screen Writers Guild, and for many years the Bureau had difficulty figuring out the connections. But it went on full alert when it learned from the Authors League bulletin that the League had formed the Writers War Board, with the particular purpose of arousing "our people to meet the present desperate need to commence the war." The FBI knew that the board, "formerly known as the Writers War committee, was organized in December 1941, at the request of the Treasury Department . . . to serve as a liaison between Writers of America and Government Departments which want writing jobs done that will in any way whatever, directly or indirectly, help win the war."

With its inherent mistrust of writers' loyalty, the FBI screened the board carefully, and became concerned when it learned that Rex Stout, who had a file dating back to 1920, would be the head of it.

In 1923, when the FBI discovered that Upton Sinclair (whose file began that year) had attacked the Authors League for not urging its members to support the American Civil Liberties Union, it decided to begin reading all of the league's bulletins, noting, however, that there were "very few articles of a controversial or political nature." In fact, it didn't find anything controversial again until a 1936 article on censorship "which condemns several federal bills pending at that time because of their 'repressive measure.' " However, the FBI also decided it might be useful to go on the offense and have the Director write for the *Writers War Board Bulletin,* and so in 1944 Hoover contributed an article entitled "The Modern Trojan Horse," which was bannered "FBI Director Warns Against Methods of Our Internal Enemies." The Director was also not so subtly warning the nation's writers that he was watching them.

During the fall of 1942, auxiliary agent Walter Winchell endorsed the drive to award J. Edgar Hoover the Congressional Medal of Honor. When a small newspaper in Lyons, New York, wrote an editorial saying that a military medal should not be given to a civilian, Hoover ordered the paper removed from "all lists"—his usual retaliation against those insufficiently appreciative of his services to the nation.

In 1944, the CPUSA, which had grown to eighty thousand members and was wholeheartedly supporting the war effort, changed its name to the Communist Political Association and announced it would no longer run candidates of its own but would support worthy hopefuls from the major parties. In *Masters of Deceit,* Hoover writes that the move was intended "to soften opposition to Communism, and make it sound a little better to Americans." To Hoover, the Party sounded even worse, if that were possible, after Walter Winchell published a report that the CP had launched a "smear campaign" against the Director.

That same year, agents recruited a librarian at the University of California in Berkeley to "produce records" on the reading habits of the poet Muriel Rukeyser, who had applied the year before for a government copywriting job with the Bureau of Publications and Graphics of the Office of War Information. (The Bureau referred to Rukeyser as "a well-known poetess who is alleged to have mixed considerable left-wing politics with her iambic pentameters.")

On February 19, 1944, H. L. Mencken wrote Hoover, "I am engaged at the moment upon a somewhat elaborate supplement to my old book *The American Language.* . . . I'd like to have a really accurate note on the term G-Man. . . ." On February 26, Hoover gave Mencken more than he bargained for in a two-page reply that includes the following: ". . . 'G-Man' . . . was first popularized and applied to the Federal Bureau of Investigation following the apprehension of 'Machine-Gun' Kelly in Memphis, Tennessee, on September 26, 1933. If you will recall the case, 'Machine-Gun' Kelly made numerous boasts that he would never be taken alive . . . agents pushed open the door, naturally expecting an exchange of gunfire. However, they were greeted by 'Machine-Gun' Kelly, not with a machine gun, but Kelly standing in the corner with his hands in the air saying, 'Don't shoot, G-Man! Don't Shoot!' These words became the subject matter of many headlines as they typify the cowardice of the boastful Kelly." Clearly, Hoover enjoyed his role as cultural reporter—and archivist—yet by helping Mencken, the Director also believed he was controlling him.

After World War II ended in August 1945, Hoover became more vigilant. As he wrote in *Masters of Deceit,* "Moscow reverted to its former hostile line,'' meaning that American Communists would start causing trouble. The Cold War was about to begin.

ROY COHN:
In 1940, 1941, and 1942, the FBI and Mr. Hoover were as militantly anti-Communist as they were anti-Nazi. The research department of the FBI understood Marxism and Leninism, understood Nazism—had read *Mein Kampf*—and it knew Hitler was out to destroy the free world. Mr. Hoover would say, "Of course we have to kill the Nazis, but you mark my words, a year later—two years later—we're going to be fighting the Communists."

The FBI saw it very clearly. It said that's where we're going, that's where we're heading. And that's why Mr. Hoover was able to build files and files and files—nobody else would have *dared* to do it!

You can say what you want about Edgar Hoover, but who else had the guts, when the Soviet Union was our ally—who else but Hoover would have had the guts to have two thousand agents out spying on the Soviet Union, spying on Communists!

Mr. Hoover would say, "They're a great ally today, we have paper for Russia drives, we have this, that, and the next thing, but they're going to be our next enemy. We don't have peace."

And after every international conference, the FBI would go crazy!

**

In February 1946, the FBI initiated an intense public relations campaign designed to impress upon Americans the seriousness of the Red menace. This sort of drive was not exactly new for the FBI, but after Churchill's "Iron Curtain" speech that year, the necessity of influencing public opinion "about the basically Russian nature of the Communist Party" in America (the FBI's phrase) became an impassioned topic at Bureau meetings. A "new" program was outlined, one that foreshadowed the March 18, 1959, "Molders of Public Opinion in the United States" report in Lippmann's file. According to Kenneth O'Reilly in his book *Hoover and the Un-Americans,* the 1946 program involved the "dissemination of educational materials through available channels." The program also included special training seminars for agents, appearances by Hoover at patriotic societies and organizations, and most important, the creation of J. Edgar Hoover, Author. O'Reilly writes that "from February 1946 until his death in 1972, Hoover published nearly 400 major items—over 200 articles . . . 37 speeches, interviews, reports, pamphlets . . . columns." The Great Enforcer took his war on words into alien territory.

On August 19, 1946, Westbrook Pegler wrote Hoover: "Apparently the move to get your job and hand it to some Communist that we observed last winter was blocked before it really got under way. I hope it is dead." It certainly was; after twenty-two years as Director, Hoover had become a Washington fixture, as immovable as the Lincoln Memorial.

Nevertheless, upon President Roosevelt's death in 1945, the Boss found that *he* had a new boss, Harry S Truman, who was not as cooperative as FDR had been. Cartha DeLoach recalled: "Truman used the FBI less than other Presidents because there was ill feeling between Mr. Hoover and Mr. Truman that stemmed from his starting the CIA. There was also ill feeling that stemmed from the old days of the Truman committee looking into racketeering. So consequently, Mr. Truman used the FBI very sparingly. But he did call upon us for quite a bit of work when they had the Greece-Turkey situation. And there was the Truman loyalty program, and the FBI was called upon to do considerable investigative work at the time. Another matter of bad feeling between the two came over the Alger Hiss matter, when the secretary of state [Dean Acheson] indicated he would not turn his back on Hiss—and the FBI later conducted the investigation and discovered considerable evidence, and Alger Hiss was prosecuted and convicted in federal court."

The creation of the Central Intelligence Agency in 1947 posed the most serious threat thus far to Hoover's power. The CIA was put in charge of all foreign intelligence, leaving the FBI in charge of domestic intelligence only. Hoover had fought to have the CIA placed under his control, but Truman refused. The Director had always considered the Office of Strategic Services, the CIA's predecessor, "a group of arrogant amateurs encroaching on his own terrain," according to Maurice Isserman. Hoover's jealousy of the CIA was a critical factor in his decision to expand his counterintelligence programs a decade later.

Former Bureau official William Sullivan writes that "Hoover's hatred of Truman knew no bounds." Sullivan also discloses that the FBI "planted stories critical of some of Hoover's favorite targets, the CIA, for instance. And of course, we placed stories about Hoover's congressional critics."

A "personal and confidential" unsigned letter dated July 22, 1954, addressed to George Sokolsky, which is included in his file, and which he passed on to Hoover because of its soundness, explains that "the only thing that is really secret about the CIA is its attitude toward Congress and the public." The letter goes on to say that "the FBI ran a very effective secret intelligence organization in Latin America during World War II and thereafter, until closed out by the CIA . . . as is always the case in secret intelligence, the public and even Congress never even heard of this organization, nor did it get any publicity, nor did J. Edgar Hoover or the men in charge get pictures in the paper entitled 'Superspy' . . .''

Possibly the only thing Hoover and the CIA agreed on was something the latter's unidentified covert propaganda director, who was in charge of its extensive book-publishing program, wrote in the early sixties: "Books differ from all other propaganda media, primarily because one single book can significantly change the reader's attitude and action to an extent unmatched by the impact of any other single medium."

RAMSEY CLARK:

Hoover couldn't be outdone by the CIA. It wasn't that he was appalled by them—they were promoting the idea that you could do ignoble things in a gentlemanly way—gentlemanly in the worst and crudest sexist sense of the word. The old CIA was very much like this, and I don't think Hoover was ever terribly upset with the means—he was upset with the competition.

I have always believed that he fiercely sought to prevent the CIA from domestic activity. He wanted to control all that knowledge, all that power; he didn't want them around.

**

There was some compensation for the Director in Truman's Federal Employee Loyalty Program, established in 1947 and designed to keep Communists out of government. The program increased the Bureau's role in screening government employees, and further legitimized inquiries into the minds of American citizens.

Perhaps not coincidentally, one year after the CIA was formed, the FBI officially inaugurated an illicit burglary or "black bag" program, under which agents broke into the offices of dubious political groups or the homes of their leaders and stole confidential material. The information thus obtained was hidden in the "Do Not File" files, also created that year. These files, of course, were not indexed and therefore no one (except the person who created them) knew the information existed.

The Communist Index was also established in 1948. This listing was separate from the Security Index, which included all citizens the FBI believed had the potential to be a danger to public safety. The Communist Index identified just those persons whom the FBI considered sympathetic to the CP.

On February 13, 1948, forty members of the National Institute of Arts and Letters disassociated themselves from an open letter criticizing the House Committee on Un-American Activities that had been signed by over 125 members, including Eugene O'Neill, Sinclair

Lewis, Edna Ferber, and Lillian Hellman. Of the forty who objected to the protest, two were writers—Robinson Jeffers, who probably did not know that the FBI had kept a file on him since 1935, and Wallace Stevens, who, according to the FBI, never had a file.

Two months later, on April 28, the FBI "placed in the Bureau library" a copy of a book that would not be found at the National Institute of Arts and Letters. It was an American Legion handbook that reported that the CP was "capturing the apparatus in publishing houses and newspapers" and that the book sections of both the *New York Times* and the *Herald Tribune* had "notorious left-wing attitudes" because "well-known Right writers would have books maltreated or not reviewed."

On March 25, 1949, the Cultural and Scientific Conference for World Peace was held at the Waldorf-Astoria Hotel in New York. A great many people believed that the sponsor of the conference, the National Council of the Arts, Sciences, and Professions, was simply a Communist front, and therefore some writers and editors withdrew their names from sponsorship. But others, such as Kay Boyle, Howard Fast, Angus Cameron, and Lillian Hellman, remained on the list.

Attendance at this conference would later become, for the FBI, a test of a person's loyalty; like the Spanish Civil War, it mattered which side you were on.

J. EDGAR HOOVER:
The FBI is as much concerned with proving the innocence of persons under charge as it is with proving guilt.
—*from "The Power of Facts," a newspaper column substituting for "The Lyons Den"; 1949*

CHAPTER TWELVE

Pound, Boyle, Hecht, and Stein

Ezra Pound, the only American charged with treason in World War II, had been in the FBI's indexes since 1911. His had been a "dead" file until sometime in the mid-thirties when new intelligence was received. However, it was not until May 9, 1942, that the Bureau actually acknowledged a "need to investigate Pound further." On that date, in reply to an assistant attorney general's memo that the Justice Department had received word of Ezra Pound's pro-Axis radio broadcasts from Italy, J. Edgar Hoover replied somewhat defensively, that "the subject, Ezra Pound, has resided outside of the United States continuously since 1911," and that "the files of this Bureau contain no further pertinent data relative to him."

In fact, the FBI had known about Pound's fascist leanings, possibly as early as 1935. A 1941 memo in his file states that "the Department of State has advised confidentially . . . that Pound is known to have been very pro-Fascist for a number of years, and to have spoken over the Italian radio system against the policies of the United States . . . [and] upon entering and leaving the Consular offices at Genoa, he was prone to give the Fascist salute." Still another memo says that "about 1939 he began broadcasting, [and] these [broadcasts] were beamed to the United States and heard by listeners in America.''

Then, again in 1941, a year before Hoover's disingenuous reply to the attorney general's office, word reached the FBI that ''Dr. Pound slanderously attacked the wife of the President.'' Hoover, who had no love for Eleanor Roosevelt, did nothing about this. Then in 1942, after that ''nudge'' from the assistant attorney general, he began an extensive investigation of Pound; in fact, one memo now said, ''It is noted that this case is considered very important.''

Bureau agents interviewed dozens of individuals. One had seen the Italian censor ''working over the scripts'' of Pound's broadcasts with him. Another told them ''that Pound had studied the writings of one Major Douglas, a well known Socialist writer.'' The FBI collected every manuscript, letter, document, article, or book that might possibly incriminate Pound. One informant revealed ''that there were only four topics of conversation on the part of Pound, namely that Martin Van Buren was the greatest president the United States ever had; that John Adams was one of the greatest men that ever lived; a strong tirade against the Jews; an equally strong tirade against the international bankers.'' Another witness reported to the FBI that ''Pound considered everyone he associated with as one of his servants, including his host and hostess.''

After the Bureau received transcripts and recordings of all of Pound's broadcasts, agents began to ask his friends and acquaintances if they could positively identify the voice on the recordings as that of Pound's. Poet William Carlos Williams told agents he had known Pound since 1910 and had attended the University of Pennsylvania with him. Williams believed that Pound ''has gone insane in order to do what he has in connection with Fascism,'' and although at one point he said that he could identify Pound's voice, he said later he ''would not like to make a definite statement to that effect,'' because in several of the broadcasts he had heard, ''the voice did not closely resemble [that of] Pound.'' He even believed that ''possibly Dr. Ezra Pound had been interned and some other individual was impersonating his voice.'' The FBI did not take this idea seriously, and continued to search for people who could authenticate Pound's voice.

In 1943, writer Kay Boyle was interviewed by the Bureau. A document in his file reports that Boyle ''says Pound defended Japan in Discussion of China Japan War and censured America as being stupid, unappreciative of poetry and culture. . . . He excoriated the Chinese for marauding and for stealing and copying Japanese culture. He declared the Japanese were justified in taking anything they could from China, but he gave no hint that he had any premonition of Japanese attack on the United States. She was rather doubtful she could identify Pound's voice on transcription due to the brevity of her association.''

Pound's publisher, James Laughlin of New Directions, told the FBI that Pound "has an unsound but brilliant mind . . . [and] is now anxious to persecute the Jews because of the fact that he, himself, has been persecuted and his genius never properly recognized.'' Laughlin also said that Pound "has actually talked himself into believing that Roosevelt is a Jew,'' and that "on one occasion Pound met Mussolini and at the time, Mussolini made it known to Pound that he had read Pound's poetry. Pound was naturally very much impressed by this fact,'' as well as the fact that he was "given a free pass on the Italian railroads by the Fascists.''

The 1942 inquiry into Pound's anti-American, anti-Semitic broadcasts—ironically, in one memo his first name is typed in as "Israel" and then corrected in ink—resulted in Pound's indictment for treason on July 26, 1943, but it was not until November, 18, 1945, that Pound was actually returned to Washington, D.C. According to Pound biographer John Tytell, "Pound had no objection" to using an insanity plea, and, in fact, "remarked that it had naturally occurred to him already." The American public was both fascinated and vindictive. Many people felt that Pound was pretending to be insane in order to avoid the death penalty.

The poet had prominent literary friends, including T. S. Eliot, Ernest Hemingway, Conrad Aiken, and Archibald MacLeish, who felt that he should be declared mentally unfit for trial. However, Pound's file shows that Hoover urgently wanted the case to come to trial so that he could make an example of Pound, and naturally Pound's friends were distressed over the possibility that he might be imprisoned instead of hospitalized. On September 9, 1943, the Office of Censorship intercepted a letter addressed to Hemingway, in Cuba, and noted that it was from an "Allen (Signature)." No doubt this is poet Conrad *Aiken:* the FBI misread "Aiken" as "Allen." The stolen letter, which is in Pound's file, reads, "I am afraid, as I told Archie [Archibald Mac-Leish] that we will have to stick our necks out for the rope after Ezra has dropped through the trap. If we do it before, we will make the case worse—if they shoot him, I suggest that a few of us get out on a limb publicly and raise hell." Presumably, Aiken felt it was best to walk carefully until after Pound's trial. In 1946, Pound was declared mentally unfit to stand trial and committed to St. Elizabeth's Hospital in Washington, D.C.

The Pound controversy did not die, however. On September 16, 1955, right-wing columnist Westbrook Pegler wrote that the "Department of Justice wanted to spare Pound's life" by asking the chief of Italian radio propaganda to "say he thought Pound was crazy." Pegler also had evidence that Pound's broadcasts were "gibberish." Hoover made a note on the column: "What about this?" On September 20, 1955, he received this reply: "Recordings and transcripts of Pound's broadcasts were obtained during the course of our investigation, and furnished to the Criminal Division of the Department. These were used as the basis of Pound's indictment and the department, therefore, apparently did not consider them 'gibberish.' " The memo also informed Hoover that "the question of Pound's insanity was never an issue in our investigation."

KAY BOYLE:

Oh, he was a dreadful man—and after all, the whole business of being in the hospital was a trick. He either pretended to be insane or got people to tell people he was. If it was pacifism, that would have been something else, but it wasn't that. He was telling the American troops to desert. He wanted American troops to lose the war.

I get absolutely furious when I think of him. I never liked his work. I never liked him as a person. I met him for the first time in Paris, in 1927. Well, he was so vain, and he wanted power so much. I mean that was his one thing. That's the only reason I think that he admired Hitler and Mussolini, because they gave him the power.

You felt that he was subjugating everybody else, and also, he was a womanizer—and there were a good number of women who were in love with him, of course. I don't like womanizers. We would eat together quite often—a number of people, four or five—and there might be an attractive young woman there, and if she went to the ladies' room, he would go and wait outside until she came out, and then he'd grab her and try to have her say she would have an affair with him.

And he didn't get the kind of acknowledgment for his work that he wanted in America, and so he went overseas. My husband, Laurence Vail, and I went to see him in Rapallo—the last time in 1938. Jonathan Cape, the English publisher, drove down with us from France, and Ezra, as usual, was out playing tennis. I don't know any of the people who played tennis with him, but people told me that he always jumped the net at the end and so every time he came in from playing he was covered with dirt, because he'd fall down when he jumped the net. And so he arrived on the terrace where we were having drinks before dinner, and he said to Jonathan Cape, "I won't sit down at this table if you are sitting there. You have to sit at another table." So Jonathan Cape, a very mild kind of man, said, "Well, I don't understand." Ezra said, "Twenty years ago you had me thrown out of your offices in London." So poor Jonathan Cape had to sit at another table during the whole weekend we were there.

Ezra wasn't broadcasting when we saw him in 1938; he hadn't started yet. He had two Japanese students staying with him, and he was saying to them that the Chinese had stolen all their culture from the Japanese, which is exactly the contrary, of course. Ezra had been so criticized by Chinese scholars for his translation that he lost interest in the Chinese. My husband, who was very well educated—he had a PhD from Cambridge—said, "Oh, Ezra, you're wrong. The Chinese were the great cultural country and the Japanese stole whatever they had from *them*." Oh, Ezra was *furious*.

It was just one agony after another because he would say, "Of course, you know what is happening is that it's the Jewish international conspiracy that's going to bring about the war," and I said, "Ezra, don't be so silly, don't be ridiculous." "No," he said, "I'll send you all the material when you get back to France." So I was deluged for weeks with all this anti-Semitic material, especially against the banks. And in one of his letters, he said, "I'm not sending any to Laurence because I have a feeling his name Vail may be remotely Jewish."

He talked about nothing but Hitler and Mussolini. Every conversation he said they were the two greatest men in history, and they were going to save civilization.

If he had only been able to get some satisfaction over here. My father was at the University of Pennsylvania when Ezra was there—Ezra must have been very young at that time—and my father said Ezra would walk with one foot in the gutter and one foot on the curb, and he'd be wearing two different colored socks. My father said Ezra did this to prove that the students would talk about nothing else but him instead of more important subjects.

When I was at a Bread Loaf Writer's Conference in Vermont one summer, in the fifties, Ezra was still in St. Elizabeth's. And I became very attached to Robert Frost. People found Frost difficult, but I didn't at all. And he said to me, "Oh, that Goddamned bastard"—speaking of Pound—"They've made me chairman of the committee to get him back to Italy. I'd like to throw him in the sea and drown him before he goes."

When I saw Ezra in 1938 I had no idea it would go so far. It just seemed impossible.

**

J. Edgar Hoover never stopped hoping that Pound could stand trial one day. In fact, a 1956 memo states that "as far as we are concerned, Pound is still under indictment for Treason as the indictment is still outstanding and if Pound is ever released from St. Elizabeth's he will be charged with treason and tried." However, in 1958, the charge was dismissed by the United States district court, so Hoover never got his chance to make an example of the poet.

The last entry in the file is dated June 30, 1971, twenty-eight years after his arrest, and concerns whether or not to get rid of some material in his file "because of space limitations" in the FBI building. "Retain," the memo bluntly states. "This is a case of historical interest. Exhibit is of recordings of Pound's traitorous broadcasts."

In an unpublished "mini-autobiography" written in 1983, Kay Boyle says, "After the fall of France in the spring of 1940, we [she and her second husband, Laurence Vail] stayed on in Megeve (which was in the Free Zone) hoping for America's entry into the war and an early defeat of Germany. I kept a day by day diary of the political and personal events of the year, which was to serve as background for my semi-autobiographical seventh novel, *PRIMER FOR COMBAT* . . .''

There was one event that would not be in the diary, because it was known only to J. Edgar Hoover: in 1940, after an informant said that Boyle was "an organized Communist," he began a file on her that would one day reach 355 pages. The informant was later called "unreliable," and when an FBI agent asked him what he meant exactly by an "organized Communist," he replied that he did not know, and admitted the information was "second-hand." Such was the evidence that began Kay Boyle's FBI file.

Although a pioneer in defending civil liberties and human rights, Kay Boyle was, in her own words, never a joiner, "because my life was much more involved with home—the children and domestic things," and, of course, her books. She adds, "I like to remain alone. The only thing I have ever joined was Amnesty International. That's different."

Boyle never did a single thing to undermine the interests and goals of the United States government, and was never a member of the Communist party, yet the FBI not only wrecked the diplomatic career of Boyle's third husband, Joseph Franckenstein, who was called before a State Department loyalty-security board because of their relationship, but had repercussions in her own career, as well, until the mid-seventies—and perhaps longer.

Boyle's FBI story is an unpleasant one, because her entire life was not only misunderstood by the FBI, but parts of it were actually fabricated by the agency. One report relies on the vague confessions of Louis Budenz, former editor of the *Daily Worker* turned paid informant, who said, "Sometime in the early forties I learned that Kay Boyle was a Communist, although for the moment I do not know the circumstances under which this was told to me." Another report said she might be a spy, when an unidentified informant accused her of being an "international courier." The only things Boyle carried back and forth over the Atlantic were her children, manuscripts, and books.

Even wilder was the report that Boyle "had a clandestine affair before World War I" with "Dr. Ezra Pound, the Italian propagandist." She was ten years old at the time. Nevertheless, on February 20, 1943, agents investigating the treason charges against Pound were requested to contact her "and determine if she could place Pound in Italy either before or after the war."

The FBI learned that the day before, on February 19, Boyle had been in Reno, Nevada, obtaining a divorce from Laurence Vail, and that on February 23, she was "going to be married in Salt Lake City to a private in the United States army whose name was Franckenstein and who was supposedly a citizen of Austria." Indeed, he was an Austrian aristocrat who became an American citizen later that year, and he not only served in the army, but risked his life as a counterintelligence officer behind the German lines.

KAY BOYLE:
I was in Reno getting a divorce, and then I went to Salt Lake City to get married, and the FBI agent had gone to Reno to interview me, and then saw in the paper that I had just gotten married, so he rushed over to Salt Lake City. And I had no idea who he was talking about at first. He just kept asking me very strange questions. My husband was in the American army, but he was still an Austrian citizen at the time, and I thought the agent was questioning me about him, and whether he should get his American papers, and all that. And then finally, the agent asked me if I would recognize Ezra Pound's voice on the radio and I said no—it would actually be impossible because he had a very nasal, mid-Western voice like so many other voices, and I couldn't possibly recognize it. The agent stayed about an hour. Well, at the end of the hour he said to me, "By the way, um, who *is* Ezra Pound?" I said, "You don't know who he is?" "No," he said. "I have no idea." I said, "Well, he's a poet and he's broadcasting, and he's a great admirer of Mussolini and Hitler, and he's broadcasting for the Axis."

**

According to the file, "sometime around 1944," Louis Budenz told the FBI that "Kay Boyle showed hesitancy about her Communist Party allegiance or wished to be relieved of obligations in that respect." Budenz told the Bureau a Party member "was assigned to straighten the matter out."

Boyle comments: "Budenz got twenty dollars for every name he turned in. He was scraping the bottom of the barrel. I had never been to a Democratic party meeting, a Republican one, or a Communist one. I'd never been to any meetings. It's frightening. It just makes you realize how the Rosenbergs were framed."

From 1945, when Budenz left the Party, until his death in 1972 from heart disease and gout, he named hundreds of "undercover" communists, as he called concealed Communists; in nearly every instance the charges were never proved.

At the time the FBI was tracking down the rumor that Boyle was a

Communist, her husband, as Boyle relates in her unpublished autobiography, had "infiltrated into Austria as a German Wehrmacht sergeant and worked with resistance groups behind enemy lines. He was eventually caught by the Gestapo, and under torture did not reveal that he was an American officer, but played the role of an ignorant Austrian peasant. He was sentenced to be executed as a German deserter from his regiment . . . but was able to escape." Boyle explains that the following year he returned to Germany in various civilian positions with the War Department—from an information control officer to news editor of the State Department's German-language daily.

The FBI continued to collect "intelligence" on Boyle, noting in 1948 that the *Daily Worker* said she was sympathetic to the Joint Anti-Fascist Refugee Committee, and in 1949 that she had participated in a Bill of Rights Conference where the FBI was "denounced" for not only "establishing American-style Fascism," but also for being a "super-snooting [*sic*] agency which commits more federal crimes than it ever detects." Agents interviewed someone who stated that she "wears the pants in the family" and that she and Franckenstein were "misfits." One unidentified informant, when asked by the FBI "for more tangible and definite information," replied, "Look into those things and then come back to see me." Another informant told the FBI that "she is inclined to be impulsive and easily swayed to interest herself in the cause of the 'underdog.' "

Although Hoover also received many reports that Boyle and her husband were loyal and patriotic Americans who belonged to no un-American organizations, Hoover kept up his pursuit. In 1952, Franckenstein was brought up before a loyalty board.

KAY BOYLE:

I was one of the charges used against my husband in his hearing, and I remember that one of the things against me was that I sent a ten-dollar check to a rally for the Bill of Rights, sponsored by Eleanor Roosevelt and Paul Robeson. Of course, just having Paul Robeson's name would be enough.

First of all, you get a notice from the State Department that you are going to have a hearing, and then they say you can resign, and then nothing will happen. So, of course, my husband said he wouldn't resign. And we decided we had to have a lawyer. We asked General Edward S. Greenbaum.

Some of the jury at the hearing were weeping when Greenbaum made the final appeal, because he said—which to me was very moving—"Here's a man, and you ask him why as an American citizen did he spend so much time in Europe? You're talking about four years he was in the American army, four years in foreign service. I think that's the cruelest thing that's been said to me here today." And then he said, "I for one am ashamed of this trial, that this had to take place. It's totally outrageous."

The first day of the hearing, I was happily in court, sitting with the lawyer, who had chosen me to be his aide. Because the charges weren't against me, I was a charge against my husband. But when people saw me in court, they immediately telephoned Washington, and then I wasn't even allowed into the hearing. They said it had nothing to do with me and I had no right to be in there.

And then Janet Flanner, who of course wrote the Paris letter in *The New Yorker*, came down and spoke as my character witness. I was an accredited correspondent for *The New Yorker,* and contributed regularly for seven years both articles and stories, as any record would show. Harold Ross had died—he was my greatest friend—and William Shawn, the new editor, sent a cable to Janet Flanner saying, "You have jeopardized the reputation of *The New Yorker* by being a character witness." Well, he withdrew my accreditation in the middle of the hearing! That to me is a blow I've never really gotten over. Well, we were in Germany at the time, and Shawn was in New York and there just didn't seem to be any point in confronting him. I never liked him anyway, and I didn't want to be reappointed under his jurisdiction. He wouldn't have reappointed me anyway, because he was too scared. But that's the way everybody was in America at that time. Terrified. Worst of all, I wrote to E. B. White and Katherine White, and then she wrote me, "Kay, Darling, You couldn't possibly be a member of the Communist party! Why don't you just forget about it all." No letter of recommendation followed from either of the Whites.

Isn't that amazing? Everyone was so terrified. The fiction editor, Gus Lobrano, also waffled, so we went into court that day in 1953 without a recommendation from *The New Yorker.* I only know that if Harold Ross had been alive, he'd have gone down and blown up the State Department or something.

I called my agent in New York and said, "Will you please tell William Shawn that I never want another word of mine to appear in *The New Yorker.*" He's twisted this story around, when people have asked him about it, and he says, "Well, I had no choice, Kay told her agent she didn't want to be published in *The New Yorker* anymore, so I withdrew her accreditation." But it was the other way around. I called my agent *after* he withdrew my accreditation.

And then my husband was cleared. Completely cleared. But two weeks later, McCarthy's two henchmen, Roy Cohn and G. David Schine, appeared with orders from the senator to go through Foreign Service files and terminate all those who had had loyalty-security hearings, whether or not they had been cleared. They were so scared over there, they fired everybody who had had a hearing!

Well, my husband's immediate superior said, "I'm not going to let you go. I'll send a cable to Washington. I can't do without you. You come to your desk every morning, and if they send somebody else over, you can both sit at the same desk. I won't let you go."

Of course, it couldn't work out that way. We left Germany.

**

WILLIAM SHAWN:

". . . About Miss Boyle, I can say the following: she has been a contributor to The New Yorker, as a fiction-writer, for the last twenty-years. In 1946, the U.S. War Department accredited her as a New Yorker correspondent. The person in our organization who directly dealt with Miss Boyle was my predecessor, Harold W. Ross, who died last December. Unfortunately, I have had practically no first-hand dealings with her. Nor have I ever discussed politics with her. Nevertheless, I have heard a good deal about Miss Boyle from Mr. Ross and others,

I have read her writings, and in my few meetings with her I have formed a personal impression, and everything leads me to have confidence in her loyalty to the United States and to our form of government. I believe her to be a woman not only of rare literary talent but of extraordinary character and of great spirituality. I have always taken her loyalty for granted, and I could only be astonished if it were to be questioned.

—excerpt from letter to the Department of State; June 11, 1952

Unfortunately, I cannot remember the details of the Kay Boyle episode. . . . The confusion, I believe, revolved around the fact that I had nothing whatever to do with arranging Miss Boyle's accreditation (the request was made, I believe, by Harold Ross . . .) and—I don't trust my memory—I did not at the time understand how Mr. Ross justified his decision, since Miss Boyle was not actually a staff correspondent. As far as I recall, I was always a great admirer of Miss Boyle's fiction and was sympathetic to her personally.

—excerpt from letter to Natalie Robins; May 5, 1987

As far as I can recall, Harold Ross asked for an accreditation for Kay Boyle because all of us at *The New Yorker* admired (and had published) her fiction, and both Mr. Ross and Miss Boyle *hoped* that she might write some reporting pieces in Europe . . .

—excerpt from letter to Natalie Robins; June 16, 1987

. . . I did not intend to imply anything beyond what I said. So the question you now ask [i.e., "Are you saying then, that *had* Kay Boyle produced some reporting pieces, her accreditation might have remained intact after you took over as editor?"] is a completely new one. If Kay Boyle had actually written an article or some articles for The New Yorker as a correspondent, even though not a staff correspondent, it is possible that the magazine would have been in a better position to ask for a renewal of her accreditation. However, I simply don't know today what I would have done in a hypothetical situation in 1952.

—excerpt from letter to Natalie Robins; July 6, 1987

**

Although Boyle's husband was eventually reinstated in his profession, Boyle was not. "As a writer for magazines, I was blacklisted," she says. By 1955, she was the author of twenty-five books.

Her passport was canceled briefly in the mid-fifties, and she was also placed on the Security Index. The FBI kept adding references to her file throughout the fifties, sixties, and seventies.

In 1963, the year Joseph Franckenstein died, the FBI removed Boyle from the Security Index. His death was noted in her file.

In 1966, the Bureau reported on her "fact-finding" trip to Cambodia. In a memo dated July 26, 1966, Cartha DeLoach speculated that the financing for her "jaunt may have come from subversive sources." DeLoach suggested to Hoover that an unnamed columnist be leaked "current information"; the Director wrote on the memo: "I concur." Boyle's trip would later cause the rejection of her application to join the Peace Corps, an application filed at the request of that organization, which wanted to recruit an older person.

Ironically, the Peace Corps used her age to reject her. "They had to find an excuse," Boyle says; "I was sixty-two in 1964, when they first approached me to join. That's not old these days. I remember they told me, laughingly, the only thing I'd have to learn was how to drive a jeep, and I said, 'Well, I already know how to do that.' "

In 1967, she was involved in an anti–Vietnam War protest and arrested for "disrupting activities and functions at the Oakland Induction Center." In 1971, it was noted that she has "many contacts in the subversive and racial [*sic*] fields."

And then, astonishingly, in 1976, the FBI opened an investigation of Boyle in order to determine if she could become an asset, or informant, for the FBI! It was decided, that because of "her background, her advanced age, and lack of asset potential," the matter would be dropped.

KAY BOYLE:
When I went to Cambodia, it was a peace group; it was not a political thing at all. I forget the names of all the peace organizations involved—the Quakers, for one. And we were supposed to follow the Ho Chi Minh Trail and the Prince Sihanouk Trail to see if supplies were coming down from China to Hanoi. And that's what we did. The prince, whom I admired very much—I think he's an extraordinary man—gave us two very old American airplanes that he'd been given. And we were taken all over the jungle—the military places. And it was very interesting talking to these men. I was the only one in our group who spoke French.

We had tea with a peasant family at one place where we went that was not a military place. The lady was eight months pregnant. There was a very interesting young man with us—an interpreter—he had graduated from Syracuse University, and spoke English very well. And he interpreted when we talked to the woman and her husband. I still have the photographs of all this.

We took a ladder up, because in Cambodia the homes of people are on stilts. This is a very important thing to remember. In Vietnam, which is on the border, the homes are not on stilts.

The prince had also supplied us with a car, and when we got down to leave, we heard helicopters coming over, and within five minutes American helicopters had bombed that house! And I have a picture of the woman lying dead.

The excuse given was that the helicopters thought they were still in Vietnam. We came back very disillusioned.

**

In 1941, after an unidentified informant told the FBI that journalist and playwright Ben Hecht was "either a Communist or a fellow traveler," his twenty-four-page file was begun.

Aside from continuing to reveal the FBI's ongoing political obsessions, the file illustrates exactly how the FBI sanitized its image on the silver screen.

In 1945, the Bureau got hold of a copy of Hecht's screenplay *No-*

torious, which was to be directed by Alfred Hitchcock. A memo reports that the Selznick Pictures Corporation said "the script was approved by the Bureau," but the unidentified person passing it on "could not believe this was so" because of the way the Bureau was portrayed in the film. According to the memo, the script had, in fact, "just been submitted" to the FBI, "and there was no opportunity for review of it." There was concern because "the individual playing the part of an agent known as Devlin [Cary Grant] drinks considerably and he falls in love with a girl [Ingrid Bergman] who is working as a Bureau agent under cover in Brazil on a mission to fall in love and marry a Nazi agent."

It is clear from the film that Hoover had his way, in a way. Not once is Cary Grant, who downs only three practically empty drinks in the film, and smokes just two cigarettes, referred to as an FBI agent; instead he is a "cop" who refers to his "chief" and his "department." Ingrid Bergman, on the other hand, is called "an American agent"—but not an FBI agent. Thus, these two can have lingering kisses on the screen without offending the prudish FBI director. Cary Grant makes an appeal to patriotism to win Ingrid Bergman over and convince her to go undercover.

Alfred Hitchcock told director François Truffaut, in the latter's book on Hitchcock, that a "producer" (not naming Selznick) had not approved "the idea of an atom bomb as a basis of the story" (this part of the plot is not mentioned in the memo in Hecht's FBI file); nor had the producer approved the idea of changing the bomb to industrial diamonds. "I failed to convince the producers," Hitchcock says, still not mentioning Selznick, "and a few weeks later the whole project was sold to RKO." (The film's trailer says it is "a Selznick release," and the movie is listed in reference books as an RKO production.) Hitchcock also mentions to Truffaut that the FBI had him "under surveillance for three months."

The atom bomb is not mentioned directly in the movie, either, although its major ingredient, uranium, figures in the plot.

The detective work by the American Legion is also visible in Ben Hecht's file: there are references to findings from its publication *Firing Line,* which had put Hecht on the lists of eight questionable organizations. (Howard Fast says that Hecht "was never a Communist.")

Hecht was among the first supporters of Israel, and the FBI clipped articles about his activities. One was a 1947 report that "U.S. Jews repudiate Hecht" because of his "endorsement" of "terrorists," meaning Menachem Begin, leader of the Irgun Zvai Leumi. A year later, in November, the FBI, now calling Hecht a "dissident," reported on his secret meeting with Begin, and a notation indicates that the reference was to be placed in Begin's file as well.

In 1953, Hecht sought the FBI's help with threatening calls he was receiving, and five years later he invited an FBI agent to be on his TV show, but the invitation was declined "because Hecht is unpredictable insofar as his remarks are concerned . . . which border on the ribald."

The following month, Hecht once again asked for the FBI's help with more threatening phone calls, and although he was told "there is no violation of federal law," the FBI offered to furnish him with the name of "a high [New York] police official." Hoover scribbled "properly handled" in the margin.

The eleven-page file of avant-garde writer Gertrude Stein was begun in 1937 with the report that "she didn't seem to be a pro–any nationality, but she was anti-Roosevelt." However, the FBI also reported that "her sympathies were not very strongly with America else she would not have stayed abroad so long"; Stein had lived in Paris since 1903, and returned to the United States only once, in 1934.

In 1941, the FBI had decided that "in the absence of more complete and definite information concerning the left-wing activities" of Stein and an unidentified person, no action is contemplated concerning these individuals at the present time." That year, a reference was added about English painter and writer Francis Rose, whose work Stein collected and promoted. The FBI wrote that "Stein considered Rose to be the greatest painter since Pisasso [sic]." (The agent obviously meant Picasso.) The much-exised document seems to concern Rose's former "press agent" and "business manager," a William Brandhove, who has two aliases in the report, as well as a U.S. seaman's number, and a U.S. Coast Guard pass. His "biography" includes the information that he "is acquainted with influential people in the U.S., French, British, and German Society," and listed among his acquaintances are Stein and Jean Cocteau. The file reports that Brandhove told authorities that Gertrude Stein "resented" his role with Rose and tried to "discredit" him with her "schemes." A document dated February 21, 1945, reports that Stein "stopped" Brandhove from accompanying Rose to England so that she would have complete control of him and his paintings.

Although the FBI indexed Stein for her purported left-wing views, it might have, had it looked further, discovered her friendship with Bernard Fay, a French intellectual who became a Nazi collaborator and a contributor to a pro-German occupation weekly. Fay was an influential figure in the Paris salon scene, where he became fast friends with Stein and her companion, Alice B. Toklas.

The Archives et Centre de Documentation Juive Contemporaine in Paris has in its possession a March 1, 1941, official memorandum sent to the German ambassador that names Fay as a candidate "who can be counted on" to take charge of rounding up French-Jewish citizens. In 1945, an unidentified informant told the FBI that Stein was "definitely pro-Nazi," but there are no follow-ups.

"I believe that Gertrude Stein and Bernard Fay were friends," historian William Shirer says, but "how much influence he had over her, I know not." Novelist and critic Elizabeth Hardwick believes that Fay and Stein "were indeed the best of friends," but added that "you can't imagine how uninterested [Stein was] in anything except herself, so she wouldn't know what he was doing, or care." Alice B. Toklas's letters confirm this: in 1946, Toklas wrote that "Gertrude completely disagreed with his [Fay's] political ideas," and in 1947 she wrote, "In the written testimony of Gertrude for Bernard Fay I found this phrase— 'he tended to the right and I tended to the radical.' "

Malcolm Cowley observes, "It's true Fay was a collaborationist, but I wouldn't call that testimony of guilt on Gertrude Stein's part. Fay was a writer and as such was respectable." Nonetheless, Kay Boyle remembers that when the Germans entered Paris, Stein and Toklas went to the south of France. Says Boyle, "I heard a rumor that they contacted a German baron whom they knew, and the baron said, 'I'm contacting Goebbels, and you'll be able to go back and live in Paris at your place.' "

During the occupation, Americans were rounded up and put in internment camps, and Boyle adds that "I also believe that it might have been difficult for Gertrude and Alice to have lived in Paris or in any big city during the war." Stein and Toklas did not return to Paris, but stayed in the countryside. Boyle says, "I heard they had German officers billeted in their house and they cooked for them and served them. Alice B. Toklas avoids the whole issue of collaboration in the book she wrote after Gertrude's death."

Although it is undeniable that Bernard Fay helped the two women, it is unlikely that a German baron or Goebbels were involved in any way. Toklas wrote in her *Alice B. Toklas Cook Book* that their papers were destroyed so the two women could be protected, and that the

German soldiers did not know they were Americans. She also wrote that "suddenly we had Germans billeted upon us, two officers and their orderlies. Hastily rooms were prepared for them in a wing of the house . . ."

KAY BOYLE:

I quoted Toynbee in an essay I wrote many years ago: "The artist, the writer must be concerned with a higher level of conduct." I still believe that. I've tried to conduct my life that way, but I don't always succeed.

I knew Gertrude Stein a little bit. We didn't get on together.

But she and Alice B. Toklas lived through the whole war in the occupied zone. Imagine! Jewish and American! When I said in an interview several years ago that their greatest benefactor was a complete fascist, I expected to be deluged with letters, but nobody wrote protesting. They probably thought I was off my head or something. But Bernard Fay was a constant companion, and after the war he was arrested by the French. He was their best friend! And when I tell people that, they just don't want to believe it. It was in *all* the French papers, but it never appeared in any paper here.

And then the Americans came in and Gertrude had the American flag waving.

CHAPTER THIRTEEN

Hemingway, Wilder, Sherwood, MacLeish, and Cowley

Ernest Hemingway's short, happy, free-lance intelligence career during World War II won him as much attention from the FBI as an enemy agent would have received. Typically, the author of *The Sun Also Rises* and *A Farewell to Arms* and the winner of the 1954 Nobel Prize for literature, first came to the FBI's notice through an imprecise report, one that began his 113-page file. In 1935, a confidential informant identified him as "a specialty writer" for *The New Masses* and the *Daily Worker*. Although he was never a Communist, Hemingway strongly supported the Loyalist side in the Spanish Civil War, which kept the FBI on his trail in the thirties.

In 1937, it clipped an item from Leonard Lyons's column saying "the report along Broadway last night was that Ernest Hemingway has sailed for Madrid . . . loyalist-bound," news that Lyons received directly from the writer. Hemingway was covering the Spanish Civil War for the North American Newspaper Alliance, but the FBI was leery, noting that Hemingway "personally purchased the first two ambulances which were sent to Spain in May, 1937." The man who would write *For Whom the Bell Tolls* had made a fiercely antifascist speech at an American Writers Congress meeting that year, receiving a standing ovation. That, however, was his last public foray into left-wing politics; in 1939, he declined an invitation to speak at another Congress, using the excuse that although he was "in complete and enthusiastic sympathy with the objectives of the League of American Writers," he was busy writing a novel and that "the most important thing I can do for American writing and for my usefulness as an American writer is to write a really good novel."

Two years later, in 1941, an informant reported that Hemingway "is on the outs with the Communists," and is only serving as an "innocent friend," and still another said that he "had broken all ties with the Communists." But the FBI remained guarded, especially since another informant reported that Hemingway was listed as co-chairman of a League of American Writers dinner with "outright Communist" Lillian Hellman.

During World War II, Hemingway would become something of a confidential informant himself. In 1942, his file reports he served as a spy for "the American Embassy in Cuba," where the ambassador was a friend of his. Hemingway, who maintained a *finca* in Cuba, planned to organize "a group of operators" to "engage in investigative work . . . activities he manages from his finca, with visits to Havana two or three times weekly." The FBI reported that "the cost of this program is approximately $500 a month."

Hoover disapproved, writing "certainly Hemingway is the last man, in my estimation, to be used in such a capacity. His judgment is not of the best, and if his sobriety is the same as it was some years ago, that is certainly questionable," but the writer set up his intelligence unit—dubbed the Crook Factory—and began collecting information on the Spanish falange, the fascist party. Tiring of that task, he used his yacht *Pilar* to hunt for German submarines.

Hoover was not only unenthusiastic about Hemingway's wartime mission; he had received reports that the writer had "severely criticized the Bureau," calling it "anti-liberal," "dangerous," and "the Gestapo." Hoover kept the peace, though, because Hemingway's then-wife, Martha Gelhorn, was a good friend of Eleanor Roosevelt.

The FBI kept track of Hemingway's activities in Cuba through reports from one or more attachés at the American embassy there. The legal attaché told Hoover personally, over lunch, that the novelist had said that Drew Pearson "made half-truths," which may have pleased the Director. Another reported two months after Hemingway started the Crook Factory that Hemingway was thought of as a Communist.

Hemingway loved his spy work, and told the legal attaché that "he had declined an offer from Hollywood . . . for $150,000, because he considers the work he is now engaged in of great importance.'' But Hoover grew alarmed when an attaché told him that ''Hemingway's activities are undoubtedly going to be very embarrassing unless something is done to put a stop to them.'' The attaché suggested that the ambassador be approached and told there was ''extreme danger'' in having someone like Hemingway given ''free rein to stir up trouble.'' But Hoover was disinclined to take on Hemingway. He told the attaché ''the Ambassador is somewhat hot-headed and I haven't the slightest doubt that he would immediately tell Hemingway of the objections being raised by the FBI.'' Since Hemingway ''has no particular love for the FBI,'' he ''would no doubt embark upon a campaign of vilification.''

The attaché continued to snipe at Hemingway's efforts, reporting to the Director that information he gave ''concerning the refueling of [German] submarines in Caribbean waters . . . has proved unreliable.'' An unnamed Bureau official went so far as to say that ''I see no reason why we should make any effort to avoid exposing Hemingway for the phoney that he is.'' But much to Hoover's relief, that wasn't necessary. He received word in the spring of 1943 that ''Hemingway's organization was disbanded and its work terminated as of April 1, 1943.''

However, another memo said that Hemingway was still ''performing a highly secret naval operation for the Navy Department'' that involved a continuation of his search for enemy submarines as well as a search for ''clandestine radio activity.''

Hoover continued to keep track of Hemingway's movements, learning that he had ''entertained Secretary of the Treasury Henry Morgenthau'' and that correspondence between the two ''passed'' through the State Department diplomatic mail pouch. The FBI also relied on Leonard Lyons's column for information, filing on September 20, 1943, a column in which Lyons wrote that Hemingway left Cuba on September 19 for ''another submarine patrol trip in the Caribbean areas . . . and expected to be gone for approximately two months.'' In the early fall of 1943, Hoover also learned that Hemingway had said ''he would never write anything about his intelligence work.''

The FBI continued to be interested in Hemingway, and in 1949 sent a blind memo about him to the secretary of defense, although for what purpose is unknown.

In 1954, the Bureau received word about a duel Hemingway might have with a Cuban columnist, and a much-blacked-out follow-up memo called ''Foreign Miscellaneous'' includes examples of other feuds this columnist had been involved in, including one with actress

Ava Gardner and her "estranged husband, Frank Sinatra, who has carried on a running feud with the press for years."

In 1959, the FBI was apprised that Hemingway had "kissed the Cuban flag" and said he supported Fidel Castro, who had just overthrown the dictator Fulgencio Batista, and "sympathized with the Cuban government." Hemingway also allegedly said he "hoped Cubans would regard him not as a Yanqui, but as another Cuban." It was also reported that Hemingway told a Cuban newspaper that "he had just come from New York, where they knew nothing about Cuba or the world—there all they talk about is [Charles] Van Doren and the scandal of the tv quiz shows."

In 1961, physically ill and suicidally depressed, Hemingway checked into the Mayo Clinic in Rochester, Minnesota, under the assumed name George Sevier. A psychiatrist at the clinic contacted the FBI to ask permission to tell his patient, who "was concerned about an FBI investigation," that "the FBI is not concerned with his registering under an assumed name."

Permission was granted.

For almost a decade, Hemingway had been certain the FBI was shadowing him. He was correct. Jeffrey Meyers writes in his biography, *Hemingway,* that some of the writer's family and friends "thought his fear of the FBI meant that he was losing touch with reality," but that his FBI file "proves that even paranoids have real enemies."

After Hemingway's release from the Mayo Clinic, he returned to his home in Idaho. On July 2, 1961, he committed suicide.

Two years after Hemingway's death, columnist Quentin Reynolds wrote the Director a letter about a proposed Cuban stamp with Hemingway's picture on it. Reynolds was concerned that such a stamp might "hurt Ernest's reputation" and "persuade people that Hemingway was a big Castro man, and again by association a fellow-traveler of some sort." Reynolds told Hoover that he knew the writer "very well," and that he was "a non-political guy" who "like most Americans in residence there" had "hated Batista," and "like millions, welcomed anyone who could oust the dictator." He also said Hemingway barely knew Castro, and had only met him once "at a fishing party," and "had talked to him for five minutes."

Hoover's marginal note on this letter is the most revealing detail in all the data the Bureau collected about the writer, because it shows clearly that for all the years Hoover spent tracking Hemingway, he did it not because of any Communist connections, but because Hemingway had been critical of the FBI.

"Knowing Hemingway as I did," Hoover wrote, "I doubt he had any Communist leanings. He was a rough, tough guy and always for the underdog."

KAY BOYLE:
In January 1945, I flew to Paris, and there I found old and beloved friends of the twenties . . . then down to the U.S. Intelligence Headquarters in Caserta, in southern Italy, where Colonel Thornton Wilder was our host, and where our friendship began.
What could the FBI possibly have against him? I mean, he was in the American army. He was head of an intelligence unit. I would doubt that he was aware of this—that he had a file—because he was very patriotic.

**

Nothing in the FBI's files is quite as bizzare as its belief in 1944 that playwright and novelist Thornton Wilder was "the mysterious Captain" in charge of German spies at an Austrian refugee camp in Keene, New Hampshire. He was also suspected of "dominating" an "elderly lady whose home was originally in Cambridge, Mass." Most of this information was received from an informant identified as "the girl at the Eskimo stand on the road leading up to the camp."

It took the FBI a year to decide that it didn't have enough to go on to "link" Wilder with any "espionage or subversive activities," although it was noted, ominously, that an unnamed person close to the case "did receive a copy of a book entitled *Soviet Power*".

The FBI had begun Wilder's ninety-two-page file after finding his name listed on the letterhead of the American Committee for Struggle Against War in 1933, six years after his Pulitzer Prize–winning *Bridge of San Luis Rey* was published. 1933 was the year Germany began burning all books by anti-Nazi and Jewish authors; the Director of the FBI, who would one day keep on display in the entrance hall of his Washington, D.C., house a marble fragment of Adolf Hitler's bookcase, was concentrating at the time primarily on his war with American gangsters, but was also proceeding with his war on words. Two years later, in 1935, agents would report that Wilder was a member of the American League Against War and Fascism, and in 1937, that he wrote, "I am unreservedly for the legal government and Loyalist government party in Spain." In 1939, the year after the debut of his Pulitzer Prize–winning *Our Town,* the Bureau detailed how he signed a League of American Writers letter that urged support of a Federal Arts project.

Thornton Wilder's mail was read by agents through 1942; one letter is described as "a friendly letter from army intelligence officer." The FBI had reported in 1941 that his name was on a list "of persons reported to be good mainly for signatures to open letters . . . but 'not much action,' '' even though ''1935 or earlier'' Wilder wrote the League of American Writers that ''I no longer believe in lending my name to the many committees of protest that are formed.'' He did, however, continue to lend his name to assorted League and other *literary* matters, which the FBI regarded as in the same category as those ''committees of protest.''

In 1948, the FBI cited him for signing a HUAC protest sponsored by the National Institute of Arts and Letters, and in 1950 for defending the Czechoslovakian producer of his Pulitzer Prize–winning *The Skin of Our Teeth*.

Wilder remained a threat to national security until 1970, just five years before his death. In the 1950s, he was subjected to three ''name checks'' (a euphemism for an outside government agency's request for a search of FBI files), by the Air Force, the State Department, and the CIA. When the White House asked for three *additional* name checks on Wilder in the 1960s, his fingerprints were requested as well.

After Pearl Harbor, writers, like everyone else, joined the war effort. They volunteered for the military, or waited to be drafted, or were deferred or otherwise avoided (or evaded) the draft. Still others went to Washington to do their bit working for one of the wartime agencies that had proliferated along with the fighting. Those who had been politically active in the thirties ran head-on into the FBI, which was charged with conducting background investigations and already had files on most of them.

The writers who achieved the greatest prominence in government service—Robert Sherwood and Archibald MacLeish—both had FBI files. Neither man was fired for his political beliefs, but even in their lofty positions and with their friends in high places they were not immune from FBI scrutiny and criticism.

Playwright and biographer Robert Sherwood, the winner of four Pulitzer Prizes and the winner of a 1946 Academy Award for his screenplay *The Best Years of Our Lives,* was President Franklin D. Roosevelt's chief speech writer, and between 1940 and 1945 he was an assistant to both the secretary of war and the secretary of the navy. He was also director of the Overseas Division of the Office of War Information.

Poet Archibald MacLeish, whose 1932 *Conquistador* won him the first of his three Pulitzer Prizes, was Librarian of Congress from 1939 to 1944, and was also director of the Office of Facts and Figures from October 1941 to May 1942, then assistant director of the OFF's successor, the Office of War Information, from June 1942 to February 1943. MacLeish was also an assistant secretary of state in 1944 and 1945, wrote some White House speeches, helped found UNESCO, and in addition, set up the consultantship in poetry when he was Librarian of Congress.

In the early forties, the FBI conducted, within the law, the required security clearances of Sherwood and MacLeish for their government positions. But both writers had records begun many years before there was any hint of government service.

Robert Sherwood's eighty-page file was begun in 1917 when "a confidential informant" told the FBI that Sherwood had enlisted in Canada's prestigious Black Watch Expeditionary Forces, news obviously deemed worthy of the Bureau's attention because the writer had gone over the border to join up. Archibald MacLeish's 602-page file began when word reached the FBI that he "enlisted in the U.S. Army Reserve Corps in June 1917, and entered active duty in August, 1917, and was appointed a second Lieutenant in December, 1917." There is no reason given why this routine, public enlistment was singled out for the Bureau's attention; perhaps, for some unknown reason, Army Intelligence forwarded it. In any case, twenty-five years later it still mattered; in 1942, the FBI would write that "an insight into MacLeish's thought processes may be gained by the following . . . references to his attitude such as going to school to avoid work . . . [and going] abroad in a hospital unit in 1917 so as to do the right thing but not be hurt."

In fact, the next reference for Sherwood, in 1919, when it was recorded that he was the "dramatic" editor of *Vanity Fair,* is still over twenty years away from his government work. The FBI also reported that he became an associate editor of *Life* in 1920, and an editor in 1924 until 1928. He has approximately ten references from the thirties, ranging from recording his membership in the Civil Liberties Union and his position as secretary of the Dramatists Guild to listing his two Pulitzer awards in 1936 and 1939. There are no references to his Loyalist sympathies during the Spanish Civil War, a point of view Hoover would regard, in MacLeish's words, "as equivalent to membership in the Communist Party." MacLeish writes of an "informal organization. . . . Bob Sherwood was a member . . . and we eventually went to see the president to protest the failure of the United States to do anything to aid . . . Spain," but here is nothing about this meeting in Sherwood's file. MacLeish's file, however, does record that he was on the Committee for American Friends of Spanish Democracy and the Washington Spanish Refugee Relief Committee, although there are no reports about the meeting with the President.

During the summer of 1941, the FBI interviewed Robert Sherwood, at his invitation, after he had written his friend, Roosevelt advisor Harry Hopkins, that "my friend Charles MacArthur" (coauthor, with Ben Hecht, of *The Front Page* and other plays, and the husband of Helen Hayes) "has come to me with a possible line on important Nazi activities here in New York." Sherwood's letter goes on to tell Hopkins that "I know that the F.B.I. is overwhelmed with crazy suggestions and false rumors which are a total waste of time, and I hesitate to add to them. But MacArthur is a veteran newspaperman and I honestly think he should at least be listened to."

But first the FBI decided to interview Sherwood, who is absurdly described in another reference in his file as "a dramatist who lives in the White House with Harry Hopkins," and he elaborated that MacArthur had told him that someone "was heard to make un-American remarks and was consorting at the [Century] Club with persons of German nationality." The FBI then interviewed MacArthur, but this report is so full of deletions that it is almost impossible to make much sense out of the interview. However, a follow-up report reveals that whatever it was that MacArthur overheard at the Century Club involved some government official who invited "someone under investigation as an espionage suspect" to come to Washington on January 20, 1941, "to be his honored guest for the Inauguration Day ceremonies." According to a letter written by J. Edgar Hoover, the FBI decided not to investigate the mysterious government official, and there are no further interviews with MacArthur.

In 1941, an informant reported to the FBI that Sherwood's play *An American Crusader* was "a radical radio broadcast" on CBS—it starred Orson Welles—and was "full of violence and stressed the thought of force, outrage and oppression. The play reportedly made it appear that it was almost impossible for a man to publish a thought or theory which was contrary to the thoughts of the majority."

It was such prescient beliefs that no doubt caused Sherwood's file to be continued until the year he died, 1955. In addition, "a highly confidential source" had named Sherwood as a Communist party member. The preposterousness of such an accusation is spoofed in Ludwig Bemelmans's satirical novel *Now I Lay Me Down to Sleep*, which depicts a "Bob Sherwood" character under investigation. One of the other characters remarks: "My God, man, that's like investigating the American flag. He practically ghosted the Gettysburg address." Ironically, it is this very anecdote in the novel that triggered the starting of the writer and illustrator's file on April 6, 1944, because an agent said it "contained a passage concerning the FBI." (However, despite his calling the FBI "the Gestapo" elsewhere in the novel, the Bureau decided not to investigate Bemelmans because "on the whole it is a well-written novel and quite entertaining in places.")

Archibald MacLeish, who is called "another long-time fellow traveler of the Communists" in the Authors League file, wrote that when he was nominated to be assistant secretary of state in 1944, there was "some opposition simply on the ground that I was a poet and that poets are unfit for public office." In fact, just two years after his appointment as Librarian of Congress in 1939, "a personal and confidential" letter was sent to Hoover from the special agent in charge of the Washington, D.C., field office saying that the poet's name was discovered on two suspicious membership lists: the National Federation for Constitutional Liberties and the Washington Spanish Refugee Relief Committee. Hoover followed this letter up with a phone call, requesting even more on MacLeish's activities. The Director was immediately informed of additional "subversive activities or associations." The Bureau already had his passport records going back to 1923; in fact this "travel to study" trip is made to appear in the record as a tenebrous and ominous venture. The Director then wrote a confidential memo to Attorney General Francis Biddle detailing MacLeish's "record," adding that "no action will be taken unless you so request."

Francis Biddle, a friend of MacLeish's, did not ask for any "action," and the matter was dropped. However, two months after the correspondence between Hoover and Biddle, MacLeish, who had no idea that his own loyalties were still being questioned and would continue to be until 1976, requested that "the FBI investigate the members of [his] staff," because "he already had several very confidential requests from the President," and hesitated to start work on these until he was definitely sure of his staff." Hoover wrote on the margin: "GIVE SPECIAL ATTENTION," but the investigations that resulted from this "special attention" were, in fact, much more than MacLeish asked for.

A memo tells some of the story: "In January of 1942 the Bureau received a letter from Mr. MacLeish wherein he criticised the investigative technique used by the Agents of this Bureau . . . and made particular reference to a phrase he had noticed in several reports which read: 'Associated with various liberal and Communist groups.' This letter was answered by the Director, and thereafter several letters and memoranda were written either to Mr. MacLeish or to the Attorney General.''

In one of the letters MacLeish had written to his friend, Attorney General Biddle, dated March 11, 1947, he said that ''Malcolm Cowley has been driven to resign from the Office of Facts and Figures by an attack carried on through Westbrook Pegler.'' Hoover saw a copy of MacLeish's letter to Biddle and taking a weak offensive wrote the attorney general that ''Cowley criticized the Bureau because the investigation [of him] was of a limited nature in that he was questioned only about the organizations declared as 'Subversive' by the Department of Justice and not by the FBI. Questions concerning other organizations were not asked as special agents are not authorized to inquire about [them].'' Cowley, who had come to work in Washington at MacLeish's behest (taking a brief leave from the *New Republic,* where he was the literary editor from 1929 to 1944), says that he ''was a peculiar pet of the Director. I represented everything he didn't like. I was an intellectual. I was a writer. I was a liberal suspected of being a Communist. I didn't have anything to conceal.''

MacLeish did what he could for Cowley, who comments about his former chief, ''Was he a good politician? He was with Roosevelt; he wasn't in respect to the situation at that time. He was wonderful to get cleared himself and keep his job.'' One clue as to how MacLeish kept his job despite his anger at the FBI over the Cowley situation—he wrote his friend Attorney General Biddle, ''I know the whole thing makes you just as sick as it makes me''—is that he wrote an extremely conciliatory letter to J. Edgar Hoover.

MacLeish has said that his years of government service ''silenced'' him as a poet—he wrote only one poem during his stay in Washington—so it is obvious that all of his energy went into being an effective politician, and thus he could write Hoover: ''Thank you for your full and helpful letter of January 29. Maybe I am over mindful of the last war [World War I], but I can't help remembering the things that happened then, and it was that memory which led me to write you. There is bound to be a wave of enemy alien feeling despite everything you and the Attorney-General can do to keep the ultimate facts in mind. I suppose there is also bound to be a wave of witch hunting in which things as far apart as liberal belief and communist membership will get wrapped up together in certain minds. But there again, as I wrote you, I thank God that we have people like you running the law enforcement agencies.''

But this praise had no effect on Hoover. In 1962, when MacLeish was being considered as a member of President Kennedy's Advisory Committee on the Arts, the FBI reported that "the appointee could be considered a 'snob' because he associates with only the highest political and social individuals . . . and does not associate with the low radicals, liberals or labor people," adding that "the appointee is not tough enough to deal with rascals."

But he did deal with Hoover, and he even risked censure when he put friendship over politics and showed Malcolm Cowley his "raw" FBI file, which MacLeish had obviously obtained from one of those snobby "high political individuals."

"I was a privileged character," Malcolm Cowley says.

MALCOLM COWLEY:

I had gone to work in Washington for one of the wartime agencies. One day the chief, whom I had known for many years, called me into his office. "Here's something I oughtn't show you," he said. "The FBI sent over your record and it's highly confidential. But I thought I'd break the rule for once and let you see it, so that you'd know exactly what they were going to bring against you."

"Can I take it to my desk?"

"Yes, if you don't tell anyone about it and bring it back this afternoon."

I'm sorry now that I didn't take full notes on it, with transcripts of the more interesting passages. My record was a document of about thirty pages of single-spaced typing. Only the last few pages had anything to do with the FBI investigation, then under way, into my fitness to endorse government paychecks; by the time that investigation was finished, it must have filled a volume. The document I saw was, for the most part, merely the dossier of a private citizen who, at the time the material went into the record, had never dreamed of working in Washington. Query to Mr. Hoover: How many private citizens who never belonged to the Communist Party or any other organization regarded by sensible people as subversive have dossiers in your files?

I wasn't even a prominent citizen. I had worked for a magazine, had let my name be used on the letterheads of several Communist-front organizations, had spoken at many of their meetings, had resigned from everything with a Communist tinge after the Russo-German pact, and had thereupon been granted the privilege of being abused in the Communist press. That was my actual story and the FBI had documented parts of it, while omitting everything about the resignations or the abuse. I began to suspect, and later became certain, that it wanted only what it regarded as incriminating evidence. One man spoke well of me, and the FBI investigator looked away with a bored air. "But don't you know anything *suspicious* about him?" he finally interrupted.

Nothing in the dossier dealt with my activities before 1935, although I had been at my reddest or pinkest during the Hoover administration. The omission didn't mean that the FBI recognized any statute of limitations; once it began to work on a case, it tried to trace a man's activities straight back to the womb. But it was handicapped in its search because it hadn't begun to function as an effective Thought Police until midway in Roosevelt's first term.

Besides the omissions in my dossier, there were a great many inclusions best described as fanciful. I was described as a prominent member of organizations I had never heard of—if they ever existed—and as a speaker at meetings I hadn't attended. . . .

. . . "Charlie (or Jim or Bob)," I said to the chief of the agency when I gave the dossier back to him, "most of this is silly stuff, but it might be dangerous. Couldn't I have a talk with the FBI and at least get the obvious mistakes and the plain lies out of the record?"

"I don't want to tell them I showed it to you," the chief said, "but maybe I could arrange a meeting."

During the next few weeks I became obsessed with the desire to set the record straight. I had decided to resign from government service, but I didn't want to leave Washington while this mass of error and allegations remained in the FBI files, to be used I didn't know how. I went to see various officials and asked their help in obtaining a hearing. Once I thought the request was granted: I was told to appear at FBI headquarters. Undistinguished young men in undistinguishable dark suits and gray snap-brim hats were going in and out of the door, as anonymous as bees. I was directed to a little office, put under oath by two of the young men, and asked for brief answers to half a dozen questions. Then I was told to sign my name.

"But aren't you going to ask me any more questions?" I said.

"No, that is all."

"Then I would like to offer a statement clearing up some of the mistakes in my record."

"Thank you, we are not authorized to receive statements." And they showed me to the elevator, with sinister politeness.

I began to feel like K—— in Kafka's 'The Trial.' I went to see high officials in the Department of Justice to press for a hearing. To one of them I made the obvious remark that most of the FBI investigators seemed pretty stupid. "Of course," he said. "You don't expect us to get *bright* law-school graduates, do you, for $65 a week?" I learned something about the sociology of the FBI. Its investigators, who have to have law-school training, are for the most part either Southerners or Catholics. Southerners are in the majority, but the Catholic influence is very strong, and some of the investigators are confused in their minds as to whether they are hunting down political or religious heresies. The word "atheist" occurs in their reports more often than J. Edgar Hoover—himself a Presbyterian and a Mason—will ever publicly admit.

In the course of my efforts to get the record straight before leaving Washington, I finally saw the Attorney-General. He was sympathetic and promised to obtain the hearing. But a few days later, as I was packing to go home to Pennsylvania, I received a letter from his executive assistant. "Since you have resigned from government service," he said, "there is no basis upon which we may continue the investigation."

. . . I left Washington with my FBI dossier still full of more falsehoods and unsupported assertions than you could find in any three of Hitler's speeches. It remains in the file with millions of other dossiers that won't be used for the time being—but who knows about the future? . . .

—From Malcolm Cowley's private papers, undated

**

Malcolm Cowley, one of the foremost critics of modern American literature, the author of over a dozen works—including *Exile's Return, The Literary Situation, Writers at Work,* two books of poetry, and many translations—was also the influential literary editor of *The New Republic* magazine and a literary advisor to Viking Press (now Viking-Penguin) from 1948 until his death in 1989.

In 1942, he went to Washington. But he had an FBI file and that's where the trouble started. Unlike most writers, Cowley actually saw his file. MacLeish showed him an unexcised "fat dossier" running to at least thirty pages. Cowley later recalled that he was "rather disappointed in reading it," although "one thing it showed was that J. Edgar Hoover kept a watch on me."

Years later, Cowley obtained an expurgated version of his file, consisting of thirteen pages of correspondence from the 1940s, plus some "confidential" sheets on the "objectives of the Office of Facts and Figures." Among the letters was the one from MacLeish to Attorney General Francis Biddle, in which MacLeish complained about Westbrook Pegler's smear of Cowley. In the letter, MacLeish expressed a suspicion about who was behind the campaign. "Pegler . . . obviously had access to information in the possession only of the Dies Committee or the FBI, and I am certain the FBI is not engaged in the business of trying its cases in the newspapers." Pegler's material may indeed have come from Congressman Dies, but Dies probably got it from Hoover.

MacLeish's March 11 letter goes on to say, "Report after report coming to me links the words 'liberal' and 'Communist' as though in the opinion of FBI investigators they were the same thing . . . and any association with Loyalist Spain is given as a basis of suspicion of loyalty to the United States." (Indeed, Cowley was first indexed by the FBI in 1936 for supporting the Spanish Loyalists.)

MacLeish also wrote a letter of protest to Hoover, telling him that "FBI agents ought to be given a course of instruction in recent history" to let them know some "facts" such as America is now at war "with the men who attacked Spain in '36 and '37" and that "President Roosevelt is a liberal." Such facts, of course, did not mean the same thing to J. Edgar Hoover as they did to Archibald MacLeish. Attorney General Biddle subsequently told Hoover that "this whole problem" concerning Malcolm Cowley "is troublesome and difficult." MacLeish, Biddle said, understood perfectly the need for "careful investigation" of government employees who would be dealing in "highly confidential material and information," such as all Office of Facts and Figures staff members would be. He had no problem with that. What he was concerned about was "investigating"—or, smearing—after the fact, as in the case of Cowley.

In an interview shortly before he died in 1989, Cowley explained,

"I became radicalized in 1932—1931 and 1932—with a trip to Kentucky. Not in 1927, as someone wrote. No, no, 1927 was the Sacco-Vanzetti case, and I wasn't really involved in that, although I wrote a poem to Sacco-Vanzetti."

Asked whether he was ever aware that the FBI kept an eye on him during his years of political activism, Cowley replied, "Oh, good God, yes." Was he aware of the FBI actually *following* him around? "Not very much," Cowley replied, adding, "I didn't give a damn because I didn't have anything to conceal. The FBI paid a great deal of attention to me, but they never got anything."

As for his resignation from the Office of Facts and Figures, Cowley says, "If I had fought the thing through as some people thought I should, I possibly would have been cleared, but it was taking up too much of my time and I wasn't interested really, and I wasn't interested in a government job. I wasn't interested in being cleared by the FBI, and I went home to Sherman, Connecticut, with a great feeling of relief! I got down and kissed the ground when I got back."

One thing Cowley did learn from the file MacLeish showed him was the names of the informants who had provided information about him to FBI men. One of these sources was Sidney Hook, an old ideological enemy. In a 1940 letter to fellow literary critic Edmund Wilson, Cowley recalled how the argument started: "Back in 1932, when [Sidney] Hook . . . et al. were going Trotskyist long before Hook had heard about democracy—there was a terrific row in an organization in which we all belonged, the League of Professional Groups for Foster and Ford. One week the league was doing a lot of interesting work, the next week and the weeks that followed it did nothing but argue about the Chinese Revolution of 1927. I got sore because it seemed to me that one faction was deliberately hindering the league from getting anything done. I made a hot speech that must have been instrumental in getting them to resign from the league. I don't think they have ever forgiven me, Hook in particular, and I have written some things that have kept the fight alive . . . these personal quarrels have come to play a major part in one sector of left wing politics."

Malcolm Cowley wrote in an earlier, 1938 letter to Wilson, that "of course the truth is that many literary Trotskyites have utterly lost faith in the revolution—not only in Stalin, but in Lenin, Engels, Marx, the Communist manifesto, the whole business . . . What is my own position? Generally pro-Russian, pro-Communist, but with important reservations. I think that the Communists have done marvelous work for the American Labor Unions, but sometimes they spoil it by getting their union mixed up in international politics. I think that Russia is still the great hope for socialism.''

Two years later, in 1940, a disillusioned Cowley wrote Wilson that ''a world run by Intellectuals would be a very unpleasant place, considering all the naked egos that would be continually wounding and getting wounded, all the gossip, the spies at cocktail parties, the informers, the careerists, the turncoats. Note that nothing I said about the intellectuals is to be construed as an attack on the *intelligence,* which remains our best and almost our only tool for making this country a better place.''

Cowley also wrote to Wilson, ''I agree with you that I ought to get out of politics and back to literature. We ought to all do that.'' This was directed at Wilson's charge that Cowley was ''being bribed or blackmailed by the Communist Party.'' Cowley had said earlier that although he ''did sign (with others) a letter about the Moscow trials, because I believe that they were about ¾th's straight, I didn't agree with everything the letter said, but I was writing two articles about the trials in which I proposed to say exactly what I thought. Have I been bribed by the CP? I had cocktails once at the Russian consulate. You ought to know better than to talk like that.''

Cowley has written, ''Sometimes I have nightmares about the use that might be made of the FBI files, and their millions of pages of hearsay and falsehood. . . . One 'informant' had seen me at a secret Communist party conference—I was never present at anything of the sort—in a city which I had never visited. This same 'informant,' whom I judged from the context to be some illiterate ex-Communist bent on earning a few government dollars by bringing more and more names into his testimony, endowed me with a long list of 'close associates.' . . . The 'informants' were not identified, but I recognized at least two of them by the phrasing of their testimony. One was a man whose last book I hadn't admired and he expressed some doubt of my loyalty to the democratic way of life. Note the equation: his book equals the democratic way of life. Another was a man with whom I had had political arguments; he accused me of being a 'transmission belt' for orders from Moscow.''

MALCOLM COWLEY:

In my case, the revelation that disturbed me was that Sidney Hook had been an informant for the FBI. This isn't general knowledge, because at that time, 1942, being an informant was a low pursuit. I found out because I got to look at my raw file, before anything was blacked out. I saw his name as the informant, but I never confronted him about it because I wasn't supposed to have seen my file. But it's something I had to say now.

**

SIDNEY HOOK:

I have never been an 'informant' of the FBI. The only time I have ever spoken to the FBI was when they did a security check on individuals who were being considered for positions in the US government. In my view, the *only* justification for any government inquiry would be in connection with the qualifications of a person—any person—for a sensitive post in government. I do not recall the names of the few individuals about whom I was questioned. I do know that on grounds of educational principle, I never answered any questions about anyone who ever studied with me.

Although I have no memory of the details, it is quite likely that I was questioned about Malcolm Cowley if he were being considered for a sensitive post in the US government. I would certainly have been willing to describe his political positions about which there was plentiful public evidence. The important question is whether what I said was true. What I probably said you will find in my autobiography *Out of Step.* There is no question that Cowley was a Communist fellow-traveller, a fervent defender of the Moscow Trials even after John Dewey's Report exposing the Moscow Trials as frame-ups. I recall Edmund Wilson referring to Cowley several times as a "Stalinist character assassin." Cowley was one of the reasons John Dewey resigned as an Editor of The New Republic, he had helped found.

It is truly extraordinary that Malcolm Cowley should ever have been offered a position in the US government. It explains something about the period in which Communist sympathizers and members (although I never believed Cowley was a member) penetrated government ranks, some of whom were subsequently exposed during the time of the Hiss trials. Cowley was a witness for Hiss.

. . . In Cowley's letter to Wilson in 1940 . . . Cowley does not mention . . . what "the terrific row" was all about between him and me and my friends. It was about our criticism of the political line of the Communist Party which Cowley strongly supported. At the meetings of the League of Professional Groups for Foster and Ford, he worked hand in glove with the Communist Party faction leaders, Joseph Freeman and Joseph Pass.

I am obviously not the "man whose last book I [Cowley] hadn't admired," since Cowley never reviewed a book of mine. If the reference to the other man is to me, I would have never accused Cowley of being a "transmission belt" because only Communist Parties could be transmission belts. Nor have I ever charged Cowley with being a member of the Communist Party. His effectiveness in attacking 'the enemies of the Party' like Trotskyists and others was all the greater because it could be said that he was *not* a member. . . .

**

After leaving the Office of Facts and Figures, Malcolm Cowley went back to writing and editing. "I got out of politics," he says. "There was no climax to the FBI investigation except my resignation. Then they started again—it could have stopped there, but the Hiss case came up. I testified for Hiss. I wouldn't duck out. So there was an investigation of everybody who testified for Hiss—that would be about 1948. And after that, I *really* got out of politics *completely.*"

CHAPTER FOURTEEN

Rukeyser, Herbst, Porter, and Fast

In 1943 Muriel Rukeyser was working for the Bureau of Publications and Graphics of the Office of War Information, a job she most likely got with the help of Archibald MacLeish, who was listed as a reference on her application. But in March of that year, the FBI initiated "a complete investigation" of her as part of a larger inquiry into thirteen hundred OWI employees in New York that were said to have gotten their jobs despite "red" ties.

But Rukeyser's name had first attracted the Bureau's attention in 1932 when she was a nineteen-year-old student, and it was reported that she took two radical courses at the "Communistically inclined" Rand School of Social Sciences. Four years later, in 1936, the FBI reported that she wrote for *The New Masses* and *The Nation,* was a member of a John Reed Club, and had written an article about the Spanish Civil War.

The file also states that "in 1936 she was in Spain when the Spanish Civil War broke out" and "is writing a novel about her experiences." But she never completed it. Was it artistic or political developments that changed her mind?

When writer and critic Diana Trilling was asked about Rukeyser's aborted novel, she revealingly described the political minefields that writers of the 1930s had to cross: "I could give you sixteen reasons why Muriel Rukeyser wouldn't have gone on with a novel about the Spanish Civil War. As time passed, we all learned in this country so much about the perfidy of the Communists in Spain—what their relations were to the Loyalists, how they shot the POUM [Partido Obrero de Unificación Marxista] people in the back. It was a dirty, dirty business, the Communist participation in the Spanish Civil War. And even if a little of that percolated to Muriel Rukeyser, she would have said, 'I simply can't cope with it.' She wasn't worrying about the FBI, she was worrying about those fellow writers who would be reviewing her book who knew more than she did about it—that would stop her, that would stop anybody from going on with a project. As you get to know what truths you didn't know, you begin to feel, 'Oh, boy, I'll go and do something else. I'll stay with my poetry.' "

In 1943, Rukeyser's FBI file became a minefield in her path to keeping her government job. On January 5, an FBI agent interviewed her. Rukeyser told the agent that "with other writers, she shared a hatred for fascism," and "admitted the presence of some communistic influence in The League of American Writers." This report, which was sent directly to Hoover, also said, "Miss Rukeyser was quite reluctant to enter into a discussion of Communism, and attempted to create the impression that her interest and knowledge of this movement were superficial and she answered all questions pertaining to Communism with hesitance and vagueness."

As the investigation branched out, the FBI learned that "she is considered one of America's outstanding younger poets," and "has excellent character," but she has written things "symbolizing the masses and the working class."

Her mentor, Archibald MacLeish, told the FBI that what Rukeyser wrote for *The New Masses* "does not necessarily reflect a political view point." One report quotes Louis Untermeyer saying that she is "instinctively a pacifist" and "against everything in any organization which represents the brutal life of enforced regimentation and national slavery."

The FBI tried to interview another poet, Steven Vincent Benét, but discovered that "he had died almost two months ago." Instead, they quote from an article in which he said that Rukeyser was "a revolutionary," though her poetry "contains no direct appeal to the proletariat, and her symbols of revolt are imaginary."

The investigation continued through 1944 and into 1945, even though Rukeyser resigned from her job on May 17, 1943.

In 1944, the FBI recruited an unnamed librarian who "produced records" from the library at the University of California at Berkeley which showed that "Rukeyser was accorded access to the library stacks as an employee of the Institute of Experimental Biology from April 5, 1944, to June 30th, 1944." A follow-up reports says "Rukeyser was not employed at the Institute," but "was accorded library stack privileges" through a friend. The FBI then initiated an investigation of the unnamed friend.

By January 1945, Rukeyser's "Employee Investigation" had changed into an "Internal Security" investigation. She left the East Coast for the West Coast, and the FBI checked her mail and telephone calls, noting that "on February 7, 1945 she obtained a renewal of her library card at the University of California library." An agent also "observed an advertisement" of a poetry workshop she was giving the following month, in March. In 1950, paid informant Louis Budenz "advised that Rukeyser was one of 400 concealed Communists."

In 1951, Rukeyser's name was added to the Communist Index; four years later, in 1955, it was removed, with no reason given. But references continued to be collected. In 1958 the FBI reported that she was one of "the celebrated leftists" whom the Westchester County American Legion accused of having "Communist-Front records" and should therefore be removed from the faculty of Sarah Lawrence College. In 1963 she was the subject of a case whose subject is blacked out, and ten years later, in 1973, she was cited for an unspecified connection to Wounded Knee, the Indian reservation in South Dakota where the American Indian Movement held a sixty-nine-day occupation to demand a Senate investigation into the conditions there. In a case that is still controversial, two FBI agents were killed during the siege.

In late 1973, with no reason given, Rukeyser's case "was closed" because of "her lack of extremist activity," even though, despite poor health, she remained active in "extremist" causes up until her death in 1980.

Josephine Herbst probably had the worst experience of any writer who worked for the government during World War II, as a result of her FBI-revealed past. Also contributing to her undoing was derogatory information provided to the Bureau by a well-known fellow novelist, Katherine Anne Porter.

In 1942, Herbst was subjected to a background investigation after she went to work on the German desk of the Office of the Coordinator of Information (OCI), precursor of the supersecret Office of Strategic Services.

Her 152-page FBI file had been started in 1924, when the Bureau noticed she had written an article for H. L. Mencken's *American Mercury*. She had also "lived three years in Paris with and later married John Herrmann, reported a Communist in 1926," and "belongs to the Leftist American writing set who resided in France in the 1920's."

Herbst caught the Bureau's eye again in 1930, when it was reported that she "sent large brown envelopes to *New Masses* and *Daily Worker* Communistic papers," and signed a 1930 "Red Scare Protest." The Bureau also reported that she contributed to the *Partisan Review* "during the period of its domination by the Communist Party," and that she and John Herrmann were involved in a farmer's strike and "numerous CP fronts" in the middle thirties. The Bureau also disclosed that she had "reported a general strike in Cuba and made a survey of Nazi Germany in 1935 as a "Communist sympathizer," and in 1937 spent "three weeks behind the lines in Spain."

Herbst's file is sprinkled with unidentified informants who gave the FBI all sorts of details about her life ranging from "Miss Herbst had an unhappy married life," and her husband "left her at a time when her writing efforts were not going well with the public" to "Miss Herbst felt the Communists were doing some good work," although "she was not the type who could discipline herself to the rules by which the Communists abide." Another informant called her "a great follower of Stalin."

A May 20, 1942, letter in her file from William J. Donovan, the U.S. Government's Coordinator of Information, to "John Edgar Hoover," says Herbst had been "giving us concern for sometime." Donovan also tells "Edgar" that he has "adequate" reasons for terminating her employment "as of noon today." But according to biographer Elinor Langer, the firing actually happened the next day: "On May 21, 1942, when Josie had been working on the German desk only a few months, she was returning from lunch with another employee when she was accosted by uniformed security guards who padlocked her desk and locker, pawed over her handbag, and escorted her unceremoniously from the building." As for the "adequate" reasons, Herbst's presence in the Bureau's indexes more than provided them.

But there was also new information that the FBI was getting from some of the people they were interviewing during the OCI investigation. For instance, Sinclair Lewis, whom Herbst gave as a reference on her job application, was lukewarm when agents talked to him, saying, "I do not want to say anything against her or too much in her favor," but also telling them she was "a good writer, apparently honest, of good character," and had "no radical or Communist sympathies" or "pro-German or pro-Hitler tendencies."

Another of Herbst's references was Maxwell Perkins, her book editor at Scribner's Publishers. A May 8, 1942, report of an FBI interview with him reveals that although Perkins said nothing negative, one or two of his answers were as lukewarm as Sinclair Lewis's, even granting the usual paraphrasing that took place when interviews were typed up at Bureau offices. Perkins said Herbst was not pro-Communist, "judging from her work," though she was "somewhat leftist," adding that he hadn't ever discussed politics with her—which the agents probably had a hard time believing. But Perkins did, however, also praise her to the sky, tell them "there was no question in his mind that she was loyal to the U.S. government," and that "in his opinion she is the most able woman writer he knows and he has a high respect for her opinion on intellectual matters and matters requiring judgment and taste."

The most negative interview was a strange, very incriminating one the FBI held with Katherine Anne Porter, who, ironically, is identified as "Applicant's friend." This interview, first confirmed by Elinor Langer in her biography of Herbst, took place just four days before the firing, although the report about it was written up three days *after* the firing. (Despite the lapse, William J. Donovan no doubt heard about the interview.)

Katherine Anne Porter, the author of such books as *Flowering Judas* and *Pale Horse, Pale Rider,* told the FBI that Herbst was a courier for the Communist party in 1934 and transmitted messages to Moscow, and that she and her husband had definitely joined the Communist party. Porter also mentioned that Herbst "has a violent temper, a revolutionist attitude, and has caused trouble whenever the opportunity presented itself" and that she has "the utmost contempt for the American form of government." Porter asked the FBI not to mention her name in any report, but the Bureau did, anyway.

According to Langer, "There is no way—there is absolutely no way—she [Herbst] could have been traveling as a courier to and from Moscow. The times and places simply do not add up." The biographer also refutes other of Porter's allegations and firmly states that her story is "purely and simply a malignant reinterpretation of everything she [Porter] knew about Josie's history."

In a recently released 1946 interview, James B. Opsatas, one of her bosses at the OCI, told the FBI it was "possible" she had been fired because of "evidence of questionable moral character" that had surfaced in another FBI "background investigation." This sounds rather lame, but given the Bureau's puritanical attitude toward women, it might have been a contributing factor, along with Porter's depictions and the weak defense by Sinclair Lewis. Yet the fact that Herbst had been known to the FBI since 1924 was the major impetus to her dismissal, which, in a letter to Malcolm Cowley, she called that "wreck in Washington . . . it made me sick of the whole eastern seaboard."

Herbst's dismissal even caught the attention of Eleanor Roosevelt, who asked the attorney general for "the real facts in the case." His letter of reply is not included in the file, nor is a letter Hoover wrote the President's wife. However, the file discloses that about a week after writing the attorney general, Mrs. Roosevelt wrote a letter to Hoover thanking *him* "for giving her the facts."

Herbst, meanwhile, wrote an article for the liberal newspaper, *PM,* which is included in the file, contending "Fundamentally I was fired . . . because I am a writer. . . ."

Five years after her firing, she became embroiled in the 1948 Hiss-Chambers clash. According to Herbst's file, "Whittaker Chambers stated she and her former husband were Communist Party members and were acquainted with Alger Hiss." On February 28, 1949, FBI agents visited Herbst, and she told them that "in Washington in 1934 she recalled meeting an individual identified to her by her husband as Carl, whom she later learned, through photographs in Time Magazine, was Chambers." She told the agents that Chambers had visited "two or three times" and appeared to be "collecting information for the Communist Party." She "denied that Chambers ever photographed any documents in their apartment" and she told the FBI agents that she did not know "Alger or Priscilla Hiss."

Nine months later, on November 7, 1949, the agents returned to interview Herbst again, and this time she "admitted that between 1932 and 1934 she had been extremely close to the Communist movement," but "that it was the fashionable thing to discuss Communism and even to be a member of the Party during the early thirties."

In 1951, the FBI placed Josephine Herbst on their Communist Index, and two years later, in 1953, even thought of "deporting" her because of additional confirmation of her Communist links that had come from "Gregory," the FBI's code name for Elizabeth Bentley, who had been a courier for Jacob Golos, one of the most important Soviet spies. Bentley aside, Herbst was probably at one time a Party member (she practically said so in that 1949 interview), and the Office of the Coordinator of Information may not have been off the mark in firing her.

**

Katherine Anne Porter had an FBI file that had been begun in 1927 after FBI agents discovered her name listed in a newspaper article describing a telegram that the Citizens National Committee for Sacco and Vanzetti had sent to President Coolidge requesting that he intervene and stay the execution of the two anarchists.

However, there are no further references for almost two decades, until 1944, when the Bureau reported that she was vice-chairman of the New York women's division of the National Citizens Political Action Committee. There is no mention of the information she gave the FBI about Josephine Herbst in 1942. Careless record keeping? No, the material is concealed in Herbst's file, probably to protect Porter's identity (although the FBI didn't blackout her name prior to releasing the file.)

Porter's eleven-page file is routine, compared to Herbst's. In 1945, a confidential informant told the FBI that Porter was a member of the National Council of American-Soviet Friendship, and had also participated in some activity (exactly what it was is blacked out) connected to the League of American Writers. In 1948, the Bureau noted that she signed an anti-HUAC letter.

But there are still questions about Porter. A February 21, 1951, CIA memo included with her file is still classified "in the interest of national defense" because it could disclose "intelligence sources and methods" and "constitute unwarranted invasion" of privacy. Could it indicate some mysterious role Porter played for both the CIA and the FBI? This seems unlikely, though most of her work, especially her 1962 novel, *Ship of Fools,* was obsessed with the collusion of good and evil. It is possible, of course, that she collaborated with the CIA or FBI to act out this obsession. But her informing on Herbst probably has more to do with an obscure hatred or jealousy of Herbst. Or it could have derived from some deeper flaw in her character. Or it may have been a sincere belief that Herbst was dangerous.

MALCOLM COWLEY:
I heard that Katherine Anne Porter was an FBI informant—that the woman who did a life of Josie Herbst came across documents in the FBI files. That was the worst thing I ever heard about Katherine Anne Porter.

But I've heard some mean things about her and she's done a lot of mean things. God knows what her motives were. She had none! Josie Herbst was her best friend for a long time.

There was a touch of meanness in Katherine Anne's character. She turned against me completely. I always thought she would. It's a complicated story and has to do with Yaddo. You don't know the background of some of these things and I would find it hard to explain, but Katherine Anne Porter is a *bitch!* She was a very close friend of friends of mine, so I have never said anything against Katherine Anne Porter in public before, but I certainly have said so in private. I was always uneasy about her.

**

In *Masters of Deceit,* J. Edgar Hoover describes Howard Fast, author of more than three dozen books and plays, including *Freedom Road* and *Spartacus,* as "one of the Party's best-known writers, later to become bitterly disillusioned." Actually Fast did not join the CP until the 1940s, though his radical career stretched back further. During an October 13, 1957, television interview with news commentator Martin Agronsky, the transcript of which is in his file, Fast said, "I have known Communists, been affected by Communists, read Communist literature and believed it, ever since 1933." According to the FBI, Fast became politically active "in the early thirties" (a specific year is not mentioned). Fast says he attended two meetings of the John Reed Club in 1933. (The FBI got the name wrong in his file, calling it "The Tom Paine Club of the Communist Party," confusing it with the name of Fast's 1943 novel, *Citizen Tom Paine.*)

Fast says he joined the Party "right after 1942, '43 at the latest," although he later changed the date to 1944. The FBI pegged Fast as "a reported Communist" in 1944, and "a key figure" in the Communist party in 1945. Compounding the confusion, in an interview with the FBI on September 4, 1957, "Fast . . . admitted CP membership from 1934 until August 1956." Now he says he left in 1958. But as Fast remarks, membership in the Party was "a fluid thing." In many instances, a writer's reaction to his own file is as inaccurate as the files themselves; both are part of their times.

Whatever his dates of membership, Fast's file is in many ways no different from writers who were not members of the Party. To the FBI, suspected Communists were the same as actual Communists. It's true that Fast's file, at 1,603 pages, is larger than most.

Another distinction is in the utilization of informants. Fast recalls, "I was followed, I was tailed. Everything I would write—articles on peace, for magazines in half a dozen countries—the FBI would pay translators and then they would pay editors in the language to compare the translation with the original! Think of the endless thousands of dollars—they did this for years and years and years." Fast's mail was monitored and read, but probably no more than non-Communist party writers.

After putting Fast's name in the index, the FBI continued to report on his activities during the thirties, noting that he was "active" in the League of American Writers and was a "writer" for the "communist-controlled *NEW MASSES*." Fast explains that he "never formally worked for it. I just did it because I thought it was a good thing, a necessary thing."

A report states that "prior to 1938, his books were received as testimonials of patriotism," and another notes that Mrs. Franklin D. Roosevelt and Harry S. Truman "praised his books before his name became linked with Communism." After Fast joined the Communist party, the FBI wrote that his "main aim in writing is to use American history to denounce America." The Bureau referred to "the warped world of Howard Fast," reporting that "he is haunted by the theme of enslavement . . . he hates it. Out of this unwavering hatred he makes books."

Comments Fast, "Hoover was as crazy as a bedbug."

The FBI reported that from 1935 to 1937, Fast "painted scenic designs on stage scenery" and was a "shipping clerk," as well as a "counsellor at a children's camp." In 1941, it noted that his local draft board granted him permission to leave the country to go to Mexico "on an alleged business of 'writing.' " Fast claims this was a mistake. "I went to Mexico in *1949*."

From 1942 to 1944, Fast worked for the Office of War Information, where, according to his FBI file, he "prepared highly dynamic pictorial pamphlets, posters, magazines, throw sheets, etc., for distribution on a world-wide basis and was responsible for the selection and verification of specific types of pictures in the preparation of material sent abroad which may have a psychological effect on the peoples of the world. . . . In 1943 [he] was responsible as Senior Script Editor for a daily fifteen minute war news and feature show."

Fast explains that it was while he was working at the OWI that he joined the Communist party. His colleagues there "were the only people in Washington who understood what the war was about, and knew what to say and do. And I was in an important position—I wrote the propaganda line of the United States every day. At the age of twenty-six, I wrote a basic fifteen minutes that was translated into every language in Europe. This started in 1942, right after Pearl Harbor. And the only people in that huge organization who knew what was going on and what to say were the people who were working with me, who were all Communists. And this, by a very understandable process, led me to join. They were very decent people, most of them—the most sincere American patriots there were—and the best force behind the antifascist struggle.''

In 1944, when the FBI first identified him as a Communist, the Bureau reported that he ''was employed by the United States Army in the Morale Services Division, as a writer and expert consultant,'' but that since he was a ''civilian employee,'' his ''case'' was being ''closed'' as of June 27, 1944. Given the FBI's increasing scrutiny of government employees in wartime, it seems odd that it would clear him so perfunctorily. Perhaps the explanation is related to the fact that on June 25, 1944, Walter Winchell broadcast that ''someone was tapping the telephone of Howard Fast, editor of 'Scope' Magazine.'' An FBI report dated June 26 indicates that Fast complained to the FBI about the tap, but apparently the Bureau attempted to stall any inquiry about it, for the memo says ''if Fast recontacts [us] and requests that an investigation be conducted . . . advise Fast that his request would be submitted to the Attorney-General for his advice and decision.''

There is nothing further in the file about the matter, but Fast remembers the incident: ''For about four or five months I was the editor of a left-wing magazine called *Scope*—it was started by the Party. We had friends who were electronically sophisticated and they told me my phone was being tapped. I called the FBI in a great rage. The tap never got removed.'' Fast also comments, ''But what could we have talked about? No one ever said anything. We never did anything illegal—we never *considered* anything illegal. One day two men came in to see me—one was a spy and the other was 'a Party member.' The spy said he had a map of the newest battleship in the American fleet and said he'd like to sell it to me. This was a very clumsy attempt to entrap me. I immediately called the cops and told them an international spy was trying to sell me the map—and I described him to the cops—the New York City cops, who are very good guys. But by the time the cops came, both men were gone. I guess it was an FBI entrapment. . . . Later, at a conference in Paris I saw the same FBI agent who brought the spy to me at *Scope*. I knew his mission was to get me—to kill me, and I let everyone know. I accused him to his face.''

HOWARD FAST:

The image of the Communist party that the FBI had is far from the reality, but in order for the FBI to be what it was it had to create a Communist party that was this terrible, deadly menace—which was laughable to anyone who was in the Party!

My group in the Party was called the Cultural Section—and just to pick a date—say 1947—we numbered about fifteen hundred people. I was in the writers branch. Everyone I knew on Broadway was a member of the Cultural Section. I would speak to the cast of a musical and either half of them were Party members or twenty-five percent were, but all of them were sympathizers.

Who were the writers? I don't mind talking about the ones that are dead—because I think the dead would want it to be known—but I can't do it with living people because some of them are important! Some of them are very important in Hollywood today!

Lillian Hellman was a member of the Party for two weeks. Steinbeck was in the Party for three weeks. Ronald Reagan, well, he's still alive, but a public figure; he wanted to join the Party desperately and Eddie Albert spent a whole evening talking him out of it because the organization said Reagan's more useful to us the way he is—he doesn't have to join the Party.

In the thirties, a half million people went in and out of the Party. It was no trouble to drop out—I mean, you didn't have to *do* anything to drop out of the party—you just ceased to be active in the Party. It was a negative act.

The Party was the anchor in my life. It's very hard to describe it today—because today it's so *unthinkable.* You would have to turn your thinking into a totally different premise. Everything has been stood on its head. Don't forget, all the good unions in the business were built by Communists—the Writers Guild West, which I belonged to, was built by Communists.

The whole resurrection of American folk music—this came from the Communist party. Woody Guthrie—*"This Land Is Your Land"*— was a member of the Party. *"The Ballad for Americans"* was written by two Party members. It's so hard today to get your thinking back into that milieu. Because even friends, even the closest people, they have to be saturated with all these years of the endless, endless, endless anti-Communist propaganda—you know, it never stops—it goes on constantly. How can you get out from under it and go back to those times? The only thing you can ask yourself is why does a list of Communists and suspected Communists include the cream of American letters and American arts at the time?

When we had the May Day Parade in 1947, we began to march at eleven o'clock in the morning and at eight o'clock at night we were still marching! I did a count: I had twelve thousand people in my block—between Seventh Avenue and Eighth Avenue. Just on that block! And we assembled on thirty blocks—this was a vast undertaking. I would see people on the block who I'd never in a hundred years dream had an inkling to do with the Party.

I was simply living my life and doing what I thought was the right thing to do. I never feared the FBI—I never went to any lengths to deceive them. Long ago, my wife, Bette, and I decided that the only way to be safe in this was to have no secrets. Absolutely no secrets. And as long as I had no secrets, they couldn't get anything on me.

But the record reads—what do they get me for? For addressing a meeting on the subject of black oppression? Addressing a meeting on the subject of the workers' pay? And on and on.

There were so many informants, so many spies and traitors in the Communist party that it's impossible to say who reported on what to the FBI. But it seems to me that when Johnny Gates—the editor of the *Daily Worker* who was one of the ten CP leaders convicted and jailed in 1950—and myself, when we left the party in 1956, no, I think it was 1958—it was probably in 1958—twenty eight thousand members of the Party left with us.

So there were two or three thousand members left, and if Hoover had two or three thousand agents out there, all that was left after that were J. Edgar Hoover's agents! So, the Communist party of the United States, in fact, at that moment, was practically a branch of the Justice Department.

So what the government finally decided to destroy was not only the Communist party, it was also the vast population which was around the Party and the artistic ideologies which they pursued. This was a terrible tragedy for America. It changed the course of American literature. It changed the course of American painting. The FBI fingered every good writer, every important intellectual in America at the time.

**

CARTHA DeLOACH:
Howard Fast, as I remember, was a member of the Party, but I don't remember any specifics concerning him.

Well, I hope the FBI destroyed the Communist party, but I think Howard Fast is giving us more credit than we deserve. It was never true that at one point there were more agents that were members of the Party than anyone else. We did have a number of informants—to give you an example, Cleveland, Ohio, when I was there, we had many Communist cases at the time, 1943, 1944—yet to my knowledge we had only two or three good informants. So Fast would be giving us a great deal more credit than we deserve. We did have some good informants, but we had some weak ones, too. But one informant, inside, under cover, is, I've always said, worth fifty agents.

**

In 1946, the FBI reported that Howard Fast "caused some disturbance in his apartment building by inviting negroes as his guests." The Bureau also reported that he was writing articles for the *Daily Worker*. Fast recalled, "We had a brownstone house and we would give parties for good causes. Once, when we were giving a party for the hospital that the Spanish Refugee [Relief] Committee maintained for the families of the sick veterans of the Republic army in Spain, someone who said he was a well-wisher sent me a letter in the mail and enclosed a picture—he said this is the FBI agent who is assigned to your party tonight. So I picked out a couple of stalwart young guys at the party and showed them the picture and said when he appears throw him out—tell him we don't want any FBI agents. Sure enough, he turned up!"

In 1947, the Bureau wrote an eight-page review of his novel, *Clarkton,* calling it "Communist propaganda at its worst," and also reported that his novel *Citizen Tom Paine* was removed from the New York City school libraries; in the early fifties, Fast's books would be removed from all the U.S. overseas libraries.

In 1948, the FBI reported that Fast had addressed students at Columbia University, telling them that "Truman . . . was obscene," and the following year, the FBI noted his participation in the Cultural and Scientific Conference for World Peace at the Waldorf-Astoria Hotel.

In 1950, the FBI reported that he was sent to jail for refusing to name the members of the Joint Anti-Fascist Refugee Committee before the House Un-American Activities Committee. "When I got out of prison, no publisher would even read a manuscript of mine," Fast says. The FBI reported in 1952 that Fast "declared that publishers were afraid to print his recent novels and that this signaled the approach of a police state." The following year he founded the Blue Heron Press to publish his own books. "They never stopped me from publishing. Not quite," he says. His passport was also revoked from 1950 until 1955, and he didn't actually get it back until the 1960s. "They dealt with me as if I were super Soviet agent number one."

In 1951, Hoover was upset because Fast's play *Thirty Pieces of Silver* "depicted an FBI agent as threatening a Treasury Department official," and "impugns the integrity of the FBI."

The following year, the FBI reported that Fast "announced his candidacy for Congress on the American Labor Party [a CP front] ticket." Fast says, "I thought it was a very exciting idea. My opponent only won by thirty thousand votes." The Bureau did not follow the campaign and election as carefully as it did some of Fast's other activities. He believes that the FBI "might have been afraid of it. You see, that's very touchy when it comes to elections and they might have been held up with criminal charges against them. [The FBI was] always afraid of incurring criminal charges."

In 1953, Fast appeared before the McCarthy Committee. He remembers how the subpoena was served: "We were all asleep, and it was a private house, and they came at twelve midnight to serve me a summons. I said, 'Get out of here—it's midnight—I'm not going to open the door.' They wouldn't go away, they kept on ringing the bell. Finally I called the cops, and they took the guys away."

That same year, the FBI reported that "a victim of Communist torture in Korea said the Reds furnished U.S. Prisoners with a complete set of the works of Fast." The victim, an unnamed lieutenant colonel, called Fast "a very vicious writer."

"I believe in the Marxist analysis of economics," Fast says. "Now, the attitude toward Russia, which led to both the Korean War and the Vietnamese War—both wars sold to the American public on the basis that we were fighting to save the world from Communism—the attitude toward these two wars connects with the attitude toward Communism that has been so carefully engineered and fostered by our present government. We are a war economy.''

In 1954, the FBI reported that Fast had been a winner of the Stalin Peace Prize. ''As soon as Stalin died, they changed it to the International Peace Prize,'' Fast says. ''I wish they had done it earlier, because the name lingers with me.''

The FBI also reported that year that an advertisement for his novel *Silas Timberman* that appeared in *The New York Times* might be a devious way of ''disseminating Communist propaganda to many unsuspecting people.''

By 1956, the FBI had received reports that Fast was dissatisfied with the Party, and considered interviewing him, but held back because ''as a writer he would possibly turn a contact . . . into an embarrassing situation.'' Nevertheless, in 1957, Fast was interviewed, ''four or five times'' according to one report. Fast says, ''They saw me only once, when they came out to my house. We were living in New Jersey, and we talked for about two hours. What could I possibly tell them about the CP that they didn't know? And *mostly* what upset them was that *we* were dying to know who the FBI people in the Party were!''

Fast would not name names of other CP members when asked, but he did tell the FBI that his just completed book, *The Naked God,* ''will assist the anti-Communist cause''—and he gave agents a set of galleys. The FBI was sophisticated enough to realize that this ''rough copy might contain data subsequently deleted by publishers,'' but noted that ''there are no startling intelligence revelations'' and ''there are no false allegations concerning the Bureau.''

According to the file, when Fast first left the Party, he called the FBI to ask: ''Am I in danger?'' A report explains that Fast ''asked this question'' because ''he was in the process of writing . . . an 'explosive' book exposing the Communist Party . . . and his friends have advised him to be careful.'' Fast comments, ''Anyone who left the Party was under attack,'' even though in a seeming contradiction he had earlier stated that there was no ''trouble'' in leaving the Party and that a member just ''ceased to be active.''

Fast says he formally left the Party in 1958, accusing it of playing ''directly into the hands of the class enemy'''; he broke with the Party over Khrushchev's 1956 exposé of Josef Stalin's crimes of mass murder and terror. Khrushchev's admissions horrified Fast.

But the FBI machine ground on. J. Edgar Hoover ordered his agents to prepare a study entitled *Communism and the Arts.* In it, American reviews of Fast's novel *Moses: Prince of Egypt* were compared to a then newly released decree about art published by a Soviet magazine. The FBI came to this conclusion: "The CP-USA is still slavishly following the dictates of the CP–Soviet Union." And in 1958, agents concocted a COINTELPRO hoax intended to stir up controversy in the CP, whereby "composite articles entitled 'Moscow Writer Denounces Fast as Zionist Apologist for Israel' and 'Fast Hits Back at "Lie" by Soviet,'" were mailed to some fifty people on the left. The FBI then sat back and waited for a dispute to heat up. The forgeries are not mentioned in Fast's file; they were concealed in the file of Dashiell Hammett, who was on the list of people who were to receive the letters. Fast only recently learned of their existence, and when asked if they surprised him, said wryly, "It surprises me because it demonstrates a degree of 'intelligence' which I have never seen in any of the functions of the FBI."

The FBI kept track of Howard Fast until 1971, thirteen years after he left the Party. The 1971 report, which still calls him a Communist, although no longer a "menace," concerns a change of residence from New York to Connecticut, where he still lives.

HOWARD FAST:

J. Edgar Hoover sent an agent to Little, Brown publishers—my publisher—and said to them, "The Director does not want this book *Spartacus* published." Little, Brown rejected the book, and Angus Cameron, the editor, resigned over that. When I had sent him the manuscript, he received it very enthusiastically, and wrote me a glowing letter saying it was the best book I'd ever done. Little, Brown held a meeting, and Cameron said, "If you don't publish this book, I'm going to resign—I will not suffer myself to be put in such a position"—so they forced his resignation.

And then I sent the book to seven other publishers—and you can be damned sure the FBI went to every publisher—with the same thing. There's no mention of this in my file! Alfred Knopf sent the manuscript back *unopened*—saying he wouldn't even *look* at the work of a *traitor*. Why was I a traitor? That's not in the file either.

Finally, *Spartacus* got to Doubleday, and they, too, turned it down. But there was a wonderful man there who ran their bookshops, and he called me, quivering with rage. He said he had been at the editorial meetings and most of the editors wanted to publish the book. He said, "I'm independent, so Fast, you go out and publish it yourself and I'll give you the first order for six hundred copies."

I went out and did this, and lo and behold, it became a best-seller. I sold thirty-five thousand copies, but didn't make any money out of it because I was plowing everything back into advertising. It came out in 1950, and since then it has sold millions of copies, and it's still in print.

Now, at that time—here's a most interesting sidelight—the feds came to the man who started the American Penguin line—he published me and he published Eric Ambler. The feds told him that he must immediately destroy—put through the chopper—all books by me and Eric Ambler. As with so many things that happened then, someone in the office called me, and I gave the story to *The New York Times,* and they published it, and the result was the books were not destroyed.

That was quite a time, because, you know, when you go off on that lunatic fringe—tangent—then you begin to believe your propaganda. You believe that books can do things. Books can wreck governments. And these were ordinary works of fiction.

**

ANGUS CAMERON:

I first met Howard Fast about 1937, and I was, at that time, an editor at Bobbs-Merrill Company, whose home office was in Indianapolis. We were holding a sales conference in New York, and one of our authors had me over to dinner, and he had this young writer there, and this young writer was Howard Fast, who, at that time, in my opinion, was a nice liberal young man. He was certainly no Marxist, and was not very radical.

As for my politics, I don't think of myself as a liberal, because I don't think that a system can be reformed. I think of liberals, generally speaking, as people who support the establishment by being niggling little side critics who can always be depended on to support the establishment when the chips are down. Arthur Schlesinger, Jr., is the classic example of that.

I had always arranged it with my colleagues that I always told them what I was going to do politically—I didn't ask their permission to do it, but I always told them.

For instance, in 1950, I told them ahead of time that I was going to speak at a big meeting in Boston against the Korean War. I remember when I told them, we had a lunch—and the lunch was at the Somerset Club, and we ate off Daniel Webster's plates! And at that time, they agreed that I had to be allowed, naturally, to take any position I wished to, and it had nothing to do with them.

Anyway, over the years I kept in touch with Howard Fast, and never published him, but in his case, as in others, I was sort of an editor at large. He would quite often bring me manuscripts that he was doing that some other publisher was publishing. So I was in touch with him, oh, on and off from, well, I went to live in New York in 1938—and all during the forties I was in touch with him.

I went to work for Little, Brown in 1938, and stayed there until 1951. We published a book of Howard's called *My Glorious Brothers* around 1948, and we took that book while he was waiting for the U.S. marshal to pick him up on his contempt of Congress charge. So you can see that, at that time at least, Little, Brown wasn't intimidated by the climate.

What happened in the case of my leaving Little, Brown was actually much more interesting, and Fast's book, *Spartacus,* had only a peripheral connection to it. It did have a connection, but it was only peripheral.

In April of 1951, I went to my colleagues and said, "I think we ought to have a meeting on how we're going to respond to this increasing climate—and how that's going to affect our policy." I told my colleagues that I thought we should resist the climate, but I thought we ought to have a general agreement on what we were going to do about it. And so, in April of 1951, it was agreed among the directors that we were not going to be intimidated, and we would continue to publish books that we damn well wanted to publish. Along about—I guess it must have been the first of September of that year . . . no, it must have been earlier: my memory is that Howard submitted *Spartacus* to us that year that he was out of jail. Anyway, it was very interesting what happened.

I was editor-in-chief and vice-president, and I recommended that we publish the book, though I wasn't quite as enthusiastic over it as Howard thinks I was. Another vice-president, Stanley Salman, wrote a report about *Spartacus,* and it always amuses me to think of it. He said, "I just don't believe that the U.S. Senate is this corrupt!"—making a one-to-one jump from the Roman Senate to the present political situation. Now, no doubt, Howard Fast *had* something like this in mind, but Salman just openly said he opposed publication.

Along about then, I went to Maine to see an author, and couldn't get back in to Boston for a meeting because the planes were fogged in. This was a meeting in which we were going to review our decision to not be intimidated.

Meanwhile, George Sokolsky wrote an article about me and Little, Brown— and mind you, by that time I'd been under fire in a lot of places, one way or another. *Counter-Attack,* which was started by two ex-FBI agents to make money out of clearing people, had devoted part of an issue on me and Little, Brown.

My colleagues got panicky, and I knew this would happen, of course. I had said to the president of the company, Arthur Thornhill, that it was going to get much worse. And then I said I think it's going to get too difficult. I had in mind that it was going to get too difficult for him, because he was simply apolitical.

Well, anyway, they went ahead and held that meeting without me being there, and because of all the things that had come up in the meantime, the board wrote me a letter which I got Saturday morning. Stanley Salman had persuaded Arthur Thornhill to write the letter—but Stanley wrote the letter, I could tell by the style, of course—and Thornhill signed it.

Among other things, the letter said I would have to submit my outside activities for the board's approval. I know for a fact that Arthur Thornhill didn't see that as any different from what had been happening, but Stanley Salman saw it as different. So we had a meeting the next Monday, and I said to them, "Well, I just don't think any free publisher can ask that and I certainly don't think that I can agree to it."

So I left.

And that was in 1951.

And Howard Fast figured in it to the extent that I just explained. It was the trouble over his book that caused me to call the second meeting, but his book had nothing to do with my leaving. The thing that had to do with my leaving was the larger issue.

CHAPTER FIFTEEN

Wouk, Cozzens, Mitford, Parker, Hammett, Hellman, and Lowell

The FBI began an eighty-six page file on novelist Herman Wouk in 1941 when he was investigated at the request of the White House for a job with the Office of Production Management. Wouk had been a scriptwriter for Fred Allen, and had volunteered his services to the U.S. Treasury, where he wrote radio scripts; he would later join the Navy.

In the 1941 investigation, the author of *The Caine Mutiny* and *Winds of War* was called "arrogant and cocky for a young man," and agents were told he had volunteered to work for the Treasury Department only to avoid the draft. The agents were also told that his "only hobby is reading classical works." In another report, Wouk is called "not Communistic," but this is crossed out in ink and the words "thoroughly American" are inserted, so the sentence can read "Wouk is thoroughly American."

That he was, even by Hoover's standards. In 1949, the FBI reported that the *Daily Worker* found the theme in Wouk's play *The Traitor* "quite unacceptable" because of his "description of U.S. Communists as atom spies." Hoover, of course, would have found it quite acceptable. Indeed, Wouk is a conservative and celebrates the military in his novels, and he describes his file as "achingly dull." Yet there is one reference in it that illustrates just how Hoover's need to control writers applied to left and right alike. On May 16, 1962, the FBI reported that Wouk's novel *Youngblood Hawke* "is reportedly critical of the FBI." The Bureau immediately "obtained" a copy, reviewed it at once, and determined that in one of the subplots an FBI agent is described as "an ex-football player gone to fat," while another agent is described as "a small man who made [the protagonist] feel that he had sinned."

A decision was made to "take action" by exerting some influence, and part of a later memo reads, "Since we knew Jerry O'Leary at the 'Star' was reviewing Wouk's book, efforts were tactfully made through him to counteract the critical part of the book. This undoubtedly resulted in the comment by O'Leary, in his review of the book several days ago, (5/20) that the attack against the FBI was unwarranted."

The inclination to retaliate against novelists who portrayed the Bureau unflatteringly in their fictions was nothing new. In 1942—the year after Wouk's file was opened, as it happened—Hoover learned that James Gould Cozzens's novel *The Just and the Unjust* made "unfounded insinuations and accusations that the FBI uses third degree methods" and that agents "would perjure themselves and withhold evidence on the witness stand during a trial."

Cozzens, a conservative like Wouk, was made the subject of a 141-page file, which contains correspondence showing that Hoover not only greatly exaggerated the number of complaints he had received about the novel, but encouraged agents pretending to be ordinary citizens to write letters of protest to the Book of the Month Club, which had offered this "most libelous" book as a selection.

Both Cozzens and his publisher, Harcourt, Brace and Company, also got the treatment; a memo "recommends" that "a letter be prepared to the publishers . . . as well as the author straightening them out. . . ." The files were checked for any previous references on both. On Cozzens there was nothing, so the FBI had to go to the latest *Who's Who in America*. As for Harcourt, Brace, the FBI established that it was "one of the better publishing houses in America," and that "in the past they have published nothing derogatory to the Bureau so far as is known."

Donald Brace, the president of Harcourt, Brace, replied to Hoover's letter by saying the company would gladly talk over the FBI's concerns with Cozzens, and that they never thought there could be a problem, since the book was fiction. Hoover's answer to this letter is reasonable enough: "Certainly it would appear that if the fiction was carried to its logical conclusion the author would have created a fictitious organization instead of naming the FBI."

However, Hoover also wrote some unreasonable letters to the editors of newspapers who had reviewed *The Just and the Unjust.* Irita Van Doren, the literary editor of the New York *Herald Tribune,* told the Director that his "argument is with Mr. Cozzens" and not with the reviewer of the book. She went on to tell the Director that "our review actually was a fairly critical review of the book and would not encourage as many people to read it as the front page, more laudatory review in the Times, though that did not mention the FBI."

Van Doren's name is marked with a check for indexing, and the words "review in the Times" are underlined with Hoover's thick black ink pen stroke. Eventually, the FBI decided not to write *The New York Times,* since the Bureau was not referred to in its review.

Finally, on September 9, 1942, Hoover received a letter from the author, who at the time of the controversy was serving as a first lieutenant in the army air force. Cozzens wrote Hoover that his novel was "misunderstood," and that it was written "as a defense and vindication of the American system of justice." He also said he realized that he implied the FBI uses "illegal means," but "the book is a work of fiction." Cozzens asked Hoover to "reread the book as a whole," and concluded his explanation by praising the mission of the FBI. In a note attached to this letter, Hoover referred to the author as a "whelp."

Eventually the Book of the Month Club caved in and sent a mild statement to its 500,000 members: "J. Edgar Hoover . . . has protested to James Cozzens . . . against certain passages . . . any unfair reflection upon the FBI . . . is . . . regretted." A more dramatic illustration of Hoover's power over the press could not be imagined.

The FBI became interested in Jessica Mitford, "one of six daughters of Lord Redesdale of England," because of suspected Nazi ties but ended up pursuing her as a Communist. And uniquely, she didn't become a writer until after she left the Party.

The FBI entered her name in its files in 1939 because her sister Unity was the "alleged girl friend of Hitler" and her sister Diana had "married a fascist Gentleman, Oswald Moseley." That information was true—two of the daughters of Lord Redesdale were indeed pro-Nazi; but not Jessica, generally known by her nickname, "Decca."

Mitford had left England in 1937 and had married Esmond Romilly, a nephew of Winston Churchill. "During the season of 1939 and 1940," an informant told the FBI, Mitford and Romilly were "employed at the Roma restaurant" in Miami, Florida. (A later FBI report called Mitford "a part owner.") The informant also said Mitford was also "employed as a clerk in the Walgreens Drug store" and as "a salesgirl at the World's Fair."

In 1942 the FBI investigated her when she applied for a junior clerk typist position with the Office of Emergency Management, a wartime agency; a report in the file states that "her services" at her earlier jobs were "satisfactory," although she "talked fluently in favor of Communist ideals" and it was "rather difficult to become accustomed to her peculiar English mannerisms." Walgreens told the FBI that Mitford had received $25 a week salary, but she says, "That's a lie. It was $16." In addition, an informant told the FBI that after Mitford and Romilly "had departed the Roma restaurant," they eventually landed in Washington, where "Jessica was engaged as an entertainer." Mitford laughs at this mistake and remarks, "How wonderful. *That* is what makes it all worthwhile!"

A 1942 memo to Hoover informs him that Romilly had fought with the Spanish Loyalist forces, and later joined the Royal Canadian Air Force. "He was reported lost in an airplane crash in the North Sea during December of 1941, at which time, his wife, Jessica, had remained in the United States and gone to work for the British Purchasing Commission in Washington, D.C." The FBI also noted that she had written articles for *The Washington Post* "which were published weekly during the winter of 1940 and 1941." Wrong, says Mitford. "Esmond wrote them, in fact. And sometimes I was supposed to write them and he really wrote them. I didn't consider myself a writer."

When Mitford moved to San Francisco in 1943, the FBI continued to observe her, reporting that she obtained jobs at the office of the Joint Anti-Fascist Refugee Committee and the United Federal Workers Alliance. The Bureau also stated that "although she was liberal in her political philosophy," she was "loyal to Democratic principles and proud of her connection with the U.S. government." And "she did not in any way share the sympathies of her sisters, Unity and Diana."

In 1944, a confidential informant disclosed that Mitford had joined the Communist party in January after a delay "due to the fact that she had just prior to this received her citizenship papers." Another report said she had been "active" in the Party while she was employed by the government but had waited until she was a citizen to join. At any rate, she and her second husband, lawyer Robert Treuhaft, did indeed become active in the Communist-party affairs in California that year.

The FBI reported that Mitford "enjoyed membership in the Communist Party because she liked to 'play games,' and that she viewed the party as an 'ornamental facade.' " The Bureau also said that she "gave the appearance of being a bit superior and above the movement," although for many years, Mitford was the executive secretary of the East Bay Chapter of the Civil Rights Congress, as well as the "full-time County financial Director of the CP."

After she entered the Party, Mitford's file swelled to 570 pages, and it includes a photo and physical descriptions of her (an observant FBI agent noted that she "has the habit of punctuating with her head by dropping her chin against her chest"), informant reports, records of passport detainments, and after she became a successful writer, reports of her articles, essays, speeches, and book reviews, as well as the FBI's own reviews of her books.

In 1945, the FBI placed her on the Security Index as "Jessica Lucy Treuhaft, nee: Jessica Lucy Romilly, with aliases Jessica Lucy Freeman-Mitford, 'Decca' Treuhaft, and Mrs. Robert E. Treuhaft." The following year a source told the FBI that Mitford said at a party meeting that "the purpose of the Communist party was to recruit members for the ultimate goal—the overthrow of monopoly capital and the democratic form of government that has failed." It was also reported that she had "inherited one-sixth of an island off the coast of Scotland . . . [and] in a joking manner stated that she might give it to the Soviet government for a naval base."

In 1947, the FBI reported that "she has been a leader in obtaining funds for the Party, especially in the recent drive for the Party's 'Fighting Fund.' " In 1948, the Bureau looked into the possibility of "cancelling" Mitford's naturalization, and in 1949, it disclosed that she was "attending Marxist Institute classes in Oakland, California."

By 1950, the FBI warned that "Decca Treuhaft was one of the group of Communist Party members in Alameda County considered to be most dangerous to the national security of the United States." It was after this report that she and her husband began to have passport difficulties.

In December of 1957, the FBI reported that Mitford "entered a building where a regional CP meeting was being held," and also that she was "reportedly disinherited by her father and cut off from his will."

The FBI records that Mitford and her husband "resigned" from the

Party in April 1958, but her file does not end. When she published a best-selling book, *The American Way of Death,* in 1963, the FBI noted that she was spending a lot of her time promoting the book, "which resulted in considerable publicity for her." This presumably bothered the Bureau, since it also reported that "she has continued to support and associate with CP front groups." Meanwhile, California congressman James B. Utt condemned *The American Way of Death* as "pro-Communist, anti-American, and another blow at the Christian religion."

In 1963, for the first time, the FBI referred to Mitford as a "self-employed writer" instead of as a "housewife." The FBI continued to conduct surveillance on her and her husband, reporting that "they had been observed at their residence, indicating they have returned from abroad." Bureau agents kept track of the stores that sold Mitford's books and whether or not they were left-oriented.

In 1961, the FBI reported that "author Jessica Mitford Treuhaft had joined the 'Freedom Riders' in Alabama and had to take refuge in a church to escape the rath [*sic*] of 'Ku Kluxers.' "

In 1968, the FBI reported that she "attended several meetings of the Women for Peace," and that in 1969 she was "gathering notes and other items in order to write an article" on the trial of "one of the members of the Black Panther Party."

The last report on Mitford is dated 1972, the year of J. Edgar Hoover's death, and is a summary of all her past "subversive" activities, including the new information that her book, *The Trial of Dr. Spock,* has just been published, and that she "is currently working on a book about prisons."

JESSICA MITFORD:

There's very little that's untrue in my file. Most of it is true.

Someone told me that a day after I was sworn in as a citizen, files had arrived from Washington that would have damned me forever! It was fascinating because I mean, I was *told* that, at the time. And in Bob's file, it said "married blank," crossing my name out to protect my privacy!

In 1967, Bill Turner, an ex-FBI agent, wrote an article for *Ramparts* magazine, and he told how he'd been at a cocktail party in San Francisco, and he'd heard a very familiar voice, a voice that he absolutely knew and couldn't put a face to the voice until he was introduced to Bob Treuhaft. He then realized that he'd been taping Treuhaft and family for a long time—wiretaps—in the fifties. We got hold of him and had lunch with him, to find out more. He had been assigned to Oakland and was part of a team of three who took an office under some pretext and then had the telephone company make connections with about thirteen people in the Communist party. And he named the people we knew, and they were not very important people, some of them. And in those knew, and they were not very important people, some of them. And in those days, they didn't have voice-activated stuff, so they had to keep the tape going all the time.

We assumed the tapping was going on, we sometimes thought we heard sounds, but there's not a single reference in my file to the taps. I asked the FBI for them, but I never got them. But never ever would we discuss anything remotely connected with security on the phone. You know, this poor wretch had to listen to me exchanging recipes with my friends.

On some occasions we knew that the FBI was taking our pictures. The FBI must have had about ten thousand employees in the fifties who were engaged in anti-Communist work. I think they outnumbered the Party!

Once we trapped them. We didn't outsmart them, but I wish we had. One of the things that the Civil Rights Congress was doing was organizing meetings—as far as we were able—in defense of the Smith Act defendants. And you can imagine that the turnout at those meetings was pretty pathetic—there had been a huge lot of intimidation and people didn't come scrambling out, you know. I mean, you could get fifty out, and that would be a lot. So we had just such a meeting planned—in one of those ethnic halls, I think it was down in Oakland somewhere—and I was the organizer of it. I was sort of in charge of having to put out the leaflets and all that crap, you know, and anyhow, we arrived on the scene, earlyish, when people were just beginning to come in.

Some of the people coming in said to me, "Look, Decca, do you see what's up there? Somebody's taking our picture." And sure enough, there was a quite obvious scene of a couple of people taking photographs of everybody as they went into the meeting. So Buddy Green—who is in my book *A Fine Madness*—and I went racing upstairs and we found at the top two obvious FBI men! Sort of gloomy-looking people, which the FBI did have. Upstairs, there's lots of offices—and we found a key, and we just locked them in! I was quite excited over this. We had them cornered, like rats in a trap. And outnumbered, too! And so, what to do with them, now that we got them? Well, we didn't quite know. Because there'd be no point in calling the police, since they were all on the same side. So I said—it was one of those ethnic halls with a kitchen—let's get all the pepper we can find and throw it in there and perhaps choke them to death sort of thing. Unfortunately, here's where the CP had a rather heavy hand on things; Mickie Lima, who was the head of the Party here, absolutely vetoed that suggestion. And so, reluctantly, we sort of let them out. Nothing happened. It's always been one of my great regrets. I mean, it's one of those things you dreamed of and nothing happened. They went slinking out—streaking down the stairs, three steps at a time, as fast as they could, with their stupid cameras. We didn't even break the cameras, unfortunately.

Howard Fast—of the I-was-duped school of ex-Party members—wrote that awful book, *The Naked God*. I never really knew him, though I may have seen him sort of glancingly at mass meetings and that kind of thing. He was tremendously taken up by the Communist party. You know, his books were absolutely sort of *must reading* in the CP—in other words, they were on every literature table—this is when the Party had a huge membership. So that's a pretty good sort of built-in sale, right? One of his books—it was the one about the slave, *Spartacus*—got a bad review or something. Most of this was extremely high level, because we weren't in those councils. It was all kind of New York stuff. Leadership stuff. And we were never in that. But we just sort of found it rather revolting that suddenly Howard Fast, just because he got a bad review, turned tail, you know.

His was an emotional attachment to the Party, and he expressed himself in emotional terms, as he does with everything he writes—that's what makes him so frightfully turgid and virtually unreadable, for me. It was the people who were *emotionally* committed to the Party, as he was, who were the most vulnerable to dropping out and breaking—and falling apart when they were under attack.

He was always redder than a rose. He was super red. And he was always highly touted and supported by the Party—the Party was very proud of him. He did all the public relations for the Party, he told Bob.

But I agree with him that the government decided to destroy not only the Communist party but the population around the Party—and the artistic ideologies.

I quite agree with all that, except why did he then join all that?

**

HOWARD FAST:
I've never met Jessica Mitford, and I know nothing about her. She's very bitter against me, though.

In the first place, I didn't leave the Party alone. I left with not only Johnny Gates and the other New York leadership, but twenty-seven thousand people left the Party in 1958. Why single me out? Why would she object to me leaving? I didn't get mad at the Party because they stopped giving me good reviews. Their reviews were always *too good.* I mean, it was overdone.

She was never challenged because no one ever knew she was a Communist. When she wrote *The American Way of Death,* nobody mentioned she was a Communist. Nobody seemed to know.

Just this week I was attacked as an ex-Communist, in a review of the play *Citizen Tom Paine.* And it's been said that along with *Catcher in the Rye,* these are the two best depictions of an adolescent in American literature—and John Leonard, in *New York* magazine, called it comic-book writing.

I'll tell you about Jessica Mitford, what has occurred to me. I wrote a book called *The Second Generation,* and I do a portrait of her sister—the confidante of Hitler—and it's totally devastating. Could she have cared for her sister? She was a very bad, bad person—at that moment in history when England was attacked—to stand up for the Nazis as she did.

But I can't think of anything else, because, as I say, I've never met Jessica Mitford.

**

The majority of references in short story writer and wit Dorothy Parker's file, which eventually grew to contain 506 pages, were collected at the end of World War II, and by this time Hoover was using "technical surveillance," such as photography or microphones, as well as "Black Bag Jobs," or surreptitious entry. One report indicates that "prior to a luncheon a confidential search of the records was made," that is, agents sneaked in while the place was empty and ransacked the premises.

Her file had started in the twenties when Parker was one of the founders of the well-known Algonquin Round Table, but not much was collected on her until 1937 when a confidential informant told

Hoover that Parker "contributed to the Communist movement." She was also reported to be "a writer for New Masses," a member of the League of American Writers, and a member of the League for Women Shoppers, which had been founded in 1935 "to provide information relative to labor conditions under which goods are manufactured." An informant also told Hoover that she was "one of the leading characters in the Communist movement in Hollywood in the early thirties," and from then on the FBI alternately referred to her as the "cream of the crop of Communists" or "queen of the Communists." It was also noted that she "has monumental scorn for the FBI."

The affiliation of Parker's that troubled Hoover the most was the Joint Anti-Fascist Refugee Committee, a relief organization founded in 1942 to help Spanish Civil War refugees. Besides Parker, its members included Howard Fast, Rex Stout, Upton Sinclair, Carl Van Doren, and Lillian Hellman, who would later become the executor of Parker's will. But the Bureau listed over fifty Communist fronts Parker was connected to. It also followed very closely her friendship with Hellman, who is called "a dedicated Communist" in Parker's file. The FBI used confidential informants to spy on both women, noting who visited whom and when.

In 1940, an informant reported that Parker and Hellman both wrote for the liberal *PM,* the newspaper Hoover described as "banal, amateurish and confusing." Eventually, he would index all its backers and board members.

The next year, in 1941, Hoover put an X by Parker's name and wrote, "the ones marked X are Communists pure and simple, no matter what their position is in the business and social world of today." The following year, he intercepted a telegram she had sent to numerous people inviting them to a publication party for the "Deluxe" edition of Hellman's *Watch on the Rhine.* The FBI also indexed all the people who received the telegram.

By 1951, Parker's name was on the FBI's Communist Index, and she was now called "an undercover Communist," "an open Communist," or "a Communist appeaser." Walter Winchell described her to Hoover as "a mad fanatic" and that year complained after he had received a form letter asking for support for victims of Spanish fascism that had been signed by her, that she had the nerve to lead "a Communist group attack on me" to get his sponsor to fire him from his radio show. "Hmf," Winchell scribbled to Hoover, who added Winchell's correspondence to Parker's file.

Winchell, too, stayed on Parker's case and sent more material involving her to Hoover. In 1951, it was a tip that "the fugitive Communist leaders" might be "in a large playroom in the cellar of Dashiell Hammett's house" (which was actually Lillian Hellman's house) and that "Dorothy Parker was also a friend of these people and that all three [Parker, Hellman, and Hammett] were in love with the four Communist leaders."

The following year, in 1952, Winchell sent Hoover a copy of another appeal letter signed by Dorothy Parker, one that also included a copy of a pamphlet written by Howard Fast called *Spain and Peace*. Once again, Hoover added this material to Parker's file, and then, three years later, in 1955, he thought about placing Parker's name on the Security Index because of Winchell's pressure. However, for reasons not spelled out, Hoover decided that Dorothy Parker was "not dangerous enough" to be included after all. She would have had a lot to say about that characterization, had she known about it.

HOWARD FAST:
I don't even remember writing *Spain and Peace*. But I'll tell you something very interesting: that pamphlet is one of those things that could make you a millionaire, if only you thought of it. The cover picture was drawn by Picasso. I wrote to him and told him I was doing this and he sent us this picture, which is one of his pen-and-ink drawings. Today, the original, signed by him, it would be worth at least $150,000. We—the Joint Anti-Fascist Refugee Committee— auctioned it off. Someone bought it, I think it was for $300!

You take Dorothy Parker, this wonderful, good woman who was one of the jewels of American culture, and she's got a file in the FBI! I mean that's so monstrous—that stinks so much—and everyone accepts it. It's a fact of life.

She was never a member of the Communist party, just as Paul Robeson was never a member.

**

ROY COHN:
They were pretty suspicious of Lillian Hellman and Dashiell Hammett. Totally suspicious. They were more suspicious of Dashiell Hammett than Lillian Hellman—they were very suspicious of Hammett.

**

In 1942, at the age of forty-eight, Dashiell Hammett enlisted in the U.S. Army as a private and served from 1942 to 1945. But the FBI was not impressed by this act of patriotism. It considered the creator of Sam Spade and other hardboiled detectives, as well as the charming amateur sleuths Nick and Nora Charles, a dedicated Communist, which he was.

Hammett's 354-page file was begun in 1934 because the Bureau thought incendiary messages might be contained in a comic strip called

Secret Agent X-9 that Hammett created for the San Francisco *Call-Bulletin.*

The FBI judged Hammett's novels "extremely lean" but said that the "pro-Communist padding gets in there, just the same." The Bureau said that he was on his "Stalinist honeymoon," and that Moscow had ordered him to begin the job of "initiating fronts." The Bureau also said that he contributed "a thousand dollars a month to the Communist Party" while working as a highly paid screenwriter in Hollywood, and had staffed *PM* newspaper (which was founded in 1940) "with Communists" such as his lover and companion of thirty-four years, playwright Lillian Hellman.

The FBI denigrated Hammett's World War II military service by reporting that "he claimed to be a Corporal in the United States army, but to date this information has not been verified." In 1951, the year Hammett went to jail rather than name contributors to the Civil Rights Bail Fund (which was set up to provide bail for arrested Communists), Hoover received a copy of a letter sent to Walter Winchell. The letter Winchell passed on was from a veterans group that was asking Winchell to answer a question about Hammett: "Why would a pro-Commy enlist in our army at his age?" In an unusual move by the head of an investigative agency, Hoover himself suggested Winchell's reply, asking the columnist not to use his name:

> You ask: "Why would a pro-Commy (Hammett) enlist in our army?" That's easy. Because our army was fighting for Russia. In other words: Only the Commies knew what the last war was all about—a war to make the world safe for Communism.
> (Don't mention me.)
> (Just call me professor.)

It has been seen in Dorothy Parker's file how Winchell tipped Hoover that four CP leaders were hiding in Hammett's house. Hammett's file contains an excerpt from Winchell's Sunday-evening radio broadcast of July 8, 1951, reporting the outcome of his tip, followed by the Bureau's own summary of the investigation:

> "Winchell: New York Mirror—The FBI searched the home of Dashiell Hammett . . . looking for his comrades, the four escaped Red leaders. They went thataway . . . and that, Mr. and Mrs. 48, winds up another Winchell . . . until then I remain your New York correspondent who is sure that the G-men would have no trouble finding those four fugitive Commies if John Edgar tried using a little cheese."

> Comment: Bureau agents went to the home of Hammett to determine
> if he knew the whereabouts of the fugitive Communists. He advised that
> he did not know of their whereabouts and invited the agents to look
> around the house if they so desired. He was advised that the agents did
> not have a search warrant, but nevertheless he said they were free to
> check the premises, which was done with negative results.

Hoover must have liked the tag line of Winchell's broadcast because
he wrote in the margin of the summary: "Please note."

The FBI sought to involve Hammett in several COINTELPRO operations aimed at stirring up dissension in the CP. First, it included his
name on the list of individuals to receive the phony articles about
Howard Fast. Six months later, in August of 1958, the Bureau sent
Hammett "an anonymous mailing" of a "leaflet" it had made up
called "Two Views of the Hungarian Executions," hoping it would
stir up more trouble in the Communist party. That same month, the
Bureau involved Hammett in a third COINTELPRO operation, sending him anonymously "page four of the 8/11/58 issue of *Labor Action*
publication of the Independent Socialist League." The hoped-for "tangible results which may arise from this matter"—as well as those from
the other two—are not included in his file.

Even after Hammett's death in 1961, the FBI stayed on his case. It
tried to prevent his burial in Arlington National Cemetery on the
grounds that he had been a Communist.

Lillian Hellman's 603-page file was begun in 1933 when an unidentified informant told the FBI that Hellman belonged to the John
Reed Club.

Until her death in 1984, Hoover pursued Hellman as if she were a
female "Machine Gun" Kelly. During the 1930s, various unidentified
informants told the FBI that the playwright—called in her file a "Jew
Communist" and accused of being assigned by the Communist party
"to smear the FBI"—belonged to a dozen or more Communist fronts,
"visited the USSR in 1936 and 1937, and spent one month in Spain
with the Loyalist forces during the Spanish Civil War."

In 1943, Hoover called Hellman a "key figure" in the Party (the
same designation he gave Howard Fast in 1945) and told his agents to
keep their investigation of her top secret "because she has a national
reputation through her writings in which she opposed Nazism and
Fascism" and "is a person who stands behind her convictions."
Hoover was nervous about tackling Hellman because she could fight

back. From 1943 on, agents continued to stalk her; sometimes using pretext phone calls to establish her whereabouts.

In 1944, the Bureau put her on the Security Index, remarking that "her lectures indicate a pro-Soviet and pro-Communist point of view and have consistently followed the Communist Party line." Another memo that year reported that the playwright "had recently remarked of Communists that their morals are too 'puritanical' for her." That remark may have contributed to the FBI's willingness to record the gossip that she had an affair with President Roosevelt's adviser, Harry Hopkins (whom Hoover greatly disliked). Hellman did enjoy flirting and had her share of romances in her lifetime, but her editor and confidant William Abrahams believes "she wouldn't have had time for her plays with all these affairs she was supposed to have had." Cartha DeLoach adds, "Hopkins was so dyspeptic and full of ulcers . . . I think he'd be too weak to do it!"

When Hellman went to Russia in 1944, agents searched every piece of her luggage, discovering such items as "a number of small blank notebooks," one copy "The Little Oxford Dictionary," and "The 10/7/44 issue of *Colliers* magazine." The agents read the magazine and reported to Hoover that "this issue contained the article by Wendell Willkie, 'Citizens of Negro Blood.' " Anything to do with the race question was automatically suspect.

What agents did not report was that Hellman's trip to Russia was a cultural goodwill mission at the behest of President Roosevelt.

In 1945, Bureau agents questioned her when she returned from an extended European trip, and a report dated May 16 says that she "displayed . . . some indignation that a person of her prominence should be subject to any questioning." A decade later, when agents successfully interviewed her, they would report that she was "quite friendly" and "very courteous."

In 1952, the FBI sent a blind memo to the McCarran Committee that contained all the derogatory material in the files, including the testimony of paid informant Louis Budenz, who said that the Politburo gave "definite directions" to Hellman. In fact, Hoover believed Hellman was still a Party member "as late as 1945," according to one 1963 memo about her.

The FBI read and watched Hellman's work, noting testily that *"Watch on the Rhine* appears to have a great social significance," and that the *Daily Worker* had called it "revolutionary." They were wary after finding out that *A Searching Wind* "is concerned with diplomacy and diplomats and some Washington people," and commented that her movie, *The North Star,* "should get more Communist friends."

Hellman's file is an example of one of the few unexpectedly beneficial aspects of Hoover's accumulation of intelligence. It is an archive, of sorts, although Hoover didn't intend it to be that. For instance, the playwright rarely talked about being a Jew, but her file contains a copy of a little-known public statement she once made on the subject: "I am a writer, I am also a Jew. I want to be quite sure that I can continue to be a writer . . . I also want to go on saying that I am a Jew without being afraid that I will . . . end in a prison camp, or be forbidden to walk down the street at night." Another item concerns Hellman's little publicized inability to find titles for her plays. "I can never think of a title, I've called Dorothy [Parker] and told her she has to come through for me again," she is reported as saying. Parker provided the title *The Little Foxes,* the item concludes.

Daniel Aaron has written that "some writers joined or broke from the [Communist] movement because of their wives, or for careerist reasons, or because they read their own inner disturbances into the realities of social dislocation. . . . Politics . . . was often the vehicle for non-political emotions or compulsions." In many ways, this describes Hellman's position. Her attraction to communism was, as Blair Clark, a former CBS newsman and editor of *The Nation,* observes, "sentimental." Clark was involved in the Committee for Public Justice, which Hellman helped organize in 1970 to advance civil liberties, and he recalls, "Lillian ran the committee in her typical style; an offhand, high-handed manner. There was a frivolity about her attitude—she was half serious and half grande dame."

In his biography of Hellman, Carl Rollyson writes that she admitted she was a CP member between 1938 and 1940, in an early draft of her well-known 1952 letter addressed to the House Un-American Activities Committee ("I cannot and will not cut my conscience to fit this year's fashions . . ."). Rollyson says Hellman described herself as a "most inactive member" and said that Party officials never pressured her to rejoin when she left. Howard Fast says she left because she "couldn't take a position of humility," and "drifted when the going got tough." Writer and critic Diana Trilling adds that, like many literary celebrities, Hellman was more useful to the Party as a nonmember. "She wouldn't be under that kind of low-grade, low-status Party discipline. I mean, she was a freewheeler. She was the person *they* turned to for help."

Hellman's politics did sometimes mirror her emotional attachment to Dashiell Hammett, who admitted to longtime Communist party membership. And so, in a way, she confirmed Hoover's theory that the sole source of all women's political beliefs was their men.

ROY COHN:

When I was counsel for the Senate investigating committee, we had Lillian Hellman on the top of the list of people who were pushing the cause of communism in the United States and in Hollywood, particularly. There was just no doubt about that at any point. And the fact that the Russians might be looking at her, too, or something like that, so what, because we *knew* in 1944—in times like that—we knew what was going to happen in the future. We knew that it was going to be us against them. I knew it by 1945. How could I know that? I knew it, believe me. I was born in 1927. I was twenty-three years old when I prosecuted the Rosenbergs. When some people were reading other things, *I* was reading FBI reports!

Lillian Hellman was a concealed Communist. I think she really believed in it. Hammett was an out-and-out, card-carrying, if you will, member of the Communist party. Lillian Hellman lived with him for years; she went to Communist-party meetings—this is by her own admission, I'm willing to stand on *her* admission—she went to Communist-party meetings with him. She gave money to the Party through him. She would give him money for the Communist party. I think it would shock people more now than then, because Lillian Hellman developed a secondary image. In other words, there was "Lillian Hellman" and there was "Lillian Hellman—Dashiell Hammett." I'm inclined to think Hammett used her more than she used him. Absolutely. I think the Party used her a lot.

But I don't think she was *that* political. I think she was sort of fifty percent an amused leftist and I think the other fifty percent a sincere leftist who believed that communism and leftism were the answers to the future of Hollywood and America.

I've never gotten very excited about her. I saw her three or four times in my life—once was at the Pierre Hotel when she was leaving, and she had a pile of Vuitton luggage that was enough to match Mrs. Marcos's shoes or something. I'm telling you. And she was always with fur coats. Jewelry. Everything like that. A Jewish Princess. No question about it.

**

CARTHA D. DeLOACH:

It was stylish in some circles during the war years to join the Communist party, and many people did it without any indication or any desire whatever to harm the United States or to aid the Soviet Union. It was just the stylish thing to do in some circles.

I knew Roy Cohn very well, but I never heard that Lillian Hellman was at the top of the list of writers who were considered to be members of the Party. If that's true, I never knew it. I know that Roy was somewhat prone to exaggeration at times, but I never heard that.

**

"Lowell is the fellow who refuses to report for induction because 'this is no longer just a war,' " a Bureau official wrote at the bottom of a September 17, 1943, report. He added that Lowell "disapproved of the Allies' methods, particularly the bombing of enemy cities." The report said that the selective service case of Robert Traill Spence Lowell, Jr., "the grandson of the president emeritus of Harvard," was being postponed until the Librarian of Congress had a chance to talk the young poet into reporting for induction. Thus began Robert "Cal" Lowell's thirty-six-page FBI file, one year before his first book, *Land of Unlikeness,* was published in 1944.

Lowell pleaded guilty to dodging the draft, and was sentenced to "one year and one day" in prison. His file includes news clippings and articles about the proceedings, because his situation was unusual. The year before, in 1942, Lowell had actually tried to enlist *twice,* but "was turned down on both occasions due to his eyes." The following year he was called up and refused to report for duty for the reasons the FBI official mentions above.

The references in the file are brief, scattered, and often confusing. The FBI seemed to have been a bit confused about Lowell, too.

In 1947, when Lowell became a Consultant in Poetry at the Library of Congress, Hoover's number two man, Clyde Tolson, asked Louis Nichols "whether the Bureau had ever investigated Lowell." Nichols jotted a hasty note to Tolson saying, "We did investigate him," as was routine for this post, but the results are not included in the file.

In 1951, almost a decade after his draft brouhaha, an FBI memorandum reports that Lowell was supposed to have served his sentence at Danbury. (This memo also notes that Lowell is "a cousin of a noted American poet" Amy Lowell, who "is not the subject" of any file.) The memo does not mention that Lowell was paroled after four months, or why the FBI waited so long to record his imprisonment.

Even more inexplicably, there is nothing about what Malcolm Cowley called "Yaddo—The Affair." In 1949, Lowell instigated what some people called witch-hunting, at Yaddo, the writers' colony in Saratoga Springs, New York. The absence of this episode from Lowell's file is completely misleading because *the FBI actively investigated Yaddo and the charges Lowell brought against one of the guest writers there.* What is more, one of the principals in the affair, the secretary to the director of Yaddo, was an FBI informant, and had been one since 1944. And a board member stated at a meeting of the directors that "the FBI have been investigating Yaddo at least beginning in 1942, if not before." The documents pertaining to Lowell's participation in the Yaddo situation are no doubt locked away in another file—perhaps in the probably still-classified file of the Yaddo secretary.

What touched off the controversy was the arrival at the colony of Agnes Smedley, an American journalist, who, according to Janice R. MacKinnon and Stephen R. MacKinnon in their biography of her, was considered "at the peak of her fame, in the late 1930s and early 1940s . . . the John Reed of the Chinese revolution for her tireless advocacy of the Chinese Communist cause." Smedley was a friend of Elizabeth Ames, director of Yaddo, and had often stayed at the literary retreat since 1944, the year the FBI began a file on Smedley. Two years later, in 1946, she was accused by the government of being a spy, and, according to her biographers, "by early 1948, the FBI's investigation had intensified." In February, according to the MacKinnons, Smedley gave a reception for a Communist official at Yaddo and the townspeople complained to Yaddo's board of directors, and "On March 9, 1948, she moved abruptly out of Yaddo." And then, "on December 31, 1948 . . . Drew Pearson wrote that Smedley was a key Soviet spy who had worked in Japan as a member of a Soviet spy ring from about 1934 to 1941." The FBI returned to Yaddo to question the guests about Smedley, and because of all the fanfare—the arguments and friction—that ensued, Lowell demanded that Elizabeth Ames be fired. Malcolm Cowley, a member of the board of directors, was opposed to such a move, as were some former guests, including Katherine Anne Porter, Delmore Schwartz, John Cheever, and Alfred Kazin.

Rumors about the literary-political battle that was brewing there that winter were extensive. Kay Boyle even heard gossip that Lowell "had gone to Washington and had given the names of all sorts of people with no political affiliations at all" to the FBI, but these rumors were untrue. Malcolm Cowley says, "I found no record of Lowell's trip to Washington—if he made it. . . . Kay Boyle often gets things wrong and repeats some rather wild stories. The truth about Lowell's part in the affair was wild enough, God knows. Allen Tate reported much of it in letters to me."

Writer and critic Elizabeth Hardwick, who became Lowell's second wife in July 1949 and was one of the guests at Yaddo, along with Lowell, writer Edward Maisel, and short story writer Flannery O'Connor, during the Smedley crisis, says that "one particular thing that has always been confused and which I have never been able to make right in the public mind is that when the FBI came up to Yaddo, they came to see *me* and Edward Maisel. The FBI had no interest in Lowell, and he didn't talk to them."

Malcolm Cowley's letters reveal more particulars, especially about who named names. In one letter he wrote on March 8, 1949, to poet

Allen Tate about Elizabeth Ames's secretary, he says: "If I heard correctly, . . . she turned over seventeen names to the FBI." Cowley wrote Tate on March 27 that "when Lowell and the other three guests thought they had evidence that Mrs. Ames was involved in a Communist conspiracy, they should have presented it to the FBI. . . . Instead they tried to hold their own investigation. . . . They acted like scared Russian writers during a purge." Another Cowley letter written on March 8 to critic Louis Kronenberger discloses that FBI agents "explained" to board member Granville Hicks "that they moved quickly into Yaddo" because they hoped "to find people off guard and make discoveries." This same letter describes how the FBI "interviewed Elizabeth Ames for two hours and a half" and they "also interviewed two of the most bitterly anti-Communist guests, Edward Maisel and Elizabeth Hardwick, who for the last three years has been finding Stalin plots in every smile. . . . They leaped to the conclusion that Yaddo had been the scene of a Stalinist plot."

After the FBI left, Lowell brought matters to a head at a special board of directors meeting on February 26, held in the garage at Yaddo. In attendance, besides board members John A. Slade, C. Everett Bacon. R. Inslee Clark, Malcolm Cowley, Richard Donovan, Thomas F. Luther, Kathryn H. Starbuck, and Everett V. Stonequist, were Director Elizabeth Ames, Lowell, Hardwick, Maisel, and O'Connor. Six other board members were absent. The following are excerpts from the transcript of the proceedings:

Mr. Lowell: The first thing, I can assure the members of this Board that this is the most important meeting in its history, one that involves its welfare and perhaps its existence. . . . I now present the petition of the four guests. . . . 1. it is our impression that Mrs. Ames is somehow deeply and mysteriously involved in Miss Smedley's political activities. 2. that Mrs. Ames' personality is such that she is totally unfitted for the position of executive director. . . . I think it is only fair to tell the Board that I myself have influential friends . . . I want to give their names—I think it is quite relevant: Santayana, Frost, Eliot, Williams, Ransom, Moore (in case you think I'm bluffing, I only know Miss Moore slightly but think she would agree), Bishop, Tate, Blackmur, Warren, Auden, Adams, Bogan, Empson. Of my own generation, Robert Fitzgerald, Farrell, Bishop, Schwartz, Shapiro, Taylor, Powers, Stafford and Berryman. . . . On February 14th, two guests at Yaddo, Miss Hardwick and Mr. Maisel were questioned by FBI. We will later bring that out. Naturally, the matter was discussed at great length among ourselves. . . . I myself have never been questioned by the FBI . . ."

Miss Hardwick: The FBI came to me first. I do not know why, since I know very little about Yaddo. . . . One thing they asked me was about Andre Lomakin, whom I read about in the newspapers as one of the most effective Soviet spies. . . . They did not want to know whether I thought any painter or writer were a communist, which I would have found difficult to answer . . . they wanted to know if Mrs. Ames had issued any instructions to guests to take any particular stand on the Agnes Smedley case. I said she had not, which was true. They asked me what I felt was her attitude toward the case, and I said I felt she was in an extremely nervous state, and I was uncertain of her attitude. They wanted to know if it was my impression that she knew more than most people about this and about Miss Smedley and I said that was my impression. . . . My relation with Mrs. Ames has been very good. I think she has been extremely nice to me. . . . I only know the sur- face. . . . I cannot read her heart. . . . The FBI did not ask me a single question about any guest at Yaddo. . . . Innocent people, due to com- ing to Yaddo, have been interviewed by the FBI. My questioning by the FBI was simply due to my presence here.

Mr. Maisel: The FBI men began by telling me they are not thought- police or Gestapo. All their questions were utterly specific, no general investigation of subversive or Communistic activities at Yaddo. It was not along the lines of the Un-American Committee questioning.

Miss O'Connor: Mrs. Ames said that Agnes Smedley had been living in fear for a long time . . .

Mr. (John A.) Slade, Board member: It's getting so you can't make a joke while riding in an automobile without having your name sent in to the FBI.

Mrs. Ames: In my early years at Yaddo, the FBI came to see me about people who are now members of the Corporation of Yaddo. They even brought you in, Granville *[she is referring here to board member Granville Hicks, who is not listed as either present or absent on the transcript]*, the other day. Even brought in Ella Winter. . . . I told the FBI I never had any affiliation with any radical party and was not in any sense a fellow traveler. For years I have been a good Democrat. . . . When the interview was about to end and they asked if they might return, one of them picked up a book called *Our Plundered Planet*, about destroying the earth for plants, and said to me, "Is this a radical book?"

Ultimately, Lowell's attempted coup d'état came to naught. On March 31, 1949, Malcolm Cowley wrote critic Morton Zabel that "Lowell and Hardwick have decided to do nothing about the charges" and that "it looks as if the great time of trouble for Yaddo was drawing to its close." On April 7, Granville Hicks wrote Cowley that "as far as I can make out, the FBI isn't at all interested in Yaddo as such." On April 16, another board member, Acosta Nichols, wrote Cowley that "a good deal of what went on at the Yaddo meeting can now be discounted in view of Lowell's condition. His insanity is indeed a sad matter . . ."

Nichols was referring to Lowell's manic-depressive episodes. Katherine Anne Porter wrote to Morton Zabel that "I hope they keep Lowell safely, poor man, he should never at any time have been left to this world on his own."

According to Ian Hamilton's biography of Lowell, Cowley managed to keep the whole incident out of the newspapers, to avoid a scandal, and thus very little has been known about the case.

ELIZABETH HARDWICK:

Cal never had anything to do with the FBI. He doesn't know the FBI from backwards and forwards! What happened up there was this thing appeared in the paper about Agnes Smedley—it was a big headline in *The New York Times*—and somehow that got Cal agitated to think she might be a Soviet spy. And he hadn't ever heard of Agnes Smedley until he read it in the paper—he didn't even know who she was! He had never been a leftist. Now, I hadn't known Cal for more than about a month then, and this is the first time he had a breakdown.

Because he seemed so formidable to me, I didn't realize just how *vulnerable* he could be at these times. After this, I would know everything. But they are very peculiar, these kind of excessive enthusiasms—and they're very impressive. People who have manic attacks tend to do these kinds of things, like try to get the president of the university fired.

I can't tell you the number of people he took up with throughout our time together—and they sort of believed him when he said "I'm going to marry you and I'm going to do this and that." And people who weren't women, when he would say, "Oh this is a wonderful poem you've written," and so forth.

Well, anyway, Agnes Smedley got him agitated, and all he had in his head then, in this grandiose, wild way, was to get Mrs. Ames fired. Then meanwhile, I was sitting up there at Yaddo and the FBI came around! They asked me if I knew Agnes Smedley, and I said, "No," which was true. I'd never seen her in my life. And they said, "Well, you are a leftist," or something—these people are as small-town as you can imagine—and I said, "Yes, but not that kind. I don't know her. And she wouldn't have been in my group." And they mentioned somebody else, who had nothing to do with Yaddo. Did I know them? They were sort of American Commie types, and I said, "No, I don't. Those aren't the people I know."

I had, myself, been a Communist when I was back in Kentucky, before I got out of college. But during the time of the Moscow trials I turned very much against it, but I still called myself a Trotskyite. That's what I told the FBI! And they said, "What is that?"

And then they spoke to Edward Maisel, a very, sort of elusive fellow. I hear from him sometimes. He feels bad that people thought Cal spoke to the FBI. He still sort of keeps up with the Yaddo case, and then you can't find him again. I don't quite know what he does now. He has some sort of job and he travels a lot. He used to write very well.

There were only four of us there at Yaddo during this period. And Flannery O'Connor. The FBI didn't speak to her either, although she was very upset over everything because she liked Cal a lot. She was just writing her first book, and was already beginning to be sick with this deathly illness that her father had had. She had no political interests at all.

I don't even remember the calling of the meeting, but I'm sure I was there. But I don't remember much about it, because we were getting rather nervous about Cal. But anyway, it turned out that a secretary of Mrs. Ames had been calling the FBI for five years, saying there were all these Communists around. But I didn't know that at the time. So they had been shuffling around up there for a long, long time. And then this Smedley thing kind of blew up and everybody thought Cal had called the FBI. Now he did behave in a most indiscreet and unfortunate manner, but then he sort of forgot about it when it was over, and got into religion about three weeks later. And his later political things were connected with war and peace and things like that.

**

Excerpts from Letters of Elizabeth Ames to Malcolm Cowley:

Katherine Anne and Agnes will be here all winter. We do have some good times together. KA is on the crest of the wave of her book's success. After a little further rest, she will be tackling the novel again. And Agnes is embarked on what I suppose will be a kind of fictionalized biography of the great Red Army General, Chu Teh . . .
—*November 14, 1944*

Agnes has left Yaddo for good. Sometime I'll give you all the details. . . . Yaddo cannot afford to get involved as she was involving it. For many months she has grown more incalculable and difficult, partly because of the book, I suppose, but partly too because of the worsening world situation. . . .
—*April 6, 1948*

Robert Lowell. All of you know of his importance up to now. He is engaged in a long poem which will not be completed for about another year. . . . He works wonderfully here, loves the combination of solitude and regularity and the sociability that is available when he needs it. . . .
—*from a letter to the Committee on Admissions; January 20, 1949*

As the days pass it is becoming clear to me and to others that the Smedley-FBI angle is mostly a strategy, and that behind it is the real move to get my resignation on other grounds. . . . And I do think the mystery behind all this ought to be solved. Why, why did four great enthusiasts for Yaddo become enemies overnight?
—*undated*

Reading your testimony in the Hiss trial, I was reminded (not that I often cease to think about it) that you so recently stood by me in my hour not unlike his. Well, quite a company of saints and martyrs is growing up in this republic

due to our wish to preserve (!) our democratic ideals. It is good to see that the press is beginning to call a halt on it . . . and I had a moment of unholy glee in reading that FBI would be raked over too. . . . The only news here is that in his last days here Lowell was calling himself King of Yaddo. . . .
—*June 25, 1949*

**

Lowell resurfaces in the FBI files in the 1960s when he would become one of the earliest prominent opponents of the Vietnam War. There is a 1962 name check which probably emanated from the White House, since that spring Lowell was a guest there for a dinner in honor of André Malraux. The file also reports that "during 1965, he refused an invitation to the White House because he did not agree with the President's foreign policy." Elizabeth Hardwick says "someone suggested it to him, 'Don't go, but say something,' because I remember they called up and he said, 'Yes, he thought that would be interesting.' It was the first kind of dramatic thing he did, and it turned out to be absolutely crucial; it was the first thing anyone had done."

Hardwick says that the FBI "has most of the things that he did, but then he would do things that nobody was much interested in, like helping Biafra. But that was not anything that concerned the government—the starving Biafrans. I have a picture of Cal and Dwight Macdonald both looking very shabby, standing someplace and saying 'Feed Biafra.' "

Was Lowell ever aware he had a file? His Harvard roommate, Blair Clark, says, "He never talked about it, but he must always have assumed he had one." Unfortunately for literary historians, the FBI left out (or hid) the best parts—what happened at Yaddo—which was an emblematic event, a portent of the McCarthy era when many writers would be highly visible targets.

PART FIVE

McCarthy's War and the Korean War

CHAPTER SIXTEEN

Sinister Influences

During the fall of 1950, Hoover launched a powerful attack on an anti-FBI book, *Federal Bureau of Investigation,* written by Max Lowenthal, a lawyer and friend of President Truman. Hoover brought his heaviest weapons to bear on the author, his family, his publisher, and many of his associates. One learns from the writers' files that Fulton Lewis, Jr., in his broadcast, announced that Lowenthal was a "red-tinted sinister influence behind the scenes" in "government circles," and still has "pro-Communist intents." Hoover even managed to get Westbrook Pegler to come on board. "I think Pegler is stirred up enough to do [something]," Louis Nichols wrote Clyde Tolson. Winchell and Sokolsky, naturally, also came to the FBI's defense in their columns. Hoover's defenders in Congress attacked the book on the floor of the House, Richard Gid Powers points out, and "HUAC investigators called on Lowenthal's publisher, William Sloan." Kenneth O'Reilly writes in *Hoover and the Un-Americans* that "The FBI Crime Records Division . . . wrote and planted critical book reviews . . . [and] FBI agents visited hundred of bookstores, attempting to persuade the owners not to stock the books."

George M. Elsey, who was an administrative assistant to Truman from 1949 to 1951, has said that after he read the galley proofs of the book, he told the President "to try and persuade Lowenthal to drop the project because the book was so unfair, so grossly biased, so sloppily done in every respect that it couldn't possibly influence anybody about the FBI." Elsey explains that Truman "just shrugged his shoulder, tended to laugh it off and say, 'Oh, Max is that way.' " Elsey also has reported that the President "recognized that Lowenthal was a little absurd" on the subject of the FBI, and did not "share" Lowenthal's "extreme" views.

But Hoover's tactics worked, for, as Powers summarizes, "It was fourteen years before another critical book on the Bureau, Fred J. Cook's *The FBI Nobody Knows,* appeared."

That same year, the FBI found out that the Authors League had not only supported the Hollywood Ten (the entertainment writers who were blacklisted for refusing to cooperate with HUAC on First Amendment principles), but had criticized the House Committee on Un-American Activities. J. Edgar Hoover wrote a letter to the special agent in charge of the New York office instructing him to "immediately institute a discreet investigation." He cautioned that "outside inquiries should be limited to confidential agents." One of the first "confidential agents" the FBI heard from said that there was "nothing subversive" in the Authors League, but the FBI pressed on until it found someone who said the league "is at least Communist infiltrated." A year later, in 1951, the Bureau would say in almost the same words it used in 1913 that the league "operates as a labor union, even though not considered in the same status," adding that "due to the Communist infiltration," it now wanted certain reports distributed to "the three intelligence Services" [Army, Navy, Air Force] as well as the "records Administration Branch of the Department of Justice." Hoover wanted a long, but "discreet," paper trail. In 1952, after receiving a detailed letter from a prominent but undisclosed league member, Hoover decided to send "two experienced agents" to question him (despite saying in a memo the year before that "no investigation has been conducted by the FBI concerning the Authors League"). During the course of the interview, the "two experienced agents" were informed that the league "is not motivated by political sympathies," and although the FBI's investigation of it would continue until 1962, the Bureau decided to concentrate its efforts on the Radio Writers Guild and the Screen Writers Guild—which "have broken away from the league." By 1955, Hoover was saying that he has "no knowledge of current Communist activity to infiltrate" the Authors League and was putting the case in "closed status." However, in 1958 the Bureau, still reading the league's newsletters, noticed that the league was trying to get Soviet publishers to pay American writers.

Nevertheless, in 1960, the *Dramatists Bulletin* would print a glowing review of Hoover's book, *A Study in Communism,* which the Director's research staff had written. It was "fascinating and thrilling," the review said, "an invaluable document every American who is interested in freedom should read and remember." Hoover acknowledged the copy of the review he was sent and included an autographed photograph of himself—a little reminder that he was still watching.

On June 25, 1950, troops of the North Korean Communist government crossed the 38th Parallel into South Korea. The ensuing war pitted the United States and its United Nations allies against the North Koreans and then the Chinese. The Cold War had suddenly turned hot, and American public opinion was told to blame Stalin. Relations with the Soviet Union deteriorated, while domestic Communists were hunted even more fiercely than before. The war against the foreign enemy intensified the war against the aliens within.

Thus it was no coincidence that the 1950s saw the rise of the phenomenon known as McCarthyism and increased measures, legal and otherwise, to stamp out the Communist party (the CPUSA had a little over forty-three thousand members in 1950), as well as its sympathizers, real or fantasized. Fueling the anti-Communist mood were sensational revelations about Soviet spy rings. Alger Hiss was convicted of perjury in January 1950 for denying that he knew Whittaker Chambers and for denying that he had given him classified documents. Ethel and Julius Rosenberg were arrested in 1951 on charges of passing the secret of the atomic bomb to Moscow. The Rosenbergs were executed in 1953.

ROY COHN:
I've seen so many memos that are phony that quote me, and a couple of them I never even heard of the subject matter! I also never heard of the person it was about!

There were some memorandums during the Rosenberg case I never saw until the mid-eighties, two or three years ago—some of which I *know* are blatant falsehoods.

**

In 1950, Congress passed the McCarran Act over President Harry S Truman's veto. Among other provisions, it mandated that Communists register with the attorney general and agree to be rounded up if a national security emergency arose. But the most significant act of 1950 belonged to Wisconsin's Republican senator Joseph McCarthy, who in a speech in West Virginia charged that the State Department was riddled with Communists.

Cartha DeLoach now says McCarthy "made up" his facts, and says "although there were at the time rare members of the CP in the State Department, a lot of those suspected were just members of the various front organizations. I recall that after McCarthy made his famous speech, when he said there are 153 members of the Communist party in the State Department, Mr. Hoover confronted him—in his office—and he asked him, 'Where did you get information of that nature? Our files certainly don't reflect that. I don't think it's true.' And McCarthy said, 'Well, Mr. Hoover, I just started talking and I heard the roar of the crowd and the applause and I just got carried away. I pulled this piece of paper from my pocket and I read off the statement.' And he said the piece of paper was perfectly *blank*. He made it up."

Former FBI official Harold T. Leinbaugh says, "Hoover had an *awful* lot of reservations concerning McCarthy. He really did." Perhaps because of them, the FBI opened a file on the senator, which eventually grew to six thousand pages. Hundreds of those pages refer to the FBI's "investigative position with respect to the 81 Communists in the State Department whose names were furnished by Senator McCarthy" to the Senate Committee on Foreign Relations—the Tydings Committee. Hundreds of other pages consist of letters filled with the names of suspected Communists McCarthy wanted the FBI to check out, internal Bureau memos about public and private meetings with the senator, articles and newspaper clippings concerning McCarthy, and summaries of radio broadcasts where he is mentioned or discussed. Some of Hoover's comments scrawled on various documents mirror his state of mind at the time. They reveal a veteran bureaucrat who doubts McCarthy's charges but fears the political heat they generated and consequently feels he must cover up for his own department and make sure he isn't personally blamed.

J. EDGAR HOOVER:
"He is just passing the buck."
  —on February 11, 1950, letter to McCarthy from John Peurifoy, deputy undersecretary of state, saying that State Department employees "have been checked and are being checked" by the FBI and any card-carrying CP members "will not remain"

"It is the usual State Department double-talk and trying to pass the buck."
—*on a February 16, 1950, memo telling him above letter also says for McCarthy to contact the FBI*

"We should make very certain we are in clear as to our investigations in these cases."
—*on March 3, 1950, memo telling him that the State Department has "identified all of the 81 cases cited by McCarthy, and approximately 68 are no longer working for the Department"*

"Strange these ardent champions of our democracy and alleged foes of subversion never stir themselves when real subversives attack the FBI, but to the contrary join up."
—*on a March 20, 1950, letter to the editor in* The Washington Post *signed by Thurman Arnold, Abe Fortas, and Paul A. Porter, saying they are "deeply disturbed by attacks on State Department"*

"Right. I want no part to review [sic] of such files or the blocking out of information."
—*on a May 9, 1950, memo from Bureau official D. M. Ladd informing him that the FBI should not help block out sensitive material for Tydings Committee*

"This checks with what I found in Wisconsin."
—*on June 10, 1950, newspaper story describing McCarthy's "uproarious welcome" in his home state*

"It is an absolute lie and should definitely be nailed."
—*on a July 18, 1950, memo telling Hoover that a journalist heard that the FBI was asked by the White House to investigate McCarthy's income taxes*

"Maybe so but I think we were stretching need for delicacy even then. If facts are facts we ought to report them in the regular manner."
—*on a July 20, 1950, memo saying that information on the homosexual activities of a State Department employee was given orally because the facts were "highly delicate" and not suitable to be put in writing. Memo says new practice is to continue to give such information orally, but to "confirm" it in writing as well*

"Allright [sic] but I dislike a discredited ex-agent calling and insisting upon an agent coming to see him. As to his turning any informant in Europe over to us, that is CIA jurisdiction, not ours."
—*on an October 2, 1950, memo telling him that an ex-FBI agent employee now working for McCarthy—the name of the ex-agent is blacked out, but because of the date it is probably Donald Surine—has "a very good informant in Europe which he wants to turn over to the Bureau"*

**

The FBI reported that there were now 31,608 members of the Communist party in America in 1951, meaning it had lost almost 11,000 members in one year. The number of members would keep going down. According to the Bureau, New York State had the largest membership—15,458—and Mississippi had the smallest—there was one lone member.

In 1951, Edmund Wilson, the preeminent literary critic, author of such books as *Memoirs of Hecate County, Axel's Castle,* and *To the Finland Station,* was visited by two FBI agents who used the ruse that they wanted to talk about someone else (not identified). Wilson was friendly but firm, and said he was a "socialist who voted for Norman Thomas." He also said that he had "tried to give Stalin the benefit of the doubt" when he visited Russia in 1935, but that he "realized that the Soviet Union under Stalin could never improve the plight of the masses and that the Russian Revolution had failed." He also voiced that "I have a certain amount of Marxist working equipment, which I use in my writing" and that the Communists in the United States "have misinterpreted the philosophies and writings of Marx and do not understand them." As late as 1987, the FBI reported that certain documents in his fourteen page file are still classified.

CARTHA DeLOACH:
    At one point the FBI knew every single member of the CPUSA. Field divisions had complete lists of members—some of the members were transitory, some of them may have come in and stayed one or two days and become disillusioned and left, and the FBI may not have had *those* names. But for the most part I think the FBI did know, because of the very definite, good number of informants, and because of the wiretaps—because Communists talked freely on the telephone. I think that whoever thinks that the lists of the Communist party members were inefficiently kept is totally wrong, because that was a source of great efficiency in the FBI—meticulously kept up-to-date.

**

Beginning in 1952, the year an FBI instructor told a class of student agents that America was fortunate that the Democratic candidate, Adlai Stevenson, did not become President because his close associates were Communists and Communist sympathizers, the passports of citizens who published or preached any form of Hoover's dreaded "isms" were arbitrarily revoked. Harold T. Leinbaugh remembers "There were broad departmental guidelines—the broadest was hate."

On February 19, 1953, a little over a month after Dwight D. Eisenhower was inaugurated as President, "six confidential directives from the State Department" began the controversial removal of several hundred books by more than forty "subversive" authors—including Langston Hughes, Lillian Hellman, Dashiell Hammett, Edgar Snow, and Howard Fast—from United States Information Agency libraries abroad. At the United States library in Tokyo, many books and periodicals were burned.

SVETLANA ALLILUYEVA:
My father had a very fine library of fiction, Western European classics translated into Russian. Everything that was published in the Soviet Union in the twenties and thirties was there, and then there was a special section of political literature and Party literature in another room—I didn't go there.

There were books of certain Russian thinkers and philosophers, and I think it was just a library which could be used for any good school or college.

But what happened to it is what happened to all personal possessions of my father, it was all removed to some undisclosed destination by all these KGB people. I don't know why. Then I humbly requested after my father's death that at least a portion of this library be given to me, because I knew it and I needed it. I thought I could own all of it, but of course that was out of the question—I had no place for all of it! But I could choose at least, the Russian classics or Western classics. But they never answered my request! I mean, they're just uncivilized. Savages! That they don't answer you at all.

I don't know where the books are. Somebody told me years and years later that my father's whole library had been given by the state to some college or university or some kind of organization. All the books were stamped with his name.

**

On March 5, 1953, Stalin died, and G. M. Malenkov became Premier of the USSR the following year. Beginning on April 22, Senator McCarthy's hearings on Communist influence in the Army were televised across the nation, vaulting his chief counsel, Roy Cohn, into prominence and giving him a notoriety that would follow him for three decades. Hoover, who readily aligned himself with Cohn's right-wing beliefs, and often defended him, nonetheless was also a little wary of him, as shown by a marginal notation he wrote in McCarthy's file: "Cohn will just doubletalk and fast."

ROY COHN:
My father, who was a strong man—he was a high court judge—he was much tougher than I am. I'm tough inwardly, and tough generally, but outwardly, I'm not tough. Every time I hear "The Star-Spangled Banner" tears come to my eyes, you know.

The Army-McCarthy hearings hit my mother and father—I couldn't believe it, because it didn't hit me. But it hit them terribly. The worst thing in our life. I thought then that if I wanted to go through life fighting like I wanted to fight, it would be much easier without a wife and children on my back, so I wouldn't have to worry that everything I did was going to affect them.

I knew my father better than anyone in the world; he was looked on as a smiling, gentle, solid jurist. He never made a frontal assault on a public official or another judge or anything along those lines. One day during the Army-McCarthy hearings—it was a Saturday or a Sunday and I used to come home on the weekends because I hated Washington—anyway, this particular weekend I was in the library of their apartment and the television was on and Senator Potter, one of the members of the committee, was being interviewed. So the reporter says to Senator Potter, "Do you think Roy Cohn is the brains behind McCarthy and that he calls all the signals? What do you think we ought to do about Roy Cohn?" My father is sitting in the armchair on the other side of the room. Senator Potter says, "There's only one thing to do with him, there's only one thing to do with someone like that—*Get him out! And get him out fast before he does any damage!*"

I look up, and my father's in tears. I couldn't believe it. I couldn't believe my father ever being in tears. And that's made such a deep impression on me. With my mother I could understand, but my father! And then I made up my mind. If I'm going to stay in this business, I better stay in it by myself. I better not do it to a family, and I never did.

**

CARTHA DeLOACH:
I believe it to be true that Roy Cohn got facts from the FBI, although it was always said by Mr. Hoover that McCarthy did not get any information from the Bureau. But I do recall Roy Cohn coming in at around seven o'clock in the evening sometimes and going up to Lou Nichols's office and talking to him for *hours.* So something was going on there—it was a very close relationship between Nichols and Cohn. Roy, for example, tried to come in one evening and the guard wouldn't let him in because he had no pass, and Nichols hadn't called down, so Roy threatened to take the guard's job; he gave him all kinds of abuse.

**

HAROLD T. LEINBAUGH:
I think Hoover felt McCarthy was very dangerous. I have that strong feeling—can't prove it, or establish it, but it's there someplace. I think in due course Hoover cut him off *completely.* I think Hoover just realized that McCarthy wasn't to be trusted.

I don't think Hoover thought that much of G. David Schine and Roy Cohn either. I'm talking Bureau gossip—there was a good underground network in the Bureau—but I think we all felt and just knew and sensed that Cohn was gay. In those days that was worse than being a member of the Politburo!

**

On May 13, 1955, the year Malenkov resigned and was succeeded as Soviet Premier by N. A. Bulganin, Associate Director Louis Nichols said, ''The most effective method of penetrating a conspiracy is to enlist the cooperation of the conspirators. If their clandestine meetings and activities are to be penetrated, clandestine methods are necessary.'' What he was acknowledging, once again, was that informants were the FBI's best weapon. He was also saying that it was okay for the Bureau to disguise certain electronic buggings—and burglaries—by calling them "informants."

On June 6, 1955, one of the Director's best weapons, George Sokolsky, wrote a history lesson that Louis Nichols called "very effective." Sokolsky's column called Revolutionary War soldier Nathan Hale, who had been sent to Long Island to retrieve information on the British (but was caught and hanged), one of the nation's first informants. "There was no FBI," Sokolsky wrote on the two hundredth anniversary of Hale's birth, "but there *were* informants."

HAROLD T. LEINBAUGH:

What motivates informants? Sometimes money, and sometimes very little money. In many cases, only the case agent could know who the person really was; we leaned over backwards to protect informants' identities. That was both good and bad. We protected them from retribution. On the other hand, you had to contend with where the case agent was coming from. Will the informant make him a hero or not? You had to trust the agent's evaluation of the informant's information. This is true in any intelligence operation, and the Bureau probably did as well as you could under the circumstances.

I specialized in this for a while because you need a con man and I guess I was a con man at one time in my life. But you go to a guy and you try to explain, "Hey, you're living here in this country now and here's an opportunity to clear your record. You're on the side of the good guys." So there's a little fear and opportunity. Many of these people were worried about an invasion of Czechoslovakia—honest-to-God liberals who were deeply concerned about the best of mankind, and they saw the tanks rolling in. So you would focus on a current event such as that and say, "We need to know what's going on and you can provide two services: we'll give you $100 a month, but you can be serving your country." The very conspiratorial nature of the relationship appeals to a lot of people—all of a sudden, "I can play spy."

Believe it or not, *patriotism* played a key part. But you never knew if the information you were getting was accurate. But you always tried to evaluate it.

**

In 1956, the FBI "officially" launched COINTELPRO, an acronym for Counterintelligence Program, as a top secret plan to dismantle the CPUSA with manufactured disruptions involving counterfeit letters and ploys, pranks and diversions that would stir up controversy within the organization. (The term *COINTELPRO* is used to refer both to the program and the individual actions carried out under the aegis of the program.) As the authors of COINTELPRO put it, "The FBI's aim [was] to turn people away from fighting the enemy and toward fighting each other." And, as General Karl von Clausewitz has written, "The aim of all action in war is to disarm the enemy." Although COINTELPRO's initial target was the Communist party, eventually its tentacles reached out to many other groups, some as forbidding as the CP, such as the Ku Klux Klan, and some not so forbidding, such as the Socialist Workers party or the New Left, which never jeopardized America at all.

Former FBI Director Clarence Kelley says that between 1956 and 1971, "There were only 2,370 COINTELPRO actions taken by the FBI." *Only?* All of them involved illegal and unconstitutional invasions of public and private lives. There were 2,370 phony letters, pamphlets, posters, poems, cards, meetings, and phone calls causing disruptions of friendships, partnerships, and marriages.

But as Kelley has written, COINTELPRO did "neutralize" the Communist party in America.

FBI AGENT "X":
COINTELPRO, among the agents, was something to chuckle about. You'd get involved in it if it was aimed at a group that we seriously considered violence prone, and really violence-oriented, although you might say, Does the end justify the means? If a COINTELPRO absolutely defused a potential bombing, you'd say, "Gee, what a coup." Although the means were somewhat questionable, the end justified it. Certainly, in other areas—COINTELPROs used against individuals—you'd have to say, "My, God, how could they have done this?"

I would say that your normal FBI agent of stability—and I'll call myself that—did not want to see somebody destroyed merely because he may have expressed an opinion to the Left.

**

On May 2, 1957, Senator Joseph McCarthy died from acute hepatitis, perhaps brought on by alcoholism. For years afterward, it was rumored that he had been poisoned. In fact, two months after his death, an unidentified correspondent from Elkridge, Maryland, characterized by the Bureau as "anti-fascist" and "anti-Semitic," even wrote Hoover that his brother, also unidentified, but characterized by the Bureau as "mentally unbalanced," had been given a copy of McCarthy's death certificate. The correspondent told Hoover that the death certificate states that the cause of death was "unknown" because his form of hepatitis was not "infectious," and therefore had to be caused by "poison."

In December 1957, the Director wrote his preface to *Masters of Deceit*, which would be published the following year. He said: "Every citizen has a duty to learn more about the menace that threatens his future, his home, his children, the peace of the world." Naturally, he was speaking about Communism. A few paragraphs later he reminded readers that "ever since 1917, I have observed . . . Communist efforts to infiltrate and infect our American way of life."

In May 1958, Martin Luther King spoke against segregation to a large crowd of followers. Shortly thereafter, the Bureau opened a file on him, suspecting Communist efforts to infect the American way of life. A reference to King in Drew Pearson's file calls King a "saintly martyr in the eyes of an incredibly deceived American public nationwide."

ROY COHN:

Hoover regarded Martin Luther King as a totally immoral person. For instance, on a mission [to Oslo] for the United States—he represented us when he picked up his Nobel Prize—he had orgies of four, five, six women going on in his hotel room, in front of all the security people of the foreign country. Hoover thought that was a disgraceful thing to do. No matter what Martin Luther King's personal desires were, he should have kept them under control until he finished his mission.

Hoover was a very moral man—he was an early Jerry Falwell, okay? He was Boy Scouts, American flag. That was a sincere belief.

If you wanted to call him a patriotic nut and say that if anyone with a Boy Scout or Girl Scout uniform came walking along he'd go ape—yes. But any immoral act on his part? No. First of all, his mind was so taken with his work, his job, his *power,* there was no way he was going to put himself out on a limb and let himself be caught. I don't think he had any real interest in life outside of his job as director of the FBI. And he loved to spy, too. I mean, he was the leading spy in the world. He prided himself on the fact that he knew every little detail and who was who and what was what in government.

**

CARTHA DeLOACH:

I don't think there was any hatred on Mr. Hoover's part against Dr. King. I think, number one, he was attempting to carry out the instructions of Bobby Kennedy to find out the extent of Communist control over Dr. King and the civil rights movement.

The Soviets for many years had given the Communist party of the United States a million dollars or over in order to carry on. The first news we had of it was from two brothers—the Child brothers—one in New York and one in Chicago, who were members of the National Committee of the Communist party. They were selected by the Party and approved by the Soviet Union to pick up a million dollars and bring it back. The FBI met with these two brothers secretly and got them to work with *us.* They would check in with us—and we would mark the money and debrief them, and then they'd go ahead and turn this money over to the Communist party. They were double agents, and we knew from them that the Soviets thought a great deal of the Communists in the United States and were trying to foster them, nurture them, and build them up. The Child brothers were the ones who informed the FBI that a prominent lawyer in New York, Stanley Levison, who also reportedly had ties to the National Committee of the CP, was preparing Dr. King's speeches and handling some of his financial affairs. And let me honestly say at this time, that as far as I can recall—well, I know for a fact: Dr. King was *never* a member of the Communist party.

I was present when Mr. Hoover and Dr. King got together—I was the only other representative of the FBI there. It went on for an hour and seventeen minutes. Mr. Hoover cautioned Dr. King to be careful of his associates because of his leadership. He alluded to the extramarital affairs by saying, "You've got to be careful of your reputation, because of your position."

Dr. King had a press release which he had written *before* he came in there—and he went right out, pulled it out of his pocket, and read it to the reporters outside.

And we made no press release.

∗∗

Masters of Deceit was published in 1958 by Henry Holt and Company, a firm owned by the Director's good friend Clint Murchison. Hoover's readers learned that "Party influence is exerted through the communist device of thought control . . .''

According to former assistant director William Sullivan, who was one of six Bureau employees who "put together" *Masters of Deceit,* the book made the Director very rich, though most people thought he had given away his royalties to charity. Sullivan adds, "I also learned that he was annoyed when he found himself in a higher tax bracket because of those royalties."

Hoover, like so many writers, saved practically every single item pertaining to the book, even the advertisements.

By 1958, the Communist party was losing most of its membership. In his book, Hoover discusses Howard Fast's departure from the Party, and quotes him as saying, "I was filled with loathing and disgust."

CARTHA DeLOACH:
Eventually the whole Communist influence wore down and communism did not become a threat from the standpoint of physical violence, for the internal security standpoint. It was still a threat by being an embryo or a potential of Soviet espionage in the United States.

Our information on the Communist party was based on the informants and also on investigation—because the FBI does not rely on informants totally. You have to very carefully measure the information informants are giving you to determine whether it's real or manufactured.

We do that to them and they do that to us——it's a war that goes on constantly, and continues to go on. We have to do that even though we're a democratic society. We're forced to do that in the best interests of the United States.

CHAPTER SEVENTEEN

Matthiessen, Untermeyer, Hughes, and Wright

The FBI's file on the critic F. O. Matthiessen begins in 1935 when he "spoke at Santa Fe, New Mexico on behalf of Communism," and ends in 1950, the year he committed suicide—a suicide brought on by his appearance before a Massachusetts legislative committee investigating communism, and indirectly—or perhaps not so indirectly—by the FBI's incessant curiosity about his activities.

His suicide note read, "As a Christian and a Socialist believing in international peace, I find myself terribly oppressed by the present tensions."

At the time of his death, Matthiessen had been working on a critical study of Theodore Dreiser, which was itself grounds for skepticism as far as the FBI was concerned. A 1947 FBI report mentions a lecture in which Matthiessen told his class that "Dreiser had admitted his Communist Party membership" to him. Agents added that Matthiessen had also commented favorably on Dreiser's work, and thus the FBI put two and two together and concluded that Matthiessen was also a Communist.

The file is almost unparalleled for its sinister tone, with such sentences as, "He was absent from Harvard University during 1938 and

1939 for what purpose we cannot say" and "Subject known as a Liberal and whenever meetings are held at Harvard University in protest of the activities of the President of the United States, the subject is usually chief worker."

In 1942, Matthiessen was marked down for "promoting the sale" of Lillian Hellman's *Watch on the Rhine,* and in 1943 for writing an article in a "negro" publication called *The Guardian.* In 1947, Matthiessen's handwriting was analyzed by the FBI laboratory in Washington, the same year his nickname, "Matty," was described as his "alias."

In 1949, the year before his suicide, Matthiessen acknowledged, to a legislative committee, membership in twenty Communist-front groups, but said "he did not consider them Communist." The FBI, in a report, accuses him of "publicly defending the USSR Communist seizure of power in Czechoslovakia," and adds that he "upholds the viewpoint of the USSR and criticizes that of the USA" in any argument.

Another report states that "Matthiessen is an extremely emotional man, and a fanatic in pursuing the ideals to which he holds"; but the report writer doubts that Matthiessen is a Communist party member because his "emotional fiber" could not "submit to the discipline." But the taunts continued, and he was called "a fellow traveller, or worse."

According to a document in the file, on April 5, 1950, just one week after Matthiessen's suicide, Earle Parks, a Boston lawyer and the person appointed by the probate court to administer the estate, contacted the FBI to say he believed Matthiessen to be a Communist, and he offered to let the Bureau go through Matthiessen's papers and belongings. The FBI stated that it "was not interested in Professor Matthiessen's affairs"—a disingenuous remark if there ever was one.

In another report, on April 13, Mr. Parks is quoted as saying he believed that Matthiessen was only a "*Socialist,*" and not a Communist, after all. This report mentions that Mr. Parks did contact the Bureau, but plays it down, and stresses the fact that he later told newspaper reporters that the FBI had not sought access to any papers, and in fact, had absolutely no interest in Matthiessen's property at all. The report concludes that "in view of the publicity" over the matter, the FBI ought not to "take advantage of this opportunity." In other words, to avoid embarrassment the FBI decided not to meddle in his papers and affairs anymore, but to let F. O. Matthiessen rest in peace.

ANGUS CAMERON:
The way the Senate Internal Security Committee—the Jenner Committee—got at me wasn't as a publisher. They said they were investigating *education* in Boston, and they had a couple of guys from Harvard, and a couple of guys from MIT. And the way they got me in front of the committee in 1948 was because I was on the Board of the Sam Adams School in Boston.

But of course they were really trying to smear me as a *publisher.*

The Boston papers were very supportive of me. I issued a statement attacking the committee, and I remember the *Herald* ran a big headline—I mean a *big* one—saying "EX-HUB EDITOR BLASTS COMMITTEE," and they ran my statement on the front page.

F. O. Matthiessen is the one who got me in all the trouble! I was a member of the National Citizens Political Action Committee, and in the spring of 1945, Matty asked me to lunch and said that he was sure I would agree that Citizens PAC's relationship with the CIO ought to be allowed to last now that the war was ending. He said he had been asked to ask me if my name could be used as the candidate for the chairmanship of it. And I said, "Why me?" And he said, "You're the only person who would be acceptable to both the right wing of the left and the left wing of the left."

So I said, "Well, all right—I'll do it." And it developed into Progressive Citizens of America, and then it, in turn, developed into the Progressive party. And I continued to be chairman—so I was chairman of the Progressive party—and then later on, titular treasurer. And of course, I came in for a lot of criticism on that account, too—and when Wallace ran, in 1948.

In a way, I was never much of a joiner, but getting involved in the Progressive party—Matthiessen convinced me to do that—I ended up getting much more involved than I normally would have.

Matthiessen was a great guy. I think his suicide was a mixture of his depression over the development of the times—our society—and also over the death of his particular friend. I think that had something to do with it, too. But I think he was in a deep depression over politics. I saw him not too long before his death, a week or so before, and he seemed concerned but not depressed particularly.

I think his death was a mixture of personal and political. He was a wonderful man—and you know, he was really responsible for the *whole* development of American studies in this country. He didn't believe you could teach literature unless you taught it in the context of the times that produced it.

**

Despite poet and anthologist Louis Untermeyer's assertion that he "unequivocally" opposed the CP, J. Edgar Hoover chose to believe the "highly confidential source" who told him Untermeyer was definitely a member. His file, of course, goes back a long way—to 1921, when the FBI found his name on that letterhead of *The Liberator*.

Hoover put his name on the Security Index in 1951, after receiving the informant's report, writing in his file that "it is to be noted that Untermeyer is currently appearing on the television show 'What's My Line?' " Eventually the producers of that highly popular panel program, which also starred Random House publisher Bennett Cerf, dropped Untermeyer from the cast, telling him, according to Arthur

Miller's *TimeBends,* "The problem is that we know you've never had any left connections, so you have nothing to confess to, but they're not going to believe that. So it's going to seem that you're refusing to be a good American."

Miller also writes that "Louis didn't leave his apartment for almost a year and a half. An overwhelming and paralyzing fear had risen in him. More than a political fear, it was really that he had witnessed the tenuousness of human connection and it had left him in terror. He had always loved a lot and been loved, especially on this tv program where his quips were appreciated and suddenly he had been thrown in the street, abolished."

In 1955, Hoover removed Untermeyer's name from the Security Index, but the harm had already been done, of course. In removing his name, the Bureau ordered "that he was not to be considered for any interviews in view of his age, his prominence in the literary field, and the fact that although he is retired, he continues to write and occasionally goes on a lecture tour." In 1959, however, his name was placed on the Communist Index, but removed a few months later.

Arthur Miller writes that in the fifties "the reassurances of the familiar past had suddenly been pulled out from under" Untermeyer, adding that "the question is whether there ever were such reassurances."

The FBI had begun its file on poet Langston Hughes in 1925. A decade later, it opened a file on another prominent black writer—Richard Wright. Hoover's FBI had a fixation about black writers, of course, and any individual or group that expressed criticism of segregation or called for equal rights was suspect. Although both Hughes and Wright had turned toward communism in the 1930s, to differing degrees, because the CP seemed to be a "friend of the Negro," both would later become disenchanted. To the FBI, however, the embryonic civil rights movement was simply a Communist plot; the Bureau remained blind to the causes and widespread nature of blacks' discontent. Consequently, it sought to pin a Red label on anyone who demanded equal rights for blacks, and all politically active blacks were considered security threats.

In 1938, the FBI recorded that Langston Hughes "supported verdict in Soviet purge trials" and that "Hughes told of the heroic work of the many Negroes from the United States in Spain's fight against General Franco." Also worthy of concern was an informant's assertion that Hughes "was suggested as a candidate in 1936 and 1938 on the Communist Party election ticket, [but] was turned down . . . because he was considered more valuable as a writer and lecturer.''

In 1941, the FBI had decided that Hughes's poem ''Goodbye Christ'' was seditious, and two years later the FBI reported that Hughes ''stated he is a believer in the Russian Soviet form of government and thereby admitted being a Communist,'' which put him on the Security Index, even though an informant told an agent that although Hughes is ''a radical,'' he was ''not a member of the Communist Party.'' But Hughes was black, and was considered subversive simply because of the color of his skin.

In 1953, he told the Permanent Senate Subcommittee on Investigations, or McCarthy Committee, that he had become disillusioned with the Soviet Union. Nonetheless, the FBI still considered him so subversive that in 1960 he was used in a COINTELPRO that sought to exploit a financial problem a Chicago Afro-American organization was having; the FBI wrote phony letters to a radical newspaper in the name of the Afro-American group, demanding a financial accounting of a meeting ''when Mr. Hughes spoke for Negro History week.''

That same year, another poem, ''One More S in the USA,'' joined ''Goodbye Christ'' as an FBI annoyance. (In 1947, Hoover had cited ''Goodbye Christ'' in a speech, calling it a ''sacrilegious poem''; later when that speech was to be included in a book, Hughes would not give permission for his poem to be included. Hoover blamed the publisher and noted, ''Make certain we furnish this outfit no more material for publication. They are too squeamish about offending the Commies.'')

When Langston Hughes died in 1967, J. Edgar Hoover still believed ''most of his work reflects his Communist persuasions.'' He always referred to Hughes as ''a colored Communist.''

LANGSTON HUGHES:
    . . . My answer to your request is that I do not grant permission for the use of the poem GOODBYE CHRIST in the book being published by the Abington Cokesbury Press. . . . The poem was written about twenty years ago, is not in any of my own books, and because it was widely misunderstood when it first appeared—irony and satire being difficult to use in poetry, it seems—I withdrew the poem from circulation . . .
    —*From a letter in his file to the publisher of J. Edgar Hoover's speech; 1948*

America's greatest and most democratic book of poems, Walt Whitman's LEAVES OF GRASS, has on occasion in some American communities in the past been banned on the grounds of obscenity. Certainly my poem GOODBYE CHRIST, is no reflection on Christ, but rather a reflection on those who use or misuse Christ for material reasons. . . . The Un-American Committee [*sic*], George Sokolsky . . . have stated that I have belonged to many subversive organizations. I am curious to know what they are. I am also curious to know why, if that be true, the FBI has not locked me up? . . .

—*From a personal statement in his file; undated*

**

AMIRI BARAKA:

When Langston would arrive to speak, there would be pickets in front. One time there was this religious nut and all these religious people out there saying that he was the Anti-Christ. When we tried to get him a hotel room, they wouldn't check him in. And then they would put out headlines, " RED POET IN TOWN."

So there was a constant harassment of Langston until they got him to submit in the McCarthy hearings. They forced him to testify—and the questioning was all around "Goodbye Christ" and another poem called "Good Morning Revolution." They made him cop out. He had to go before them and actually say he was sorry he wrote that poem. And the poem says, "Goodbye Christ," you know, "get out of here. You've been using me all these years, I'm looking for somebody else. I ain't looking for you, Christ." It's a whole put-down of Jesus Christ.

Langston submitted. He said, I'm sorry I wrote that poem. I won't do it again, but the reason I did it is because America was a bad place then but it's a good place now. And it's getting better. And he had to say that. Now *that* broke him in spirit.

But for a lot of us—and myself definitely—that was something they never should have done. That was the evilist shit in the world. So when Langston saw a group of young poets coming up who had, you know, some kind of militancy and a spirit about them, then he was very, very pleased. You know he sort of adopted us in the sixties. It gave him the spirit to come back. And you'll find his last book of poems is much, much stronger, much more poignant. Because what the FBI and the committee was trying to do was cut his balls off. That's really what they wanted to do.

**

The FBI began its 181-page file on Richard Wright, the author of such books as *Uncle Tom's Children, Native Son,* and *Black Boy,* in 1935, when he worked on the Federal Writers Project in Chicago, although the Bureau later reported that he had been a Communist party member since 1932.

The Bureau's distrust of Wright, who they reported was a Communist party member until 1942 (he says he left in 1940) reflects its distrust of blacks, already alluded to, and further elucidates Hoover's strong antiblack prejudices, which culminated in the formation of the COINTELPROs against some blacks that began in 1956 and did not end until 1971.

In 1937, Wright came to New York to become an editor of the Communist *Daily Worker,* and the FBI had informants spying on him when he was employed by the New York Federal Writers Project from 1938 to 1939. In 1941, the Bureau reported that his *Twelve Million Black Voices* "appeared to be seditious," and began an "immediate investigation," which resulted in his being a candidate for the Security Index.

In 1944, the FBI reported that he now believed that Communists were "narrow-minded, bigoted, intolerant and frightened by new ideas which don't fit into their own." Hoover decided to take advantage of these remarks, and recommended that the special agent in New York attempt a "discreet" interview, possibly to attempt to recruit him as an informant, warning him that Wright's anticommunism was probably not like theirs, but rather more along the lines that the Communists were not revolutionary enough, especially regarding race relations. As another report put it, "His interest in the problem of the Negro has become almost an obsession." In fact, the following year, in 1945, Hoover referred to Wright's "militant attitude toward the Negro problem" and recommended that his name remain on the Security Index.

There is no indication in the file whether any "discreet" interview ever took place in New York. Two years later, in 1947, the FBI recorded that Wright had moved to Paris.

The Bureau (and the CIA) continued to follow him abroad, and became uncomfortable because "wittingly or not [Wright] has been serving Communist Party ends" by contributing to left-wing French publications. Four years later, in 1951, the FBI was still receiving reports that Wright was participating in "Communist fronts" overseas, and that, in fact, he was "active in the French Communist Party."

For the rest of the fifties, Wright was periodically interviewed by the U. S. consul in Paris, and asked the same questions over and over again. In 1954, he told the consul "he could not fix the exact time of his joining the Communist Party" because "their recruiting is of such a nature" that exact membership dates are not possible. In 1958, after four more years of harassment, he told the U. S. consul he had been a member from 1932 to 1942.

In 1960, the year of his death, he was still being listed as a "possible subversive among US personnel in France."

In a 1956 letter to Wright, Kay Boyle writes, "There is a story, a rumor, about you that is going about . . . that you are known to be working with the State Department, or the FBI, I don't know which, and that you give information about other Americans in order to keep your own passport and be able to travel. . . ." Boyle later said she had heard the rumor that he ''was put out of the way by the government.''

Was Wright an informant? Could he have been murdered by ''the government''? And if so, for what reason, especially if he was ''working'' for the government?

There is information in a 1956 Department of State document that is part of Wright's FBI file that indicates he did cooperate voluntarily to some extent with officials. A confidential memo declassified in 1986 states: ''On his own initiative, Mr. Wright called at the Embassy to express certain concern over the leftist tendencies of the Executive Committee for the Congress [the First Congress of the Présence Africaine—an organization composed of scholars of the Negro world]. He believed the members of the committee were liberal thinkers and he thought there was a distinct danger that the Communists might exploit the congress to their own ends. Many members of the Présence Africaine, he said, were in search of an ideal they could not obtain. . . . To counteract such a tendency, Mr. Wright wondered if the embassy could assist him in suggesting possible American negro delegates who are relatively well known for their cultural achievements and who could combat the leftist tendencies. . . .''

Wright's suggestions to the embassy for members of the congress are hardly right-wingers, however: Langston Hughes, Chester Himes, and Ralph Ellison. It may have been that Wright was simply trying to get the government off his back.

Wright biographer Addison Gayle writes that ''the temptation to draw conclusions in line with those who believe the FBI and the CIA were directly involved in Wright's sudden death are great. To do so, however, based upon the facts of the documents would be wrong. . . . What I found was a pattern of harassment by agencies of the U.S. government, resembling at times, a personal vendetta more so than an intelligence-gathering investigation. I discovered that the government was guilty of producing anxiety and stressful situations, which would have produced severe hypertension in most men, let alone one so sensitive as Wright. . . . In retrospect, this may well have been a crime of the magnitude of assassination. . . .''

CARTHA DeLOACH:
I think it could be highly exaggerated, that Wright was assassinated. I have never heard, certainly not during my time, that anyone was assassinated by the FBI.

Mr. Hoover had his many faults, there's no doubt about that, but he was a strict disciple of the law. He was a very, very religious person—and he was raised in the Presbyterian Church, and almost became a minister before he went into law school.

**

AMIRI BARAKA:

Addison Gayle, who's a black literary critic, stopped short of saying that the FBI had actually murdered Wright. But I don't see any reason to rule that out. Wright's whole life was peculiar—you understand that. Early Richard Wright—*Uncle Tom's Children*—you find that it's different from those things that happened after *Native Son*. After *Native Son* you see his consciousness goes through a real weird shift.

He came to Paris and started hanging around with Gertrude Stein and Jean-Paul Sartre—and he changes a lot. And he no longer is the same kind of very relentless revolutionary voice of the early days, at least of *Uncle Tom's Children*.

CHAPTER EIGHTEEN

Adams, Shapiro, and Williams

The FBI's history with poets was long (starting with Ezra Pound in 1911) but not beautiful: in 1941, when an unidentified friend sent the Director a recording by actor Ronald Colman of Edna St. Vincent Millay's "Poem and Prayer for an Invading Army," Hoover thanked his friend for the gift—"I will count it among my treasures"—and then because Millay had been called a Communist he sent the gift to the FBI crime laboratory. Hoover, when he picked up poetry at all, read Robert V. Service and Edgar Guest.

In 1944, (Harold) Witter Bynner, whose file was begun in 1937 when his name was found on the letterhead for the American Committee for the Defense of Trotsky, was caught in the FBI's net of suspicion because he attended a party with nuclear physicist Robert Oppenheimer, the head of the Manhattan Project's Los Alamos, New Mexico lab, who was declared a security risk in 1953 because of his left-wing associations. Edgar Lee Masters was indexed in 1938 because he wrote, "I am for Republican Spain, of course," in the *Daily Worker*. His eleven-page file contains five pages that are still considered too secret to release. One undated reference indicates that the

Bureau did not like the fact that Mike Gold, a writer best known for his column, "Change the World," in the *Daily Worker,* said that the Red Scare was even spreading to Lewiston, Illinois—a town Gold said was featured in Masters's *Spoon River Anthology.* Masters's Spoon River is, of course, fictitious, and Gold uses Lewiston (where Masters did live during his childhood) as a metaphor in the same way that Masters uses Spoon River as a metaphor for Middle America. But the FBI did not understand this. Louis Zukofsky, a distinguished but underrecognized American poet, came to the attention of the FBI after an anonymous letter writer described him as a "Communist writer" in 1935. In 1951, Whittaker Chambers told the FBI that he had personally recruited Zukofsky for membership in the CP, although he "only stayed one month." The Bureau also opened a file on Marianne Moore in 1935 after receiving an anonymous tip in "a plain envelope" that she was a Communist. In 1949, agents evaluated her poems, reporting that their reading "failed to indicate anything on [Moore's] political sympathies." Robinson Jeffers, who disassociated himself, along with Wallace Stevens, from the National Institute of Arts and Letters' 1948 letter condemning HUAC, was also discovered by the FBI in 1935 when it noticed he was a contributor to *Pacific Weekly,* a forerunner of *People's World,* the West Coast Communist newspaper. But as he turned more and more to the right, the Bureau began referring to him as a "loyal American," and in one report, "a definitely loyal American."

In 1936, the position of Consultant in Poetry at the Library of Congress was established, and since that time there have been thirty-one American poets who held the post, either for one or two terms. Most were routinely investigated because the post is a government one, although not all were aware they were examined. For instance, Robert Penn Warren, the third consultant (1944–1945) said shortly before he died in 1989 that he "was never aware of any FBI interest in him at all." Louise Bogan, the fourth consultant, has an FBI file that was begun in 1937, but it does not contain any mention of or any investigation into her government post. And Louis Untermeyer, in the long run, managed to outfox Hoover. Despite his past, he was appointed a consultant in 1961, proving that Hoover didn't destroy him in quite the way he wanted to.

But here is how three poets who were investigated fared:

Léonie Adams was the FBI's first woman writer. Her 128-page file was begun in 1921 after she published some poems in *The Liberator.* No new data was added to her file until 1932, when the FBI learned "she was affiliated with the League of Professional Groups for Foster and Ford."

She was appointed Consultant in Poetry in 1948, and held this position for one year, as did most appointees, with the exception of the first one in 1937, who held the job for four years, and the appointees after 1950, who held the job for two years.

What is exceptional about Adams's appointment is that an FBI loyalty investigation was requested by the Civil Service Commission in 1949, *after* she was already on the job. The FBI instructed its agents to handle the investigation "in a most discreet and circumspect fashion," because new information had been found to link the poet with the Communist party. This "new" information consisted of the Foster and Ford connection, and the poems that had been published in *The Liberator*.

In the course of this new investigation, agents could find no one who questioned Adams's loyalty. In fact, most people told them "she believes the Communist movement has stifled free thinking and affected the poetic movement in Russia."

Eventually agents discovered that Adams was "a descendent of President Adams," and then, just as her one-year term as poetry consultant was ending, reported "she had terminated employment prior to a decision on loyalty." In other words, the FBI made it appear that Adams had quit her job because she was not cleared.

In 1940, an FBI agent reported that poet Karl Shapiro, the editor of *Poetry* magazine from 1950 to 1956, and *Prairie Schooner* from 1956 to 1966, "produced an edition of *The Exiles Anthology*" which had a three-paragraph introduction that "may be of interest to the Bureau."

It is probable that these are the lines in the anthology that "interested" the agent who read them: "For one the poet is comfortably a policeman. He polices with some Bohemian credulity the criminal acts of the politicos in power. Yet owing to the quality of his illegal imagination, he defies the civil savants and accepts no dictation." The last section contained this line as well: "Since we are not exiles from this planet of disorder, our participation amid its ruins is one of pamphleteering for the valid activities of a demilitarized world."

Shapiro says, "I don't remember the book and can't imagine what 'produced' is supposed to signify. It may mean 'reviewed' or 'had it reviewed' in *Poetry* magazine." But the latter cannot be the case, since Shapiro didn't take over the editorship there until 1950.

From 1945 until 1966, the FBI cited Shapiro, who one informant said was "as red and radical and they come," for participation in over twenty-five activities believed to be seditious.

Shapiro was Consultant in Poetry at the Library of Congress from 1946 to 1947, but the inquiry is not included in the file (43 pages out of his 117-page file are still classified, so his investigation may be still secret for some reason.) Shapiro recalls that "at my first meeting with the Librarian of Congress, Luther Evans, he made a personal and obscene remark about Communists. I came in and the first thing he said to me was 'Shapiro, we don't want any Communists or cocksuckers in this library.' I almost fainted."

Shapiro also says that during his term, he was asked to persuade Ezra Pound to participate in a Library of Congress recording program, "but I wasn't about to do that. The other poets were going over to St. Elizabeth's all the time—Robert Lowell was practically an inmate over there. But I wouldn't do it. When Pound was finally asked if he would record, he said no, he wouldn't do that while he was in jail." Shapiro adds that "in 1948 I was the only dissenter from the Bollingen Prize to Pound, except Paul Green, who abstained. Eliot, Auden, Tate, Lowell—all voted the prize to Pound. A passel of fascists."

In 1965, the Bureau reported that Shapiro participated in a Vietnam protest teach-in at the University of Nebraska, and in 1966 that he demonstrated against apartheid. In the report on the latter, the agent observed that "most of the marchers were a motley group, many dirty-appearing and sporting beards. One had a black motorcycle jacket and blue jeans and another carried a guitar and sang most of the march." The agent also noted that "one of the group was heard to state that at 'ten a.m. Shapiro asked what the march was about. He was reminded he was to speak this afternoon. He had somehow forgot.' "

Shapiro, who was a professor of English at the University of Nebraska from 1955 to 1966, says "I don't know who it was who spied on me and reported my presence. The U of Nebraska wasn't exactly Berkeley. When I first came there, the Communists invaded Hungary. And I was being interviewed by the local paper and I complained about the apathy of the students and why they didn't protest or do something about it. So the students hung a sign on my door, 'Shapiro—go back to Hungary.' I didn't have a side—I was against the whole apathy, and then in the sixties, I was against the vandalism. During the sixties, I was considered a right-wing dissident because I didn't like what the rioters were doing, even though I had invited Allen Ginsberg to come on the Nebraska campus. He turned the town upside down! And I helped him do that. But I can't remember speaking at a big rally. It's possible, but I don't remember that they asked me. I wrote a novel, and the way I re-created it was I went home and watched the rally on my TV! I couldn't get through the crowds.''

KARL SHAPIRO:

I'm delighted to have the FBI reports on my waywardness. It's a rather pitiable affair, what there is of it. I imagine the good stuff is what they blacked out.

But it never affected my career and I was never aware of any surveillance. Nobody ever obstructed my getting jobs at any university, or lectures, or anything. And the government sent me abroad to lecture, so I figured they didn't consider me an enemy of the government. The State Department sent me on a couple of wonderful trips. In 1955 they sent me to Ireland, Italy, and India—all countries beginning with *i*. I was supposed to go to Israel, but the plane couldn't land in Israel because it was going to land in Beirut. But anyway, I spent most of the time in India lecturing on Walt Whitman. I carried around a big photograph of Whitman, which was part of the lecture. I finally got tired of carrying it around and pushed it off a train into a jungle in India!

My only encounter with FBI agents was after I got my first teaching job at Johns Hopkins in 1947. Two agents came to see me about a girlfriend of mine that I had gone to Tahiti with, in 1936. They were checking on her because she was a major in the WAC, and she was up for another promotion. The agent's question to me was, "This woman goes away every summer. What does she do with her furniture, because she doesn't have any other place to live?" Well, she and her sister lived together and they would store their furniture in friends' basements. The FBI wanted to know *my* relationship with her—Tahiti was no hotbed of Communists! Except that the time we were there, the Spanish Civil War broke out.

I have a vague recollection that the FBI came some other times, too. But I had such unfriendly feelings about it. I would never have told them anything. The only other thing—this might have turned up in their files—there was a man who came to see me after the Bolligen Prize. But I don't think that had anything to do with the FBI. The *Saturday Review of Literature* sent a man down to see me to write an exposé of fascism in Capitol Hill. And I refused to do it because that isn't the way it was, or at least, that isn't the way I saw it.

When I was in Australia, in 1942, '43, and '44, off and on, my friends were writers, and a lot of them were Party members. They belonged to the Australian Writers Federation, and I would go to meetings—and I was in an American uniform. A lot of this stuff was real pro-Marxist stuff, and I'd sit up on the stage with them. So I'm quite sure that my career in the army is colored by my association with them.

But I don't think they thought I was of any importance.

I was never active in any direct way. I signed petitions and things like that. I even satirized a lot of the things they were doing. At the John Reed Club they asked me to give a lecture one time and I defended James Branch Cabell—it was sort of a satire—and I got attacked viciously for this insult.

I went to all sorts of meetings, but I don't think I ever was an officer mostly because I have an aversion to committee work. But I would certainly attend meetings and rallies. This was all in Baltimore, which was pretty radicalized in those days. Huge strikes at Bethlehem Steel. And I remember a Nazi battleship came in to Baltimore, and we were all outraged because the society people were entertaining the Nazi officers—and, in fact, if I have this right, I think the Bethlehem Steel workers had a terrific strike going on partly against this ship being in the harbor.

In the army I worked on a spy case, which I think was just an exercise. I was supposed to write a report about a German woman who lived in Manhattan whose telephone was tapped, and I was supposed to find out whether she was working for the Nazis. And I never got anywhere with that.

But the other thing I remember doing was writing—helping Selden Rodman with a poetry anthology called *War and the Poet,* which was edited by Rodman and Richard Eberhart. Our department—in the army—was called Foreign Nationalities—we would get all the foreign newspapers and translate them and then brief them and send the briefs to the State Department. When I got out of the army, my chief wanted me to stay in because they were going to become part of the CIA. I could have been in the CIA!

**

The 166-page file of poet and physician William Carlos Williams was begun in 1930 when a letter from him appeared in *New Masses.* Part of the letter reads: "I like the John Reed number. Here's money. Send me more. The only thing is, what the hell? I feel in a false position. How can I be a Communist, being what I am. Poetry is the thing which has the hardest hold on me in my daily experiences. But I cannot, without an impossible wrench of my understanding, turn it into a force directed toward one end, Vote the Communist Ticket, or work for the world revolution."

The FBI, believing that the impossible could become the possible, kept alert to Dr. Williams's "wrenches of understanding," reporting that he "wrote for the Partisan Review during the period of its domination by the Communist Party," and that he signed the 1937 Golden Book of American Friendship with the Soviet Union, as well as a statement the following year, in 1938, calling for greater cooperation with Russia.

In addition, the FBI reported that "again, in 1939, he signed an open letter calling for closer cooperation with Stalin Russia," and that he also urged support of the Federal Arts Project, which was an acceptable endorsement until it became tainted when the *Daily Worker* looked favorably upon it.

Since 1921 the FBI knew that one of the Communist party's rules for members was "don't carry or keep with you names and addresses, except in good code." On September 2, 1942, an FBI memorandum recommended that William Carlos Williams be temporarily watched because an informant had turned in "seventeen sheets bearing typewriting of a suspicious nature." An agent believed that some of Williams's poems might be a clandestine code, commenting that "they appear to have been written by a person who is very queer or possibly a mental case.'' In ordering an investigation of the poet, the Bureau advised that it should be "conducted in such a manner as to avoid embarrassment for the informant," probably an employee in Dr. Williams's medical offices.

It took five months for the FBI to determine that William Carlos Williams, "a sort of absent minded professor type but certainly 100% American," uses "an 'expressionistic' style which might be interpreted as being 'code.' ''

In the course of this investigation, the Bureau also learned that although Williams believed that Ezra Pound was "ga-ga," he "admired his verse as 'some of the loveliest of our century.' ''

In 1943, when Kay Boyle was interviewed by the FBI about Pound, she had mentioned that Williams "was an old friend of Pound's," and was "absolutely loyal"; but her words did not change Hoover's assessment, and the FBI remained suspicious of Williams—a suspicion which eventually had a damaging effect on his career.

In 1951, he was investigated in connection with his appointment as a Consultant in Poetry at the Library of Congress, a position he never actually held.

After an announcement of the appointment was made, the FBI received a report that some of his poems contained "the very voice of Communism." Lines from a 1948 poem, "Russia" were cited: "O Russia, Russians! Come with me into / my dream and let us be lovers . . . / These I dedicate now to you . . . I hold back nothing, / I lay my spirit at your feet . . . / Among many others, undistinguished, / of no moment—I am the background / upon which you will build your empire.''

Shortly afterward, the FBI leaked derogatory information to columnist Fulton Lewis, Jr., who accused Williams of "association with some of the smelly outfits that have been peddling Moscow propaganda in the U.S. for 25 years . . .''

As the FBI's investigation continued, agents interviewed all of the poet's associates, and even used a wide array of informants from the departments of State, Navy, and Air Force.

Agents interviewed poet Richard Eberhart because he "was acquainted" with Dr. Williams when he was a "visiting poet at Harvard around Nineteen Fifty." According to a report in the file, Eberhart told agents that he had "no reason whatever to question [Williams's] loyalty," and that he "believes him to be an outstanding American and extremely pro-American." Eberhart also told the FBI it was possible that Williams's writings were "misinterpreted" because he is a "free-thinker, who writes with an open mind and heart on any subject." (Indeed, Williams's poem "Russia" is quite critical of the Soviets.)

In the end, the FBI succeeded in preventing his appointment, although many other reasons, including ill health, were given for his failure to be selected. Indeed, one memo in the file reports, "Dr. Williams had recently suffered several heart attacks [and] the family was apprehensive about another." The memo concludes that "the investigation could not be continued while he was in poor health," although Dr. Williams later told Luther Evans, the Librarian of Congress: "Who's sick?"

In 1953, the *Washington Star* reported "the appointment revolves around clean bills of health, both political and physical." Dr. Williams himself said in a 1954 interview: "I don't know a thing. What did they find? They never did give me any indication. I received a communication from the FBI to be fingerprinted and replied to all sorts of preliminary inquiries. Then I wasn't even given the courtesy of a reply. For heaven's sake, what kind of country is this?"

This is the kind of country America was at that time: The file contains a document confirming that the delay and subsequent denial of the appointment had absolutely nothing to do with the poet's health. According to a November 22, 1954, report sent directly to J. Edgar Hoover: "APPLICANT WAS NOT APPOINTED BECAUSE OF UNFAVORABLE REPORT."

KAY BOYLE:
I first met William Carlos Williams in 1921. I was a secretary at *Broom Magazine,* and every Thursday afternoon the editor would have a tea—I was very young then, and I'd just pass the cakes and tea. Three East Ninth Street. A sacred address in my mind. John Dos Passos used to come. Waldo Frank. I met everybody there. There was also a wonderful woman from the *New Masses*—I can't remember her name.

It's simply unbelievable about William Carlos Williams—those notes that the FBI found—well, maybe as he worked in a hospital, someone got into his desk. I don't understand it. It's incredible.

I saw William Carlos Williams just a few months before he died. No, it was longer than that. I drove over with a friend to Rutherford to see him. A place that I had been so many times as a young woman. And he opened the door, and the tears were coming down his cheeks, and his wife said to me, "It's the first time he's opened the door in months—because an old friend was coming, and he had to do it himself." He had I don't know how many strokes. And he said—it was absolutely pathetic—he said,"I can read the separate words in a newspaper, but I can't put them together to make a sentence. I don't understand the sentence. I can say this word and I know that word, but it doesn't make any sense." Imagine that happening to a writer and a reader.

**

FBI AGENT "X":

Can this happen again? That we're concerned about codes and code books? I'll tell you, I'm not clairvoyant. That's one thing I'm not. Now, could it ever happen again? I don't know and I don't even know if it was true *then*.

But I don't read it as censorship. In the case of William Carlos Williams, this was just something that they found and they wanted the laboratory to go through it. If there's reasonable suspicion, we're concerned. They could be sending it to the laboratory for fingerprints, too. You really don't know. Suppose they were secret writings, or something like that? Or invisible ink?

**

RICHARD EBERHART:

I note that my name is misspelled in the FBI account. It was my first call from the FBI, and my only one. I remember it vividly. The agent was not nervous, neither was I. I think the agent only talked about Williams—of course memory is faulty that far back. I don't think the agent knew Williams; he was just doing his job. I think the visit was right after lunch. He stayed probably half an hour, not longer than an hour. The FBI never later contacted me about anybody else. I can't recall whether the agent took notes—I should think not, he was just taking in what was said. He was civil and courteous and it would probably not have been his style to scribble notes, but I may be wrong. He was alone.

The idea that Bill Williams would be considered "un-American" seemed to me so wrong that I suppose I was prejudiced against the agent but did not show it. I probably told him to go and read all of Williams's poetry, a lot, which I guess he had not done, and which I suggested in this stanza from a poem entitled "Vignettes," included in *The Long Reach,* my new and uncollected poems 1948–1984. It goes

> In 1952 I was sitting in my office, in Seattle,
> When in came the F.B.I., truculent and bristling.
> Did I know a poet named William Carlos Williams?
> He had written a subversive poem called "The Pink Church"
> in which he called the Russians commrades. Weren't they?
> We were shoulder to shoulder in the war. I said he was
> As good an American as they were or I was,
> Investigate America, go back and read his poetry.

**

KARL SHAPIRO:

I was very surprised by the controversy over Williams, and never really got to the bottom of it.

He had very strange political opinions—he was an extremist—but it was hard to know which side he was extreme at.

His career goes so far back that he first sympathized with the Russian

Revolution and all that—like all the intellectuals did in the twenties. He was always on the side of the underdog and against whatever government was in power. And anyway, he made himself unpopular when he was appointed to the poetry consultantship—I guess the FBI had so many things Williams had written that they either didn't understand or felt suspicious of him that I think they said, This guy is not a good risk.

**

ALLEN GINSBERG:

You know, Williams was basically such an upstanding Americanist—like Grant Woods. He was so much a part of the American landscape that was America, that *is* America. The idea of the FBI investigating him makes them very un-American.

It's sheer paranoia—"Williams uses expressionistic style which might be interpreted as being a code"! "The expressionistic style," or whatever the FBI called it: that sounds like a terrible buzzword. Did they mean the literary movement of expressionism or did they mean he was expressing himself by self-expression that bohemians do? It's used in the most loose terms, like a very amateur way of saying he was writing poetry. "Oh, gee, I wish I were a poet, I could *express* myself."

It would take extreme paranoia for them not to know he was a famous poet expressing himself and that he used a notational style based on American speech. They would have to ignore all of his actual published writing not to realize that what he was doing was a famous, celebrated attempt to notate the language of Paterson, New Jersey, or the hospital.

Williams wrote a few poems about a marriage between Russia and America. And they're such obviously imaginative, charming little poems—a poet's view of Russian people and American people getting married and going to the circus. And to take that seriously and think that was subversive—it's parallel to the mentality of the Russian "bureaucracy," it's the same kind of party-hack-bureaucratic-unimaginative literalism that doesn't understand anything. It's obviously a waste of taxpayer's money, but it's also an intrusion of the government on literary and private life that if it were known at the time would have been scandalous.

The FBI's overt, announced objective is against the Soviet-octopus-enemy. Of course, they had real good reasons to be scared of it in the thirties.

Williams is such a completely different kettle of fish—not left wing exactly: middle class. Solid. Real small-town USA physician. Family doctor.

CHAPTER NINETEEN

Trilling, Agee, Capote, Gardner, and Miller

Lionel Trilling is one of the twentieth century's most distinguished literary critics, the author of a study of Matthew Arnold in 1939, a study of E. M. Forster in 1943, a collection of essays, *The Liberal Imagination,* in 1950, followed by five other essay collections, as well as a novel about the social and political conflicts of the thirties and forties, The *Middle of the Journey.* In 1949, someone in the Bureau wrote "not merely gossip," on the margin of a report stating that this novel "contains the answer to a key problem of the current espionage cause celebre," referring to Chambers and Hiss, and that "among intellectual circles" it is believed that Lionel Trilling "must have had an intensely clairvoyant imagination." Thus did the FBI, for the first time, turn to a novel for help in solving a case.

Diana Trilling says that the handwritten words "not merely gossip" on the report "could mean one of two things. Either that it's not merely gossip that this book has a key to the case, or the fact that it is thought to be very important is not merely gossip. In other words, it's taking it seriously in that regard."

Indeed, another 1949 report, entitled "Jay David Whittaker Chambers, Perjury; Espionage," asks whether "the information contained in the novel could possibly be of use to Hiss and his attorneys." The report concludes that the novel could not aid Hiss, "although there is some similarity to Chambers' activities after he had broken from the Communist Party in 1938."

The report also mentions that "Mr. Trilling was told of rumors that the FBI had sent a couple of agents to ask him about the characters in this book and Trilling had stated that he read something somewhere to that effect in the newspapers and he understood that they were reading this book assiduously."

The report also quotes Trilling as saying that "he had known Chambers and that portions of his book were written on the basis of his knowledge of Chambers' background." It is not clear from the report, which was sent to Hoover from the New York office, whether the FBI actually interviewed Trilling or got its information from an article that appeared in the New York *Herald Tribune,* which is also mentioned in the report. In any case, the report seems purposely evasive on the subject of an actual interview, so that J. Edgar Hoover could interpret it either way. Diana Trilling at first thought she remembered the FBI questioning her husband about the case, but then remembered that "it was not the FBI. It was Hiss's lawyers" who had interviewed him.

The file includes a copy of a report of the "background and personal history" of Chambers in which he speaks of his "first two years at Columbia" University when he was "convinced" that his "mission in life was to be a poet." He mentions that "through my literary efforts I met a number of other students, including "Trilling, who is now an English professor at Columbia."

Sidney Hook writes in his autobiography that Chambers asked Lionel Trilling to be a letter drop for him; it is not mentioned in the file. Diana Trilling says that Whittaker Chambers came to *her,* and not to her husband, and that she told him, "I'll have to talk about this with Lionel." But, she adds, "I had no intention of receiving mail, but I was scared to say I don't want to do it. It's very complicated and will be in my new book, but by the time Whittaker Chambers called me for my decision, we had broken with the Communists—all in the next forty-eight hours. It was a very, very strange period. So Whittaker said 'I know your answer,' and I said, 'I would like to tell you my reason,' and what I wanted to tell him was I didn't want to betray my country. He thought it was because I was mad at the Communist party."

In 1950, the FBI began its "discreet" investigation of Communist infiltration into the Authors League, and a memo about the investigation is in Trilling's fifty-seven-page file, although his name is nowhere on the document. Mrs. Trilling doesn't remember her husband being investigated about the Authors League at all. A newspaper article from the New York *Compass* about the Authors League statement that the Supreme Court's refusal to review the case of the Hollywood Ten would generate widespread censorship is also in the file because Lionel Trilling's name appears in the article as a member of the Authors League "council," along with that of Lillian Hellman, Elmer Rice, Rex Stout, and John Hersey. However, Diana Trilling says she doesn't have any recollection of her husband being on that council, although he was a member of the Authors League. "He wasn't as famous as those people on the council," she says, "and *The Liberal Imagination,* which would make him famous, wasn't published until that year."

Two years later, in 1952, another document involving a Communist security matter entered the file, and it quotes from the *Daily Worker*'s 1947 review of *The Middle of the Journey*: "a cold calculated slander of the Communist party . . . every detail, every incident is put into exactly the right focus to leave the reader with one single impression— and that is that the Communist party in the United States is an 'innocent front' for another sinister force."

"Well, it's true," Mrs. Trilling says.

The following year, in 1953, still another Internal Security report that does not list Lionel Trilling's name anywhere was put in his file, and two years later, in 1955, the FBI reports that Trilling, along with Reinhold Niebuhr, Norman Thomas, and James T. Farrell, signed a telegram to President Eisenhower protesting the deportation of an Indonesian official.

In 1958, according to Trilling's file, the FBI set up a COINTELPRO against the Communist party, using for the first and possibly only time a group of America's preeminent writers. In an effort to stir up trouble, the Bureau used, in an unauthorized manner, a perfectly legitimate open letter than had been published in a newspaper. The FBI's actual plans are not made clear in the document other than its intention to "photostat" the letter and mail it to undisclosed places. In any case, the FBI not only exploited the motives of the letter writers, but interfered with their freedom of speech.

On January 9, 1958, Lionel Trilling, Saul Bellow, Leslie Fiedler, Irving Howe, Alfred Kazin, Philip Rahv, and Robert Penn Warren signed a letter that appeared in *The New York Times* that protested Soviet treatment of Jews. The letter, which asserted that "no other minority in the U.S.S.R. has been singled out for such complete obliteration," urged that Jews be allowed to emigrate to other countries. It was a strong, forceful, and well-documented letter, and the FBI, without permission, decided it could also be useful in its private campaign to wipe out communism and the Soviet Union. The FBI intended to arouse discord, if it could, beyond the stated intent of the letter itself, which was anti-Soviet-treatment-of-Jews and not anti-Soviet, even though some of the signers might have held that position. But the point of the letter was to attack the Soviet's treatment of Jews and not be an overall attack of the Soviet Union.

Its authors intended the letter to appear in a public forum, and did not intend that it be used in a clandestine campaign that they had no control over. The FBI attempted to distort the original purpose of the letter in order to use it in an unauthorized manner. What did the FBI really hope to accomplish? What was the effect, if any, on the signers?

Diana Trilling did not recall any problems, although she was "appalled" by what the FBI did; "when they take a perfectly simple, decent protest and turn that into a way of creating mischief—it's just disgusting!"

Robert Penn Warren said he "had no recollection" of any kind "concerning the letter or similar matters," and Alfred Kazin said he didn't remember "any 'hate mail' in response to my signing. The only 'hate mail' I've ever received as a Jew has been from the ultraright fanatics, some of them connected with 'Cobra,' an anti-Semitic 'the-holocaust-was-a-hoax' organization."

However, Leslie Fiedler said, "I have only dim memories of having signed that 1958 letter, though I have of course continued through the years to do what I can to help the situation of Jews in the Soviet Union. The only response to the letter that I remember were charges from Communist party sources of my being—along with the other signers—a 'Red-baiter.' This seemed to me at the time ironic, since right-wingers in Montana were accusing me of being pro-Communist. But even then, both terms were blurring out toward meaninglessness."

Certainly, then, the FBI's mission to stir up trouble among individuals and groups was accomplished if the signers were called "Red-baiters" by the CP. This is confirmation that wherever the original letter was sent by the FBI, and whatever was done with it by agents, the FBI's first major literary COINTELPRO "worked" to some extent.

There are close to a dozen more references in Lionel Trilling's file, covering the years from 1959 to 1965. None are as dramatic as the

COINTELPRO report, but they are nonetheless significant—primarily because of their inaccuracies.

There are two 1959 documents. One is marked "no dissemination at this time" and is totally blacked out except for its "character," which has to do with Internal Security: Russia and Poland. Trilling did go to Poland for the Ford Foundation, but not until 1962. The other is an unreleased CIA memo dated October 1959 that the FBI says is still classified.

Diana Trilling remembers that "1959 was the year in which Lionel's friend Elliot Cohen, who had been the editor of *Commentary*, committed suicide—that's what I associate with 1959. I can't think what was going on politically." She did, however, recall a trip to England and France "in the late fifties," and says that "Lionel was held up for a long time at the airport in England. And he never found out what it was. Our guess was that he was held because of his name—there was a Trilling in London and another at Cambridge, relatives, and they were very strong fellow travelers."

There is a 1960 document that requests security information because Lionel Trilling "is a potential participant in an exchange between Columbia and Moscow University." Diana Trilling says, "That's madness! That's absolutely *mad*. They put it as fact, and that's dumb. Maybe there *was* a suggestion to begin with, but Lionel was not in Moscow. He was in Poland, in 1962. It's very interesting, extraordinary, extraordinary. They miss all the really important things. I mean on that trip to Poland, Willy Brandt of West Germany wanted to meet the group, and Lionel refused to go, and it was very tense. That would be much more interesting to put in a report."

There are two documents dated in 1961. One concerns the Fair Play for Cuba Committee, and is totally blacked out.

"He was *totally, totally* opposed. Lionel did not want *any part* of supporting Cuba. That's one for the books!" says Diana Trilling. "Lionel was absolutely anti-Castro, anti the Cuban Communists. It's inconceivable to have his name on a Fair Play for Cuba Committee. It's absolutely insane."

The other document concerns a "Communist Security Matter and Fraud Against the Government." This mentions a book review by Trilling that appeared in *Commentary* magazine, and indicates that copies of it were sent to Naval Intelligence. Diana Trilling believes this could be her husband's review of C. P. Snow. "The FBI would have been very suspicious—and rightfully suspicious—of C. P. Snow because he was very deeply involved with the travelers at that time."

One of the last documents is a name check requested by the United States Information Agency in 1964, and the FBI reminds the USIA that Trilling was listed on the 1937 letterhead for the Trotsky committee (the reference that began his file).

"In 1964, we went to England," Diana Trilling remembers. "Lionel was at Oxford."

There is a final name check requested by the White House, in 1965. This one asks for a fingerprint check as well.

Diana Trilling was astonished by the fingerprint request, but says, "There are a couple of possibilities in 1965. When T. S. Eliot died, which was in January 1965, President Johnson asked Lionel to represent the U.S. government at his funeral—he was buried in Westminster Abbey. Actually, this I'm sure was not because of Johnson, but because of Cleanth Brooks, who was our cultural attaché. He probably told President Johnson it would be the appropriate thing to do. And it may be there's some automatic way which demanded clearance. Another possibility—even more likely—they wanted Lionel to be cultural attaché in England and France. It was done through sources. They wrote to the university and asked if the university would mind letting him go. *I* considered it because I wanted to go to Europe! The duties of a cultural attaché are very onerous. You have to promote American culture in that country, and what you do is you go around lecturing—on this or that aspect of American life, and you set up a lecture series, and you meet distinguished visitors. When Lionel was Eastman Professor at Oxford in 1964 and 1965—I lectured at the American embassy at the invitation of the cultural attaché who was stationed in London. And then the attaché in Holland invited Lionel to give a lecture at the University of Utrecht, and he invited me to do a lecture at the University of Amsterdam. And we were paid a pile of dirty bills, you know, out of somebody's pocket. It's very family-like."

Despite the disparate, as well as questionable, material collected on her husband, Diana Trilling says, "I don't remember his having a hostile moment with either the FBI or the CIA."

Unquestionably, any effect was invisible.

Yet the impact of collecting documents in a secret file, and making many of them ominous because of their omissions—in content and context—and the discovery that one of America's great critics was used in a COINTELPRO scheme, has now become "a hostile moment" in Lionel Trilling's life as drawn by the FBI.

DIANA TRILLING:

Well, all I can say is that the file sounds crazy, which doesn't surprise me *too* much. And it just goes to show that one cannot really rest with this unless one has enormous corroborative evidence. One must not take anything said by the FBI as being an accurate statement about anything.

It surprises me that they left out the National Committee for the Defense of Political Prisoners in 1933, and working on the Scottsboro case—going to all those meetings in Harlem for the Scottsboro boys. And being associated by marriage with me and by friendship with many people to the activities that were going on. I would have thought the thing about Lenny Bruce would be in the file. Lionel at some point was in trouble for defending Lenny Bruce in the sixties. I guess the FBI never got into that.

During World War II, I would be interviewed from time to time, although I was never interviewed by the FBI—but I was interviewed by other agencies. I would be questioned about the security of this one or that one who wanted a post that was connected with our military or naval situation. They always knew an enormous amount about me, and they knew it in a kind of friendly and favorable way—it may have been a device. They were very intelligent.

**

Another insight into the principals of the Hiss-Chambers confrontation appears in the file of novelist and film critic James Agee. He came to the notice of the FBI five years after he graduated from Harvard University because of an article and poem he wrote for the June and September 1937 issues of *New Masses*. Agee biographer Erik Wensberg comments that he published in *New Masses* because of a "general and hazy political sympathy, and a great liking for Fred Dupee," who was the literary editor. Wensberg explains that what appeared in the magazine when the FBI discovered Agee were two book reviews and a poem "on the pathos of love and death. No politics."

In 1942, the year after his *Let Us Now Praise Famous Men* was published, Agee is referred to as "formerly a Liberal fellow traveler, but now in opposition to Communist Party." This eighty percent blacked-out Internal Security report also relates that he once "considered joining the Communist Party, but never did so." Wensberg says Agee had been approached to join in 1936, "but was in fact an anarchist," which the FBI did not know.

In 1943, when he was being interviewed about the loyalty of an unnamed government employee, Agee told FBI agents "his outlook had changed." Wensberg comments, "As for his disappointment in the Party, I place it as beginning while he and Walker Evans were in Alabama doing the tenant-farmer research—when they saw Communists at work in the union movement—and as having been completed by Whittaker Chambers, Agee's colleague at *Time* and rather emotionally dependent friend."

In 1949, during an investigation of the Communist influence in movies, the FBI was concerned because Agee's film script for *The Quiet One,* about the experiences of a ten-year-old boy from Harlem, "reportedly carries great social significance." Wensberg explains that Agee had also "spent November and December of 1948 in Hollywood doing research for a signed *Life* magazine article on silent comedy stars." The FBI was no doubt troubled about his relationship with Charlie Chaplin, who has a large FBI file. Wensberg says that Agee "already knew Chaplin from New York and spent time interviewing him," adding that Agee, "probably through Chaplin, hung out at the gemütlich Sunday salon kept by Salka Viertel, a non-Communist, long-time anti-fascist émigré screenwriter who entertained many of the European writers and movie people . . . CP and non."

The FBI visited Agee again in 1949, but not to ask about *The Quiet One.* This time it was interested in a letter he had written to Assistant U.S. Attorney Thomas Murphy stating that "as a friend of Whittaker Chambers I want to inform you of the following, for whatever use it may be." In the letter, which never figured in the Chambers-Hiss trial, Agee discusses the theory of a well-known Boston psychiatrist, Dr. Harry Murray, who believed Hiss was innocent and that Chambers "acted out of 'envy.' " The report indicates that the agents had spoken to Whittaker Chambers before seeing Agee, and that Chambers had told them he had known Agee at *Time* magazine and that Agee had "an excellent reputation." Before Chambers became an editor, both men wrote for the Book Section, and even briefly shared an office.

According to the file, Agee told the agents who came to interview him on December 1 that "he had no further information" to add to his letter and that he had a "high regard" for Chambers and had "absolute faith in him and believed that he was telling a truthful and complete story with regard to Alger Hiss." Agee told the agents that in 1946, after a photograph of Hiss had appeared in *Time,* Chambers said of it, "Yes, he is a very able man and at one time was my best friend." Agee also said that Chambers told him that when he knew Alger Hiss, sometime in the thirties, he was a Communist, and that "he could not understand how Alger Hiss could deny he was a Communist." Agee also reported to the agents "that Chambers thought perhaps Hiss had reformed and now he believed that since he refused to admit he was a Communist that he must have been acting under instructions of the Communist Party."

The FBI report concludes, "Chambers also told Agee that he could not understand how Hiss could maintain such a position since he must well know that he, Chambers, knew that Hiss was not only a Communist but that he had done some terrible things. Agee advised that Chambers never did state what these terrible things were. This statement was made prior to the time that the microfilms were found in the pumpkin at Westminster, Maryland."

Erik Wensberg explains that Agee's writing the letter to the U.S. attorney was "an uncharacteristic intervention" and an "amazing departure for him" because he "feared and disliked all bureaucracies and agencies of authority," but that Agee was "extraordinarily steamed up" over the Hiss-Chambers situation. Wensberg adds that "what brought him to this pitch seems to have been his respect for personal privacy, his compassion for Chambers, and his outrage at Dr. Murray's apparent abuse of professional authority and ethics."

In 1954, the year of Agee's death, and three years before his novel *A Death in the Family* would be published—and win a Pulitzer Prize—the Security Screening Board of the U.S. Naval Photographic Center requested "additional" information on the writer.

There is no follow-up. Wensberg says, "Agee was deep into screenplay work" at this time, and a year before, he had wanted to go to the South Seas, but the movie never worked out." He recalls that "around 1954, director John Huston wanted Agee to write a screenplay for *Moby Dick,* and that Agee had an offer to work on a screenplay in the Philippines, but I don't see where the Navy comes into it at all."

So, the last reference in his thirty-nine-page file remains a puzzle.

On December 13, 1956, the FBI became anxious after learning that an unidentified subject under investigation had "obtained" *The Muses Are Heard* by Truman Capote, a nonfiction account of the Soviet tour of the *Porgy and Bess* company.

The report quotes a passage from *The Muses Are Heard* about the troupe's interpreter breaking the rules to take photographs and then "hurling himself" back on the train, and altering his appearance so the Soviets wouldn't know it was he who had jumped off the train in the first place. The FBI was very suspicious of this information, and felt it held some clue, although it is hard to figure out what that clue might be, since the Bureau called the book a novel and did not at the time seem to know it was a work of journalism. But the Bureau might have believed or known that the interpreter was a spy, and worried because Capote had blown his "cover." In any case, this reference put the author of *Breakfast at Tiffany's* and *In Cold Blood* in the FBI's index and began his 185-page file.

During the winter of 1959, Capote sought the FBI's help in his attempt to get research material from Kansas law enforcement officials for his then book-in-progress, *In Cold Blood*. Actually, some unnamed person from Capote's publisher, Random House, called on his behalf, telling Cartha DeLoach that Capote hadn't brought any credentials with him to Kansas and was "crushed" that officials out there didn't recognize his name. But the FBI's position was that it "could not insert itself in a local murder case." DeLoach recalls, however, that "Mr. Hoover liked *In Cold Blood* very much."

On April 18, 1960, the Bureau received a report that Capote "supports the Revolution" in Cuba. On April 26, Hoover wrote a note asking for "summaries" on all the members of the "newly-formed Fair Play for Cuba Committee": Waldo Frank, Norman Mailer, Simone de Beauvoir, Jean-Paul Sartre, Kenneth Tynan, and Capote.

Most of Capote's file concerns Cuba, although by 1963, Fulton Lewis, Jr., announced in a column—he sent an advance copy to the Director—that Capote, as well as Mailer, Sartre, Tynan, and James Baldwin, were no longer members.

The file includes a copy of "a proposed press release" regarding publisher Lyle Stuart's Senate testimony about his involvement in the Fair Play for Cuba Committee. Cartha DeLoach describes Stuart in a memo as "a New York publisher whose book lists are dominated by earthy novels, sex-technique manuals and pro-Castro works." In fact, the press release, instead of keeping strictly to the subject of the testimony, lists some of Stuart's titles: "*Pleasure Was My Business, Diary of a Nymph, Transvestism,* and *The Marriage Case.*"

The file of trial lawyer and novelist Erle Stanley Gardner, the creator of Perry Mason and the author of over 140 mystery books, might be subtitled "The Case of the Overzealous Amateur." Gardner was something of an FBI groupie. A Bureau report observes that he "associates with law enforcement officers in order to pick up material for his novels." Many of the reports in Gardner's file concern requests for information on cases he was using as grist for novels and for newspaper and magazine articles. And, the Director was a fan of Gardner's: "Mr. Hoover loved his books," Cartha DeLoach says.

Gardner entered the FBI files on November 4, 1943, not because of his political beliefs but rather because he was writing about a case in which the Bureau was interested. A memo says that "information was received by the Foreign Travel Control Unit . . . that [Gardner] is scheduled to arrive in Miami, Florida, by clipper plane." Gardner is identified as "the reporter assigned to cover . . . the de Marigny trial in Nassau," the November 1943 trial in the Bahamas of the accused murderer of wealthy British socialite, Sir Harry Oakes.

In 1950, Hoover undertook the role of critic of a magazine article he had helped Gardner put together. The Director reprimanded the novelist for saying that a suspect had been "hounded" by the FBI. Hoover ordered his agents to interview Gardner in order to stress "that our files are confidential." A report of the interview is not in the file, but a later memo mentions that Gardner's "faith in the Bureau had been restored by the interview." But not the Bureau's in Gardner.

In 1953, the novelist wrote Hoover requesting data for a talk he was giving on "the huge number of cases where persons who should have been convicted are turned loose by the courts because there was inadequate proof." Hoover sent him some material, and Gardner then mailed the Director a "rough draft" of his speech, requesting that "a public relations secretary" read it. The file does not disclose whether this was ever done, but Gardner's letters show no letup in his requests for information and favors.

In 1956, when Gardner was proposed as an associate member of the International Association of Chiefs of Police, Hoover jotted in the margin of the memo, "Okay, but basically I don't like the idea of associates nor [sic] honorary memberships."

Sometimes Gardner sent information *to* Hoover, such as his 1956 tip on an unidentified engineer who was "dealing with sabotage." Agents decided the material "presented nothing really new."

A few weeks later, Gardner asked Louis Nichols to read a "rough draft" of an article he was writing on crime trends, for an encyclopedia yearbook. Nichols sent a three-page letter of corrections to him. One of his "suggestions" was changing Gardner's statement that "crime statistics can be misleading because they are based on information from law enforcement agencies" to "crime statistics can be misleading unless we use care in interpreting such figures." Another correction concerned Gardner's statement that "law enforcement is not a game to be conducted according to the rules of fair play." Nichols commented that "I wonder if this might not be subject to misinterpretation. I frankly think that you did not intend to convey the impression that law enforcement must engage in anything other than fair play to catch a crook."

Gardner accepted the criticisms gratefully—and then proceeded to write the article his own way. For example, he amended the crime statistics sentence to read "police can and sometimes do make their crime statistics read like complete fairy tales."

During the summer of 1959, the irrepressible Gardner wrote a letter to Hoover claiming that the man the FBI had arrested in a little-known 1950s kidnapping case was innocent. This claim activated Hoover's self-protective instincts, for he penned a marginal note on the letter: "I think we should for our own satisfaction analyze point by point the issues raised by Gardner."

The FBI went over its work in the case quietly, because as a memo explained, "An active investigation would tend to indicate to Gardner that we were not sure of our position in the first place." The FBI also commented that for Gardner, "there is little doubt in his mind that the suspect is innocent." In addition, a Bureau official complained to Clyde Tolson in a memo that he believed that "the purpose of Gardner's letter is to try to have the FBI prove that he is right." The official also passed on gossip that another FBI official "was not at all impressed with [Gardner's] sincerity," warning that "he has made serious allegations against the Bureau."

J. Edgar Hoover decided that these "allegations must not only be met head-on, but it is felt that certain things should be done to tie up loose ends to strengthen the Bureau's position in regard to the case."

What those "certain things" were is unclear, but one of them was an interview with Gardner, who seems to have been clinging to his theory with Perry Mason–like tenacity. A report states that he was "most difficult to interview" because he "appears to be possessed of a disjointed personality," and "he is capricious, wasting time talking about himself and his opinions while he refuses to get down to facts." The report concludes by saying that although his "intense egotism made him utterly intolerant of accepting any facts that might deprive him of his deeply rooted feeling of the kidnapper's innocence . . . the discussion with Gardner believed [sic] worth while, if only to straighten out his thinking in regard to Bureau jurisdiction and operations."

Ultimately Gardner apologized for the "erroneous impression" of the Bureau's original investigation of the case. But he had gone too far. Clyde Tolson suggested that his letter not be acknowledged, and Hoover wrote, "I concur."

Two years later, Gardner wrote Hoover a friendly letter about another matter, mentioning that he was "still working" on the kidnapping case. Hoover replied coolly, and a typed note at the bottom of a copy of his answer says, "We have experienced considerable difficulty" with Gardner.

Playwright Arthur Miller was perhaps the most famous writer to be grilled by the HUAC about his political convictions. Miller's refusal to cooperate in 1956 almost resulted in his imprisonment.

The FBI began keeping records on Miller in 1938, when he was still in college. He was found to be a member of the American Youth Congress, a sponsor of the American Relief Ship for Spain, and a signer of a cable sent by the League of American Writers. The following year, he wrote a protest letter to President Roosevelt, which was not answered by the President's office, but for some unknown reason, by the FBI. However, there is no record of this correspondence anywhere in the playwright's 654-page file. Arthur Miller says the letter, written just after he graduated from the University of Michigan, "had to do with the Spanish Civil War," and that he got a "form letter from the FBI, with a number on it, saying the letter has been deposited at the FBI. I'll never forget it. I thought, the FBI? I wrote the President a letter!"

The Bureau also searched the records of his Selective Service board, culling for his FBI file such details as his being classified 4F because of "weakened and impaired use of wrist due to accident. Swelling and stiffening of right knee joint as of 3/17/41." In 1942, the Bureau reported that he was a member of the American Labor party, and by 1944, the FBI was using confidential informants to spy on the playwright. The FBI found witnesses willing to smear Miller. One person said that "like Miller, he had found Communism in the sifting search for a philosophy of life." As early as 1944 the FBI also used frequent pretext phone calls to check on Miller's whereabouts.

In 1947, the FBI knew about his participation in a weekly discussion group of writers organized by a senior editor at Simon and Schuster, Jack Goodman. Miller writes in his autobiography, *TimeBends,* that "Jack managed to collect a couple of dozen stars of the magazine and fiction worlds," who attempted "to conceive a countertide in the media to the overwhelming propaganda of the right." When Jack Goodman appeared before HUAC, the committee knew all the members. Was there an informant?

Miller, who was questioned by HUAC about the meetings, says, "I'll tell you what happened. We are piddling along with a dozen people, eighteen maybe—it varied weekly. Suddenly, one time—I had missed one or two meetings—I arrived and the place was jammed with people, many of whom I didn't know. They were not all writers, and I have a feeling the informant may have been one of those new people. I doubt that it was one of the writers that I knew. Of course, the FBI could have also had a real spy. Nobody stood at the door and said, 'Where are your credentials?' I mean everybody came, and was welcome. It was like a big party."

Miller's first play, *All My Sons,* about an engine manufacturer who knowingly sells a defective shipment to the Air Force, was produced in 1947; the FBI called it "party line propaganda." *Counter-Attack,* the Red-baiting newsletter of the forties, considered Miller a Communist, and was incensed when a production of *All My Sons* was scheduled in Germany, saying "it would help Stalin in his efforts to convince the Germans that the U.S. is controlled by heartless plutocrats." It even accused the playwright of "twisting the facts in a central situation in his play!"

In 1948, the FBI reported that Miller wrote an article entitled, "Concerning Jews Who Write" for *Jewish Life* magazine, and then noted that he was a speaker at a "Salute to the Jewish State" rally at the Polo Grounds. The FBI reported that "the large audience responded with thunderous applause" when the Soviet Union was mentioned. The following year, in 1949, the FBI reported that Miller's *Death of a Salesman* received an award from the American Committee of Jewish Writers.

ARTHUR MILLER:
Jewish Life was a left-wing Jewish magazine, if I recall, but the FBI was trying to smear the whole thing with that magazine. Clearly. This is a mind-set. It's just what you know, of course, of that far right—from the Nazis to the people in Central American countries. It's all one pot.

The birth of Israel—I remember that quite well—was a big event at Yankee Stadium or the Polo Grounds, which had absolutely not the slightest connection with any left-wing thing!

It was all the synagogues, and if there ever was a total Jewish community in this part of the country appearing, it was to that. I hadn't seen so many people with yarmulkes since I was a *child.* My father was there with me. I remember that occasion because I spoke for a minute or two.

I hadn't connected that many religious Jews with Israel because so many of them still said this can't be the real Israel because it's not being established by the Messiah. But, *a lot of them were there!* Now that's why it was noteworthy to me.

**

In 1949, Miller's Pulitzer Prize–winning *Death of a Salesman* was unfavorably reviewed by the FBI: "[Although] you won't find any overt Communist propaganda in *Death of a Salesman,* it's a negative delineation of American life. . . . [It] strikes a shrewd blow against [American] values." The Bureau was receiving reports that the National Commander of the Catholic War Veterans had "a detailed file" on the subversive activities of the playwright, and that Miller had participated at a Bill of Rights conference, a conference that "would bluntly speak up against the police state methods of certain Army and FBI officials."

In 1950, Louis Budenz testified that Miller was a "concealed communist," and the Bureau reported ominously that a house Miller had bought in Connecticut in 1949 was not just a "summer place," but was "sufficient for all year round living." Soon the Connecticut, as well as the New York, field office became active in investigating Miller's activities, and agents had him under surveillance, though to what extent is not known.

In 1954, the American Legion put pressure on the FBI to do something about Miller's "red ties," and later that year, the playwright was denied a passport "because of believed CP support." Although there is nothing in the file to indicate that the Legion directly influenced the U.S. Passport Office, it is clear that an accumulation of many pressures led to the denial.

In 1955, the FBI, calling Miller "one of America's greatest writers," made a decision "not to interview him" even though it said "he was a member of the CP in 1946 and 1947." As with Lillian Hellman and other stars, Hoover felt an interview might embarrass the Bureau because of his "position as a well-known writer." Miller recalls that no friends told him that they had been questioned by the FBI, either, although he remembers being questioned by the FBI in the early 1940s about someone else. "A friend of mine from college got a job writing—let's say, a documentary for the Public Health Department, or whatever—and he was being investigated by the Civil Service. I remember clearly once one of these guys asked me about this man. So we met in my house. He started using terminology which made me realize that he was investigating me—he wasn't investigating my friend. It was an entrapment."

The Bureau also recorded in 1955 that Miller was "rejected by the New York City Youth Board as a writer of a film on juvenile delinquency," noting later that "the project was held up by New York City Mayor Robert F. Wagner, after accusations that Miller held left-wing political beliefs." Miller says that the Youth Board won his dismissal by "one vote," and that indeed Wagner "ultimately made the decision to disassociate from him as a result of the vote."

By the time Miller testified before the House Committee on Un-American Activities on June 14, the FBI recorded that it had "over two hundred" references on him in their files.

On May 29, 1956, Richard Arens, staff director of HUAC, called Clyde Tolson to say that Miller would be appearing before the committee sometime in mid-June. Arens "stated that the committee knows he was a member of the party in 1943 but is unable to find a live witness that can put him in the Party." Arens asked Tolson for help on getting a "photostat of Miller's Communist Party (CP) card."

Tolson then revealed to Louis Nichols that the Bureau did not have a card, although the files showed Miller was a CP member in "1945, 1946, and 1947." Hoover penned "Right" next to a suggestion that the Bureau defensively tell Arens that "due to a new departmental ruling," the FBI cannot help, and that "in the future," the chairman of the committee should write a letter to the attorney general for any information. A final afterthought adds that Arens should be told not to write a letter, though, because "it would be fruitless since the data desired is not available."

At the time the Bureau reported on Miller's June 14, 1956, committee appearance (where on top of everything else, committee members tried to confuse and smear him because he disapproved of what they referred to as Ezra Pound's anticommunism), it was also reported that "Miller's name had recently been linked romantically with actress Marilyn Monroe."

Actually, a few months earlier, in February, Hoover had his friend Walter Winchell leak an item saying that "America's best-known blonde movie star is now the darling of the left-wing intelligentsia, several of whom are listed as red fronters. I do not think she realizes it."

Three months later, according to Miller's file, Winchell did it again, this time saying, "One of Marilyn Monroe's new romances, a long-time pro-lefto, will be asked to testify," and then, four days before Miller's appearance, Winchell wrote, "Next stop—trouble."

Arthur Miller was cited for contempt for refusing to answer two questions that HUAC put to him. Miller remembers, "I went to trial on the basis of contempt for refusing to answer who was in the room in that [1947] meeting—that was the whole charge. I was acquitted of everything." (When an attorney in the Internal Security Division asked Hoover's staff for a copy of "all of the constitutions of the Communist Party, USA," for use at Miller's contempt trial, the Director bridled, scrawling on the memo, "I thought the Internal Security Division of the Dept. were the 'experts.' ")

Yet after the acquittal in 1958, the FBI remained on Arthur Miller's trail. In 1960, the FBI reported that Miller and William Faulkner "were honored by Polish critics" in a magazine called *NWR,* which was regularly reviewed by agents. The FBI also reported that a Soviet journal said "*A View of the Bridge* [i.e., *A View* from *the Bridge*] is one of the greatest anti-American plays ever written in America in recent years." The Bureau also noted that "by keeping track of Soviet journals and newspapers" it can be shown that Miller has achieved "first place" in the Soviet Union ever since the termination of "relations between American writer Howard Fast and the Kremlin leaders."

Two years later, in 1962, the Bureau received a report that a dramatization of Miller's novel, *Focus,* which appeared on NBC, "was strictly Communist propaganda" because it attempted to "foster race hatred between Jews and Gentiles."

In 1965, the Bureau infiltrated a conference on Vietnam which was held at the University of Michigan, and monitored Miller's speech. It also monitored the Vietnam peace march in Washington, which was held that year, and indexed three writers from the sponsor list: Miller, John Hersey, and winner of the 1976 Nobel Prize for literature, Saul Bellow.

The FBI also noted in 1965 that Miller was elected the president of the American Center for PEN, the international association of poets, playwrights, editors, essayist, and novelists, which had been founded in London in 1922. The Bureau clipped and translated articles about the group that appeared in the foreign press, including an interview Miller gave to the Soviet news agency, Tass, in which he "demanded closer contacts between Americans and Russians."

Miller comments that, "I thought—it passed through my mind— that the government might have wanted me to become president of PEN because they couldn't otherwise penetrate the Soviet Union, and they figured that traveling behind me could be their own people. They wouldn't expect me to do it, I don't think. One of the early people who approached me about PEN—I can't remember his name now—but people later would say about him, 'Why that guy was an agent all the time.' Now I have no evidence of that—it was gossip." Miller held the post until 1970.

In 1967, the FBI monitored the activities of another Vietnam War protest group that included, besides Arthur Miller, Ray Bradbury (whose name was marked for indexing), Albert Maltz and Alvah

Bessie, two of the Hollywood Ten, and writers Jessica Mitford and Alfred Kazin. (Some others indexed from the document as it appears in Miller's file include actors Tony Randall, Robert Vaughn, and Janice Rule, and producer Carl Reiner.) Another Vietnam protest group document in the file indexed, besides Miller, writers Robert Lowell, Norman Mailer, Susan Sontag, Joel Oppenheimer, Alan Dugan, and Stanley Kauffmann.

In 1968, the Bureau observed an antiwar rally in New York, noting that Miller was a speaker. "That's the last thing" in the file, Miller says, adding that "maybe it went over to the CIA. This I don't know."

ARTHUR MILLER:

Envy of creative people is a very important element in this whole FBI and HUAC business, because if you consider that they went after a large number of Hollywood people, many of whom had no particular political connection, it comes down to a simple thing. An artist, an actor, a writer, gets an audience voluntarily to come to his plays or read his books or whatever, and the HUAC committees have to break their necks to get a line in the press or else they have to pay for ads in order to get into the press. That was a big job; that was almost all the committees were doing all the time—trying to get in the papers! And it's natural that they should envy and fear the artist.

I could leave their hearing and go write a play, and tens of thousands of people could come into the theater. *They* can't do anything like that—they can issue a statement which nobody reads.

The FBI and the committee were very publicity conscious. They were adept at using the press when they were hungry. Later on the press got soured on them and they wouldn't necessarily use in any prominent place a handout the committee gave them. But for years, everything that came out of that HUAC committee was front-page news, and then it began to die off and the committee had to compete with a lot of other news.

The Un-American Activities Committee—*the whole thing was basically, fundamentally, a brutal deception!* From the beginning. I mean, anybody who was around the left knew that the *real* left guys were never bothered! Because they weren't famous, because they weren't known—so what the hell was the point of it? Why waste a day grilling some janitor from some union which was a Communist union if you can talk to someone who can get on the front page of the *Daily News*? And with their picture!

I mean, the payoff was the chairman of the committee, Francis E. Walter, saying that he would call off the whole thing if he could take a picture with Marilyn. That was perfect. You know, in the theater you always try to get the "significant action," the action that needs no explanation—the theme and the emotion are together—and suddenly there it was!

PART SIX

The Continuing Cold War and the Vietnam War

CHAPTER TWENTY

The 1960s Aliens

FBI AGENT "X":
The sixties writers weren't marching arm in arm with other *writers,* they were
really part of the whole milieu of the *activists.*

**

During the 1960s, the FBI would add the names of more than 250
writers, editors, and publishers to its files—more than in any previous
decade. Most of those writers/activists still do not know they have
files.* The FBI's justifications for indexing them were that their activities involved ''some phase of intelligence under FBI jurisdiction'' or
''a possible violation of the law.'' Such was the Bureau's attitude
toward writers who spoke out on the Vietnam War and other issues
during the sixties.

---

* Their names were found in the files of Ginsberg, Baraka, Dupee, Hellman, and Mailer, which
contain lists of supporters of organizations to which the subject of the file belonged; the names
of all the supporters have been marked for indexing. For example, the last reference in critic F.
W. Dupee's file, dated 1968, mentions his sponsorship of the International Committee to Defend
Eldridge Cleaver. Every single name is marked for indexing; among them are book critic Christopher Lehmann-Haupt, publishing executive Alice Mayhew, book publicist Selma Shapiro, and
writers Robert Coover, Martin Duberman, Herbert Gold, George Plimpton, Adrienne Rich, and
Kurt Vonnegut.

What were the laws that writers/activists might have violated? According to the FBI's *Foreign Counterintelligence Manual,* there are more than thirty-one "crimes likely to impact upon the national security, defense or foreign relations of the U.S." These include sabotage, espionage, communicating classified information, neutrality offenses, being an unauthorized agent of a foreign government, aircraft piracy, counterfeiting U.S. obligations, making false official statements and carrying false official papers, perjury, and obstruction of justice. With the exception of the last charge, which was used from time to time to remove many writers/activists from picket lines, the likelihood that a writer might be involved in the listed crimes was remote, yet the suspicion that he or she might commit such crimes—as evidenced by his or her political beliefs—was the sole justification for placing the writer's name in the indexes.

The most outspoken writers/activists felt Hoover's power of suspicion most keenly. Moreover, they were subject to all kinds of harassment—surveillance, pretext telephone calls, and COINTELPRO operations. During the 1960s the COINTELPROs would become bolder, more brazen, and more bizarre.

As an example, in 1967, J. Edgar Hoover received a memo from the special agent in charge of the FBI office in Albany, New York, describing "a new counterintelligence endeavor" that was going to "expose, disrupt, misdirect, discredit, or otherwise neutralize the activities of Black nationalist, hate-type organizations or groupings . . ." A later memo plumbed new depths of racism, suggesting that in order to be "more effective," the planners of COINTELPROs "should bear in mind that the two things foremost in the militant Negro's mind are sex and money." Also, that "Negro youths" must be told that it is "better to be a sports hero, a well-paid professional athlete" than a "revolutionary."

Frequently, the COINTELPROs were devised to sow dissension among black groups or foment rivalries with whites on the left. For instance, a 1969 COINTELPRO sought to drive a wedge between white radicals and the Black Panthers with a phony "angry Brother" letter that asked, "Since when do us blacks have to accept the dictates of the lilywhite SDS" (i.e., Students for a Democratic Society). A purported letter from student activists in Newark, New Jersey, called Jersey City Panthers "pussycats." On February 17, 1970, the FBI created "caricatures attacking a white contributor and supporter of the Black Panther Party," and a "second caricature depicting [black activist] Huey Newton as a homosexual."

Louis Untermeyer (*second from left*) on *What's My Line?* panel. Host John Daly greets New York Mayor William O'Dwyer, 1950. THE BETTMANN ARCHIVE

Roy Cohn (*left*) gestures to Senator Joseph McCarthy (*right*). Columnist George Sokolsky is in the middle. THE BETTMANN ARCHIVE

A sampling of J. Edgar
Hoover's marginal notes

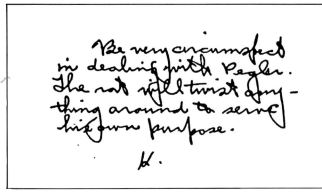

From the file of Westbrook
Pegler, May 17, 1940

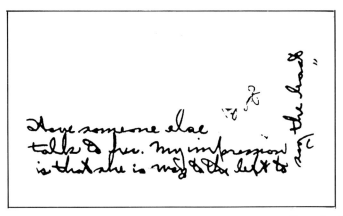

From the file of Pearl S. Buck,
November 17, 1950

```
Director's Notation:
"Make certain we furnish this outfit
no more material for publication.
They are too squeamish about
offending the commies.
                    H."
```

From the file of Langston
Hughes, June 29, 1948

Find out where this
is. It is now 3.30 P.M
Sunday & I haven't re-
ceived it yet.

J. E. H.

9/16/34   OK

From the file of Upton Sinclair,
September 19, 1934

Let me have
memo on Ernest
Hemingway.

H.

From the file of Ernest
Hemingway, April 27, 1943

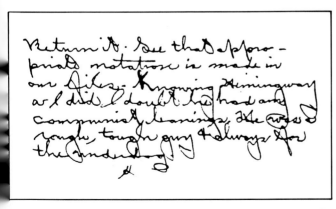

Return it. See that appropriate notation is made in
our files. Knowing Hemingway
as I did, I doubt he had any
Communist leanings. He was a
rough, tough guy & always for
the underdog.

H.

From Quenton Reynolds's letter
to J. Edgar Hoover, January 6,
1964, in Hemingway's file

White women's delegation to
Mississippi in Willie McGee
case, 1952. *First row, right,*
Jessica Mitford.   PHOTO
COURTESY OF JESSICA MITFORD

BELOW: Document confirming
that William Carlos Williams
was not appointed to Poetry
Consultantship of the Library of
Congress because of
"unfavorable report," 1954

TO: Director   DATE: November 22, 1954
    Federal Bureau of Investigation
    Washington 25, D. C.   FILE: DISO:SJM:jwk

| NAME: WILLIAMS, William Carlos | DATE OF BIRTH 9/17/83 |
| POSITION, ORGANIZATION, AND LOCATION Applicant for the position of Consultant in Poetry Library of Congress Washington, D. C. | |

Your Bureau conducted investigation in this case under provisions of
Section 8(d) of Executive Order 10450. The disposition made of the case
is indicated below:

EMPLOYEE OR APPOINTEE:

☐ Retained

☐ Separated because of unfavorable report

☐ Resigned or otherwise separated from Federal service prior to
 decision on investigative report (See explanation below);

APPLICANT:

☐ Favorable security determination

☒ Not appointed because of unfavorable report

☐ Applicant withdrew from consideration prior to decision on
 investigative report.

☐ Not appointed for reasons other than unfavorable report (See
 explanation below):

CHIEF, INVESTIGATIONS DIVISION

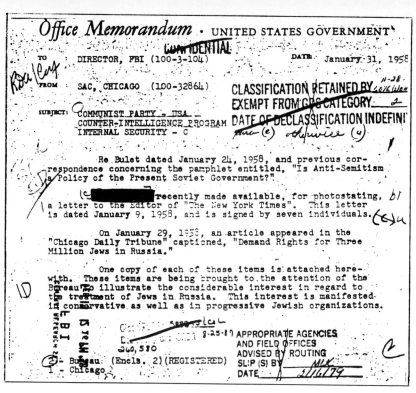

Office Memorandum · UNITED STATES GOVERNMENT

CONFIDENTIAL

TO : DIRECTOR, FBI (100-3-104)

DATE: January 31, 1958

FROM : SAC, CHICAGO (100-32864)

SUBJECT: COMMUNIST PARTY - USA
COUNTER-INTELLIGENCE PROGRAM
INTERNAL SECURITY - C

CLASSIFICATION RETAINED BY
EXEMPT FROM GDS CATEGORY ___2___
DATE OF DECLASSIFICATION INDEFINIT

Re Bulet dated January 24, 1958, and previous correspondence concerning the pamphlet entitled, "Is Anti-Semitism
a Policy of the Present Soviet Government?"

[███████] recently made available, for photostating,
a letter to the Editor of "The New York Times". This letter
is dated January 9, 1958, and is signed by seven individuals.

On January 29, 1958, an article appeared in the
"Chicago Daily Tribune" captioned, "Demand Rights for Three
Million Jews in Russia."

One copy of each of these items is attached here-
with. These items are being brought to the attention of the
Bureau to illustrate the considerable interest in regard to
the treatment of Jews in Russia. This interest is manifested
in conservative as well as in progressive Jewish organizations.

APPROPRIATE AGENCIES
AND FIELD OFFICES
ADVISED BY ROUTING
SLIP (S) BY
DATE

2 - Bureau (Encls. 2)(REGISTERED)
1 - Chicago

ABOVE: FBI memo about 1958
Cointelpro involving letter
signed by Lionel Trilling

Letter written by Lionel Trilling
(et al.) that was used in 1958
Cointelpro   FROM LIONEL
TRILLING'S FBI FILE

Letters to The Times

Soviet Treatment of Jews

Liquidation of Their Culture Cited
Freedom to Emigrate Asked

TO THE EDITOR OF THE NEW YORK TIMES:
Ten years ago, on Jan. 13, 1948,
Solomon Mikhoels, director of the
Moscow Jewish State Theatre and
chairman of the Jewish Anti-Fascist
Committee, died in an accident under mystifying circumstances. The
Kremlin ordered an imposing funeral and then denounced him post-
umously in 1953 as a "Jewish
bourgecis-nationalist conspirator."
Jewish escapees from the Soviet
Union have since brought out the
grim story that he was assassinated
by the Soviet secret police.

His death presaged the last—and
most severe—phase of a deliberate
campaign by the Kremlin to extin-
guish the culture of more than
3,000,000 Jews in the U. S. S. R.
This was another example of the
fundamental inhumanity of this
system.

Within several months padlocks
had been placed on the last of the
Jewish cultural institutions in the
Soviet Union. Hundreds of leading
Jewish artists, writers, actors and
scientists were rounded up by the
secret police. Approximately 400
writers alone perished between 1948
and 1952.

Toward Extinction

In 1937-38 there were eighteen Jewish theatres in the Soviet
Union. In 1948 the last of these was
padlocked. In 1918 there were eleven
Jewish dailies in the U. S. S. R. In
1948 the last Jewish periodical with
a national circulation was shut
down by Government order. In short,
by the time of Stalin's death a
small civilization, compact with
accomplishment, was on the way to
extinction. No other minority in
the U. S. S. R. has been singled out
for such complete obliteration.

To this date no public apology
has been made to the families of the
liquidated Jewish writers and artists.
In his address to the Twentieth
Party Congress, Nikita Khrushchev
called out the roll of minorities persecuted in the last years of Stalin's
rule. Soviet Jewry was not included.
Mikhail A. Suslov, member of the
Presidium of the Central Committee of the Communist party, told a
Canadian Communist delegation
bluntly: "We have no intention of
calling back to life a dead culture."

Concomitant with this liquidation
of a culture the Soviet Union has
been guilty, under Stalin and now
under Khrushchev, of a policy of
deliberate discrimination against
Jews in the professions, civil service
and education. The existence of an
unofficial but effective quota system for Jews was conceded by
Nikita Khrushchev to a French
Socialist delegation and a Canadian
Communist delegation.

Captive Nationality

Under these circumstances there
can be only one equitable solution.
Soviet Jews who refuse to counte-
nance this humiliating inequality and
persecution of their culture should
be granted by the Soviet authorities
the elementary right of freedom of
movement, the right to seek a home
elsewhere. Such emigration would
not actually set new precedents in
Soviet law and conduct. In the past
the U. S. S. R. has solicited the
"repatriation" to the U. S. S. R. of
Russians, Ukrainians and Armenians
from all over the world, and also has
permitted the repatriation from the
Soviet Union of Poles, Spaniards
and Greeks.

The Soviet identity card identifies
the Jews as a nationality. They are
evidently an unwanted and captive
nationality. Israel has indicated
readiness to receive Soviet Jews.
Other countries also would welcome
their talents.

SAUL BELLOW, LESLIE FIEDLER,
IRVING HOWE, ALFRED KAZIN, PHILIP
RAHV, LIONEL TRILLING, ROBERT
PENN WARREN.
New York, Jan. 9, 1958.

Arthur Miller (*right*) testifying
before H.U.A.C., June 21,
1956   THE BETTMANN ARCHIVE

Allen Ginsberg, whose file was
opened in 1957   PHOTO BY
HANK O'NEAL. COURTESY OF
HARPERCOLLINS

Svetlana Alliluyeva, 1969
THE BETTMANN ARCHIVE

BELOW: William F. Buckley,
Jr., addressing some
Connecticut judges at "Law
Day," an annual celebration
held in New Haven,
1969   PHOTO COURTESY OF
WILLIAM F. BUCKLEY, JR.

The Feds snare yet another subversive in their library awareness program dragnet.

Political cartoon by Chan Lowe, 1987   COURTESY OF TRIBUNE MEDIA SERVICES

FBI Director William S. Sessions, 1991   PHOTO COURTESY OF THE FBI

On October 30, 1970, the FBI had a State Department attaché in Sweden mail a phony letter to Amiri Baraka. The letter was supposedly from a U.S. Army deserter, a black power advocate who hung around with homosexuals and was waiting for the day he can "kill the pigs" back home. This particular letter has an elaborate subplot involving the deserter's homosexual affair with someone "who works in a Swiss bank handling numbered accounts." The deserter implied that perhaps some American BPP members had been stealing from the Party and "stashing funds" with the help of his lover. Still another FBI hoax letter advised the Jersey City Panthers that someone was "pocketing donations for their breakfast program."

The Bureau's provocateurs went to almost schoolboyish lengths to make their missives look authentic. They stipulated that one counterfeit letter be written on "5 & 10 store–type paper." Another carried instructions that "to look even more authentic," the paper should "be stepped on several times to give the appearance of having been trampled on while laying on the street."

Of course blacks weren't the only targets of COINTELPROs. The Bureau continued to harass the Communist party, even though its ranks were depleted. In 1965, Bureau strategists created a phony organization called the Committee for Expansion of Socialist Thought in America and published a newspaper in its name attacking the Party. Another enemy on the Bureau's list was the Fair Play for Cuba Committee, formed in 1960. In a COINTELPRO called Cuban Matters, letters and pamphlets were dispatched to Cuban-exile businessmen in Miami and to leaders of the FPCC. U.S. citizens doing business with Cuban firms were harassed by "publicizing through established sources" their personal affairs. It is not clear whether these "established sources" refer to friendly columnists or friendly politicians. At the offices of one Cuban businessman, FBI agents "buried some records beneath the floor . . . in order to delay production. . . ." A November 30 memo reports that a hoax involving the FPCC leadership had a "humorous aspect." What this was is not described. Finally, the Bureau provided names of some FPCC leaders to "the local vice squad" to cause them "embarrassment."

On November 22, 1963, President John F. Kennedy was murdered in Dallas. Vice President Lyndon Baines Johnson, a Hoover friend of over twenty years, was sworn in as President and elected the country's thirty-sixth President the following year. Johnson was the only American President whose autographed photograph hung on the living-room wall of J. Edgar Hoover's home. The Director also kept a bust of Johnson in his dining room.

The Civil Rights Act of 1964, which mandated that any outbreaks or riots be handled through negotiation and concession put the director on the defensive. On November 20, 1964, he asked Cartha DeLoach "to discreetly" ask "our friends in newspaper circles" to publish stories about the "FBI's accomplishments in the civil rights field." According to the memo "13 friends" were asked to do the Director a favor.

The FBI also continued its electronic surveillance of suspect writers. At eleven A.M. on February 8, 1965, agents tapped a telephone conversation in which the architectural historian and critic Lewis Mumford (whose file was opened in 1923) was asked to speak at a civil rights convention to be held in April. Mumford said although he "was very sympathetic," he was "working on a book and I've had to say no to every such outside call on my time."

SOPHIE MUMFORD:
I think Lewis would have been amused at how stupid the collection of information on him was. I remember once someone read into *The Congressional Record* that he was a friend of Communist party official Earl Browder. But my husband never set eyes on him! He once attended a meeting of the Writers Guild when it was first formed, but he walked out after discovering it was under Communist influence.

During World War II he was called to Washington to be interviewed for a possible job in intelligence. He was down there for a few days, but it didn't work out.

**

In 1967, the year Ramsey Clark became attorney general, Svetlana Alliluyeva arrived in the United States, where she remained until 1982, when she moved to England. In 1984, she returned to the Soviet Union, but eighteen months later returned once again to America. In 1987, she moved again to England. "I do not consider myself a Russian," she said in 1986.

SVETLANA ALLILUYEVA:
I know from my Russian experience that if people want to suspect someone of something, they will make the case. It would not necessarily be a famous writer—they can choose anyone they want and there will be a file.

When my aunt was sentenced to ten years of solitary confinement—she was released after my father died and after KGB chief Beria was removed—and she said, "My God, I signed." And I said, "But why? What was your crime?" And she said, "Oh, there was a whole file on me—I did this, I did that. I signed everything. If you don't sign, you will be dead, I was told."

Do you think that maybe there are FBI files on me? In connection with my going to Russia and coming back in 1985?

Well, I don't care. Oh my God, I don't care if they have a file or not. I lived forty years in Russia where there are files on everyone. There were always files against *writers* because they were considered the most important enemies, even in the time of Pushkin—God, so long ago!

**

CARTHA DeLOACH:

I would doubt there's a file on Alliluyeva. I'm sure there are references in various internal security files concerning her, because there's a natural suspicion directed toward any defector. The Soviets practice treachery in that regard—the Soviet disinformation service—in planting rumors, et cetera, or sending defectors over here who have no desire whatever to be a United States citizen, but they go through this scenario of saying "I want to defect," and they come in and try to learn everything they can concerning the United States—take pictures, get maps, and then decide to redefect and go back to the Soviet Union.

**

RAMSEY CLARK:

I think beginning in 1965 there was much greater care on the part of the Department of Justice and FBI in dealing with, for instance, writers' files—which weren't designated as "writers" files—they weren't kept in a separate place.

Suddenly the FBI was being looked at. I remember members of Congress becoming very concerned about files on them, and I delved into it at the time and said you could not keep secret files on public figures, unrelated to a criminal investigation, in a criminal investigative agency.

It was very difficult for Hoover to be rejected. Take the most sensitive area—like wiretapping: I turned him down on *scores* of wiretaps. He never had been, really, rejected; I think I found there were two times that Francis Biddle had rejected him. One was a bookstore in Philadelphia, a radical bookstore. Probably some Communist or somebody thought to be a Communist had had Communist literature in bookstores, so the FBI wanted to put a tap on him, and lo and behold, Francis Biddle turned it down. And there was one other time.

I never found—and haven't to this day found—that Hoover had, in fact, put on a wiretap when it was prohibited. When I say wiretap, I mean bugs, too—I mean electronic surveillance. Nor have I found evidence that Hoover caused somebody else to do it, or that they engaged in what I used to call "suicide taps"—it's your neck if you get caught. Anyway, I never discovered any of that. Now, it could have happened and just not have been disclosed. How do you find out about those things?

My reading was that in those years, Hoover, either out of a sense of what he ought to do or out of a sense of self-preservation, didn't do it. I'm pretty sure of it. There may have been exceptions I haven't discovered.

But Hoover would sometimes be *very* insistent. The FBI had a code they couldn't break—this was national security—and they claimed they had spent something like $800,000 trying to break the code, and they wanted authority to slip in and steal it. Hoover probably came back three or four times, and I always said no. And I don't think they ever did it.

**

For Hoover, there were always aliens to be watched. In the tumultuous sixties it was the hippies, with their beards, beads, bell bottoms, and bandannas, their spontaneous, easy-going conduct, their drugs, nudity, and subversive music. The hippies, the legacy of the fifties Beat generation, offended not only Hoover's inflexible rules of patriotism but also his rules of fastidiousness. The independence and uninhibited styles of the hippies were as odd, unkempt, and out of place as any alien group could be for the authoritarian Hoover. The passionate, radical writers of the sixties became as threatening and ominous to him as the passionate radical writers of the teens. The youth of America seemed on a subversive course, and this was evident in the late 1960s when a wave of anti–Vietnam War protests flared up around the nation. On December 11, 1969, the FBI taped a Yippie meeting in Wisconsin at which one of the participants said, ''What do I think about what? Capitalism? Capitalism? I just don't understand the question, what do I think about capitalism? It should be destroyed, root and branch.''

Between the late sixties and the early seventies, the FBI ''must have spent a million dollars maintaining informants in the antiwar movement,'' according to former FBI official William Sullivan.

The counterculture of the 1960s produced a rash of underground newspapers, catering to the hippie lifestyle but also noisily political and critical of the war. The FBI tried to destroy these rebel sheets, much as it had sought to silence *The Masses* and other publications in the teens. But this time the Communist influence excuse was a flimsy one because there was no real threat anymore. No. It was strictly personal now. The hippies offended Hoover's sense of order. What J. Edgar Hoover wanted destroyed was a group of ''despised aliens'' that he believed, once again, were the ''source of evil'' in America.

ALLEN GINSBERG:
During the time of underground newspaper strength in America, there was an attack on the underground papers, illegally, by the FBI. And there exists a very good report on that—by the PEN Club—a white paper called *Un-American Activities*. There was a destruction of about sixty percent of the underground newspapers in America—or the attempted destruction. That's quite well documented by the PEN Club. I remember when we inaugurated this book and held

a press conference, the only people who came were the underground press! Nobody from the *Times* or *Time* or NBC or CBS.

I've had recurrent censorship of my work, beginning with *Howl*. English printers refused to print some of the words; put in dots. Then, when it was brought over here from England, the first volumes that were printed there, by City Lights—Customs seized them from City Lights Bookshop and arrested the poet Lawrence Ferlinghetti, the owner of the shop and the publisher.

If you're going to have a society dominated by war, by war gestures, the erotic gesture, which is sincere and genuine—or even a parody of the erotic gesture—cuts through the democracy and opens up a whole area of mental frankness and straight forwardness and candor and humor that a good deal of the military or patriotic bullshit tries to hide, or covers over. And so ultimately you might also say sexual humor itself is an antidote to totalitarian chauvinism.

If you attack people in the emotional nexus, the deepest biological effective urge which is eros; if you censor their public communication on the subject of love—eros—, certainly you can extend your network of hazy censorship into all other areas, the most sensitive areas certainly. If you put a figleaf over people's minds as to what sex is—good or bad—if you mystify that, then you can mystify all other areas of emotion. So the Nazis had their book burnings—anything that does not follow the party line.

Yes, we've conquered the immediate censorship of books as of now, but that can always be rolled back. I think it's possible to roll back the clock. All it takes is money. I don't think it will, but it's not impossible. Start a war and you'll move back the clock easy. Back to the Stone Age.

Cardinal Spellman—the great gay cardinal of New York, who helped start the Vietnam War—mentally sucked off the Pope. He vowed to roll the clock back. I think J. Edgar Hoover vowed to help him.

You don't have to censor political writing in the sense that there's self-censorship. I read *The New York Times* to find out what the middle-class party line is. If I want to find out what's going on in El Salvador, I might pick up occasionally the *Wall Street Journal* or Noam Chomsky or some very specialized work. In that sense, there's no need for political censorship. And when there was a need, which is to say during the time of the underground-newspaper strength in America, there was then a great attack on the underground newspapers—illegally, by the FBI.

INTRA-FBI CORRESPONDENCE:

To: Director, FBI   5/23/69
From: Special Agent in Charge, Newark
Subject: COINTELPRO—New Left

There are enclosed for the Bureau's perusal an issue of a newspaper published in NYC called "SCREW" dated 2/7/69 containing a type of filth that could only originate in a depraved mind.

It is representative of the type of mentality that is following the New Left theory of immorality on certain college campuses. Officials at Rutgers are at the very least condoning its distribution since no curtailment of its sale or distribution has been imposed by them. This paper is being given away and sold inside Conklin Hall, Rutgers University, Newark, by "hippie" types in unkempt clothes, with wild beards, shoulder length hair and other examples of their non-conformity. . . .

. . . A short story titled "Tea Party" published in "Evergreen Review" . . . was distributed by professors of literature to students in composition classes at Paterson State College. It contained 79 obscene terms referring to incest, sexuality and biology, four dozen "cuss" words and a dozen instances of taking the Lord's name in vain. . . .

To: Special Agent in Charge, Newark   6/4/69
From: Director, FBI
Subject: COINTELPRO—New Left
Authority is granted to prepare and anonymously mail the letter suggested . . . to State Education Committee. . . . Assure that all necessary steps are taken to protect the identity of the Bureau as the source of this letter . . . which would purportedly be from a concerned student who is offended by the obscenities being distributed at the state institution. . . .

**

One of the most prominent organs of the New Left was the San Francisco–based magazine *Ramparts,* which was read attentively by the FBI. Indeed, a lengthy 1967 memorandum on *Ramparts* is concealed in the file of Djuna Barnes, an avant-garde writer of the 1930s and 1940s, author of the novel *Nightwood.*

The memo covers issues published between May 1962 and May 1964. It reports that the magazine "was primarily a literary, artistic, and Catholic magazine during its first two years. The change into a Communist-line, New Left publication came rather abruptly, in May 1964, when Warren Hinkle II, the present editor, rose suddenly from director of promotion to executive editor."

The next twenty-five pages analyze the "topics and themes" of the magazine, in order to make plans to harass it, presumably. The FBI concludes that "a dominant theme in *Ramparts* is that only the rebellious young of America offer hope to the country." The report describes a review of *A Fine Madness,* a novel by Elliott Baker, as "not a review but a series of satiric thrusts against a number of American writers: Nelson Algren, Norman Mailer, J. D. Salinger," and ends with the preposterous pronouncement that "it appears highly probable that neither *A Fine Madness* nor Elliott Baker exist" and that the reviewer "invented them" in order to take his "swats."

Why was such a damaging and inherently embarrassing report concealed in Djuna Barnes's file? Apparently it was chosen because *Ramparts* had published a poem of hers. Along with ninety-three other contributors to *Ramparts,* her name appears in the magazine's glossary. A CIA report attached to the document states that twenty-four of the writers on the list had "most frequently and most vehemently expressed major Communist themes in their published articles."

EXCERPTS FROM *RAMPARTS* MAGAZINE MEMORANDUM:
 • "Vol. I, No. I . . . Pp. 47–52, 'J. D. Salinger's Glass Menagerie,' by Warren Hinkle. Page 49 is missing, which doesn't help one to follow Hinkle, whose pedestrian theme is that Salinger is principally concerned with sensitivity and estrangement from society."
 • "Pp. 81–85. 'The Goldfish,' a short story by L. W. Michaelson. A mood story without significant ideational content."
 • "Vol 2, No I. Pp49–53. 'THE WELL,' a short story by N. Scott Momaday. A drunken Indian murders an old hag. (The Indians in this story are not the noble and abused people that became a RAMPARTS stereotype later.)"
                                                —from file on Djuna Barnes; 1967

**

Another movement that accelerated in the 1960s was feminism, or "women's lib," as it was usually known. As women became a strong political and social force, the FBI began watching organizations advancing their agenda.

Generally, Hoover's attitude toward women spilled over into the material he collected about them, and he often blamed the men in their lives for introducing them to subversive thoughts. Léonie Adams's file reports that she "would follow the beliefs of her husband in matters of a political nature."

The writers' files are overwhelmingly male, reflecting not only the fact that there were more well-known male writers than female writers, but also the FBI's viewpoint that women were meant to be protected and not harassed. Ironically, if such a point of view weren't purely sexist, it might be appropriate.

Between 1969 and 1979, the FBI amassed a file of nearly three thousand pages on the women's liberation movement, comprising reports on meetings, conferences, workshops, demonstrations, magazines, membership lists, and so on. One target of the inquiry was "evidence of affiliation and/or sympathy with other organizations" such as the Black Panther party, Students for a Democratic Society, or the Socialist Workers party. Sexist attitudes tinged agents' reports on demonstrations. One report says, "The Women, in general, appeared to be hippies, lesbians or from far-out groups. Most of them were colorfully dressed, but the majority wore faded blue jeans. Most seemed to be making a real attempt to be unattractive."

To Hoover, equality for women was an affront to basic American values, and he refused to hire women agents.* Cartha DeLoach recalled, "Hoover's mother was such a strict, religious individual, and he was so close to his mother and had such respect for womanhood that he thought it would be wrong to put a woman out on the front line and

---

* In 1991, the FBI employed only 1,064 women out of a total of 10,035 special agents.

make her deal with criminals—rapists—the seamy side of life. That was one thing. And another thing was he didn't think that they had the muscular ability to make arrests.''

Hoover not only believed women were to be protected, but he idealized them and felt that they were meant to be kept on a pedestal at all times. In his personal art collection, statues and paintings of women far outnumber those of men; his house in Washington was full of statues of nude women, and there was even one painting of geisha girls that hung in his living room.

SVETLANA ALLILUYEVA:
I want to write a book for the granddaughters, and pick up all these characters, these characters of my maternal line—my mother, my grandmothers, and my nanny. You wouldn't find any more characters like *that*—this belongs to a different era. These people are gone forever.

Well, I'm not a feminist, but I simply want to make a point. I'm making the point because people just can't listen; they're so obsessed by the figure of my father that they forget that I even had a mother! Something came from that side, too.

The twenties and the early thirties was a time of great liberation for women. And my mother was one of those—and all the wives of the other party leaders— they were always working and studying and living under their own maiden name, as part of liberation. Ah, well, I think my father was simply very conservative about it. He was very Asian in many ways—it takes a lot of changes in generations for an Asian man to come to the concept that wives—that women— should have lives of their own and achievements of their own.

**

Now in his seventies, the Great Enforcer was increasingly out of touch with the times. In 1970, he rejected President Richard Nixon's ''Huston Plan,'' a joint FBI, CIA, NSA, and Army Intelligence project to spy on the antiwar movement as well as the civil rights movement. Hoover repudiated it because it impinged on his sovereignty, and in the climate of unpluggable news leaks, covert activities could no longer be hidden. This decision led the White House to employ the ''plumbers,'' leading to the Watergate break-in, and, finally, to Nixon's exile.

CARTHA DeLOACH:
I think Nixon really wanted to get rid of Hoover. A short time after I'd left the FBI to join PepsiCo in 1970, John Mitchell, who was the attorney general at the time, called the chairman of the board at PepsiCo, Donald Kendall, and asked him if he would mind if I came down to see him—Mitchell—at the Justice Department. And Kendall asked me, and I told him I'd be glad to, so I went down at five o'clock in the afternoon. Mitchell had me come in to his private, small office in the back—not the large office—and he said he wanted to talk in con-

fidence. He asked me what would be the best way to get rid of Mr. Hoover. And I thought to myself—I was astonished, but I thought to myself—if they're going to do it anyhow, let's try to work something out so Mr. Hoover can leave in grace. So I suggested to Mitchell that he make him director emeritus, let him keep an office, albeit a small one, let him keep his secretary, Helen Gandy—because Mr. Hoover didn't know how to order groceries, he didn't know how to handle correspondence and so on, and Helen Gandy could continue doing that. It would give her a job. Let him keep his car—his bulletproof Cadillac (and Mr. Hoover didn't know how to drive, either). And I said, let the President do it, not you. Make him director emeritus and call upon him for consultation every once in a while on matters of espionage or organized crime. Mitchell said it was a good idea and said, "I'll do it."

Two weeks later he called me personally in New York and he wanted to know if I'd come down to Washington again. And I got down there at the same time—late afternoon—and there were only the two of us there. Mitchell said, "I told President Nixon what your suggestion was, and he thought it was a good idea." Mitchell said the President had had Mr. Hoover over for breakfast that morning and he had told Mr. Hoover exactly what I had said to tell him, and Mr. Hoover kept right on talking. Mitchell said President Nixon didn't have guts enough to tell Mr. Hoover himself that he wanted a new director. And he said, "The President and I think that *you* should go in"—meaning me—"and tell Mr. Hoover we want to get somebody else and he should be made director emeritus." And he asked me, "Will you do it?" And I said, "No, I won't do it." Mr. Hoover was very kindly disposed toward me, and even though I liked him—well, I loved him, but I didn't like him, on a day-to-day basis—but I said no, it would frankly make him very angry because he would think it was coming from a subordinate.

And so Mr. Mitchell said, "Well, I guess I'll have to do it *myself.*"

But he never did. He never did it.

CHAPTER TWENTY-ONE

Mailer, Ginsberg, and Frank

In 1960, the FBI noted for its records that Norman Mailer had said on a Chicago radio show that "J. Edgar Hoover has paralyzed the imagination of this country in a way Joseph Stalin never could." The novelist recalled, "The reaction to the show was fascinating. The switchboard lit up, and there were twenty-eight calls against me and twenty for me! It was my first intimation that the sixties were coming."

Mailer was perhaps the most prominent of the activist writers of the 1960s and the 1970s. His 1968 *Armies of the Night,* an account of the peace demonstrations in the nation's capital, became the classic text of the anti–Vietnam War movement.

But Mailer's name had entered the FBI files well before the 1960s—in 1949, to be precise, when his name appeared on the sponsor list of the Cultural and Scientific Conference for World Peace at the Waldorf-Astoria Hotel. This reference inaugurates his 466-page file.*

---

* Mailer received 364 pages of the file in 1975 but misplaced them. Since then, 102 pages were added, of which 56 were declassified and released in 1988. These pages are the basis of the present assessment.

Three pages of undated electronic surveillance have been "withheld in their entirety."

Mailer says that he remembers "for a long period, maybe a year or two, I just took it for granted my phone was being tapped. There were all sorts of odd noises on it." He can't put a specific date on the bugging, however, and says, "There are so many periods when it could have been. But my feeling is that it's been off and on for thirty years." During the Cold War 1950s, the author of such books as *The Naked and the Dead, Deer Park, The Executioner's Song,* and *Ancient Evenings* indirectly felt the chill.

NORMAN MAILER:
My father at one point during the McCarthy period was in danger of losing his job. He was working for the government as an accountant, and he had a reasonable government level, GS-13, nothing very high. And he was not a young man, anymore—this was back in about 1952. And my father came up before a loyalty board and was found a risk. And the reason was—this is engraved forever in my mind—"because of your continuing close association with your son, Norman Mailer, who is reported to be a concealed Communist."

And the definition of a concealed Communist was someone who would not admit to being a Communist!

I thought it was a lost cause, and we should save time and just walk away from it, but Cy Rembar's attitude—he was the lawyer—was that there's going to be a judge somewhere at the end of it who will think of himself as a judge, not a bigot, and why don't we appeal to his good side and try to present some arguments? I wrote a brief, together with Cy Rembar.

We actually won that. My father was reinstated in his job, though he wasn't permitted access to certain kinds of confidential papers. So his job really had a shadow cast upon it.

That was where it all began, I think. In other words, during the period that I belonged to the Progressive party in 1948 I think I probably got on an FBI list, and I've been on it ever since. I went out to Hollywood in 1949—I can't swear to this—but I had some *very* odd experiences there. I had an agent who was particularly calm and was very sure of my getting work. But very often people would want to hire me—this was after *The Naked and the Dead*—and at the last moment the job would fall through. I said to my agent at one point, "Do you think it could be a political thing?" At the beginning he said, "Gee, I don't think so," but by the end he said, "I don't know anymore." And this guy was a Republican, or if not a Republican, he was a conservative.

I was in Chicago for the Liston-Patterson fight—it was 1961 or 1962. It was one of the most bizarre weekends of my life. I was staying at the Playboy mansion. The rooms were bugged. Let us say, in the CIA sense. I have a ninety percent certainty. To begin with, I was told they were bugged by a whole bunch of people who said, "Watch out what you're saying." And then someone else said, "I think there are movie cameras, as well."

At one moment, I did get this incredible feeling I was being photographed, and I froze. There was a lot of subtle stuff, but I could never swear to it in a court of law.

**

In June of 1962, the FBI sent a top secret memo to a person or agency whose name is blacked out. The message: "We respectfully report that a visa has been authorized for Norman Mailer, a United States citizen, and writer for the Macmillan Company publishing House." Where in the world was he going that the FBI cared so much? Mailer explains that he "went to England in '62 with [his then wife] Jeannie Campbell. We went to London and we went to Paris, and then we went to the Riviera." Mailer says there was no literary conference or writers meeting of any kind, and he has no idea why this trip was singled out by the FBI.

On April 26, 1966, the year his *Cannibals and Christians* was published, and one year before *Why Are We in Vietnam?* would be published, the FBI decided to attempt to exploit Mailer in a COIN-TELPRO against the Communist party. The scheme was to mail forged letters signed with "the printed name of Gus Hall with the terminal notation 'Comradely' " to people critical of America's Vietnam policy. Mailer was on the list to receive this "typewritten note," plus a copy of "The New Draft Program of the CP, USA." It was hoped that he would write Gus Hall, questioning him on why he was sending him CP plans, and then it was hoped Mailer would get mad enough about being considered "in the CP's eye" that he might write a public protest.

In the end, this COINTELPRO was not used, because Hoover felt the FBI's "technique might be compromised" because "the Communist party plans a broad distribution of their draft program" and some people on the list might get two sets of draft programs, one accompanied by the phony letter, and then become leery. There are two other names blacked out, and Mailer speculates that one of them could have been Robert Lowell, "given the year."

He also speculates that one reason Lowell's file was so brief, compared to his and those of other writers engaged in anti–Vietnam War protest, is that "it could have been cleaned out." He adds, "Don't forget, I'm a parlous figure. Lowell was much more respected than I was. With me, people just shrugged and said, 'Well, how not?' "

Mailer's race for mayor of New York City in 1969 is *not* reported in his file; nonetheless, at the time, he "had his suspicions about a couple of people" who might have been spying on him. He says there were "odd things that happened," including a "too good nuts-and-bolts guy" who somehow managed to sabotage certain "little" things having to do with the timing and planning of some meetings. Mailer also received reports that the man was rude to certain groups, and says, "This guy was too smart for that, so afterwards I began to think that perhaps there were people trying to sabotage things. And the more I've read and studied and learned about this over the years, the more this makes sense to me. That's the way they do work: small petty stuff."

During the spring of 1969, the year after his Pulitzer Prize–winning *Armies of the Night,* as well as *Miami and the Siege of Chicago,* the FBI used Mailer to counter an ad which appeared in *The New York Times* which "claims the recent controversy over black anti-Semitism is a fake."

The FBI concocted a long memo to be sent to "Honorable Henry A. Kissinger and the Attorney General" saying that Mailer, "the negro Bayard Rustin [*sic*]," was among a group of "Negro-watchers" who spoke "sickening obscenities." Many of the phrases in the memo were taken from the February 1969 issue of *Liberator* magazine, a black nationalist publication. There was also a reference to "the vicious anti-Black sentiments expressed by Norman Podhoretz." These phrases were quoted by the FBI to illustrate how and why "black nationalist anti-Semitism has been building up since 1966." The FBI also quoted from an "anti-Semitic" [it was released with the title *Beyond the Law,*] poem by Amiri Baraka, and this particular reference does not appear in Baraka's own FBI file.

In 1970, the FBI believed that Mailer's "16 MM black and white featured [*sic*] length film 'Bust 80' " [it was released with the title *Beyond the Law*] demonstrated Communist influence. Mailer comments, "From their point of view it *was* subversive, since it mocks the police." The following year, the FBI reported that Mailer's "*The Prisoner of Sex* would be published by Little, Brown," and that "it had been selected by the Book Find Club, proving that it, and Little, Brown, know how to find incendiary books."

Says Mailer, "Incendiary? God Almighty! Well, the FBI was always after the Book Find Club because it was seen as a sort of left-wing outfit. But, Little, Brown, good God! Of all the stodgy firms in all the world! Angus Cameron used to work there years ago, and that's what got Little, Brown on the list originally."

In November of 1973, the FBI monitored all the participants—including Mailer—of a conference held at Georgetown University sponsored by the Committee to Investigate Assassinations. Mailer remembers it as "an odd occasion," and he "took it for granted that there were all sorts of secret policemen there."

In November 1974, the FBI entered in the file a report that Mailer had recently formed his own intelligence committee to join forces with the already existing Committee for Action/Research on the Intelligence Community (CARIC). The FBI said Mailer's plan was "to link CARIC with his idea of a Fifth Estate," explaining that "his idea of a Fifth Estate means groups of citizens who have banded together to research, watch and prevent the type of Orwellian, 1984, concept of 'Big Brother is watching.' " The Bureau concocted a threat to national security because Mailer and the others could "come in contact with classified material" that could be used against the FBI.

Mailer says, "There was an organization in existence already, and I said to them if you call it the Fifth Estate, I'll join with you. I wanted the words *fifth estate* to get some standing. The organization was called the Fifth Estate for a while, but then I dropped out after about six months because I really wasn't too close to these guys, and I didn't feel comfortable with them. A little ultra, shall we say? They fingered that CIA man in Greece who got killed. My name was read out in Congress as one of the people responsible for the death of a CIA guy in Greece. I hadn't intended a citizen's group to go round fingering CIA men to get knocked off—that wasn't my idea how you do it."

A large majority of the various reports on Mailer were "disseminated" to field offices all around the country, as well as to Army and Naval Intelligence and the Secret Service. Mailer believes that this is because when he was living in a building in Brooklyn on Fulton Street, Rudolf Abel "had the studio under me." Abel was a Soviet spy who was apprehended and exchanged for U.S. pilot Gary Powers in 1962. He resided in Brooklyn for many years passing himself off as an artist and photographer while he was communicating American secrets with Moscow via shortwave radio.

Mailer moved in the building in 1953, and had his studio there for seven or eight years; the building was torn down in 1962. "Abel was a silent man—you'd see him occasionally in the elevator, and he'd kid around very slightly with the elevator man. Anyway, there I was, above him all that time. And who knows what waves went up from him into me, so that I'm now spending all these years on a novel about the CIA." (The novel, *Harlot's Ghost,* was published in October 1991.)

NORMAN MAILER:
   I've spent most of my life thinking about that funny double life that secret policemen lead. In fact, I've thought about it so much, I've ended up with a special theory for my new novel. I've got a psychiatrist in the novel—a woman

who's married to one of the top people in the CIA. And she's in the CIA. She's come up with a brand-new psychological theory to explain that double life that they all have.

Policemen and intelligence officers lead a double life as fully as spies. Intelligence officers and spies have the same umbilical relation that policemen and crooks have. It's like older brother, younger brother—it's a deep, familial relation. I think intelligence officers are tremendously complex people under all the rhetoric. In the rhetoric, they usually often sound like idiots, but under that they're complicated, wily, interesting people with very good sides, very often.

I think that for a great many people psychic health consists of having a double personality.

**

SVETLANA ALLILUYEVA:

The effect of this obsession with my father is an obstacle for me. There's great resentment, because people hated him. You know, I just want to make one thing very plain and I want it to be on the tape. Is it going there? I wrote about my father as a man in my first book, *Twenty Letters to a Friend*; and in my second book, *Only One Year*, I wrote about him as a politician—his work, his power as a Communist leader.

He would turn one minute to you as a human being and absolutely charm you, and then he would turn around to another person and be a Communist dictator, and absolutely knock the person down by words or something. Well, he had this double kind of character—but I always divided these two things. And when people talk to me about him as "your father," "your father," "your father"— this is *one* thing to me: this is his human character. And then I speak about him as a different thing—as a Communist dictator. To me, it's *two* different things, *two* different sides of the same man. And I think it's true in every politician, because every politician is one thing in his work, and another at home.

**

FBI DIRECTOR WILLIAM STEELE SESSIONS:

The mission of the Bureau is investigative, and it has to be an investigative agency. When you are talking about an agency going about its business, doesn't it sometimes role-play? And the answer is yes. It does role-play. Every agency in the world that I know role-plays in certain instances, and role-playing is not truthful. When people are role-playing, they are pretending to be something that they are not in order to get the job done.

**

Allen Ginsberg's file—and career as an activist writer—bridges the cultural gap between the 1950s and 1960s, between the Beats and the hippies. His poem *Howl,* which had its first public reading in 1955, became the most famous lyric protest of the Beat generation, and his magnetism as a poet and as a spokesman carried over to the hippie movement of the sixties. In the files the "Beat poet" would become "the New Left poet."

The Beats were the latest incarnations of the aliens Hoover had been tracking for forty years. As a 1960 memo said, "The Beat generation is an accusation of the system," a system that Hoover had dedicated his career to preserving.

The first reference to *Howl* in Ginsberg's file is hostile. On October 4, 1957, the Bureau reported that it was published by Lawrence Ferlinghetti, who "had been acquitted on charges of dealing with obscene literature." Describing Ginsberg's publisher as a merchandiser of dirty words is typical of the smears that characterize the FBI's intense, harsh relationship with the writer. Obscenity and subversion were indissolubly linked in the Director's mind, and he was profoundly offended by Ginsberg's open and candid homosexuality. Ginsberg's file is full of aspersions on his personality and his way of life. He is described variously as "a hippie movement leader," the "beat poet" and an "entertainer" who "chants unintelligible poems." He wears a "fuzzy beard" with his "hair long, combed back and untrimmed." His personality is "extremely eccentric" and "extremely revolutionary and inflammatory."

Not only was Ginsberg unceasingly watched by the FBI ("He was met at the airport by three 'hippie type' individuals"), but his writing and lecturing were obstructed, his mail was opened, his passport questioned, and he was often detained for rude interrogations. On one such occasion in 1965, Ginsberg says he was stopped by customs and subjected to a "detailed intensive search, all my luggage fine-tooth combed, the lint out of my pocket sifted for suspicious weed, et cetera, made to undress to my underwear—all the dull humiliations of a Kafkian trial."

In 1967, according to a report in the file, a photograph of him "in an indecent pose" was placed in "a locked sealed envelope . . . for possible future use." Ginsberg has no idea what it is or how the photograph was obtained.

Ginsberg not only has an FBI file, but a record at fifteen other agencies, including the CIA, the Defense Department, the U.S. Postal Service, the Treasury Department, and Drug Enforcement Agency.

The only criminal conduct alluded to in his approximately 919-page file is dated 1949, when FBI agents from the New York office visited him at the New York State Psychiatric Institute, where he was undergoing treatment, to interview him about a stolen car, part of the "approximately $18,000 worth of valuables and personal property" that had been stolen from a Long Island family by a friend of his. Ginsberg told them "he knew nothing whatsoever about the origin of the car" (although the police report indicates he admitted he had been in the car). Ginsberg was a student at Columbia University at the time, and through the help of some professors there, including Lionel Trilling, he was hospitalized instead of imprisoned for his role as an accessory to a crime for which he was ultimately never indicted. Diana Trilling comments that in addition to her husband, Jacques Barzun and the dean "undertook to save Allen. They got him a very brilliant forensic lawyer who helped, so they got him free psychiatric treatment for a whole year instead of going to jail. I don't think Allen ever forgave Lionel for treating it as psychiatric rather than criminal."

There are also two even earlier references, but these came to the attention of the Bureau only in 1968. One is a 1942 job application to the Defense Council of Paterson "N.Y." ("N.J." is meant) when he was a sixteen-year-old boy, and another is a 1954 California vagrancy charge, of which he was found not guilty.

The political and literary references date from 1957, when the Bureau also recorded that Ginsberg was "a friend of Jack Kerouac and William Burroughs." Curiously, the FBI says it has no file on Kerouac, whose *On the Road* had been published that year and is described in Ginsberg's file as a "manifesto of the beat generation." Ginsberg comments that "Kerouac constantly said nice things about the government and about the FBI. He never attacked the FBI." He adds that Kerouac sometimes complained that the FBI "was after him," and that he seemed "a little paranoid" about it, but Ginsberg believes "his patriotism was unassailable."

In 1959, the FBI reported that Ginsberg's mother was "a psychotic and a Communist." (She was confined to a mental hospital.)

On December 20, 1960, and eight days later, on December 28, the FBI intercepted two letters Ginsberg sent to the Soviet writer Elena Romanova, in care of the Writers' Union in Moscow. In one, he tells her he has been invited to Cuba. In the other, he confided that he'd like to visit Russia and live there for a while.

Ginsberg did not visit Cuba until 1965, when he was invited to judge a poetry contest. On that occasion he was expelled from Cuba by the government. Nevertheless, after that trip, he was labeled by the FBI "potentially dangerous" because of "emotional instability," "strong anti-U.S. sentiments," and "prior acts indicating a propensity for violence." In addition, the FBI had recorded that he was a member of the Fair Play for Cuba Committee in 1960.

ALLEN GINSBERG:
I was expelled from Cuba for fighting the Communists, for denouncing Castro's antigay policy, for hanging around with younger writers, for criticizing Cuba's monolithic press, for talking "strange," and for saying I thought Che Guevara was *cute,* and that Raul Castro was gay.

What it boils down to was that I was very vociferous in behalf of the younger people—they were putting people in jail for having long hair and pegged pants and listening to the Beatles.

So the police picked me up in my room about two days before I was supposed to leave anyway. They locked me in and said, "You are being held incommunicado." And then they took me downstairs through the hotel lobby—so I started shouting to everybody: "I'm being arrested by the secret police!" They were scared shitless. They were all frightened to death—they thought I was an eccentric anyway. So I didn't have any credibility because I was a beatnik and they were all sitting there with their tails between their legs, eating whatever propaganda the master race served up for them! I asked the immigration people, "What am I being expelled for?" And the guy in the green uniform said, "You'll have to ask yourself that." Classical, total, bureaucratic Communist answer. Then he said, "For breaking the laws of Cuba." Then I said, "Well, what laws did I break?" *"You'll have to ask yourself that."*

So I hadn't done anything, actually, as far as I know. I'd slept with one boy—barely—but that's about it. I don't think it's against the law.

**

During the summer of 1960, the FBI's suspicions were aroused when it heard that "the works of Ginsberg were read to jazz accompaniment" at a "Greenwich Village type" café in Czechoslovakia.

The following year, the FBI reported that the magazine of the League of Militant Poets published a letter from Ginsberg in which "he admitted using narcotics, having homosexual experiences and homosexual love affairs." The report also said "he indicated his background as Jewish, Left-Wing, Atheist, and Russian." Ginsberg later wrote in a note to his lawyer, Ira Lowe, who was helping him obtain all his records under the FOIA, that the report "makes no mention of my criticism of Marxist consciousness. If the FBI research had as its justification an attempt to describe my 'connections with communist dominated organizations,' it was sloppy, prejudiced, and selectively biased in summary of materials."

In 1963, the Bureau reported that Ginsberg "passed through South Viet Nam after a stay in India," and that some Vietnamese monks "felt sure that the man was a spy" because he had "a long beard, hair very long in back and curly, was a poet and a little crazy and liked Buddhists."

In 1964, the Bureau reported that Ginsberg was in favor of legalizing marijuana, and had founded an organization called LEMAR to promote its legalization. Ginsberg says that "following the publication of *LEMAR* newsletter, a series of burglaries occurred" at one of the editor's apartments, and papers were stolen. He suspects documents were stolen by the DEA or FBI for the file. "I was suspected of international drug peddling," he says. That year, the FBI also reported that Ginsberg and LeRoi Jones "appeared to use [a] radio program as a soap box for communist propaganda, by interjecting remarks from time to time without much bearing on what was being discussed, mainly "censorship" in the United States."

When Ginsberg traveled to Czechoslovakia, the FBI followed his movements closely from Washington. It later reported that he was "chosen 'King of May' of all Prague universities, but that a few days later he was expelled from Czechoslovakia." The Bureau quotes from an editorial in a Czech paper that "certain young people were aroused and disturbed . . . that he had overstepped his limits." His crime was keeping a diary which "freely described in detail his sexual adventures with a series of young boys he met in Prague." The diary had been stolen from his hotel room. Ginsberg later told his lawyer that "very little 'sympathetic' accounting of my clash with communist authorities is included, but only communist party line accounts of the situation accusing me of 'bisexuality, homosexuality, narcomania, alcoholism, posing & a social extremism verging on orgy.' There is a striking affinity between the Prague communist account of my social behavior & previous FBI reports. . . . In other words, under rationalizations of investigating me for subversive pro-communist associations, material was gathered from communist police state journalism attacking my character in terms similar to FBI thinking."

Another 1965 memo reports that although Ginsberg's activities "are bizarre," he does not qualify for the Security or Reserve Index because nothing he has done is "inimical to the interests of the U.S." The memo also says that agents are never to interview Ginsberg without authorization, because of "his narcotic and sexual proclivities" and his "connections with mass media." Although Hoover discouraged interviews with prominent writers who he feared might raise a public fuss and had a greater media clout than he did, this is the first time the FBI concluded that a writer's "proclivities" were potentially embarrassing to them. Perhaps Hoover feared his agents would be seduced.

On April 19, 1966, the FBI reported that the "Free University of Detroit" was teaching traitorous works by Ginsberg, Pound, Zukofsky, Robert Creeley, and Robert Duncan.

Two years later, on March 28, 1968, a confidential informant told the FBI that Ginsberg "chanted unintelligible poems in Grant Park."

"The poem in question was in fact Blake's "The Grey Monk," tuned for harmonium and sung for the first time," Ginsberg explained. He also said that another informant report that said he had given an "extremely revolutionary and inflammatory speech" was false, because "as a matter of fact, my voice was almost gone and all I said was one 'om.' "

The Bureau also reported that Ginsberg, known by the name "La Poesia," was a sponsor of the Yippie Festival of Life, and was also a sponsor of "an LBJ unbirthday party" at the 1968 Democratic Convention in Chicago when police cracked down on peace demonstrators.

Ginsberg explains that he was covering the convention for a magazine. "I had proper credentials to enter the convention Hall. On Wednesday, August 28 . . . as I was going to cover a Democratic caucus, I was intercepted with a photographer companion near a Coke machine by a uniformed Chicago policeman, badge #309, who ordered me to follow him. On my protesting, he said, 'Shut the fuck up or I'll wipe the fucking beard off your face!' I was taken to the Secret Service headquarters . . . and detained for an hour without explanation."

During 1969, the FBI tracked "the bearded apostle of opposition and resistance" as he spoke at various college campuses. An array of student informants was used to monitor his speeches and readings.

In January 1972, Ginsberg's CIA file reported that he accused that agency of being "tied in with the drug traffic in Southeast Asia." Three months later, the FBI recorded that Ginsberg read "an original poem dealing with the recent bombing of North Vietnam" to a South Carolina "Walk of Life" rally. On September 7, the Bureau reported that Ginsberg's civil rights might have been violated during his August 23 arrest at the Republican National Convention in Miami Beach, Florida. However, the file indicates that "inasmuch as civil rights complaints arose from arrests . . . no further investigation is being conducted." In other words, since his civil rights were violated as a result of being arrested and not for some other reason, the matter could prove embarrassing to the Bureau.

On May 3, 1976, the FBI reported that Ginsberg's name was mentioned in a *New Times* magazine article entitled "Commune Children." The last line of the article, which also happens to be the last line of Ginsberg's file, reads: "This Community, where all are one, is a very real and viable way to deal with this thing called Life; it is . . . one way to make it sanely through a world that, from all appearances, is clearly going mad."

ALLEN GINSBERG:
   I always thought that the reason J. Edgar Hoover was kept in is because he denied that there was organized crime. My theory was that the Mafia had got him in a basement and some big hairy goon was screwing him and had pictures of him—so they had blackmailed J. Edgar Hoover to deny that there was any organized crime. Someday the tapes will emerge out of the Freedom of Information Act! It's certainly a fantasy on my part, but on the other hand how could Hoover be so dumb or so neurotic as to say there's no such thing as organized crime—at a point when everybody in New Jersey that comes from Paterson knows that the longshoremen's union is riddled with organized crime? They've got *On the Waterfront,* with Marlon Brando, in the fifties, and Hoover's still saying there's no such thing as organized crime.
   How did they keep him quiet? Or was he such a neurotic nut? You see, *The New York Times* party line was that he was just such a nut—obsessed with communism, and had blinders on. It's sort of like saying Stalin didn't understand what he was doing. They wouldn't take a line like that with Hitler, or with secret policemen somewhere else. They wouldn't let the *Communists* get away with a line like that—they'd see a plot.
   One thing I've always thought, they're very eager to report when the Russian poets get in trouble, but when the American poets get in trouble, they don't report it. That's why Hoover could get away with this all his life—because it's ultimately the middle class. The question is how did he deceive himself, but also the question is how did the middle-class media allow themselves to be deceived all along?

**

   The FBI's great interest in the Fair Play for Cuba Committee brought new trouble to an old radical who never hid his Communist sympathies: Waldo Frank, best known as the author of the 1925 *Virgin Spain* and the 1943 *South American Journey*. His record dated back to 1932. In fact, by the late thirties he had already accumulated a hefty FBI file. But in the 1960s, when he became chairman of the FPCC, the FBI singled him out for intensive investigation.

   He had long been involved in Latin American affairs as a vigorous critic of U.S. imperialism in the region, before such sentiments became a central doctrine of the program of the American left. During the 1940s, when the FBI carried on intelligence operations in Latin America, it had monitored Frank's activities, reporting, for example, that in the summer of 1941 he lectured in Argentina and Chile, and the following year in Brazil, Peru, and Uruguay. An agent was in the audience taking notes when Frank spoke at the University of Puerto Rico in 1948. According to his report, Frank urged the Puerto Ricans to "retain their Spanish language and resist cultural absorption by the United States," which was "an imperialist nation." However, the FBI also reported that the Communists had criticized Frank, on another occasion, for telling "Latin American youth" that they can "learn more from Gandhi than from Stalin."

The Fair Play for Cuba Committee was considered a front for Fidel Castro's Communist regime, and the FBI made it a COINTELPRO target in an effort to break it up. Soon, Frank's activities in its behalf attracted the Director's personal attention. "Press vigorously," he scribbled on a 1962 report.

An article that appeared in the Cuban newspaper *Hoy*, included in Frank's file, reported that on September 25, 1959, he "would accompany Prime Minister Fidel Castro on a tour of the country." *Hoy* quoted Frank as saying, "I am not afraid of communism, and I will not join hands with the anti-communists."

When Frank became chairman of the Fair Play for Cuba Committee in 1960, the FBI opened a new investigation of him under the heading "Waldo Frank/Internal Security—Cuba." It placed a network of informants in the committee, noting in May 1961 that "all information hereinafter referred to as being from 'Hoy' is attributable" to an informant. This is another example of how the FBI concealed informants' reports in other files, in this case the file on *Hoy*.

That year, the FBI looked into possible violations of the Registration Act by Frank as a way of curbing his pro-Castro activities. The FBI wanted to explore the possibility that he was an unregistered lobbyist for a foreign country. On June 15, 1961, it reported that the "investigation to date has not disclosed nature of Frank's relationship with Cubans, although we have learned that it involves writing a book," and that Frank "had a contract with the Cuban Ministry of Education to write a book favorable to Fidel Castro for which he received a final settlement of $5,000." A report in November states that the FBI "will remain alert to secure copies of Frank's book 'CUBA—Prophetic Island' " (i.e., *The Prophetic Island: A Portrait of Cuba*) when published. It was decided to send a "blind memo" to the Internal Revenue Service requesting a copy of his tax forms, "in a further effort to resolve subject's connections with Cuban officials."

A State Department document forwarded to the FBI discloses that "Mr. Justo Carrillo, recently-resigned chief of propaganda for the Cuban Revolutionary Council . . . stated that he had a letter or a photostatic copy of a letter from Armando Hart, Cuban Minister of Education, to an official at the Cuban 'National Bank' ordering the bank to pay some $5,000 to Waldo Frank, leftwing American Author, for services connected with writing a book on the Cuban Revolution. The latter also purportedly mentioned a previous payment to Frank for his work on the book. Carrillo wanted to turn this letter over to a Senate Subcommittee investigating Cuba, so the subsidization of Frank's book could be publicized." The FBI decided "it might be useful evidence to use in any case against Frank as an unregistered agent of a foreign government."

After Frank's subsidy was revealed in the press, Frank announced on October 31, 1961, that it had been "no secret," and that "it is an insult to suggest that my opinions can be bought, and I refuse to answer these insults." He also said that "in the book he shows himself to be . . . critical," and he also "recalled that one of his previous works, *Birth of a World—Bolivar in Terms of His People* [*sic*], was commissioned by the Venezuelan Ministry of Education . . ."

Another report says that *The Prophetic Island* was published by the Beacon Press in Boston, and a note at the end tells Hoover that the publisher "is affiliated with American Unitarian Association which in late 1940s and early 1950s was critical of loyalty program" and that an "official publication" of that association, "in November 1958, carried an article which was critical of . . . *Masters of Deceit*."

But Frank's widow, Jean, can't recall that Beacon Press had anything to do with the book. Indeed, the book was published by Marzani and Munsell, and another report says that "reputable publishers would not touch" it, and "Frank had to turn to communist publishers," possibly because the FBI exerted some pressure on "reputable" publishers, as it had done with other books it considered dangerous.

The FBI's review of the book described it as "a rambling account" that was more like a "literary essay" than a "chronological account of Cuban history," and said that it dealt "only intermittently and incompletely with such issues as communist infiltration."

In 1963, the FBI asked an unidentified scholar to read the book. This "expert in the field of Latin American History and politics" told them that "he did not consider the book to be an example of scholarship, nonetheless he could not testify that the book was in fact propaganda rather than an expression of the author's personal view of the events." The scholar also told Hoover that "the book is typical of the non-objective style of writing for which Waldo Frank is noted," and "that to his knowledge the book had not received any literary plaudits, but conversely, neither had it been generally condemned by the academic community."

The FBI also began to "review newspapers and periodicals" to see "whether Frank has attempted to influence public opinion of the Castro regime."

On March 27, 1963, Frank testified before an executive session of the Senate Internal Security Subcommittee, telling it that "he has never been a communist and that his activities on behalf of subversives are matters of principle.'' Two months later the FBI decided to put the registration matter into ''inactive status'' because of Frank's ''advanced age''—he was seventy-four. However, in 1964, Frank's name was put on the Reserve Index, probably because, as Jean Frank recalled, ''he maintained contact with Castro and saw him when he was in New York.'' Frank's name remained on that list until his death in 1967.

JEAN FRANK:

I went with him to Venezuela when he was doing his book on Bolívar, but I didn't go to Cuba with him. He knew he was under surveillance, but I don't think he knew his phone was being tapped or that his mail was being read— good heavens, I don't think he knew *that*. Or that he was put on the Reserve Index. It does surprise me that his file is over five hundred pages—that *does* surprise me.

But actually, the surveillance was going on long before the Cuba book. He had gone to Kentucky in 1932—and got hit in the head there—but the conditions in the coal fields were the kind of social issues he was concerned about. He joined a lot of committees, but he was never a Communist. It was all done by guilt by association—that was how it was done.

It colored his life. He knew the surveillance was going on and that it was affecting the publication of his books. But the blacklisting never affected the contents of his books—what he wrote.

I don't think he ever felt he had been cleared. Even though he was never convicted under the Registration Act, he never felt he had been cleared.

And his granddaughter is now studying medicine in Cuba, and I'm sure her interest in Cuba was sparked by her grandfather. He'd be proud of her.

**

CARTHA DeLOACH:

The Communists were very clever and the Nazis were very clever in having organizations which had patriotic- or religious-sounding names. The Ku Klux Klan, too. If a petition were passed around in your neighborhood and it said, "Would you support the Knights of the White Camellia?" you might think it was a horticulture society. But it's a branch of the Ku Klux Klan.

The Fair Play for Cuba Committee had a name like that—and a lot of people thought at first that Castro was not a Communist, philosophically. But later on they found out differently.

But nevertheless, to make a long story short, the Fair Play for Cuba Committee didn't get off the ground and amount to anything. It was a very weak outfit, and never gathered any great strength in the U.S. because the Communist party, while it may have supported the committee, wasn't strong enough to lend any great strength or support to it.

I guess one of the most famous members—and he was just a guy who handed out handbills on the street corner—was the fella that assassinated John Fitzgerald Kennedy. He was a member in New Orleans. Lee Harvey Oswald.

CHAPTER TWENTY-TWO

Baldwin, Baraka, Schwartz, Roethke, Stout, Williams, Paley, and Doctorow

The first mention of novelist, playwright, and essayist James Baldwin anywhere in the FBI files occurs in 1951—in Richard Wright's file. At that time, the twenty-seven-year-old Baldwin, whose first novel, *Go Tell It on the Mountain,* would be published in 1953, had been living in Paris for two years, and had become friendly with his fellow black expatriates.

According to the December 1951 report, an unidentified source reported that "one James Baldwin, a young Negro writer who was a student in Paris," had "attacked the hatred themes of the Wright writings." (Baldwin had, indeed, at one time assailed Wright's *Native Son* as being too full of anger.) The source also said that Baldwin did not like the "attempt of the Franco-American Fellowship group," which "was organized almost entirely by Richard Wright," to "perpetrate 'Uncle Tom Literature methods.'"

The reference to Baldwin is ironic because "Uncle Tom methods" were not what bothered the FBI (or Baldwin, for that matter) about Wright or any other black writer. On the contrary: militancy in behalf of equal rights was what caught the "FBEye," as Walter Winchell would have said. But there is symbolism in the young Baldwin's FBI "career" beginning in the file of Wright—thus was the bias toward black writers that had begun with Hughes in 1925, and continued with Wright in 1935, passed to Baldwin, the leading voice of the new generation of black writers.

Baldwin's 1,429-page file remained "dead" until 1960, when the FBI recorded that he was a "prominent member" of the Fair Play for Cuba Committee. The following year the FBI got on track, reporting that Baldwin "supported organizations supporting integration" and participated in a rally to abolish the House Un-American Activities Committee. Once again civil rights was equated with insurrection.

The FBI also reported two damning pieces of information: Baldwin had said that "only in revolution could the problems of the United States be solved" and that he had "criticized the Director." Not long after this, Hoover wrote in the margin of a memo: "Is Baldwin on our Security Index?" The answer came back that he was on the Reserve Index for the time being. As he became more vocal in criticizing segregation, his status was changed to "dangerous" and he would be placed on the Administrative Index.

The FBI employed a great many confidential informants to shadow Baldwin, people who attended rallies and meetings with him, and reported what he said and did, as well as neighbors who were willing to keep a surveillance on him, or monitor his mail for any change of address. The FBI also telephoned him under various pretexts to ascertain his whereabouts, and photographed him. One report says that he and James Foreman, the president of the Congress of Racial Equality, were photographed entering the "Dallas County courthouse on October 7, 1963." (Foreman was actually the executive secretary of the Student Nonviolent Coordinating Committee (SNCC). James Farmer was the national director of CORE.)

By 1964, the Bureau stepped up its harassment of James Baldwin, targeting him in a COINTELPRO operation called "Disruption Program Aimed at the Socialist Workers Party." He was to be one of eight recipients of an anonymous letter "designed" to "bring discredit" to the SWP in the "Negro civil rights field." Other recipients were unnamed editors at *The New York Times* and the *National Guardian*. There was also a plan for a "follow-up disruption to generate further suspicion," which consisted of a four-line mischievous jingle that someone in the FBI wrote about a defense committee in North Carolina: "[*blank*] down in Monroe,/Found himself alone with the dough,/Called the cops, and what did he say?/'Bad guys came and took it away.' "

The FBI was as interested in Baldwin's writings as it was in his life; for instance, in 1962, the FBI decided to have the General Crimes Section review his novel *Another Country* because it was reportedly "similar to the 'Tropic' books by Henry Miller." Baldwin's novel was controversial, and was banned in some places for its "obscenity": it contained interracial and homosexual sex scenes. Surprisingly, the FBI did not go along with the censorship this time. The General Crimes Section concluded that the novel "contains literary merit and may be of value to students of psychology and social behavior." Despite this apparent magnanimity, in a later 1969 summary of the author, the FBI reported that an informant suggested that "klansmen obtain copies of [*Another Country*] to determine whether it is suitable reading for college students."

In 1963, the Bureau reported on Baldwin's "disastrous sortie" to the office of Attorney General Robert Kennedy. This was a meeting held to discuss the racial situation, which did not go well, according to the FBI, because of Baldwin's "integration now" philosophy. But the real reason the report called the meeting "disastrous" was because Baldwin had told Kennedy, among other things, that he should fire J. Edgar Hoover.

The FBI also reviewed Baldwin's book of essays, *The Fire Next Time,* published in 1963, which warned that the patience of black people was running out. The Bureau's reviewer wrote, "Baldwin does not regard the Negro as inferior to the whites and says the only thing the white man has that the Negro needs is power." Underlined in Hoover's familiar pen stroke is this line: "He refers to Christ as a 'disreputable sunbaked Hebrew.' " To Hoover, such blasphemy was as bad as communism.

On May 2, 1963, the FBI reported that the author was "caustic" and "uncompromising" in a speech delivered at the Staten Island, New York, chapter of the Congress of Racial Equality. An informant told agents that there were "close to one thousand persons listening to him."

Five months later, on October 28, the Bureau received word that the writer "contemplated protesting certain deletions made by the U.S. Information Agency in a videotape of a round table discussion about the March on Washington." The deletions involved an attack on Hoover and the FBI. Word of Baldwin's alleged protest was forwarded to the USIA, and Paul McNichol, its director, wrote Hoover that he had not received any such request from Baldwin or his lawyer, although he had prepared a statement saying time limits made certain deletions necessary. It seems obvious that since Baldwin did *not* protest, that Hoover used him as an excuse to bully the USIA into removing the criticism of the FBI from the tape. But the USIA seems to have been more than willing on the pretext of time.

In 1964, the FBI learned that Baldwin was "contemplating" a book about "the FBI in the South." An agent had also read a recent interview in which Baldwin "referred to Bureau personnel as *The Blood Counters*," and explained that the term was the "Negroes' nickname" for FBI agents. Later, the Bureau learned that this was going to be the title of Baldwin's forthcoming book, to be published by the Dial Press. According to the report, the "irresponsible and unreliable" *New Yorker* was going to run excerpts from the book. Not only had *The New Yorker* written critically of Hoover, the memo continued, but it had "published articles of a satirical nature concerning FBI tours." Hoover's note on this memo reads: "Isn't Baldwin a well known pervert?"

Hoover's query got an equivocal answer: although "the theme of homosexuality figured in two of his three published novels . . . it is not possible to state that he is a pervert," even though he is "sympathetic" to homosexuality and has "a very definite hostility toward the revulsion of the American public regarding it." This reply suggests the Bureau wasn't reading its own files, for a 1963 report, which asserted that Baldwin's political activities were part of a Communist plot, included a comment from a confidential informant that "Jimmy's sexual propensities are known." In case there was any doubt, the report stated that "information had been developed by the Bureau that Baldwin is a homosexual."

In 1966, the FBI returned to the subject of Baldwin's sexual preferences. It recorded an Air Force Office of Special Investigations report stating that "during the summer of 1966" Baldwin was evicted from an apartment in Istanbul" for "having homosexual parties." The informant in this particular report was identified only as a "young man who worked with Baldwin at Roberts College" in Istanbul.

During the summer of 1964, the FBI said that "one of its contacts in publishing" was going to "secure" the galleys of *The Blood Counters* and Hoover was told that the matter "is being closely followed." However, Richard Baron, the former president of Dial Press, who is now an independent publisher and writer, says no such book was ever published, although Baldwin "may have once thought about such a project" because "he had a bitter feeling about the FBI." Baron believes, though, that it was only "a passing fancy," adding that "we put a bunch of titles on a contract once and that might have been one of them." James H. Silberman, who was the editor in chief of Dial from 1960 to 1963, and who is now with Little, Brown and Co., has "a vague memory" that Baldwin talked about an FBI book "before 1964," but also says, "Baldwin lied horribly. He had a story for everybody."

On April 9, 1964, Baldwin was included in a report on the "Negro Question," whose subtitle said it all: "Communist Influence in Racial Matters." With Baldwin now firmly adjudged a Communist, the FBI, which was still investigating Communist influence in the radio, television, and movie industries, warned that he might write the screenplay for a history of blacks from 1619 to 1968.

In 1971, the Bureau's reviewer quoted from a colloquy between Baldwin and anthropologist Margaret Mead published as *A Rap on Race:* "Baldwin believes our society is on the edge of absolute chaos." Mead, "who was associated with several Communist fronts," asked 'what about the Italians who are picketing the FBI as being unfair to Italians because they are persecuting the Mafia?' " Baldwin "had no comment" to this question.

The FBI summed up its case against Baldwin that year: he "was an advocate of Black Power, and due to his position as an author, is likely to furnish aid or other assistance to revolutionary elements." In other words, the most dangerous fact recorded in his file was that he was a writer.

AMIRI BARAKA:
The sixties reemphasized the questions of the twenties and took them a little further, although not really, because revolution was in the air in the twenties. But in the sixties—particularly because of the African liberation movement—all the liberated African countries suddenly had a whole international effect. The civil rights movement changed in the middle sixties and black people started calling it the Black Liberation Movement.

It is not like in the twenties—not merely, we are beautiful people and we have a right to all the good things. No, by the sixties—after the early part of the civil rights movement—it became "This society is going to be burned to the ground." A whole different consciousness.

**

The FBI began its over two-thousand-page file on Amiri Baraka, née LeRoi Jones, author of some two dozen books of poetry, drama, and essays, because he was on the guest list of a reception for Fidel Castro on September 24, 1960, in New York City.

The Cuban connection marked the poet. The following year, the FBI reported that he was a member of the Monroe Defense Committee, which another informant told them "is overtly sponsored by the same sponsors of the Fair Play for Cuba Committee." The informant was misinformed. Baraka says the Monroe Defense Committee was "for the defense of Robert Williams, framed by the police." The FBI did get it right when it recorded that on November 9 of that year, Baraka was elected president of the New York chapter of the Fair Play for Cuba Committee.

Baraka was a supporter of Castro and went to Cuba for a couple of weeks in 1960, "right after the revolution." He went with an international group of writers, and recalls the celebration: "It was like two or three million people up in the mountains, and they brought intellectuals from all over the world. What was amazing to me is that after all the adventure we went through, when I got home—we landed in Miami—I picked up a newspaper and it said 'CUBAN CELEBRATION RAINED OUT.' So they wouldn't have to report on it. You see what they call disinformation."

In 1968, the year Baraka founded the Committee for Unified Newark, the bureau also reported that he "was sentenced to 2½ to three years and fined $1000" for possession of "two revolvers during the Newark riots of the previous summer." (There is no record of his serving time in prison.) That year the FBI said that Baraka's main theme in his public lectures had been "the conflict between the races and his hate of the white man." The FBI also reported that agents "observed a Black Community Defense Training session in Connecticut" on May 25; however, Baraka's name is nowhere on the much-blacked-out document, so why it is in his file is unclear.

Another document, dated May 2, 1968, contains a stunning revelation: "A representative of another government agency" told the FBI that "two lightweight brown envelopes measuring approximately 9" by 12" arrived in the U.S. via air at Kennedy airport" from Stockholm, Sweden, addressed to Baraka, and that "enclosed in each envelope, covered by two pieces of carbon paper, were five 8" by 10" pages of instructions on the manufacture and use of improvised explosives and incendiaries." The pages listed such recipes as "Sawdust and Wax: Molten wax or tar added to sawdust makes a long burning effective incendiary." In addition, there was advice for making "fuses, igniters and delay devices." A note at the bottom said "suggested targets: Government or public buildings, especially police stations, banks, courthouses, post offices, schools, transportation systems, gas stations, radio and telephone buildings, newspapers, *all* communications facilities.''

This is, of course, an alarming document, and in light of the targets mentioned, it is obviously appropriate that it reached the hands of the FBI. Baraka denies requesting such information, and says the document was a setup: ''If you ever get busted, then they can say well, he received this mail—they're making a case against you.''

In 1971, Baraka became chairman of the Congress of African Peoples, which had been founded in 1970 with the ''basic goal'' of ''global expression of black nationalism through the promotion of Pan-Africanism.'' Agents monitored a radio show that Baraka moderated, reporting that he spoke about the goals of the Congress. Another 1971 report indicates that a close associate of his had been recruited as an informant.

The following year, on January 27, the FBI reported that Baraka condemned U.S. policy in Africa; it also reported that ''fifty black ministers in Newark'' had charged Baraka with intimidation and extremism. The FBI was always on the lookout for such conflicts among black groups to exploit in its COINTELPROs. Posters bearing Baraka's picture and the message that he was ''wanted'' as a CIA agent were put up all over Newark, presumably by the FBI. Baraka says, ''We had just won the election [Kenneth Gibson became the first black mayor of Newark] and they feared we were going to have too much to say in how the Newark city government was going to develop.'' He explains that the later dissension with Gibson ''was caused by all this,'' which culminated in a disagreement over a cable franchise the two were organizing. Baraka believes someone got to Gibson and ''frightened'' him, because ''he turned around completely,'' that is, he turned against Baraka. Baraka comments that ''these are the kinds of things I'm interested in. What was the conversation? What was said to him?''

Baraka was the victim of many COINTELPROs. On November 11, 1970, for example, the FBI forged a letter from the minister of information of the Black Panthers in Jersey City that attempted to discredit him. The letter, which was sent to newspapers and Baraka's colleagues, called him a ''Tom Pig'' who ''uses people's money for liberation soul power to line his pockets.'' It included a sartorial dig: ''Even Africans laughed at Baraka's homemade daisheckis [*sic*] in New York.''

''When we looked at it we laughed,'' Baraka recalls. ''They got black FBI agents. Why didn't they let them earn their money—'cause whoever wrote that letter was obviously someone who didn't know the Afro-American speech.'"*

AMIRI BARAKA:
The FBI is full of diletanttes. I asked them one time about our phone being tapped. So the FBI and the sheriff came to our office and they said, "Mr. Baraka, we believe that the Black Panther party is tapping your phone." So I said, "Oh, really? You think the Black Panther party is tapping us? Well, why don't we go down and trace the line right to them, and then, why don't we all come in to the office together and we'll get the newspapers to take photos of us finding the tap." They said, "No, we don't want to do that."

They spend taxpayers' money, too, to make some clandestine copy of a newspaper that you could go buy on the street. If they had come to me and said, "Give me a paper," I'd say, "Here, you can have it." But they have copies of plays, poetry, newspapers, as if it's some stuff you couldn't get a hold of, as if it's some secret stuff.

What is so interesting to me is that you don't hear in any of the COINTEL-PROs any attempt to analyze real problems or any attempt to arrive at real human-oriented solutions. What you hear is attempts to *hoodwink* people—kill 'em, eliminate 'em, separate them from their peers and their people.

**

In 1974, Baraka joined the Communist party, though there is no mention of this in his file, and he remains a Party member today— "whatever that means, with Gorbachev selling his ass," he says.

He became a Communist after he was followed, harassed, embarrassed, and policed for over a decade. Ironically, this might have seemed the only way out of the mayhem.

Poet Delmore Schwartz triggered his own file on September 13, 1961, by sending a telegram to Attorney General Robert Kennedy: "I need help badly Please Please help." The following day, agents visited him, and after showing them a listing of his publications and accomplishments from a 1960 *Current Biography,* he "related a rambling disjointed story of personal problems relating to marital difficulties and inability to obtain work." Schwartz biographer James Atlas comments: "I can say with assurance that Delmore had no real reason to fear the

---

*But within the FBI itself, racial tension was a way of life for years and continued into the 1980s. In the late eighties, it took a lawsuit to achieve equality in one instance, in which a black agent accused the FBI of discrimination.

As of April 1991, the FBI employs 477 black special agents out of a total of 10,035. Although Hoover's attitudes are responsible for the FBI's antiblack bias for fifty years, the fact that prejudice still exists—twenty years after his death—indicates a more deeply rooted cause. It is one, however, that is being faced, it seems, in the nineties. FBI Director Sessions says that "it is absolutely essential that our nation's racial and ethnic composition be reflected in the FBI," and has given such recruiting "top priority." No director has so publicly taken that position before.

FBI; he was clinically diagnosed as paranoid, and paranoid ideation often has a common motif: Rockefeller, the Empire State Building, and other images of power and authority. I would imagine the FBI is one of these motifs. In his last, tragic years, Delmore did send a number of telegrams to government officials, among them Adlai Stevenson, to whom he once sent a telegram from the Earle Hotel. Robert Kennedy would have been another likely focus of his hallucinations. Like many intellectuals and writers in the early sixties, Delmore was obsessed with John F. Kennedy. He had been invited to his inauguration, but he was drifting from one address to another by then, and the invitation arrived four months late. But he was not visibly political, and signed few letters of protest.''

The agents reported that the poet appeared ''aberrant,'' as well as ''dirty, slovenly and unkept.'' There is no explanation as to why his telegram was answered so promptly, but the FBI decided to take ''no further action'' after the agents' visit. Two years later, however, according to the file, Schwartz called the FBI again to say ''he had been instructed to report his whereabouts at all times.'' Schwartz told the FBI he was staying at the Hotel Commander in Cambridge, Massachusetts, and when asked how long he expected to be there, he replied, ''When one starts doing what the FBI says, one hasn't a very clear sense of how long one will stay anywhere.''

Another poet who had what the Bureau delicately termed ''mental trouble,'' was Theodore Roethke, whose file was begun in 1941. Curiously, he too had an obsession with the FBI. In 1949, his file reports that he frequently called the Seattle, Washington, FBI office because ''he fancys [sic] himself as a highly placed espionage agent in close contact with Army and Navy intelligence.''

The FBI refers to Roethke as ''a near genius . . . nationally known in educational fields'' who believes ''himself working for the Bureau.'' The Bureau's main concern was to establish that he was ''mentally unbalanced''; ''because of his reputation'' he might embarrass the Bureau with his complaints of mistreatment.

There are no other reports until 1963, when it is noted that he and Norman Mailer ''expressed disparaging comments'' about J. Edgar Hoover in *Harper's Bazaar* magazine. These remarks were noticed when an FBI employee read the magazine ''at a local hairdresser's.''

The article in question contained ''the anathemas of five noted Americans.'' Roethke said his was Hoover, ''head of our thought police—a martinet, a preposterous figure, but not funny.'' Mailer said that "the worst celebrity in America is of course J. Edgar Hoover."

"Check files on Norman Mailer and Theodore Roethke," Hoover jotted in the margin of the article. The Director was given a one-paragraph summary of Roethke's, which left out all the information obtained from confidential informants, but surprisingly included his long list of prizes and awards. But Hoover underlined four phrases in the summary. The first, that "as of 1963" Roethke "was at the University of Washington." The second, that he had become a "mental defective"; the third, that "at one time he was placed in a local sanitarium for the insane." The fourth, that he was "an ardent pacifist."

The veteran mystery writer Rex Stout, who had been in the files since 1920, popped into prominence in 1965 when he published a mystery entitled *The Doorbell Rang*. According to the FBI, the novel "presents a highly distorted and most unfavorable picture of the FBI in its operations as they relate to the plot of the book." Hoover ordered a detailed study to be "prepared." It concluded that "this is a vicious book which puts the FBI in the worst possible light. Within its scope as fiction, it is almost as scurrilous an attack on the Bureau as Fred Cook's *The FBI Nobody Knows*."

Stout was unrepentant. Six months after the publication of *The Doorbell Rang*, in a television appearance on *The Today Show*, he called Hoover a "tinhorn autocrat" who was "on the edge of senility." Stout also told the audience that "the FBI retains dossiers on thousands of individuals and through the FBI's possessions of these dossiers they have an implied blackmail threat against numerous citizens." This criticism caused Hoover to retaliate with his most vindictive epithet: "Stout is nothing more than a bearded beatnik looking for publicity," he wrote on a Bureau memorandum.

By making Stout's wisecrack about his senility an issue of vanity, Hoover showed how personal his literary battles could become. A handwritten marginal note on a transcript of *The Today Show* says, "Stout has a nerve in referring to me as close to seventy and on the edge of senility. He was born in December 1886." Stout was seventy-nine when he appeared on *The Today Show*, and Hoover was seventy-two at the time.

Playwright Tennessee Williams, unlike Arthur Miller, his contemporary and chief rival for the title of America's leading playwright in the post–World War II era, was an unpolitical man. His file runs only seven pages, and the references in it are, for the most part, routine, even boring: the *Daily Worker* praises his play *A Streetcar Named Desire* when it is published as a book in 1947. Williams sends "greetings" to the Moscow Art Theater. He defends the Hollywood Ten. He is called "a top cultural name" by the *Daily Worker*.

But a 1961 reference stands out in this litany: "The Bureau ascertained that Thomas Lanier Williams has the reputation of being a homosexual. Further, the Office of Naval Intelligence, in a separate inquiry, secured statements from individuals who admitted participating in homosexual acts with Williams."

Did one of these "individuals" kiss and tell? Did the Bureau interrogate these individuals in order to obtain the information? Or is it possible Williams was the victim of an entrapment by informants or agents?

The FBI's attitude toward homosexuals, and Hoover's attitude in particular, is well-known. His Official and Confidential files are crammed with homosexual references ranging from the anonymous reports alleging that Hoover "was a queer" to "information furnished by Senator Dirksen (deceased)" that an unidentified "prominent person" was "a homosexual, and Communists were using this to blackmail him."

Former FBI official Harold T. Leinbaugh explains, "homosexuals were considered a security risk, because they were subject to blackmail." But Tennessee Williams was not involved in any government work of any kind, so why would the FBI be concerned if he was a security risk?

A CIA-FBI memo on the magazine *Ramparts* sheds further light on the intelligence community's attitude toward gays in the 1960s; after describing a review of a book by Christopher Isherwood, there is a parenthetical aside saying he "is a homosexual, and the early *Ramparts* seems to have a predilection for the topic."

The FBI had a similar predilection, though its attitude was the opposite of tolerance. Cartha DeLoach says there were "two or three agents during my years in the FBI who were found to be homosexuals, and they either resigned or were dismissed from the service," adding, "but out of nine or ten thousand people, that's not a bad average."

ROY COHN:
Times have changed enormously since those days when homosexuality was a way-out thing which people couldn't understand. Today, in the eighties, homosexuality is somebody's private life.

When I was on the *60 Minutes* program, there was nothing I really minded except the way it could be applied to other people. I thought when Mike Wallace asked me about homosexuality and AIDS, once he got a denial from me, and he had no proof to the contrary, I thought it was a very good time for him to drop it.

I made up my mind that the worst thing I could do was blow my top and say "I'm entitled to my right of privacy." What effect does that have on the audience? I'm claiming the Fifth Amendment, and sure, the answer is yes.

And so, I just made up my mind I would smile when he introduced the subject and say, "no." He just wanted to be the one to come out and publicly say what some people privately said. He wanted to be the hero. But he wasn't the hero!

"Mike," I said, "my constituents—the conservatives—don't care if you find a life with a muskrat or a woman or a man or this or that. All they care about is what are you going to do to get rid of the Soviet Union and what are you doing to strengthen America. That's all they give a damn about."

**

Grace Paley, author of highly praised collections of short stories, including *Enormous Changes at the Last Minute,* once referred to herself as a "somewhat combative pacifist and cooperative anarchist." The FBI called her "dangerous."

It had discovered her in 1941, reporting that she was a secretary of New York University's Young Communist League. Paley recalls: "I don't think it *was* the Young Communist League. It was the Karl Marx Society of NYU. It was a school organization, and I remember being surprised by the FBI calling it the YCL. I mean, I think most of the people in it *were* Communists as a matter of fact. But I was a wide-open member—that's another thing. A lot of kids were going on to medical school, and the society had to have five members in order to be in business. I knew I was going to be a writer and never have to worry about things like getting into medical school—I must have been eighteen at that time—so I agreed with four others that we would be the open members of the Karl Marx Society, because the others did not want it on their records. I don't even think it was five—it was three of us, and we felt very generous. *We'll* do it because we're not going to relate to the state the way other people do."

Her file remained "dead" until 1967, when she became involved in antiwar activities. (Actually, her name did surface briefly in 1948 in the Department of Justice's Criminal Division, which noted she was a member of a group called the New York Emergency Committee on Rent and Housing.)

But from 1967 on, the FBI followed her relentlessly, noting her presence at demonstrations, rallies, meetings, and marches, keeping up to date on her movements with pretext phone calls, surveillances, and reports from dozens of informants. Her seventy-eight-page file contains detailed descriptions of her activities—signs she carried, speeches she gave, the time she arrived and the time she departed. Always her primary identification was "writer": "Grace Paley is the author of a book (Viking Press) entitled 'The Little Disturbances of Man' ''; "Paley would be the next guest at the New Yorker Bookstore's writer-reader session." She is often quoted; one report notes that she called *draft cards* "death cards."

In 1969, she was followed and watched when she traveled as part of a peace delegation to visit American POWs in North Vietnam; the FBI obviously had an informant in the group. An unidentified person told the Bureau that "an individual who has been meeting with North Vietnamese officials in Paris . . . said Paley would be a desirable asset" to such a delegation. Another memo said her passport was not valid for travel to North Vietnam, and the FBI sent her photo to the passport office in New York in an attempt to stop her. However, she did travel as planned. The FBI later reported that she said the prisoners were receiving "favorable" treatment, and sent fifteen copies of this statement to "the military intelligence agencies" as well as to the Secret Service.

It was decided that she should not be interviewed by agents, and also that she "did not qualify" for the Reserve or Security Index because she "does some writing" and is an English professor at Sarah Lawrence College.

In 1971, a summary of Paley's file was sent to the Office of Naval Intelligence, which requested a report for reasons not given. A copy of this report was also sent to the CIA, the first time information on her was shared with this agency. Now the Bureau said that she would be recommended for inclusion on the Administrative Index (which began that year) because a confidential informant told the FBI that Paley was an official of the National Emergency Civil Liberties Committee, which the Bureau considered a Communist front.

The FBI also decided to try to interview her, using the pretext that it was seeking information about the whereabouts of one of her former students. Paley, however, "adamantly refused to continue the conversation," an FBI agent reported.

"I notice in my file that they're always telephoning me," Paley says, "and I tend always to tell them certain things. Somebody called me, oh God, it was in 1985—the United States Information Agency woman in Paris. And she said, 'Why don't you let us send you on this trip?' And I said, 'But I feel so bad about the administration, and I really don't like to take the money.' I was very honest with her. And she said, 'Well you don't have to speak for the administration,' and I said, 'In a way, that's bad—you go to one of those countries where we are tormenting people economically or something, you know, and you say to them this is such a free country—look, here I am—I mean, it's true we are tormenting you economically, but isn't democracy wonderful?'

"There are things I won't ever tell them, but on ninety-nine percent of the conversations I have with anybody, it's my politics to speak truth to power. It's an old Quaker idea—I'm not Quaker, but . . .

"I'm wrong in the sense that once I made up a leaflet saying that when the *FBI* calls, what do you say? What should you say? *Nothing.*"

In 1972, her photo was "disseminated to the Secret Service" and she was called "potentially dangerous because of background, emotional instability or activity in groups engaged in activities inimical to U.S." She was also "okayed" for the Administrative Index, but by the following year, one year after Hoover's death, she was removed from the list and her "case closed."

But it was not exactly closed, because the file became an obstacle for Paley in the late 1980s, when she was "disinvited" from a writers' conference because of it.

GRACE PALEY:
People in other countries are afraid that they're going to be put in jail—people here are afraid that somebody will call them a Communist. People in this country are more afraid of being *embarrassed*. In certain situations, they lose jobs. I mean, the number of people who keep quiet in jobs! All those whistle-blowers—they're very brave. But most people are afraid of losing prestige, and they're afraid of losing *things*. So it's economic fear which is very great.

As for the other things, like making a statement or giving out a leaflet, what people fear there is that someone will see them doing it. In this country, people will write a letter, but they'll sign another name. Back inside of them is this fear from twenty years ago when the FBI was a great menace.

When we established the Greenwich Village Peace Center, people would come in and say there are Communists here, and I'm not going to work with you. We'd have to decide whether to say we didn't care whether there were Communists or not, or decide to get the Communists out. A lot of public peace centers, which were established by the Society of Friends around the country, made the second decision, to get the Communists out, and they went out of business very fast. We said we didn't care if the Communists were there. And, as a matter of fact, we were part of the whole Left movement—we didn't know it—which was saying, Forget it, you can't tar us and we don't care if you do, it doesn't bother us. I mean we were part of that post–McCarthy period, where people said, Listen, we've got to answer this stuff back.

Well, we felt there were a couple of people who might be informants. You just really got a feeling about it, and I'm sure we missed plenty. Plenty. But you see, we were in the nonviolence part of the movement, and the FBI sent most of their people to the ones who were beginning to talk a lot about armed struggle. But it was always the FBI who suggested bringing a bomb—because as radical as some of these people were, it just didn't occur to them half the time to go blow up this place or to do this or that. It was usually an informer who made the suggestion, and then appeared in court ten years later.

We tended to say what we were going to do, usually. Now there were things we did that we really could keep secret, but they really weren't terrible things. I mean we kept them secret because we didn't want the newspapers to know it. Once we planted 340 crosses right at City Hall at five o'clock in the morning. About four of us sat there building crosses—that was a funny kind of thing to have been very careful about, but we did a lot of resistance work and we were very careful how we handled things. We had people in sanctuaries—resisters or deserters.

There really were four or five people you could trust with your life. But in general, we tried to act as though everybody was pretty trustworthy. There was one guy who I felt was definitely an informer, and he fell in love with one of the women there, and he really got to like us, and one day he said, "I'm going to California," and we said, "Well, write to us," and he said, "I'm going to try to, but if I don't, just remember me."

I think he left because he didn't want to do it anymore; I guess there's always guys like that. We used to say, if they're willing to lick envelopes, they can stay, *whoever* they are!

The FBI is the least free of all of us—they're probably the most imprisoned. They have to behave in a certain way. They've completely lost touch with what they really think, or, if they know what they really think, they can't act on it. Like that guy who ran away to California. I think all people who are somewhat imprisoned get angry at others, whether they're writers or not.

I remember one of the first times I did a vigil on our local green up in Vermont—a very tiny town—and seven people stood opposite the church. It was a very forward thing to do. A plain old simple vigil. And on the anniversary of Hiroshima, nothing even fancy, like Central America or something like that. There was one guy from the church who was berating us, and he was the *one* guy who really agreed with us! But he couldn't make himself do that, so he kept yelling at us, saying, "What makes you think you're the only people who think like this?" Two or three years later, he was standing with us. But it took him that much time to free himself from his fears. And I've seen that before.

It's a freedom envy.

**

The twenty-four-page file on writer E. L. Doctorow, author of such prize-winning novels as *The Book of Daniel*—based on the Rosenberg case—*Ragtime, World's Fair,* and *Billy Bathgate,* was opened on February 13, 1968. Ironically, it was not his outspokenly left-wing politics or concern for civil and human rights that brought him to the Bureau's notice. At the time, Doctorow was editor in chief of Dial Press, and in that capacity he wrote Hoover a letter requesting that the Director provide an advance comment on a soon-to-be-published book about an international narcotics conspiracy written by Alwin Mosow, who had helped Nixon write his memoir, *Six Crises*.

Hoover responded with his usual line, "Long-standing policy precludes me from furnishing comments on material not prepared by this Bureau." Of course, Hoover did issue comments on books favorable to the FBI when he chose to. (He praised books on the FBI by Don Whitehead and Quentin Reynolds.) Because part of his reaction to Doctorow's request is blacked out, it is not possible to know why he did not choose to comment this time, on what Doctorow described as "the first authoritative book available to the general public" about the illicit drug trade. One can surmise, however. Doctorow mentioned that his author had help from the Bureau of Narcotics; perhaps Hoover didn't want to step on or around anyone else's toes, or perhaps he didn't want to boost a rival agency. What is more, as a memo states, there are only "several passing references" to the FBI.

Three pages of what Doctorow refers to as his "insubstantial" file are still classified—the reasons given are "in the interest of national defense," and "constitutes an unwarranted invasion of the personal privacy of another person." Doctorow says that "I was a relatively quiet guy. I don't think I signed anything until the sixties."

The remaining nine pages of his file "originated with the Department of State," and concern Doctorow's 1980 participation at the Fourth Soviet-American Writers Conference, held in Los Angeles "despite the unwillingness of the U.S. government to fund or facilitate the meeting." The latter phrase is contained in a nine-page report from the American embassy in Moscow to the Department of State that is actually an "informal but accurate" translation of a 1981 article by Nicolay Fedorenko about the conference that originally appeared in a Soviet journal. The embassy said that it was "being submitted to keep the record complete and for background when the U.S. Government is considering future requests for funding or other assistance to the writers conferences which apparently will follow." The State Department had reported on the conference previously—reference is made to an earlier report—though this document is not included in Doctorow's file.

Doctorow recalls that "someone from the State Department was there"—at the conference—"and translated it." He also remembers that Fedorenko asked, "Do you know who speaks the best English in the Soviet Union? Our Jews.' I remember he said it just like that. 'Our Jews.' "

The 1981 article states that the "remarkable event"—which was also attended by Elizabeth Hardwick, playwright Edward Albee, novelist Ray Bradbury, and journalist Harrison Salisbury—"had the theme Universal Spiritual Values and Literature."

Doctorow remembers that he delivered a speech about how Russians treat war as an epic and how Americans treat it with irony. He recalls that "a KGB agent who was posing as a writer said, 'Mr. Doctorow, if you had a bayonet in your stomach, you wouldn't speak of irony.' "

Fedorenko's article, which Doctorow says "is the equivalent of a company report," hews to the Soviet government line. He writes that "the writers conference was carried out under conditions of serious aggravation of Soviet-American relations. . . . More hotbeds of conflict have appeared in the world, and a new spiral in the arms race (not started by us) has been triggered, and the danger of war has grown." He also writes, "*worth nothing* is the fact that the participants . . . criticized the new, extremely dangerous nuclear war strategy of the U.S. Administration that stipulates, according to Directive 59, the possibility of 'limited' nuclear war" (italics added).

The phrase "worth nothing" seems odd. Surely Fedorenko wrote "worth *noting*." Was the State Department's version the result of a misprint or mistranslation? Or was it deliberate? Such negative phrasing could sow mistrust between American and Soviet writers. Perhaps that was the point, especially if the translation was meant to be read by people outside the State Department and the FBI.

In any case, the article goes on to analyze some "U.S. writers of democratic and progressive views" who did not participate in the 1980 conference but who are well-known in the Soviet Union. The author writes that "Saul Bellow stresses that art moves from disorder toward order, but the majority of American writers go in the opposite direction—toward disorder, more and more destructiveness, drug addiction, savageness, and barbarism, affirming a primitive culture within technological society. The book market in the U.S. is flooded with spy books, criminal police stories and pornographic comics, with the dissemination of the latter going on at a monstrous rate."

The article also says that American publishers "are more concerned with reaping profit than with literature." It concludes by claiming there was no mention "of the contents of the conference in any American mass medium. So much for the boasts of 'freedom of information' in the U.S.' "

But the Freedom of Information Act sanctions a translation of Russian criticisms of American writers and publishers. Perhaps by the year

2000, the Soviets will have passed a similar law and be able to see a critique of them by Americans.

Better still, maybe there will be only open evaluations on both sides—and reprimands on neither side.

SVETLANA ALLILUYEVA:

I'm not surprised that Carl Sandburg once described Russia as "immense, chaotic, and fog-like." It's a very true word, "fog-like," and for most Americans, Russia *is* one big piece of fog. You cannot see anything there. Neither can Russians really know America as part of their vision.

PART SEVEN

After Hoover

Memorandum : P..

TO : Director, FBI (105-174254)
Attention: Counterintelligence and Special
Operations (Research Section)
DATE: 10/13/70

FROM : SAC, Detroit (100-35108) (P)

SUBJECT: COUNTERINTELLIGENCE PROGRAM
IS - DISRUPTION OF NEW LEFT

Detroit is proposing the disruption of the physical plant of the Radical Education Project (REP), 3908 Michigan Avenue, Detroit, Michigan. REP is a full time publishing outfit of the New Left through whose auspices numerous virulent revolutionary treatises reach the Left.

In addition, the Black Panther Party (BPP) in Detroit receives BPP publications from San Francisco. Detroit has easy access to these papers after they arrive in Detroit.

The Bureau is requested to prepare and furnish to Detroit in liquid form a solution capable of duplicating a scent of the most foul smelling feces available. In this case, it might be appropriate to duplicate the feces of the specie sus scrofa.

A quart supply, along with a dispenser capable of squirting a narrow stream for a distance of approximately three feet would satisfy the needs of this proposed technique.

: \\

REC-15

2 - Bureau (RM)
2 - Detroit
(1 - 157-3214)
CRO/cc
(4)

5 OCT 15 1970

CHAPTER TWENTY-THREE
A Broader Outlook: 1970– Present

In an extraordinary 1970 document prepared "in response to the Director's request," the FBI expressed great concern about playwright Lillian Hellman's "support of New Left and antiwar groups." Hellman, considered a Communist, had helped organize the Committee for Public Justice to investigate the FBI because, she said, "some of us thought we heard the voice of Joe McCarthy coming from the grave." Hoover immediately asked that the Bureau files be searched for derogatory information on the ten members of the executive council, and that files be opened on those who didn't have them. The Bureau was not only worried about the existence of such a committee, and Hellman's ties to it, but it wanted to link the Old Left with the New.

In a report dated November 19, 1970, the FBI presented the result of its file check on the members of the executive council: Blair Clark, associate editor of the *New York Post*, was "liberal and independent"; Dr. Robert Coles, a research psychiatrist at Harvard, had been "active" in the Mississippi Summer Project of 1964; Norman Dorsen, general counsel of the American Civil Liberties Union, "has supported the [National] Emergency Civil Liberties Committee, a cited organization" and has appeared on television with sixties rebels "Abbott

Hoffman, Jerry Rubin, and Rennie Davis''; Burke Marshall, former assistant U.S. attorney general of the Civil Rights Division, ''was not considered a friend of the FBI'' and ''in 1964 he made false allegations to the White House that we leaked information on Martin Luther King,'' regarding which the Director noted ''Marshall is a liar''; Telford Taylor, professor of law, Columbia University, ''admitted membership in the National Lawyers Guild in 1942'' and ''associated with members of the CP and fellow travelers''; Dr. Jerome Wiesner, ''internationally known scientist,'' admitted membership in a Communist front organization and ''allegedly indicated sympathy for communists in the mid 1940s,'' and ''more recently has been outspoken in opposition to an antiballistic missile system for the U.S.''; Roger W. Wilkins, director, Community Relations Service, had ''exchanged friendly correspondence with Mr. Hoover'' (the next two or three lines are blacked out); Harold Willens, ''millionaire businessman,'' had helped organize a ''protest against the U.S. involvement in Vietnam among the business community'' and was ''reportedly born in the USSR and his father was a Communist labor organizer''; and Robert B. Silvers, editor of the *New York Review of Books,* ''used individuals with 'leftist tendencies' to review books dealing with security matters and the U.S. Government'' (although ''allegations that this publication was directed or controlled by the CP were not substantiated'') and was on the board of the Center for Cuban Studies.

The voice of McCarthy could indeed be heard from the grave.

Robert Silvers, who still is editor of the *New York Review of Books,* said he was not surprised by this memo, because ''we have published articles that are extremely critical of the Bureau.'' Silvers added that when he obtained his file a few years ago, this particular document was not included. His ''brief, very blacked out file'' did contain a CIA memorandum listing all the contributors to the *New York Review of Books*—''every writer and every subject.''

As though vindicating Hoover's original concern, in 1971, the Committee for Public Justice organized a conference on the FBI at Princeton University. The FBI, highly critical and suspicious of this enterprise when it learned about it, once again prepared ''thumbnails'' of the ''executive council'' of the committee in a memo; in addition, it warned nine FBI officials and the Crime Research Division that the conference ''was stacked against the FBI because most of those involved are liberals and Democrats.''

In the 1971 ''thumbnails'' memo, Blair Clark's name is blacked out, but the others are left in. Clark, who attended the conference, which he called "a useful exercise" although "it had the flavor of Spanish Civil War protest without much clear political objective," says he "hasn't the slightest clue" why his name would be blacked out and not the names of any others, adding that although it's "very odd," he doesn't think it's "sinister."

Stephen Gillers, the director of the Committee for Public Justice and its Princeton conference, says that "we invited conservatives and Republicans, as well as J. Edgar Hoover, who chose not to come." Instead he sent two agents to "observe" what was going on.

On May 2, 1972, J. Edgar Hoover was found dead in his bedroom by his "three black servants." He had died of hypertensive cardiovascular activity; "the immediate cause was probably a heart attack."

The Hoover era was ending. Gradually, his loyal cadre would die or retire. Clyde Tolson—"the Killer"—was frail and sickly from a series of strokes. He died in 1975 of natural causes. Number three man Cartha DeLoach had retired in 1970 to join PepsiCo as an executive.

CARTHA DeLOACH:
I think many of us followed FBI rules and policies—it definitely was the thing to do—and I have no apologies to make for that at the present time.

I admit we made mistakes. I think that Mr. Hoover had many eccentricities. He was jealous of his turf, yet he was a man who sacrificed his life for the FBI. But I do think he stayed on too long and I think society outran him and he was living somewhat in the past at the very end.

It's a different America now. We have different enemies. We have different friends.

Today communism represents no physical threat to the United States. The last I heard, they had fewer than three thousand members. The Ku Klux Klan represents more of a physical threat. The Ku Klux Klan outnumbers the Communist party and is more active from the standpoint of potential physical violence—although you still have the faint specter of communism hanging over your head.

The Klan is not a political threat to any extent. They put out a lot of misinformation—they claim to be close followers of God and to be deeply religious people, yet how can you be deeply religious and be so filled with hatred and bigotry?

I have a much broader outlook on society and life in general now. I'm a member of the Catholic Church and have been for many years. I guess I'm more religious now than I was then, mostly because of the fact that I'm older and more mature.

But I think when I entered the FBI, I was very patriotic and I was as good an American as I hope I am now.

**

A "new" FBI was struggling to be born, but it first had to pass through a long transition period, when, it seemed, the ghost of the

Director still hovered over it. After Hoover's death, former assistant attorney general L. Patrick Gray III was appointed acting director, but he was denied confirmation because, as *New York Times* reporter Philip Shenon explains, "He was never able to shake off Congressional suspicions that he was working too closely with [President] Nixon. . . . [Gray] acknowledged having burned potential evidence in the Watergate inquiry along with the Christmas trash." William D. Ruckelshaus, administrator of the Environmental Protection Agency, was acting director after Gray, until July 1983 when Clarence M. Kelley, the police chief of Kansas City, Missouri, was confirmed as director, a post he held for five years—years that saw the end of the U.S. involvement in Vietnam, the abolishment of HUAC, and the discontinuation of the FBI's Administrative Index.

With Hoover gone and times changed, the Bureau was no longer sacrosanct. In 1974, Idaho Democratic senator Frank Church, chairman of the Senate Select Committee on Intelligence, held hearings on FBI abuses. According to a transcript, the committee "tracked a pattern of FBI misdeeds—beginning with the Roosevelt administration— when the agency was ordered by the President to compile lists of citizens who cabled the White House protesting FDR's war policies."

Partly as a result of the probe, in 1976 the first set of FBI domestic security guidelines were established by Attorney General Edward H. Levi. These guidelines, a series of rules governing the parameters of investigations and procedures, were formulated in response to the widespread criticisms of the Bureau for doing the things that enabled the writers files to be assembled. For instance, according to the *Legal Handbook for Special Agents,* "An agent is an observer and reporter, not a judge. . . . Derogatory data developed through interviews or witnesses and other sources must be completely proved or disproved, and accurately and factually established as applicable to the person under investigation."

Levi says, "You can't make changes unless you have a lot of support," and he believes that Director Kelley "deserves a lot of credit." Levi adds that "I think the Bureau wanted to make changes, and did so," but he maintains that the "guidelines had to be flexible."

In February 1978, William Webster, a federal appeals court judge, replaced Kelley as director of the FBI. William M. Baker, assistant director of the FBI's Office of Congressional and Public Affairs under Webster, says that after the Church Committee hearings, the Bureau began to "evolve," and when Webster arrived, "he refined it and put more emphasis on relevance. Webster had a great concern for the protection of the Constitution." As for writers files, he says, "there would not have been any," because there "had to be a relevancy for a name to enter in a file; it had to relate to a crime."

FBI AGENT "X":

The FBI is much more open now than it was under Mr. Hoover. We're doing everything *within* the law—we don't have any secrets to hide.

Communism, or the Communist Party United States of America, used to be a top priority, investigated within the realm of domestic security. Right now, our predicate on domestic security cases would really have a *criminal* predicate—it would be more in the realm of domestic terrorism.

What we try to do in domestic security since the mid-seventies is determine if in fact individuals, groups, or organizations are engaged in or have the propensity to engage in a truly criminal act—sabotage, for example, which would be an act of terrorism.

The guidelines are fairly stringent in order to prevent overbroad investigations that would have a chilling effect. I welcomed the guidelines because nothing was left in a cloudy Washington mist of "could you do this or couldn't you do this," and in my opinion, the guidelines did not stop us from conducting a thorough investigation. And like any bureaucracy in government, it would take a very courageous or crazy man to violate those guidelines.

**

When Webster left to head the Central Intelligence Agency in 1987, William Steele Sessions, a federal district court judge and former U.S. attorney from Texas, was chosen to be Webster's successor. In view of Hoover's ultrasensitivity to criticism and the excesses to which it led, Sessions was asked in an interview how he reacted to negative publicity. He replied:

I find myself to be sensitive to it personally. I don't get mad; I understand it. The press and the media have a very definite responsibility to the American public, and First Amendment rights are extremely precious, and the ability to comment, the ability to disagree with your government, the ability to express yourself is an *absolutely essential* ingredient of our way of life!

When you read something about yourself, you tend to be defensive about it. If it's unfair or you perceive it to be unfair, you're even more defensive—and the worst would come when you *know* you didn't do that which you are accused of doing. It's kind of like your mama accusing you of stealing cookies and you know you haven't stolen a cookie, because Johnny did it. Or you didn't know it was done at all. So I would say, you know, we're all human. You have the same reactions that I do, basically. I want the Bureau to be run in a fashion that it could be as criticism-free as it could be, and yet I recognize criticism as a part of the function of our whole society, and it's very important to us, so I don't get angry about it.

The director's respect for his critics' right of free speech is commendable, and he seems determined to avoid Hoover's sins of personal vanity and vindictiveness. But his estimable personal qualities aside, some FBI watchers, such as the Center for Constitutional Rights or the National Security Archive, still wonder if Sessions has the strength and staff required to change the institution and purge it of deeply embedded antidemocratic qualities.

The Bureau's critics contend that the word *"terrorism"* has been used by the new FBI much as "communism" was by the old—as a pretext to repress radicals and dissenters. Director Sessions was asked about this charge: "I would have to say that terrorism and the conduct that falls from it is a crime. Terrorist acts are criminal acts, and we always—in domestic situations—have an interest in violations of the law that are terroristic acts. When American citizens are abroad and are dealt with by terrorists—we also, under the law, have jurisdiction in that area. Congress gave it to us and we use it. And I hope we will continue to use it to protect Americans abroad."

And yet, from 1981 to 1985, despite the supposedly "stringent" guidelines, the FBI spied on individuals and groups that opposed U.S. policy in Central America. The Bureau compiled a file of nearly four thousand pages on the activities of CISPES, the Committee in Solidarity with the People of El Salvador. The Center for Constitutional Rights sued the FBI to obtain the CISPES documents, and in 1989 the Bureau agreed to purge its files of the names of the Americans involved in this illegal investigation.

Terrorism posed increased security problems during the 1970s and 1980s, as did foreign espionage. In 1986, Director Webster told the House Subcommittee on Civil and Constitutional Rights that the FBI prevented twenty-three planned terrorist acts in 1985 and took "a number of terrorists out of circulation." In a 1986 newspaper interview, Thomas L. Sheer, the head of the FBI's New York office, said that counterintelligence was the top priority of his office, adding that "there are roughly 4,000 of what we consider hostile-nation diplomats in New York City, and of that, probably one-third are intelligence officers." Nevertheless, Sheer took pains to say that "the FBI has changed. . . . We're not the FBI of the 70's or the 60's or the 50's . . ."

A test of that change would be the FBI's attitude toward writers. Are the practices of the Hoover era still going on? Director Sessions says, categorically, "There are *no* files being kept on writers. If there are writers that are involved in criminal activity or there is a preliminary inquiry or a preliminary investigation or an investigation, then that would be a different matter. But I know of *none*.

"Whatever your judgment is about the Hoover years, we now operate under guidelines. I would think that as long as the guidelines are what they are, you can be guaranteed that what happened before will never happen again."

But what of the preexisting files on writers? The case of Grace Paley suggests they might still be active. In 1987, Paley was invited by the United States Information Agency to participate in two writers' festivals, one in Australia and one in New Zealand. In October, not long before she was to leave, she learned from an Australian playwright friend that her invitation "was rejected on what I believe are political grounds."

Paley says, "We probably won't ever find out why, but I really think it relates to this whole business of my protesting Secretary of State Shultz at the PEN meeting in 1986." Norman Mailer, the president of PEN at the time, had invited the first government official ever to address a PEN congress, and instead of seeing this as an opportunity to have doors opened for PEN endeavors, many members, including Paley, protested Shultz's appearance and walked out on his speech.

Grace Paley's Australian friend also wrote her that "I thought artists were allowed to be radicals. It seems terribly inconsistent, while you are being honored by the State of New York." (Paley had just been named the first State Author.)

Eventually, Paley would learn that her invitation was not rejected by Australia or the USIA, but by the American embassy in New Zealand. In the meantime, her difficulties received a great deal of publicity, which, she says, "was very effective" because as a result of it, "people were falling all over to *help* now," and she received "lots of international invites."

But why did this happen to her in the first place? Why was Grace Paley singled out by the State Department—in 1987? She was not involved in any criminal or terrorist activities or organizations. She is a pacifist and a feminist who supports various social and political causes.

Did one of the "private organizations" that civil libertarian Aryeh Neier says are now doing political surveillance report on Paley? In his *Surveillance as Censorship,* Neier writes that one of the private organizations doing such work are "electric companies that use nuclear energy. . . . They justify the compilation of dossiers by the dangers to public safety if a terrorist organization . . . was able to blow up a plant. The large 'anti-Nuke' movement is the prime target of this political surveillance on the theory that such a terrorist group might emerge from within it." Paley is involved in the antinuclear movement.

FBI Director Sessions says an interviewer who asked him about Neier's contentions "was the first person who's brought me information that there are private companies that are in fact cleared to do investigations for the FBI." Sessions also says that he "knows nothing, absolutely nothing about any investigation or preliminary investigation of Miss Paley at all. If it exists, I don't know about it." He pointed out that "there are a great number of indices that are kept by various agencies in the country—Immigration, the State Department."

But Paley also had an FBI file going back to the 1940s. Was it still following her around? Was it part of the "indices that are kept" by other agencies—the State Department, for example? Director Sessions emphatically says he does not know where the State Department got whatever information it has on Paley: "I presume that it did not come from us," he says, "but I don't know that."

In the eighties, the Book Review Section of the FBI, which had begun life in 1920 as the Publication Section, was placed under the Public Affairs Section. During the 1950s, book reviews had been handled by the Central Research Section, and in the 1960s, by the Research Satellite Section. In the 1970s, they were back under the Central Research Section.

Today, FBI deputy assistant Milt Ahlerich says that certain books are of interest to the FBI "not from an investigative standpoint necessarily," and that "in a very limited fashion we will review five or six books a year." The FBI is no longer looking for subversive writing, but "technique or new research that's being done—maybe a current work on terrorism, a current work on foreign counterintelligence."

In addition, according to FBI special agent Susan Schnitzer, "The authors of books reviewed are not indexed, because it is not done for investigative reasons."

What interested the FBI in the eighties? Thirteen books:

In 1980, *Playing Dirty: The Secret War Against Beliefs,* by Omar V. Garrison; and in 1981 *The Last Mafioso: The Treacherous World of Jimmy Frattiano,* by Ovid Demaris, *The Sting Man: Inside Abscam,* by

Robert W. Greene, and *The FBI and Martin Luther King, Jr.*, by David Garrow. There were no 1982 books reviewed, but in 1983, the FBI looked at Richard Gid Powers's *G-Men: Hoover's FBI in American Popular Culture* and Kenneth O'Reilly's *Hoover and the Un-Americans*. (For the O'Reilly book, the FBI listed the publisher as "House Committee on Un-American Activities." The publisher is actually Temple University Press, in Philadelphia.) In 1984, the FBI reviewed *Inside Hoover's FBI*, by Neil J. Welch and David W. Marston, and *Seven Silent Men,* by Noel Behn. In 1985, they reviewed one book, Margaret Truman's *Murder at the FBI*—a mystery!—and in 1986, *The Federal Bureau of Investigation* (in the Know Your Government series) by Fred L. Israel, and *Hitler's Last Soldier in America,* by Arnold Krammer and George Gaertner.

Between January 1986 and January 1988, the FBI reviewed seven books: *The New Blue Line: Police Innovation in Six American Cities,* by Jerome H. Skolnick and David H. Bayley; *The FBI-KGB War: A Special Agent's Story,* by Robert J. Lamphere and Thomas Schachtman; *The Underground Empire: Where Crime and Governments Embrace,* by James Mills; *Secrecy and Power: The Life of J. Edgar Hoover,* by Richard Gid Powers; *Echoes in the Darkness,* by Joseph Wambaugh; *Lost Undercover,* by Ron LaBrecque; and a book whose author and publisher are not available: *The Kidnap Business.*

In 1989, the Bureau reviewed *Interference,* by Dan E. Moldea, and *Donnie Brasco: An FBI Agent Undercover in the Mafia,* by Joseph D. Pistone and Richard Woodley. As of May 1990, no further books were reviewed.

CHAPTER TWENTY-FOUR
Spies in the Stacks

In a front-page article on September 18, 1987, *The New York Times* reported that agents of the FBI has asked "fewer than twenty" New York City libraries for help in catching spies who might be lurking in their stacks. According to reporter Robert D. McFadden's account, "The contacts have been under way since last spring as a result of a sensational espionage case in which a Soviet employee of the United Nations, Gennadi F. Zakharov, recruited a Queens College student as an agent through contacts made at a library." Under this Library Awareness Program, technical libraries were being requested not only to be on the lookout for spy-recruiting activities but also to report on the reading habits of foreigners who might be copying information allegedly harmful to national security.

Was the FBI trying to turn librarians—the caretakers of writers—into informants? What was the significance of the LAP, or as it was first called, the Development of Counterintelligence Awareness Among Librarians, or DECAL?

The *Times* did no follow-up article, and aside from local stories and one in *The Washington Post,* there was little coverage until *The Nation*

375

magazine published an article, "The FBI's Invasion of Libraries," in its April 9, 1988, issue.

Why were libraries, of all places, the targets of an FBI investigation? The library does have a long history as a setting for clandestine meetings of all kinds—from assignations to espionage contacts. In 1917, Walter Lippmann was part of a secret military intelligence unit that met at the New York Public Library on Forty-second Street.

The FBI has also long been interested in books read by people it was investigating. As has been shown, in the mid-forties the FBI looked at Muriel Rukeyser's library records. A professor at Oberlin College in Ohio recalls that sometime in the 1950s, a Russian history professor told his class that he couldn't put a certain book on reserve because the FBI was keeping track of who used it. An official at Princeton University says the FBI visited the library there "sometime in the mid-sixties. [The agents] were looking for records of the types of books someone read. Of course, we did not cooperate." Also in the sixties, the Alcohol and Tobacco Tax Division of the Internal Revenue Service checked library records for the users of books on explosives. So there's a precedent.

The FBI's incursions also inevitably evoke memories of the invasion of U.S. overseas libraries in the 1950s by Senator McCarthy's aides Roy Cohn and G. David Schine, who forced the removal of books by such writers as Theodore Dreiser and Pearl S. Buck. In 1988, the FBI denied any similarity. Supervisory Special Agent Susan Schnitzer said, "We're not telling people to censor." FBI agent "X" commented that the FBI is "not looking at authors. We're looking at people who want to read authors." In fact, Agent "X" doesn't like the term Library Awareness *Program* because "it's not a program like COINTELPRO or the Ghetto Information Program of the early nineteen seventies. It's more of a counterintelligence investigative technique—it's used for movement analysis," that is, tracking the whereabouts of espionage suspects.

Sven Holmes, majority staff director and general counsel for the Senate Select Committee on Intelligence, said that the FBI "appears to have a legitimate reason to make carefully selected contacts with specialized technical libraries of the type known to be frequented by Soviet-block intelligence officers." Nevertheless, committee members believed such investigations imperil First Amendment rights and "should be subject to strict controls and should have a compelling justification."

In the spring of 1988, the FBI stated that its "compelling justification" was "the potential hostile presence in this country of 20,000 students from Communist countries, 9,000 visitors from Communist countries and over 4,000 Communist diplomats and commercial representatives based in the United States." The Bureau said that one third of the Communist diplomats "are believed to be involved in intelligence gathering efforts, and we do not have enough personnel to keep track of everyone who comes into the country with an intelligence gathering mission, and therefore public awareness is important to our efforts."

But the American Library Association, which has been the central forum for libraries and librarians since its founding in 1876, charged that the Library Awareness Program was "an unconscionable and unconstitutional invasion of the right of privacy of library users," and issued an advisory alerting its more than forty-five thousand members to "unwarranted government intrusions." Judith Krug of the American Library Association's Office for Intellectual Freedom complained that the Bureau "thinks libraries are an untapped mechanism to enhance law enforcement."

Edith Tiger, director of the National Emergency Civil Liberties Committee, called the program "harassment of librarians." Jaia Barrett of the Association of Research Libraries wondered, "What's the next step? Classifying road maps because they show where bridges are for terrorists to blow up?"

Such criticism did not seem to deter the FBI, which countered that "the Zakharov case shows our theory was correct, and we stepped up our program." Agent Schnitzer added that "we're not asking librarians to play 'Junior FBI.' " But Congressman Don Edwards, Chair of the House Subcommittee on Civil and Constitutional Rights, believed that the Bureau was doing exactly that. "We have protested mightily," he said. "We have to stop it."

There was very little public support for the LAP; aside from one or two editorials in small-town papers, a 1988 *USA Today* article by the conservative antifeminist Phyllis Schlafly, and another pro-LAP article by Bill Gerz in the right-wing *Washington Times,* the Bureau had few sympathizers.

In an interview in January 1988, FBI Director William Steele Sessions was asked about the program. He said it was both "true" and "routine" that the FBI "has historically depended upon the American public's assistance in carrying out its investigative responsibilities."

When it was mentioned to him that seeking librarians' help in this way seemed a desperate move, Director Sessions said he "would not characterize it as a desperate move,'' but rather ''as a logical move, that is, a move that should be understood very clearly by the American public and by any person who is aware of it.''

Is it possible that in the eyes of the FBI, going from the surveillance of writers and the surveillance of books to the surveillance of the place where books live and take on a life of their own is seen as a *logical* move because there is a link between the impulse behind the Library Awareness Program and the impulse behind the writers' files? In 1950, in answer to Soviet criticism that FBI agents were ''as obedient as a corpse,'' the Bureau replied that an ''agent exercises the obedience of a free American not a corpse.'' But isn't it possible that even though J. Edgar Hoover has been gone for more than twenty years—and five directors have succeeded him—his skeleton lingers amazingly? Isn't it possible that the FBI is like a corpse that continues to grow fingernails and hair? Or is the link between the LAP and the writers' files plain old institutional callousness toward freedom of expression—a callousness that showed itself in the efforts to chill writers? After all, the Bureau showed an insensitivity to civil rights by such intimidation, and is showing the same insensitivity by invading libraries where the *products* of writers are stored. The LAP casts a pall of suspicion over the free circulation of information in a democracy. Whatever threats America faces, or has faced, there is no greater threat to national security than ignoring First Amendment rights.

FBI DIRECTOR WILLIAM STEELE SESSIONS:

For several years now—maybe as many as ten years—the FBI has sought the assistance of librarians in connection with specialized libraries where there are people who come to gather technical research. Believe it that these are places where foreign, hostile intelligence persons seek both to gather information and recruit people who will be their agents in this country! I think it's a totally understandable circumstance, that if a librarian is *aware* that this happens, and that information and persons are dealt with in this fashion, that they would want to be aware of it, and then, if they *want* to give information, *fine*.

I find nothing threatening about the Library Awareness Program. I guess it's in the mind of the beholder. If, in fact, I came to 'Librarian Robins,' and came in a secret, unpublicized fashion and said, 'Now we want you to spy on these people,' I think that's an entirely different circumstance! What we're asking for is intelligence that comes by way of awareness and their observations. For instance, if you saw and were aware of recruiting activities that were taking place where people were being encouraged or were being solicited.

We do not expect the librarians to keep an eye on the books on the shelves—not at all. We expect librarians to be aware of things that in their minds are in fact foreign, hostile intelligence-gathering efforts.

**

In March 1988, the FBI expanded on Director Sessions's January statement that the LAP had been around "maybe as many as ten years," stating that "it's ongoing, and it's been more than ten years, but we'd rather not give out the exact date." However, Congressman Major Owens of New York, the first professional librarian ever elected to Congress, said that he was told at an FBI briefing on February 10, 1988, that the Bureau had been infiltrating libraries "for twenty-five years." Owens also said that the FBI told him there had been fifty incidents in the past twenty-five years of foreign agents stealing information from libraries.

What, exactly, can American libraries have in their open stacks that the FBI considers so dangerous? Mainly "sensitive" scientific, technical, and economic data that are *not* classified and are available worldwide to the general public in scholarly journals and books. The possibility that technical materials and ideas were being leaked to America's adversaries had been widely discussed since the mid-seventies. In the 1980s, the Reagan administration suggested publicly that restrictions on the use of this "sensitive but unclassified" material must be implemented, and suggestions ranged from changes in the Freedom of Information Act to voluntary censorship. At one point, the National Security Council's definition of "sensitive but unclassified" was so sweeping that it literally included *everything*. Strong opposition by scientific and library groups helped rescind this indiscriminate definition—much to the dismay of Reagan-administration officials. In fact, the Reagan administration wanted nothing less than a closing down of the United States' technical resources, including not only placing limitations on the very act of sharing scientific research among scholars, but even possibly requiring that the authors of research books and articles might need government approval before publication.

The Library Awareness Program was a logical outgrowth of all this, or as Congressman Owens put it, "another example of President Reagan's info-phobia."

Although in a 1988 briefing to the Senate Intelligence Committee the FBI said that only libraries in the New York City area were being contacted, this was not the case.

Fifteen libraries across the country had been targets of FBI inquiries from 1982 to 1988. Five of them were in New York State; the others were in California, Florida, Maryland, Michigan, Ohio, Pennsylvania, Texas, Utah, Wisconsin, and Virginia. Some had reported the visits to the American Library Association, the New York Library Association, or the Association of Research Libraries.

These libraries had a total of twenty-two visits from FBI agents. One occurred in 1988, but the vast majority occurred in 1986 and 1987, with the rest in 1982 and 1985 and no reported visits in 1983 or 1984.

Librarians said that agents invoked "national security," "counter-intelligence," aid against "hostile foreign agents," or "antiterrorism" in asking for cooperation. One agent flashed a copy of a 1982 *US News and World Report* article entitled "Drive to Keep Secrets Out of Russian Hands."

On October 16, 1987, an FBI agent asked a librarian at Pennsylvania State University's main library about an interlibrary loan of a dissertation requested by the East German embassy. At the engineering library of the University of Cincinnati, agents inquired about the borrowing habits of a Russian scholar because, although he was studying mining engineering at home, in Ohio he sought material on robotics. At the University of Michigan's engineering-transportation library, agents asked about a visiting Russian math professor studying graph theory who was spending too much time at the photocopying machine.

"There was a heavy patriotic theme," University of Michigan engineering-transportation librarian Maurita Peterson Holland recalled. "The agent appealed to my sense of adventure," said University of Cincinnati reference librarian Margaret Lippert. (Agent "X" says that "an agent's going to impress upon librarians that the free world will fall unless the library cooperates. He cons a person.")

University of Cincinnati head librarian Dorothy Byers says she "resented being pulled into this. The information community shuts down if you try to limit it."

"I felt intimidated," recalled Sylvia Evans of the University of Maryland's chemistry library. "The agent said these people are not U.S. citizens and should not be protected." The agent who approached director Selma Algaze of the Broward County Library in Fort Lauderdale, Florida, "tried to appeal to my sense of patriotic duty, and there was an implied threat that I should do what he asked. He said, 'We know for a fact that there are agitators in this area who are using the library for information.' When I asked for specifics, I was told that it was privileged information. He wanted to look at our computer. I said that 'what you're asking is privileged information to us, too.' "

Alexander Rolich, a Soviet and East European bibliographer at the

University of Wisconsin, Madison, reported this vignette of the FBI in action: Two agents watched a Soviet scholar, whose specialty was the Chinese economy, while he took a break to read *Pravda*. Then, Rolich said, "There were two more people by the library elevator and they were wearing raincoats and boots and it wasn't raining. A couple of days later, the FBI called to say this Soviet scholar had been identified by a defector as having been present at a meeting with the KGB. They wanted to know if the newspaper he was reading looked funny, or like it had been marked up."

According to FBI documents, Rolich was the subject of a May 1988 memo that said a former local FBI agent "now assigned to headquarters . . . may have additional knowledge" of him. Nothing beyond this vaguely ominous statement was included, however.

When FBI agents asked to monitor books checked out by interlibrary loan at the University of Houston, counsel Scott Chafin told them, "Absolutely no! If they have a problem with Soviet scientists, they should not let them in. Librarians are not going to do the work of the FBI." An agent also wanted to track patrons' computer database usage there and told the librarian, "Certain Russians are acquiring economic materials which could benefit them." Commented one librarian on this: "It's preposterous—you can dial up these library data bases from Moscow! It's all material in the public domain. I reject the FBI's theory that putting it all together in a computer makes any difference."

Up until 1988, the FBI had the greatest success with library clerks, most of them students. Head Librarian Dorothy Byers of the University of Cincinnati recalls that in a 1986 visit the agent was "pushy" and "went to a clerk who was all excited and caught up in the mystery of it."

Leanne Katz of the National Coalition Against Censorship says, "The clerks rarely know the laws." She believes that the FBI took this approach in the beginning for this reason; "the more informal, the more reports they can get," she says. Judith Krug of the American Library Association confirmed this: "The clerks are almost defenseless. The agents flash their badges at . . . nonprofessionals who have the mentality of 'you want the records, here they are.' "

Sometimes agents were vague in their requests. At the Brooklyn Public Library's Science and Industry Division, a polite young agent asked a librarian "to look out for suspicious-looking people who wanted to overthrow the government." The FBI later said the incident "was blown out of proportion."

When asked how librarians were supposed to recognize "suspicious-looking people," Special Agent Susan Schnitzer said, "You know when you see them. Someone who is looking for students, for instance. We're asking librarians to report this. If you spot it, tell us, and we'll take it from there."

At New York University's Courant Institute of Mathematical Sciences, the FBI asked to monitor photocopying and date-base usage. "Two or three months later," according to Courant's head librarian, Nancy Gubman, "I received a phone call from another agent who stated that he was following up on 'you know what.' " At Columbia University's mathematics and science library, the FBI tried its approach-a-clerk routine, but Paula Kaufman, then acting vice-president for information services (she is now a dean at the University of Tennessee), overheard the conversation, interrupted it, and told the agents—two women in their late twenties—to leave.

FBI Agent "X" comments, "We don't have people who remember the past. What, are they crazy? How can they go to Columbia University Library? It was ill-advised."

It is important to note that the targets of FBI requests for information about data-base users have not always been limited to librarians. In October 1986, agents paid a call on Mead Data Control, the suppliers of Nexis and Lexis. Nexis is an on-line library that contains material from eleven major newspapers, thirty magazines, ten newswires, forty newsletters, the *Federal Register,* and the *Encyclopaedia Britannica.* Lexis is an on-line legal library that is mostly used by lawyers and legal scholars to research court decisions.

Gerald Young, vice president of government relations, said FBI agents wanted to learn about the company, and "they asked if any Eastern bloc countries were served by us and we said no. They asked for our customer list, and we said no, it was confidential. There was subtle pressure, but no arm-twisting." Nonetheless, some self-censorship occurred. The *Wall Street Journal* reported on February 5, 1987, that Mead planned to drop research published by the government's National Technical Information Service. "We've drawn the battle line," Mead Data Control told the *Journal;* "With NTIS out of our system, we're saying that's it."

Dialog, the other large data-base system in the United States, located in California and owned by the Lockheed Corporation, has had no FBI visits, but that's because Lockheed probably had one under the special FBI awareness program that educates defense contractors.

According to Maureen Fleming of the weekly *Information Industry Bulletin,* the FBI's visit to her publication's offices was "strange." She adds, "We were surprised they thought we were unarmed but dangerous. The agent said one of his moles saw our bulletin on the desk of a Soviet U.N. employee. He asked why a Soviet would read it. He [the Soviet] could have gotten it *anywhere.* The mole got our name wrong and the agent was slightly embarrassed because he had to track us down. He mentioned he was visiting other companies."

FBI AGENT "X":
There is a great deal of information open to the public in all of our great libraries—and many Third World countries and Communist countries go there to see it. We have a lot of information because we are an open society and foreign operatives can take advantage of this. One of the most important gathering places is libraries.

From the perspective of the FBI, we're asking a United States institution to help in identifying, say, a Russian agent. If a Russian intelligence agent goes into a particular restaurant—or a library—it is the FBI's responsibility to ensure that this agent does not gather or develop additional sources. We are asking librarians to say when this person comes in.

The Library Awareness Program is a counterintelligence technique adopted by certain segments of our office; it's not universally adopted by everyone in the FBI.

I don't know who's using it. There are certain squads—and it's classified who does what, so I can't say what squads.

Personally, I don't think movements are that important, so I'm not using it. It's asking for trouble, and there's not that much of a reward.

The end doesn't justify the means. Nonetheless, there's nothing wrong with it, because American people are supposed to help American agencies. Libraries don't have to cooperate, but if it were my spouse who was a librarian, I'd say do it.

But you have to know you'll get burned if you use such a technique. It's catchy, and you *could* make something out of it, although it is perfectly legal. But the consequences of being in libraries is not good.

To tell you the truth, the first I heard of it was when I read it in the papers.

**

RAMSEY CLARK:
I remember William Webster said that anyone who's old enough to read and go into most good public libraries in the United States can obtain sufficient information from which he or she—he didn't say "she"—but he or she could construct atomic weapons you could carry on your back.

Now they've also had the mentality for many years that we're an open society, and the Soviets are a closed society, and that we're terribly disadvantaged by it, because you can go into our sources of information and gather up all you need to know—whereas we can't find anything about what *they're* doing.

If you really want to know what's going on in the Soviet Union, you don't use spies, because spies warp things; the very technique warps. You gather public information. It's like body counts in Vietnam: Who's doing the counting? What motives do they have? If you're a spy in the Soviet Union, you're not going to say "What lovely people, you can always trust them, they're not doing anything harmful, there's nothing to be afraid of"—you'll put yourself out of business. You're always going to see the worst side, you're always going to enlarge the possibility of danger—you've got a warped perspective.

People who rely on that are influenced by it. It may be subjective.

But I think where they come up with this library stuff is because we're an open society, people take advantage of us. They can come into our public libraries, our university libraries and get a lot of information. We don't want that. We want to find out if that's what they're doing. We want to cut it off.

I think it's awful. It's really saying that we're an open society only for Americans. Real Americans.

That's not an open society. That's a select society.

**

At most libraries, FBI agents were told that the information requested could not be divulged because of state laws governing the confidentiality of library records. Since 1970, thirty-eight states have enacted such statutes. Most agents did not press their requests; a few, however, returned again and again. In one city, they kept calling weekly, even after the ''suspect'' had left the country. Their final message was, ''Look out for anyone else suspicious.'' At the engineering, mathematics, and sciences library of the University of California, Los Angeles, an agent said, ''Everything can remain confidential—it's your duty to cooperate.'' And at the Broward County Library in Florida, the agent said, ''Don't you think we could just bypass all this nonsense?''

But the FBI did not become concerned about the library-records laws until after the Library Awareness Program began receiving negative publicity. Documents obtained under the Freedom of Information Act in 1989 by the National Security Archive, a public-interest scholarly research institute, revealed that in 1988, well after the LAP got under way, the Bureau asked various Bureau field offices to send information on state legislation concerning ''the confidentiality of library records.'' Evidently, there was some haste involved, for the field offices were instructed to send the material ''by appropriate overnight delivery,'' and in a few cases ''no-name pretext checks'' were made at certain libraries to obtain the legislation.

Up until that time, the FBI had never really worried about the possible illegality of obtaining library records. For instance, in 1988, a visitor to the FBI's own library in Quantico, Virginia, was told about the sophisticated computer searches available to student agents. The FBI librarian mentioned that one student needed an article on drugs that had appeared in *Rolling Stone* magazine and had been able to obtain it via the computer. The visitor thought this was an unusual magazine for an FBI agent-in-training to request, and murmured to the librarian something like, "That's quite an intriguing student. I'd like to see what *else* he has ordered from you."

"That's none of your business," the visitor was reprimanded by the FBI librarian. The visitor then politely remarked, "Well, that's exactly what the librarians across the country feel when you—the FBI—approach them for such information." There was a long silence.

Several months later, the story was related to Nancy Kranich, director of Public and Administrative Services at New York University's Bobst Library, and she said, "You know, that reference librarian shouldn't even have told the visitor *about* that student's computer search." Professional ethics had been breached. The ALA policy manual states that "Librarians must protect each user's right to privacy with respect to information sought or received, and materials consulted, borrowed, or acquired."

One government official said that the FBI is not aware of ethical issues, "because the Bureau feels that librarians can say no to them—so how can it be a problem?"

The guidelines governing investigations under the LAP are classified. Agent "X" explains that, as a general rule, "You don't let the opposition see how you play the game. Other intelligence operations would like to know, so guidelines are kept secret." However, in the case of the LAP, he confessed there "are no guidelines to it, per se." Others outside the FBI say they *have* seen some LAP guidelines, but described them as "quite general," and "nothing much."

Some of the documents received by the National Security Archive suggest that the FBI later tried to clarify and update whatever vague guidelines existed before the adverse publicity, and that it believed that most of its "problems" (the FBI's word) with "educating" (again, the FBI's word) librarians were brought on not only by the lack of firm guidelines, but by the lack of trained personnel. In short, the FBI believed that if it had just been more discreet, there might not have been any "problems." The wrongness of the program was never an issue.

The FBI said in 1988 that some institutions were secretly participating in the LAP, although it would not reveal their names. Special

Agent Susan Schnitzer explained that "librarians can't admit they're cooperating with us, due to the program's controversial and confidential nature; plus there's the risk of alienating people. A librarian won't say—it would make them suspect."

The FBI did say that the head of one library association was coordinating agents' visits. The organization was subsequently identified as the Specialized Libraries Association. When this organization was contacted, a spokesperson there vigorously denied that the organization was cooperating, and the FBI backed off, explaining that "specialized libraries association" was actually a "generic" name. There was no point in naming the real association because there was "probably not an association that would say [it is cooperating] . . . [none would] admit it because it would be confidential. There'd be no advantage to exposing it."

On May 18, 1988, in response to critics of the LAP, the FBI released an unclassified version of a thirty-three-page report, *The KGB and the Library Target, 1962–Present.* According to a memorandum dated May 5, "Secret and Top Secret versions of that report were being prepared and would be available by May 10th, 1988." (The "Top Secret" version actually was not ready until June 29.)

The *Foreign Counterintelligence Manual* describes "secret" information as that which, if disclosed, "could be expected to cause serious damage to national security"; while "top secret" information, if disclosed, "could be expected to cause exceptionally grave danger." FBI agent "X" admits, "Sometimes I don't understand" the differences.

In any case, the declassified version of *The KGB and the Library Target* concludes: "The FBI must logically pursue any contact between a Soviet national and an American citizen regardless of where the contact occurs . . . and that would include libraries. . . ." One high government official objects to this conclusion and calls it "staggering."

The report accuses the Russians of "significant penetrations" and "blatant disregard for American laws and the personal rights of American citizens." It includes quotations from a 1981 book entitled *The KGB: The Eyes of Russia,* by a former CIA agent, Harry Rositzke. When the book was first published, it received mixed reviews; *Choice,* a publication of the Association of College and Research Libraries, wrote that "this is not an academic book. Much of its contents cannot be verified by independent scholarly research."

The report also charges that the Soviet Intelligence Service (SIS) attempted to recruit public librarians "and encourage them to seek employment at more attractive targets'' and that it compiled lists of librarians "by ethnic background." The FBI report disclosed that the SIS attempted to recruit the librarian wife of a U.S. Army officer, and that ''over one hundred specific libraries have been the target of the KGB.'' It quoted from a 1985 study entitled *Soviet Acquisition of Militarily Significant Western Technology* that said state secrets were being stolen from such targets as ''defense contractors, manufacturers, foreign trading firms, academic institutions, and electronic data bases.''

The report stirred up trouble again with the Specialized Libraries Association by stating that ''the Soviet Intelligence Service has utilized clandestine means to obtain large volumes of documents'' from the SLA. Executive Director David Bender said, ''Nothing's been stolen.'' An FBI spokesman refused to divulge exactly what the Soviets had taken, saying this was ''classified, and if we were to answer that publicly, it could disclose to the KGB just how much we do know.''

For several weeks in the early summer of 1988, there were a great deal of Keystone Cop–type antics, with David Bender denying that anything had been taken from the offices of the SLA, and saying, ''I'm not sure where the FBI is coming from.'' The FBI countered: ''We're not saying who we talked to. It's certainly not *him*.''

Another high government official believed that the FBI's ''saying we're not going to tell who it is is a way of backpedaling, and saying it *is* the SLA is two-faced of the FBI.''

But some people felt the SLA was ''doing some backpedaling, too,'' because by the end of June 1988, it still hadn't taken a stand on the LAP. Bender admitted at the time that he ''couldn't get a firm stand'' because he is ''governed by a board of directors'' that wanted to remain ''neutral.'' Nonetheless, he insisted that the SLA and the ALA were working ''toward the same ends,'' and were ''just using different means.''

A library group that did publicly support the LAP was the National Commission on Libraries and Information Science (NCLIS), a board created in 1970 to advise the President and Congress on library policy. On January 14, 1988, FBI official Thomas DuHadway gave a ''nonclassified briefing'' about the LAP to the commissioners. DuHadway said, among other things, that the Soviets have recruited professional librarians and ''think it's better to recruit two librarians . . . [than] three engineers.''

DuHadway's presentation was well received. One commissioner

told him that "we all should read a book by J. Edgar Hoover called *Masters of Deceit*" because it "opens your eyes to so much." The FBI man thanked the commission member for his "guidance." Gerald Newman, chairman of the commission, defended the LAP and said "the real problem . . . is the Intellectual Freedom Committee [*sic*] of the American Library Association." DuHadway commented, "We're not attempting to speak to libraries that are controlled by them."

One librarian, who prefers not to be identified, says, "I've always thought, frankly, that perhaps someone from, say, a group like the National Commission on Libraries and Information Science (NCLIS) could be helping the FBI, either directly or indirectly. In fact, a lot of us feel this way because we know of people connected to the commission who were once involved with the real Specialized Library Association, so it would have been easy for SLA's name to be used as it was by the FBI." This librarian also asks, "Did you realize that the National Commission was worried that the minutes from their January 1988 meeting would get released under FOIA? Is that the way for a *government agency* to behave? Just who are they protecting? Themselves, perhaps?"

GERALD NEWMAN:

. . . I have to tell you, and I'm supposed to be impartial, but I am inclined on behalf of what the Bureau is doing. . . . The Soviet intelligence threat in our country is only rivaled by [that of] the Red Chinese. . . .

—*excerpt from transcript of a National Commission on Libraries and Information Science meeting; January 14, 1988*

**

A Short Conversation at a NCLIS Meeting:

Commissioner: Would you want the librarian to tell you what a person is wearing, and the person's appearance, glasses and hair?

DuHadway: No.

Commissioner: Well, how would you know what person to start looking for?

D: By description we'd probably know; we'd have an idea.

Commissioner: You do want a description then?

D: Physical description. I don't want to know that he has a gray and red checked tie. You give me a general description of who he is and I'll be able to tell.

Commissioner: But you'd want to know the color of hair, glasses, or height or something?

D: Whatever.

—*from transcript of NCLIS meeting; January 14, 1988*

**

Whether or not the Soviets actually recruited librarians as spies, the documents obtained by National Security Archive suggest that the FBI recruited some of them as informants. There are excised reports from some librarian "assets" and other evidence indicating that the Bureau attempted to recruit over thirty librarians. It is not known how many cooperated. In 1988, an FBI spokesman emphatically said the Bureau "was not trying to make librarians assets," which was not the truth.

What is true is that the Bureau made a total of 266 background searches in *1989* on individuals connected "in any way" with the LAP. The FBI said these searches were done "in an attempt to determine whether a Soviet active measures campaign had been initiated to discredit" the program. In other words, the FBI was trying to find out if any of the librarians or others who had criticized the LAP were being manipulated by the Soviets. Congressman Don Edwards said there was "absolutely no evidence to support this theory either in any of our private briefings or public testimony by the FBI."

The file also indicates that at one point the LAP was recommended for suspension because it doesn't "warrant a substantial expenditure of manpower," but that in 1985 the program was "reinstated." The dates on the suspension documents are blacked out, but Sheryl L. Walter, associate general counsel for the National Security Archive, believes it occurred "during the 1970s."

The LAP file confirms the FBI's resistance to listening to librarians, or placing any importance on their right to speak their mind. For instance, after an unsuccessful FBI visit to the Brooklyn Public Library in 1987, the New York field office wrote headquarters that the library's attitude that what the Bureau was doing was illegal and improper "should not go unchallenged."

Paula Kaufman, who had been approached by agents when she was at Columbia University and did not cooperate, was preposterously singled out at the January 14 NCLIS meeting as an opponent of LAP. Gerald Newman called her "the principal Vietnam anti-war person on campus" and opined that she became a whistle-blower about the LAP because "the FBI didn't do their homework and know who they were asking." In an editorial in the *Library Journal,* editor in chief John Berry called Newman's charge "totally inaccurate."

It happens that the FBI had recruited an informant at Columbia in 1982, a student employee at the engineering library who informed for the FBI over a period of "many months." After graduation, the student confessed his activities and said he had been bullied by the FBI into cooperating. He was amazed when told that the university could have taken legal action to protect him from the FBI's threats.

A college official in Virginia admitted that the college he works for did not "turn the FBI down firmly enough." The Bureau wanted the library to suspend the borrowing privileges of a Soviet patron who was reading material about missile sites. This college official said, "Many of our money people are those who would say we should have cooperated. We didn't do anything, one way or another. I was told by our president to 'not be in' " when FBI agents called.

In another instance, a library gave the FBI permission to observe suspects' "habits" as long as the surveillance did not disrupt service to other scholars.

On May 4, 1988, FBI agents visited the library at the University of Utah. According to Julie Hinz of the documents division, "The agents wanted to talk about a specific situation," a letter from a Soviet embassy official, who wrote as a private person asking about the capabilities of the library's NTIS (National Technical Information Service) data base. FBI officials later testified that the library's assistance had helped them catch their spy. Roger Hanson, the university's director of libraries, comments, "The FBI is concerned about NTIS because Russians will be living out here monitoring the [INF] missile treaty. We're concerned, too."

But specific situations aside, most libraries refused to go along with the LAP.

A few FBI agents threatened to obtain a court order when they met resistance, but only at the research library of the State University of New York, Buffalo, did they actually obtain the court order. The library was compelled to turn over the data-base search list requested by an Iraqi student—who by that time, the Bureau claimed, had already returned home. According to Stephen Roberts, associate director of libraries, "The agent remained very confident. I once asked him, 'Where did you park?' because parking is often a problem around the library. He answered, 'I parked wherever I wanted to.' "

Although the September 18, 1987, *New York Times* story that provided the fullest report to date on the LAP suggested that the New York Public Library had not been approached by the FBI, and a Bureau official corroborated this after the story appeared, this was not the case. In the spring of 1987, agents had asked the Economics and Public Affairs Division at the Forty-second Street branch about a specific person. The FBI concedes that this visit happened, but said it had to do with another "ongoing" investigation that had nothing to do with the Library Awareness Program.

Nonetheless, according to Paul Fasana, director of research libraries for the New York Public Library system, the agents returned in November of 1987 and inquired about two staff members who no longer worked at the library. The agents told Fasana that the LAP "has been misrepresented." A week or two later, on November 24, 1988, a lone agent spoke to top library officials, who once again refused to cooperate.

Meanwhile, around this time, two Hispanic agents went to the home of a New York Public Library employee on a Saturday afternoon to inquire about some documents—"not subversive"—that had been recently donated by the Cuban mission to the United Nations. The FBI agents referred to telephone conversations and photographs, leading the employee to believe that a phone tap and a hidden camera had been used. (The library later determined that there indeed had been a tap on an unidentified Cuban national's phone, and the library employee's name had been *heard* on the tap.) According to Fasana, to whom the original story was told, the library employee became flustered and started speaking in Spanish, but the agents refused to acknowledge that they understood him. The visit lasted forty minutes.

Even if the FBI had good reason to investigate in this case, they didn't handle it professionally. In addition, a member of the library's senior policy group says, "The FBI was told not to contact anyone and they went ahead and did it anyway." The official added, "They are escalating this library awareness thing."

Why did library officials and FBI agents have to be at such cross-purposes if the FBI had a legitimate reason to be in the New York Public Library? Because the Bureau erred and used a bona fide investigation as a jumping-off point for its LAP. The Bureau grouped the Cuban investigation with the LAP, and befogged library officials by misrepresenting both.

The House Subcommittee on Civil and Constitutional Rights held a special hearing on June 20, 1988, chaired by Congressman Don Edwards. Valuable testimony was given by several library groups, although it did not end the debate. And there were still serious aftershocks. In July 1988, a patron of the Brooklyn Public Library wanted to acquire the published proceedings of a recently concluded Communist party congress, but "wondered" if she'd be reported to the

FBI. "I just don't want to get in trouble with the government," she said.

On August 1, 1988, two months after Edwards's hearing on the LAP, the FBI declared that "pressure groups are having no effect on us because it's a worthy program," although a spokesman conceded that the many newspaper political cartoons on the subject "bother us."

As the eighties came to a close, the FBI was convinced that the LAP controversy would "die out. These things come in waves," it insisted. But the FBI had come to resent the time it was taking to defend itself, and a spokesman would concede that "maybe things should be modified."

In fact, a Bureau official told a reporter that "the American Library Association agreed to stop criticizing the LAP if the FBI stopped being proactive about the LAP." In other words, the ALA agreed to stand aside *if* the FBI stopped being aggressive in its library visits, and went into libraries only when there was a specific suspect or situation, used court orders, and showed respect for the laws governing libraries.

However, C. James Schmidt, head of the ALA's Intellectual Freedom Committee, said there *was no truce,* and the FBI official's statement "was absolutely not true." Schmidt says that the FBI and the ALA "agreed to disagree," and that "the FBI thinks they're on the side of the angels and we think they aren't." Was the reporter who was told about the truce being used as a messenger by the FBI to sound out the ALA for a possible cease-fire? Was the FBI, wanting to save face, saying enough is enough?

On March 1, 1990, Congressman Edwards's subcommittee once again heard testimony on the LAP, this time from two representatives of the National Security Archive who spoke about their efforts to obtain the LAP file.

The LAP file had also shown that the Criminal Investigative Division of the FBI opposed Vermont Senator Patrick J. Leahy's 1988 Video and Library Privacy bill, "which attempts to ensure that the choice of books we read and the movies we view will be protected against unlawful disclosure." The Bureau objected to the fact that in order for a law-enforcement agency to gain access to such records, a court order would be needed, as well as "clear and convincing evidence that the subject of the information is engaging in criminal activity." The file also indicates that the FBI was worried that the congressional hearings "will result in new guidelines restricting investigative contacts at libraries." A May 1988 memo suggested that the FBI ought to "aggressively handle" the hearings and "resultant publicity" so they serve "as a platform from which to alert all librarians nationwide of the threat faced by the U.S. from hostile intelligence services." It was business as usual.

But there have been no reports of FBI visits to libraries since 1989. The ALA believes the FBI "has pulled in," although Judith Krug says, "Once things have calmed down, it will start up again." In fact, she thinks "the LAP has gone underground." A government official says, "This LAP thing is just hanging there." Another government official agrees: "The FBI has not abandoned the LAP."

When Director Sessions was asked in 1988 that if he believed the LAP was "logical," did he then see a "logical" end to it, he replied that "our efforts to identify and neutralize the threat posed by hostile intelligence services and their agents in the U.S. must be continued as long as a threat to our national security exists. . . . This is a continuing process." In short, the end is not in sight. Or as Special Agent Susan Schnitzer put it, "There's no logical end as long as there's something out there to be aware of."

And for the FBI, there has always been "something out there."

AN AMERICAN LIBRARIAN:
It's kind of like a witch hunt. And there was an implied threat that I should do what the FBI was asking.

It's just a shame that such truly important matters got rolled around in the mud. Why did it have to be that way? It was like McCarthyism all over again!

I consider myself a patriotic American, but I will not break any laws. I will not compromise in any way the American Constitution, and that seems like what the FBI wanted us to do for them.

If they have a security problem, I want to help, but within the law, and within official library regulations. They told the commission that they were very concerned about recruitment of spies, so if this is a genuine problem, why didn't the FBI plan it out more carefully and ask us to deal *just with the recruitment aspect*?

Why ask about confidential records? Why ask us to break the law?

If librarians become deputy FBI agents, they can also be recruited to spy on the reading habits of ordinary Americans and—though now I'm going to extremes—even to volunteer information that a certain Arab-American, say, is checking out books on bombs or Sister Mary is suddenly reading a lot of Marx and Lenin. There are good reasons for the privacy statutes—reading habits should not be subjected to official scrutiny. That's an invasion of privacy and it's just the kind of thing that they did in totalitarian countries. Is the next step going to be to ask us to pull out "dangerous" volumes? Am I going to be told not to buy "controversial" books?

Does the FBI think we're pushovers?

PART EIGHT

Preparing for the 2000s: Is the Past Past?

CHAPTER TWENTY-FIVE

"Most of the Damage Was Invisible"

The bulk of the people examined in this book would not be in the FBI's files if they were not writers. Certainly, from the FBI's viewpoint, many of them were political activists as well, and were not so much singled out for their ideas or writings as they were for political acts or at least membership in groups like the Communist party. But none of the writers were actual physical threats to national security at any time in their lives. None were imminent threats to public peace. Many were not angels, and a lot of them did or thought foolish and pointless things, had messy private lives, betrayed others, and behaved irresponsibly, illogically, and dangerously. But none of that was any business of the FBI's. In no way are they individually or collectively an objective correlative of the investigative crusade, the hostile spirit, and the overhanging sense of threat and menace that shadowed the FBI's efforts (financed at considerable cost to the taxpayers). Their only crime, as defined by the FBI, was deviant thoughts.

There was a personal animus that held the drive together, of course, and that came from J. Edgar Hoover's determination, need, and obsession to control American opinion, especially when it criticized the Federal Bureau of Investigation. One man, because of his fears and envies, enforced laws which were not necessarily those of his country. One man tailored the meaning of the word *alien* to fit *writer*.

How many writers were adversely affected by the FBI's power of suspicion? Can this ever be tallied? How can it ever be accurately measured? Our best gauge is the subjective experience of the writers themselves, who are the witnesses to this extraordinary aberration in a democratic society.

There was sometimes very little visible effect. Most of the damage was invisible. Should we be grateful for this? As diplomat, economist, author, and professor at Harvard, John Kenneth Galbraith wrote in an article about his file: "While the impression of other people's paranoia is great, my own was diminished by the fact that while [my] documents are full of deeply damaging intentions, virtually nothing unpleasant ever happened as a consequence."

That "virtually nothing unpleasant" ever happened to such a prominent liberal Democrat is perhaps not surprising. That "virtually nothing unpleasant" ever happened to such a well-known writer on the right as William F. Buckley, Jr.—is not surprising. "They haven't interfered in my life," Buckley affirms.

But what of the consequences, however remote, on a fledgling or an unknown writer who might have heard rumors or chance remarks (meant to discourage his or her works-in-progress) at a lecture, class, meeting, or literary conference? How many writers with files suffered financial loss? William Carlos Williams lost a government salary when he was not cleared for his Library of Congress poetry consultantship. How many less-experienced writers lost jobs, grants, fellowships, or scholarships? How many writers were censored, even in vague, dimly perceived ways, by nervous editors, publishers, teachers, or administrators who may have received visits and or questions from FBI agents, or simply had heard of the writer's reputation as a "radical"? And how many, knowing that relatives, friends, neighbors, acquaintances, or colleagues were being interviewed by the FBI, engaged in some form of self-censorship? Or became what Max Eastman called a "self-confessed criminal"? Will we ever know whether a particular character, scene, locale, or plot direction was a result of either conscious or unconscious self-censorship? Or that a book or play or article was aborted by fear? Or indeed, that an entire generation of writers and a genre of writing became suddenly "unfashionable" because of the tales of suspicion borne by the FBI to a society that had grown fearful and wary of ideas? Jessica Mitford asks, "How many books *never* saw the light of day? How many writers *stopped* writing?"

HOWARD FAST:
The terrible thing the FBI did was to destroy social writing in America. Today, even from the so-called best of American writers, there is no social writing. The whole great American tradition of social commentary that produced all of our great writers, right up to World War II and the few years after World War II, this is over. Either a person writes as Updike does in terms of the minuscule thing or he writes in terms of nerves, obsessiveness, sex—Philip Roth. The social view of the writer has been terrified out of existence, and that is a great tragedy for American literature.

**

CARTHA DeLOACH:
I think it's absolutely false to say that the FBI destroyed social writing in America. In the first place, the FBI does not have the authority to destroy social writing, and as far as Fast's statement or allegation that the FBI caused a phobia which prevented or terrified social writers, it is not true. Because you do have social writing today. You have many individuals who are responsible for social writing.

**

JESSICA MITFORD:
I think it's true what Howard Fast says about the FBI destroying social writing. It's very true.

**

DIANA TRILLING:
Did the FBI have an effect on whether writers used certain characters, or a plot, or a locale? The answer is no. I've never known anyone that's been stopped by the FBI. Never. Not even unconsciously.

Well, you know whom it affected? Norman Mailer. He wrote a book, *Barbary Shore,* which is really involved with such things. He is absolutely paranoid on the subject of the FBI. He is more concerned than almost any writer I ever heard of.

As for Howard Fast saying the FBI destroyed social writing, well, he might say that. He was a committed, energetic, overt Party person—he wasn't just a fellow traveler. If you are an out-and-out Communist, then you have to believe that every move you make will be countered by a move by the FBI, because the Communists have always been under constant inspection by the FBI. So if Howard Fast says the FBI stopped social writing, he is talking about social writing as done by Communists. He doesn't mean as done by non-Communists. Nobody that's not a Communist is worried about the FBI.

I wouldn't say that the FBI destroyed the Communist party, either. It was one factor of very many. The Communist party self-destructed. All the negotiations with the Soviet Union are now on a very, very much higher level of negotiation. Once Roosevelt recognized the Soviet Union, it all got to be a different kind of enterprise. You didn't have to have your Communist party and all your little fellow-traveling groups and clubs to do your work for you. You now were able to work within the framework of the recognized relations between the two sovereign powers.

**

FBI AGENT "X":

At a point, there were probably more informants within the Communist party than certain cells of the Party. I've heard stories that they may have had cells of seven members of the CP and four of the members were informants. Now, is that called demolishing the Communist party? When you have four or five members of the CP and four are informants—they were informants to begin with, that is, somebody came and asked them to tell the FBI what was going on—is that destroying the CP?

Now certainly you can say we destroyed the Ku Klux Klan's activities against blacks. In certain klaverns we had three out of the ten members as FBI informants. The FBI is very proud of having destroyed the Klan, although there were many things said against the FBI.

But I don't think we destroyed the Communist party. The CP doesn't have a cause anymore—they had no cause and they passed away—like the New Left.

**

GRACE PALEY:

I think there's a lot to the idea that the FBI destroyed social writing in America. It's complicated and I think a lot of people don't even realize it. What the FBI had to do is create the Cold War forever, and what they had to do is underpin, backup, and enlarge and enhance the raging anticommunism of the country. So they did that, and then culturally they had to help in the development of the anti-Communist literary world. I mean there is a whole literary world because of that. Even when they were right about Russia, which they often were, in that literary world the movement against what would be considered close to Russian socialist realism or anything like that—I mean, people were simply terrified to be found writing like that. They would feel it's very inartistic of them or that they're missing the trendy boat of the period. But the *self-censorship* that happens is so much a part of it.

The attitude is so American that you can't write politically even when you *are* writing politically, and if they like it, they'll say it's not political. I'll give you an example which is irrelevant almost. I just read a couple of the most remarkable Chinese stories in a magazine called *Fiction.* The guy who writes the introduction says that of course these people are not writing political stuff. One story is on a woman and he calls it an absolutely nonpolitical story—but it is the most fiercely political story you ever read in your life! So you have two things happening: you have a kind of literary class—like this guy who wrote the introduction which when they like something they don't want it to be political—and then you have another class that really talks only in terms of form and Marx. So you have two things happening and it's very peculiar.

I began to write stories in my thirties, and I only began to write what I wanted to write. I couldn't write what it seemed to me the period wanted me to write—I already was a failure! I couldn't do it, not that I wouldn't have tried—I would have, but I couldn't. I mean, the whole history of my life is more of an anarchist one than a Communist one—and that I really felt.

I just never lived life asking permission, and when I wrote, I wrote. I wrote out of a good deal of internal pressure, and the writing really served me more than anything else. It served my own internal anxieties, and I don't mean private ones. I mean political anxieties, and women anxieties, and gender anxieties, and everything like that. I didn't finish school because I couldn't handle the whole thing—I couldn't write the papers the way they wanted me to. I mean, I'm a cooperative person—I happen to like people a lot—but I'm not *obedient*. Except in small matters, like anything my sister tells me—I do! On the other hand, you can't be naive about it—you're a part of your culture, no matter what. Whoever you think you are, you run the barricade. All our movements are a barricade.

**

FBI AGENT "X":

I don't think we've ever held ourselves out as great book reviewers. I don't think the FBI would ever put itself in a censorship-type mode or even suggest that certain books would be on some kind of blacklist. We're interested in the *people*. Now the *people* may be writing books, and maybe the names of the books that they write appear someplace—but it's almost incidental. We're talking about *people* and what they said or have written that would tend to prove they were Communists or Communist sympathizers.

The FBI did indeed separate the dancer from the dance—it did separate the book and its author. They could investigate the writer, but not what the writer produced. The FBI is not in the business of blacklisting or trying to change or restrict any works of art, any writings, any opinion. That's not our business.

Hoover was a very opinionated man and I think he genuinely wanted to protect First Amendment rights. He was a unique man, really. A strange man, nevertheless. He was a man who probably got to the point that he so enjoyed power that you could almost say that power was a substitute for sex. This man was *married*—the FBI was his organization. It may have given him every thrill in the world, too. He considered himself a cabinet member in the greatest country in the world.

A blacklist? Hoover might not have intended the signals to be that way, but other people might have read them that way and it became known.

Now, what happened as far as information that was in the file—in effect, the destruction of a particular individual who happened to be an author, and therefore the destruction of his *works*, *or*, a man who never wrote another book because of what happened—well, we go back to that *chilling* effect.

There was no *conscious* effort aimed at writers. Writers were considered a special group in that you wouldn't want to go out and interview them without getting approval from headquarters, because they *were* considered a sensitive group. What it really came down to was not trying to convey a feeling of duress on a writer because we didn't want it to backfire in our face. It depended upon how a writer or member of the media interpreted the visit by the FBI, because there's one thing I think you *can* say—and I've heard it said in a court of law—that the mere fact that the FBI comes to talk to you, it *does* have a chilling effect: just the FBI or the police coming to talk to you! It gives you tingles! The question, of course, becomes, Is that chilling effect so great as to constitute a violation of your individual constitutional rights? That's when it becomes, what you would say, an incorrect act.

**

Many writers and editors felt Hoover's power of suspicion and the chilling effect without even being visited by the FBI. Most who succumbed to fear did so unwittingly. Most writers were not consciously aware of being monitored. But the concealed way the Bureau operated left some writers feeling as if they *might* have been violated instead of feeling they *were* violated. The dread felt by people who suspected but didn't know they were being investigated was almost worse than the visible harassment. There was always the "I *think* I might have heard odd noises on the phone," not "I am certain I heard odd noises on the phone." Often the FBI interviewed a person about someone else, when it was really seeking information on the interviewee. Or, conversely, the questions to the interviewee would be a pretext for obtaining information about others. The poet Stanley Burnshaw recalled this technique very clearly:

> The interesting aspect of all the FBI inquiries was a kind of fishing-expedition attempt to get me to talk, not of myself, but of others—from William Blake to Christina Stead to Archie MacLeish and a good many well-known writers—names—contributors to *The New Masses* weekly during my years as an editor, 1928 through the first eight months of 1936.
> The agents seemed to indulge in distastefully personal questions concerning people of essentially no "importance," among them a man who had once taught at Boston University. . . . We had had a falling out, and the [purpose of the] questions I was asked was all too obvious to me: to test the validity of some of the answers I'd offered in earlier and more specifically political sessions.

The power of suspicion at work in specific people's lives, with varying degrees of hurt, has been documented: Before he died in 1961, Ernest Hemingway believed the FBI was after him, and it was. John Steinbeck suspected he was being followed, and he was being followed. Richard Wright felt harassed, and he had been harassed. F. O. Matthiessen, Maxwell Bodenheim, and Theodore Roethke were worried about the FBI, and had reason to be. Jessica Mitford and Howard

Fast believed their phones were being tapped and their footsteps followed, and they were. Ella Winter and Kay Boyle suspected they were being scrutinized, and they were. Arthur Miller, Grace Paley, and Malcolm Cowley were wary of informants, and they were right to be. Vincent Sheean and Norman Mailer thought they were under surveillance, and they were right. Allen Ginsberg suffered through a virtual government plot to immobilize him, and only when it was "over" did he know for sure that it had indeed happened the way it had felt.

During the McCarthy years, only the strong—the famous and successful writers like Arthur Miller and Lillian Hellman—could survive that withering fire. "The capacity for scaring people is tremendous," Miller says of such procedures. And during the 1960s the Bureau used a new kind of psychological warfare, an array of "dirty tricks" known as COINTELPROs that created a Kafkaesque world for a few writers. Lionel Trilling—the butt of a COINTELPRO! Norman Mailer, as well; Dashiell Hammett, and Howard Fast. William F. Buckley, Jr.: manipulated by COINTELPRO? Amiri Baraka was the victim of a series of COINTELPROs against blacks, COINTELPROs that attempted to discredit him with his colleagues and his family. Baraka, like Donald Ogden Stewart, was often under twenty-four-hour surveillance. "We thought so," he says. "We thought they were there all the time, all the time."

Grace Paley observes that what the FBI "really did was destroy the black movement. They let those guys kill each other." She also believes that "a lot of the black power politics allowed it to happen, allowed informants in easily—because all you had to do was out-power or out-radical somebody."

In fact, by setting certain events in motion and then just letting things happen, the FBI accomplished what it couldn't have done any other way. With politically active writers such techniques enabled the FBI to act secretly and avoid overt measures which might backfire, as Agent "X" attests. The fake letters about Baraka and Fast. The bogus letter sent to Buckley, meant to stir him up about black radicals at Yale University. The exploitation of Trilling and company's serious and scholarly letter about Soviet anti-Semitism.

FBI AGENT "X":
You have to draw the line between true expression of one's individual opinions, protected by the Constitution, and what is *not*. Very, very few of those individuals that were involved in antiwar expression and civil rights expression were guilty of crimes, yet the investigations continued, and that's why I think the

FBI came under great criticism—and justified criticism, I think. Not in *all cases,*
but certainly in many.

⁂

ELIZABETH HARDWICK:
You know, you're shocked just to see any file.

⁂

RAMSEY CLARK:
The FBI is not a Who's Who Agency, and you ought to prohibit the accumulation of information by federal criminal investigative agencies that is not
maintained in a form that is available to the public.

It's legitimate to prepare unauthorized biographical data on individuals in the
private arena, and I can see a reason to do it in the public arena. I can imagine
it could be helpful, for instance, to the Department of Agriculture to have biographical data on great agronomists who are working all around the country.

But you can't just say "I don't like this guy" and investigate him. You can't
say his name is on the wrong list.

Writers are shakers and the police will always fear writers because of their
capacity to destabilize. I think it's always been true. Writers are more dangerous
than others; they're the undercover agents of the other side, in a way.

⁂

What of the future? Former attorney general Edward Levi believes
"these things tend to go in cycles." Ramsey Clark believes that even
the congressional oversight committees that are supposed to keep the
FBI in line "don't ask the basic question: What ought a criminal
investigative agency at the federal level, under our constitutional system, do? How ought it to function?" Furthermore, he adds that if the
United States "begins oversight with the proposition that it's a terribly
dangerous world and we have to have a lot of trust in agencies like the
FBI, and there are many areas where you just have no right to know
and no business knowing, then you never really oversee—you're always standing off at a distance." Clark believes that often the chair of
the oversight committee "may be the only one who hears a lot of
information and wields power over other members of the committee
through that information." If the chair "is of a particular ideological
bent, where's the objective oversight?" Clark asks.

Over the past decade, the oversight committees have been reason-
ably vigilant and effective in making improper practices public. Still,
many people believe there should be an FBI charter that would clearly
define the FBI's duties. The Center for National Security Studies says,
"The FBI is controlled only by Executive Order and Attorney-General

guidelines, both of which are open to indiscriminate change and interpretation.''

During the past twenty years there have been calls for the formation of a citizens' advisory commission to oversee the FBI, but this has never been implemented. Many government officials are in favor of such a group. Others contend that the best antidote is keeping the FBI in the news and placing its performance under a public microscope for the world to examine, and certainly the Freedom of Information Act—despite the attempts to limit its effectiveness*—is still a key tool for opening the files to the light. So long as the Bureau exercises its power in darkness and secrecy, it can never be checked.

In this regard, Director Sessions admits that it's difficult for "a writer, or for any person, to get information" about the FBI because it "doesn't go and share it." Nevertheless, he is sympathetic to the attempt to try to get certain information, and believes "the struggle to understand" is "good." He believes that the FBI is not unlike the courts, "which may many times deal with things that are not public record, and it's easy to think ill of them or to think that they are hiding something when what they are doing really is being responsible under the law." Sessions underscores the importance of the FBI always being "available to the media." He says the Bureau does its "best" to "answer questions that we can answer—they're answered openly—they're opened as far as we can answer. And when my answer is that 'I'll look into things,' I may or may not discuss them later with the media. *But,* I expect to be held accountable for why I would not discuss them."

America does need an FBI; but an "intelligent" one, as *Partisan Review* editor William Phillips says. Newspaper editor and writer Bob Woodward, whose recent book *Veil* is about the CIA, agrees that over the last decade both the CIA and the FBI have been "battered," yet they have to get on the right track because "both agencies need to know what is going on" around the globe. But, Woodward emphasizes, "It would be bad if the intelligence agencies didn't have bad times, because they're almost antidemocratic."

There will always be uneasiness in America about intelligence operations, because they run contrary to our belief in the right to privacy and free speech. What about the "antidemocratic" aspect of the FBI's mission? How does one balance on the line that divides protecting

---

* A 1991 release from the State Department says, "The enclosed material includes documents from which the FBI has deleted its marginalia." This is a new—and ominous—development. Are in-house notes now classified?

America's security and protecting America's Constitution? That question goes to the heart of our system of government, and the answer is that it can never be finally answered but rather must be answered again and again, each time it arises in a new guise.

Director Sessions describes the "constant evolving problem" of "give and take and trust between the media and an agency." But this "constant evolving problem" can be widened to include the "give and take and trust" between "an agency" and the Constitution of the United States of America.

The impulses to control writers preceded the man who took advantage of them for almost fifty years. John Reed, Ezra Pound, and Walter Lippmann were already indexed by the time Hoover entered the picture, and dozens more were indexed before his powers became potent. J. Edgar Hoover created an imbalance that was unique—yet it must be emphasized that those same impulses he abused existed before his arrival. Will they now be held in check? And why now, if not before? Director Sessions argues that all investigative agencies "automatically have a chilling effect"—one of the more detectable consequences of the impulse to control. He explains: "For instance, when one leaves a meeting, if a red light goes on and a siren comes on and you say, 'Oh, no, what did I do?' and the police car goes right on by you and stops the car ahead of you, you say, 'Whew.' Is that a chilling effect? Yes. You'll be more careful about the way you drive."

There will always be sirens to warn us of danger. But a warning may be more than anyone needs, no matter how great the threat. Even though for a time in the thirties and forties the Communist party was plotting to win over American minds, there was no cause for any government official to counter with an even more vicious attempt at mind control. After all, as Diana Trilling has said, the CP "self-destructed."

Americans "will be more careful" about the way they drive, not because the car ahead of them is stopped for speeding, but because they want to live just and longer lives—lives free from chilling effects of any kind.

What of the future? Can the excesses that have been the subject of this book happen again?

ARTHUR MILLER:
I think all this *can* happen again, because in principle, it hasn't really been thrashed out. It really hasn't. And there's a lot of reasons why. One is that it's like the Iran-Contra thing, and our government obviously didn't want to dig too

deep into that, and so they took the easy way out and made conclusions which apparently left out a hell of a lot of stuff. The other thing is that the principle of a secret government, so to speak, has not been discarded. The United States is still in the throes of believing that it's going to stop—or control—a social change in the country by this means. The government really believes that—and I think the liberals do, too. Everybody, to one degree or another.

There's no question in my mind that it could happen again. But it won't be the same. It never is. There'll be some other issue. You know, there's the utter hypocrisy—the blatant, brutal hypocrisy—of the way they are now perceiving Nicaragua. My mind is being injured by all this. Like the Un-American Activities Committee, the whole thing depends upon lying.

**

GRACE PALEY:
Things come back in different forms.

**

HOWARD FAST:
I don't think the kind of terror they mounted will ever occur again.

**

WILLIAM F. BUCKLEY, JR.:
It was plain stupid for Hoover to get sore at me, plain dumb. Suppose I had gotten sore at him? I could have done him much more damage than he could have done me.

**

KAY BOYLE:
The FBI will always think of excuses.

**

MURRAY KEMPTON:
I think the collection of files—that kind of squirreling mind—is incurable. If they have collected files, they go on collecting.

**

FBI DIRECTOR WILLIAM STEELE SESSIONS:
Am I willing to confront the FBI's history? I've done it. I have no information about any list of writers that is being maintained. I categorically deny that we have any files on writers simply because they are writers.

**

AMIRI BARAKA:

I would imagine I'm still under surveillance. I've got lots of hints—the same hints we had in the sixties.

∗∗

JESSICA MITFORD:

I mean, the point is that they—the FBI—live in a dream world, don't they?

∗∗

ALLEN GINSBERG:

All totalitarians have had the need to control the minds of the populace—censorship, propaganda—but mainly censorship and book burnings, or throwing authors in jail.

The same guys who want to censor, press the button and start the war, I think.

∗∗

NORMAN MAILER:

Drugs and foreign policy are going to create endless possibilities for intelligence. I think the drug dealer will replace the KGB agent as the figure of attention—drugs, terrorism, and foreign-policy manipulation form a pretty potent triad.

∗∗

FBI AGENT "X":

Could there be a time when books would again be removed from shelves? I don't know.

Appendix A: Writers, Editors, Agents, and Publishers Indexed by the FBI Because They Signed Civil Rights and/or Antiwar Protests During the 1960s

Donald Allen
Walter Arnold
Aaron Asher
Dore Ashton
Eliot Asinof
Richard Baron
Thomas B. Barry
Elizabeth Bartelme
Sally Belfrage
Francis Bellow
Larry Bensky
Eric Bentley
Albert Bermel
Joyce Bermel
Sidney Bernard
Sara Blackburn
Paul Blackburn
Robert Bly
Florence Bonine
Ray Bradbury

Frederick Bradlee
Harry Breverman
Thomas K. Brooks
Dan Brown
Susan Brownmiller
Hortense Calisher
Emile Capuya
Jerome Charyn
Lois Chevalier
Noam Chomsky
Robert Claiborne
Arthur Cohen
Fred J. Cook
Robert Coover
Thomas Cornell
Robert Creeley
Frederick Crews
Joseph Cunneen
Guy Daniels
Amy Dave

David Dellinger
Barbara Deming
Stanley Diamond
Digby Diehl
Laurence Dietz
Candida Donadio
Diane DiPrimi
Edward Dorn
Alan Dugan
Robert Duncan
Martin Duberman
Whitney Ellsworth
James Whitfield Ellison
Barbara Epstein
Jason Epstein
Richard M. Elman
Jules Feiffer
Leslie Fiedler
Eliot Fremont-Smith
Norman Fruchter
Lawrence Ferlinghetti
David W. Fisher
Harold Flender
Isobel Fox
Joe Fox
Jean Todd Friedman
Betty Friedan
Barbara Garson
Marvin Garson
Maxwell Geismer
Herb Gold
Mitchell Goodman
Arlo Guthrie
Graham Greene
Ralph Ginsberg
Todd Gitlin
Saul Gottlieb
Dan Green
Josh Greenfield
Harold Greenwald
Ronald Gross

Richard L. Grossman
William H. Hackett
Richard Hammer
Elizabeth Hardwick
Curtis Harnack
Michael Harrington
Dianne Harris
Mary Heathcote
Nat Hentoff
Bernice Hoffman
Lamar Hoover
Warren Hinckle
John Hopper
James Leo Herlihy
Richard Hudson
David Ignatow
Will Iman
Paul Jacobs
Martin Jeyer
Stanley Kauffmann
Alfred Kazin
Ken Kesey
Galway Kinnell
Howard Koch, Jr.
Hans Koning
Andrew Kopkind
Richard Kostelanetz
Norman Kotker
Zane Kotker
Paul Krassner
Tuli Kupferberg
Peter Kemeny
Edwin Kennebeck
James Kirkwood
Max Kozloff
Christopher Lasch
Keith Lampa
Al Lee
Elinor Langer
Denise Levertov
Christopher Lehmann-Haupt

R.R. Laing
John Leonard
Janice Lloyd
Louis Lomex
Dick Lourie
Eric Lasher
Sidney Lens
Jackson MacLow
Martha MacGregor
Paule Marshall
Robin Morgan
Leonard Melfi
Jonathan Miller
Henry Magdol
George Mandel
Richard Marek
Charles Lam Markham
James R. McCawley
John McDermott
David McReynolds
Harold Mehling
Merle Miller
Henry Misrock
Howard R. Moody
Kelly Morris
Carl Morse
Erika Munk
Jack Nessel
Michael Novak
Jay Neugeboren
William Noble
Robert Nichols
Peter Nevramont
Jack Newfield
Bink Noll
Robert Ockene
Joel Oppenheimer
Ned O'Gorman
Conner Cruise O'Brien
Peter Olovsky
Charles Olsen

Joel Oppenheimer
Kenneth Pitchford
George Plimpton
Francis Fox Piven
Thomas Pynchon
Philip Rahv
Jules Rabin
Ismael Reed
Anne Reit
Adrienne Rich
Henry Robbins
Richard Rhodes
Barney Rossett
Alan Rinzler
Richard Rovere
Frances Ross
Bertrand Russell
Philip Roth
Marshall Sahlins
Ed Sanders
Faith Sale
J. Kirk Sale
Gertrude Samuels
John P. Scanlon
Gertrude P. Schafer
Hal Scharlatt
Richard Scheehner
Andre Schiffrin
Janet Schulman
David Segal
Robert Sherrill
Paul Showers
Jules Siegel
Alvin Simon
Joan Simon
John J. Simon
John Simon
Bennett B. Sims
Robert Schier
Selma Shapiro
Susan Sherman

Wilfrid Sheed
R. B. Silvers
Gary Snyder
Theodore Solotaroff
Susan Sontag
Peter Sourian
A. B. Spellman
Peter Spackman
John Speicher
George Starbuck
Christina Stead
Gloria Steinem
Sam Stewart
I. F. Stone
Harvey Swados
Dave Swaney
Hope Taylor
Norman Thomas
Hunter Thompson
Caroline Trager

Tomi Ungerer
Edward Victor
Kurt Vonnegut, Jr.
Gerald Walker
Arthur Wang
Andy Warhol
Arthur Waskow
David Walsh
Arnold Wesker
Ruth West
Wallace White
Roger Wiesenbach
Judith Winkler
Anthony West
Richard Wilbur
John Wilcock
Richard Yates
Sol Yurick
Jose Yglesias
Howard Zinn

Appendix B: Additional Files (Some are mentioned briefly in text*)

Conrad Aiken. 1889–1973. Poet, critic, novelist. *Charnel Rose, Blue Voyage,* among others.

His twenty-page FBI file began on December 12, 1945, when the FBI sought an interview about the trial of Ezra Pound. Agents were particularly interested to find out ("discreetly") whether Aiken had been approached to be a character witness for Pound.

There is nothing in the file pertaining to his holding the post of Consultant in Poetry from 1950 to 1952, although the Bureau once described one of his poems that appeared in *Ramparts* magazine: "Life is a wonder imprisoned in the humdrum. Above all it is brief."

Nelson Algren. 1909–1981. Novelist. *The Man with the Golden Arm, A Walk on the Wild Side.*

Algren joined the League of American Writers in 1935, marking the beginning of a 568-page file. He later became executive secretary of the League's Chicago chapter. "He was always chased [by the FBI] because he was such a natural," fellow Chicago writer Studs Terkel comments about Algren. "He was like a character in one of his books. And he was a clown in a big way. The FBI clowns in a lower class way."

---

* These files have been placed in the appendix not because they lack significance or because the authors are not important, but because of space considerations in the main text.

An example of Algren's clowning "in a big way" was listing his lover, Simone de Beauvoir, in a local Indiana phone book as the sole occupant of Algren's address there; thereon, the FBI referred to "de Beauvoir" as Algren's "alias."

For thirty-five years, until 1969, the FBI kept track of Algren, recording his travel plans, subjecting him to mail covers, pretext phone calls, and actual physical surveillance. In one 1958 report, the Bureau calls him a "publicity agent for the Rosenbergs, executed Communist agents" and in another, it worries about a report that he is a "correspondent" in Vietnam. The FBI considered him a leader in the Communist party, a charge he denied. The FBI, however, insisted that he was "working actively" for the Party but "is not known by the name Algren" and writes "cleverly and with great facility left wing slanted articles."

KAY BOYLE:

I think that Nelson Algren, like William Carlos Williams, didn't know he was under FBI surveillance. And the FBI's saying he wrote left-wing articles for *Holiday* magazine. *Holiday*! I thought they were going to say *The New Masses*.

He knew, actually, *nothing* about politics. He was hopeless.

He stayed with me before he went to Vietnam—either *Harper's* or the *Atlantic Monthly* was sending him there to write stories about the GIs. He told me he was sailing on a Communist ship called the *Empress of China*. And I said, "Nelson, a Communist ship could not be called *Empress of China*. It must be from Taiwan." And he said, "No, it's a *Communist* ship." And he was taking all these books—*Red Star Over China* and all. And when we took him down to the ship, in San Francisco, of course it was Taiwan—with a very conservative crew. They looked askance at these books that he had.

When he was in Vietnam he never saw a GI. He stayed in the Chinese quarter and played poker all the time. He never wrote a thing.

**

Fred Allen. 1894–1956. Humorist and vaudeville and radio comedian; his popular radio show had twenty million listeners.

It was a radio sketch that brought Allen to the attention of the FBI, in 1936. The skit was based on an article by an FBI agent about changing third-degree methods. Another agent who head the broadcast wrote Clyde Tolson about it. Tolson decided the sketch was very funny and made the Bureau look good, so he told Hoover about it. The Director was very pleased, too, and wrote Allen for a complete copy "to be included in our files." He also asked permission to reprint it in *The Investigator,* the Bureau's in-house magazine, saying "the employees of this Bureau would find much amusement in reading your version of third degree methods.''

The sketch was a slapstick routine that had obviously appealed to J. Edgar Hoover's sense of humor. (He had no patience for satire or irony.)

The agent who had first brought the sketch to Tolson's attention summed it up in a single paragraph:

> There followed a portrayal of old third degree methods of the rubber hose type, wherein one of the lines was as follows: "He's trying to talk but he can't because his jaw is dislocated." Then, the scene shifts to a very facetious new method of treatment of a killer. He was offered cigars and then a portable bar was brought up in the cell and drinks served. The killer finally stated that he just could not stand it any longer, that he was breaking down, that this kindness was getting the best of him, that they should give him a chance to tell them that he had killed the man. Whereupon the officer replied, "No," they should finish their drinks first. Then the prisoner begins to choke and cannot confess, due to the fact that the olive out of the martini got stuck in his throat. The scene closes with the usual sound effect of clapping and fadeout.

Such was the broad humor that pleased the Great Enforcer, who became Allen's friend. "Mr. Hoover thought a great deal of him, and liked him very much," Cartha DeLoach recalls.

Two years later, in May and June 1938, Allen asked permission to mention Hoover's name in two skits. Hoover gave his permission both times, responding with a collect telegram. These skits are also slapstick—in one an Indian accuses someone of taking a porcupine from his gift shop and says, "Chief want porcupine, call J. Edgar Hoover," and in the other, some G-men arrive somewhere and a man and woman are surprised to see them, so the man says, "But this is hardly a case for the G-Man," and the woman says, "It sure is, the thieves stole my radio, Mr. Hoover, and it's Town Hall Tonight" (the name of Allen's radio show at that time).

Once Allen saw that Hoover enjoyed being part of his show, he often put him in sketches. Nothing about Allen's routine seemed to bother the Director, not even "Inspector Bungle, the poor man's J. Edgar Hoover." However, in 1947, his threshold of tolerance was reached. After receiving some letters complaining that actor Edward G. Robinson said in a sketch with Allen that "Crime does not pay and neither does going straight," Hoover protested that "clean living not only pays dividends but is the only decent pattern of human endeavor."

Allen's sponsor tried to explain that this particular sketch was "pure farce and hokum" and that "as straight comedy it was not offensive," but Hoover did not agree. Some things weren't funny.

Maxwell Anderson. 1888–1959. Playwright. *What Price Glory?, Both Your Houses* (Pulitzer Prize), *Winterset, High Tor;* adapted *The Bad Seed* for the theater.

Anderson was indexed in 1938 for being a member of the Committee to Save Spain and China, information that was used against him four years later, in a 1942 blind memo "in connection with Alien control work." Hoover kept seventeen pages of references on Anderson, "a person interested in social legislation," until 1956, three years before his death in 1959. In 1942 he was a candidate for "custodial detention," because of his numerous front activities, but his case was eventually put in "deferred status."

S. N. Behrman. 1893–1973. Playwright. *Rain from Heaven, No Time for Comedy.*

Behrman was also indexed in 1938, because he signed a protest letter to President Roosevelt requesting an embargo on the Nazis.

His seven-page file ends in 1957 after Hoover pens "right" next to a sentence which says that Behrman is "*not* the type of person" the FBI "would want to be identified with." An unnamed producer's aide had told the Bureau that Warner Brothers thought "from a craftsmanship standpoint Behrman was one of the best writers in the field." But Warner Brothers wanted to check first to see if "it would be embarrassing" to the FBI to assign him to write *The FBI Story.* Hoover looked, and found it would be embarrassing because of Behrman's front activities, and nixed the project.

Stephen Vincent Benét. 1898–1943. Poet, short story writer, and novelist. *John Brown's Body, Western Star,* among others.

Benét's file began in 1938. But in 1954, years after his death, the FBI was suspicious because a Thanksgiving Day script that he wrote for the Writers War Board for use in a Department of Agriculture broadcast, was *rebroadcasted* on CBS. (Benét's older brother, poet and critic William Rose Benét, who died in 1950, was indexed in 1938 or 1939; his name appears on a list of writers supporting Spain that appears in James Thurber's FBI file.)

Louise Bogan. 1897–1970. Poet. *Body of This Death, Dark Summer,*

The Sleeping Fury; also poetry editor of *The New Yorker* for thirty-eight years.

She was indexed because she contributed to the September 25, 1937, issue of *The Nation.* There are eleven name-checks in her file, all involving national or international poetry festivals or conferences, and each "check" brings up the same 1937 reference. Missing, however, is any mention of her appointment as the Consultant in Poetry at the Library of Congress in 1945. Probably these reports are sequestered in some other file.

LOUISE BOGAN:

... to be perfectly frank with you, Malcolm, many people disliked you because they thought you were party-lining like mad, for awhile. In my own case, I took a dreadful beating, through the 1930–1940 period, because I wouldn't take the Communists seriously for a moment. . . . I was never taken in by the League of American Writers, for example . . .
—*excerpt from a letter to Malcolm Cowley, March 7, 1941*

**

Jane Auer Bowles. 1917–1973. Novelist and playwright. *Two Serious Ladies, In the Summer House.*

The FBI started collecting information on Bowles in 1945, when her name came up in the course of an investigation of someone else. She lived in Tangier, Morocco, most of her adult life, with her husband, writer Paul Bowles, who died in 1991. (Whenever she referred to herself as Mrs. Paul Bowles, the FBI called it her "alias.")

Her file remained "dead" until 1958, when a new investigation of her was opened under the heading "Security matter—Communist," despite her having told officials of the U.S. Passport Office that she had been a Communist from December 1938 to March 1939 but "was willingly dropped from the party" because she was not "serious enough."

Van Wyck Brooks. 1886–1963. Literary critic and historian. *The Ordeal of Mark Twain, The Flowering of New England, The Confident Years.*

Brooks's seventy-two-page file began in 1935. His name was spied on the membership list of the League of American Writers, and the FBI remained curious about him until 1963, the year of his death. It listed every petition he signed and every organization he joined, from the

1937 Golden Book of American Friendship with the Soviet Union, to his 1958 membership on the National Association for the Advancement of Colored People (NAACP) Legal Defense and Educational Fund Committee of One Hundred.

Most of the information in the 1958 memo concerning his involvement with the NAACP is from a secret memo from HUAC's files, which, of course, was supplied from time to time with FBI references, making it hard to know what originated where. This memo lists over one hundred "subversive" activities on Brooks's part, accusations that led the FBI to note ominously that he "reputedly received" a Pulitizer Prize. He had indeed won the award for his 1936 study of early American literature, *The Flowering of New England*.

HOWARD FAST:
Van Wyck Brooks's whole critical position in *The Flowering of New England* was accepted Communist party position, which doesn't mean that it was pro-Russian or anti-American. It was very pro-American, but it was a point of view that the Communists accepted, and which the crowd that developed out of *The Partisan Review* and The *New York Times Book Review* section rejected violently. So in that sense, there was even then an extreme left wing and a center and right wing in critical literature.
But I don't know that that's any reason to call a person a Communist.

**

Heywood Campbell Broun. 1888–1939. Journalist and critic. *Pieces of Hate, Gandle Follows His Nose.*

Broun was one of the most popular and controversial left-wing columnists of his time. Founder and first President of the Newspaper Guild, he was an unsuccessful Socialist candidate for Congress in 1930. Broun has a one-page FBI file. Given Hoover's obsession with the press, why would he let someone like Broun slip through his net? Probably there are more documents on Broun in the Newspaper Guild's file, or hidden under the names of informants or other organizations; clearly Hoover would have given Broun more than a single page. But that one page spans seventeen years—from 1935, when the FBI said Broun was a member of the Communist party, to 1952, when it reported he might have been "a Communist in 1935 or 1936," and circulated a carbon copy of this information to the House Committee on Un-American Activities, even though he had been dead for twelve years.

Pearl S. Buck. 1892–1973. Novelist. *The Good Earth* (Nobel Prize, 1938).

The FBI opened a file on her in 1937 because she was a member of the Women's International League for Peace and Freedom, and because she attended a dinner in support of the Spanish Loyalists. J. Edgar Hoover argued that Pearl S. Buck was "a little too liberal" and had to be watched for the good of the country.

Hoover also did not like that she was "a champion of the colored races" or that she "has been against universal military training and militarism," although he was sympathetic to her views about kidnappers. In a September 8, 1938, letter, he told her that "a friend has called my attention to your article entitled 'Ransom' which appeared in the October issue of Cosmpolitan magazine. . . . It immediately impressed me with your keen understanding of human nature, as did your book, *The Good Earth.*"

J. Edgar Hoover showed a side of his personality he rarely displayed when he wrote Buck that "I suffered with the young parents," and "as I read the story of the young people and their children I again lived the horrors of kidnapping as I have on innumerable occasions in the past through actual cases." That year, legislation was pending which would prohibit the payment of any ransom in kidnapping cases, and Hoover also wrote that "it is hard to tell a parent whether he should or should not pay the ransom. . . . I feel it would be most difficult to successfully legislate in matters involving human nature."

Hoover was so overcome by the emotions that Buck's story aroused in him that he even invited her to tour headquarters. However, by the time she actually decided to visit twelve years later, in 1950, those emotions were long forgotten. He wrote on a memo. "Have someone else talk to her. My impression is that she is way to the left to say the least."

Their past communication was even more of a distant memory in 1956, when he was asked to be part of the Kraft TV theater's production of *Ransom*, the story he was so moved by in 1938. His reply? "Certainly not in anything Pearl Buck has anything to do with."

(Harold) Witter Bynner. 1881–1968. Poet. *Grenstone Poems, Against the Cold,* among others.

He was indexed in 1937 when his name was found on the letterhead of the American Committee for the Defense of Trotsky.

Bynner, who was also known for his translations, as well as a well-known literary hoax he was part of in 1916 (a volume of poetry that parodied imagism), was noticed by the FBI again in 1937 because he was a member of the Medical Bureau to Aid Spanish Democracy.

In 1943, on a list of one thousand individuals who called for the abolition of the Dies Committee, Bynner, along with Dreiser and Van Wyck Brooks, is designated a "writer." (Some others, but not all, are also designated by their professions—"teacher," "artist," "scenic designer," or "actor.")

The Bureau also sent its information on Bynner, whose description was expanded to "American poet, very much interested in all things Chinese" to the El Paso (Texas) Office of Censorship, after that office had "opened" a letter in which Bynner's name was mentioned.

Bynner, who was watched until 1954, fourteen years before his death in 1968, also had his name on one of the FBI's oddest lists: it appears along with such names as "Cozy Inn Bar," "Courtesy Hotel," and "Cat Gang."

Erskine Caldwell. 1903–1987. Novelist and short story writer. *Tobacco Road, God's Little Acre, Trouble in July.*

His 212-page file was inaugurated the year *Tobacco Road* was published, in 1932, because he was "one of the leaders" of the League of Professional Groups for Foster and Ford. He was cited in 1935 for participating in the League of American Writers, and called a "fellow traveller of Communists" in 1938.

That same year he received a threatening letter and turned to the FBI for help. The letter said, "To every thinking adult who has seen your play 'Journeyman' they will wonder what kind of person you be, they will either curse you, or pity you, in my case I condemn you, as being a man of base intention. I challenge your right to air your individual opinion in public . . .", and was signed "C.Y.A." At the time, Caldwell was producing *Journeyman* at the Hudson Theatre in New York, and the play's frankness, like that of his novels, was controversial. An FBI agent went to the theater to interview him, and Caldwell said "he was at a loss to understand who could have written the letter to him."

Eventually the FBI decided there was no violation of the law, and put the letter in its Anonymous Letter file. In 1952, Caldwell again called the FBI when he received another threatening letter, which the FBI decided was written by "a typical crack-pot" and was not a violation of the law, although this time the FBI told Caldwell that the sheriff's office had been alerted.

Early in 1940, the FBI received a tip from an "unknown outside source" that Caldwell and his wife, Margaret Bourke-White, "noted photographer," "have been members of the CP for a long time." Hoover took this warning seriously, and recommended the following year that Caldwell be considered for custodial detention in the event of a national emergency. That same year, Hoover also became leery when Caldwell gave the original manuscript of *Tobacco Road* to the Librarian of Congress—Archibald MacLeish.

But what upset Hoover the most was Caldwell's popularity in the Soviet Union.

In 1942, the FBI decided that *The New York Times*'s book review of *All-out on the Road to Smolensk,* with photographs by Bourke-White, "was a typical example of the reviewer's sly manner of boosting the Soviet angle and at the same time leaving himself an out with his superiors on *The New York Times.*"

The Bureau had also reviewed it two weeks earlier, and its reviewer could be accused of similar things: he concludes that "on the whole the book is interesting" and "shows the determination of the Russians to win this war," but he stresses the irritants Caldwell discovered in Moscow.

The FBI persisted in calling Caldwell "an outstanding propagandist for Communism," and was extremely disturbed when it learned he was "well-acquainted" with Kenneth Durant, who, the Bureau said, "was one of the most important members of the CP in America," and was head of the Tass News Agency "from the early twenties to the early forties." Durant and Caldwell even "visited in each others homes."

In 1961, Caldwell called the agent in charge of the San Francisco field office "to keep clear" his position on a State Department Soviet translator he had given a reference for in 1959. But what Caldwell really wanted to clear up was the possibility that the person he was acquainted with might not be the person who was now living and working in the United States, but might be an "imposter." He told the agent that he had recently read that the person he thought he was acquainted with had been killed in Russia, so how could he then be in the United States? A report indicates that there were two people using the same name, though it is never quite made clear what the FBI did about reassuring Caldwell or itself about this coincidence. Possibly Caldwell had stumbled into a spy operation.

Dale Carnegie. 1888–1955. Author of inspirational self-help books, lecturer, columnist.

On August 5, 1936, J. Edgar Hoover asked the Communications Section to purchase a copy of Carnegie's *Public Speaking and Influencing Men in Business,* which one of his agents had advised him to read. In 1937, Hoover "suggested" that Carnegie's most famous book, *How to Win Friends and Influence People,* be "adopted for parallel reading by all new Special Agents during the original training school."

The following year, in 1938, Carnegie volunteered his newspaper column space to Hoover "in your fight against crime." Hoover liked the idea, and invited Carnegie to come to Washington "to discuss this matter," and offered him "a tour of inspection." Hoover told Carnegie that he "enjoyed following his activities . . . through his columns."

There is no indication in the file whether Carnegie ever toured headquarters or visited Hoover, although in 1942 Carnegie asked to interview Hoover "next time you come to New York," for a book he was writing "on conquering fear and banishing worry and developing courage and self-confidence." Helen Gandy, Hoover's long-time personal secretary, wrote Carnegie that her boss's "duties with the war program have made it impossible for him to tell when he would be in New York again," so Hoover missed out on giving his advice for the 1948 best-seller *How to Stop Worrying and Start Living.*

In 1942, presumably to stop worrying about him, Hoover added Carnegie's three-page entry from *Current Biography* that pointed out that "Carnegie provided an engagingly simple solution to a problem that has long baffled world economists. Depressions, he said, can be overcome by confidence," to his twenty-eight-page file, which didn't end until 1955, the year Dale Carnegie died.

CARTHA DeLOACH:
Dale Carnegie and Mr. Hoover had a speaking acquaintance.

∗∗

Willa Cather. 1873–1947. Novelist. *O Pioneers!, My Ántonia, One of Ours,* among others.

The FBI says her six-page file (later revised to three pages) must be withheld from public disclosure because most of the material in it pertains to someone else.

Cather would have approved of this secrecy, since she herself stipulated in her last will and testament that none of her papers could ever be directly quoted. However, she would not have approved of such secrets being kept behind her back.

John Cheever. 1912–1982. Novelist and short story writer. *The Wapshot Chronicle, Bullet Park,* and *Falconer.*

At one point in the sixties, the Bureau tapped his phone. The reasons for this are bewildering, considering that Cheever, according to his widow, poet Mary Cheever, "was not political." He never lent his name to anything, she says. "Civil Rights? John? Forget it." Nonetheless, Cheever has a four-page file that was begun on June 18, 1965, a file that Mary Cheever says "would not have made him mad." She adds, "I don't think they had anything on him, they were just being the way they are."

In fact, one very blacked-out 1965 document does not mention Cheever's name anywhere, nor the subject of the report, although copies of it were sent to the legal attachés in Bonn and London, and to field offices in New Orleans, Louisville, Washington, and New York. Mary Cheever recalls that her husband "may have gone abroad in 1965."

He also went to Frankfurt for PEN, Mary Cheever says, but there is no mention of this organization anywhere. He went to Russia in 1964, "the day after Khrushchev went out of power, and I remember John stopped in Germany. When he went to Russia, he had to be debriefed," she says. "He went to Washington before and after the trip," she recalls, adding that he went to Russia three times altogether—in 1964, sometime later in the sixties, and in 1977.

Mrs. Cheever finds it "utterly mysterious" that the FBI sent copies of the 1965 document to Louisville and New Orleans. "John had no connections there," she says. "I can't imagine what it means."

A 1969 two-page document emanating from Cleveland, Ohio, contains two brief mentions of John Cheever; the first part of one is blacked out but concludes with "Mary Cheever and John Cheever, who were then residing on Cedar Lane, Ossining, New York." The second mention is also blacked-out, except for the end, which states that some unidentified person "advised he did not know the Cheever family personally." Mary Cheever says she "knows one person in Cincinnati," but it would be "too farfetched" to connect this person with the document.

e. e. cummings. 1894–1962. Poet and novelist. *The Enormous Room, Tulips and Chimneys, 73 Poems.*

Cummings served as an ambulance driver in World War I, visited Russia in 1931 and returned unimpressed with communism. The FBI began his six-page file in 1955 after it learned he had translated "a small paperback publication called *The Red Front,*" which was by the French Communist Louis Aragon. In order to read *The Red Front,* agents went to the University of North Carolina Library in Chapel Hill. "The poem inferred [sic] the revolution would be bloody," their report said. The agents also uncovered who donated the book to the library and then indexed the donor's name. The Bureau also investigated the publisher of the Cummings-Aragon pamphlet, Contemo Publishers, and wrote a report saying that another of Contemo's books contained an article by Norman Thomas, which said, "Communism is a great principle. Democracy was a great principle." The agents ended their ominous-sounding report by saying, "Further [pamphlets] support Communism by inference."

T. S. Eliot. 1888–1965. Poet. *The Waste Land, Four Quartets;* winner of the 1948 Nobel Prize.

In March of 1949, the FBI began a two-page file on Eliot, after agents clipped two references from *The Daily Worker*. The first, dated March 15, calls Eliot "the anti-Semite primarily responsible" for giving the Bollingen Prize to "Ezra Pound, one of the most discredited and disgraced men of letters in the United States." The other, dated March 23, is an "open letter" asking Eliot, "Do you think it possible there is some causal connection between the vicious asininity of your views and your receiving at this moment the Nobel Prize . . . ?"

Eliot had already been vilified by the Communists over a decade earlier, when he was called "anti-people, and fascist-minded." Yet that meant nothing to the FBI, which indexed Eliot not for his political or literary beliefs, or his friendship with Ezra Pound, but because his name was mentioned in *The Daily Worker*.

William Faulkner. 1897–1962. Novelist. *The Sound and the Fury, Light in August, Absolom, Absolom!;* winner of the 1949 Nobel Prize.

His file began on February 7, 1939, after agents found his name on the list of writers asking that the embargo on the Spanish Republic be lifted.

In 1951, confidential informants reported that the Civil Rights Congress had "procured" a statement from Faulkner on behalf of Willie McGee, the black man accused of raping a white woman in Laurel, Mississippi, in 1945.

Jessica Mitford and her husband, lawyer Robert Treuhaft, were prominent members of the Civil Rights Congress. Treuhaft says that "in the late forties and the early fifties, the Communist party played a major role in the struggle for civil rights within the U.S. The Party helped create the congress—and the branch in Oakland was one of the most active and most effective in the entire country." Concerning Willie McGee, Mitford says, "I immediately called a meeting and said how many white women want to go to Mississippi the day after tomorrow? Four of us did travel . . . to save the life of Willie McGee. Mrs. Hawkins, the white woman he was accused of raping, had in fact been having an affair with Willie McGee for a long time—she was the one who initiated the affair, and when her husband began to find out about it, she screamed 'rape.' "

According to Faulkner's eighteen-page file, in 1957 he, himself, was involved in an affair that was inadvertently brought to the FBI's attention by executives at Random House, his publishers, because they believed someone was attempting to extort money from Mrs. William Faulkner.

Publisher Donald Klopfer told J. Edgar Hoover that a caller had asked Mrs. Faulkner "for five hundred dollars" in exchange for information "about a Miss Stein and [Mrs. Faulkner's] husband." William Faulkner told FBI agents that he felt the caller to his wife was "possibly a young writer he had offended in some manner."

It has now been acknowledged in Frederick R. Karl's biography of Faulkner that Faulkner did indeed have an affair with the writer and editor Jean Stein, described in the report as a Faulkner "family friend," who is "age 22, and the daughter of Jules Stein of the Music Corporation of America."

After Donald Klopfer asked the FBI to investigate for possible extortion, the Bureau did so willingly because "Faulkner, one of the foremost authors of the day . . . at one time had a brother in our service." However, the case was eventually dropped after the FBI decided the caller was only attempting to "sell information to Mrs. Faulkner" and made "no demand for money," so there was no basis for a charge of extortion.

When apprised of the contents of Faulkner's file, Jean Stein, now the editor of a small literary magazine, *Grand Street,* said she was "disturbed by the information" in it, but knew "nothing about the situation," adding "unfortunately Donald Klopfer is no longer alive." She declined an opportunity to review the documents concerning her, saying "I am not interested in seeing it or discussing it."

Edna Ferber. 1887–1968. Novelist. *So Big, Show Boat, Cimarron;* in collaboration with George S. Kaufman, the plays *Dinner at Eight* and *Stage Door.*

One of the most discussed crimes of the thirties, the kidnap-murder of the infant son of Charles and Anne Spencer Morrow Lindbergh in 1932, is responsible for bringing Ferber's name to the attention of J. Edgar Hoover.

On December 28, 1935, Hoover wrote a letter to his special agent in charge of the New York office about "the conduct of the crowd at the trial" of Bruno Richard Hauptmann, who was later executed for the Lindbergh crime. The Director wanted his agent's comments about the trial, and in fact asked him to "submit" them to him, because he had read in a New York newspaper that Ferber, one of the spectators at the trial, had commented that "the revolting faces of those who are watching this trial [are] an affront to civilization."

This comment began her eighty-nine-page file. It is not known what happened to the New York agent, since his comments are not included anywhere.

Two years later, in 1937, Hoover reported that Ferber was a member of the Women's International League for Peace and Freedom, along with Pearl S. Buck, actress Helen Hayes, and philanthropist Mrs. John D. Rockefeller, Jr., whose names he indexed. Another document, listing 150 names, has 25 checked or circled for indexing. These include musician Benny Goodman, actor Orson Welles, and violinist and composer Efrem Zimbalist, whose son would star in a popular sixties television series about the FBI.

F. Scott Fitzgerald. 1896–1940. Novelist and short story writer. *This Side of Paradise, The Great Gatsby, Tender Is the Night.*

His four-page file was begun on August 21, 1951, eleven years after his death. The occasion was a report that one of his stories, "A Diamond as Big as the Ritz," was going to be made into a musical. The report includes the comment that Fitzgerald "was merely heard to be a Red," but that was enough in the McCarthy era to alert the FBI to possible treason on Broadway—by a dead author. However, Howard Fast says, "Sure Fitzgerald was a member of the Party. John Howard Lawson, the cultural dean of the Party, finally convinced him that his only way to salvation—especially literary salvation—was to join the Party."

Robert Frost. 1874–1963. Poet. *A Boy's Will, A Further Range, A Witness Tree.*

Frost's twenty-six-page file began as a "dead" file after agents clipped his 1942 *Current Biography* summary and indexed his name for future reference. Sixteen years later, in 1958, the Bureau reported that "America's favorite poet" would become a Consultant in Poetry at the Library of Congress; but there is no record of his investigation included among the documents. His name is also mentioned in a 1958 internal security reference about someone else who is not identified, and handwritten in the margin (but not by Hoover or Tolson) is one word: "Communist"—with an arrow pointing to Frost.

Perhaps the notation explains why the Bureau clipped a 1962 United Press dispatch reporting that Frost and Soviet poet Yevgeny Yevtushenko disagreed on whether Marx's *Communist Manifesto* was poetry. " 'Was it ghost-written?' Frost asked with a twinkle," the dispatch concludes.

The Bureau also reported on Frost's impressions of Russia and Nikita Khrushchev, noting that the poet "advised that he is not a Communist or a Socialist but he believes that Socialism is the only system that can deal with the economic problems" in the world. That same year, in 1962, Frost was honored with a Congressional Gold Medal, just one year after his memorable poetry reading at John F. Kennedy's inauguration. Frost once said of George Washington that he "was one of the few in the whole history of the world who was not carried away by power." If Frost had known about his file, he would have recognized the handiwork of a man who *had* been "carried away by power."

Horace Gregory. 1898–1982. Poet. *Chelsea Rooming House, Another Look,* among others.

Much of Gregory's poetry criticizes middle-class life, but it was not for this reason that the FBI began a fifty-six-page file on him in 1930. His file was opened after agents read in the May 19 *New York Times* that Gregory, "among others of the John Reed Club of New York," had signed a protest against "alleged anti-communist propaganda."

Gregory was not a member of the Party, although he wrote, "My poetry has contained social implications that can be resolved only by the success of the Communist Party."

Two years later, in 1932, the FBI reported that he was a member of the League of Professional Groups for Foster and Ford, and because he supported the Communist presidential ticket, the FBI reported on Gregory's activities every year for the rest of the decade, dubbing him a "Revolutionary writer" and detailing where and when he published various articles and poems.

In 1948 and 1949, and again in 1953, the poet who said, "Ever since I left college, my political interests have been centered in the work of the Communist party,'' was the subject of a loyalty-security hearing, although documents from the Department of Army indicate that the 1953 inquiry concerned only his son-in-law.

John Gunther. 1901–1970. Journalist and writer. *Inside Europe, Inside Asia, Inside Latin America,* and others.

Gunther would have been surprised to find himself inside the FBI files. He was put there in 1936 after agents read in *The Daily Worker* that he had "attended a dinner sponsored by the American League Against War and Fascism."

In 1939, Leonard Lyons wrote Hoover that Gunther "would like to see you and your Bureau, so if you're not too busy donning those fancy pants for the King and Queen, call him and invite him over" because he "is a very high class guy." Hoover did just that, but later wrote "Len" that "unfortunately I was tied up at the time of his visit" and was unable to meet him. According to a report in the 104-page file, Gunther still enjoyed his tour, particularly "the experience of shooting the machine gun in the Range."

Although Hoover felt that "Gunther certainly slips in some subtle pleading for the U.S.S.R.," he kept up "cordial" relations because *The Daily Worker* had called *Behind the Curtain* (or as the FBI named it, *Behind the Iron Curtain*) "anti-Communist," and "anti-Soviet." He even granted him an interview in 1957 concerning a case identified only as having to do with "the Sterns."

In June 1958, the Bureau received information from the "indices of the House Committee on Un-American Activities" concerning "a white male author"—John Gunther. Included was such new material as his 1937 sponsorship of the Friends of the Abraham Lincoln Battalion [*sic*], which the FBI had missed the first time around. Hoover also learned from this report that Gunther's books were on sale at a Communist bookstore, but surprisingly, he kept no further records on Gunther, who died in 1970.

Moss Hart. 1904–1961. Playwright and director. *You Can't Take It with You, The Man Who Came to Dinner* (written with George S. Kaufman), and others.

Hart's file was begun in 1938 after his name was found on the letterhead of the American Committee for Anti-Nazi Literature. His thirty-two-page file is filled with references from the thirties and forties concerning his involvement with Loyalist Spain and American-Soviet friendship causes. In 1951, the FBI was concerned because the playwright had signed an open letter calling for the abolition of HUAC. In 1958 the Bureau received an inquiry from the United States Information Agency asking whether or not Hart's work was suitable for use overseas.

Howard Fast jokes that Moss Hart "wouldn't know what a Communist is if you were to explain it to him," a remark which the FBI would not have believed, since they kept the file open until 1968, seven years after his death.

What was the worry in 1968? It was whether performance at the White House of excerpts from the musicals *My Fair Lady* and *Camelot,* which Hart directed, would cause any embarrassment to the President.

Robert Herrick. 1868–1938. Writer and teacher. *The Common Lot, Together, The End of Desire.* Called by critic Alfred Kazin "one of the most distinguished moral intelligences in the early history of twentieth-century realism."

Seven out of the eleven pages of Herrick's FBI file are still considered too sensitive to declassify. The released four pages have to do with his membership in the League of American Writers.

It is difficult to understand what Herrick could have done to be in such a serious category: still classified. Perhaps the FBI got him confused with the corrupt and depraved Robert Herrick who appears in Robert Louis Stevenson's tale *The Ebb Tide.* Farfetched? But the genteel Herrick's having a file seems farfetched, too.

William Dean Howells. 1837–1920. Novelist, poet, critic, and editor. *A Boy's Town, A Modern Instance, The Rise of Silas Lapham,* among others.

In the course of his distinguished literary career, Howells encouraged such renowned writers as Twain, Henry James, and Stephen Crane. Howells's FBI file was begun in 1941, twenty-one years after his death. Why was his name put into the indexes? Because of a report that one of the new owners of *The Daily Worker* once "sat at the feet of Boston's great Novelist, William Dean Howells."

This information led the Bureau to discover that Howells had been a charter member of the National Association for the Advancement of Colored People in 1909.

Fannie Hurst. 1889–1968. Novelist. *Appassionata, Five and Ten, Humoresque.*

The eighty-four-page file on Hurst was begun in 1930, when the Bureau learned of her association with four questionable groups: the Non-Partisan Committee for Heywood Broun for Congress; the National Unemployment League, the "Norman Thomas New York City Election," and something the FBI called the "Recommending Book League of America."

But of the dozen or more organizations that Hoover knew Hurst was involved with during the decade, none bothered him as much as her 1934 support of the Welcome Home Tour of Emma Goldman. Here was a new alien holding out her hand to an old alien he had worked so hard to discredit.

Even though Hoover knew that Fannie Hurst "has been very close to Mrs. Franklin Delano Roosevelt for many years and is acquainted with many prominent people," he watched her vigilantly. In 1952, when she was nominated to be a delegate at the Fifth World Health Assembly, he initiated a "special inquiry" that included interviews with her family, friends, former teachers, employers, neighbors, and colleagues. A handwritten note discloses "this is a 'White House Special.' "

Hoover also received information about Hurst from the United States Passport Office, as well as "another Government agency which conducts personnel and security type investigations": the Civil Service Commission. According to a notation in the file, the commission showed the FBI a 1934 "souvenir program" of a dinner in honor of the "Ambassador of the USSR," which Hurst attended.

The FBI also reported that Hurst "has been connected with the National Broadcasting Company for about eight months, appearing on a television show, *It's a Problem,* with Ben Grauer." Hoover was wary of such national attention; however, his agents also reported to him that she "has also indicated her dislike for certain Communist front organizations," and that "she does not capitalize on her fame as a writer."

Hurst's last reference is dated 1956, and involves some undisclosed documents that were sent to the CIA, the Department of State, and to something called "RAB." According to the 1981 book *Are You Now or Have You Ever Been in the FBI Files?*, the meaning of "RAB," a code or abbreviation, "is not yet known with certainty."

William Inge. 1913–1973. Playwright. *Come Back, Little Sheba; Picnic; Bus Stop; The Dark at the Top of the Stairs.*

His four-page file was opened in 1957 because his work was mentioned in a Department of State intelligence dispatch called "Czechoslovak Communist Regime Attitude Toward Cultural Expression and Informational Activities." The report said that some "inroads" are being made to loosen things up in the country and that signs of it are the staging of *Bus Stop* by Inge, as well as *Autumn Garden* by Lillian Hellman and two plays by Arthur Miller. However, the report went on to say that Czechs were having difficulty receiving permission from Inge's and Miller's agents (Hellman's evidently said yes right away) because of the possibility of the text being "altered enough to produce quite a different effect from that intended by the author."

Randall Jarrell. 1914–1965. Poet. *Little Friend, Little Friend; Losses; Sad Heart at the Supermarket* (essays); among others.

His 322-page file began in 1944, when a surveillance on some suspected Communists turned up a car registered in his name. Jarrell, the agents reported, was in the army at the time, and some unidentified person had borrowed his car.

By 1948, the FBI knew he attended a World Congress of Intellectuals, and that he was an "advanced-guard" poet (the report is corrected in pen to "advance-guard").

The rest of his file consists of 1956 reports on his security investigation, which turned up such unremarkable things as the fact that no one in his "neighborhood" could say anything "unfavorable" about his conduct, that "a woman" who knew him had once "attended a Communist Party," and that in 1952 he was divorced.

His investigation for the Consultant in Poetry position he held from 1956 to 1958 *is* included among his reports. Jarrell filled the post after William Carlos Williams was turned down, and the new appointment sparked the Director's curiosity enough to ask to review Williams's file and "anything we have on Randall Jarrell."

Two years after Jarrell's death in 1965, an outraged parent of a high school student in California wrote the Director a letter complaining that Jarrell's "gobble de gook" had been assigned in her son's English class. "It is contrary to my long-standing policy to comment upon material which has not been prepared by personnel of this Bureau," Hoover wrote the distressed mother.

Robinson Jeffers. 1887–1962. Poet. *Flagons and Apples, Tamar and Other Poems,* and *Solstice and Other Poems.*

Jeffers, who along with Wallace Stevens disassociated himself from the National Institute of Arts and Letters' 1948 letter condemning HUAC, was first noticed by the FBI in 1935, when he contributed to *Pacific Weekly,* a forerunner of *People's World,* the West Coast Communist paper. The following year, in 1936, the FBI noted that he attended the funeral of Lincoln Steffens, "a well-known member of the Communist party."

Jeffers's file indicates that any association with him was considered questionable; one very blacked-out page reports that some unnamed person under investigation was "a good friend," and another very blacked-out page mentions someone else under investigation had "several books of poems by Jeffers" in his "library of one thousand volumes."

The FBI remained interested in "the famous poet," as it referred to him, until 1961, the year before his death.

James Jones. 1921–1977. Novelist. *From Here to Eternity, Some Came Running, The Thin Red Line.*

The FBI indexed Jones on August 22, 1963, because he participated in a civil rights march—led by James Baldwin—that picketed the American embassy in Paris. Eighty other American writers—not identified—also participated in the march, which totaled more than five hundred Americans living in France.

There are no further references on Jones, although his widow, Gloria Jones, says they also marched against the Vietnam War. She adds that not only did he "sign everything" because he was "a big liberal," but "Jim did a lot for kids—we were helping deserters. He played poker with the ambassador, and I guess they thought he wasn't dangerous, and he wasn't," Mrs. Jones says. "We had two friends in high places—the ambassador and General Weyand."

Joyce Kilmer. 1886–1918. Poet. *Trees and Other Poems.*

Although an FBI official once observed that he didn't "know *her,*" meaning Joyce Kilmer, his name had been in the files since 1941, when Kilmer's wife's entry from *Current Biography* was used to begin a file on *him* that ended when the FBI realized he had died in World War I, four years after his most famous poem, "Trees," was published in the August 1913 issue of *Poetry* magazine.

Joseph Wood Krutch. 1893–1970. Writer, critic, and editor. *Edgar Allan Poe: A Study in Genius; The Measure of Man.*

Krutch was on the book committee of the American Society for Cultural Relations with Russia when the FBI put his name in its files in 1928. The file remained "dead" until 1941, when the 1928 reference was reinvestigated. There is no follow-up included, however. In 1945, an unidentified former student was investigated by the CIA, but an FBI report indicates that "we failed to contact Professor Joseph W. Krutch." In 1951, the CIA investigated the visa of an unidentified person, but the individual's relationship to Krutch is not given. In 1960, the loyalty of a United Nations employee is questioned, but there is no indication why this report is in Krutch's seventeen-page file. There is, however, mention of an "interview" with Krutch by FBI agents, but a report is not included.

Mary McCarthy. 1912–1989. Novelist, short story writer, and critic. *Memories of a Catholic Girlhood; The Company She Keeps; The Group; Venice Observed; Vietnam.*

Before her death, McCarthy wrote NR several letters explaining her file (she did not send the actual file).

MARY McCARTHY:
Unless they were holding back something when I requested to see what they had under the Freedom of Information Act (and I asked the CIA and the State Department too), the result was disappointingly slight. It mainly had to do with my marriage to James West, then a USIA employee—we had met in Poland very late in 1959—and maybe with my going to Vietnam. Nothing on the thirties or forties or most of the fifties. There was one report, I remember, relayed from some State Department person in Poland, saying that I had described myself to Polish journalists as a 'Marxist' and/or Libertarian Socialist. Probably I did, but that was the most shocking thing in the file. There was nothing about my anti-Stalinism. Indeed I wondered whether they even identified me as the same person who had been on the Trotsky Committee, etc. I wasn't even sure that they knew I was a writer. This may have had something to do with my changes of surnames, since I may have first come to their notice as Mary Johnsrud, then as Mary Wilson [McCarthy was once married to critic Edmund Wilson], then as Mary Broadwater and finally with my present identity. Some bits of the CIA file, if I recall right, were listed as censored, 'to protect the identity of an informant,' I think.

. . . I have never been a sympathizer of the FBI's, have never let myself be interviewed by them, did not like what I heard of their methods. But, much to my surprise, these methods were certainly not evident in their treatment of my case.

—from letters to Natalie Robins; May 25 and June 23, 1987

**

Carson McCullers. 1917–1967. Novelist and short story writer. *The Heart Is a Lonely Hunter, Reflections in a Golden Eye, The Ballad of the Sad Cafe,* and others.

McCullers has a one-page file begun on a request by the USIA for her "subversive references only." There were none.

Thomas Mann. 1875–1955. German novelist. *Buddenbrooks; Death in Venice; The Magic Mountain;* winner of 1929 Nobel Prize.

Mann came to the U.S. in 1939 and in 1944 became an American citizen. He is the subject of a 153-page file, consisting of "approximately 800 references." The FBI first became suspicious of him in 1927 "when information was received that he was a member of the American Guild for German Cultural Freedom," which was, according to the FBI, "a racket."

The Bureau followed Mann, whom they called "a warm defender of Moscow," very closely, even reading all his mail. In 1951, just four years before Mann's death, Hoover was sent "new" evidence consisting of "several hundred clippings, letters, speeches, articles, etc." The Director was also told that this "material goes back prior to World War I and is rather complex and not easily understood unless one understands the political setup in Europe since prior to World War One."

THOMAS MANN:

. . . The great achievements of the American spirit in the field of the social novel, symbolized by such names as Theodore Dreiser, Sinclair Lewis, Upton Sinclair, Ernest Hemingway, John Dos Passos: all this belongs to the cultural possession of mankind and to my own intellectual past; it actually helped me to find the way to my personal work. . . . The American mind has the inestimable advantage over the European, in being practically immune to the germs of fascism. . . .

—excerpts from his speech to the Third National Congress of the League of American Writers; June 2, 1939

**

John P. Marquand. 1893–1960. Novelist. *The Late George Apley* and *H. M. Pulham, Esquire,* as well as a popular series of stories about a Japanese detective named Mr. Moto.

Marquand was indexed when FBI agents located his name on a list of writers who had signed the February 7, 1939, appeal for the lifting of the embargo against Loyalist Spain.

There are no further references for four years, when an October 19, 1943, memo to Hoover related that Marquand, "one of the country's better known authors'' as well as the director of information, War Research Service of the Federal Security Agency, wanted to meet with the Director concerning ''his interest in suppressing the publication of stories'' having to do with bacteriological warfare. The memo reminds Hoover that the FBI has given Marquand material on the subject, and that he is anxious ''to prevent public hysteria and speculation'' over anything that might appear in his ''Mr. Moto'' stories about a Japanese detective that appear in the *Saturday Evening Post*. The memo, also, surprisingly, refers to Marquand as a ''technical advisor to the FBI'' and states that he was once involved in a highly secret assignment concerning bacteriological warfare that was not known to ''the public nor, in fact, to Government agencies generally.'' The memo adds that Marquand ''might possibly be inclined toward the Communist viewpoint.''

The FBI continued to collect fourteen pages of references on Marquand until 1956, four years before his death. This last, June 29, 1956, document is an investigation into his background to determine whether or not he might be a subversive influence on the editorial board of the Book of the Month Club.

Henry Miller. 1891–1980. Novelist. *Tropic of Cancer, Black Spring, The Books in My Life*.

The Bureau, which called Miller ''a phoney writer,'' had opened a nine-page file on him in 1945, after Walter Winchell sent Hoover a tip about Miller's ''collaboration.'' Someone had observed Miller telling a group of students at Dartmouth College ''that the Nazis were just the same sort of people as the Americans and they were fighting for the same thing.'' The Bureau investigated these charges but could find no evidence that Miller, who the FBI was told ''has a following among pseudointellectuals in this country,'' had made any seditious statements. There is nothing in the file about the pornography controversy Miller's novels created; most were banned in the United States until the 1960s. The only thing agents came up with was that Miller ''is considered somewhat of a pacifist as is the case with practically all of the true artists.''

Marianne Moore. 1887–1972. Poet. *The Pangolin, What Are Years;* also *Predilections* (essays).

In 1935, the Bureau reported that Moore is ''a descendant from Revolutionary heroes,'' and then opened a file on her after receiving ''a plain envelope'' containing a ''list of Communist writers.'' For thirty years the FBI kept a file on the person they called the "Poetess of Brooklyn," reporting such things as her signing a 1948 protest against the prosecution of Chilean writer Pablo Neruda.

The FBI also noted that she signed the 1948 anti-HUAC letter that Robinson Jeffers did not sign. The following year, agents evaluated her poems, reporting that their reading "failed to indicate anything on [her] political sympathies."

Lewis Mumford. 1895–1990. Writer and social critic. *The Culture of Cities, The City in History, The Myth of the Machine.*

In the entry that marks the opening of Mumford's forty-seven-page file, he is described as "a writer by occupation." The entry goes on to report that Mumford fits this description because he "has been engaged in that type of work and its associated ramifications since approximately 1923." It was that year that Mumford, who said of himself, "If I have any field or specialization at all, it is the all-inclusive one of the social philosopher," cofounded the Regional Planning Association of America, which is not mentioned in his file, nor is his earlier association with *Dial* magazine, nor his service in World War I.

For J. Edgar Hoover, the "associated ramifications" connected with being a writer, meant, of course, groups such as "The Advising Council Book of Union," which the FBI called "the Communist Book of the Month Club," as well as the American Academy of Arts and Letters, of which Mumford was president in the early sixties, when his *City in History* was published. Sophie Mumford, his widow, says she has no idea what the "Book of Union" is.

The FBI listed Mumford as the head of a City College of New York committee formed to aid the Loyalist forces in Spain, a position Hoover believed made an individual a Communist. Mumford's good friend, critic Van Wyck Brooks, says in his *Confident Years* that Mumford "did not side with the loyalists." However, Mrs. Mumford says Brooks is "wrong," and that her husband "most definitely" sided with the Loyalists, adding "there's no doubt about it, although he didn't do it publicly."

Mumford believed that "there are three facets necessary in any form of government—cooperation, competition, and socialism." He also favored socialized medicine and was against loyalty oaths. For Hoover, such views made Mumford "well known to the Bureau as closely associated with Communist and liberal causes and fronts for years."

On March 3, 1941, the FBI wrote a three-page book review of Mumford's *Faith for Living*. Hoover underlined the last line in the review: "For what Mr. Mumford proposes is a brand of medicine that looks, smells and tastes like fascism." Mumford's daughter, Alison Mumford Morss, remarks that "this is more interesting about Mr. Hoover than about my father." She also adds that the family "had heard that he was in the files as a premature antifascist."

On February 26, 1942, Mumford was made the subject of a blind memo "prepared on various left-wing individuals." The file does not indicate where this anonymous memo was to be circulated.

Mumford died on Friday, January 26, 1990, and always suspected he had a file. His daughter says that the "actual file simply shows how little the FBI was to be trusted," adding that nonetheless, her father "was always able to keep on teaching and writing and wasn't black-listed."

Ogden Nash. 1902–1971. Writer of light verse. *Free Wheeling, Everyone But Thee and Me,* among others.

The Bureau used Nash's entry from *Current Biography* to begin his "dead" file in 1941. The "master of bouffe rime, adroit user of Americana as spoken in subway and cocktail conversations" was not reported on again until 1956, concerning a speaking engagement, and then in 1962, when information on him was requested to determine if he was suitable to participate in a National Poetry Festival.

George Jean Nathan. 1882–1958. Drama critic, editor. Coeditor, with H. L. Mencken, of the *Smart Set* magazine from 1914 to 1923; and cofounder with Mencken of the *American Mercury* in 1924. Also the author of *Autobiography of an Attitude,* as well as a collection of his reviews, *The World of George Jean Nathan.*

Nathan's file was opened in 1922, as has been shown, because of the irreverent article he co-wrote about Prohibition. The file remained inactive until 1937, when Nathan was listed as a member of the Committee on Civil Liberties in Jersey City, which had been formed to help organize workers in that New Jersey town. The FBI decided that Nathan and some other committee members, such as Walter Lippmann, Rex Stout, and Sherwood Anderson, were "hiding behind labor as a screen for their communistic activities."

That same year, according to a column written by Walter Winchell, Nathan had asked J. Edgar Hoover to arrange access for him and one other unnamed writer to Alcatraz Prison for a series of articles. Winchell said that when Hoover told Nathan "that's not my department," Nathan replied, "You fix it up for me and I'll play ball with you."

Hoover, of course, leaked the story to Winchell to discredit Nathan. He was probably offended by Nathan's implication that he "played ball." He did, of course, but only with favorites like Winchell.

Three years later, in 1940, the FBI reported that the *Daily Worker* had denounced Nathan (as well as Max Eastman) for being "birds of a feather"—"phony socialists" and "phony liberals." In 1946, the FBI reported that the *Daily Worker* had denounced Nathan for alleged bias against blacks.

Anaïs Nin. 1903–1977. Novelist and diarist. *House of Incest, Winter of Artifice, Cities of the Interior,* among others; also *The Diary of Anaïs Nin, 1931–1966.*

The FBI opened a "dead" file on Nin in the hopes of catching her at some subversive undertaking in the near future. But it never did, although Howard Fast says he "always presumed she was a Communist." Cartha DeLoach says that "sometime or other she probably made some reference to the FBI or about Mr. Hoover, or perhaps she was a member of the party, and the FBI put her up as a possible source of information."

In any case, her sole reference is a *Current Biography* entry, which quotes from her "personal friend," novelist Henry Miller, who praises her work.

John O'Hara. 1905–1970. Novelist. *Appointment in Samarra, Butterfield 8, From the Terrace.*

The FBI began a ninety-eight-page file on O'Hara on June 14, 1939, after agents saw his name on a list of the Hollywood branch of the League of American Writers. This was a full decade before the Bureau would have a legitimate reason to investigate the writer, when he applied for a job in the CIA in 1949.

During the course of that 1949 investigation, the FBI received word that O'Hara had resigned from the league after the Soviet Union invaded Finland in 1939, and he is subsequently called a "loyal American."

O'Hara "had been associated with the Office of Strategic Service for a short time" in 1944, and confidential informants told the FBI that he was "free of any leanings toward Communism"; however, other sources told the Bureau he was "a very heavy drinker," "hot-tempered and temperamental," "quarrelsome," "highly opinionated," and "a little wild." Various "neighbors and acquaintances" told the FBI that "the O'Hara family were at one time highly respected members of the

'Mahantonga Street blue bloods' '' and that "certain prominent" Pottsville, Pennsylvania, citizens "would enjoy painting a black picture" of O'Hara because of his "expose" of them in *Appointment in Samarra*. In fact, one person told the FBI that after O'Hara "sought the opinion of the book" from a friend, and received a bad review, O'Hara "punched him in the face."

On July 18, 1949, the FBI assigned a "mature, experienced and well qualified agent" to interview *New Yorker* editor Harold Ross about O'Hara. The Bureau was wary of Ross because he had once said publicly that agents "need an elemental education in politics" and objected to being interviewed about his staff or contributors. However, there is no report in the file of an actual interview with Ross, so it is possible—and probable—that it never occurred.

In any case, O'Hara, called "in the class with such authors as Ernest Hemingway and Faulkner" and a person who "would not be intrigued by such asinine concepts as Communism" by other references on his CIA application, did not get the job.

Ernest Taylor Pyle. 1900–1945. Journalist. *Ernie Pyle in England, Here Is Your War,* among others; Pulitzer Prize winner.

Pyle caught Hoover's eye in 1937 when he wrote a newspaper column entitled "Ernie Discovers He's Old Pals With Alaska's New G-Man." On July 1, the Director wrote him a letter "expressing appreciation" for this article. As it turns out, Hoover's message wasn't a simple thank-you note spontaneously composed because of a sweet column about the FBI in the *Washington Daily News*. The note had a hidden agenda.

About three weeks before the column appeared, Hoover had received a letter from his new Alaskan special agent divulging that he had met Ernie Pyle on the boat trip from Seattle to Juneau, but did not reveal his identity as an FBI agent. Later, the agent wrote, after Pyle read news accounts about the new field office, he stopped by and "commented" that his newspaper bosses "felt to some extent ill will toward" Hoover because "the Scripps-Howard management" feels that Hoover "discriminated against their representatives" and "favored particularly one Rex Collier who is connected with the Washington Star," the *Daily News*'s chief rival in the capital. The agent also wrote that Pyle said that "the animosity his paper felt was due to [Hoover's] desire for personal publicity," but that he had a "heated" discussion with Pyle and told him no one was being "discriminated against unless it was because of some good reason,'' and ultimately Pyle "left the office apparently in the best of humor.''

A memo in Pyle's file reveals that Hoover's hidden agenda was to prove "that it is untrue" that he "favors any particular representative of the press," although these words were not in his polite note to Pyle; instead they were in the letter of reprimand to his agent.

John Crowe Ransom. 1888–1974. Poet and critic. *Chills and Fever, Selected Poems,* among others; founder of *The Kenyon Review.*

Ransom's three-page file began in 1962 because he was a participant in the National Poetry Festival, and the report indicates that his name had previously never been in the indexes—so in this case, his file was started because he didn't have a file.

Damon Runyon. 1884–1946. Journalist and author of stories about Broadway characters. *Guys and Dolls, Blue Plate Special,* among others.

On April 19, 1946, Hoover wrote down his reaction to Runyon's column about New York mayor William O'Dwyer's new drive on gamblers and gambling: "a very cleverly written article and certainly a true slant on the hypocrisy of the N.Y. 'drive.' '' What is extraordinary about his comment is that it concerned one of his best and most famous friends. The year 1946 was that in which Damon Runyon died. His sparse, nine-page file shows, once again, the often unreliable facet of the FBI's intelligence gathering. It is simply not possible that the nine pages released are all that exist on Runyon, whose cousin was once accused of subversive activity by an informant in 1953, according to a letter in the file.

William Saroyan. 1908–1981. Playwright, short story writer, and novelist. *The Daring Young Man on the Flying Trapeze, The Time of Your Life, The Cave Dwellers.*

Saroyan was discovered by the FBI the same year, 1940, that *The Time of Your Life* won the Pulitzer Prize, which he turned down. An unidentified informant reported that the playwright spoke at "a committee of Publishers Pan-American Dinner for Writers in Exile," which was described to Hoover as "an extremely left-wing affair" because "all the speakers were in one way or another known front people for the Communist party." However, "at the last moment," some unnamed prominent writers "refused to participate" when they discovered the CP was behind the planning of the event.

Saroyan's forty-five-page file continues until 1970, when there is an Internal Security memorandum, which is, however, totally blacked out. There is also an undated CIA document that is considered too sensitive to release publicly, and it is possible that these are connected. They might in some way have to do with Saroyan's 1950's tax problems "that drove him out of the United States" by 1960, the FBI reported. In 1970, Saroyan was living in Paris.

Irwin Shaw. 1913–1984. Novelist, short story writer, and playwright. *Bury the Dead; The Young Lions; Rich Man, Poor Man.*

The FBI started Shaw's twenty-eight-page file in 1935 because he was "engaged in Communist activities." Three years later, the FBI reported that Shaw's "hopes are completely with the people of Republican Spain," and, in 1942, cited him for being part of the American Committee for the Protection of the Foreign Born.

Another 1942 report uncharacteristically praises Shaw as a "Lieutenant," along with Lillian Hellman, in the "furious fight against the 'fascists' (meaning anyone who objected to Communist domination)" and even refers to "the brave attempts of the Authors League to wrest the Hollywood section from the Stalinist group."

In 1943, an unidentified informant told the FBI that "the motion picture industry is the greatest medium for subversive activity there is. It is in the writers' hands and comes under the guise of a story." The informant singled out Shaw as a writer who needs "watching."

In 1944, when Shaw was a colonel in the U.S. Army, Hoover warned the War Department that he should not be writing for *Stars and Stripes,* because of his Communist sympathies. Two years later, in 1946, the Bureau reported that Shaw had finally admitted he had "Communist connections."

Booth Tarkington. 1869–1946. Novelist and short story writer. *The Gentleman from Indiana, Penrod, The Magnificent Ambersons, Alice Adams.*

Tarkington was indexed by the FBI on December 9, 1936, for being a member of the Authors Guild. Two years later, the FBI reported that Tarkington was also a member of the League of American Writers. In fact, his ninety-page file includes part of the League's constitution. It also includes a telegram from Donald Ogden Stewart, president of the league, asking J. Edgar Hoover to write a five-hundred-word statement on anti-Semitism. Stewart tells Hoover that Tarkington will also be a contributor. The Director's reply is not in the file.

In 1940, the Bureau was apprehensive because of Tarkington's interest in the North American Spanish Aid Committee, as well as the American Defenders of Freedom, a group which Stephen Early, the secretary to President Roosevelt, asked the FBI to investigate. Agents even searched "The New York Times Index morgue" for information about it, although there is no indication whether this was done surreptitiously or with permission from the editors.

In 1941, the FBI registered Tarkington's interest in the Negro Cultural Committee, and two years later, someone at headquarters marked "index all names" next to a news clipping about a resolution sent to President Roosevelt to stop race riots that were occurring in Detroit, Michigan. Besides Tarkington, others who signed the petition included Albert Einstein, James B. Conant (president of Harvard), Alfred M. Landon, and R. J. Thomas (president of the United Auto Workers).

In 1946, the year of his death, Tarkington's name came up in the 1932 Lindbergh kidnapping case when Colonel Charles A. Lindbergh forwarded two letters to the FBI from someone whose name is blacked out who wrote that "it is high time to dig into Booth Tarkington's past." The rambling letters suggest that Tarkington had something to do with the ransom money, but are quickly disposed of by the FBI as the work of a mental case.

Allen Tate. 1899–1979. Poet and critic. *Mr. Pope and Other Poems, Jefferson Davis, Memories and Opinions*; founder of *The Fugitive* literary magazine.

Tate, who once wrote Malcolm Cowley that he had "never signed anything but a small check," had a one-page file begun on August 26, 1956, because of a name check request from the United States Information Agency, which was checking on possible subversive affiliations. There were no references available, not even reports of his compulsory investigation when he was appointed Consultant in Poetry at the Library of Congress in 1943. That part of his file, like the investigations of so many other poetry consultants, is filed elsewhere.

James Thurber. 1894–1961. Humorist, cartoonist, playwright, and short story writer. "The Secret Life of Walter Mitty," *The Male Animal, The 13 Clocks,* among others.

In 1938, exactly eleven years after Thurber convinced *The New Yorker*'s E. B. White in 1927 to put him on the magazine's staff, the FBI put Thurber's name in the index and began his 105-page file. He was indexed after his name appeared on the list of writers attending the Third American Writers Congress that was sent to the Director by an unidentified correspondent. The note accompanying this list read: "Dear Edgar, Here's a pretty good dictionary of Communists."

One name among the *S*'s has been blacked out by the FBI, and it is, no doubt, that of the "unidentified correspondent." The Bancroft Library of the University of California at Berkeley houses the papers of the League of American Writers, and has in its possession a copy of the same document the FBI has, but in its copy all the names are intact. The one blacked out by the FBI is that of one Leland Stowe, the author of three books, *Nazi Means War,* published in 1933, *While Time Remains,* published in 1946, and *Conquest by Terror,* published in 1952. Stowe is quite possibly the mole who forwarded information on league business to the Bureau. (In a California HUAC document in Thurber's file, Stowe's name is again blacked out in 1946.)

In 1939, Hoover noted that Thurber donated some of his cartoons to an auction whose proceeds were going to Spain, and also reported that he signed a letter asking for closer cooperation with the Soviet Union. Thurber signed this letter along with four hundred others, including Langston Hughes, Granville Hicks, Dashiell Hammett, Ernest Hemingway, and F. O. Matthiessen. (Some prominent nonwriters were also indexed from this letter: composer Marc Blitzstein, producers Harold Clurman and Herman Shumlin, and artists William Gropper and Rockwell Kent.)

In 1940, Hoover's secretary, Helen Gandy, typed an office memo saying that "Mr. Hoover wants to be sure all names in this memorandum are indexed thoroughly." Why the added emphasis—the "thoroughly"? Because Hoover was furious at a letter "125 people in all walks of life" had sent FDR defending the Abraham Lincoln Brigade's participation in the Spanish Civil War.

In 1946, the FBI reported that Thurber was a member of a committee calling for "a clearcut break with Franco Spain"; others on the committee included Thomas Mann and actress Judy Holliday. (The FBI was concerned in 1950 because Thurber's short story "The Catbird Seat" was going to be made into a movie starring José Ferrer, who was also under fire as a fellow traveler.)

The following year, in 1947, the FBI clipped a gossip column from the *Daily Worker* that mentioned Thurber was "disgusted" with the red-baiting activities of Elliott Nugent, his collaborator on *The Male Animal.* In 1946, the Bureau reported that Thurber was helping to raise money for the ten Hollywood writers and directors fired after being cited for contempt by HUAC.

The Bureau also noted Thurber was fighting another "C": censorship in the arts.

Mark Van Doren. 1894–1972. Poet, novelist, critic. *Henry David Thoreau, Nathaniel Hawthorne, Collected Poems* (Pulitzer Prize, 1939).

Carl Van Doren. 1885–1950. Editor, critic, and biographer. *Benjamin Franklin* (Pulitzer Prize, 1938).

Mark Van Doren's 246-page file was begun in 1927, when the FBI reported his connection with the American Society for Cultural Relations with Russia. Mark Van Doren was literary editor of *The Nation* from 1924 to 1929, the year the FBI discovered his older brother, Carl, who had been the literary editor of *The Nation* from 1919 to 1922. Carl Van Doren was also a member of the American Society for Cultural Relations with Russia, but it took the FBI two years, until 1929, to discover it. By the late twenties, lists were becoming so plentiful that careful attention was not always paid to them.

Younger brother Mark Van Doren, whom the FBI referred to as "a Red-ucator at Columbia University," was not reported on again for five years, until 1932, when the FBI discovered that he supported the National Student League, which the Bureau suspected was a Communist front. Two years later, the Bureau reported that he was a member of the National Committee for the Defense of Political Prisoners, and in 1936, it reported that "he made statements approving the employment of Communists as teachers." It was also reported that he was, as they put it, a "writer" for the Book Find Club. In 1938, it was reported that he was "in agreement with the Communist viewpoint in the Spanish situation." In 1942, it was reported that he wrote a letter to the FBI suggesting that the Bureau investigate some person whose name is blacked out; whatever it was, "the matter" was "referred" to the "Postmaster General." It is highly unlikely that he knew this letter was being added to his own file. In 1945, an "anonymous source" told the Bureau that Mark Van Doren "was one of the nice cozy Reds that are around most all intellectual outfits," and an "undated typewritten report received from an unidentified source" but "probably written in the early part of 1945" said he was part of a "High Toned Red Group."

In 1945, both Van Doren brothers, along with Howard Fast, were cited for being part of a citizen's committee that "urged that the U.S. accept the Bretton-Woods Economic Plan for the recovery of Europe," after an article about the group appeared in the Communist *Daily Worker*.

In 1951, a "new main file" was opened on Mark Van Doren, marking the beginning of what the FBI called "a security-type investigation" on the writer. The FBI searched its index using fifteen variations on his name, ranging from "M. Doren" to "One Van Doren." The Bureau later referred to these names as aliases. The search revealed that nine of the name variations actually contained material on the writer. In other words, intelligence information was discovered in nine *separate* files, intelligence information that came, of course, from a variety of sources.

In 1953, Mark Van Doren was recommended for the Security Index, and his name remained on the list until 1955, when it was decided that he had never been an "actual member of the Communist Party." But he was watched until 1965, seven years before his death.

Older brother Carl Van Doren's next reference after 1929 was in 1937, when it was reported that he attended a banquet raising funds for "the defense of the Spanish government."

In 1938, the year his Pulitzer Prize biography of Benjamin Franklin was a best-seller, the FBI reported that Carl Van Doren was a sponsor of the American Committee for the Protection of the Foreign Born. Two years later, in 1940, the FBI became suspicious of his lecture about Franklin when a copy of it was sold at an auction benefiting exiled writers.

In 1939, the FBI again reported that Carl Van Doren participated in the Third National Congress of the League of American Writers, stating that "of the 72 signers," "at least fourteen" were Communists and "the others" were "fixtures on Stalinist manifestos and whitewash documents." Among those listed are Upton Sinclair, Dorothy Parker, Vincent Sheean, Malcolm Cowley, "Lilliam" [*sic*] Hellman, Irwin Shaw, and William Carlos Williams. The file does not state exactly which are "communists" and which are "fixtures."

The FBI often referred to Carl Van Doren, whom they watched until 1948, two years before his death in 1950, as a "dupe." Agents became suspicious when they learned in 1941 that he, Clifton Fadiman, Alexander Woollcott, and Sinclair Lewis were reviewing books for the Readers Club, which would make well-known books available to the public for a dollar a copy.

Hoover was afraid that books he considered subversive would become too accessible to Americans.

MARK VAN DOREN:

I have never knowingly joined any Communist or Communist front organization. I was a liberal in the thirties and I am a liberal today. I am opposed to Communism.

—*statement in his file, undated*

**

Gore Vidal. 1925–. Novelist, playwright, and essayist. *Visit to a Small Planet, Myra Breckinridge, Lincoln, Empire.*

According to Walter Clemons, Gore Vidal's biographer, Vidal's thirty-eight-page file was begun in January of 1948, when agents reported that the *Daily Worker* had reviewed *The City and the Pillar,* his vanguard novel that candidly and realistically dramatizes homosexuality.

The Bureau shadowed Vidal's activities for three more decades, calling him "on the pink side," and reporting in 1960 that his play *A Best Man* took an "unnecessary jibe" at the Director.

The following year, in 1961, the FBI noted that he was anti-HUAC, and three years later, in 1964, it was reported that Vidal was critical of the Bureau during an appearance on a David Susskind television show, *Hot Line.* According to the file, agents were encouraged to write letters of complaint to the network, and were also told to request that *Hot Line*'s contract not be renewed.

In 1970, the FBI watched television again, this time *The David Frost Show,* and reported that Vidal made some "unnecessary remarks" concerning Vice-President Spiro Agnew.

That same year an unidentified correspondent told the Bureau that he had heard Vidal say that in order to battle the system, one could "blow up the Capitol." The FBI's reply to the distressed letter writer said only that the FBI was "strictly" an investigative agency, and that officials could make no comment about any alleged advocacy of violence.

Nathanael West (pen name of Nathan Wallenstein Weinstein). 1904–1940. Novelist. *The Dream Life of Balso Snell, Miss Lonelyhearts, The Day of the Locust,* among others.

The FBI says no file exists for West, even though his name is marked for indexing on a copy of the 1935 League of American Writers list that is in Robert Herrick's file.

Edith Wharton. 1862–1937. Novelist. *The House of Mirth, Ethan Frome, Old New York.*

Edith Wharton lived most of her life in France. In 1945, the FBI indexed Wharton because her 1920 Pulitzer Prize–winning book, *The Age of Innocence,* was on the list of books owned by an unidentified person undergoing a security clearance.

E. B. White. 1899–1985. Humorist, essayist, contributor to *The New Yorker. The White Flag, Is Sex Necessary?* (with James Thurber), *Charlotte's Web, Stuart Little.*

White's name came up during a 1956 USIA "name check." There were no references in his file.

Alexander Woollcott. 1887–1943. Drama critic and journalist.

Woollcott was a drama critic for *The New York Times,* and later for *The New York World.* He was also a *New Yorker* contributor, and a member of the famous Algonquin Round Table. Woollcott's two-page file was begun the year of his death because of two United Press releases. The first reported that he had "collapsed at a broadcast," and handwritten on this was a note that Woollcott had been "previously removed from the mailing list." No reason is given, no "previous" correspondence is included, and the name of the FBI official responsible for the measure is blacked out. Woollcott had recently edited *As You Were,* a "portable library of American prose and poetry for members of the armed forces and the merchant marines"—an anthology that included the work of Hemingway, Parker, Tarkington, and Nash. It is clearly this anthology and its "suspicious" contributors that was behind the FBI's interest in Woollcott's illness and death.

Louis Zukofsky. 1904–1978. Poet. *All: The Collected Poems,* and *A,* among others.

Zukofsky came to the notice of the Bureau in 1935 after an anonymous letter "described him as a Communist writer." The FBI immediately started a file and learned that he wrote articles for *The New Masses,* and was also a member of the League of American Writers (the Bureau would have found him on that list eventually without the anonymous tip).

Six years later, in 1941, he "filed an application for employment with the Bureau as a translator" but did not get the job. Ten years later, in 1951, the Bureau renewed its interest, after Whittaker Chambers told agents that he personally had recruited Zukofsky for membership in the CP in 1925. When the FBI could find no further corroboration, and learned that Chambers had qualified his remarks to say that "Zukofsky only stayed in the Party one month," it reluctantly ended its investigation two years later, in 1953, because it knew that the poet could not lead them directly into the Party. The final report, however, calls Zukofsky—and his wife—"guarded in their answers."

Appendix C: An Epilogue

On February 14, 1989, the Ayatollah Khomeini issued a death sentence on writer Salman Rushdie for writing a novel entitled *The Satanic Verses*. The Ayatollah considered the book blasphemous to Islam, and a grave insult to all Moslems.

The assassination threat not only sent the author into hiding in England, where he lived, but brought danger to his publisher, Viking Penguin, and many other writers, as well as publishers, booksellers, and libraries—worldwide—who came to Rushdie's defense.

There were protest marches, speeches, and readings. At a symposium held in Roxbury, Connecticut, during the summer of 1989, Arthur Miller told the audience that "the publication of this book reminded the world that the power of words is still enormous."

In the spring of 1990, Rushdie wrote in a pamphlet entitled *In Good Faith* that his novel was "a work of radical dissent and questioning and re-imaging. It is not, however, the book it has been made out to be, that book containing 'nothing but filth and insults and abuse' that has brought people out on the streets across the world." In early 1991, Rushdie reaffirmed his Moslem faith in an effort to end his death sentence, and also called for a halt to a paperback edition of *The Satanic Verses*. But during the summer of 1991, Rushdie's Japanese translator was murdered in Tokyo, and his Italian translator was stabbed in Milan.

Earlier, many bookstores that sold *The Satanic Verses* were subject to threats and harassment from fundamentalist Moslems. Several were firebombed, as was the office of a local prize-winning Bronx, New York, newspaper.

On February 28, 1989, fourteen days after the Ayatollah's threat, a bomb blew up the offices of the *Riverdale Press* because it had published an editorial in defense of Rushdie.

Copublisher and editor Bernard Stein had written on February 23 that "to suppress a book or punish an idea is to express contempt for the people who read the book or consider the idea. In preferring the logic of the executioner to the logic of debate, the bookburners and the Ayatollah Khomeini display their distrust for the principle on which self-government rests, the wisdom and virtue of ordinary people."

Stein says that on the morning of the bombing, "The FBI was there by 6:30 A.M.—I have no idea who called them"—adding that news of the attack had spread "rapidly": "it was a total media firestorm."

He recalls that the FBI agents on the scene were "genuinely appalled" and he was "very impressed" with the degree of outrage they showed. One agent said, "God, if they can bomb *newspapers!*" Stein says "I began to shift my idea of the FBI right there. I really felt they were on my side."

This was not always the case.

As a political activist at the University of California, Berkeley, in the mid-sixties, Stein was once on the FBI's list of undesirables for signing a Free Speech Movement petition, and he has a twenty-five-page file that was begun in 1965. The FBI also tracked Stein in the late sixties when he was on the staff of an underground newspaper in San Francisco called *The Movement*, which was affiliated with the Student Non-Violent Coordinating Committee and the Students for a Democratic Society.

He remembers a burglary of the paper's editorial offices and is "now convinced it was the FBI" who was behind it. In 1968, he was put on the FBI's Reserve Index, because, as was written in his file, he was "in a position to influence others as a writer."

Twenty years later, things would be different.

"I haven't changed," Stein says.

He describes the FBI in 1989 as "scrupulous about our rights and concerns as journalists. They even asked permission to tap the office phones for tracing, and had to get special clearance from the Justice Department to interview the staff—because we are a newspaper. I was *bowled over* by that."

Is it possible that the FBI was now legitimately looking for aliens—actual outsiders and/or foreigners who might be involved in all the

Rushdie-related bombings and threats—and that America had at last come full circle because the FBI was now protecting our writers' freedom of expression and First Amendment rights?

Director Sessions says that "anybody who is involved in and pushing for social change is not at risk of being investigated for terroristic activities."

The FBI, it would seem, has changed.

On March 1, 1989, a delegation of publishers and booksellers met with Director Sessions and Attorney General Richard Thornburgh. According to the March 17 issue of *Publishers Weekly*, a publishing trade magazine, "Thornburgh promised that the FBI 'will utilize its ongoing intelligence-gathering activities to aid in protecting against attacks on bookstores and publishers. In addition, the bureau will vigorously investigate such incidents and the U.S. attorney's office will prosecute any case on a priority basis.' " The magazine also reported that the FBI had directed its field offices " 'to get acquainted' with local booksellers and to treat the Rushdie-related threats with a high priority."

When questioned if perhaps the Library Awareness Program had been stepped up in an effort to gain intelligence information from foreigners who might be connected to any Rushdie-related terrorist acts, Director Sessions replied that the LAP "was not designed" for this purpose, "nor is it utilized to protect bookstores or publishers from attack." He added that "naturally, though, such attacks would be investigated were they to fall within our investigative jurisdiction."

The Director was also asked if the FBI considers the writers who have protested the Rushdie incidents to be part of the "public assistance" that the FBI "has historically depended upon" in "carrying out investigative responsibilities," and whether or not any of these writers groups are under surveillance. Many people feel that the possibilities for such surveillance are even greater as America becomes more and more of an electronic society.

However, the Director did not reply to the first part of the question, about whether the writers groups are part of "public assistance," but did say that the FBI "would not conduct surveillance of any group protesting such attacks or threats, based just on their protest."

The implication is that there could be a surveillance based on other reasons, possibly the fact that where Rushdie-related protests are being held, there is a likelihood that Rushdie-related terrorists could be standing by.

Here the FBI is, in fact, standing right on that hard line of protecting individual rights and protecting society from terrorists. But at least this time writers are not under suspicion for supporting the right of a person to write what he or she thinks and feels.

Notes

For frequently cited books, only the author's name is used after the first identification.

Unless otherwise noted, all quotations from "formal witnesses" are from interviews (and sometimes follow-up telephone calls and letters) with NR. The dates of the interviews are as follows:

Svetlana Alliluyeva: 11/16/86; 11/19/86; 12/3–12/5/86
Jack Anderson: (telephone interview) 12/11/89
Amiri Baraka: 2/3/87
Kay Boyle: 6/30/86; 10/1/86; 2/18/87
William F. Buckley, Jr.: 9/21/88; 6/25/89
Stanley Burnshaw: (letter) 7/29/89
Angus Cameron: 10/10/89
Ramsey Clark: 1/25/89
Roy Cohn: 4/29/86; 5/12/86
Malcolm Cowley: 7/14/87
Cartha D. DeLoach: 9/16/87; 4/12/89; 11/9/89
E. L. Doctorow: (telephone) 4/12/89; 11/8/89
Howard Fast: 7/23/86; 4/26/88; 5/5/88; 5/22/88
Allen Ginsberg; 4/14/87
Elizabeth Hardwick: 4/21/87
Murray Kempton: 10/7/89
Harold K. Leinbaugh: 1/12/88
Sylvia Lyons: (telephone) 5/2/88
Norman Mailer: 1/19/89
Arthur Miller: 1/20/88
Sophie Mumford: (telephone) 5/21/90

Jessica Mitford: 5/19/87
Grace Paley: 9/18/87
William Phillips: 8/86
FBI Director William Steele Sessions: 1/11/88
Karl Shapiro: 5/23/89
Diana Trilling: 5/2/89

Prologue

Page

15 "Two or three weeks later . . .": I am grateful for the advice and sample letters contained in the "FOIA FILES KIT" provided by the Fund for Open Information and Accountability, Inc., P.O. Box 022397, Brooklyn, New York 11202-0050. In addition, its newsletter, "Our Right to Know," was a helpful resource in the preparation of this book.

16 " 'FBI Intelligence has its roots in war . . .' ": Morton H. Halperin, Jerry J. Berman, Robert L. Borosage, Christine M. Marwick, *The Lawless State* (New York: Penguin Books, 1976), p. 93.

17 " 'The FBI could make a best-seller . . .' ": For more details, see William C. Sullivan, *The Bureau: My Thirty Years in Hoover's FBI.* (New York: W.W. Norton, 1979).

17 "67,744,000 index cards . . .": Letter to NR from Assistant FBI Director Milt Ahlerich, Office of Congressional and Public Affairs, September 26, 1988. Mr. Ahlerich wrote: "As of June 30, 1988, FBI headquarters was maintaining 26,744,000 automated index records. Approximately 41 million cards are being retained in our inactive manual indices." Since most of my FOIA requests go far back and might be considered "inactive" now, I added both the automated and manual figures together for the total.

18 "Later on a file could also be opened as a dead file . . .": NR interview with FBI Agent "X," a current agent who requests anonymity.

18 " 'We get conflicting information . . .' ": Ibid.

19 " 'The FBI builds its files . . .' ": From a column by Drew Pearson, as quoted in *The FBI-KGB Wars* by Robert J. Lamphere and Tom Shachtman (New York: Random House, 1986), p. 114.

20 "Richard Gid Powers writes . . .": Powers, p. 591.

20 "A former special agent says . . .": NR interview with former FBI official Harold Leinbaugh.

20 *Secrecy and Power: The Life of J. Edgar Hoover* by Richard Gid Powers (New York: Free Press, 1987) is frequently cited in this book. It helped me enormously in fitting the pieces of my story together and led me

toward my interpretation of the writers' files. However, any mistakes in said interpretations are mine, and mine alone.

Chapter One

32   " 'as the numbers of immigrants rose . . .' ": Powers, p. 33.

32   "After the flood of immigrants . . .": William Preston, Jr., *Aliens and Dissenters* (Cambridge, Mass.: Harvard University Press, 1963), p. 4.

32   "Socialism was rampant . . .": Albert Parry, *Garrets and Pretenders* (New York: Dover, 1960), p. 100.

32   "According to William Preston . . .": Preston, p. 5.

32   " 'revolutionary remarks are heard everywhere.' ": From the FBI file of Max Eastman.

32   "entered a reference . . .": I have chosen the first reference *sent directly to the FBI* as the opening date of a file. For instance, if in the course of an investigation, someone in the FBI reads *Who's Who in America* and discovers from that reference book that the subject of the investigation went to Spain two years before the investigation began, that would not be considered a reference sent directly to the Bureau. However, if the information on this trip to Spain reached the Bureau separately, say from the State Department, then it would be a "legitimate" reference. In John Reed's case, the information on his connection to *The Masses* was sent directly to the Bureau, and in Ezra Pound's case, the information on his whereabouts came to the FBI directly from the State Department.

33   John Reed's very early references are at the National Archives (Washington, D.C.) They are on the old German microfilms, reel 585, #182787. A lot of the material did not reproduce well on the microfilm and is unintelligible. In 1989, I received from the FBI 115 additional pages on Reed that contained assorted references from 1920 to 1950.

33   " 'A magazine with a sense of humor . . .' ": See Henry F. May, *The End of American Innocence* (New York: Alfred A. Knopf, 1959).

33   "Ezra Pound first left the United States in 1908 . . .": John Tytell, *Ezra Pound: The Solitary Volcano* (New York: Doubleday, 1987), p. 35.

33   "As Kenneth O'Reilly writes . . .": Kenneth O'Reilly, *Hoover and the Un-Americans* (Philadelphia: Temple University Press, 1983), p. 17.

35   "Louise Bryant told the 'incredible story' . . . ": Theodore Draper, *The Roots of American Communism* (New York: Viking Press, 1957), p. 287.

37   " 'This class struggle plays hell . . . ' ": See Van Wyck Brooks, *The Confident Years* (New York: Dutton, 1952).

37   " 'originator of Communism' ": J. Edgar Hoover, *Masters of Deceit* (New York: Henry Holt, 1958), pp. 18–21.

37 " 'even the head librarian . . .' ": for more details see Ronald Steele, *Walter Lippman and the American Century* (Boston: Little, Brown and Co., 1980).

38 Excerpts from letters of Max Eastman to Floyd Dell are from the collection at the Newberry Library, Chicago, and are used with permission.

39 " 'that journal of fun, beauty . . .' ": May, op. cit.

39 " 'a who's who of artistic and literary America . . .' ": For more details see Draper.

39 "Max Eastman even went to Washington . . .": Parry, passim.

40 "Jack London . . . best-known and highest-paid . . .": See Alfred Kazin, *On Native Ground* (New York: Harcourt, Brace, 1942).

41 The 1917 and 1918 references pertaining to Jack London are at the National Archives, in the Bureau of Investigation 1917–1918 files. However, they are not listed in the catalog and I found them by chance when I was looking up something else on the microfilm. In addition, twenty pages on London (out of a total of thirty-two) were released to me under FOIA by the FBI; the dates on these range from 1923 to 1955.

41 Lincoln Steffens's FBI file is also at the National Archives, in the Bureau of Investigation 1908–1922 files. His first reference is located on OG (Old German) 167. His name is mentioned in sixty-nine references on fourteen separate index cards.

42 "President Theodore Roosevelt . . . proposed idea . . .": Richard E. Morgan, *Domestic Intelligence* (Austin: University of Texas Press, 1980), p. 24.

42 "are recorded by Post office officials . . .": According to ex-FBI agent Jack Levine, incoming mail was often watched through contacts at the U.S. Post Office, as per taped interview courtesy. Pacifica Radio Archives.

42 Agent J. F. McDevitt's report is entitled "People's Lyceum," and concerns a radical bookstore by that name.

43 Re Scott Nearing. His widow, Helen, wrote NR on October 8, 1987, that she had requested her husband's file, but had so far received only three letters from it. However, the July 1917 references mentioned are from a dissertation on Nearing written by John Saltmarsh. The relevant pages were sent to NR by Ellen Laconte, Helen Nearing's secretary.

43 " 'Agents of the Bolsheviki and I.W.W's . . .' ": Preston, p. 5.

43 "Another memo helps explain the Bureau's excitement.": Found in the FBI file of Max Eastman.

43 Some Authors League information is from the FBI "see-reference" file of Lillian Hellman.

46 Re Carl Sandburg. There are entries for every single decade up until his

death in 1967, so it is possible to follow certain FBI fixations. In Sandburg's case it is overwhelmingly Russia. In 1923, just five years after his notes and manuscripts were impounded, the FBI wrote that he "was reported to be a well-known Communist in Chicago," and that his activities "were reported to be in a technical capacity." In 1932, Sandburg's 1918 experience would surface again and the FBI would ask the War Department for all its files on the matter. In his letter about this, Hoover called Sandburg "Charles," instead of Carl, which may account for the lack of any follow-up. In the late thirties, the FBI noted that Sandburg told a crowd that "to the outside world Russia had been 'immense, chaotic, foglike,' but that now we are acquainted with Russian courage."

46   For more details on Sandburg and the Comintern, see Draper, op. cit., pp. 237–338.

Chapter Two

47   " 'disloyal utterances' ": For more details, see Halperin, op. cit.

47   "this wartime experience . . .": Powers, p. 55.

48   " 'had completed a classification of over 60,000 "radically inclined" . . .' ": Powers, p. 68.

48   "With the nation troubled . . .": Powers, p. 91.

49   " 'enforcement technique . . .' ": See Hoover, *Masters of Deceit*.

49   "William Z. Foster, a former chairman . . .": Quoted in Bert Andrews, *Washington Witch Hunt* (New York: Random House, 1948).

49   Quote from Clarence Kelley, from his autobiography, *Kelley: The Story of an FBI Director* (Kansas City, Mo.: Andrews, McMeel & Parker, 1987), pp. 58–59.

50   "guest columns . . .": In 1920, J. Edgar Hoover even published his own newsletter, a confidential bulletin concerning radical activities that he circulated to government officials. However, it included information on only one writer: Walter Lippman.

50   Quote about Publication Section is from an August 17, 1945, FBI memorandum from the file of Witter Bynner.

50   "Once, to illustrate . . .": From the FBI files of Sinclair Lewis, John Dos Passos, Thomas Wolfe, Howard Fast, and Truman Capote.

50   "The FBI also singled out the following complex line . . .": From the FBI file of Robinson Jeffers.

50   "The one writer Hoover revered . . .": "Inventory, Appraisal, and Reappraisal," document #967-72 pertaining to the estate of J. Edgar Hoover (U.S. District Court for the District of Columbia, 1972).

50 "G-Man and Tarzan comic strips . . .": See Fred J. Cook, *The FBI Nobody Knows* (New York: Macmillan, 1964) as quoted from a profile of Hoover by Jack Alexander in *The New Yorker* magazine.

50 "westerns (which he swapped with . . .)": NR interview with Cartha DeLoach.

50 "personal library included . . .": Observation by NR after visit to the FBI Library at Quantico, Virginia, where part of Hoover's personal library "is housed as a museum," as an official there described its current status.

Chapter Three

55 "a party that 'in the beginning seemed little more than a freak . . .' ": Hoover, *Masters of Deceit,* p. 53.

55 " 'complete and unquestioning . . .' ": Ibid., p. 55.

56 " 'informants reporting on informants.' ": NR interview with FBI Agent "X."

56 " 'The recovery of the self . . .' ": During NR's interview with her, Kay Boyle said, "I'll read you some of a speech I gave recently. It's called 'Writers in Metaphysical Revolt.' " This is part of that speech.

56 "On September 5, 1922 . . .": This document was found in the FBI file of Lincoln Steffens.

56 "As he later wrote . . .": Hoover, *Masters of Deceit,* p. 312.

56 "the Bureau 'is not to be concerned with political or other opinions . . .' ": For more details, see Halperin, op. cit.

57 "Actually, Stout had resigned when he learned . . .": Rex Stout to Dies Committee on Un-American Activities, 1942. Stout had been called a "prized exhibit" by the FBI. From the FBI file of Rex Stout.

58 " 'Its overriding theme was . . .' ": See Carl R. Dolmetsch, *The Smart Set: A History and Anthology* (New York: Dial Press, 1966).

59 "it 'saw nothing to gain in continuing . . .' ": Powers, p. 126.

61 Re Fast on Dos Passos: *The 42nd Parallel* was completed in 1930, *1919* in 1932, and *The Big Money* in 1936, so if Fast is correct, Dos Passos was a party member around the time the FBI put him there.

62 The FBI report on O'Neill is in the National Archives. #61-529. At one time I believe there must have been more to the file because Robert Sherwood's file has O'Neill's name checked for indexing on a 1938 letter to FDR that is not in O'Neill's file.

63 "Negro Activities.": National Archives. #B52202600-558.

63 "Racial hostility so strong . . .": Powers, p. 128.

64 " 'The desire to destroy Garvey . . .' ": Powers, p. 128.

65   "As William Preston, Jr., writes . . .": Preston, p. 236.

65   "Hoover—who referred to the clock . . .": Hoover's "Inventory, etc.," op. cit.

65   " 'a trifle to the Left . . .' ": The FBI "stole" this description from a 1940s *Current Biography* entry.

66   " 'Clyde joins me in sending . . .' ": From Hoover letters to Leonard Lyons (1950s). FBI file of Leonard Lyons.

67   "Contained, principally, printed pornographic . . .": Athan G. Theoharis and John Stewart Cox, *The Boss* (Philadelphia: Temple University Press, 1988), p. 95.

67   "Hoover identified political radicalism . . .": Ibid., p. 17.

Chapter Four

71   " 'The appeal of Marxism . . .' ": Kazin, p. 41.

72   Information on Theodore Dreiser is from NR interview with Richard Lingeman.

72   Sinclair Lewis quote from Mark Schorer, *Sinclair Lewis: An American Life* (New York: McGraw-Hill, 1961), p. 610.

72   "Lillian Hellman, who admitted . . .": Carl Rollyson, *Lillian Hellman* (New York: St. Martin's Press, 1985), pp. 319–320.

72   "As Daniel Aaron comments . . .": *Writers on the Left* (New York: Harcourt, Brace, 1961), p. 392.

73   "As Maurice Isserman writes . . .": *Which Side Were You On?* (Middletown, Conn.: Wesleyan University Press, 1982), p. 24.

73   "But, as Kenneth O'Reilly writes . . .": O'Reilly, p. 16.

73   Information about the 1934 executive order is from Halperin, op. cit., p. 96.

73   "the President issued secret oral instructions . . .": See Richard E. Morgan, *Domestic Intelligence* (Austin: University of Texas Press, 1980), as quoted from the 1976 Church Committee report.

74   " 'Such a very great man as Franklin . . .' ": Quote by Sullivan is from Cathy Perkus, ed., *COINTELPRO: The FBI's Secret War on Political Freedom* (New York: Monad Press, 1975), p. 28.

75   " 'Hoover got the idea . . .' ": See William C. Sullivan, *The Bureau* (New York: W. W. Norton, 1979).

78   "The cryptic effusions of poets . . .": From FBI file of William Carlos Williams.

78   As Harvey Klehr writes in *The History of American Communism*, pp. 357–358.

79   Martin Dies quotes are from his book *The Trojan Horse in America* (New York: Dodd, Mead, 1940).

Chapter Five

84   "In the September 1932 issue of *The New Masses* . . .": Aaron, op. cit., p. 192.

84   " 'Dear Comrades.' ": Letter from Cowley Collection of Newberry Library. Used with permission of Malcolm Cowley, the Cowley estate, and the Newberry Library.

85   In Upton Sinclair's letter to Mrs. Roosevelt, the underworld source mentioned could be Al Capone, because another report in the file mentions a request for an interview with Capone for either Lewis or a friend (it is not clear because of the deletions). Also, the last reference in Sinclair's file is dated 1939.

87   The FBI released only five pages of Sherwood Anderson's file. However, a 1956 name check by the Coast Guard (fifteen years after his death!) indicates that there are other references besides the released ones. These are 1938 and 1939 references from the Dies Committee. However, the FBI did not release them because it said it lacked "identifying data" on Anderson!?

89   William Phillips received his FBI file in 1991. He reports that it is "not shocking," although it "says I'm a Communist."

91   For Odets's testimony, see *Thirty Years of Treason*, edited by Eric Bentley (New York: Viking Press, 1971).

92   Re Donald Ogden Stewart: " 'a secret party member . . .' ": Harvey Klehr, *The Heyday of American Communism* (New York: Basic Books, 1984), p. 355.

99   Bodenheim letter to Hecht is from *The Chicago Reader*. Newberry Library. Used with permission.

101   "Farrell . . . who supported . . .": Alan M. Wald, *The New York Intellectuals* (Chapel Hill: University of North Carolina Press, 1987), p. 83.

101   "By 1937, Farrell had joined in the defense . . .": See Klehr, op. cit.

101   "it was Farrell who 'exerted the most influence . . .' ": From an essay by Malcolm Cowley in *Six Decades at Yaddo,* a pamphlet published in 1986 to commemorate Yaddo's sixtieth anniversary.

103   "Hicks believed 'the Communism to which . . .' ": From an article in his FBI file: "The Ex-Communist Novel," *The New Leader,* 7/23/51.

104   For Hicks's HUAC testimony, see Bentley, ed., op. cit.

Chapter Six

109   " 'When creating the Obscene file . . .' ": Theoharis and Cox, p. 94.

Chapter Seven

115 " 'I know Winchell as well as . . .' ": Marginal note in Winchell's FBI file.

115 "Richard Gid Powers says . . .": Telephone interview with NR, August 1990.

Chapter Eight

135 " 'If you publish J. Edgar Hoover . . .' ": Robert Bernstein, former CEO of Random House, to NR, winter 1987.

138 Statements by Jeffrey Lyons: Telephone interview with NR, May 1988.

Chapter Nine

145 "In his diaries . . .": The ex-employee is Harry Costelolo. *Drew Pearson's Diaries* (edited by Tyler Abell) (New York: Holt, Rinehart & Winston, 1974), p. 191.

151 According to his file, the conversation between Edgar Snow and the State Department took place "during a four hour visit" with State Department staff official Allen S. Whiting, at St. Cerque, Switzerland.

Chapter Ten

168 "Crime Records Section, the 'chief producer' . . .": For more details, see Ann Marie Buitrago and Leon Andrew Immerman, *Are You Now or Have You Ever Been in the FBI Files?* (New York: Grove Press, 1981).

170 Letter of Hoover to Attorney-General Biddle, 1941, is from FBI file of Archibald MacLeish.

Chapter Eleven

188 "In November the FBI began using . . .": O'Reilly, op. cit., p. 87.

188 "(In the fifties, Hoover would ask Cartha DeLoach . . .)": Ibid., p. 80.

188 "In 1941, the Legion passed . . .": From the FBI file of William Saroyan.

188 "In 1941, the FBI decided . . . Langston Hughes . . .": From the FBI file of Langston Hughes.

189 "Clifton Fadiman . . . says . . .": Letter to NR, 9/9/88.

189 "In 1923, when the FBI discovered that Upton Sinclair . . .": From the FBI file of Upton Sinclair.

190 "During the fall of 1942 . . .": From the FBI file of Walter Winchell.

190 "That same year, agents recruited . . .": From the FBI file of Muriel Rukeyser.

190 "On February 19, 1944, H. L. Mencken . . .": From the FBI file of H. L. Mencken.

192 "On August 19, 1946, Westbrook Pegler . . .": From the FBI file of Westbrook Pegler.

193 "Possibly the only thing Hoover and the CIA agreed on . . .": Halperin, op. cit., p. 48.

194 According to the FBI, these writers have no files: Ring Lardner, Fannie Farmer, Grantland Rice, Elinor Wylie, Hamlin Garland, Ellen Glasgow, Vachel Lindsay, James Whitcomb Riley, Edward Arlington Robinson, Jack Kerouac, Amy Lowell, Sara Teasdale, Flannery O'Conner, Sylvia Plath, Bernard Malamud, Wallace Stevens, William Sydney Porter (O. Henry), and Robert Benchley.

Chapter Twelve

196 "Poet William Carlos Williams told agents . . .": Williams's name is blacked out in Pound's file; however, the report number is not and it matches the one in his own file.

196 A clue to Kay Boyle's (blacked-out) identity in Pound's file was located in William Carlos Williams's file. Boyle has confirmed her FBI interview concerning Pound.

197 "Pound's publisher, James Laughlin . . .": Because John Tytell's biography of Pound quotes from Laughlin's interview with the FBI, I was able to go through Pound's FBI file and piece together the rest of the interview from the clues in Tytell's selections.

197 "According to . . . John Tytell . . .": Tytell, op cit., p. 285.

198 "The Pound controversy did not die . . .": Column found in FBI file of Westbrook Pegler.

208 Memo about Bernard Fay is from the Archives et Centre de Documentation Juive Contemporaine, Paris, March 1, 1941. Many thanks to Alice Yaeger Kaplan for locating this document for me.

208 William Shirer on Gertrude Stein: Letter to NR, 4/8/87.

208 Excerpts from Alice B. Toklas letters are from *Staying On Alone: The Letters of Alice B. Toklas*, edited by Edward Burns (New York: Liveright, 1973).

Chapter Thirteen

211 Hemingway letter to League of American Writers from League file at the Bancroft Library, University of California, Berkeley.

213 "Jeffrey Meyers writes . . .": *Hemingway* (New York: Harper & Row, 1985), p. 543.

213 Reynolds-Hemingway material and Hoover's note are from the FBI file of Quentin Reynolds.

214 Kay Boyle on Thornton Wilder: Most of this is from Boyle's interview with NR, but some lines are excerpted from an unpublished chronology she wrote and gave to NR. It is used with her permission.

214 "the Director of the FBI, who would one day . . .": From Hoover's "Inventory," op. cit.

215 Thornton Wilder letter to League of American Writers from League file at Bancroft Library, University of California/Berkeley.

217 "The Century Club . . .": In his FBI file, Sherwood is listed as belonging to "the Harvard and Century Clubs." In the report concerning MacArthur, I deduced it was the Century Club that was meant here since it was described as "a very exclusive club located in New York City."

218 " 'Some opposition simply on the ground . . .' ": From *Archibald MacLeish: Reflections*, edited by Bernard A. Drabeck and Helen E. Ellis (Amherst: University of Massachusetts Press, 1986).

220 The previously unpublished essay by Malcolm Cowley is in the Cowley Collection at the Newberry Library and is used with Malcolm Cowley's permission and the permission of the Cowley estate and the Newberry Library.

223 Letters from Cowley to Wilson: The Cowley Collection, Newberry Library. Used with permission of Malcolm Cowley, the Cowley estate, and the Newberry Library.

225 Testimony of Sidney Hook: Letter to NR, January 26, 1986.

Chapter Fourteen

229 "But, according to biographer Elinor Langer . . .": See Langer's biography of Josephine Herbst (Boston: Atlantic Monthly Press, 1984), pp. 249–259. Also notes on pp. 355 and 356.

230 "A May 8, 1942 report . . .": Perkins's address on Herbst's application is c/o Scribner's, New York. Since file #77-4400 is the only 1942 report marked "New York," I deduced that the statements in it are Perkins's. (Also, even without the clues mentioned, the words sound like what an editor might say about one of his writers!)

231 Herbst letter to Malcolm Cowley, March 29, 1943: Newberry Library, Cowley Collection. Used with the permission of Malcolm Cowley, the Cowley estate, and the Newberry Library.

232 Porter wrote in a December 31, 1960, letter that when an an FBI agent interviewed her "years ago" she was "floored" that the agent thought the person under scrutiny was a "conspiratorial character": *Letters of Katherine Anne Porter,* edited by Isabel Bayley (Boston: Atlantic Monthly Press), pp. 582–583.

233 " 'one of the party's best-known writers . . .' ": Hoover, *Masters of Deceit,* p. 107.

233 In an interview (and follow-up phone call when an excerpt from this book appeared in *The Nation* in 1987), Howard Fast told NR he left the CP in 1958. However, he changes the date to 1957 in his autobiography, *Being Red,* published in 1990. In Fast's interview with NR he also said he joined the Communist party "in 1942, 1943 at the latest." In his autobiography he changes the date of joining to 1944. I believe he meant what he said the first time.

Chapter Fifteen

244 " 'achingly dull . . .' ": Letter to NR, 2/6/90.

253 Hoover's reply to Walter Winchell re Dashiell Hammett was found in the FBI file of Walter Winchell.

255 William Abrahams on Lillian Hellman: Telephone interview with NR, 1989.

256 "Daniel Aaron has written . . .": As quoted in Wald, op. cit., p. 14.

256 Blair Clark on Lillian Hellman: Interview with NR, 1989.

256 "In his biography of Hellman . . .": Rollyson, op. cit., pp. 319–320.

258 "secretary to the director of Yaddo . . .": Ian Hamilton, *Robert Lowell: A Biography* (New York: Random House, 1983), p. 148.

258 " 'The FBI has been investigating Yaddo . . .' ": From the minutes of the Special Board of Directors meeting at Yaddo, 1949, courtesy of Cowley Collection, Newberry Library. Used with permission of Malcolm Cowley, the Cowley estate, and the Newberry Library.

258–259 Agnes Smedley quotes are from *Agnes Smedley: The Life and Times of an American Radical* by Janice R. MacKinnon and Stephen R. MacKinnon (Berkeley: University of California Press, 1987), pp. 317, 320, and 325. This book provides an excellent background on the Yaddo case.

259–261 Cowley letters re Lowell and Yaddo are used with the permission of Malcolm Cowley, the Cowley estate, and the Newberry Library.

262 Katherine Anne Porter to Morton Zabel: Zabel Collection, Newberry Library. Used with permission.

262 Elizabeth Hardwick initially agreed to order her FBI file for this book, but then changed her mind. "I have a reluctance to see it," she said.

263 Elizabeth Ames's letters to Malcolm Cowley are from the Cowley Collection, Newberry Library. Used with the permission of Malcolm Cowley, the Cowley estate, and the Newberry Library.

Chapter Sixteen

267 "Richard Gid Powers points out . . .": Powers, p. 307.

267 "Kenneth O'Reilly writes . . .": O'Reilly, op. cit., p. 141.

268 George M. Elsey's comments are from his May 1974 oral history interview conducted by Charles T. Morrissey and Jerry N. Hess of the Harry S. Truman Library, Independence, Missouri. I thank the Truman Library for providing me with this material.

272 "the year an FBI instructor told a class . . .": From 1962 taped interview with ex-FBI agent Jack Levine. Courtesy Pacifica Radio Archives.

275 "The FBI's aim [was] to turn people . . .": Perkus, ed., op. cit., p. 139.

275 "There were only 2,370 Cointelpro . . .": Kelley, op. cit., p. 190.

276 "In fact, two months after his death . . .": From the FBI file of Senator Joseph McCarthy.

Chapter Seventeen

282 Arthur Miller on Louis Untermeyer: *TimeBends* (New York: Grove Press, 1987), p. 264.

285 Letter from Kay Boyle to Richard Wright, 1956: Courtesy of Southern Illinois University Special Collections, David Koch, Curator.

286 "the temptation to draw conclusions . . .": For more details, see Addison Gayle, *Richard Wright: Ordeal of a Native Son* (New York: Doubleday, 1980).

Chapter Eighteen

289 Information re Consultants in Poetry via Sophie Wilkins.

289 "For instance, Robert Penn Warren . . .": Letter to NR, 4/16/87.

290 There is an interesting story attached to very-much-alive Karl Shapiro's appearance in *Alien Ink*. His name was on NR's original list to the FBI that included both living and deceased writers. His name remained on the list and in 1989 the FBI forwarded his file to me. I wrote Shapiro for

permission to include it in my book and he granted it immediately, commenting, "*The New York Times* called me a late American poet in a crossword puzzle, so why shouldn't the FBI also think I was dead?" Shapiro adds, "I'm the only poet who sued the American Medical Association and beat them! Around 1979 their journal listed me among the poets who had committed suicide."

293 "Since 1921 the FBI knew that one of the . . . rules . . .'': Draper, op. cit., p. 207.

Chapter Nineteen

301 Re COINTELPRO: Robert Penn Warren, Alfred Kazin, Leslie Fiedler, letters to NR, 1989.

304 "Erik Wensberg comments . . .'': Letters and telephone interviews with NR, 1990.

Chapter Twenty

320 FBI's Foreign Counterintelligence Manual: Appendix 7, p. 353 (excised 6/21/82). Available at FBI Reading Room, J. Edgar Hoover Building, Washington, D.C.

320 Most of the COINTELPROs discussed are from the files of Allen Ginsberg and Amiri Baraka. In addition, 6,106 pages of Black Extremist Hate Groups COINTELPRO pages have been released via FOIA and are available at the FBI Reading Room. Material concerning other types of COINTELPRO operations is also available at the reading room, and a list is available upon request.

321 "Cuban Matters.": Available at the FBI Reading Room.

321 "Johnson was the only American President . . .'': Hoover's "Inventory," op. cit.

322 "According to the memo, '13 friends' were asked . . .'': Some of these names are mentioned and not blacked out. They include Jerry O'Leary, Victor Riesel, Tom Waring, Lou Harris, and John Montgomery.

322 "At eleven A.M. . . . Mumford . . .'': From the FBI file of Lewis Mumford.

324 "Between the late sixties and the early seventies, the FBI . . .'': Sullivan, op. cit., p. 129.

327 Ten Sections of the Womens Liberation Movement file are available at the FBI Reading Room.

327 "One report says . . .'': "The FBI Was Watching You," by Letty

Cottin Pogrebin, *MS.* magazine, May 1977. I am grateful to Jessica Mitford for giving me this article.

Chapter Twenty-one

336 "Ginsberg says he was stopped by customs . . .": From a letter among Ginsberg's papers, used with his permission. I thank him for giving me access to all his file cabinets, which contained not only his government records but personal documents pertaining to those records. I also thank AG for introducing me to his lawyer, Ira Lowe, who also provided me with many FBI documents and letters.

340 "Ginsberg explains that he was covering the convention . . .": From private papers of Allen Ginsberg. Used with his permission.

343–344 Information from Jean Frank: Telephone interview with NR, 1990.

Chapter Twenty-two

345 "(Baldwin had, indeed, at one time assailed Wright's . . .)": James Baldwin, "Many Thousands Gone," which first appeared in *Partisan Review*, and then in book form, *Notes of a Native Son.*

348 Richard Baron on Baldwin: Interview with NR, 1990.

349 James H. Silberman on Baldwin: Interview with NR, 1990.

349 Amiri Baraka's file consists of 759 pages, but 632 are still classified. In addition, there are approximately 2,000 pages of LAP papers he has requested but not received.

352 James Atlas on Delmore Schwartz: Letter to NR, 1990.

355–356 Roy Cohn, who publicly denied he was gay up until his death, died of AIDS on August 2, 1986.

Chapter Twenty-three

366 "In an extraordinary 1970 document . . .": From the FBI file of Lillian Hellman.

367 Robert Silvers: Telephone interview with NR, 1990.

368 Blair Clark: Telephone interview with NR, 1990.

368 Stephen Gellers: Telephone interview with NR, 1990.

368 "On May 2, 1972 . . .": Powers, op. cit., pp. 480–485.

369 "Philip Shenon explains . . .": "Wanted by F.B.I.—a New Director," in *The New York Times*, March 15, 1987.

369 *Legal Handbook for Special Agents*, April 28, 1978, 188pp. Available at the FBI Reading Room.

369 Former Attorney-General Edward Levi: Letters and telephone interview with NR, 1990.

369 William M. Baker: Telephone interview with NR, 1988.

371 Thomas L. Sheer: Article by E. K. Shipp, *The New York Times*, December 7, 1986.

372 Aryeh Neier's *Surveillance as Censorship* is from the PEN American Center report, "The Campaign Against the Underground Press," published by City Lights Books (San Francisco: 1981). I am grateful to Allen Ginsberg for sharing this book with me.

373 FBI Deputy Assistant Director Milt Ahlerich: Interview with NR, 1/11/88. Also follow-up letters 1988–1989.

373 FBI Supervisory Special Agent Susan Schnitzer: Interview with NR, 6/29/88. Also follow-up letters and telephone interviews, 1988–1989.

Chapter Twenty-four
Note: In some cases, government officials have requested anonymity.

376 "The FBI's Invasion of Libraries," by Natalie Robins, *The Nation,* April 9, 1988.

376 "A professor at Oberlin College . . .": Letter to NR from Richard Ohmann, Department of English, Wesleyan University, Middletown, Connecticut, 5/18/88.

376 "An official at Princeton University . . .": This person has requested anonymity.

376 Alcohol and Tobacco Tax Division information: See Paul Cowan, et al., *State Secrets: Police Surveillance in America* (New York: Holt, Rinehart & Winston, 1974).

376 Sven Holmes: Letter to NR, 2/8/88.

377 Judith Krug: Telephone interviews with NR, 1988.

377 Edith Tiger: Telephone interviews with NR, 1988.

377 Jaia Barrett's comment is from a 1988 interview with the College Press Service.

377 Congressman Don Edwards: Telephone interview with NR, 1988.

378 "In 1950, in answer to Soviet criticism . . .": V. Minayev, "New Times," Moscow, February 1950. From the FBI file of J. Edgar Hoover, #67-561, section 5.

379 Representative Major Owens: Telephone interview with NR, 1988.

380–393 All the librarians quoted were interviewed by NR via telephone between 1988 and 1991.

381 Leanne Katz: Telephone interview with NR, 1988.

382 Gerald Young: Telephone interview with NR, 1988.

383 Maureen Fleming: Telephone interview with NR, 1988.

384 "For instance, in 1988, a visitor . . .": The visitor was NR.

384–393 LAP file via National Security Archive.

388 Transcript of NCLIS January 14, 1988, meeting was obtained by Toby J. McIntosh of the Bureau of National Affairs, Inc.

391 1988 Brooklyn Public Library information from news release by Ellen Rudley, Brooklyn Public Library, 7/19/88.

393 "An American Librarian": The combined voices of seven librarians. They were combined into one voice because two requested anonymity.

Chapter Twenty-five

398 John Kenneth Galbraith. "My Forty Years with the FBI," *Esquire* magazine, October 1977. I am grateful to Jessica Mitford for showing me this.

404 "The Center for National Security Studies says . . .": From a column by David Corn and Jeffrey Morley, *The Nation,* 1989.

405 Bob Woodward: Telephone interview with NR, 1988.

Appendix B

413 NR telephone interview with Studs Terkel, 1988.

423 NR telephone interview with Mary Cheever, 1990.

424 Jean Stein letters to NR, 1989.

427 Horace Gregory quote from Irving Howe, et al., *The American Communist Party* (Boston: Beacon Press, 1957), p. 294.

432 NR interview with Gloria Jones, 1989.

437 NR telephone interview with Alison Mumford Morss, 1990.

446 I am grateful to Walter Clemons for his willingness to share Vidal's file with me.

Selected Bibliography

Books

Aaron, Daniel. *Writers on the Left*. New York: Harcourt, Brace, 1961.

Anderson, Sherwood. *The Letters of Sherwood Anderson*. Howard Mumford Jones and Walter B. Rideout, eds. Boston: Little, Brown, 1969.

————. *The Portable Sherwood Anderson*. New York: Viking Press, 1972.

————. *Sherwood Anderson's Memoirs*. New York: Harcourt, Brace, 1942.

Andrews, Burt. *Washington Witch Hunt*. New York: Random House, 1948.

Barron, John. *KGB: The Secret Work of Soviet Secret Agents*. New York: Reader's Digest Press, 1974.

Benson, Frederick. *Writers in Arms: The Literary Impact of the Spanish Civil War*. New York: New York University Press, 1967.

Bentley, Eric, ed. *Thirty Years of Treason*. New York: Viking Press, 1971.

Biddle, Francis. *In Brief Authority*. New York: American Heritage, 1962.

Bouza, Anthony J. *Police Intelligence: The Operations of an Investigative Unit*. New York: AMS Press, 1976.

Boyle, Kay. *This Is Not a Letter and Other Poems*. Los Angeles: Sun and Moon Press, 1985.

————. *Words That Must Somehow Be Said: Selected Essays*. San Francisco: North Point Press, 1985.

————, and Robert McAlmon. *Being Geniuses Together*. San Francisco: North Point Press, 1984 (originally published in 1968).

Braden, Anne. *The Wall Between*. New York: Monthly Review Press, 1958.

Branch, Taylor. *Parting the Waters: America in the King Years 1954–1963*. New York: Simon & Schuster, 1988.

Brooks, Van Wyck. *The Confident Years*. New York: Dutton, 1952.

Buckley, William F., and L. Brent Bozell. *McCarthy and His Enemies.* New York: Henry Regnery, 1954.

Budenz, Louis Francis. *This Is My Story.* New York: McGraw-Hill, 1947.

Buitrago, Ann Marie, and Leon Andrew Immerman. *Are You Now or Have You Ever Been in the FBI Files?* New York: Grove Press, 1981.

Caute, David. *The Fellow Travellers.* New York: Macmillan, 1973.

Cavins, Huntington, ed. *H. L. Mencken: The American Scene.* New York: Knopf, 1965.

Childs, Marquis, and James Reston, eds. *Walter Lippmann and His Times.* New York: Harcourt, Brace & World, 1959.

Clarke, Gerald. *Capote: A Biography.* New York: Simon & Schuster, 1988.

Clausewitz, Karl von. *On War,* Vol. I. London: Routledge & Kegan Paul, 1968 edition.

Cohn, Roy, and Sidney Zion. *The Autobiography of Roy Cohn.* New York: Lyle Stuart, 1988.

Cook, Fred J. *The FBI Nobody Knows.* New York: Macmillan, 1964.

———. *The Nightmare Decade: The Life and Times of Senator Joseph McCarthy.* New York: Random House, 1971.

Corson, William R., and Robert T. Crowley. *The New KGB.* New York: William Morrow, 1985.

Cowan, Paul, et al. *State Secrets: Police Surveillance in America.* New York: Holt, Rinehart & Winston, 1974.

Cowley, Malcolm. *Exile's Return.* New York: Viking, 1951.

Demaris, Ovid. *The Director: An Oral History of J. Edgar Hoover.* New York: Harper's Magazine Press, 1975.

Dilling, Elizabeth. *The Red Network.* Milwaukee, Wis.: C. N. Caspar Co., 1934.

Dolmetsch, Carl R. *The Smart Set: A History and Anthology.* New York: Dial Press, 1966.

Draper, Theodore. *Abuse of Power.* New York: Viking, 1967.

———. *American Communism and Soviet Russia.* New York: Macmillan, 1960.

———. *Present History.* New York: Random House, 1983.

———. *The Roots of American Communism.* New York: Viking, 1957.

Dubofsky, Melvin. *We Shall Be All: A History of the Industrial Workers of the World.* New York: Quadrangle, 1969.

Dupuy, R. Ernest, and Trevor N. Dupuy. *The Encyclopedia or Military History.* New York: Harper & Row, 1986.

Earnest, Ernest. *The Single Vision.* New York: New York University Press, 1970.

Eastman, Max. *Journalism Versus Art*. New York: Knopf, 1916.

———. *Since Lenin Died*. New York: Boni & Liveright, 1925.

Elliff, John T. *The Reform of the FBI Intelligence Activities*. Princeton, N.J.: Princeton University Press, 1979.

Fast, Howard. *Peekskill U.S.A.* New York: Civil Rights Congress, 1951.

———. *The Pledge*. Boston: Houghton Mifflin, 1988.

Frank, Elizabeth. *Louise Bogan*. New York: Knopf, 1985.

Frost, Robert. *Letters to Louis Untermeyer*. New York: Holt, Rinehart & Winston, 1963.

Robert Frost: Poetry and Prose. Lathem, Edward Connery, and Lawrence Thompson, eds. New York: Holt, 1972.

Garrow, David J. *The FBI and Martin Luther King, Jr.* New York: Norton, 1981.

Gayle, Addison. *Richard Wright: Ordeal of a Native Son*. New York: Doubleday, 1980.

Goldman, Eric F. *The Crucial Decade and After, 1945–1960*. New York: Vintage, 1960.

Green, Bernard. *The Timetables of History*. New York: Simon & Schuster, 1975.

Halperin, Morton H., et al. *The Lawless State: The Crimes of the U.S. Intelligence Agencies*. New York: Penguin, 1976.

Hamilton, Ian. *Robert Lowell: A Biography*. New York: Random House, 1983.

Hicks, Granville. *John Reed*. New York: Macmillan, 1936.

Higham, John. *Strangers in the Land: Patterns of American Nativism 1860–1925*. New York: Atheneum, 1973.

Hofstadter, Richard. *The American Political Tradition and the Men Who Made It*. New York: Knopf, 1948.

———, and Beatrice K. Hofstadter. *Great Issues in American History*. New York: Vintage Books, 1982.

Hook, Sidney. *Out of Step*. New York: Harper & Row, 1986.

Hoover, J. Edgar. *Masters of Deceit*. New York: Holt, 1958.

———. *A Study of Communism*. New York: Holt, Rinehart & Winston, 1962.

Howe, Irving. *Politics and the Novel*. New York: Meridian Books, 1957.

———, Louis Coser, and Julius Jacobson. *The American Communist Party*. Boston: Beacon Press, 1957.

Ickes, Harold. *The Secret Diaries*. New York: Simon & Schuster, 1954.

Isserman, Maurice. *Which Side Were You On?* Middetown, Conn.: Wesleyan University Press, 1982.

Jones, Howard Mumford. *The Theory of American Literature.* Ithaca, N.Y.: Cornell University Press, 1966.

Kaplan, Justin. *Lincoln Steffens.* New York: Simon & Schuster, 1974.

Karl, Frederick. *William Faulkner: American Writer.* New York: Weidenfeld & Nicolson, 1989.

Kazin, Alfred. *On Native Ground.* New York: Harcourt, Brace, 1942.

Kelley, Clarence. *Kelley: The Story of an FBI Director.* Kansas City, Mo.: Andrews, McMeel & Parker, 1987.

Kempton, Murray. *Part of Our Time: Some Monuments and Ruins of the Thirties.* New York: Simon & Schuster, 1955.

Klehr, Harvey. *The Heyday of American Communism: The Depression Decade.* New York: Basic Books, 1984.

Lamphere, Robert J., and Thomas Schachtman. *The FBI-KGB War: A Special Agent's Story.* New York: Random House, 1986.

Langer, Elinor. *Josephine Herbst.* Boston: Atlantic Monthly Press, 1984.

Lingeman, Richard. *Theodore Dreiser: At the Gates of the City.* New York: G. P. Putnam's Sons, 1986.

————. *Theodore Dreiser: An American Journey.* New York: G. P. Putnam's Sons, 1990.

Lippmann, Walter. *A Preface to Politics.* Ann Arbor, Mich.: The University of Michigan, 1914. (Paperback, 1962).

Lynn, Kenneth. *Hemingway.* New York: Simon & Schuster, 1987.

McCarthy, Eugene. *Up 'Til Now: A Memoir of the Decline of American Politics.* New York: Harcourt, Brace, Jovanovich, 1987.

Macdonald, Dwight. *Against the American Grain.* New York: Random House, 1962.

————. *Memoirs of a Revolutionist.* New York: Farrar, Straus, 1957.

McKelway, St. Clair. *Gossip: The Life and Times of Walter Winchell.* New York: Viking Press, 1940.

MacKinnon, Janice R., and Stephen R. MacKinnon. *Agnes Smedley: The Life and Times of an American Radical.* Berkeley, Ca.: University of California Press, 1987.

MacLeish, Archibald. *Reflections.* Bernard Drabeck and Helen Ellis, eds., Amherst, Mass.: University of Massachusetts Press, 1986.

McLellan, David. *Karl Marx, His Life and Thought.* New York: Harper & Row, 1973.

Marx, Karl. *Early Writings.* New York: Vintage, 1975.

May, Henry F. *The End of American Innocence*. New York: Knopf, 1959.

Meeropol, Robert, and Michael Meeropol. *We Are Your Sons: The Legacy of Julius and Ethel Rosenberg*. Second edition. Champaign, Ill.: University of Illinois Press, 1981.

Mencken, H. L. *The Diary of H. L. Mencken*. Charles A. Fecher, ed. New York: Knopf, 1990.

Meyers, Jeffrey. *Hemingway: A Biography*. New York: Harper & Row, 1985.

Miller, Arthur. *TimeBends*. New York: Grove Press, 1987.

Mitford, Jessica. *The American Way of Death*. New York: Simon & Schuster, 1963.

―――. *Daughters and Rebels*. New York: Simon & Schuster, 1961.

―――. *A Fine Old Conflict*. New York: Knopf, 1977.

Morgan, Richard E. *Domestic Intelligence: Monitoring Dissent in America*. Austin, Tex.: University of Texas Press, 1980.

Murray, Natalie Danese. *Darlingkissimi: Letters to a Friend—Janet Flanner*. New York: Harcourt, Brace, Jovanovich, 1988.

Murray, Robert K. *Red Scare*. Minneapolis: University of Minnesota Press, 1955.

Navasky, Victor. *Kennedy Justice*. New York: Atheneum, 1971.

―――. *Naming Names*. New York: Viking, 1980.

Nearing, Scott. *The Making of a Radical*. Harborside, Maine: Social Science Institute, 1972.

Nicosia, Gerald. *Memory Babe: A Critical Biography of Jack Kerouac*. New York: Grove Press, 1983.

Nixon, Richard. *Memoirs*. New York: Grossett and Dunlap, 1978.

―――. *The Real War*. New York: Warner Books, 1980.

O'Neill, William L. *Echoes of Revolt: The Masses 1911–1917*. New York: Quadrangle, 1966.

O'Reilly, Kenneth. *Hoover and the Un-Americans*. Philadelphia: Temple University Press, 1983.

―――. *Racial Matters: The FBI's Secret Files on Black Americans 1960–1972*. New York: Free Press, 1989.

Orwell, George. *Homage to Catalonia*. New York: Harcourt, Brace, 1952 (originally published in 1938).

Parry, Albert. *Garrets and Pretenders: A History of Bohemianism in America*. New York: Dover, 1960.

Drew Pearson Diaries 1949–1959. Tyler Abell, ed. New York: Holt, Rinehart & Winston, 1974.

Perkus, Kathy, ed. *COINTELPRO: The FBI's Secret War on Political Freedom*. New York: Monad Press, 1975.

Porter, Katherine Anne. *The Collected Essays and Occasional Writing*. New York: Delacorte, 1970.

Powers, Richard Gid. *G-Men: Hoover's FBI in American Popular Culture*. Carbondale, Ill.: Southern Illinois University Press, 1983.

————. *Secrecy and Power: The Life of J. Edgar Hoover*. New York: Free Press, 1987.

Preston, William, Jr. *Aliens and Dissenters*. Cambridge, Mass.: Harvard University Press, 1963.

Pyle, Ernie. *Here's Your War*. New York: Henry Holt, 1943.

Rips, Geoffrey, coordinator. *Unamerican Activities: The Campaign Against the Underground Press*. San Francisco: City Lights, 1981.

Rollyson, Carl. *Lillian Hellman: Her Legend and Her Legacy*. New York: St. Martin's, 1988.

Rukeyser, Muriel. *The Collected Poems*. New York: McGraw-Hill, 1978.

Schott, Joseph L. *No Left Turns*. New York: Praeger, 1957.

Seager, Allen. *The Glass House: The Life of Theodore Roethke*. New York: McGraw-Hill, 1968.

Shorer, Mark. *Sinclair Lewis: An American Life*. New York: McGraw-Hill, 1961.

Sinclair, Upton. *The Brass Check*. Published by the author. 1920 (revised, 1936).

Spanier, Sandra Whipple. *Kay Boyle: Artist and Activist*. Carbondale, Ill.: Southern Illinois University Press, 1976.

Spender, Stephen. *Journals 1939–1983*. John Goldsmith, ed. New York: Random House, 1986.

Spiller, R. E., et al. *Literary History of the United States*. New York: Macmillan, 1974.

Starobin, Joseph H. *American Communism in Crisis, 1943–1957*. Cambridge, Mass.: Harvard University Press, 1972.

Steele, Ronald. *Walter Lippmann and the American Century*. Boston: Little, Brown, 1980.

Steffens, Lincoln. *The Autobiography of Lincoln Steffens*. New York: Harcourt, Brace, Jovanovich, 1968.

Stein, Gertrude. *Wars I Have Seen*. New York: Random House, 1945.

Sullivan, William C., with Bill Brown. *The Bureau: My Thirty Years in Hoover's FBI*. New York: W. W. Norton, 1979.

Swanberg, W. A. *Dreiser*. New York: Charles Scribner's Sons, 1965.

Szulc, Tad. *Fidel: A Critical Portrait*. New York: William Morrow, 1986.

Taylor, Robert. *Fred Allen: His Life and Wit*. Boston: Little, Brown, 1989.

Theoharis, Athan G., and John Stuart Cox. *The Boss: J. Edgar Hoover and the Great American Inquisition.* Philadelphia: Temple University Press, 1988.

Thomas, Bob. *Winchell.* New York: Doubleday, 1971.

Thomas, Hugh. *The Spanish Civil War* (new edition). New York: Harper & Row, 1986.

Toklas, Alice B. *The Alice B. Toklas Cook Book.* New York: Harper & Row, 1954.

————. *Staying on Alone: The Letters of Alice B. Toklas.* Edward Burns, ed. New York: Liveright, 1973.

Townsend, Kim. *Sherwood Anderson: A Biography.* Boston: Houghton Mifflin, 1987.

Trilling, Lionel. *The Middle of the Journey.* New York: Viking Press, 1947.

————. *Sincerity and Authenticity.* Cambridge, Mass.: Harvard University Press, 1972.

Truffaut, François. *Hitchcock.* New York: Simon & Schuster, 1983.

Tytell, John. *Ezra Pound: The Solitary Volcano.* New York: Doubleday, 1987.

Ungar, Sanford. *FBI.* Boston: Little, Brown, 1975.

Untermeyer, Louis. *From Another World.* New York: Harcourt, Brace, 1939.

Von Hoffman, Nicholas. *Citizen Cohn: The Life and Times of Roy Cohn.* New York: Doubleday, 1988.

Wagner, Linda, ed. *Interviews with William Carlos Williams: Speaking Straight Ahead.* New York: New Directions, 1976.

Wald, Alan M. *The New York Intellectuals.* Chapel Hill: University of North Carolina Press, 1986.

Watters, Pat, and Stephen Gillers. *Investigating the FBI.* New York: New Directions, 1973.

Weintaub, Stanley. *The Last Great Cause: The Intellectuals and the Spanish Civil War.* New York: Waybright and Talley, 1968.

Welch, Neil J., and David W. Marston. *Inside Hoover's FBI.* New York: Doubleday, 1984.

White, William, ed. *By-Line: Ernest Hemingway.* New York: Charles Scribner's Sons, 1974.

Wilson, Edmund. *The Fifties.* New York: Farrar, Straus & Giroux, 1986.

Wise, David. *The American Police State.* New York: Random House, 1976.

Woodward, Bob. *Veil: The Secret Wars of the CIA 1981–1987.* New York: Simon & Schuster, 1987.

Woodward, C. Vann. *Thinking Back: The Perils of Writing History.* Baton Rouge, La.: Louisiana State University Press, 1986.

Wright, Richard, ed. *Whose FBI?* La Salle, Ill.: Open Court, 1974.

Zabel, Morton D., ed. *Literary Opinion in America.* New York: Harper, 1962.

Articles, Pamphlets, Tapes, Films, Unpublished Manuscripts

Draper, Theodore. "Long Ago and Far Away: A Memoir." *Dissent,* Summer, 1986.

————. "Nuclear Temptations." *New York Review of Books,* January 19, 1984.

Inquiry into the Destruction of Former FBI Director J. Edgar Hoover's Files and FBI Record Keeping. Washington, D.C.: Government Printing Office, 1975.

Pacifica Radio Archive–WBAI tapes. BB1397a, BB1397b, BB1397c, Jack Levine, ex-FBI agent, interviewed 10/10/62, Los Angeles, California, by Dick Elman and Chris Koch.

O'Keeffe, Mike. *College Press Service,* vol. 26, no. 31 (January 18, 1988).

Evans, Steven, and James Morgan. Documentary film on Jessica Mitford. KQED Project with the Berkeley (California) Graduate School of Journalism, 1986.

Lichtenstein, Allen. Documentary film on Allen Ginsberg. Sponsored by Brooklyn College, 1987.

Rappaport, Richard. *Joe's Boys* (unpublished manuscript about Roy Cohn and G. David Schine).

Index

479

About the Author

Alien Ink is Natalie Robins's sixth book. She is the coauthor of *Savage Grace,* which won an Edgar Award for the best fact crime book published in 1985. Robins lives in New York with her husband, writer and *New York Times* book reviewer Christopher Lehmann-Haupt, and their two children, Rachel, a college senior, and Noah, an eighth grader.